About the Author

Wanting to live a life worth living, Stephen has exhibited a talent for doing research that, more often than not, has been unfunded. Intermittent income. Then was generated by being a ferryboat skipper, wildlife walks and sea cruises leader, local newspaper nature columnist and above all as the scientific observer aboard Norwegian Antarctic krill trawlers in the Southern Ocean and aboard Japanese and Taiwanese refrigerated cargo vessels collecting tuna from the tropical Indian and Atlantic Oceans' tuna fleets. While seal studies have been his primary interest, he has made many smaller studies of the seals' neighbours and also was a pioneer of studies into marine debris impacts on wildlife and wild places. He lives with his lady in Cornwall, had two daughters – one of whom died following a heart operation – and two grandchildren. He continues to study the seals, but is grateful most of all for the love and friendship that underpins everything

Somerledaa's Tale
A Story of Grey Seals

Stephen Westcott

Somerledaa's Tale
A Story of Grey Seals

Olympia Publishers
London

www.olympiapublishers.com
OLYMPIA PAPERBACK EDITION

A CIP catalogue record for this title is
available from the British Library.

ISBN: 978-1-78830-564-8

This is a work of fiction.
Names, characters, places and incidents originate from the writer's
imagination. Any resemblance to actual persons, living or dead, is purely
coincidental.

First Published in 2020

Olympia Publishers
Tallis House
2 Tallis Street
London
EC4Y 0AB

Printed in Great Britain

Dedication

To the loving spirits of the people of my heart and, most especially, to
Katie

On stark slabs of glinting, pale-brown rock that might have been rough-hewn by an axe wielded by a savage god, Mornalas lay at rest. On a platform where no barnacles grew, under the tall, faded stalk of a lighthouse bearing a famous name, she lay drowsy in summer sunlight. Neither quite awake nor asleep, she retained a sun-drenched awareness of the ever-intrusive gossip of the ocean. Just now it was decorated by the distant crying of herring gulls and the crude corkscrew-creaks of gannets muttering to themselves as they prepared to fold their wings and plunge into the sea.

These waters, their voices, the touch and taste of them: they patterned her radar continuously. They fed her an endless stream of information about her vast, multi-dimensional water-world; her home. Not far north of her rocky resting place scoured entirely clean of barnacles, the most powerful of tide races was growling, ravening, as it bowled headlong southward like an express train. Not far south of the same rock, another race of slightly lesser potency was ripping northward. The two races never moved in the same direction. Their relative potencies waxed and waned, not only with the growing and shrinking of moons, but on the turning wheel of the winds.

Their strident voices, the bickering of them, were a comfort to Mornalas. Upon her and her kind, they conferred a rare sense of security. Hauled out and mainly relaxed on this solid, inaccessible place about which the wild races roistered, they luxuriated in a vibrant charmed circle. Few, indeed, were the boats or kayaks that ventured close to the seals' rocks and fewer still the people who attempted a landing there.

Once, and for long years, men had lived in the Longships lighthouse that loomed like a stern mast over the north end of the fleet of rocks. During hundreds of years before that, fishermen had seen and hunted seals basking in the summer months on the same evocatively-named rocks. Here, then, was an ancestral haunt of considerable antiquity.

The movements of keepers to and from the dressed-granite stalk, topped by its spinning wheel of light, had been attended often by a sonic commotion sufficient to send her forebears slithering into the sea. True, at other times, when keepers emerged to stretch their legs or cast a fishing line, the seals learned they need not startle after all. For their part, the keepers enjoyed the neighbourly company of the seals, the sight of them, and the evocative music of their mournful gossip. There had been times when they responded in kind, sitting on the steps leading to the iron door of the lighthouse, regaling them with music conjured from fiddle, squeeze box or pipes. Of such times, the keepers enchanted their wide-eyed children with simple stories during periods ashore.

Now, the keepers were long-gone; only their ghosts remained. Somewhere to the north-west of their old home, crewmen of a crabber were hauling in and sorting their strings of plastic pots, attended by a small flock of herring gulls. Their distant, occasional voices competed hardly at all for the attention of the seals. Neither did the little aeroplane, flying from the nearby airfield under Chapel Carn Brea. Full of holidaymakers, passing overhead its white livery drew little more than a passing glance as it droned by, outward bound for the Isles of Scilly.

There was an intention... perhaps, more, a stirring of appetite... drifting into her consciousness. She thought to slip from the rocks, go hunting when the waters rose again. She was in no hurry, having no desire to dive from such a height above the unsteady waters. She would wait until the tide was sufficiently high that she could just roll lazily into the summer-warm waters. Her hunger — she was often famished, now — was associated with that other life quickening inside her. This was not because the pup she was carrying was her first. Already, she had delivered four white-coated pups on sea cave shores not far from where she lay. It had always been so easy. Not that it was like that for all seals. Take elderly Morlaira, for example. The last two had been stillbirths. Perhaps her time for producing little ones was drawing to an end.

For Mornalas, it was pleasure. Raising the little white one to the time of weaning and independence, she was suffused by a vast sense of tranquillity and well-being. It ruled the days of her active motherhood even in the face of occasional territorial aggression encountered in other mothers sharing the same rather cramped darkness of the nursery beach.

A snarl, a sudden movement, blundered into her reverie. She lifted her head sharply, looking toward the source of the disturbance. Nearby, six or seven other females had become, likewise, alert. Tyrian and Meinek, two great males, had engaged in an ongoing trial of strength that had become unsettling for the females and younger males sharing this same vast rock. So far, they had confined themselves only to the theatre of aggression. No blood had been spilled. The volcano had rumbled, not yet blown, but the time would come and the females knew that; when it did, there could be a battle-royal. In which case, woe betide any other seal in the vicinity.

It had been similar last year and for several years past, except in the identity of the challenger. Meinek was an exceptionally powerful and potent dark-brown seal. Countless were the males he had bullied into fleeing from him without a fight. Of those who had made a contest of his authority, every single one had been bloodily vanquished and then hotly pursued for a considerable distance. Having cleared the locality of rivals, it had subsequently been his pleasure to father most of the next year's cadre of pups before the local seal mothers left the nursery grounds.

Tyrian lacked the fullest bulk of Meinek. He was slightly less massive and entirely black. Over the recent seasons of his maturing, he had seen this great seal holding sway, knowing they must meet sooner or later and had dreamed it would be for him to put an end to his savage reign.

Close up, the two seals had been leaning one against the other. It was a form of seal arm-wrestling, the last chance to avoid a battle-proper. It served to make both seals aware of how their strength measured against that of the other without the risk of bloodshed and even maiming.

Tyrian felt his disadvantage and came to a wider recognition of what Meinek was. He had felt the superior strength of the great male, recognised the malevolent battle wisdom in the pitiless eyes that stared through his own. He had even felt the strength growing in his rival, as if brazenly burgling strength from the weakness he assumed was his private, shaming secret. Amid the tangle of unwelcome awareness, his will broke. Fear gushed in. He broke physically free and, with all the power in his two fore-flippers, launched himself from the chest of his rival away toward the lower ledges, travelling as fast as he had ever travelled over rocks.

Tyrian had noticed even in peaceable times the laboriousness of the heaviest males whenever stampeding into the sea. Always, they were the slowest movers in any seal party, needing to stop for breath between short bursts of acceleration, so heavy was the weight they were dragging toward the sea. The females and even the yearlings moved much faster and more freely.

His fear outran Meinek's fury; just. The black seal made the great dive of about four metres straight down into the sea while the all-powerful brown god of these terrible rocks paused at the brink. There, silhouetted against the sky, he bellowed his triumph even as Tyrian fled directly out into the noisier tide race that was also a favourite hunting ground. He had no sense of all the females diving into the sea in his wake, fleeing the frightening savagery of the atmosphere.

A kilometre distant from Longships light, he surfaced and imposed a kind of calm upon his clamorous heart, slowing the beat of it right down. He rested there for less than a minute, taking deep breaths before striking out westward toward other lighthouses and far islands behind which the sun set. There, he knew, a haven awaited him.

Before the sun dipped below the sea horizon, he was asleep in the shallow, kelp-floored sea close to a long rocky islet well-known to him. Called The Rags, it is situated inside the outermost shield of the Western Rocks. It functioned as a sanctuary rock, a place of refuge for any seal defeated in combat or desiring to avoid it. Such refuges exist in every locality where seal pups are born and males fight. During the late afternoon, his spirit humiliated, Tyrian arrived exhausted in the gentle swell of the adjacent shallows.

It was not his first visit to the sanctuary. In the very first winter of his life, battered by a run of big storms, ravenously hungry from the inadequacy of his earliest hunting efforts, he had been swept up on to its gaunt slabs in the surf of a broken wave and then sucked immediately back, bowled over seemingly endlessly in the raging backwash. It happened again and then again. Some remnant of memory recalled a group of male seals already safely hauled out at the top of the slope, under a tower of rock. They watched him. In brief flashes, while the salt water cleared from his eyes, he saw heads turned toward his rolling, struggling form. It had felt like indifference, magisterial indifference, like the eyes of all the seals that had ever been; watching how he dealt with the challenges of first independence, first dangers: survival or not.

Rolling back down the rocky slope on the thinnest mattress of surf, sight failed and vision intervened. Already, in his short span of weeks, he had seen his half-brother, Ralicon, stretched in premature but final rest on a pile of kelp decorating the shoreline of Mount's Bay. Before that, they had travelled together, in amity, the hundreds of sea miles from the north Wales cave upon whose sandy beach they had been born.

Tyrian had been bobbing just outside the wave break, watching a late afternoon diesel train moving slowly out of Penzance railway station. Behind the windows of the carriages, he could make out the pale blurs of passengers faces, pressed against the glass and soaking up their last close-up sight of the ocean before they disappeared into the Cornish hills.

While the brightly-coloured train began its long journey to Paddington, a lone person had been walking across wet, compacted sands, preceded by a black and white border collie. It alarmed a greater black-backed gull, a great pirate of a bird, from its bloody-billed perch on top of some item of flotsam. In turn, the dog stopped to examine the item, sniffing it before lifting one hind leg quite delicately and peeing on it. Strange.

That evening, when the tide was high, he remembered the strange behaviour of the bloody-billed gull and the territorial activity of the indelicate dog. He came in through the surf near the place where the strange theatre had been performed. The run and suck of the surf was rolling the object into the shallows, over and over. A seal pup, head lolling down in the water. It seemed almost alive again, but for the strange odours of, and losses to, scavengers and the shocking gaping red hollows where his dark eyes had once been; his half-brother, Ralicon.

Ralicon, Loy, Morran and Vellien: companions of his nursery places, playful in their brief lifetimes; aggressive or reticent, too slow to learn. In the first few weeks of his dispersal from that first home, they came to seem like stepping-stones of death. Something mournful afflicted his outlook during that period. It occurred to him that one day, one of his few surviving peers would likely chance upon his own lifeless form cast up on some other unfamiliar shore.

Was this gaunt place, here among the westernmost stones of this edge of Europe, to be that shore? The Rags. Tiny Tyrian, so small then compared with what he was to become, rebelled against the thought with all that was left of strength and will. At the far reach of the next bruising drenching wave, he managed to jam his long claws into a crack in the rock and there to brace himself. The white water sucked and tugged. He felt himself weakening so he dug deeper. A claw broke then another but, of a sudden; he was free and almost too dazed to move with necessary haste toward the fearsome, watchful males. Unevenly, then, because of the keen hurt to his left fore-flipper, he made his bid for life. Closer, closer to the community of males he hobbled until he was almost there. A big, brown male shifted a little, making room in the shield-wall of bodies. Panting, near the end of strength and courage, fresh heart was gleaned from that small gesture.

Trembling, he came into the offered gap. He collapsed and, despite the horrors of the wave action and the drama of the magisterial males, tumbled over a precipice unseen into the healing oblivion of merciful sleep.

Again, but with less effort, he came to this old place of sanctuary where, perhaps, the spirit of all he had it in him to become had been truly wakened. This time, huge bodies shuffled more readily to yield space to the wild-looking seal. He did not reward them. This time, while he slept, he dreamed uncomfortable, haunted dreams. He gave battle to demons and, as he fought, he thrashed about, groaned and roared, so that the others slept but, fitfully, wondering at the company they kept.

***

Mornalas relaxed again very soon after rolling herself under the consuming waters close behind Tyrian. Meinek's ire, even when it was just the noisy business of bellowed triumph, was directed exclusively against his rivals, be they imagined or real. Normally, no female trembled at his size or proximity for with them he was unfailingly courteous. The conflict destroyed all hope of restfulness. The site was emptied of females and males alike; only Meinek remained.

Something of her previous drowsiness remained upon Mornalas as she propelled herself vertically downward, parachuting all the way to the seabed. Slipping down through the water column, her heartbeat slowed and slowed until it reached a settled rate at six beats per minute.

Her drifting gaze was caught, held in passing, by the rays of turquoise flashes splaying over small, gleaming, honey-coloured mounds: the shells of blue-rayed limpets. They had quarried into and studded the stipes of the kelp. Reaching the bottom, she drifted in the bottom current as if performing some stately dance with the granite roots of the islet upon whose roof she had rested so recently. It was a slow progress, coiling languidly among waving fronds of kelp. Following the barely discernible sloping of the seabed she idled, her body silvering with air bubbles trapped in the hairs of her coat, down to a place of shorter algal turfs. The kelp forest thinned, then failed entirely. Here, the dominant colours ceased to be shades of brown. Now she cruised over shades of red, maroon, crushed blackberry stain. Deeper still, the waving was no longer of fronds, but the tiny feathery arms of interlinked brittle stars. Farther to seaward, sliding away from the roots of the islands and their living distractions, Mornalas lazily summoned the power of her hind parts. She drove away through a gap in the rocks, gracefully corkscrewing along before electing to continue upside down, scanning the shell-sand bottom.

As she went, she scanned automatically for tell-tale signs that a flatfish — a sole, perhaps — might lie under the shallowest camouflage of sand. Hoping to detect flatfish was a game she had played since she had disturbed the first fish, part-hidden in sand, not more than a day from the nursery site where she had entered the world. She loved glimpsing the first betraying trickle of sand that would initiate her stealthy hunt. She righted herself, feeling real hunger now, continuing her foraging glide. Her head was down. The long mystachial whiskers along her muzzle were stroking the pale-coloured shell-sand seabed, the very lightest of brushings, trickling along like the lightest of ploughs, searching for life much as an experienced safe-breaker listened for clicks announcing the discovery of the combination in an old black-and-white movie.

A massive, rusted bent iron sheet reared in front of her. A relic of a boat that had struck the Longships reef and foundered one hundred and forty-two years previously during a long January night; it startled her. Concentrating on her sand-ploughing, having forgotten previous such encounters, she veered away and upwards, up to the surface of the sunlit sea. Her heartbeat quickened on the ascent just as it had slowed at the outset.

Bursting through the almost magical surface layer that kept apart two mainly incompatible elements, she exhaled explosively, noisily. A lone gannet that had been gliding along with never a wing-beat just above the surface lost poise at the eruption and flapped five times before regaining it, gargling a brief gaggle of affronted words that were lost on the silver seal. Starting to breathe air again, her eyes followed the surf-bright, surf-white bird with the great wingspan and wingtips dipped in blackest ink. Rra'ik was far from home, not for the first time. Her young of this year was a bloated woolly hungry scrap in a nest decorated with old pieces of fishing net, high up on one of the Saltee Islands, off the south-east corner of Ireland.

In fact, seal and gannet had seen one another without registering the detail quite recently. Ten days previously, Mornalas had been resting with other seals on the Irish rocks just above the reach of the gentle sea swell, but far below the crowded slum of noisome nests and the cacophony of noise that spilled down from them. Rra'ik had glanced down at the small group of seals, noticing how well they blended with the rocks, now their coats had dried. It had been a fleeting perception made as she glided in toward the nest burdened with the latest offering of mackerel caught for her voracious chick. One seal, Mornalas, touched by her passing shadow, felt the passing scrutiny and glanced up. A fleeting moment for seal and gannet, both, unremembered in a life of memories that existed without signifying.

The Mornalas who noticed Rra'ik was hardly recognisable as the creature of ten days since. She was wet, sleek and casually lithe where the other Mornalas might have passed for a fat stranded slug of a thing, dressed warmly in the padded velvet of her dryness. This Mornalas sparkled with life where the other might have been but one more wreck on some lonely shore.

Hunger.

The growing familiarity of the movements of her unborn young.

Joy of this sea life, under the summer sun.

Exhaling one last time, she peeled over and lazed downward again from the skylight to waters growing darker the deeper she drove. Southward she ran, with the tide, foraging casually without success over great sparkling deserts of shell-sand. Too deep to leave a shadow telling a tale of her passing, she surfaced only with the occasional compelling need to take breaths. Down below, all breathing stilled, her heart followed its familiar rhythm. It slowed quickly, then more slowly, before finally settling at six beats per minute. That whispered, sepulchral rhythm fitted well the deep glooms of the depths.

Her senses matched her heartbeat. Her entire way of sensing the depths differed from the way she saw the world from the surface. It was as if all her senses fused into some marvellous Rubik radar. It was not primarily about what she saw but what she sensed, all flowing in through the several stations of cupped whiskers along her muzzle, the few erect whiskers above her eyes and the pair at the centre of her snout.

As a seal pup, there had never been another seal, not even her mother, to teach her how to swim, hunt, make a map of the world or locate other seals. There had been no booklet explaining how to be a seal: the when, where, how and why of anything. There had been perilous adventures, experiment and — now and then — the grace of good luck, especially during the first year. As for all seals, survival had been her Grail during the hungry, weary, learning and often painful odyssey of that first year.

Now, in the ninth year of her life, she was soon to give birth to this fifth pup.

Amid so much that was wonderful, the most wondrous aspect to her own self was her whiskery world. She loved the way she could feel the void, locating and tracking the invisible, able to discern where fish had been fifteen minutes before and so embark on the age-old pursuit. She loved the marvel of sensing the world and all life down here in its multiplicity of dimensions.

Mornalas surfaced once more; this time, in white water piling over the Runnelstone Reef, more than a kilometre off Porthgwarra. She did not know — it was not her own language — that, many centuries since, the reef and its emergent low water stone had been named for the seals by people using a Celtic language closely akin to Welsh.

The seal reef was extensive. Not far below the surface spread the roof of a rocky plateau bisected by many steep-sided gullies wide enough to allow for exploration. Here, all about, she could feel the ocean thrumming with life. She was in precisely the place where the Atlantic divides to become the channels that run eastward along the Cornish coasts, north and south.

A short distance to the east, she could see a flotilla of five cove-boats working the inshore waters. They had come around from the little fishing haven of Penberth, poles set in diagonals to left and right, trailing lines for bass. On the stern of one boat, she made out the name *Grey Seal*, but the words meant nothing to her. While she watched, a man in the nearest boat called across the water to the skipper of the *Grey Seal*, pointing toward the sleek silvery head gazing their way from a place now slightly south of where the ocean divided. The fisherman turned, shading his eyes. Seeing her, he raised an arm in friendly salute.

Heedless, Mornalas approached them gradually, working along the roof of the plateau, but surfacing every time a little closer to the small fleet. She had gullies to explore. Brushing by below the holdfasts of the kelp forest, she tested the walls of those narrow, dark places the fishermen had worked over for so many years without ever seeing them. It proved to be a bad time for fish relying on camouflage. Several startled blennies were swallowed. Several congers remained prudently still and hidden in their lairs.

One huge conger did not trouble to hide. He was grown to an age and size beyond fear of any seal. He was alive, despite the scars along his scale-less grey body that showed the interest seals had taken in him in earlier times. Moreover, despite all those scars, he knew the taste of seal pup. Now, he noticed the movement of Mornalas outside the coiled, sea-sculpted boat iron that partly-concealed him on the plateau. He watched her awareness of him flicker on and, out of all the long years of his learning, now refined to cunning, he sensed the mood of her. She sought no life-or-death combat. Here was a seal restless with the young he sensed in her; hungry but not famished.

Guarn was his name. He was over one hundred years old and he knew Death had forgotten him. He was the horror of the gullies, the breaker of fish hooks; the doom of the unwary. Watching her, glancing back at him with disinterested, fearless curiosity, he wondered where she might give birth to the young one. They took long to learn the ways of the sea, he had learned. They grew hungry during autumn and winter storms, losing co-ordination, losing strength, losing the sense — so dangerous in their elders — of the water-world about them. They would pass his way, weary, alone, maybe injured; too weak to put up much of a struggle in the end.

Guarn guessed right. Mornalas saw the size and strength of him and gave no thought to challenging such a monster in his lair. Neither did the memory of him linger for, five dives and half an hour later, her radar picked up the distant movement of a large shoal of fish to seaward. This was the thrilling signal she had been seeking: Pollack. Moving along in the far distance in travelling rather than hunting mode just above the bottom, she locked on to their position. She swerved lazily to adopt an intercepting course, but careful to generate no excitement that might communicate itself to her targets.

Fish had their own marvellous awareness of what was going on about them, their own counter-measures available to help them evade the lethal stalkers.

She came nine more times to the surface to breathe the breaths she needed to replenish essential oxygen supplies in her blood. She was hoping they would continue to head toward the pink float she had first glimpsed some minutes before. She planned to use the line below the buoy as a form of scant cover to conceal her final descent to the bottom, and in that she was successful. Nothing indicated the shoal was aware of her proximity.

Slowly, her speed increased with the apparently leisurely flexion of her hind flippers and the hind half of her body. The increase in speed was deliberately gradual. Now she could see what she pursued, dimly: distant, silver glimmerings. She mastered the desire to accelerate a third time, maintaining a speed and angle of approach almost directly behind and below the shoal. Very soon, now, she knew they must glimpse or sense her.

Now! The evolution of all her senses locked on to the one particularly large pollack that had taken her attention. The few whiskers above both her eyes bristled and, like the sights of a gun, linked with the two on the bridge of her snout and those clustered around her muzzle. The large fish became huge and she knew herself close enough to accelerate. Too late, the shoal was scattering in all directions. The marked fish scattered, too, not knowing its plight. It was as if, having locked on to her prey, she had become of one mind with it. Other fish, closer to the tail of the glimmering column, were barged in passing by Mornalas, but she gave them no thought. Her mouth opened, then snapped shut on the pollack that had been in her sights and already she was beginning to swerve away upwards toward the surface and the light when she ran into a huge spider's web.

Startled, not yet alarmed, she strained onward and upward, and when that did not break the light constraint, she surged more fiercely; and found it was to no avail.

She paused, became entirely still, trying to read her accelerated, panicked senses and discover what had happened. The pollack, broken in two halves, dropped unnoticed from her jaws. Vibrations faintly registered around her neck, causing her to scan left and then right. In so doing, she became aware that all around her, pollack were behaving strangely. Perhaps due to the shock of the event, her sensory world had shrunk to her immediate locality. There, she found she could make out glimmerings that were not pollack but strands of fine, plastic fishing net. Dread overran her and strength gushed from her.

Primordial fear, such as she had never felt in all the years of her life, possessed her now. She knew the purpose and peril of nets. Had she not taken fish trapped in them in her time? She recognised the lethal danger into which she had blundered. These were monstrous things deployed from fishing boats to catch everything: fish and crabs, coral, seals and porpoises. Everything died; this she had learned.

Bottom set nets, such as these, she had seen often enough. It was impossible not to, in Cornish waters. Always, she had been wary approaching or cruising alongside them, knowing the necessity. True, there were often rays or pollack to be burgled from them, but soon after her departure from her nursery site she had found a seal caught in a net such as this. It had seemed large, though perhaps it was only two years old. It had been a shock to see it held there, upright in the gloom, unnaturally still, the meshes cutting into his neck. He had seemed so alien in death.

She had seen nets enough, in her home waters and farther off, in some of the renowned sea areas named daily during radio shipping forecasts. In some areas, they were hard to avoid, here more than anywhere. It was as if every piece of seabed was covered with static trammel or tangle nets. Where they were absent, larger boats using heavy gear destroyed the seabed flora and fauna as well as the benthic environment, even out to the edge of the Continental Shelf, with bottom trawls, but Mornalas gave them no thought.

She knew which frontier she had reached in her own self.

She did not wonder whether her own unborn young had any sense of it; although, the little creature was now as vivid in her mind's eye as had been the pollack she had caught the moment before the world changed.

She knew what she had to do. Employing every last atom of her strength, looking to the sunlit surface of the quiet sea above her, she accelerated toward it.

The net was much, much heavier than she had assumed. Nine days had passed since it had been winched to the surface and checked. The skipper had left it set while hand-lining for mackerel and the premium prices they fetched, but the force in Mornalas was as blind as her spirit was strong. She drove past the first shock of resistance, the second, the third, when she felt something snap. In that moment, she could not tell whether it had been part of her skin, something in her heart or even the net itself. Her whole being was given to the blind drive for life, up to the light and the saving air. She must not falter. She knew she had but one chance. If anything, she had to find more strength and then more, beyond the possible. Something agelessly ancient inside her knew she was taking the only chance there would ever be.

Life itself was reduced to improbable slow motion, real or imagined. Something else snapped, snapped again, lurched, snapped some more, all in a dance of rainbow coloured specks of light. Was this death? Were the specks of light the specks of her own departing life; the life of her pup so nearly born; going out from her to be re-absorbed into the Universe? It was the only thought registering in her primordial miasma of effort. Out of her almost dream state of being, she felt the last constraining meshes snap without knowing what it meant for her. She flared on upward to the light — upward, through the surface layer of the sea, entirely clear of the water; unexpectedly reprieved. A strained growl escaped her, unlike any sound she had made before; hardly of triumph. Her cry was the tail end of the greatest exertion of her life, uttered even as the last of her power leached away.

She crashed back down into the sea.

It took her a long time to recover her bearings. The little essential tasks that needed be addressed were performed automatically. She rested at the surface, limp, drifting with the current, eyes open but unseeing. As the short hairs of her face dried, she began to feel again the warmth of the sun but her mind remained numb with shock and fear. She feared she might be broken beyond repair. Small wavelets slapped her face and once, as she flinched slightly, with a shock of fear she saw the return of the coloured specks of light somewhere out of the uttermost corner of her eye.

It was only a very small hook, but it drew her back to the moment. She glanced sideways, again just making out the specks. They seemed real but, no matter how hard she tried, she could not make them materialise properly. Looking in the other direction: yes, they were there, too.

Exhausted, she drifted and drowsed, snout pointed toward the blue sky, not yet feeling any return of strength, neither of reality. She did not stir even when the white-painted passenger ferry *Scillonian III* passed by close to the black and yellow painted Runnelstone Buoy where it moaned as it rocked on the swell. That drear music had enlivened many a misty winter's evening in Porthgwarra homes.

***

The rails of *Scillonian III* were crowded with passengers all watching skimming shearwaters or the famous landmarks around the Land's End. Soon, not far beyond the Runnelstone Buoy, they would see specks of people wandering about the open-air Minack theatre, cut into cliff slopes above one of the finest bays among all the fine bays of the world. Already, local people among the passengers were naming the Land's End coves when a child cried out and pointed a compelling finger. Immediately, a battery of binoculars was trained on what he had been quickest to identify. There was a swell of comment, of excitement.

Among the people enjoying the late afternoon sunlight on the top deck, Amaury Valneuve had spent the trip enjoying seeing everything other than seals. There had been the wave-mirroring, narcissistic passage of shearwaters, the glorious javelin-plunges of surf-bright gannets. There had been distant glimpses not far beyond the Eastern Rocks of a boisterous party of common dolphins, gannets plummeting into the sea amongst scything dorsal fins as they conducted their own joyous, ferocious hunt. Now, with a rueful smile that was also dutiful, he glanced about him. So dense was the crowd of people trying to glimpse the seal the child had discovered that the ferry was tilting over noticeably to port. He was not going to see it unless he could find a high point, so he clambered up to a conveniently adjacent part of the superstructure at the end of the row of seats.

Below him, an elderly couple who had remained attached like clams to their hard-won seats glanced up at him with nervousness and some irritation. They were clearly not convinced it was allowed, or that they were entirely safe.

He trained his binoculars on the small speck in the sea.

"Is it a seal? There is something strange about it! What's wrong with it?" someone cried.

Amaury did not at first recognise the peculiarity, being more than anything surprised that she was so close, seemingly indifferent to the passage of the white ship. He focussed. Yes, it was a silvery female with beautiful black markings along her neck, appearing and disappearing as she bobbed up and down with the swell; sleeping. Sated after feeding, he supposed casually? One marking caught his attention, on the left side of her neck. It looked like an inverted number 'seven' except that it had two horizontal bars at the bottom rather than the one. He had seen many patterns on the necks of the thousands of seals he had monitored and, as ever, this one would be unique. The detail was registered. If he saw her again, he would recognise her.

So well-schooled was his eye to identify the sex and age of any seal, to scan for patterns, that he failed to notice the fine shawl of monofilament fishing net she had acquired at the earlier hour. He failed to make out the deep, strangling indentation in the profile of her neck. Indeed, for the most part, it was hidden below the swell. It was only while his binoculars lingered that a wave larger than the others lifted her before draining away so fast that the greater length of her neck was exposed. Sunlight glinted on the deadly plastic strands dangling there. He winced.

When he ceased to watch her, she was so far distant that all detail was lost from the silhouette of her. He squatted down on the iron-based eminence where he perched like some enormous gull. Drawing a notebook from his pocket, he sketched the outline of the seal, detailing the inverted, double-topped seven and then the strands of net. At the top of the page, he added the date, time, location and a few notes about sea and weather condition. 'Viewed from the *Scillonian,* 18:25, at a minimum distance of sixty metres; homeward bound.'

Having eased his way back down to the deck without further disturbing the elderly couple, he made his way back to the largely abandoned seaward rails of the ship. He was wondering whether he might chance upon the netted female at one of the seal nursery sites he would be monitoring during the impending breeding season and, if he did, would he be able to do anything to relieve her of the cruel shawl?

It was a continuing problem. He had met such seals before and nearly always failed to help them — or to help the adults, for they were too powerful for a solitary man to constrain. A couple of immatures he had managed to cut free of nooses cutting deeply into their neck blubber. It was the unexpected strength and agility of seals that was the biggest problem, along with their ability to telescope their necks at will. At close quarters, there was nothing playful or winning about a seal desperate to reach the sea. At such times, reality was raw snarling power, the driving strength of the heaviest wild mammal breeding ashore in the British Isles. He grinned, remembering the time he and a friend had struggled to release a small, juvenile seal they had discovered in one of the sea caves. They achieved a rare happy outcome but had recognised the need, thereafter, to experiment with other methods.

It was a plan overtaken by events, crowded out by the onward flow of life. Exasperated by his inaction, he was still thinking about how it might be done while *Scillonian III* ran across Mount's Bay and came very slowly in alongside the North Pier at Penzance. Mooring ropes were cast ashore, taken in hand and walked to be secured around iron bollards while the white ship edged closer to the quayside. During the final slow, careful movements, he scanned the waiting crowd, remembering the times when Isobel Trevenna used to stand on top of the wall, her long dark hair constrained into beribboned braids wrapped and pinned around her crown. He remembered, especially, a long blue armless dress and the red T-shirt that she used to wear underneath it — coloured gaily as a gallipot, he had suggested appreciatively. It was not her usual style but she had dressed to be noticed by someone and, as it turned out, to be remembered.

It was a warm memory, though time had done its worst with them. They had struggled valiantly with the lack of money in their lives and what that did and did not translate into. In the end, recognising he was not going to give up his studies, which she knew were also a way of life, they had strayed from love and, somewhere along the way, been scattered on the busy winds of what might have been.

Not long thereafter, in a terraced road leading up from the sea, he unloaded his rucksack and carrier bag into his reliable old VW campervan. He found it randomly decorated with gull compliments that also betrayed how long it had been standing there unused. The small task done, he returned slowly to the quay to collect the wave ski he used for island-hopping from seal haunt to seal haunt. This more awkward piece of luggage he carried on one shoulder to its customary resting place on the roof rack.

He was smiling and relaxed as he settled behind the wheel, having it in mind to buy a vanilla ice cream from Jelbert's. After making the short drive and the small, necessary purchase, he strolled seaward over the humped bridge toward Newlyn harbour. As he idled along, he quarried out of the tub small spoons heaped with familiar vanilla ice cream, transferring them to where they belonged. While he walked, never far from his feet, busily purposeful it seemed on the dressed granite blocks at the edge of the quay, a few seemingly fearless turnstones pattered. Despite the lack of stones to turn, it was their habit, these being town turnstones rather than the beach turnstones who pattered just along the coast across sands behind the sea walls at Mousehole. Overhead, harbour gulls cried as they wheeled. Below them, lined along the quayside, rusty-looking beam trawlers rested placidly on still waters at their moorings. About them, the early evening air remained warm though the sun had disappeared behind Chun hill and its terraced rampart of residences by now. Well-fed cats abandoned recently-shaded ledges that had been sunny for the greater part of the day but the mice failed to tremble.

Afterwards, the dusty VW strained up Chun Hill meandering westward toward the low sun. He drove slowly, simply happy to be home, soaking up its atmosphere. At peace with the world, he was in no hurry to be going anywhere. He was precisely where he wanted to be.

In another part of his mind, he was closing another summery Scilly chapter. It had been a good trip, sunny, the seas mainly quietly allowing. He had been able to paddle out to the seal islands every day. A couple of the boatmen had been generous to him; the usual ones. They had carried him close to all the most distant places, notably the outer stones of the Western Rocks. In return, he had given commentaries on wildlife and what he knew of histories of the more remote islands. In a way, those were the best times. It was always good to feel less than a total stranger. It was the same every Wednesday evening, when he rented the Masonic Hall to give illustrated talks about seals and other island wildlife. At such times, he forgot the sense of being the lone wolf circumstance seemed to want him to be.

He had found no grey seal pups. He had been surprised to have found none by the time his visit concluded at the end of August, having been discovering pups being born since May along the Cornwall coasts in all the predictable places. Of course, they were all born in sea caves... he had discovered the first pups of every season were born, unfailingly, in the sea caves. On Scilly, natal sites seemed to be uninhabited islands; exclusively.

There were very few sea caves on Scilly, only one was reckoned to be a seal cave. That site, understandably, remained yet unconfirmed. It was situated at — under — Menawethan. It was said to be accessible to seals via a submerged entrance. Various unconnected people had described hearing the cries of seal pups filtering through cracks in the granite from some presumed cave in the heart of the island. Divers had described to him a claustrophobic, seal-shaped passage leading into the 'possible' cavern. The thought of it haunted him. He could not help but wonder, did he venture into that seal-shaped passageway, what would happen if he came face to face with the battering ram any emerging seal must inevitably be? He knew it was something he would never attempt.

He followed the familiar road home, shadowing the mainly bare rim of West Penwith by way of bends above and below Lamorna, the ancient battlefield and the dancing stones beyond, ancient roadside stones bearing crosses or a human figure fashioned from granite long ago, by the turnings to the small villages of Penberth, Treen and Porthcurno, before coming between the winter cauliflower fields toward lovely Porthgwarra, remote but so well-known to bird-watchers.

He was bound for the farm cottage where he lived as a tenant.

Handsome hens and strong-thighed cockerels with glorious golden or iridescent-green mantles above gaudy plumage scattered as he turned into the dusty farmyard. A small, familiar, black and white border collie bitch danced out, harrying the car but not barking until it drew to a standstill just under the cover of the barn roof. He was tolerant when Tess leapt up, committing affectionate importunities, and while strolling across the farmyard and down the green lane. The hedges were tall, spangled with blackberries, bryony, ivy tangles, sloes, butterflies, dragonflies and the flowers of late summer, among which figured prominently the striking yellow spires of common toadflax. Tess flushed a skulking cock pheasant to a clatter of frosted wings from the green shadows, gliding beyond the hedge when certain he was no longer pursued.

Swallows dressed in finest dark blue satin were swooping low over the fields on the far side of the hedges, chirruping now and then, just as they had been doing before he departed. They wove mazy aerial ways between the grazing South Devon crosses, a herd of bullocks that would be sold on before long to someone farming richer ground farther up the line. A very low-flying swallow came down the dusty lane, circling him twice as if to spin invisible thread around his ankles. As it flowed along, he could make out every detail of the lovely body, especially the array of white specks near the base of the needle-forked tail. He remembered them making a specialty of doing this sort of thing out on the football pitch on St Mary's.

It was a happy way to return home. The small cottage lay ahead, about fifty metres short of where the lane came to an end. No paint coloured the granite but encrustations of deep yellow *Xanthoria parietina* lichen prettily blotched the old slate roof while the granite walls supporting it carried a less intense, but more flourishing pale green bearding of a more florescent lichen: *Ramalina siliquosa*.

The cottage was a plain, rectangular place, with four window frames painted white — two up, two down — a faded lovage-green door between the two downstairs windows. The seaward windows with the main door faced south-westward to Lizard Point and another singular lighthouse. The long line of the peninsular was clearly picked out along the horizon. In another direction, the Isles of Scilly stood so clear against the setting sun he could even pick out the trees growing there by eye.

Once, the family of the last farm labourer had called the cottage home. Now, in the brave new world that often made no sense, there were no permanent labourers working on the farm.

A small garden was neatly hemmed in by low dry-stone walls that yet allowed the evocative views. Inside their perimeter, he had planted a mixed hedge of blackthorn and hawthorn that would take many years to mature — something he would never see. Closing the sturdy wooden gate behind him, he walked around the house to the ocean door, as he called it. Along that side of the cottage, last summer he had built a veranda substantial enough to support an outside table off which breakfast or supper could be taken. Already it seemed it had been there forever, so much use had it seen.

Once settled in, he made a small supper whose constituent parts he had bought on St Mary's and which now he ate at the table on the veranda. It was a reflective time for him, now that his interesting adventure was done. Here he had begun the greater adventure, more than anything for the sheer romance of seeing whether a real life, worth the name, might be made at the very edge of the world. He had never imagined quite how much romance really might be awaiting him.

Within weeks of arrival, to his enormous surprise, the seal scientist he admired above all others had invited him to work on a seal photo-identification project up at the University of St Andrews. Even though it was only a tiny three-month contract, he had felt enormously buoyed at having been noticed.

Amaury was captivated by the brilliance and potential of the programme. It was made possible because every grey seal has a pattern of pelage markings unique as a human finger-print. In females, this was represented by a pattern of black markings of all shapes and sizes against a white, creamy or rust-coloured background — or even grey, sometimes, in the case of their dorsal surfaces. Conversely in males, typically they were without a discernible pattern except for maybe a very few white markings on a dark background; but some had scarring and all had snouts that varied marvellously in shape.

Stripped to essentials, it was based on taking quality photographs of, at least, the head, neck and chest of grey seals — the parts that always showed whether they were in the water or ashore. Especially when shared, these allowed initial insights to be made into seal life histories in a way that had been, previously, almost impossible.

With high hopes, returning from Scotland, he invested a substantial part of the money he had saved from the project into the best quality photographic tools he could afford.

Not long afterwards, his mentor, well acquainted with the ambition of his protégé, travelled south, making a surprise visit. He stayed for three nights in the cottage. Together, they strayed down to the seal caves or across to high headlands overlooking the several seal sites in the locality. There, they watched, silent for the most part.

At evening, there had been much talk, thinking aloud, between the man who had done absolutely everything and was peerless in his field and the younger, more naïve, man in love with every fragment of the life he lived while studying the seals.

On the last evening, his mentor had spoken of the possible.

"Make yourself an expert in the seals of the Land's End. Stay small for now. Follow them everywhere, every day. Discover which terrestrial and inshore aquatic sites they use — the important ones but also the lone-star places. Monitor them around the entire year. Never think you know it all because they are individualistic and will surprise you. Monitor a sequence of breeding seasons, major as far as possible on the identity of the participants, including the moulted pups. Find out where they moult, when, in what numbers, with what sex ratio. Go to the local haul-out sites and take good photographs there.

"Be a monk for two, three years, but before you begin any fieldwork, send the methods you plan to use to me. I will review them and send them right back, knowing how eager you are to begin. But whatever you do, whether as a naturalist or scientist remember: everything you do must be repeatable and comparable. Whatever you read about seals, no matter how trivial it may seem at the time, always write down the title of the paper or book, the author, the year of publication, the name of the publisher. Make sure you record everything you do and why you are doing it. Be truthful. Never try to bend what you observe to make it fit what you want to claim, or what you want to feel, is happening. Your mission is to explain — justify — everything you assert about everything. Those references must be in your journals ready to be dusted off, and ready to back up every reference you make to the work of others as well your own discoveries."

That advice became his guiding star. What he remembered he wrote down on sheets of paper he pinned to the board above his uncluttered desk.

That had been four years previously.

He had played the monk, learned from his improvised, teach-yourself-seals course conducted around the exposed, unsafe places of the entire Land's End peninsular. He had come to know the sea caves they used, the rocky haul-out sites, the inshore water resting places, the occasionally used places and he had come to recognise where human pressures threatened them. He acquired fluency, presenting slide shows at localities around the West Country and even in selling postcards to supplement his irregular church-mouse earnings. He learned to use a sound recording unit to such effect that he had created a regular niche on a Radio Cornwall show, thanks to the kindness and interest of the presenter. In turn, regional television took an interest, and a bare sufficiency of monetary crumbs was generated.

Elsewhere, since he had been a teenager and through his university years, he had worked through the summer holidays as a deck-hand on pleasure boats in Devonshire, on the River Dart; more recently, having secured his skipper's ticket, he had persuaded the family company to let him run wildlife cruises. The income was poor but was the largest component of his annual earnings.

Sitting alone under the brightening stars above the brightening Morse flashes of the famous lighthouses, Amaury was aware a condition of happiness existed in him. Inside his skin, relaxed, he felt very well. He listened to the ocean whisper.

***

For a few days of peaceful weather and attendant quiet seas, Mornalas remained troubled by the dance of bright sparks flickering perpetually just beyond the edges of her vision. The maddening flickering ceased only when she dared return to hunting mode, powering along over the floor of the sea; but this new anxiety made her life a misery. All her natural and lifelong self-confidence in what she was and, crucially, her faith in her own natural instincts was in tatters.

Now, even as she closed in on the fish, she needed to hunt down to assuage the hunger of her own self and the pup who seemed to draw ever more heavily on her reserves, the nightmare-anxiety repeated itself. It was a nightmare of entanglement in an invisible web with the lightest of initial touches; that lightest touch then intensified to the point of cruel partial suffocation she was suffering every time she hauled out seeking rest on the rocks. It made for restlessness, continual movement. It disturbed the seals around her, causing them to shuffle away leaving her isolated on the outermost fringe of their assemblies.

At this horrible time, the fact she continued to hunt successfully, over-riding haunting fears and self-doubt, was entirely down to the mother in her. Beset by anxieties, upset and traumatised, she never realised just how trustful of her own instincts she did indeed remain.

The first four pups she had borne had all been a pleasure for her. Whatever the sea conditions, whatever the company she found herself in on the nursery beaches, whatever the nature of her pup — and they had all seemed different to her — she had relished each experience. They allowed her to exercise something of her natural, unique self, not apparent during the remainder of the year. Each time, with the pup somewhere nearby, somewhere safe, she found herself enjoying a unique tranquillity of inner being

Why?

She brought the latest fish to the surface held crossways in her mouth. It was a ling, large as a college scarf and not unlike one as seen by the pair of walkers noticing her from the cliff-top, forgetful of the hive of jackdaws swarming noisily in the airs above. The seal seemed to be 'standing' upright just off the headland; the power of the water movement was not disturbing her.

Despite everything, would the tranquillity return this year, or had she experienced some emotional rock-fall in the core of herself? Was she still Mornalas or had she become something other, something diminished?

Her imagination snagged on rockfalls, Mornalas remembered vividly that about thirty miles along the coast, beyond a shallow, sandy-bottomed bay beloved of bottlenose dolphins, lay a succession of headlands. The holes in the cliffs between them had been popular with seals for as long as they had swum in local seas. For a long time, this was a remote place, just a few threads of fishermen's paths leading down to favoured headland fishing places. At the end of a day's labour, working men would tramp down there for a spot of night fishing; a spot of peace and room to breathe without being beholden to any other. She wondered whether she might take refuge there, now.

There were few safe ways down to the beaches between the headlands except by landing from a boat. Here, the savage peace of the Cornish shore remained yet secure against human intrusion. However, there was another tribe of humans than the solitary anglers who knew all the nooks and crannies of this coast. These were the local children.

Through the long years until the end of the Second World War, little gangs of them explored the old coastal mining country, delving into great, overgrown holes in this ground. They came from as far afield as St Ives, Hayle and Camborne, running wild, doing things that would have terrified their unwitting parents even in those more virile times. Groups of brothers, sisters, cousins and friends from St Ives had a favourite place: the Adit. It had served for a drain from a watery clifftop mine before it fell into disuse.

In 1929, a girl of nine and her brother, two years older, entered that dark mole-run with two torches. Having served his time among a slightly earlier group of young explorers, their oldest brother had warned them specifically against seeking out this place, blissfully heedless that he would have been as fascinated by the prospect of it as they showed themselves to be on their very next trip. Moths to the flame, they had the feral-child instinct to follow the thread of a track near the cliff edge to the hole in the ground that their brother had described. They took some rope with them, entering the hole without initial enthusiasm but growing in confidence as they worked their way along the secret tunnel by torchlight. They progressed until they reached the hole in the floor of which they had been forewarned. Below them, unexpectedly clearly — it was a bright day — they could make out the jumble of massive boulders on the floor of the great sea cave that they knew ran deeper still into the cliff.

Anchored to a stake driven deeply into the adit floor, a rope used by earlier explorers including their eldest brother, dangled to the cave floor. Its length was marked by a series of knots designed to help the climber shin back up again.

To the horror of his sister, the boy decided to complete his adventure by descending into the cave. Rudely cutting short her protests, he drew up the rope, took a strong handhold just above the highest knot and simply made a dare-devil drop into space over the lip of the hole. Hardly daring to look, the little girl opened small fingers that had automatically covered her eyes and watched with horrified admiration as he shinned down to the boulders below.

There, he scanned about him by the light of his small torch whose scant light was totally gobbled up by the darkness and shouted: "Wow! It goes a long way in; really long. It has huge entrances. They're miles away. I think I'll explore to the back. Someone might have stowed treasure here. You wait there."

"Davie; don't go. It's dangerous. There might be creatures of the dark or even dead men." Bedtime stories had, in her case, sometimes been chosen more for the pleasure of the reader than his impressionable daughter.

More alarmed by the warning than he cared to admit, Davie retorted hotly: "You just shut up. I'm going and that's…"

He never finished the sentence. To their ears, simultaneously, came the prolonged unearthly, mournful moan. Had they been sitting at home, it might have sounded more like nature itself making choral music, but they were very young, far from home and farther still from safety. All of a sudden, the boy peering up from the cave floor was no longer the hero of the adventure books he liked to read. He was just a small, frightened boy with a white face and legs that had started to tremble uncontrollably.

The moaning continued. A second voice swelled sounds that were being amplified by the cave acoustics. It was supported by a percussive sound, faint at first but growing louder as it drew closer. It was a slapping sound, as if something wet was making its way out of the deep interior of the cave.

"God! What shall I do, Jenny? Oh God!"

"Listen." Suddenly their worlds switched, everything changed between them: "It can't be a monster. They don't exist. Mother is always insisting on that. Flash the torch around you and climb up on the highest rock."

Despite his terror, he managed to do as she bade without dropping the torch, to which he clung tightly as his hope of continuing life. He wanted to whimper with fear as the slappings of the creatures drew closer but dared not, for fear of betraying his position — as if it had not been betrayed already by his shouted conversation with his sister and the flashing of his tiny light.

In among the slappings, there were occasional quite savage growls.

Up above, in a frenzy of fear for her stupid brother, Jenny peered down, eyes wide, as the dim forms of the seals went humping, barging by below. One even paused and, apparently sensing her wide-eyed scrutiny, looked up to the hole in the ceiling and its frail lifeline of knotted rope. Her stillness interrupted the flow of seal bodies. Another seal started to clamber over her back, causing her to challenge the impropriety with an open-mouthed snarl before resuming her breathless trek to the safety of the sea, where all fear of intruders could be irradiated.

In the wake of the seals came a silence scented with fish, but unbelievably soothing. It was a long silence, broken by the movement of a lone seal from the back of the cave. His eyes adapted by now to a darkness that was far from entire. Davie made out its smaller form, humping and squirming over rocks, between gaps, splashing noisily through shallow pools.

He waited for quite a long time after it had passed before daring to move. It was time well-spent, steadying his heart, stilling his trembling. There was nothing to be done about his dry throat. He waited until after he heard the laggard seal follow its companions into the sea, lapping at the huge boulders some twenty metres inside the twin entrances one hundred metres from where he stood.

Relieved to have been neither squashed nor spattered underneath the flow of monsters, Davie readily set aside thought of further exploration. Tucking the torch inside his cotton shirt, he began to shin up the rope. He climbed slowly, puffing with exertion. Even as he laboured upwards, a little thought yammered at the back of his head, reminding him he had surrendered most of his strength to the terrors of the dark, even if they did not seem quite so terrible, now the seals had gone crashing into the sea and the sunlight beyond.

Close to the top, the rope rested taut against the small overhang. He had got around the problem earlier without even noticing it by leaping into space. The jolt as the rope had become still had almost broken his grip, but he had made no mention of it to his sister. Now, coming as high as the rope allowed, just short of being level with the floor of the adit, he stopped. He stopped for at least five minutes, the sweat standing out cold on his brow, sharing a curt, not entirely friendly, conversation with his little sister. Having steadied his nerve while he was on the cave floor facing the avalanche of huge, slapping, moaning monsters, she seemed to have developed a new habit of telling him what to do.

At length, in turn, she lost patience with her block-headed brother and shouted shrilly: "Either go down and rest your feet on the first knot, or all the strength in your arms will seep out and then you'll never get up here. Just do it, stupid. Then, while you're there, I'll try to wedge my torch between the rope and the wall. When you have your strength back, you'll have to make a dash for it. Come up fast and grab this stub of rope tied to the top bit. I'll make a loop for you with a knot that won't slip. I'll catch your free hand and you'll make it."

Incredibly, her idea worked, although the wedging torch was lost, dropping down among the boulders. Perhaps more improbably, he was grateful for what she had done. He never forgot it. Theirs was one sibling friendship that lasted the length of their lives.

That same cave and another dangling, knotted rope was the one known to Mornalas. Some seals like to sleep under the open sky with good views of anything that might approach. Others have a fondness for caves. Mornalas was one such and it was to the adit cave she sometimes returned after hunting adventures. This was especially so in early winter, when the adjacent sea area was her favourite recuperation ground, the place where she remembered how to hunt and feed after the starvation of the nursery period.

The sea caves of this coast were never overcrowded with adult seals. Adit cave was often a fair place to rest when south-westerlies were coursing in off the ocean. She did not know, but it was not instinct alone that brought her there. She had no way of knowing that the female seal who had paused amid the torrent of seals on that secret day so many decades ago in 1929 had been a maternal ancestor, nor that their association with these holes in the cliffs stretched far back into the glooms of long-forgotten history through their abiding blood-line.

But what she did look for, whenever she swam into that great chamber, was the ever-changing shape of its ceiling, caused by repeated crumblings of unstable rock. It troubled her to see each latest rock-fall wondering, as she did, if she might sense the imminence of such a fall, make good her escape and thereby escape the horror of a doomed living immurement. Of all the sea caves known to her around the Western Approaches, this was the most crumbly.

Little wonder that at the time of the greatest instability in her own life, she remembered adit cave with its rock-falls. Little wonder to her, but to the two people continuing to watch her from the clifftop, it would have been the greatest surprise to know the thoughts just then of the seal wearing the fishy college scarf.

***

As with Amaury aboard *Scillonian III*, it was only near the end of their interlude of observation that the woman cried out: "Oh look! It's got net cutting into its neck! The poor thing!"

It was very hard to see, but the man persevered. In time, he glimpsed it too, catching the light. They were left feeling frustratingly powerless. There was nothing they could do about it and there was nothing they could imagine anyone else doing.

The next evening, they visited a crowded pub in St Just to listen to some Celtic folk music performed by a collection of local musicians gathered around a large circular table. Being full up with what they had seen, they shouted the story of the strangled seal above the hubbub to the barman. When they were done, he nodded his head toward Amaury, who had just taken his place near the end of the bar, waiting to place his order.

Whenever he was free on a Monday night, which was usually, he came to enjoy this music and to meet with Harry Trevissett, who he regarded as the best naturalist he had ever met. Typically, he would arrive after they had begun to play and leave before the end, walking the long miles home for the pleasure of it or because that way he saved the petrol money.

Eager to do anything that might help the seal, overcoming reticence, the woman asked the barman to introduce them. That was how they came to pour out their tale to him. He teased out the essential details, especially the name of the headland where they had made their observations. It mortified them that they couldn't name it, but he had them describe it and recognised it readily enough.

***

While they talked, just outside the wave-break in Porth Ledden, at the bottom of the Kenidjack Valley below the pub, Mornalas bottled under the stars, upright and asleep just outside the wave break. Without knowing, she twitched restlessly all the while.

Despite the lack of surf exploding against the skirts of nearby Cape Cornwall, she was agitated and her breathing came in laboured gasps. She could feel the imminence of the birth of the pup she had carried, in one form or another, for almost the full year. Something in her was quickening in response to its great leap for life that she sensed was imminent inside her. They had lived as part of one another for so long that their harmony of sensation seemed entirely natural.

On the dark side of her outlook, the tightness of the shawl of netting, glittering with light even in the moonlight at the edges of her vision, was beginning to feel like the grip of death. It frightened and depressed her. It was ever-present, inescapable. The sounds of her own laboured breathing disturbed her.

Her thoughts blurred together erratically. In her stronger moments, she determined to give birth to this fifth pup and, if it was to be her last, to give to it all that was in her to give, a parting gift to the lovely life she had been allowed before she faced whatever must be faced. Strange it was to be having such thoughts when all life had flowed so easily, even happily, to the recent event of bizarre error.

Later in the night, on the ebbed tide, she swam to Longships. There, on the wet granite rocks, oftentimes she stretched, telescoping out her beautifully patterned neck to ease the continuous torment of it. It was the only way she could achieve brief ease, but the restlessness left her feeling haggard.

The other seals recognised her predicament and made space for her, recognising the decoration about her neck. She was neither the first nor last to be so encumbered. Hauled out closest to the sea though she was, Meinek, king of the Longships seals and terror of his rivals still lifted his head to sniff near her tail, just checking — as was his habit — whether she was in mating condition when he cruised by her resting place. He was not exclusively interested in her condition. All females were subjected to the same passing scrutiny, but he had not forgotten the pup she carried was his and that its time of birth had become imminent.

The next day, as the quiet, sunny conditions persisted, a female seal surfed up out of the sea close by Mornalas, causing her to come sharply to the alert. Irritation evaporated the moment she recognised Ithian. She telescoped her neck toward her old friend and sent her a feeling of pure warmth.

Ithian was a strange one. That is, she was strange insofar as she seemed to be unable or unwilling to have pups. She also seemed strange in that, being so dark, at first glance it was never immediately clear whether she was a male or female. They had first met just before the birth of Mornalas' firstborn. She had hauled herself out of white surf at the bottom of the cave sand hill. Careful to move in slow, short bursts, she had made her way up the sandy sea cave fairway to where Mornalas tossed and twitched, fearful of the imminent-unknown. Settling peaceably nearby, Ithian had started, quite softly, to sing. In fact, she had sung her to improbable sleep.

Later, when she wakened, the strange female was still close by, still singing softly. No other seals were present, but the atmosphere was totally altered. Instead of wrestling with flimsy demons, feeling pressures and anxieties associated with the unknown, she found herself bathed in a sense of security the like of which she had long since ceased to feel. She was reminded of the time when her own mother had extended her great body broadside on against the run of high tide surf during the first storm of her life, the scrap of her own self snug, safe and snoring behind that living bulwark.

It was a detail especially precious to her, one that flared up, now and then, in her dreams and, sometimes, even in drowsy and sun-drenched memory while basking on the summer rocks. Life had never been so safe since and she guessed it never could so be again. What did not occur to her was that perhaps it was the reason she drew so much pleasure from being a mother herself. Amid all the caring for the little pup, initially so helpless, she could leave that special, secret mark. She could leave behind her a sense of loving, caring warmth that, to her, meant as much as all the other important things in life put together.

Now, she turned in all her restlessness and distress to acknowledge the arrival of dark Ithian. Sleek, wet, dark and salt-stained, Ithian saw the shawl immediately. Moving close to Mornalas, closer than ever she had before, she leaned forward to sniff with greatest delicacy at the plastic strands; then she edged away again, giving breathing space to the stricken seal.

She saw how deeply wounded was Mornalas and was shocked by it. She had seen many shawls or bands of plastic caught around the necks of many seals. There were likely to be at least four entangled seals, sometimes many more, in every hundred using resting places such as this at any given time. Some survived, some dwindled and many died horrible unnoticed deaths, the mesh snagged on some inescapable underwater hook. The young ones suffered more than others because they lacked the strength to drive free of entanglement. Their under-developed lungs were inadequate to the task. If they did escape, the shawls they acquired inhibited their fledgling hunting efforts, helped tip them down the slope to starvation and death.

She saw nothing to inspire the hope that Mornalas could survive this.

She read very clearly the thoughts of the beautiful, free-spirited, silvery seal. She knew how urgently she craved to see her little one enter the world. She had recognised the same look in other female faces across the years.

Ithian?

Ithian glanced sideways, directly into the tortured eyes of Mornalas, startled to hear her name, though no sound had been made. It was a long time since she had heard her name articulated in such a way, and that she heard it uttered at all showed the extremis to which Mornalas had been driven in herself.

Grey seals do not talk. They sing, and when they do, it is one of the most evocative, soulful sounds in the entire natural world. That they do not talk is not because they cannot. Indeed, when they are very young, they are remarkably talkative. But once they leave the security of their first home, they are faced with the challenge to survive for a day, a week, a month; the first year. It is an enormous shock to be suddenly alone, hungry, perhaps famished and without safe havens. It is a shock experienced by most seals and means they learn, from the age of about four to seven weeks, to shut down systems such as speech just like Grimm's little mermaid, as an inherent part of learning the craft of survival.

Just as its heartbeat slows while it dives down to the seabed and begins a hunting quest along the bottom, or rests in immobile ambush, so other systems close. Perhaps at the nursery cave, there was a pool where a pup played with others using the same cave. Life was water chases, water dances; hiding, pouncing, threatening; enjoying sunlight, moonlight, the colours of the inter-tidal life growing on the cave walls; the scent of mother's milk, the sound of her voice as well as her comforting warmth and solicitude.

Afterwards, alone after this brief time of plenty, the vulnerable pup feels hunger, cold, incomprehension, fear of irritating larger seals, fear of the sea that it yearns for in its blood and disorientation. Cramped up inside itself, the pup learns to concentrate on whatever is essential to survival.

Silence becomes habitual.

"Ithian?"

"Mornalas?"

"Am I going to die?"

"We all die."

"Who are you?"

"I am your friend."

"I believe you were my friend before ever you knew me. Who are you?"

"I think you know what I am. I am the midwife seal. I try to help make everything right. I come to paint the atmosphere of the birthing places".

"But you do not come for everyone?"

"When welcome, I attend the time of firstborns. The first birth is often a frightening occasion. No-one has been shown the way, and wild seas have washed away all the marks from before."

"What of your own pups?"

The dark midwife seal stirred a little at her place of rest, lifting her head a little higher and turning her attention to the sea, to some distant point out there in the ocean darkness. Mornalas looked that way too, alert as her companion.

"I had a pup, long ago. I was not a good mother. That surprises you, I see. I was frightened and had no idea what to do. My pup failed and died. I was glad to escape from the nursery place. I made the greatest journey of my life, east toward the sunrise and then north until I reached the place of ice and long nights swept with veils of coloured light. It was lonely but beautiful. I was unhappy, I think. I did not like myself. Often, I was hungry.

"I meandered, without thinking where I was going, into another sea. The taste of everything there was very different; not nice, but I did not care. I became acquainted with snow, ice, wind and darkness. There was even a time when I had to keep open a hole in the ice into which I would slip to do what hunting needed to be done. I think that was the northernmost limit of my odyssey.

"Everything was stark and beautiful there. Some nights I saw the sky swept by great green and yellow swishing veils of dancing light, and one night, during such a dance, while lost in my visions, a huge white ghost-bear crept up and almost slew me. That was how I realised the stories we learn as we suckle our mother's milk are true, after all. The Ghost Bear of the Icefields really does exist. I felt the cool draught of air under the swish of his great paw as I dived into the black waters. Afterwards, I played cat and mouse for a long time, breathing when I dared, fearful that as I came up he would be there, waiting.

"After that drama, I decided to move closer to the edge of the ice. A big ice-breaking ship appeared soon thereafter, made it easy for me to cruise through the big lead it opened. I shared the ice places not only with seals of our own tribe but also with a tribe of very small seals — smaller even than those harbour seals so common along the coasts of Scotland and Ireland.

"They are like us — or like you — in quite a lot of ways. They are grey-coated, patterned with the same black markings as us on their backs, except their marks are often ringed with a lighter colour. They have tiny heads, unlike us, but when their pups are born, they are as white as ours. They have them at roughly the same time as us but instead of using rocky sea caves, as you have chosen to do, they use little snow-caves part-melted by the heat of their bodies, suckling them much longer than we do. It seems awfully risky to suckle them for so long, but they have survived this far... they must be doing something right.

"They were not unfriendly, but there was never much communication between us. We seemed to be interested in different worlds. Who knows; perhaps the truth was they feared me because of my size?

"Spring came, but I felt no stirring to depart. The snows melted, the icefields started to shrink, flowers sprang up in places where that great weight of ice had rested. The seals there spoke another language and there was an old one with the patience to teach it to me. Her teeth were worn down and she was quite thin. We hunted together and the fishing was good. I shared what I caught with her as I learned the new sounds and grew plump again.

"Ours was a strange friendship. Hi'umaa was her name. She was a wise one; very wise. She was forever singing. I breathed it all in because the magic of it coiled about me and belonged. I found myself imitating her, repeating some of the songs. I think I can explain it to you. As I sang one day, the whole world changed, like seeing one world out of one eye and another world out of the other one, and then there was just one vivid merged world seen by the two eyes of me!

"It was like hunting — that moment when something happens not because you will it, but simply because it happens. No longer are you following the silver stream of a shoal of fish, but just the one fish stands out, extraordinarily clear; from that moment, you are no longer on the trail of any fish. It is as if you have received from it all that its instincts make it. You know what will come next. It is a knowing deeper than knowing. It is a seal thing, I suppose. We don't really know much, do we?

"One moment, I was singing her song and the next, an entire chamber of my being illuminated inside me. The songs and all their words were there, arrayed and ready to be sung. They are still there, in her language and in mine. As if they had always been there, like the buried treasure for which those few humans come searching in our caves.

"I looked at Hi'umaa. I could see she knew what had happened. She said: 'You see how thin the differences between us can wear at times? It wears so thin that holes appear and things start leaking through! Welcome, Ithian seal singer.'"

Again, the dark midwife seal stirred, remembering where she was as well as those faraway places where she had been. It was the middle of the night. The great wheel of stars, the Milky Way that — to seals — is the Seals Strand and the bright moon were turning slowly, the way they did every night. Far off, she could just hear the fins of a pod of eleven bottlenose dolphins cutting through the surface waters, even as a twelfth leapt and fell back through the ocean's topmost membrane with one great, meaningful splash.

The gunmetal-grey travellers drew together and briefly milled before heeding the guidance of the great leaper, turning about and heading back the way they had come, north along the west coast of Penwith. The glitter of phosphorescence made by their wheeling brought the sleepless gulls about them in vulgar enquiry. Was something to be scavenged? With a small chorus of gay or derisory whistles and puffs of expelled air, the dolphins dived, surfaced, dived again. They had eaten well. They were of a mood for merry-making.

Mornalas did not dare try calling forth more of the story Ithian was weaving for her. Eager to know more, glad to be able to forget for periods of time the unrelenting pain of neck and throat, the rasping effort to breathe, she was aware of the passing of the night. She was hugely glad no longer to be so entirely alone.

Ithian glanced about her. Under the great lighthouse and along the skirts of the great rocks, she could see no seals. They lay on the more low-lying rocks around which the flooding tide was inching. Forty or fifty of them, a mixture of colours and ages, lay all about. Most of them were relaxed. Night time was the time of least disturbance on these ancient rocks and in the nearby caves. Men kept far away and, apart from them, there was almost nothing to fear.

Summer was when the maximum number of seals would be present at the remote islands. Most seals preferred to keep far from the crowded shores and fishless shallows of summer. Among them rested not only local seals, but visitors hailing from Brittany, Ireland, Man, Wales and sometimes even farther afield. There was just such a Babel of dialects now.

On Longships Reef, the great brown seal sensed Ithian's alertness. Stirring, he lifted his massive head, stared at her, his attention dark and grave. Looking back into such a gaze, it was easy to imagine you were peering into something intimate with the mysterious knowledge of the darkest chasms of the deeps as well as the sun-shadowed kelpy shallows. Meinek: fearless hunter, fearless warrior. Meinek: father to so many pups. To be sure, the tireless wheel of time would humble him, soon or later, but it would have no power to steal away what he had been, what he had lived, what he yet remained.

Ithian watched the massive head return to rest, and noticed that though he rested, his eyes did not. They watched her still.

It took her a little while to return from her rich treasury of memories. Glancing at Mornalas, watchful as Meinek on rocks quietly lamplit by the few stars with sufficient reach, she reverted to the singing that was all the roosting shags, herring gulls and the returning turnstones heard of what passed between them.

"You must take your rest now, Mornalas. There will be more times for sharing. The next time, you must tell me something of how you came to this night across all the years between. But when the sun rises again, your special day comes with it. You will need your wits and strength. Let me find a special song for you. You will not have heard it before. It comes from the snowfields of the faraway Gulf of Riga, where first I found the gift of songs. You do not believe me and I do not blame you, but you will sleep."

Quieter than an ear might hear did she begin. It welled in the telling. It grew and dwindled, grew and curved and tingled. One great, long, lavish saga of a song she sang, her head and half-opened mouth lifted to the stars above the head of sleeping Mornalas. As much a song of healing as could be made, Ithian contrived, bringing necessary peace to body and soul; for the silvery seal mother would need all she could save for her. That much was certain. Singing for another seal depends on touching that seal — not the simple touching of snout to mouth or flank to flank. A song began as a key. You tried it in the lock and if it failed, as often it did, you tried another and another until the key turned. And turn it always did, despite her misgivings.

She sang until the song was singing itself, which was when she knew the key had turned. Thereafter, she trusted the song to become whatever it was meant to be. Here, tonight, the desire was upon her to make the greatest music. Here was a naturally loving seal mother in the greatest need of her life, the drear clouds of death gathered, hovering over her head.

"Am I going to die?"

"We all die."

It had been an evasion. With luck — which is never a little thing — the pup might be saved.

**

When Mornalas wakened, she was bobbing upright in the sea, her whiskered snout pointing toward the sky. From afar she looked like a bottle bobbing on the ocean. Around her, other seals slumbered, likewise bobbing. The tide had crept up in the night and lapped all of them into the sea. Only Meinek and Reefer, a lesser male who had long since decided never again to challenge Meinek, had wakened and slithered into the sea of their own volition. Ithian bobbed now close by Mornalas after successfully hunting mackerel along the edge of the race.

She had not been alone. She had encountered a small group of three harbour porpoises hunting for the same prey, having heard the gentle piffing of their brief surface blows. They were two adults accompanied by a calf already more than a year old but still being suckled. The meeting had been by chance and was without rancour, a brief awareness of one another while continuing to pursue each their own hunting lines. But not before Ithian sensed that the porpoise-mother was heavily pregnant and would be giving birth to another calf before the next new moon.

She had glimpsed a sunfish, a pale grey fish larger than a dustbin lid, resembling a flatfish without a tail but swimming upright. Where the tail might have been, the skin was pinched, resembling the place where the pastry is joined on a pasty. Ithian had seen such fish before but found the sight of it and the way it moved so peculiar that she made no effort to hunt it and test the succulence of its flesh. In fact, something about it repelled her and usually if something affected her like that, she had learned there was reason to leave it alone.

Now, Mornalas articulated one fore-flipper so that she swirled slowly upward to rest horizontal at the surface, facing southward. She glanced at dark Ithian, knowing she would follow, and the two of them set out on an easterly course, heading directly inshore at a leisurely pace, side by side. Up above and beyond them, no crowds featured on the cliff tops at Land's End; just one or two perpendicular matchstick figures moving along behind their dogs.

Easterly, then, the two female grey seals swam, never far apart. They were noticed by a succession of small troops of gannets, solitary shags and equally solitary fulmars that sheared by, skimming low over the surface of the sea and the blurred reflections of themselves. Often, the fulmars would circle the seal heads, once, maybe twice, subjecting them to what felt like the cruel regard of their large, mascara-darkened eyes. Where seals hunted, there tended to be a treasury of scraps on which to thrive; but not this morning, it seemed. This was recognisable from the casual regularity of shallow dives by which the two female seals proceeded.

The fulmars straightened out of their circling enquiry and glided onward. Perhaps plankton would have to suffice, after all, to assuage the hunger of each, their solitary, bloated young. In just a few more days, the great labour of the year would be over for them. They could leave the narrow ledges, with the hollows at the back, where achieving landfall was always difficult because their legs were set so far back. Leaving was greatly easier. They would spread their straight wings, lift off for the final time from a breeding ledge selected and guarded, ten months before. Free, then, they could glide out and range far from memory of land. Free, gorging themselves over lonely seas that heaped over the central oceanic ridge where it marched north-south along the dark floor of the Atlantic.

Others would drift north into chill and sometimes frozen airs. There, the ocean was patterned with icebergs creaking along like some ancient rheumatic fleet bound on a final voyage to the breakers yard. They would remember the rare sounds of silence as well as the screeching demons of the wilder storms. They would become again one — for a time — with the spirits of wave, spray and wind out of which, in their most ancient stories, they understood themselves to have been made. Thereby, they could lose rust accumulated like an invisible clogging of their feathers from uncomfortably prolonged contact with the edge of the land. Blasted clean again, they would be reduced to nothing more than themselves.

The farthest-travelled would go skimming by occasional Inuit hunters yet paddling their kayaks in the style of their forebears. They would regard them with a dark eye; circling back, they would subject them to a similar regard with the other eye; hunter to hunter. The Inuit hunters would offer some small salute to a bird important among the deities of their people. Returning home, where the old stories were held in high regard, they might weave a story of what they had seen to the children who welcomed them back. The happenings of the day would be woven into the ancient tales, refreshing them.

Perhaps, also, the brief lingering of the fulmar above the seals had about it something of the passing of a baton, one breeding season almost over, another about to begin; fulmar and grey seal.

The seals swam on in a slow northerly curve toward granite cliffs and great headlands that presented a seemingly inhospitable shore. They made no speedy headway but lazed by places grown familiar. By Land's End, by the gaunt islet of the Armed Knight where scores of razorbills and guillemots had done with raising their young of the year more than a month since. By grass-topped Enys Dodnan, the roof of its sea hall rudely littered with relics of another nesting season. On that sloping place, a gang of cannibalistic greater black-backed gulls dwelt; untrusting, untrustworthy neighbours, even to their own kind. If the opportunity occurred, they would swallow the new-born young of absent neighbours; they would kill and eat the older young. To survive they had learned they must be savages.

Theirs was a roofless lair of brutal, bullying bandit birds whose thatch of short grasses had wilted in the scorching Cornish sun where the next generation of bandit birds had survived their neighbours, making each their own leap from being cared for to swaggering independence.

Beyond were extremely exposed low tide ledges where only maroon coralline algal turfs grew. The seals paid them no attention. They swam under granite castle towers, over vast acres of shell-sand, endlessly re-arranged over millennia. Along their way, they were speeded or hindered by familiar threads of tidal races. Sometimes, a boulder or encrusted piece of broken ship appeared below them, marked by the waving of algal fronds hold-fasted there.

Closer inshore, they travelled comfortably just outside the ripple of the small wave-break. A gentle late summer easterly wind had laid a timely, calming hand upon the sea, though it did not necessarily make life easier for the seals. It made the place for which they were bound less accessible to those who might disturb their privacy when the rocky shores were no longer whitely surf-girt. Two shadows ghosted along the bottom, keeping them company.

The sun was high in the sky by the time they came to the last great headland with its well-remembered scattering of enormous rocks tumbled seaward. Here a seal might play in surging unsettled waters for the most part of any year. Play, haul out, corkscrew lazily down to the shell-sand submarine floor, pursue and capture fish or depart on adventures? The seals passed by without pause but not without memories of such times.

It was still very early on a Tuesday morning. Mainly due to the earliness of the hour, but also because the school holidays had ended on the previous day, they arrived unseen at their destination. Had anyone been looking down into the bay, they must have delighted in the seal-shadows, gliding darkly in so great and lovely a spread of green-turquoise water. They passed by four dark cave entrances as well as five islets of varying size before arriving at a final insignificant promontory. One unwitting, immature seal awaited them, asleep close to the final small islet. As they cruised by the small, beige seal, he sensed them. Immediately submerging, he steered away in haste over the glittering sands, recognising their purpose. They were the heralds of the advent of pupping time. No seal, no matter how young, old or ferocious, would have done other than yield to seal mothers the sites they elected to use in this crucial season. Not even savage Meinek, who was exceptionally well-acquainted with this place.

There is a remarkable culture of courtesy among grey seals demonstrated from beginning to end of breeding seasons at remote sea cave breeding places all along the sunset coast of the British Isles. Sea caves, even the largest of them, are mean, cramped places compared with the vast, fenceless sea acres of their daily roaming. Mean and cramped, also, compared with the long sandy beaches of east England that, in relatively recent times, had become so populous with seals and the thousands of people drawn to watch the marvellous spectacle of them.

The dark seal caves are places where, at the most relaxed of times, seals tend towards politeness to one another. Alone, their preference is to rest at the base of walls, keeping to the edges of the main fairway or snug in little tunnels off to the sides. The main fairways are left for the comings and goings. Even so far from likely disturbance, there the seals maintain their age-old wariness of being ashore, ever-careful to keep open their line of retreat to the sea.

Larger groups of seals do gather at the time of the great winter assemblies, from the end of November through to March and even as late sometimes as May. Then, rather than spreading like some huge hairy, moth-eaten rug across the cave floor, they lie close together without quite touching, creating of the small spaces between their great bodies a maze. Except when the sea is most restless and threatens what remains of their beach at high tide, such gatherings remain mostly free of jockeying for position or attempted hectoring. In the prevailing relaxed atmospheres of winter, disputes are rare and brief.

During these periods, the seals might rest ashore for days on end. For that while, they give no thought to entering the sea unless driven to do so by alarm, and then tending to do so in the one great stampeding cavalry charge.

A similarly peaceable atmosphere prevails during the season of pup births. Once the season begins, any cave used as a nursery site is almost always abandoned by all other seals — a seemingly formal arrangement that allows mother and pup utmost peace. Accidental crushing of pups by seals moving to and from the sea is thereby avoided. Neither is there disturbing or stressing of the mother.

There are two exceptions to this custom, primarily where more than one mother uses the same site. Then, anxiety and inexperience can intrude to such a degree that mother might fight mother to some bloody compromise or else to a deeper impasse resulting in one mother and pup departing the caves for a more peaceable nursery.

The other is where a midwife seal attends a birth.

The same does not hold true for the males. Before they return to participate in the great drama of the year, many will have travelled long, far and sometimes painfully. Yet, despite the sometimes-marvellous stories they could tell, at best they are barely tolerated by the seal mothers. They have to keep their distance and this the males respect, although over a period of days they will try to edge ever closer as if worming their way into the confidence of the seal mothers.

The two seals felt sand beneath their bodies as they flowed, later bumped, to a standstill in the sea cave shallows. Both recognised the time had come to turn from being spirits of sea-grace into the velvet slugs they became on land. All the force of gravity came to bear upon them as they took the first few paces up the beach, their great eyes adjusting to the gloom.

They entered the cave on the half-tide of a neap tide. Moving now on sand, both were doing an awkward uphill breaststroke with their fore-flippers, each movement forward accompanied by a humping of their backs. Their hind flippers they did not move at all just dragging them along behind them, not realising how like a caterpillar moving along a twig they looked just then.

They panted with the exertion of it, that of Mornalas being much more laboured and frantic than that of Ithian, who was leading the way. Hearing the ragged strain and fear in her companion, Ithian stopped. Looking about her, she started once more to sing a simple song of encouragement, speaking of the time of peace and fulfilment waiting at journeys end.

It took a little while to work, but such was the faith of the younger female in Ithian that she forced herself to hear and thereby unlock the door so the healing might be done; however, there was, as she was beginning to recognise, a limit even to the power of song and the magic of its healing. Use it too much, too often and, like any other drug, it would begin to lose its efficacy. It would wear her thin.

Very slowly, then, the two seals moved up the straight sandy fairway beyond a great boulder that mainly blocked their way about halfway in. Here, the two of them splashed through a shallow pool that had not existed during the four previous breeding seasons. It had a gleaming brown mattress of sugar kelp, tangle and sea oak at the bottom that felt slippery under their flippers.

Thus, they entered the age-old birth chamber, under cathedral-high walls of sheer granite. Here and there, blue-turquoise marks - copper carbonate - leached down, thinly streaking the granite. Here, the quiet dark was soothing. The sand-hill was empty but for the two of them. Near the back of the cave, they could make out something huge and pink that proved to be a plastic buoy deposited by storm surf almost a year previously. Before being torn from its anchorage, it had marked the place where a string of crab pots was set out near Wolf Rock lighthouse, some eleven miles offshore.

As well as the buoy, there were seven empty plastic water bottles and many fragments of white Styrofoam used in the manufacture of fish boxes. There were smaller coloured floats that kept the top sides of trammel nets upright just above the seabed and pieces of fishing net of various colours and weights. All the way up the sand-hill lay a heavy scattering of kelp fronds and stipes under which sand-hoppers feasted. A rock pipit had been feasting on them in turn but had flown out of the cave when the seals appeared.

This fairway was mainly between three and four metres wide, except near the back it narrowed substantially while some distance in from the rock stack they had passed, it bellied out briefly to become five metres wide. As such, it was the largest chamber in a generally narrow cave. Off one side of this chamber ran a narrow little cubby-hole. It was a tunnel with room enough only for two seals to lie, where they oftentimes did rest, end to end.

Mornalas fell asleep for a time, overwhelmingly relieved to have reached her destination. Perhaps she felt the ghosts of the old sense of security she had experienced here, at the very outset of her life. Of all the places in the world, this one was dear to her, holding all the best memories.

Slightly below her, Ithian did not sleep, but kept watch through the gap between the toothlike rock stack and the cave wall. She watched the light dwindle. Only for part of the morning did the sun shine directly through the entrance. Light dwindled, the tide drained away. To the discerning eye of a seal mother, this was the best of nursery caves.

It was remote. People did not think to explore it during autumn or winter, particularly with the entrances stormbound. People were the most disturbing things that could befall a seal ashore. They all knew the stories, learned with the suckling of each their mothers' milk. Burning torch brands, smidging in the damp cave air. Big men, the smell of beer. A shout! Clubs raised high, seals suddenly desperate to reach the cave entrance and the succouring sea; the hedge of booted legs. Seals splashing, snarling, through cave waters, clubs thrashing, a dropped torch hissing then smoking as water quenched it. The crying and dying of stricken seals or the breathless strangeness of escape. How could they be yet alive. Old stories, they decorated the cave as physically as the maroon algal turf near the entrance that caught the sunlight during the earlier hour

There were newer stories of young ones snatched from nursery places, packed into cages, carried across beaches and up cliff paths. Caged pups loaded into vans, driven away. Some brutal overlord, it seemed, was taking an annual tribute of their young.

Other than people, there was nothing here to fear but the violence of the surf.

At low tide, the cave floor was not everywhere revealed. There remained from all the years Mornalas could remember a great pool. It measured, usually, some twenty metres long, a metre deep, and stretched from a few metres below the big rock toward the bright entrance. A seal might sleep comfortably there, completely submerged. At the seaward end, the floor briefly reappeared. Here was massed a pile of boulders covered with a pale reddish-mauve encrusting alga, *Lithothamnion*, below the far side of which the floor disappeared again to become the base of a much smaller entrance pool of lesser depth.

Beyond the entrance, the foreshore widened as granite bedrock and a clutter of huge boulders. Here, even the largest boulders rocked under the pummelling of heaviest waves breaking. Smaller boulders only shivered below a passing flipper.

Here was a small inlet of the sea. It was mainly sheltered to seaward by the combination of the small islet by which the juvenile seal had been sleeping when the females arrived. It lay just beyond a small promontory. These features offered sufficient but essential protection to the cave entrance against oceanic wave action. They made the sea cave habitable by the seals.

They offered protection, and to the pair of rock pipits, one of whom even then flittered across the bright entrance. They had made a nest in a crevice near the top of the left entrance tower of the seal cave where it joined the lintel. In that shallow place, lined with a fine cup of moss and grass, the pair had produced three broods of hungry young this year for which they had foraged tirelessly all summer long. Quite recently, the last of those young birds had departed to try its hand at surviving its first year.

Four had not escaped beyond the confines of the great bay outside.

Part way across the bay, not visible from the ground, was a ledge that was the brooding place of a savage prince among birds. His name was Pellitras; his kind were the peregrines. They acknowledged no peers.

For fun, in March, with his mate, O'Sîana, he had come slashing down out of the heavens, to the doors of which they climbed in their marvellous flight. From those doors they fell, wind thrumming through their wings, close by two ravens become statues in their anxiety. The male raven often perched hunched at the edge of the nest of woven gorse stems containing, in their innermost woollen cup, the four eggs of their young. The female was incubating them, shrinking deep inside herself every time the peregrines streamed by. Like birds on a pulley, they repeated the action, over and over again until they tired of it; and all the while, the ravens remained at anchor. They could not take up the challenge laid down by their age-old enemies. They dared not lumber out on the wing to challenge such ferociously uninhibited enemies at such a time. They had tried it once, in the beginning. For their rashness, they had been driven to land on the cliff slopes above, there suffering an extended period during which the two deadly, beautiful falcons swept over and back over their heads, daring them to attempt to lift off again. It had been a bitter humiliation.

The same birds knew of the pipit's nest. Four young pipits followed in the wake of plumper birds. Taken on the wing, slain at the moment of impact, the light weight of each of them in turn carried to the banqueting table, as local birdwatchers called the peregrines plucking post. Their feathers and a few small bones including one small skull yet remained. The peregrines might have taken more of them, but they made a scant meal. A time would come when the peregrines ceased to notice them.

The tiercel, Pellitras, was there even now. He had watched the arrival of the two seals. That the cave was a seal place, he knew. It had ever been. There was nothing between the seals and peregrines: not enmity, not fear, not friendship. All they shared was the sense of home in this great, granite bay where the sea was always some glorious shade of turquoise no matter how grey the weather.

Watchful by the stubby stack, Ithian could see the vertical white smear of him. She recognised him for the wild aristocrat among the flying ones that he was; but she knew others she deemed worthy of an equal regard. Not least among these were tiny wave-top dancers, the storm petrels who lived nearly all their lives above the far places of the deep ocean. She had seen them come to land. By night, they had flown to burrows among pale granite boulders in the Western Rocks, laying their eggs and nursing the young to independence. Storm petrels; manx shearwaters; gannets or black-eyed fulmars; marvellous travellers, marvellous lives, one and all, but none — for all the skills at their various hunting ways — remotely so deadly as this neighbour standing so still in the sunlight. Pellitras was wild and free as can be and it was something she could recognise.

Behind her, there was a small sound in the gloom. She turned her head. Was Mornalas dreaming or was the great drama beginning at last? No. Still asleep, she twitched a little, as if with her dream. At her hindermost end, she was still and relaxed. Ithian settled again and, for a while, she dozed.

A sharper cry wakened her from dreams of icefields and wavering green veils swishing across the night sky.

Her gaze locked with the widened eyes of Mornalas. A pure flash of knowing passed between them. This time, here was no false alarm but a beginning. A low moan, the spontaneous beginning of the song she needed to sing this day for this unique pup escaped Ithian. Pitched deeper, it developed, feeling its way around the atmosphere of the cathedral-high cave, around the personalities of the two females and, more tentatively, around the sense of the new one beginning its journey into a world become recently so unexpectedly perilous.

At times like these, she might have appeared to those for whom she sang like some pedlar reaching into a raggetty sack of songs slung over her shoulder drawing forth some pretty bauble. Mornalas knew otherwise. They knew, both knew — since last night, at least — that the song was born of the place, time and personalities there present. It was strained out of everything, making itself, growing into itself and dreaming out of that self.

Mornalas did not forget the great peril in which she stood. There was risk to her life stalking menacingly around the edges of her perception, here in the gloom of the cave; side by side, pace for pace, stalked hope. Hope was decked out with the bouquet of closest friendship between these two females. More even than the song, the presence of such a friend gave her courage along with a sufficient tranquillity that allowed the large female pup to come flooding out on to the sands so easily, shockingly easily, at the end.

In a flowering of radiant joy, Mornalas turned to gaze upon the little yellowish package smeared here and there with blood, part-burst from its amniotic sac. Turning more completely, she nudged the package with her snout causing it to tear even more and the damp little yellow-coated seal pup to flop weakly on to the sand and fully into life. She watched her try to lift her head from the sand and fail. The damp, tiny pup tried again, failing again. Several times, she tried and failed but, in the end, she did indeed lift it up and, in so doing, came more certainly into life. Wobbling, she had already tried a few shallow breaths. Now, she managed a bubbling first cry, a thin bleat that both quavered and strengthened in the making.

Reaching down over her, a gentle whiskered muzzle nudged her once again and a warm tongue licked the dampness of her. It was the point when Mornalas and Ithian both recognised that here was not one of those pups that came into the world only to fail without drawing a breath. Here was one with the will to life.

Ithian watched or listened for the next hour as mother and pup nuzzled each the other, as the little one discovered her own flippers and what they were for; as she discovered her voice. Such a voice! For mother and midwife, there was joy in hearing the utterance of those half-forgotten sounds — sounds they had made, themselves, when life had been the simplest it would ever be and had contained nothing at all to fear.

The point came where Mornalas keeled over on one side and guided the pup, with gentle vibrations of her upper flipper down toward her nipples. Normally, they never showed but now, in their eagerness to sustain the little one, they had popped out through the slits on her pale, mottled underside, down near her tail.

For some pups, discovering first the teat and then its purpose was a long, bungling, frustrating mystery. It can grow to become an insurmountable problem because a pup cannot be forced to feed though, as Ithian had seen, it might be not the fault of the pup but of the mother. In some cases, the mother is fretful and unhelpful as, indeed, Ithian had been. This is the second fence at which new life can fail.

The pup was guided by a flipper, vibrating fussily, down toward the sand in the direction of a pair of relaxed tail flippers which, had she known it, were portrayed as seaweed attachments in certain surviving mediaeval drawings. Every so often, she kissed her mother's exposed belly, or so it seemed as she quested without quite understanding why for the elusive, eager nipple. Mornalas curled her tail flippers around just a little more, as if to ensure the little one would not stray beyond the end of her body in her essential quest.

It was a moment of profound relief and happiness when the final baby kiss located the nipple. Neither mother nor pup noticed the seal song sung by Ithian dwindle to silence, or a silence suddenly noisy with eager but initially inefficient sucking and gulping.

That first feed, punctuated by the need to breathe before rediscovery of the source of warm, thick soup of seal milk, was a noisy, lip-smacking affair. All the while, despite the suffering she was enduring from the tightness of the shawl of fishing net, Mornalas managed to rest quite still on the damp sand. All the while, her eyes rested on the new life that had so suddenly erupted into the world. Her expression was calm and indulgent. Her eyes shone, brightened by refreshed happiness.

The feeding went on until Mornalas became aware that, though the teat remained in the small mouth with its proud display of small, sharp teeth, the sucking had been ceased for quite a while. Very slightly, she moved. The chin of the little one slid down her abdomen, came to rest on the sand. Somerledaa had glutted herself to sleep. Indulgently, the seal mother reached around, sniffing the face of her baby. Her scent had not been abroad in the world one hour previously. Now, it was the heart of the world. Now, no matter how many pups might crowd around her, clamouring for a feed, this scent would be unique. By this means even more than by sight, she would recognise Somerledaa.

Where did that name come from?

Where did any name ever come from, but within? The pup stirred, looking suddenly directly, dark-eyed, into the eyes of this great silvery mother and sang formally, quite gravely: "My name is Somerledaa, Mornalas-mother, and for this chance of life, I thank thee."

The wonder of it never faltered. Mornalas heard the gravely formal greeting spoken just as it had been spoken now four times previously with only the new names differing. Just as on each previous occasion, she was struck dumb, her own warm heart overflowing with love and contentment.

Remembering they were not entirely alone, remembering Ithian was not far distant, she lifted her head and gazed directly at her. The dark midwife seal sang, almost gaily: "Some seals are mighty fighters, like Meinek, who fathered Somerledaa. Some seals explore great tracts of the world, for the pleasure of being able to return to anywhere and be not a stranger. Some seals sing; others collect, remember, retell the old stories. Most seals swim and hunt and rest ashore on rocks or sand or mud, living their lives the age-old way without ever colliding with the mysteries.

"You are none of these, Mornalas, for you are love. I know you do not think it any more-or-less-than-normal to be so, and that is as it should be, but I tell you that you are the hope of the world. The loving kind, caring beyond themselves because they know no other way, acknowledging true things when they meet them: that is the heart of where you belong. The loving kind, there are not so many of you. You are needed. Promise me that you will not forget that?"

In the heart of a happiness that had forgotten the rest, who begrudges an easy promise? She gave it.

Somerledaa's coat, still stained yellow by the amniotic fluid in which she had twitched, shifted and rested for the months before her birth, was increasingly speckled with sand. Four times she suckled on the first afternoon and evening of her life. Between-times, she slept. The atmosphere of the cave, of all she knew of the world, was restful. Slow, regular droplets of freshwater fell straight from the cave roof into the low water pool and later into the sea when the tide came in, licking up toward where they lay. The tiny wavelets that melted into scant surf between the great boulders outside the cave sounded surprisingly loud, considering how small they were, but Mornalas explained it was due to the acoustics of the cave, which served to exaggerate every sound.

While Somerledaa moved about, dragging her frail, baggy-coated body behind her soft-haired head, she grew fluent in the use of her disproportionately large fore-flippers, developing a first weak breaststroke action. Very soon, she learned to make her way about the cave, learning soon enough to move almost as well as her mother. Where she had passed, small marks left by her flippers were dwarfed by the larger ones made by Mornalas. Her body was so light that it left hardly any mark but for a line so fine it might have been traced by a twig. This contrasted with the churned wake left by her mother's body, flanked by its chevrons of flipper tracks.

For now, however, the little pup did not think to venture beyond the stack, even toward the temptation of the low water pool and the often-changing light beyond.

***

Another lovely morning of quiet winds, one more day under the tyranny of the sun. Amaury felt happy, standing barefoot in the kitchen at six in the morning, the door wide open, sipping warm tea from a mug. He was watching an unusually early short-eared owl questing over maritime heathland that spread between the edge of the farm fields and the cliff edges. The same owl — was it the same owl? — returned every autumn. Most often, he glimpsed it on the ground, but this was the kind of sighting he enjoyed the most, except it was being harried by a pair of jackdaws.

Once the buoyant bird had drifted from view, he turned to resume the packing of his dry-bag with the tools of his trade.

In the painful past, cameras, lenses, a flash unit and binoculars had been ruined before he learned all the precautions required to protect them against misadventure, learning to take greater care. The key lesson had been to use one dry bag packed inside an outer one so that any puncture of the external skin still left the inner skin safe from water-the-destroyer.

The loaded rucksack on his back, he followed a track across the spread of maritime heathland. The great blaze of tartan colour that had been a feature of July and August was dimmed. Now, many flowers had faded or browned, but there was still a brave show of heathers, gorses, tormentil, bedstraw, milkwort, eyebright, lousewort and others. Because of the fair weather, there was an equally brave show of butterflies and moths with the ubiquitous silver-Y moths prominent among several familiar butterfly species. What pleased him most this day was the very latest arrival. This was a gorgeous immigrant with a penchant for landing on yellow flowers and flaunting wonderful butter-yellow wings, edged with black. It was the anticipated and most welcome clouded yellow. Fresh in from Brittany, he counted six in all, hoping the birds would not catch them too soon. In his photographic lingering, he almost forgot the finger-tapping drumbeat of the remorseless tide; but not quite.

The peregrine Pellitras now brooded on a shallow, approximately triangular, watchtower of granite rock erupting from the sea of heathland that might, at another time, have served for some ancient sacrificial slab. About him, there was a dearth of small birds and their songs, for in the peculiar way that all Nature senses some flaw in the rhythm of the day, all were aware he had not yet hunted and killed. In the distance, there were six ravens. They were the two adult birds he had shamed in the spring and their young who had been, at the time, safely sheltered from sight of it all if not entirely safely inside their eggs in the woollen nest cup. It was in their minds to make mischief of their enemy, but the fact he had yet to make a kill made the adult birds nervous knowing, as they did, that he was capable of absolutely anything. They knew, also, that their four youngsters, even together, were no match for his aerial prowess.

While continuing his passage amid the confetti of butterflies, Amaury paused abruptly in the dry tractor tyre rut that served for his path, for a female adder basked a few metres ahead of him. It had a brown body with a darker zigzag pattern. He wondered whether it would be the last one he would see this year.

The pictures taken, the adder having slithered into the heather, he proceeded along the track until he could see not only the crude brown granite fins of the Longships Reef but also the skerries below the tip of the headland around which Ithian and Mornalas had swum twelve days before. Seeing no trace of white around any of them, his spirits soared. Yes! Today is going to be a special day! I can reach all the caves. There is no surf. He skipped on and broke into a jog-trot in his pleasure. He was happy: today, life was easy. He was aware his surfer friends would have disagreed utterly.

Having made the damp, precipitous descent, making use of the gravel and stone bed of a tumbling stream, he reached his launch point. There, on a bare ledge of bedrock promontory bisecting the boulder beach, he removed his land clothes, stowing them in bags where they could not be seen from the cliff tops.

He set off fast over the boulders strewn beyond the ledges and pools. You dance over them, he had always described to those who wondered. That way, you don't give your body time to teeter and fall. You school your balance in ways that work. Don't take infinite care. Dance! You dance from boulder to boulder, keeping part of your attention on what you are doing and part on what lies ahead, way-finding. You think you might fall? Always have some notion of how you are going to fall if you were to do so with your very next step. Make sure when you do fall, you do so in the way kindest to yourself. But the truth is that once you slot into the rhythm and the confidence that rhythm breeds, you are not going to fall. The momentum carries you beyond the little errors and doubts. If you are determined to interrupt the dance flow, don't fall: subside!

It was nonsense, wasn't it? Not to him.

On the far side of the bay, he was aware he was watched by O'Sîana, Pellitras's mate. Although he glanced up at her, glad to see her where he hoped she would be, he was unaware she had taken a feral pigeon in the first hour of daylight. His mind only really noted her in passing, being focussed on the nearest cave entrance where, in due course, he squatted. Unaware Somerledaa was asleep within, he drew the dry-bag from the rucksack. Reducing the chance of betraying a silhouette to any watchful seal in the cave, he moved toward the sea, as ever planning first to explore the farthest cave.

Into the sea he eased himself, wading deeper awkwardly as he half-stumbled his way over vari-sized submerged boulders partly patterned by algal decorations. Deeper still he waded, stumbled, until surrendering to flow with the suck of a receding pulse of water that took him swiftly out around the promontory.

It was not always so, not often so, but this day the swim was sweet and lacking in the challenging drama brought by breaking waves.

Unthreatened by wave action, he drifted languorously around the promontory as the sun came up hearteningly over the cliffs on the far side of the bay. He accelerated with the squeezed waters between a small islet and the tip of the promontory toward the entrance to the Great Seal Hole. He had no seals for company this day although sometimes they idled here. No gulls screamed abuse above his head, drawing down upon him the attention of the world. Considering how forbidding the waters could be here, he recognised he was having the easiest of swims and took it for a good omen.

Arriving among great, jagged-edged boulders rudely dumped by storms-past in the huge cave entrance, his horizontal body grounded on a large, flat-topped, submerged boulder. The sea drained from his body quietly while he rose slowly, achieving some teetering measure of comfort in the perpendicular. Once upright, he moved without awkwardness farther into the cave, moving diagonally toward the left wall, as was his habit.

The mantra remained the same. Don't be seen. Don't be heard. Hope you are not scented. If you are glimpsed, try to appear as little as possible like a human. Give them no clues, no reason to stampede; before above the jumble of mainly huge boulders, reared a great, unmarked whale-back of pale shell-sand. It offered the prospect of easy progress after the clamber over jumble of boulders and bedrock outcrops in the sea cave foyer. Ornamenting his roof were patches and spreads of rusty-back ferns and damp pale-green lichens.

He edged up the sand-hill, forever keeping close to the wall, moving with a soundlessness of long practice. Just below the summit of the whaleback, he stopped, squatted, and opened the dry-bags. This time, not seawater but a towel emerged first, to be draped about his neck. He wiped his fingers on it, making sure no grains of sand adhered to them before he handled camera and lens. Once they were hung about his neck, he reached in again.

It was like opening a Christmas stocking full of his much cared-for necessities.

In succession, he withdrew headphones that he slipped over his head. A small sound recording unit followed, into which he plugged an external microphone before attaching both to his belt. Lastly, he picked up his rather heavy but powerful lamp before moving over the brow of the whaleback and down the far side without resort yet to its great illumination. To any onlooker, it would have seemed the most absurd progress. That progress froze immediately as he startled to a sound, loud and extraordinarily clear, reminiscent of… what exactly? Imagine the offspring of a marriage between a very slow turning, old-fashioned football supporters rattle and metallic burping. Peering up and then further up into the dark, he knew very well what he sought. Sure enough, there was a glossy-plumaged shag. Perched on a narrow ledge about six metres up, neck craned forward, its crest was flared erect in fullest alertness.

Taking a deep, muted breath, he continued until the far sand-hill, pale in the general gloom and rising to the very back of a cavern one hundred and twenty-five metres long, came fully into view. He continued to edge forward, but more slowly than before until he had almost reached the place where bright light came gushing in from the left where the other tunnel ran to the sea. There, he dropped to his knees. However, here was no moment of prayer. He continued shuffling forward on his knees, low enough now to be concealed behind a rampart of very large boulders from the possibility of being seen by any seals on the fairway.

Slowly, he shuffled across the bar of brilliant daylight until he reached the shadows beyond where all cover ended. Here, he was at the foot of the interior sand-hill. A few small rocks that were bedrock protuberances spoiled the pale perfection of these sands, but none stood so high that a seal might hide behind it or even, in deep shadow, be mistaken for one. There were seal tracks marking the damp, otherwise smooth sand running down from the high-water mark, where all the marine debris appeared to be concentrated. These he had expected.

For Amaury, one of the great joys of studying seal cave sites was taking account of the amazing mobility of the substratum: the sea cave floor. Unless the weather and the accompanying sea conditions were quiet, he never knew in what respect the cave floors would have changed from the time of his previous visit. In times of wild weather, oftentimes it was transformed overnight. Hundreds of tons of sand might have been sucked from the cave or else shovelled in by wave action. The angle of a sand slope might be radically altered. On the exceptional occasions when sand was sucked entirely from the cave, only bare bones — the boulders and bedrock — remained. The atmosphere was totally altered, infinitely bleaker. This apparently exposed cave in fact was subject to least change thanks to the orientation of its entrances and the sheltering islets beyond them, conferring considerable shelter against the prevailing wave direction.

As his eyes grew accustomed to the lowering ambient light levels, he managed to ascertain at least one small seal was present, near the top of the hill. It seemed to be asleep. He edged out on to the fairway, tentatively. Had the seal been awake, he would have been seen. Always seeking deepest shadow, he moved very slowly up the slope. He had not yet switched on the torch because there was still just enough natural light by which to maintain progress without inadvertently blundering upon a rock that might not be a rock. Walking on damp sand was certainly the luxury end of this kind of fieldwork. The misadventures occurred most often in caves whose floors were made from boulders covered either with mucous or slippery brown fucoid seaweeds. In such places, he had moved oftentimes as an accomplished dignitary of the Ministry of Silly Walks

Lightly brushing the damp wall with its oblong feldspar windows and its glinting speckling of mica, he concentrated his attention on the seal. It was a small one. Dry, it had become the colour of honey. It was a yearling, sleeping as deeply as any young mammal that had not yet learned enough of the wicked ways of the world might sleep.

He was rewarded. At the top of the hill, and likewise asleep, lay a huge seal, a large sheet of skin missing from the front of his throat. It was a recent wound, still suppurating. When close, Amaury knelt and attempted to focus the camera lens in on his head and neck. Very carefully, he lodged the torch between his knees, angling it so that its beam was trained just beyond the area he wanted to photograph. He switched on the torch, chose the option of the dimmest beam.

Immediately, the reluctant camera, previously confused by the dark, came to life, focussing as he wished. He took the first 'gunfighter's' shot, fearful the seal would waken, but he had made no response to the sudden luminescence. Taking a little more care, Amaury now composed the picture he wanted; snapped, zoomed out, took a full seal shot. Immediately he switched off the torch and, returning it to hand, began to melt back down the hill. Above him, the exhausted male snored quietly on, undisturbed. His nightmare was Meinek, not the paparazzo.

Slipping back, he studied the yearling. There were no significant distinguishing marks, no justification for taking more pictures, risking wakening it and maybe both seals. Having been in this situation countless times before, he knew precisely how lucky he was that neither had been wakened by the lamplight or the brilliant shock of the camera flash.

He departed, leaving all behind him undisturbed and returned to the sea. There, after another bout of sunlit drifting, he came floating to a discreet landing place where there was no possibility of being glimpsed from within the cave outside which he had left his rucksack. He moved quietly toward the right side of the entrance under a lintel hung with grasses, ferns and pale lichens. There, where he could not be seen had a seal been peering toward the bright entrance, he repeated the sequence of equipping himself.

Entering this cave, the procedure was more complex though no swimming was required. This cave was totally different to its more remote neighbour. His approach began by hugging the right-hand granite entrance post and slipping in as close as possible to the wall, again offering no human profile to any watchers within. He waded slowly, therefore silently, through the entrance pool. A maroon seaweed resembling a crinkly lettuce except in colour was catching petrol-blue light; *Chondrus crispus*. He delayed long enough to take two photographs, having no need of betraying flashlight in the sun-bright entrance before wading out of the shallows on to rocks covered with the lovely pale blackberry stain of encrusting *Lithothamnion*. All around the rocky coasts of Cornwall, this lovely alga paints the skirts of inter-tidal rocks near the bottom of the retreating tide. The colour of it was not brazen as, say, the flash of kingfisher turquoise, but he found it exquisite. In passing, he brushed against a considerable cluster of soft orange sea squirts anchored to walls that did, as their name suggested, squirt little jets of water in response. A goby-like fish darted for cover at his passing. He knew it for a Father Lasher, watching as it become first still, then almost invisible.

Another much longer pool spread before him. Its waters were clear in the nearby shallows but murky farther on. Here, he forced himself to pause for ten minutes, enough to allow any submerged seal to surface for air. When the waiting time had been observed in full, he shuffled quietly on as far as the waters were clear before switching on the lamp, again using the dimmest setting. Holding it below the surface, slowly he panned the partly-shielded light of it from side to side.

This was a most famous pool.

Before Amaury had identified this place as a cave regularly used by seals, it had been unknown as a breeding site. When first he had entered it, his thoughts had been no more than to explore its depths, looking for signs of seals.

At that time, he had been exploring his way, cave by cave, around the coasts of south-west England. That questing odyssey, spread over more than four years, had been the essential preliminary to his work, along with the review of all literature pertaining to seals. Now, looking back, he realised the work in which he had taken such pride could never really be finished. Cliffs collapsed, sea cave roofs collapsed, interiors altered and became more or less attractive to seals. Probably, he had completely and wrongly disregarded sites, being limited as to how many he could subject to the regular, year-round study that allowed the occasional surprising detail to be detected.

The pleasure of exploration and discovery had been everything at the time. Sunny days, snowy ones; tranquil seas, marginal ones; sheer pleasure to such fear that he had too often turned aside from wave-bound sea cave entrances. Encounters with seals or the discovery of their distinctive tracks in the sand: it all merged into a great spread of retrospective happiness — a living of his life so much more than an existence.

The length of this cave, the Lesser Seal Hole, had surprised him and even then, when he knew less than he had come to know about the relationships between grey seals and the caves they most favoured, he had imagined that if he was a seal, this would be the kind of site where he would hope to be born. The cave was another natural cathedral along a coast where such cathedrals proliferated. The form of it and the acoustics were wonderful. It seemed incredible that in all his copious researches, trawling through literature and anecdote, there was no mention of it attracting the attention of seal hunters of the past. He felt local people must have explored it but no-one had recorded anything of the battues that likely had occurred there — at least in any records he had found.

Scanning underwater with the torch, he was searching to discover, as ever, whether a seal might be lurking in the murk. He was wondering, as ever, whether the shape of the bottom had changed since his last visit — had new boulders been introduced or pits appeared: impediments to his progress. Always, he was nervous at this point. He found himself wishing he had charged the torch battery before coming out, frustrated and a little worried by the weakness of the illumination it was throwing out.

Seven years previously, having studied the pool for no more than two wary minutes, he had set foot in the shallows and started to work his way along the right-hand wall, moving only slowly because the floor of the pool was covered not with sand but boulders of all sizes. He was no more than five paces in when the head of a seal surfaced silently about three metres ahead of him. In the shock of the moment Amaury roared with surprise, the seal roared with surprise, both thrashing the waters in their alarm having turned tail, fleeing fast as they could in their opposite directions.

Gaining the security of the slippery shore within reach of the cave entrance and pressing himself against the wall, he had come to a standstill and looked back at the pool. Where that lone seal had been, now there were five. All lay approximately broadside-on to the cave entrance, heads turned toward it. They looked like spaced out railway sleepers. Additionally, they gave the significantly more potent impression of being entirely impassable.

As they made no move to rush the entrance of the cave, Amaury grew calmer and studied them more closely. There was sufficient light to be able to recognise four of them were females while the fifth was the male who had roared. All five continued to watch him. If one submerged into the unknown depths, whenever it reappeared it was still facing directly toward where he remained standing.

How long this continued, he could not judge because he lost track of time, but while he watched he became aware that there were other seal noises issuing from within. They emanated from behind a tall, massive rock resembling an incisor tooth that largely blocked the main fairway some distance in from the far side of the pool. Tooth Rock, he called it. In those days, he was still learning about seals; feeling his way. He had not yet learned enough to be confident about what he was hearing, but he suspected pups lay in the deeps of the cave. To test his theory, he moved across to the opposite wall.

Leaning against it, the lamplight picked out a gentle sand slope that continued beyond the incisor rock for tens of metres before being engulfed by darkness. On the small spread of sand, he had been able to see, he made out two scraps of white and recognised them as pups.

Satisfied but thwarted, realising how stressful his presence must be, thereafter he had departed the cave. Outside, he dried himself and, being in no hurry, settled to enjoy the tranquillity of the view before him while being serenaded — as he had chosen to feel it — by at least two hungry pups. He was totally unprepared for what followed. There was a commotion in the pool followed by some snarling and some slapping sounds that seemed to be drawing nearer. They were drawing nearer, he corrected himself belatedly.

Even in those earliest days, he had command of his wits to an extent that allowed him to absorb surprise or fear and remain functional. During periods of stress, it was as if real time slowed down to a fraction of its normal speed for him — like a sort of reactional bradycardia. Picking up his camera, briefly checking it was switched on, he had run seaward from the cave entrance immediately to a point of partial concealment where, nonetheless, he held a fair view of the cave entrance. There was even time to ensure the focus was good.

The drama consisted of five seals emerging in a straggling line, one behind the other. Great leviathans, jerking, hunching, bunching and bumping along, they looked about them while they hastened to the sea. One stopped. The one behind bumped her inadvertently, causing them to bicker. There was a brief exchange of snarls before the caravan rolled on and, one by one, they went crashing into the sea. All the while, Amaury reeled off shot after shot of seals some of which were destined to become very familiar over the succeeding years.

Some days, everything you do goes right. That had been such a day. He took great pictures. The pictures identified part of a cadre of seals, some of whom continued to use the bay through the full year and in succeeding years. More than that, he learned he would never dare cross a pool full of seals; and he learned that if you meet seals in a cave, and thereafter leave, they do not simply settle down again. Rather, they pause for the long moment, which is variable, before usually following the intruder out into the light. The place has been made to feel temporarily unsafe for them; but only temporarily. He learned that, too.

Seeing them go, he had remained aware of the pups, alarmed at what he might have done but also riven by curiosity. Re-entering the cave, he hastened through the now empty pool. He hurried up the shallow sand-slope beyond, slowing as he neared the Tooth, being yet uncertain whether there were other adult seals in the interior. But there were none. He found and photographed four seal pups, all being white-coated. In addition, he found and photographed a moulted pup in a cubby-hole off the main fairway. He wondered if it found it wisest to keep out of the way of the adults using the nursery. Then he beat the hastiest retreat and noted he had been within the cave for about four minutes.

He departed the locality immediately, dancing back over the boulders this time with an honour guard of watchful seals shepherding him along from adjacent waters. They continued to watch while he clambered up the trackless cliff and disappeared over the top.

A few minutes later, he had back-tracked along the coast path to a point from which he had an excellent view into the entrance hall of the cave, being able to see in about as far as the near shore of what he decided to call the Great Pool. It was easy to make out the five seal-specks in the sea just outside that perpetually open door.

He watched. Minutes passed, the tide rose. After an hour, three seals had returned into the cave. When another half hour had passed, a fourth seal entered, but the lone male remained outside. As Amaury watched from behind his binoculars, he wondered if the male had drawn the short straw, being left there to watch for his return; but he was reassured by the outcome.

The principal lesson of that day was that he must always stand by any deep seal-cave pool for as long as twelve minutes before assuming it to be empty of seals — this because he had never counted a seal submergence lasting longer than twelve minutes. Now, here he stood again before the anticipated murk of the same waters. Their impenetrability never engendered confidence.

The minutes ticked by. He made several false starts, attempting to flush out any seal in hiding, but no head appeared at the surface. Thereupon, as happened sometimes, he grew impatient with his fears and ventured forward decisively, leaning the hand with the lamp against the wall to better keep his balance. Deeper and deeper he waded until the waters were up to his chest, that proving to be the high-water mark, this day. Thereafter, the pool became rapidly less deep until he emerged on the far shore where he examined tracks in the wet sand. They suggested two adults and one pup, all heading for the interior.

At that point, Somerledaa uttered a quavering cry of hunger, stoking the tension.

Camera in hand, Amaury moved toward the narrow gap between the stubby stack he called the Tooth Rock and the left-hand wall. Insinuating himself around the rock, immediately he made out one adult seal high up the slope beyond, unexpectedly close to the back. Normally they were clustered within ten metres of where he stood now, where the chamber was widest. There was just sufficient light to make out she was female. The pup was hauling itself up toward her in short bursts of activity. At each pause it cried, wheedling for food. Just like a lamb or a human child, it was a breathy, plaintive sound. He estimated it must be about fourteen days old, over-estimating by two days.

Below the sleeping mother and a little above the labouring pup, a second seal lay just outside the cubby-hole off to the right. A dark seal, it had come to the alert and was watching him; but he could not make out what sex it was. If it was a male, then it was remarkably small to be locally dominant. It was exceptional for any male to be tolerated so deep inside a nursery cave. If it was a female, as logic suggested, what was she doing here? He had learned much of seal etiquette. Nursery beaches were for mothers and pups. A male might be tolerated, sometimes but not always. He is supposed to keep utterly out of the way of nursery life, preferably near the water and more preferably in it.

Was she pregnant, then, if she was a female? Was the birth of another pup imminent? Surely, she was a female; a dark female? Equally powerfully, though, her shape suggested she was not pregnant.

Trawling through his memories, something from the past nudged him, asking to be noticed. It did not necessarily have anything to do with this breeding station, but it was to do with the nursery grounds and a dark seal. What was it?

That was the point at which she began her song.

She was not aggressive. She made no threatening movements although she had edged forward until half the distance between them had been covered. Now, her body lay between the intruder and Somerledaa. Was that deliberate? Her body had paused although her song continued. By the shape of her head, Amaury decided she could not be a male; she must be a dark female.

There was something strikingly unusual about her personality. No surprise in that. He had long since recognised grey seal personalities were incredibly variable. This one: I could swear she is not afraid of me. Is she calling or is she singing? Why is she singing? What does it mean?

Then he had it.

Far up the north coast, the greatest sea cave of those used by the large seal tribe frequenting the locality north of Boscastle: that was where it had been. Early one June he had managed to gain access to the longest, darkest sea cave that ever he had explored. Paddling in on his wave ski, the lamp clenched like a spotlight between his knees, he had no idea of the depth of water under or ahead of him. He could see the illuminated eyes of seals swimming so close he could have reached down and touched them. He could half see, half feel, them diving around him languidly, repeatedly, under the ski without ever quite brushing against it. Improbably, even in the deep, cloying darkness, his will held and he kept going. He did not panic even when, two hundred metres into the cave, a seal fell out of the darkness from what must have been an overhead ledge presumably reached on the high tide. It crashed just ahead of him, sending up a geyser of water that caused the ski to rock violently and the luminous eyes to disappear.

He paddled ever deeper into the cave. It seemed to curve forever into the cliff, this way and that, until eventually it yielded on to a beach of compacted sand. Upon landing, immediately, he located two seals. They lay, as so often with their kind, at the place where the foot of one wall met the sandy fairway. One seal was silvery and clearly a female; the other was dark. The dark one had started to sing even while her head was resting on the sand, even before he had landed.

It had distracted him, that beautiful and haunting evocation of a wild seal place and of any moment in all seal time. It was enchanting. Where normally he would have landed, whether seals were present or not, this time he turned the wave ski broadside on to the landing place. He sat for a while, legs dangling in the water on either side of the ski, taking in all that was there. Now he saw the unexpected breeze that had played on his face while he paddled in came from a second entrance too narrow for him to essay but probably not too narrow for seals to use. He had been blind to it while paddling in but once arrived off the beach it was clearly and comfortingly visible. It was only when turning purposefully to the beach, having decided to land, that he noticed the new-born pup sleeping on its side between the silvery seal and the cave wall. The raspberry-coloured afterbirth lay close by, just up the shallow slope from the pup. Later, he found it warm to the touch, so recent must the birth have been.

Since then, there had been a very small number of other early season occasions when he had noticed a dark female with no pup on the nursery grounds. Surely it could not be the same one, over such a great distance and span of time. But then, seals had always taught him to expect the unexpected. He had taken photographs of her but comparisons had been inconclusive; and even if she was the same seal, what was she doing?

The answer to that, he had guessed before. It was entirely improbable, of course. Other seal researchers would laugh themselves silly had he proposed it to them. There is no such thing as a midwife seal. But it did strike him that whenever he happened upon recently-born pups in Cornish sea caves, as in Welsh and Manx caves he knew, it was no longer unexpected for the first seal mother of a new season to come ashore and experience her ordeal accompanied by a companion. If that was true, then perhaps it was her role to sustain some sense of security for the seal mother, perhaps including the deterrence of intruders. What else could she do?

Now, her song quietened and the magic quietened, too. Abruptly, he became aware of the formidable slapping sound that bespoke a seal charging down a sand-hill toward the enemy.

He switched on his torch, loosing off the first picture of the mother charging toward him. He caught her on the up while she resembled a heavy little boat breasting a rough sea.

Whether it was the sudden shock of the bright light of the torch or weariness, Mornalas came to a heavy-breathing standstill, throwing up a small spray of sand. Still on one knee, the torch shining first just to one side of her, then to the other, he continued to reel off shots, hoping that as he did so her head would turn to reveal enough of the unique patterns on her neck to make his intrusion and her inconvenience worthwhile. He had learned to avoid shining the beam fully upon any seal not primarily for kindness or courtesy but because full beam irradiated the patterning on images so captured. Neither did he forget the dark seal holding position at the station she had taken up. Although the photographs were of Mornalas, he was taking them with both eyes open because if the dark seal moved any closer, he knew he must retreat, fast as he could, back across the pool.

It was only later that evening editing the photographs on his laptop, that he noticed the monofilament net drawn tight around the neck of the seal mother and recognised the inverted number seven pattern on her neck.

Immediately, his thoughts ran all over the question of how to release her. Recognising she was bound to the cave by her pup for a few more days, he quickly ran together an idea entailing the use of hoop nets, traditionally used by research groups to capture seals on land or in the shallows. It meant he must locate some heavy-duty plastic piping, work it into a circle and secure the place where the two ends met. That would serve for the entrance to a dwarf's hat, an elongated cone of small mesh, heavy-duty fishing net.

The plan of action needed little thought. His team must enter the cave on a falling tide, ensuring a maximum window of time in which to work. Ideally, the seal would come galumphing toward the cave entrance and run through the hoop into the net, which would then need to be tightened to prevent it from becoming a point of exit, thereby facilitating the cutting of the monofilament netting... as if life was ever that easy.

He knew it must be done soonest. The pup was but a few days from weaning and thereafter the netted mother would abandon the locality. There was a risk, though he doubted it, that the disturbance caused by any effort to liberate her would be sufficient cause for her to abandon the pup. The thought failed to inhibit his planning. The risk was worth taking.

He knew a sane option was to contact the RSPCA, but knew it was probable they would contact a seal sanctuary. He disliked the regime under which pups were kept — the length of their stay in captivity, the degree of exposure and potential habituation to people and dogs. Had he been anywhere near the facility at Portaferry in Ulster, beside Strangford Lough, he would have had no such qualms.

In any case, close by were friends who would help him. That evening, he contacted them.

***

Restless, Tyrian was fresh back from Scilly, drawn back to this place to which he felt he belonged but where he feared he might meet again his Nemesis. He shuffled uncertainly ashore in the headland cave. Hythar, a little belatedly, resisted his arrival with a song of warning against approaching more closely. To her amazement, because she had never warned off a male before, the handsome male halted courteously.

To one side and looming above him were the angles and ledges of brown granite walls. On the pale submerged sands, his body looked sparklingly dark. Enormous power and good health radiated from the stillness of him.

She sensed his reserve and uncertainty, but not how unique it was for him to have crossed the threshold of a nursery place. She could not know that for ten years, this black seal had wandered the world mainly alone, a nomad; in any case, her imagination was mainly focussed on her pup, Aleutia, who remained close by and yet asleep. The same pup reminded Tyrian of his earlier days. Then, excitement had been confined mainly to marking on the cave walls of his questing soul a map of the world as he was discovering it, day by day.

Wherever he went, among the sunlit-moonlit calms or the extreme violence of storms winter raging, he felt he was leaving indelible luminous trails. He found he could always find them, follow them, again. He discovered himself incapable of losing his way. Whatever the secret, it lay between the mysterious inner compass he followed, the patterns of land masses, the movements of heavenly bodies, the tastes of the seas and rivers he explored. It seemed he had compiled, unwittingly, a library of sights, tastes and sensations.

In time, having survived his first year, growing in size, awareness and power, confidence found life inside him. It grew through the adventures, across the years. Initially, he tried to be friendly with other seals but found himself rebuffed repeatedly by suspicious males or disdainful females. Being yet small, they recognised with clarity hurtful to him that he was a no-hoper. He had not even the status of inadequate challenger.

There were other immatures, of course. They always seemed willing to play, having not yet acquired the weighty, often pompous, gravitas of the older seals. But there came a time when he realised, quite literally, he had outgrown them. Increasingly, they showed themselves wary of him, of his increasing size, of his aura of ocean-wisdom that was the accidental burgeoning fruit of his far travels.

Now delivered back to the present in all his recovered power, fresh from the healing grounds of the Western Rocks of the Isles of Scilly, Tyrian was watching Hythar. This was not the female he sought. She was too small, but something of the brightness of her spirit pleased him. Her curiosity had shone betrayingly bright through the growled warning with which she had stayed him.

The tide flooded, ebbed. The two seals rested companionably on the drying cave sands, maintaining their distance but refraining from making any effort to heckle one another. Heckling was a commonplace nursery ground theatre in the seal world, but there was no joy in it; only custom. It was a little like a gang of street-corner boys whistling after unattainable girls passing by, or vice versa. Neither of the two seals here present had yet developed a nursery ground personality. Simply, they were themselves.

The wind whipped up. The waves grew bigger, heavier.

Before the next high tide, which occurred during the night, Aleutia was washed into the surf and bowled about there by the weight of it while Hythar slept. She had fallen asleep offering the bulk of her body as a breakwater against the surf, feeling the scrap of white-coated warmth that was her pup, safe against her black-blotched silvery back. It was Aleutia who, unnoticed, went exploring, chasing the receding flow of spent surf back around the body of her mother.

Tyrian observed all that befell. Since his arrival from Scilly, feeling peculiarly alert, the taste for sleep had been fading in him. Now, rather than be slapped and made generally bedraggled and restless by the runs of surf, he had driven his black body into the surf and was dancing with the water movement. The vibrancy of it all matched the sense of being alive that he was feeling. It felt good to be at home in the exploding heart of it all.

Amid his play, he caught the white, bedraggled movement of Aleutia and, no sooner had he noticed her than the next wave bowled her heavily up the beach. The wave hit the rocks at the back of the cave so hard that they cushioned Aleutia against what seemed the inevitability of being battered and immediately broken. Suddenly turned to a sodden scrap, the white rag of her was dragged brutally back, rolling over and over with the powerful ebb of the wave. Five times, backwards, forwards, she was bowled and dragged, before she was no longer on the beach, but in the sea being sucked outwards up the dark escarpment of the next wave. For a few saving moments, Tyrian intervened. His great black head became a dark island sheltering her against harm. For a few seconds, the confused pup was enabled to steal some breaths before the next roller coaster buffeting.

Three times the woebegone pup was sucked out to sea and three times the dark seal protected her with his bulk. The last time he saw the pup cart-wheeled ashore, he surged in behind her and offered a substitute breakwater against the confusion. He remained so for a while, until he felt the incorrigible pup begin to follow the lure of another spent wave. This time, he nudged her away from the course she sought to follow, reinforcing the communication with a low growl.

As growls go, it was unimpressive. He intended only a pup-sized warning. To the little pup, it sounded terrifying. Having cleared the air, they remained thereafter paired as protector and protected against whatever the sea saw fit to send to shore, until the tide had ebbed and Hythar wakened with a start.

Her first awareness was that no scrap of warmth nestled into her back. It was followed immediately by the sight of Aleutia nestled into the back of the handsome black seal. Confused, frightened, she drove angrily toward the two of them with an ululating cry. He did not flee immediately, wondering what was amiss. His very stillness caused her onward charge to falter, although she continued to ululate almost hysterically. Pausing, she lay with neck tensed as it extended towards him. Her mystachial whiskers along either jowl were cupped towards him, seemingly charged by the electricity of her emotions. Her dark eyes were fixed upon him.

The pup tried to make her getaway toward one side of the cave beach. She assumed Hythar's anger was directed at her for her foolish forays into the surf. This distracted Hythar for a moment; but then she resumed her charge toward Tyrian, causing him to wheel away into surf that, initially, exploded in all directions against his body.

Once consumed by the seething water but while yet stranded on the sand, he glanced once over his shoulder at her. There was no reproach. It was not his place to feel reproach. At the nursery grounds, as he had learned with his own mother's milk, seal mothers were queens, the only law.

He was sorry to be leaving. He liked this lively, brave, able female who, until the last, had been so good-natured. Gathering strength and focus, he dived powerfully into the breaking wave steepling before him and was gone from view. It did not occur to him that the little female he had so casually admired might soon become aware of regret that he was gone.

For a little while, she watched where he had gone, guessing wrongly and wrongly again where he might come to the surface. She did feel regret, but she was not yet sorry. That came later when the silent language of their kind passed between mother and pup. Then, Hythar learned a story that shamed her, making her sorry to lose so staunch and peculiarly modest a companion. He seemed unlike any male she had met before. At their wave-bound refuge, Hythar achieved the surprising insight that males are not all alike and may have thoughts in their heads unconnected with mating, fighting and hunting.

***

Unaware of the improvement of his reputation with Hythar, Tyrian swam powerfully across the shallow bay, through the big swell. Heavy waves rolled over like green wheels, so tall they were. Had he been in highest spirits, he might have responded to the temptation to roll with them, but instead he tracked along outside the great thunder, hiss and fizz of it all.

Part of what kept him behind the wave break was that he sensed the proximity of Meinek but he felt no fear. Rather, he was content to avoid him, knowing he yet lacked the pitiless, primitive violence that Meinek could deploy at will. He had roamed this length of coast during several late summers and autumns past. In fact, it was directly from the Land's End that he had explored the Western Approaches during the winter of the previous year. He had paused at Scilly, swum on in travelling mode north-westward until he had come to the inshore waters of Ireland and, in due course, to the Blasket's.

Before departing this coast, the year before, he had tentatively explored every cave. In the Great Cave, a lone female with a pup of just a few days old had driven him from the waters-edge with aggressive rushes and another song from the Book of Ululations. The singing females, these seal mothers, had songs which had the power of binding spells at this time of year. Pool Cave being empty, he had crossed the bay, drawn to the sound of seal-song and the crying of pups emanating from Waterfall Cave. Into it he had ventured, travelling quiet and carefully. For his reward, he found four seal mothers, each lying close to a pup and otherwise spread across the wide sand hill. Closer to the water's edge than any of them lay Meinek, whose head was not alert this once for whomsoever might be approaching from the sea but turned toward the seal mother beside the oldest of the pups, recognising the signs. She was coming into season, into breeding condition, and so his personal hunting radar had locked on to her.

He did not notice the younger male come to a standstill, upright in slightly more than his own depth of water, close to the granite wall. It was one of the seal mothers who noticed him, or thought she had. She came to the alert, stretching higher on her fore-flippers and peering intently toward him, her head craning to achieve a more certain view. The nearest female to where she lay noted this change in the demeanour of her neighbour and, likewise, grew alert. That was sufficient to alert Meinek. The great brown head swung around. His pitiless black eyes immediately picked out the black male. Without pause, he lumbered into movement, accelerating rapidly down the sand-hill and into the sea.

Tyrian had departed at the first sign of movement on the part of Meinek, submerging and swimming out of the cave and on as far as an islet that only showed above water at low tide. There, he twisted around the plateau of rock and surfaced to assess what was happening. He surfaced with the crest of a wave, peering intently toward the beach within the cave and felt immediate, acute alarm. Only two females remained, along with all four pups. Most alarmingly, he could not see Meinek.

He slipped back under the surface where he was immediately aware of a thrumming through the waters from the direction of the cave. It meant other seals were following his submerged getaway track. Thereupon, he powered away to seaward, travelling at his fastest speed, remaining submerged as long as he dared. It was as he paused that he felt Meinek. The remorseless male was not making a token chase. Now, he drove into Tyrian, or to where Tyrian had been taking breath the moment before. Like a matador before a bull, there was just enough strength in his body to eddy to one side and escape in the opposite direction to that of Meinek's lunge.

The chase went on longer than Tyrian feared, but he had drawn from himself all the guile at his command, which was greater than it had ever been, repeatedly changing course to eke out every fragment of advantage. Only when well beyond the northerly headland of the neighbouring cove did Meinek pull out of the chase. The great male had bidden farewell with a savage roar promising great ill to Tyrian, did he return. The latest fruit of that warning was the anxiety now nibbling at the edges of Tyrian's imagination.

He had been following no compass within himself when he returned to the place near where Meinek had roared the challenge of his farewell, the year before, and so recently reinforced by his humiliation. With initial shock, thinking Meinek was upon him again, unexpectedly now he met a male similar in size to himself. Pharos was extremely wary of him at first, but Tyrian made a few languid passes of the other, signalling he had no aggressive intent. Encouraged, Pharos relaxed his defensive posture.

Both were glad of the company. More relaxed than otherwise they might have been, they slept overnight in white waters surging around and over the headland stones across the bay from Hythar's nursery cave. When daylight returned, the two males remained on station. It was by the light of day that Tyrian saw the massive wound quarried into the nape of his companion and the shock in his large eyes.

It emerged that, on the previous day, Pharos had met Meinek for the first time. Like Tyrian, he had fled. Like Tyrian, he had been amazed by the speed and power of the paramount male who had not only overhauled him, but had taken a great chunk of hair and blubber out of his nape in the ferocious, one-sided battle that had ensued. Pharos described how he was forced to play dead for several minutes underwater before Meinek released his hold and went upon his way.

The wound had begun to heal already, but it would be a long time before Pharos would seek another battle. For this season, he had been rendered hors de combat. Soon, he would depart to find one of the sanctuary rocks, there to lie up and allow the healing to proceed. Tyrian asked him whether he had heard of Guthensbrâs Island, south along the coast.

Pharos had not heard of it by that name, for it had others, but it turned out he had already spent three low-water sessions resting there in the company of a small group of males and juveniles. It was the nearest local place of retreat available to seals wanting to be left at peace in this season of conflict.

However, before he made that coastwise passage, he travelled in the opposite direction across another great, sandy-bottomed bay backed by more pale granite cliffs. Above the cliffs, grassy slopes were patterned with spreads of the ever-flowering gorse, which served as a perch for stonechats, dunnocks, wrens and linnets, and lesser spreads of the maritime heathland. The pair of seals travelled across the greater part of the bay, two black submarine shadows. Their underwater passage ceased at the seaward entrance to a small maze of low-lying islets. There, they spent some time standing tall in the water to see if they could locate other seals. Finding none, they drifted into the main water channel between the rocky shore and the main trickle of islets.

Here, the sea was mainly calm, just an occasional sheet of seawater slopped over the islets, spilling into the main channel. Tyrian made a leisurely, slow-paced dive and drifted alongside a vertical wall of rock that was the underwater root of the largest islet. As he drifted, the sun came out from behind the scant cumulus clouds, brightening the waters and illuminating all the encrusting life there.

The effect was hypnotising. Every colour was brightened. There were green and mauve tentacles of snakelocks anemones waving beside the shorter maroon ones of beadlets; the strong, stubby tentacles of the large daisy anemones and the deceptively frail white tentacles of orange-tubed *Sagartia elegans*. There were glistening orange sea squirts. The swollen orange, red and sulphur encrustations of sponges appeared like some blotching condition intermittently covering especially overhanging tracts of rock. In other places, there were iridescent seaweeds: a clump of blue-green *Cystoseira tamariscifolia;* the beguiling petrol blue of the *Chondrus crispus.*

Farther along, where the islet ended and the full power of the ocean drove in during storms, there was an untidy pile of quite large boulders gathered about a ridge of bedrock. Because they had been long-settled, kelp holdfasts used them for anchorages, growing up from them while their fronds waved gently with the leisurely currents. There were clumps of dark-green, felt-like *Codium tomentosum*, whose fronds resembled the antlers of deer. There were fern-like fronds of the pale, honey-coloured *Desmarestia ligulata* and longer, much sturdier fronds of the laminarians, smooth-stemmed *Laminaria digitata*, rough-stemmed *Laminaria hyperborea* and the sea-wrinkled scabbards of *Laminaria saccharina*.

Most colourful of the life studding these rocks were the gorgeous jewel anemones in their arguably-lurid pinks and greens, flaunting their circlets of tentacles, each one culminating in improbably hard knobs.

The same algae were clamped by their holdfasts to the channel slopes. Together with the fronds growing from the seabed of great granite boulders, they conspired to make a three-dimensional kelp canopy, down through which the black seal coiled. Entirely devoid of hunting intent, he was enraptured by the riot of light, colour, and texture. He did not threaten the various wrasses he glimpsed disappearing surreptitiously into the sea forest.

Sometimes, along the edge of his vision, he glimpsed the long shadow of Pharos. Later, the other seal drifted upright down to the sea floor where his hind flippers wrapped around a protruding boulder of no great size. With no great strength of grip, he slept. It was as if that solid fragment relaxed him, made him feel safe while he slept, dreaming his troubled dreams.

All the while, the tide drained away.

Offshore, gannets tracked by and, for a while, hunted when a shoal of mackerel, looking like miniature tuna, tracked northward with the tide across the bay. Time and again they stalled, for the long instants hanging there, folding their marvellous, black-tipped wings back along and beyond their white flanks before spearing down into the sea. They pierced the marvellously elastic surface membrane of it with the appearance, weight and purpose of javelins. Five seconds, maybe six, seven, eight, nine, ten, they would disappear below the surface before making buoyant re-emergences. Some swallowed mackerel; more did not. For brief interludes, then, they would bob there before stirring their wings and, slowly at first, generate power and momentum to achieve lift-off. At the last, their black feet would be pattering fast as they could run across the sea surface.

While the surf-bright, surf-white birds plunged and plundered the gleaming shoals, passing flocks of dainty kittiwakes, also with ink-black wingtips, danced prettily just above the reach of any spume wind-scuffed off wave crests. If a piece of fish was lost in the hunting of the gannets, a kittiwake would see it, manoeuvre down deftly, and take it.

The gulls were warier than the smaller kittiwakes, fearing the spears of bills wielded so deftly by the gannets, who knew no real oppressor in these southern waters. Farther north, in the years of his far-wanderings, Tyrian had seen them tormented by brown-plumaged pirate birds above the ferocious tidal streams of the Pentland Firth and off the Monachs in the Outer Hebrides; great skuas and the hardly less fearsome Arctic skuas. Landing on the backs of food-laden gannets homeward-bound to their young at the nesting station, they startled them into regurgitating whatever they had won. As soon as the fish fell free, the gannet would lose its rider who would swoop down with brutal but exquisite grace to recover, examine, swallow the swag before it was reclaimed by the sea and lost to the seabed scavengers.

Inshore, a young kestrel, born that year, hovered over the cliff edge, elegant in black-barred chestnut. There was nothing about her remotely as dangerous and unbiddable as her slate-grey cousins, the peregrine falcons, whose nest was in the neighbouring bay. The jackdaws would never even dream of trying to torment the peregrines. Kestrels were a different matter.

Ever since Ar-Laran had become independent of her parents in late summer, she had been harried by the local robber band of jackdaws. Many were the lizards and voles who escaped her patient, controlled, stealthily murderous descents because of bullying jackdaw ambushes. They would slither acrobatically down the slopes of the wind, screaming abuse, forcing the graceful little huntress to tip her wings and slide out of their way. She did not fear them, but had grown to hate their ubiquitous noise, as well because they seemed to have selected her as a favourite target.

She had begun to tailor her hunting schedule to take maximum advantage of times when the jackdaws were elsewhere, bullying someone other or exploiting some item of carrion on cliff-top or shore.

Having taken a slow worm, she had brought it to a sea-facing perch just below a clifftop facing out over the Mermaid's Pool. There she feasted despite the sound of the jackdaws roistering by, somewhere over the heights behind her. This time, they did not guess at her presence, leaving her to feast in peace above the watery place to which the seals almost always came at low tide.

Today, there were just two males. One was sleeping while the other drifted lazily beside the underwater walls and through the waving weedy fronds; tireless in slow motion. Some way along from the kestrel, which he had seen perched there this day as well as on other occasions, a barefoot man in faded shirt and baggy trousers rolled up almost to the knees picked his way over the lip of the cliff and down a steep, trackless slope. Below the grass, he trod over crumbs of granite, passing by occasional gleaming black bosses of tourmaline. Beside one such clump, he turned to peer closely at it. In so doing, he drew an eyeglass from his pocket to aid his examination. He was a man who carried an odd variety of tools in rucksack and pockets.

The eyeglass he had carried since being persuaded of the need of it by his friend, Martin. Of necessity, and after so many years of plying his trade as a wildlife tour leader, Martin was formidably well-informed about the renowned geology of Cornwall, and so, too, its flora. Part of it had come by endless personal exploration of the world he had always loved. Part came because he had the vision to bring in specialists to work with him for one day in a week with the holiday groups he introduced to those places and things he loved. He would drink in what they said, in part because finding out about things is fascinating of itself, but also to be able to add something extra to the future holiday adventures stretching before him. Nowadays, the eyeglass was ever-present, being whipped out to peer at a vug of minerals in the rock, at the detail of the petals of a flower, this before the initially bemused, subsequently enthused, holidaymakers.

Such a simple tool, it added to the quality of the day; for Martin and, at that moment, for Amaury, influenced by his friend. He peered with pleasure at the closely-packed spindles of black in their granite setting as he had done so often before.

Having pleasured his eyes, Amaury extracted the new camera and lens combination that had consumed one-quarter of his scant savings and took a close-up shot of the tourmaline. Then he moved to the bottom of the slope, where he stood just below eye-level with the black vug — as the Cornish called crystal-laden hollows in the rock — to take a more distant shot. Looking seaward, having scanned the view beyond and below, he packed away his camera.

Now he settled into the stone depths of a natural granite throne cut into the edge of a small sea tower. Here, he had often rested before. It gave him a perfect seat, with arm-rests, from which to observe the seals below in their favourite water resting place. In such a seat, a god might have sat, looking about himself with greatest satisfaction.

This was his favourite such place in all Cornwall. Here, as at the nearby islands, islets and sea caves, he had taught himself seals. Initially, he made a list of the range of their behaviours, ashore and in the sea. Having drawn up that list, leaving space for a few extra behaviours, he had drawn up a table with a long row of cells beside each behaviour and finally a plan view of the locality. Thereafter, he made observations of what every seal was doing at intervals of two minutes for several hours each day over a period of several weeks.

This had yielded a fair insight into what the local seals were doing. Even in so short a time, it was clear that behaviour as well as the sex and age ratios of the seals varied from site to site. He repeated his labour through successive seasons.

It was hard work. In the winter, he got wet and cold, but he found it all interesting and worthwhile. He learned eagerly.

It became clear that their behaviour varied not only between sites but between individuals. Some identified seals remained locally-based for the greater part of the year. Others appeared to return only for the breeding period. Still others returned intermittently, in cycles that, via reference to the photo-catalogue toward which those early studies had inclined him, he came to recognise.

Fitting together the jigsaw pieces was the principal excitement. Encouraged by his distant mentor, he persevered and slowly began to tease out part of the story here to be told, about the seals of Land's End. But it was a slow process. He came to regard it as a form of alternative brass-rubbing: slow emergences.

Now, he was aware of a frisson of excitement as a familiar black male seal surfaced and, with their weird-wild facility for feeling themselves watched, turned three-quarters of a circle to return his stare.

He recalled readily those three days since, down near Headland Cave, he had captured an image of this seal. Running through his records that evening, the wanted poster of this latest seal image on one side of his computer screen and the reel of images already catalogued rolling by on the other, he had experienced the excitement of a matching image. He had photographed him last year, also outside Headland Cave. He was not easy to mistake for another male. Clearly, he must be moving up the male social scale into the fighting years. His present location suggested he was still not quite strong or wilful enough to see off paramount males like the brown colossus currently dominating the entrance waters of Waterfall Cave. Or did it?

As usual, there were many potential assumptions, but too many pieces missing from his personal jigsaw of confirmations. As much as he could, he tried to think like a seal without ever being entirely certain that he was succeeding; but it felt like the best way to study them.

Tyrian lingered all day at the Mermaid's Pool but, when the dimpsey hour arrived, swam back across the bay for one last time with Pharos. The man who had noticed them had long since trotted home along the coast path. Ar-Laran had hunted successfully thrice more and was now perched on a ledge above the entrance to a small, dog-legged sea cave that opened into the Mermaid's Pool. Farther in on the same ledge were the collapsed, guano-painted remains of the nest made by a pair of shags who had raised two grey plumaged, blue-eyed young to independence by the end of June. Between the nest and the kestrel lay a scattered pile of small bones, mainly having once belonged to mice but now all belonging to the crypt of kestrel-slain.

Across the bay, the two males came to the parting of their ways, there making a friendly farewell. The day of quiet company had allowed Pharos to recover some equilibrium, some confidence. When he was gone, in the direction of Guthensbrâs Skerry, Tyrian continued to dive and roll in the white waters around the headland rocks, aware that though he had retraced his morning route there was no thought in his head about what to do or where to go.

Simply, he loved this bay, its caves and islets. They exerted allure, somehow reminiscent of his own birthplace in the far north-west of Wales. On the north-west tip of Ynys Môn, in the greatest cave of Ynys Arw on the shores of the Irish Sea, he had been born. His first swimming lessons had been in a porpoise-haunted tide race bowling wildly along just outside the cave entrance.

This was a gentler place despite the power of the ocean brought to bear on these shell-sand shores. There were safer inshore hiding places from storm seas and the tide races felt less potent. Here, also, more varied shoals of fish awaited discovery and pursuit.

On the other side of the ledger, there was infinitely more human pressure on this coast. More people came ever-closer to the nursery places. Infinitely more killing nets were set just above the sea-floor and many more boats dragged the offshore seas even down to their floors with vast nets.

He wanted nothing more than to rest on a beach. It was not a privilege for which he wanted to fight. Just to lie on sand in a cave, out of the showers that were threatening, and out of reach of the surf. With no other thought in his mind, he went with the flow of the steep swell, along the side of the headland into the cavernous entrance of the nearest sea cave. To one side, when he glanced up in passing, he noticed the remains of a raised beach. This year, yet another pair of shags had nested there.

He drifted with the swell into the cave. Ahead of him, its main fairway bisected his line of approach, but he went with the curling of a secondary wave. This swerved abruptly toward the greater darkness of the interior, to the left. The unexpected acceleration of it brought him to a rude grounding on the wet, hard-packed sand-slope within.

There was no sense of Meinek having been here, but as his eyes adjusted to the lesser light, he found himself far from alone. On either side of the sandy, seal-tracked fairway, a female seal lay close by her pup. His attention rested first with the female with the older pup — Tyrian guessed it to be about fourteen days old though, in truth, it was never easy to guess the age of any pup, so variable was the quality of maternal care. Here, it was not so much the female who commanded attention but the pup. The mother must be close to mating condition. Reluctantly, then, his attention slid down the cave fairway to the male seal who lay between him and her.

He recognised him. Balanec had been resting on the neighbouring islet on the day he had been humiliated and chased away by Meinek. Born among ferocious tidal streams such as Tyrian might have found familiar off the west coast of Brittany, he moved between Brittany and Cornwall regularly. Always he came north in midsummer to be close to the Cornish breeding grounds. Very few grey seal pups were born on Breton shores so opportunities to mate there were scarce. More pertinently, males nearly always find their mating partners away from the locality where they were born. He was no exception.

Here, Balanec was wise enough not to challenge or provoke Meinek. He was content to live quietly, aside from the mainstream and here was a justification for that strategy. These two females would soon be in mating condition and, Meinek being preoccupied in

Waterfall Cave, Balanec would mate with them, probably becoming the father of pups born here next autumn.

The two females had become alert. Alora, the one with the younger pup, was singing softly, not yet feeling too anxious about the seemingly respectful newcomer lingering at the far reach of the surf.

Balanec had expected no new arrivals. His back had been to the sea but now he was looking over one heavy shoulder, growling at a low pitch. At the growling end of his body, his nostrils told him Er-Erie was close to breeding condition. The perfume of hope pre-occupied him, making him reluctant to turn from her. He had the choice taken from him. A wave larger than any that had gone before surged in, soaking the newcomer and causing him, quite helplessly, to be swept farther up the sand-hill than he had thought to move.

This was unacceptable, bringing him much closer to the two seal mothers. Balanec whipped around and, extending his neck, began a sequence of savage snarls, making blood-curdling promises threatening the future of the younger intruder.

Tyrian stared back at him, entirely unimpressed by this display. He was far-travelled and had known, despite prolonged interludes of solitude, many kinds of seal companions. In all the years of his life, he had never initiated a brawl with another seal. There seemed no natural inclination to fight in him. However, the attitude of this Balanec irritated him. Meinek he feared because there was reason to fear him. Meinek was more than just a physical colossus. He was steeped in the lore of battle, a living encyclopaedia of battle. He would remain feared long after his power was eventually broken and much longer after lesser seals had lost their aura of invincibility. Even in his fear of Meinek, Tyrian felt a profound respect and appreciation for his enemy.

Balanec lacked similar mettle. Somewhere inside himself, as he returned the aggressive stare, he was certain he could outfight and drive off this blustering male. There was even the inclination in him to take up the challenge because he found himself suddenly weary of being pushed around. He had no desire to swim after Pharos to the safe-haven off Gwennap Head. On the other hand, he was the intruder. Here, he had inadvertently blundered into a safe, orderly little out-of-the-way world. That much he could concede.

The jumbled intensity and indifference of his feelings communicated themselves. The snarling fell silent and the bigger seal bunched up his body as a prelude to making an attack. Yet he was in two minds because his instincts always veered toward caution.

The initiative was taken by Tyrian, swinging away peaceably into the shallows. This triggered Balanec into launching a chasing, harrying probe, but as suddenly as he departed the disputed shore, Tyrian whipped around, his body grounded on hard-packed sand under the thin layer of water. There, silhouetted against the swiftly-fading light behind him in the cave entrance, he appeared impressively massive. Daunted, Balanec drew up short, with difficulty. Now, in turn, Tyrian spoke. The words he used were not blood-curdling but to the point. If Balanec chose to make an issue of his departure, they could fight it out. Otherwise, he could remember his manners.

With that, Tyrian turned and, without haste, swam out to the lesser darkness waiting around the corner. Left in possession of the unexpectedly bloodless sand-hill, Balanec allowed himself a snort of relief. Belatedly, he recognised the youngster had a formidable way about him. Glad not to have been put to the test, he lumbered around and made his way slowly back up the hill, settling again just below Er-Erie and her milk-fat pup. He noticed she exhibited a sense of withdrawal as if she, too, had sensed the untested quality of the black seal, and was feeling some regret at his departure.

Meanwhile, Tyrian returned the way he had come, swimming down the tunnel back out into the swell. Still not prepared to abandon the bay, he let the swell determine where he went. It washed him farther inshore. He passed four islets. The one with the steepest slopes was crowded with roosting shags, the many brown ones among them having been born this year at nest sites about the bay on cliff ledges and inside the several sea caves. Many such sites were still highlighted by great name-plates of thin, smooth chalk whitening the vertical cliff-faces below them.

Approaching the last of the islets, just offshore from a small promontory, he heard something on the wind, or thought he did. It sounded like the singing of a seal. Around the last islet, the surf was piling, breaking, hastening Tyrian inshore and forcing him once more to beach abruptly, without grace, on massive honey-coloured boulders. Even as he struggled and failed to achieve secure landfall, he heard the sounds again, this time more clearly. For some time thereafter, he was struggling in churning white water and so the singing was roughly punctuated by intended and unintended submergences.

There is always a lull in the percussion of the surf, sooner or later. That much was common knowledge to seals and surfing people. Therefore, when it came, he hauled himself out of the sea, awkwardly up over the first fence of boulders and the jumble of lesser rocks beyond. This brought him under the sea cave lintel into the first and smaller of two cave pools. He was nervous of his reception, but because there was no sense Meinek had been present in recent days and because he was growing weary, he decided to proceed.

The main cave pool reached nearly all the way to the Tooth Rock, allowing him a relatively easy passage deep into the cave. He drifted in with strong pulses of water, the memory of it returning. Previously, his visit had been made on a slightly higher tide. He could remember the cubby-hole beyond the Tooth, and smaller boulders partly obstructing the widest part of the fairway.

He reached the gap between the Tooth and the cathedral wall, resting there for a while in a shallow pool. Just around the skirts of the Tooth, a fat, white-coated pup stared up at him without knowing what to make of him. His bulk and much shortened white hair made him look about a fortnight old.

Having taken some small notice of the pup, Tyrian looked beyond into the deepening gloom of the interior and there, indistinctly, made out two figures.

They were difficult to see clearly because a great tangle of kelp lay strewn across the interior fairway, in stark contrast with the bare sands on to which he had hauled himself from the long pool. Here was a great kelpy mattress of a sea cave floor. In fact, it looked like a moment in the life of a stormy sea, frozen in an instant of time into gleaming kelpy peaks and shadowy, slithery troughs.

His first reaction, however, was irritation. After all, he was going to have to fight for the pleasure of resting here. Illumination followed swiftly on the heels of first impressions. Neither seal was a male, but there was no leisure to relax. One of the females was moving directly toward him as swiftly as the mattress floor permitted. The sounds of her breathing were so tortured and horrible that he was almost unnerved, so strange it was, but he did not allow his lapse of confidence to show. Rather, he drew himself up to his fullest bulk.

Mornalas stopped just short of him. Extending her neck to the limit, she began to sing, to wish him away, reinforcing the measure by vibrating one of her fore-flippers against his mighty chest. To his surprise, the second female joined her, joining her own song to that of her companion. The sounds they achieved were powerful indeed, but more than the power of it, Tyrian sensed that the second seal, improbably, was not a seal mother or about to become one. To his own surprise, he even identified what she was. He recognised a midwife seal.

Even among seals, which often have a fine way of overlooking details of the lives of outlandish seals living outside the mainstream, few knew of midwife seals. This was true even for many of the seals who had been supported by them at the needful times. Courtesy of his travels along the Irish west coast, Tyrian had met several of them by now, becoming steeped in their lore and loving their stories. In not quite every case, they were celibate females, or females who would bear nevermore bear young. He had found them to be wise, gentle and thoughtful. In addition, he was aware of their burden of history. Frustrated by nature or mischance from becoming what it was most natural for them to become, for consolation they had won a deep knowledge of seal lore as well as a nomad-knowledge of the wideness of the world.

On the west coast of Ireland, more than anywhere else, they were the ones keeping alive the memory of what it had been in time-past to be a grey seal. In the Baltic, in the Barents Sea, around the seal cave riddled coasts of the Faeroe Islands and the volcanic coasts of Iceland, they said there were other midwife seals keeping other lines of seal memory alive in the face of severe hunting pressures. He heard how, on the edge of the Russian and Greenland ice-fields, rumours came of yet others who were custodians of fragments of the same story.

In their company, Tyrian became once more a very young seal. Usually quite frail, modest and always poorly marked though they were, he was warmed by them. That they had made time to include him he found particularly humbling: especially, that they should have sensed some quality in him to which they desired to sing.

Tyrian, like Mornalas, was born into natural self-confidence and well-being, but the regard of the midwife seals had deepened and enriched that confidence. With them, he experienced the only sense of true kinship he had felt since he had been a white-coated pup, drunk at his mother's nipple.

He had expected to emerge from his circumnavigation of Ireland a more knowledgeable and a more interesting seal. No-one needed point out, either, that he was on the brink of participating in the great mating drama. He was bowling along toward that lovely point in life when he became a bold, merry, wicked seal. He had an expectation of winning his battles and, thereafter, appearing blackly beautiful and irresistible to the seal mothers at the nurseries.

In the end, he had emerged from the Irish sojourn a quieter, more reflective male. He had lost nothing of the desire to be bold, merry and wicked, but somehow his recent experiences had left also an uncontrived atmosphere of mystery clinging to him.

Consequently, he endured the harangue of the two seals peaceably until they fell silent, puzzled before the massive silence of him. As a behaviour, it was reminiscent to them of the most confident of supposedly dominant males, but it was shocking in one this young. Shock was to follow on the heels of shock. He had no singing voice worth the name but in Ireland, because he had spent so many evenings with midwife seals, he had learned some of their simpler songs. Now, to offer his goodwill to them and proclaim his peaceable intentions, he raised his own voice. At the outset, it was pitifully off-key, but it grew with the telling. That he sang in the dialect of the Gaelic seals betrayed by whose flippers he had done his learning. That he should know anything at all from the world of the midwife seals was amazing indeed to Ithian.

In response, she shuffled a little closer in the dark, singing much more softly and personally now:

"Here is a surprise indeed! How is it you know something of the secret of our songs?"

Something akin to a sigh of relief escaped Tyrian: "It is a long story but, if you have the patience and space for me, I hope I can make it interesting for you. My name is Tyrian and I am very weary. May I share these sands with you?"

Ahead of him, the two females did now confer. He tried not to listen to the music passing between them although he sensed the resistance in the seal mother who had initially challenged his entry. The well-fed pup, Somerledaa, had wandered away, making a laborious progress up the sand-hill. Behind him, Tyrian could hear the flooding waters.

It took a long time but Ithian prevailed. Mornalas retreated almost to the back of the cave, albeit not out of earshot. There, her tortured breathing would remain painfully audible for the remainder of the night. Meanwhile, in her wake, Tyrian followed Ithian up the beach to a point just above the cubby-hole and on the opposite side of the widest part of the chamber.

"Here we should remain out of the reach of the surf, come high tide, leaving you free to begin your story?"

Tyrian gazed back at Ithian, searching for a place to begin and then grunting:

"It begins long ago and faraway, like so many stories, beginning where the wind itself begins." Ithian recognised his words for the traditional form of beginning that they were.

***

They did not sleep that night. Because it was what she had really asked, Tyrian recounted for her the story of his life and, most particularly, of his recent travels, the places he had visited, the seals he had met, the companions who had shared small journeys along the way. Sometimes, she took over from him, elaborating some detail that he had not understood or filling in details he could not possibly have known. Sometimes, they fell silent or as silent as the breathing of Mornalas, or the snoring of untroubled Somerledaa permitted, dreaming her milk dreams.

***

Most recently, he had returned to some early haunts. Just as Ithian had swum high up into the horribly polluted stew of the Baltic Sea, Tyrian had swum out to his favourite stretch of the Shelf edge. During winter last year, he drifted west along the coasts of southern Ireland. That coast had always held fascination, serving as a haven or a launch pad for him into the vastness of the ocean.

It seemed perfect, seen through a seal's eye. There were haul-out sites, potential nursery caves and coves, proximity to the richest hunting grounds and, most especially, there was the greatest allure of the Shelf edge itself.

At the end of a bright December day, he had paused to sleep outside the tiny haven of Dunquin, nestled under its long peninsular, the domineering peak of Mount Brandon looming behind. Earlier, coming across Dingle Bay, he had melted discreetly past a small swarm of crowded boats. They were full of people, bound toward or circling around or come to stillness near the famous hermit-dolphin, Fungie, who had been expelled from the pod to which he belonged for having slain a dolphin calf during overly boisterous play. News of his aberration travelled so that all dolphin pods turned their faces from the sickness in his spirit. On occasions, when he was driven to seek out their company, he was brutally repulsed. The dominant dolphins in the pod would lead the attack, repeatedly raking him with their teeth.

The lonely dolphin had seen the seal. In his peculiar, busy loneliness, he had hunted for Tyrian who, for no conscious reason, sought without effort to evade his sonar curiosity. The dolphin, bulky and almost twice the length of Tyrian, traced him to the sea floor where he was swimming along upside down, swerving effortlessly through a maze of large bedrock protrusions.

The beak of the questing dolphin probed toward the seal. Tyrian coiled his body about for some moments so that coarsely his whiskered snout tickled the smooth grey beak.

It was something unique for Tyrian, but not for Fungie. The dolphin, having ascertained the identity of this visitor to his home bay, lost interest and powered away. Shortly afterwards, he surged gloriously up into the air where, before falling back, he heard familiar, American-style whooping of delight coming from boats that had drifted a little apart during his prolonged underwater absence.

Nobody in the boats saw Tyrian surface to draw the breaths he needed. Neither did he desire to be seen. He was shy of people and boats, recognising danger in a precautionary sort of way. When boats approached places where he was resting, he never lingered, always sliding into the water without waiting to check the intentions of the boat or the people it carried.

Near Dunquin, he met a seal he might have been seeking across all his lonely years. He was yet small, a youngster in the fourth year of life teetering on the brink of the Rubicon of sexual maturity. Called Iolair, he was named improbably after the eagles that once spread their vast wings in the boisterous, cloud-haunted airs above the peak of Mount Brandon and had lately been noticed at Sneem by Tyrian when swimming far up the Kenmare River.

Iolair was, like Tyrian, completely black. Each was mildly surprised by the rare coincidence of colour, prompting them to take more note of one another than otherwise might have been. Iolair, approaching the much larger male, had enquired courteously whether he minded if they continue swimming together for a while.

Lacking strong feelings, Tyrian agreed. It had been a very long time since he had found himself travelling in the company of another seal and wondered, not very seriously, whether he would remember how to communicate in the seal's way after so prolonged a silence. That evening, he learned the answer. They had settled at Dunquin, idling in the sea close to where they had met. Both were watching a tall sailing boat with a dark blue hull paused at anchor but planning to sail on to Dingle harbour. The name on its side was Sailfish. The skipper was a sailor of some renown, presently hunting for sightings of turtles and other marine megafauna. Since May, he had been transecting along a great arc of the Shelf Edge from a point south-west of Cape Clear to a point between Scotland and Iceland. The crews he carried consisted of a mix of volunteers and paying passengers, each new crew working for a week or two as a makeshift research team. For everyone, it was a glorious adventure.

The smaller seal remembered aloud, crooning quietly:

"It is noisy with people tonight. It is not always like this. Noise is a summer phenomenon. For the remainder of the year, it is quiet and only the fishing boats and maybe the divers to be wary of."

Few places compared for tranquillity, even in the seal world, with these far south-western headlands, coves and islands.

"Where do you come from, Tyrian?"

"Far to the east, beyond all the shores of Ireland. On the far north-western shore of an island called Ynys Mon by some, Anglesey by others; but my nomadic home is a promontory culminating at the place called Land's End, in Cornwall."

"Ah, yes! I have heard of it. I see why you smile. Is it true people are numerous there as stars in the night sky and yet still there are places for the nurseries and the moulting? How can that be?"

"I know; it is strange to me, also. People are strange. They drive in boxes along roads and leave the wide fields empty. They lie like seals at haul-out sites on all the sandy beaches but hardly visit the rocky places. They walk along the cliff paths, backwards, forwards. They see us and we see them. At some places, they come in boats seemingly to stare at us. Only rarely do I see them swimming, except from the fast boats, and then all dressed in black with big drums on their backs, glass in front of their faces and fins on their feet that feel hard and taste strange."

"Here it is different. As different as that fine boat from the ones they launched from Dunquin harbour the long years since. Before, they used no fuel to make the waters taste so unpleasant. Then, they used boats made of timber laths over which they stretched and tarred canvasses. Light as feathers, they seemed, in the waters of the Sound. Fast and light and true. Those boats were like kin to us; distant kin. They were at home on the sea."

Tyrian turned his great head and looked enquiringly at the small, black seal:

"You tell the story as if you had been there when the first such currach's were made."

"I suppose you could say I was, in a way. It is the tradition of the seals of these parts to remember the past as far back as it can be remembered. All our young ones are taught to remember. That is, the ones who stay and do not set forth, a-roaming, in the fine, grand manner of yourself."

"Are you made to learn?"

It was the turn of the smaller seal to be amused:

"The opposite! Do you remember how it was for you, when you left the nursery ground for the first time? Not knowing where to hunt, how to hunt, what to hunt? Perhaps, not even knowing how to swim? Not knowing where it might be safe to haul-out, especially among other much larger seals? Friendless, in great danger."

"Indeed, although it was not as awful as you describe, for I could swim from the third day of my life. I had no choice. There was a storm. I was dragged into the sea despite my best efforts — which, as I recognise now, were puny — and there I learned. My mother, from time to time, offered me her back, that I might use it for an island. I suppose she protected my life for just as long as it took me to learn to protect it for myself. But, for the rest, it is true that it is a tough beginning."

"Do they still hunt for pups there, at Ynys Mon and the Land's End?"

"Not hunt to kill. They do tell stories of pups being stolen from the shore and taken away in cages. Some of the stolen have returned to us. It seems they are held in human places, where more people come to stare but not to kill, and never in boats. Why do you ask?"

"Because we always try and evade the men who come to kill us here. As far back as the storytellers can remember, men have killed seals with clubs in the quiet places where we rest by the sea. They do it during the fair days of summer and most of all on the autumn nursery grounds. And you know how important to our kind those grounds are. We could change, move elsewhere, but very strongly we prefer not to. There is the deepest belonging to place, especially for us of the far-west."

99

Now both were silent. Tyrian asked: "Why do they try to kill you?"

"I don't know. No-one knows. Perhaps it is part of their tradition, as storytelling is ours. Perhaps they have always been hunters? Though I have tried, I cannot put my mind into theirs. We hunt for fish. They hunt for fish. I believe they want no rivals. So, they come with clubs or shoot us with guns. For our part, we try to become invisible. We teach the new-borns to be wary of boats, nets — especially the invisible, almost unbreakable ones that the sea-people set. We teach them to be wary of human sounds and the sounds of their dogs. So, when we leave the nursery grounds, those of us who do not become nomad seals find ourselves welcome at the haul-out sites among the old ones — the ones who fight no more and produce young no more. They make us welcome. They encourage us. They tell stories of our ancient history, hundreds and hundreds of years ago; and they teach us how to remember them. That is the tradition here in the far-west."

"But how does it help?" demanded Tyrian. "Does it stop the killing?"

"No. Ask yourself, then: when the world becomes a dangerous, frightening place, where death swoops without warning, what happens to true things and especially what happens to the seals? I will tell you. They change. I will tell you something else. Their ways do not change quickly enough, so life becomes confused, unhappy, restless, pointless; degraded. The old ones teach us what we have been and tell us something of what we are and what has always been worthwhile." He paused, and then went on more quietly: "Tyrian, what is life for us? We are the dwellers at the edge of the world. We rove beyond the edge of what is known. It seems to me there is no great harm in us except, occasionally, when males are in their prime and eager to fight. Yet everywhere we dwell along these coasts, they try to kill us."

Both fell silent reflecting on that. Later, they slept. In the night, however, they were wakened by the sounds of powerful outboard motors and glimpsed the silhouettes of two boats crowded with men bulkily clad in dry suits and hats. A little afterwards, they felt the disturbance of waters churned by their passing.

Iolair was instantly alert, his face looking now suddenly much older than his few years. He looked as if he was going to crash-dive in his anxiety. It seemed an extreme response to something so normal, but Tyrian forbore to comment. He was, after a fashion, the guest of the smaller local seal.

Now staring, wild-eyed, at Tyrian: "Will you come with me?" he enquired abruptly, nervously.

"Where to?"

"Across the Sound, after that boat. To the Blaskets."

Tyrian felt no desire to be chasing shadows, but Iolair had given him a fine evening and, out of courtesy, he quelled his reservations: "So be it!"

Imperceptibly, the atmosphere lightened and forthwith Iolair led him out past the silent yacht, its light shining dully at the masthead, mainsail furled loosely, neatly, around the boom. The folk aboard were sleeping but for the watchman huddled in the stern. When the fast boat had gone tearing by, he had glanced at his watch. Just after three o'clock: strange time to be setting out. He supposed they were fishermen but, being unfamiliar with the customs of the locals, he made an entry in his notebook to record the incident. Then, unscrewing the stopper of his flask, he poured himself a small, sustaining cup of black coffee.

It took the seals more than half an hour to cross the Sound, to come under the looming shadow of a massive island. In times-past, people had been cut off there periodically, especially during the winter months, for many weeks at a time from the nearby mainland, just three miles yonder. The seas were reminiscent of those parting north-west of Porthgwarra, off the Land's End coast. Shallow, strewn with rocks perilous to shipping; dramatic tide races and over falls.

That night, the moon was full. The tides ran particularly strongly, hindering even the two tide dancers. It had been otherwise for the fast boats full of men. One empty boat, the seals discovered, drawn up on a long, white moonlit strand striped with dark lines of kelp marking the twice-daily reach of successive high tides.

Onward, south-westward, the two seals flowed; Iolair forever peering toward the shore, scenting the air, listening. They swam all the way to the southern tip of the island, and beyond to the isles of Inis na Bró and Inisnacileáin. At Inisnacileáin, there was a great sea cave into which they trespassed, sensing seals resting within, but they did not land or linger. They headed back to the long, white beach with its empty boat and where, now, they scented something they preferred not to name even to themselves.

Approaching the far southern corner of the beach, the hairs were erect on the back of their necks. Ahead of them in the dark, they could smell blood. Quite close to shore a hoarse, lingering cry of lamentation rang out. Two voices, three together, all took up the note, developing it. There was something frantic about the sounds.

All the instincts Tyrian had honed so keenly were screaming at him to flee for his life. Reason did not prevent him but the extraordinary foolhardiness or courage of his small companion. Iolair truly was well-named after the eagle, for now he stranded on the shore and was forcing himself up toward the horrible sounds.

The reality was worse than the fear. Following reluctantly, Tyrian flinched back violently the first time he touched a peculiarly inanimate but still warm body. Sniffing it, he recognised it was a pup, or what remained of it. The white coat was damp, saturated with blood, its head misshapen from the blow it had taken from a club wildly swung.

Tyrian knew how to count, but this night he lost count of the number of broken-bodied pups found ruined on this beach where seals had borne their young for centuries.

Nor only pups. Among the slain, lay five dead seal mothers; dead and worse than dead. They had not been beaten solely with clubs. Clubs would have been bad enough. No; these seal mothers had been beaten with clubs into which great nails had been hammered. The cruelty of it, the soullessness, was enough to drive sanity into hiding.

Tyrian found his mind swamped by horror, trying to hide from any more horror. Iolair had to bump into his head to attract his attention. The smaller black face looked grey with the ugliness of what he had seen, and him just four short years in the world:

"You are stronger and faster than me. It is probably too late, but I implore you to run with all speed to the north end of the Island. There are more mothers there; more pups…"

Tyrian was gone already. Now, at last, Tyrian the Nomad grew fully into his own skin. Faster than ever he had swum before, submerging as soon as he was in waters that were sufficiently deep enough, he drove through short, steep seas freshening with the coming of the dawn. He used all his considerable water-wisdom, hitching a ride wherever chance presented itself on this piece of tidal stream, then that. Most of the time, all thought blanked, he drove along just above the seabed. He did not watch where he was going but drove blindly for the precise place Iolair had described for him.

Gannets were diving off the pale strand when he reached it. They were making a fine catch among a glittering shoal of herring. A few seal heads turned at the furious arrival of the great stranger. Among them, a bull the size of Meinek moved to block his passage to the beach, but Tyrian did what he would never have thought to do had he arrived at any other time. He just barged through him as if he had not been there; such was his intensity of purpose. He drove to the end of his swimming strength to that pale shore. Where he landed, he found himself gazing down at a live little pup with huge dark eyes just beyond the second empty boat. Was it three, four days old? Not thinking, he grabbed the shocked scrap by the baggy nape, tossing it over his shoulder into the sea.

Then he went rampaging up the hill, finding his song and singing voice, both. It is not often given to male seals to sing and certainly, it had never been given to Tyrian in his wanderings. Most often, he forgot he had a voice, so solitary were his haunts.

Halfway to the back of the strand, he had to pause to catch his breath. It was not in his mind to try to sing out his warning, but that was what befell. Deep and wise, the bass notes came rumbling out, rusty and awkward at first, then growing in authority. Dimly, higher up the beach he saw men pause in the act of wielding their clubs in the developing dimpsey light. Two seals came charging down the beach followed more slowly by a pup. The song continued. Two men came running towards him. Suddenly, his ears and nose began to work and the shock of it hit him again. Here was death, cruel and bloody death, once more. The white rags: the dead pups, all less than three weeks old; the red rags, the darker, inanimate mounds that marked the last resting place of their mothers. One bull, surrounded by three flailing men, still roared his defiance, but they were weakening until there rose not the ululating lamentations of the mothers but the more savage roar of triumphant men as the great bull seal fell at last to whimpering and then to silence. They had reasserted the only real authority on this farthermost fringe of Europe.

Let the sentimental folk of southern England or metropolitan Holland and Germany raise their ignorant, bleating voices in sentimental complaint. What did they know about edge of the world realities? This was the way things had always been done here. This was the way things would be done. Who would have the courage, be they ever so sentimental for the cause of seals, to challenge a bold Munsterman with a nailed club in one hand, a fist for the other and the fighting spirit within to command them both?

The two bulky men running toward Tyrian were hindered, else his must surely have been the fate of the bull seal that had stood his ground and fought to the end. At the end of this same day, the gang would toast that bold fighting boy in their drinking place. Now, in the lightening dimpsey hour, the lead runner fell, measuring his length on the sand, having tripped over a pup. The other man drew up, glad to catch his breath. The faller back on his feet, they turned toward the pup and beat it with renewed savagery, not realising it was dead already.

The falling of the lead man broke the spell and the folly binding Tyrian to his ground. He wheeled, fleeing the field. A shout rang out from somewhere else. Tyrian did not stop to look where but rippled on down to the sea, desperate to feel the saving waters close over his head. He did not see the man waiting there until it was too late. By then, he was fully committed. He did not pause or alter direction but undulated onward at full speed.

Just above the tideline, another bulky man wearing a woollen hat waited, the butt of the rifle tucked snugly into his shoulder. He wanted a point-blank shot. When the seal — by the god's he was a big bugger — was three metres distant, he gently squeezed the trigger as he had done so many times before in his life.

Tyrian went bowling on, crashing in a great commotion of waters through the shallows and then sliding telescopically into and under a wave. Behind him, the bulky man with the gun growled with bitter anxiety. It was the first time ever that his trusted rifle had malfunctioned. He did nor swear, as he might have done. He valued no possession more highly than this gun with its singular history.

The two chasers were upon him now. The one who had fallen enquired sarcastically: "Was that a family member, Rory? I never took you for a seal hugger."

Rory returned the gaze of his would-be tormentor with equanimity. He had always been able to handle the talkative fellow that Tomas O'Riordhain was and now was no different:

"And yourself, was it, who thought he was on this beach to be scoring a try for Ireland?" he enquired, his eyes running over the sand clinging yet to his front. He shrugged and turned toward the sea. He might have taken a shot at the heads bobbing out there, beyond the messy wave-break, but he would not be using the rifle again until he had taken it apart and located the cause of the malfunction. After all, they had achieved what they had come here to do.

Noticing everything was getting easier to see in the gathering light, he called out:

"Lads! Back to the boat! Time to be gone".

When the boat was launched, but before he pulled the cords and set the twin outboards running, he drew the other two men close and cautioned them: "OK, lads! We'll not be careless on the homeward run. I am thinking of that environmental boat moored up outside of Dunquin. I think we take the boat home by way of Ventry. Nobody will say anything there. My sister will take me to pick up the land rover and trailer and I'll be back by the time you have finished eating breakfast at Drenagh's."

***

It was only by chance that Hugh MacPherson had brought the boat to Dunquin, having decided to test whether hearsay was true and there was an adequate fair-weather mooring here. Over an early breakfast that morning, they discussed the day ahead and, not surprisingly, everyone fancied stretching their legs on one of the Blaskets remote shores. There was magic in treading on some of the most westerly sands of Europe. There would be seals and seabirds with, perhaps, a few harbour porpoises in the Sound.

By just after eight o'clock, Sailfish was under sail.

By nine-thirty, they were standing with the scavenging gulls amid the remains of the seals. Standing to one side of them all, Hugh was putting through a stream of telephone calls. A call to his office let Mike know what was going on, instructed him who to contact. A call to the company supplying the team for the current week ascertained whether they wanted their name mentioned when the media people started to circle down; a call to a friend at the BBC who had told him to be in touch whenever a good story surfaced; a call to another friend would ensure the story was circulated to the national newspapers. He would mail through a press release, along with the photographs that, even now, were being taken. That way, the story would remain, as far as possible, accurate.

Aware that two television companies were already airborne and heading out to the Blaskets, Hugh rang Amaury. That he was not in some communications black hole or seal hole — therefore, incommunicado — was a small miracle in itself: "Amaury? Hugh here. Can we talk?"

Amaury was surprised by the unaccustomed urgency of the introduction: "Hugh! Are you speaking from Sailfish?"

"Not exactly! I'm on the Blaskets."

"OK! I'm jealous. Is that it?"

Hugh chuckled: "Not quite. Bad news. I am standing on a beach on the landward side of the island covered with dead pups — grey seal pups. Plus, there are seal mothers among the dead. We are not sure if this is the full picture, but we have counted six adult females, one adult male and thirty-six pups. They have not been shot, as far as we can make out. They appear to have been clubbed to death. There is a concentration of damage in the region of the skull, in every case — so far as we have seen. I'm phoning to ask what I should be doing. You know I am not a seal person. What data is useful to you?"

"You must be on Tra Ban, I think. White Beach. Do you have people with you?"

"There are six paying guests, plus Siobhan, Robbie and myself."

"Then get a scenic view, if the topography permits. I imagine you will have a camcorder with you as well as cameras, so double up on everything you record. I assume there will be television interest?"

"They're on the way."

"Get them to circle the scene before they land. That will secure the aerial view. That is about all they might contribute. Try for close-up photographs of each animal, with a ruler or some item included that clarifies scale. Detail the wounds of every animal. You say they have been bludgeoned to death?"

"One moment, Amaury." Hugh turned to Marie, one of his guests. She was signalling violently that he come and look at one of the adult females so he trotted across and squatted beside the hulk, nose wrinkling at the unpleasant, overwhelming smell. Batting away an aerial cloud of flies, he said:

"Each adult seal seems to have holes in the skull," she said decisively, pointing to one of the holes in question. Because he was still focussed on taking in the things that Amaury was advising he did not immediately follow her, so he prompted: "So you are saying?"

"They used clubs studded with nails; paramilitary-beating style."

For seconds his eyes closed, lips tight, before raising his mobile phone to his ear:

"Did you catch that, Amaury?"

"Yes."

Hugh grunted, then made the effort to clear his head: "Look; there will be mayhem here shortly, so tell me what else I need to do before they arrive and muddy the waters."

Amaury made his suggestions before adding: "One more thing. I think there are a couple of large islands south-west of the main island. On one of them, I believe there is another traditional grey seal breeding site. You should check there as well, if you are willing and sea conditions permit."

"Thanks, Amaury. Will do! I'll send Robbie right away in the tender. I know you'll find it frustrating but, believe me, you wouldn't like it here. I will be in touch later regards what Robbie finds, then also when I'm back."

"When will that be?"

"Near the beginning of October, probably, about ten days. Anyway, good luck. I'll be in touch soon as I am back."

"Thanks. Good hunting."

Even before the final peroration of their conversation, Amaury faintly picked up the sound of a distant helicopter coming around into the Blaskets skies.

***

Amid all the furore in the skies, and along the shore, there was also a litter of the living seals in the sea. Shocked by the terror that had befallen them, bereft of their young, their world was upside down and the steady, the normal rhythms of their body clocks were in ruins. This held most true for the seal mothers. Two had given birth only the day previously but the remainder had been at all stages in the suckling calendar.

Even the males were disturbed. In the extended aftermath of it all, they forgot to squabble and lacked, for once, the heart to try to mate with the very few receptive females.

Tyrian was exhausted, drifting alone in a tidal stream, not bothering to look up even while a helicopter hovered overhead. A film cameraman was focussing on the great, dark seal, leaning outwards in his safety harness to improve the angle.

Tyrian had a shadow, though he had no sense of it. Iolair was retaining visual contact with the seal that had done everything asked of him.

At evening, having drifted into the entrance to the mighty Shannon, Tyrian stirred enough to go hunting. The bass made it easy for him. He took four, all varying in size. He ate three but dropped the fourth, not bothering to retrieve it. It was not lost but became a prize on the seabed over which crabs quarrelled. The bass shrank before the crabs were displaced by a large and supremely well-armed monkfish.

Calmed and quietened, now Tyrian recognised small Iolair swimming toward him through the gloom, exuding welcome without concealing he felt weary to his bones.

"Now you understand why our stories mean so much to us. You see why we must remember? The killing, the endless killing. It has always been so. Travellers like yourself bring stories of times changing elsewhere, like in your Cornwall and Scilly; but not here. Here, the killing always was and maybe always will be. Our edge of the world is a place in need of strong, wise seals." He hesitated, uncertain whether he was pushing Tyrian too hard.

Wearily, his senses unexpectedly but intensely open to all the fine currents of life, Tyrian helped him, saying:

"Go, on, Iolair the wise. It has been a bad day; by far, the worst of my life. The memory of it will abide forever. The only relief from the horror has been the company of yourself, and what I have learned — I admit it — to my great surprise, from one still so extraordinarily young. It wasn't the first time, was it, that you have seen such sights? You sensed it immediately, didn't you?"

"It is the fate laid on me, I think. I'm not going to grow into a big, bold seal; ever. I shall never be like you, Tyrian. It shines out of you that you were born to have pups, to carry forward the gleaming line of us. Me? It is for me to see and know, to understand and remember, and then to keep the old stories alive."

"Their power grows and grows," Iolair continued. "Once upon a time, they had gods who exercised some control over them, but it is as if they have burgled the keys to the Heaven's from the pocket of some careless god. They have unlocked the doors and either butchered their gods the way they butcher us or else they have corrupted them. That is how it feels to me. What, then, are we?"

Again, he both posed and answered the question that clearly was the maypole around which all his questions danced.

"Truthfully, I do not know. Yet what seems clear to me is there is little of harm in the seal's way, so many of us perish in the dreadful first year of life, every year. So many others fail along the way. We die our unseen deaths in the remotest places, at and beyond the edges of the world. Neither are we numerous, abroad on the face of the Ocean; or so the few far-travelled seals I have met have told me.

"It seems to me that to be a seal is a good and even wondrous thing. I love my life and almost everything that bears upon it. Must we change to accommodate people who come as slayers among us or wish to make unbarred zoos of our resting and nursery places? Must **we** change? I would say it seems we are well as we are, as we have ever been.

"How good it would be just to be able simply to fade away before the attacks of those who it would be just to be able simply to fade away before the attacks of those who it would be just to be able simply to fade away before the attacks of those who would wipe all that we are from the face of the Ocean.

"The trouble is we have faded and faded and now we are left with nowhere left to fade to. A grey seal pup needs be born on the land. We are not the little harbour seals who can give birth on some sandbank or in inaccessible shallows. How can we survive in a world with no more hiding places?"

"Once headlands and islands were private places; remote, as all the old stories you tell. Now, they are open to all manner of access — even your Blaskets, from which, for a while, the high tide of humanity appeared to have ebbed. I cannot answer your questions, Iolair. All the voices in me seem quiet set beside the wisdom in voices so articulate in you. Yet, it does seem to me thus: there is no sense in thinking of fighting humanity. We would lose. We are just these few on the face of the ocean; they are numerous as plankton. What remains of the way of the seal? If the wide world is suddenly so lacking in privacy, should we perhaps be seeking another form of privacy, somewhere inside our own selves?

"We are not made of rock or metal. It is not written that, as we are now, so must we remain forever. Think of the rainbows. Not more than seven colours have I counted there. So, I ask myself: what colour am I travelling on and how might it be if I travelled on another? And if I have that choice, how different might it be to travel on indigo rather than yellow?"

After hearing that, Iolair was for a long time silent. It was a companionable silence that ended when he said: "Tell me true, Tyrian; would it trouble you to take me for a travelling companion for a while? I know it is not your way, but if we share worlds for a little while, who knows what good might become of it?"

Humour is a rare trait in a seal, even in the privacies of their intimacies. Tyrian showed a glimpse of it then: "Iolair, I thought you would never ask!" After letting it sink in, he added: "I shall head north. These are coasts unknown to me. I have long intended to explore them."

"And you will not mind sharing thoughts?"

The big, black seal was not yet capable of looking magisterial; one day, whether he intended it or not, he would acquire that look. Now, though, he still looked young, friendly and eager for life, despite the bloody misadventures and gruesome memories of this day: "I would be glad."

***

Having described to Ithian meetings along the way shared with Iolair, including all that had befallen with the midwife seals and the storytellers, Tyrian fell silent. Ithian remained silent, reflecting on novelties.

All the while, the waves ran in, piling ever more seaweed on dunes already created, and then they grew quieter before finally the noise of them retreated outside into the night.

Morning light returned, insinuating itself so that at first it was hardly noticed. Creeping along high, vertical walls, the south face first, it was a grey light. But the brightening drew little Somerledaa toward it, slithering eagerly into the placid waters of the long pool, there to play.

In the thirteen days of her short life, already Somerledaa had spent long hours playing there. It was where she had learned to swim. She had also spent hours in the entrance pool, which was the same depth but, otherwise, much smaller and frothier with the fronds of various brown, red and green algae. There, she had several times tried to burrow into a little tunnel that led toward the entrance so that only her hind end, her waving flippers and her stubby little tail, showed to the world. She had also made many unsuccessful attempts to capture the sunlight whenever it was playing on the little pool.

The long pool was different. It was her main playing place. There were great slabs of rock that never moved on the right-hand side, emerging more than halfway across the pool as angled shelves. On the left, the waters were deeper, the bottom more varied, being a mobile mixture of small boulders and sand. There had been hardly any rough surf within the cave this far into the suckling period. She did, however, notice small changes — the minor rearrangements and turning of boulders that were wrought. She was not consciously aware that thus her map-making had begun.

In the long pool, she had learned to swim, to open her eyes under water, to nudge the smaller rocks and the sand on the bottom, eager to see — without yet knowing why — whether her initiatives disturbed anything.

Here, under the water and an overhanging ledge, she had first hidden from her mother when she came searching. She had followed, without yet hunting, the small fish that sheltered under rock and among weed. She had met a small shoal of sand eels, gleaming like slivers of sunlight horizontal in the still waters at low tide. When she stirred, the shoal read the message of the waters and, as one mind, scattered in all directions, disappearing into the sands below. Mystified, she had swum lazily down to the bed of the pool and trailed along, sifting the sands with bristling whiskers and the lightest touch. To her amazement, one sand eel emerged and darted away. Then another emerged, darting in another direction. It was enchanting for the young seal, these flashes of light teasing something yet dormant in her, calling to the hunting instinct that was alive in the essence of her.

That morning she had harried the sand eels who, for the most part, knew themselves safe in the cave pool, despite the presence of the adult seals. The pup killed none of them but, on the next tide, they swam from the cave into the sea of greater peril rather than endure any more dangerous curiosity from the small white seal.

Now, thirteen mornings old, the pup watched the spreading sunlight illuminate the right-hand wall of the cave, her world. She watched one of the little miracles she had already seen several times before. The wall was black, then brown in the growing light, but with the gleaming of the sun, it became vibrantly maroon as all the stubbly

112

fronds of the red algal turf growing there were revealed in lovely velvet luminosity. Somerledaa just stared entranced, heedless of all else, heedless even of the great black seal who had arrived last evening and sung, on and off, all night long.

She lay horizontal and still, except for occasional lazy sidewise brushing of her hind flippers, at the tranquil surface of the pool. At three different points, large droplets of water tumbled irregularly from the wrinkled roof of the cave, so much less smooth than the walls. Where they struck salt water, the plops rang loud and clear. Outside the cave, waves were breaking, flooding in among the boulders. In their irregular, muffled booming, the waves sounded grave and sonorous as oceanic church bells. Their surf roistered on to rocky shores, delving among cracks between the boulders, overwhelming some, moving others, lapping around others; surge and ebb, so slowly at the turn, then faster, shallowing before colliding and making the next wild challenge to the next flooding wave.

These were the sounds of her world; these, and the tortured breathing of her mother that had never sounded strange to her because it was all she knew.

Every day added to her curiosity about the world and to her comfort inside her own skin. Yes, the big black seal had been a shock. That huge head with its great bowed snout, the great gleaming eyes and even his whiskers had seemed massive as they cupped toward her, looming above and disturbingly close to her own tiny, fragile white skull that might be so easily broken. Something of that she had sensed. Daunted, she had slipped away from him, making a slow, discreet escape back up the sand-hill even as her mother and the midwife seal confronted the stranger. Glad to be no longer noticed, she grew more content when her mother returned, settling close by. The proximity restored confidence in her before she tumbled again through velvet darkness into sleep and dreams.

The sun moved on, making stars dance on the pool waters. The pipits came to play, foraging in the entrance again. The pup drowsed at the surface of the pool. Already, she had learned to sleep in the water, bobbing up whenever there was need to breathe. In fact, she had come to prefer sleeping in the sunlit water of morning to any other kind of sleeping. It was the most comfortable mattress. The sands were all right except they got everywhere and, after a while, every position became uncomfortable. That is, in the early days, when she had been little else but skin and bone. Plumper, now, kelp had come to provide a more comfortable bed as well as strange sea-smells that stimulated her dreams.

It was a prejudice, one of the earliest lessons she had learned. She had not yet noticed that in her growing plumpness she was no longer a skeletal thing dressed in a coat too large and baggy for her. Neither had she forgotten that the pool at morning was more luxurious, warmer, than at any other time of day or night. There she lay, keeping her contented tryst with her good friend, the autumn morning sunlight. Nor did she know that, did she survive the first year of life and then a second, not only the sands would forever offer her a comfortable resting place but so too, improbably, would barnacled granite and the sharp fins of slates and shales. But even had she known, that lay many ifs and buts into the future. It was not just a gift awaiting her if she learned the lessons she was required to learn. Rather, it was chance — perhaps a matter of entertaining adequately gods so ancient their names were long-forgotten.

***

Unable to sleep longer, like Somerledaa, Amaury had risen even as first light appeared in the eastern skies. Outside, he found the weather dry and the wind improbably light but the stars were nowhere to be seen for the cloud cover was almost total. Back inside, he ate an early, light breakfast and his companions started arriving two minutes after he had washed the glass from which he had drunk his juice. Having had farthest to travel, Martin opened the door, poked his smiling head around it and asked:

"Am I too early? I thought you might like a hand getting everything together."

Martin gave his friend one of his hallmark lavish hugs. After dwelling on the cluttered surfaces distinguishing the kitchen for the long moment, he looked to Amaury, enquiring: "Is this everything? Are you sure you haven't forgotten anything? What is this for?" He always wanted to know everything about everything.

His other victims arrived thick and fast soon thereafter. Amaury had taken a uniquely serious line with all the volunteers, stressing the importance of arriving on time, stressing that the tide was the crucial factor that could not accommodate late arrivals.

Once everyone had arrived, they made their way from the cottage out across the maritime heathland. Amaury had seen the white lace surf worrying around the distant granite reef of Longships. He knew it promised there would be surf in the bay. Closer to the bay, the small clutter of indicator skerries were likewise worried by white water.

It was no hardship to be out on such a September morning. The blue and white, skies painted the sea blue rather than pale turquoise or green. The usual flock of unruly jackdaws had been roused to life by the fresh breeze out of the south-west and were scudding about the sky like black embers from some recently extinguished fire.

When they reached the cliff edge, they watched bright gannets gliding low over a swell heavily daubed with white horses of all sizes. In the bay, no birds rode on predominantly white waters. Where the waves broke, they were dragging behind them long white tails.

The wave-break this day, failed to excite the imagination of the surfers: Rory, Tom and Neil. They looked, as each of them knew for certain the others were looking, with surfer's eyes at the messy crumbling of the wave faces. Each saw lots of pain and minimal reward for struggling through the surf and outside the break, imagining a chaos of short rides and unexpected wave collapses.

The straggling company came to a ragged standstill, bunching together at the cliff-edge having come down by way of a lovely old-fashioned mattress of Cornish coastal grasses that yet survived. Looking at the waves, Neil glanced beyond Tom, catching the eye of Amaury: "I thought the waves worked here."

"Oftentimes they do, but this year too many strong winds have blown out of the south-east — unusual for these parts. They seem to have shovelled stupendous quantities of sand into this and neighbouring bays, re-shaping and adding to the extent of the mobile sandbanks over which you know the waves rear and break."

Having clambered down the cliff and reached a bedrock spur without misadventure, they spread out their gear. Once it had been decided who would carry what, they moved from boulder to boulder, heads carefully bowed, eyes alert. In this early phase, they found themselves teetering along a narrow crest of one massive boulder just before stooping through a tunnel created by another enormous boulder balanced at a steep angle against several others. In a straggling line, they climbed to a surf-girdled promontory of castellated bedrock. Behind the high places of the faulted point of the promontory, deep rock pools were densely decorated with pale mauve encrusting algae. Small fish were plentiful, darting between the many gullies that offered seclusion.

Onward, they trekked until they came to what Amaury had called the tripwire point. Here, they gathered again and heard him emphasise the need for quiet.

Thus, by ways sometimes precarious and, near the very end, surf-threatened while they traversed gingerly a stretch of smaller boulders mainly under or awash with surf, they approached the cave entrance. Surviving their main test unscathed, they arrived at one side of that entrance without misadventures or giveaway sounds. Their gear they set down on the rocks to the right of the entrance — out of sight of any watchful seal within.

Amaury drew his five companions around him where they formed as regular a circle as the rough-hewn boulders and bedrock permitted. There, he showed them a plan view of the cave and then repeated:

"If there are seals in the long pool, we can achieve nothing — or, at least, I've never dared slip by them in so narrow a watery place. I think all our hope of freeing her comes down to crossing that pool and catching her in the interior of the cave. If we achieve that, we will have the advantage of working on sand. Let us assume she is waiting in near total darkness on that interior beach. Then, it is imperative we do nothing to alert her. I'll come to the specifics of what I would like each of you to do next but before that are there any questions?"

He looked around the circle, from face to familiar face. More than one of them was beginning to feel the effects of adrenalin, now the denouement was imminent; but no-one spoke.

"Good!" He ran through his plan for their adventure and then everyone changed into wetsuits and picked up the equipment they were to use. He said: "Mount and havoc, then; probably, especially havoc!", and led the way from the sunlight into the cave, immediately intensely watchful. As he waded slowly, silently, through the first pool and faded over toward the right-hand wall, he was watching the surface of the long pool ahead for ripples, shadows or a watchful head, anything that betrayed the presence of a submerged seal. He saw nothing, yet. As he made his slow progress, he did hear the strong cry of a pup, broadcasting its hunger somewhere beyond the Tooth. Involuntarily, he clenched one fist, hoping he was hearing the pup of the entangled mother.

Trusting the wall to keep him steady, he trod lightly over sharp-edged boulders covered with the mauve encrusting *Lithophyllum* algae until he reached the shallows of the long pool. He was pleased that while waiting there he could hear almost nothing of the progress of his companions drawing themselves up in close order just behind him.

He turned, looking at Martin who was at his shoulder, signalling he was going to check whether any submerged seals were present in the long pool. However, before edging forward, he pointed out to him a huge strawberry anemone, tentacles fatly waving, clamped to the wall just below the surface. Having oftentimes visited the cave together, they were intimate with its collection of permanent residents. This anemone was a particular favourite. They had been noticing it through all the six years of their shared visits, for it was a wonder to them that never did it appear to move, grow, be rudely scoured from its anchorage place no matter how ferocious the seas seething into the cave. Looking into the friendly face of this companion in so many adventures, Amaury was glad he was the man at his shoulder. He knew him to be brave and whole-hearted. With a wink, he turned and, a net and its long handle trailing behind him, moved deeper into the still water.

Although the main torches were with Tom and Neil, Amaury and Martin both held rather inadequate rubber torches, which now they checked. The small illumination they offered was greedily gobbled by the vast dark space. The two of them exchanged an eloquent glance.

Amaury glanced around him, at Tom, Rory and Neil. His heart was beating fast. He had never attempted anything remotely like this before, preferring to eschew all contact with the seals and keep the disturbance to a minimum. Not all people liked seals. Some would do them harm — had, historically, come to such places to do them greatest harm. Furthermore, he had a healthy fear of their power. Now, his voice tightening, he whispered:

"Smash and grab time. All of us drive in. We try to pin the female to the base of a wall, so that if there are other seals that want to make a getaway, we are out of their way. Next, I think, we spend some relaxing moments without light, trying to keep things calm. Then maximum light from Rory will help Lucas do his slicing. You ready, Lucas?"

Lucas Vennor exuded the greatest calm of them all, holding up the instrument he was going to use to slice through the netting. It was a blade, wickedly sharp, that he had honed himself before leaving home that morning. He had many abilities. Of these, most useful at the present was his time spent working as a volunteer-doctor in overseas wars during which he had mended a remarkable number of people.

His first glimpse of the interior of the cave was a shock, though from experience he should have known better.

During the current week, there had been a spell of three days and nights when a big south-westerly blow had churned up the seas. Acres of kelp had been torn from their holdfasts and driven through the water column. Much of it was heaped now on all the windward shores of the West Country, making first a strewn patterning on rock and sand, then a carpet and finally heaping up brown, glistening dunes that marked the far reach of successions of high tides.

By some mysterious process of apparently magnetic attraction, the largest deposits of seaweed were often channelled into sea caves, along with storm-driven fishing floats that became wedged ultimately in fissures at the very back of the caves. That was what he saw now, while he knelt and peered around the rock — a great, undulating spread of kelp dunes except at the very back of the cave, which lay beyond the reach of the tide. There, the sand hill had been radically reshaped since his last visit, rising steeply at the last to a roof seemingly much lower than usual.

On that fragment of sand, he made out dark blobs that were two adult seals. One of them looked large enough to be a male. Partway down the same narrow section of fairway, he could make out a third adult asleep on her side. Without shining his inadequate torch in their direction, he could not be sure what sex they were, or even whether the netted seal was present. The two comforts lay in having seen no seals in the sea outside the cave, greatly increasing the probability of meeting the encumbered seal mother within. And there was only the one fat pup present.

In the foreground, he could see the bloated seal pup, resembling a barrel of lard, swollen by the fat-rich, protein-rich milk of its mother. Snug against the base of the far wall, it snuffled while it slept.

Amaury looked around at his friends, eyebrows raised, thumb raised, whereupon he trotted round the Rock into the much darker interior, closely followed by Martin. He had run six or seven paces, taking him in beyond the pup, before he switched on his torch. It was comforting to hear he was not alone, that the team was trotting in, single file, behind him. It was especially comforting to have the extra lights coming on, illuminating the primordial darkness, bringing colour and hope as well as light.

Scanning, he made out the strands of monofilament netting catching the light where they dangled from the neck of the nearest adult seal. He shook the netting free of his hand so that now he was holding only the big, pale blue entrance-hoop of plastic tubing. He watched her stir as he bore down on her. He tried and failed to close his mind to the sound of somebody falling behind him, bringing down a second person in the process, aware that it did not leave him quite alone.

Perhaps it was the number of them and perhaps it was the impression they gave of a phalanx of people driving in. All the seals were awake now but dithering, uncertain how to respond. Mornalas lay with her head only slightly raised, as if she was in the confusion that comes with emergence from deep sleep. At the back of the cave, Tyrian was poised at his full height but Ithian moved first, initially to the left, then right while continuing to lie broadside on to the approaching people.

Aware he had the best chance of making the capture, Amaury found himself trembling. He was frightened of being bitten, of being run down by blindly fleeing seals. He was frightened of running out of courage at the last moment, not daring to pull hoop and net back over the head of the needy seal.

At the last, Mornalas reared up and partly around, as if to face her assailants. She could hardly have made things easier for Amaury who darted in, tugging the hoop over and around her extended neck, his fears forgotten. That was as easy as she made it. During the next few seconds, Amaury was pushed, tugged, shaken and bucked. He dropped his torch and lost his footing. He was thrown across her body against a wall as she made the supreme effort to work herself into motion and momentum. By now, she had turned entirely about and was undulating powerfully but terribly slowly while also making tortured breathing sounds down the fairway. Clinging on like the rider of a bucking mustang, Amaury was struggling to dig his heels into the sand, to put the brakes on, giving no thought to the two seals trapped at the back of the cave.

Behind him, someone else had managed to settle astride her, slowing her still more; then a third arrived to stop her altogether.

With their backs to the interior, Amaury and Martin had no idea what the other seals were doing.

Lucas moved in, knelt fluently, began probing with his knife while Rory provided a steady stream of brilliant torchlight from his side but, suddenly, the three surfers, never having stood before charging seals before, turned and ran. Ithian and Tyrian had found their courage. Amaury and Martin could hear the formidable heavy slapping sounds as the two seals came barrelling down over the dunes of kelp. By now, their fingers were irretrievably hooked in the hoop net mesh. There was no possibility of moving out of the way. Torchlight sprayed erratically now. Lucas was forced to retreat to the Tooth, seeking concealment behind it from the bullocking seals.

Martin was more in the firing line than Amaury, having been dislodged down one side of the captured seal and having nothing left with which to cling on except his thighs. Hearing the horrible, frightening sounds, his eyes were shut tight. He was hoping against hope he had left room enough for the seals to pass. It was his good fortune that Ithian, the lighter seal, was in the lead and as she sought to accelerate past him, she struck him only glancingly.

Light, though the blow had been, his grip on Mornalas's body was loosened. It was enough to inspire her to make a renewed effort to escape their clutches. She bucked, snapping her teeth, catching the finger of Martin who had tumbled forward by her head. He let out one, agonising cry of pain, truncated as he clenched his teeth before he was launched into aerial collision with Amaury having been sent flying by Tyrian, bludgeoning his way by him toward the narrow gap.

Amaury, battered by his friend, tiring, alarmed by Martin's cry, not daring to imagine what might have happened, yet clung on mightily, his heels dug deep into the sand, still slowing Mornalas. She was undulating her body, jerking her head backwards and forwards in her effort to achieve traction and escape. In the confusion, her back jolted Amaury forward, her head collided with his, dealing him an explosive blow almost fully on the eye. His entire upper body was slammed sideways against the wall. Fireworks exploded all around him and he weakened disastrously but, even as his grip failed, his will kicked in. He dug his feet slithering through the shallow carpet of seaweed into the sand once more, slowing Mornalas yet again.

Beyond the looming Tooth Rock, he could hear the escaping seals entering the long pool, splashing loudly through the sandy shallows. Somewhere on the far side of the rock, a light came on. Beside him, Martin had returned, taking a grip of the net with one hand. Concentrating on holding his current position, through the failing exhibition of fireworks in his head, Amaury whispered tautly:

"Are you OK? You still have all your fingers?"

"Think so. She nipped me. By the gods, it stings. Where the hell are they?"

As if in answer, people and light came flooding around Tooth Rock. Two more people arrived to straddle Mornalas. Glancing sideways through an eye that felt as if it was swelling into a balloon, Amaury made out Tom and Neil.

He could make out Rory close by, directing the torchlight where he was bidden by Lucas who knelt uncomfortably on the damp stipes of kelp. His voice was preternaturally calm amid all the confusion and drama:

"It would be ideal if we could get her to extend her neck because then I'll not have to slice so deeply into her blubber. Dare we risk trying to behave as if we are removing it, giving her the chance to extend her neck telescopically?"

"That is what we were hoping you'd ask," Neil answered: "Something nice and simple."

"OK... now!" Lucas continued, heedless of the humour, entirely unruffled, apparently calm.

As one, three people removed themselves from pinning Mornalas to the ground while Amaury fumbled to comply.

It didn't work. Amaury was thrown forward through the air again, on to the ground immediately below the still-netted head of Mornalas even as she escaped, surging forward. Briefly, though it felt longer to him, she undulated over his chest and shoulder, pinning him heavily to the sand. In passing, she breathed into his face drawing from him a grunt of repugnance as he found himself briefly trapped in a nightmare miasma of fishy breath. Then other hands waylaid her, catching the net before she could work entirely free of it. Having rolled free, Amaury focussed wearily on the tableau of seal-with-attendant-figures and resumed his position behind the shoulders of Mornalas, renewing his grip on the hoop net.

Feeling himself subject to a rather direct scrutiny from Lucas, Amaury glanced as directly back and said quietly: "I'm OK!"

"Then let's proceed: I'm going to make a deep, direct slashing cut. She is going to buck, probably more violently than before. Everyone ready? Rory, focus on my side of the top of her neck. I think that is where I will do least damage."

He did as he had warned. The wickedly sharp blade cut through the netting and the blubber. For an instant longer, all was quiet and the trapped female made no response, but then she roared and bucked at the same time, casting people off in all directions. This time, not only did she lose her human parasites but also the net, which came flying part-way off. In the next moment, she was entirely free of it. Not waiting, finding traction at last, she moved fast, rippling toward the gap between the Tooth and the cave wall. Close behind, Lucas led the chase, trying to see if he had cut the netting entirely free, closely followed by Tom and Rory and then by the taller figure of Neil.

Amaury, no longer in the chase, rose slowly to his feet, covered in sand and some blood, holding his head. Martin was bent double, clutching one bloody hand. Only very slowly did they begin to follow the others toward the bright cave entrance.

Mornalas was across the long pool on the small rocky field that lay inside the small outermost pool. Here, she was almost caught by Rory and Tom, the latter shouting: "One strand is still holding. Shall we hoop her again?" Somehow, he was holding the second net and waving it airily for all to see.

Rory had overtaken Lucas in crossing the pool and now made an incomprehensible cry. As it burst from him, he lunged forward, drawing up the college scarf of trailing, tangled monofilament netting, running on now as fast as he could go, and leaping over the tail flippers of the seal as she turned to face him.

Come to the far side of her, he had drawn his own diver's knife from his leg sheath. Fast as he could move, he changed his grip, holding the netting as near as possible to the bloodstained blubber wound in her neck. Lifting the net, he slashed blindly.

His knife was less sharp than Lucas', but the strand was severed. He held on, pulling it free from where it had started already to become sealed in by the partial healing that had occurred. He held on only for as long as it took to come bloodily free of her flesh before leaping sideways out of her way.

Back in the cave, slowly wading through the pool, Martin had his fingers raised before his eyes, daring at last to examine the injury and only then discovering the seal had nipped off the nail from one forefinger.

Tom and Neil, hurrying to his side, helped him on through the shallower of the two pools and out into the light.

Having anticipated people might be hurt, Lucas had come prepared. Sitting Martin as comfortably as possible on the uncomfortably knobbed granite in the welcome sunlight, he administered an injection of Doxycyclin to combat the effects of the potent bacteria inhabiting the mouth of the sea monster. Then he set about covering the wound with a dressing, which he was continuing to apply while an unusually pale and silent Amaury emerged into the grey light of day. He settled placidly on a less than comfortable rocky seat near his hunting companion, heartened by the wonderful unroofed light.

Although Lucas was concentrating on the dressing he was applying to Martin's finger, he said: "There is a soft ice pack in the cold box. One of you could apply it to his eye."

Not having taken in that the doctor was speaking of him, Amaury looked across and down at the bandaged digit of his friend but spoke to Lucas: "Is he going to be all right? I take it you know all about the nasty bacterial flora?"

Of course, he did: "I double-checked yesterday with the Sea Mammal Research Unit to make sure I was carrying all that might be needed in my bag of remedies. He is all right though the wound will sting. The seal nipped off a finger nail. It may be a long time before it grows properly again. Still, it will confirm whatever story you choose to tell of this day hereafter."

"What happened, in the end? Did we get rid of all the netting? Do you think she is going to be OK?" Martin asked, looking first at Lucas, because his face was closest, and then around at the others.

It was Tom who answered: "She looked to be entirely free of netting when she emerged from the cave, going like a bat out of Hell toward the sea." After a prolonged pause, he asked, uncertainly: "Do you think she will come back to the pup or do you think she has had enough of drama and nightmares?"

He was looking to Amaury, whom drive and animation had drained entirely away. When the silence stretched a little, he glanced up, realising he was the one being questioned: "Your guess is as good as mine. I guess she will return. The mother-pup bond is well-established by now and I think her presence ashore today, so close to the time of weaning, indicates she is one of the more caring mothers."

Martin was watching his friend while still clutching his hand tightly because it seemed to keep the pain manageable.

When Lucas came across to attend him, through his pallor Amaury grinned suddenly. Animation flickered in eyes that, previously, had been dulled: "Great, to have your own personal physician on an expedition like this!"

While Amaury was being treated, Rory poured tea from a flask for Martin, who seemed more energised than deflated by his injuries. The remainder of the company watched the seals.

One hundred metres offshore, the black male and dark female were keeping watch, albeit riding low in the water. They had relaxed, relieved to be in the sea where they could be sure of eluding their human oppressors. Of Mornalas, there was no sign, which was troubling because the repeated hunger cries of the all-but-forgotten pup sounded heart-rending.

In the meantime, having satisfied Lucas that he was not concussed and was seeing clearly from the good eye as well as the one that was closing fast, despite the icepack ministrations, Amaury was back on his feet. He was unaware that yet he looked grey-faced under his tan.

Much more rag-tag than before, but still burdened by their baggage, everyone began to depart the stage where the drama had been played out; except for the netters. While the others embarked on their long, awkward return across the boulder beach and up the now sunlit gully, Amaury and Martin left the vicinity of the cave and made their way halfway across the beach to where a massif of bedrock reared out into the sea. Here, they clambered to a flattish high point and trained their binoculars back the way they had come, then all around, scanning for the freed seal.

For all their scanning, all they could see were the seals whose bullocking departure from the cave had left so much pain in its wake. When he was not scanning, Martin was gripping his wrist and grimacing, striving to quiet the fearsome throbbing that had set in.

"You know, we are going to have to rename that cave," Amaury remarked, gingerly feeling around the edges of the impressive swelling around his eye.

"Freedom field?" Martin offered, experimentally.

"Martinsfinger Cave, surely," Amaury amended: "You were heroic in there."

With one of his huge grins, Martin spread his hands and amended: "We were heroic in there, seal rider! You brought to mind one of those mosaics on the wall or floor of some Cretan palace! Well, less good-looking, of course!"

Amaury grinned: "You were the one who hung in and made the difference. Today was a big day. So, we must pay another visit to Martinsfinger Cave quite soon, if only for old time's sake."

"Martinsfinger Cave? I like the ring to it."

They gripped hands in the enthusiasm of the moment — in Martin's case, the one that had suffered no injury.

They lingered on their rocky crow's nest for a quarter of an hour, both relishing a time to be tranquil in the wake of the brief, intense drama of noise and activity. Now and then, as was their way, one would point out some detail to the other. Both were observant and both were inveterate sharers of their swag of sightings.

Above all, they relaxed and found their separate ways back from melodrama into their own selves. Relaxing, they felt the flooding weariness Lucas could have predicted for them; but the day was turning a darker grey and the wind was picking up. Still without having glimpsed the liberated female, the two men rose and, more slowly than was usual for them, made their way across the boulder field to the rock ledges, the pools and the discreet track up through the crease in the cliff to the green world above.

Having made the wet, weary ascent, they stopped and spent a few more minutes scanning for Mornalas, but of her there was no sign. Slightly disconsolate, they trudged back along the same maritime heathland trail, putting up occasional brown and orange small heath butterflies and the bigger painted ladies and red admirals. Near the pond, or the place where the pond would reappear once the rains returned in earnest, they followed a faint trail out of the tractor ruts and inland through a dense spread of willow carr. The willows were the haunt of mysterious small brown songbirds and the telescope and tripod laden twitchers' who peered after them every spring and autumn.

In fact, there was the beginning of a shallow winter pond in a depression at the corner of the shallow space that soon the fuller pond would swamp. Even as the two men noted it, a lone snipe erupted giddily into zigzag flight, low at first and then steepling upward above the spread of leafless branches. There it corkscrewed onward through the wind, predicting autumn for all who saw her.

Last of the company by far, the two of them came over the threshold into the kitchen of the small farm cottage.

The surfers, Rory, Neil and Tom, declined to linger for lunch, leaving almost immediately to answer the daily call, promising to return soon to call Amaury to join them in scrawling graffiti on Sennen wave faces.

Lucas remained long enough to run a discreet but concerned professional eye over his two patients before he also slipped away. That left the two of them. They sipped the prawn and avocado soup he had made; both secretly marvelling that it tasted so good. Afterwards, they lingered over more tea, but then Martin excused himself so that finally Amaury was alone again.

Amaury had offered to drive him to the hospital. He had been insistent, but Martin said he was fine for driving and any alternative would just complicate things, so he had prevailed. In any case, both men trusted Lucas's ministrations would prove sufficient.

Fifteen minutes later, Amaury lay immersed in a hot tub. Had he so chosen, he could have watched the green view down toward hidden Pol Ledan, in which case he would have seen a vixen strolling along under a blackthorn hedge in the middle distance. However, his attention was given to the book he was reading about the history of the Welsh princes of Gwynedd. The subject matter was part of a prelude to a visit to North Wales he was hoping to make in late autumn or winter to that region where remarkably little seemed to be known about the seals.

Later, dried and fragrant, dressed with care, he came down and began to write up his seal notes into the database and afterwards into his hand-written journal.

***

Very faintly, under the sound of the freshening wind off the ocean, the seals in Martinsfinger Cave made fragments of music. Black Tyrian and dark Ithian lifted their heads and resisted the temptation to shuffle seaward. Little Somerledaa fretted. Her food-begging was hoarse, quieter, after a restless night with inadequate sleep.

It was light. Mornalas had not returned.

Tyrian had felt all the flaring power of her when she had flowed blindly seaward through the unsteady waters outside the cave.

More than three hours later, he had forced himself back to the unquiet shore, followed more warily by Ithian. They had been restless, peering about trying to locate where the people were hiding. In short bursts of movement and long spells of watchful waiting, they re-entered the cave where hungry Somerledaa was crying.

The hours passed. The rising tide drove them deeper into the cave. Tyrian had not forgotten dread Meinek nor unfriendly Balanec, but still he went back to the cave entrance to thwart efforts by little Somerledaa to swim from the cave in search of her mother. When she sought to elude him, he re-positioned himself repeatedly until the pup was persuaded back into the cave.

Back ashore, after her prolonged search, weary, cold and hungry, the pup fell into a disturbed sleep. Her dreams were full of the strangeness of the day. Woven in among them was the biggest question of all. She had no conception of death and so she did not dream what would have been the worst of her fears, but she did wonder if the people had driven her mother away forever after trying to kill her with their lights and nets and knives.

Not far from the restless pup, Tyrian slept fitfully with kindred dreams. He was a powerful seal on the threshold of his prime, yet he had been able to do nothing. He tossed and turned, growled and wailed in his sleep, just like a huge version of little Somerledaa.

Ithian did not even try to sleep. She sang, willing Mornalas home, willing her to mend the tear in the fabric of her deep-rooted trust in place, so fundamentally, important to any seal mother. Her song was sung and hung as a lantern over the entrance to the cave. A small, insignificant light, Ithian willed it to brightness by the force of her supportive will against the darkness of the bay.

The waves of the restless sea added a thunderous backdrop to the small sounds she made, swallowing them entirely. Walls of black water came driving in. For a while, they slopped heavily against the base of the cliffs, but as the great, relentless wheel of the tide began to fall, the waves broke just short of the walls of the cliffs. White water made rolling thunder. The walls of the cliffs themselves seemed to shudder as the black waves peeled entirely over. They evolved into massive, ragged geysers of spray bursting up the granite walls of all the Lands End cliffs before they were spent.

The winds screamed as they drove thinly through tens of thousands of clefts of rock. Along the peaks of the endless march of waves, the winds were constant, pushing from behind, hurrying them to the fractured shores.

Mornalas?

Grey light of morning. Ithian fell silent, sleeping at last behind a dune of kelp that spanned the full width of the fairway. In ancient song, she had reached far into the night for a seal mother who seemed worth saving, worth calling back. Never had she sung so long a song before. Perhaps the Mornalas who had flared so swiftly away through the sea after all the traumas of being captured and attacked with nets, knives and sprawling men had been mortally wounded, after all. It had not seemed so at the time. She had sensed confusion and pain, yes, but it had not seemed she was leaking away her life's-blood.

In the cave entrance, Somerledaa continued to cry hoarsely, if at reduced volume, for her next meal. Ithian knew the odds were beginning to pile up against the plucky little pup.

***

Wearing thin green cotton overalls supplied by an army surplus warehouse in Plymouth, Amaury made his way from the cliff path down through big boulders protruding from the cliff slope and the coarse, springy grasses. The overalls were not the colour of grass but they muted his visibility, both to people above him and, he hoped, any seals in the sea below.

The pup was easy to locate when he reached his secluded observation roost. Initially, she betrayed herself by her heart-rending cries. Amaury used them to track her to a flat rock just short of the easiest point of access to the sea. They sounded weary and strained. With a deep sigh, Amaury recognised them as confirmation the seal mother had not returned. Nearby, from the sea the black male seemed to be watching her. No other seals were visible.

He spent a quarter of an hour scanning the inshore waters and their adjacent shores for glimpses of a seal that might be resting or watching, but to no avail.

Under normal circumstances, he never returned to a site on consecutive days. His impression of seal cave use, was that if they suffered disturbance, they would not use it on the following day. The only exception was during the breeding season, when they strayed little from the nursery site. Now he was breaking his principal rule. He had to learn the fate of Mornalas and Somerledaa.

Settling, he waited. Hours passed. The tide rose, driving the pup into the cave, followed without haste by the black male. The crying continued, weaker, more intermittent. Three stranger-seals came to the cave entrance but all continued onward. Amaury managed to take a photograph of one of them — a mature female — at least the right side of head and neck. He marked her down as a possible imminent mother, for she headed on toward the Great Seal Hole.

Around five, another possible Mornalas appeared on the far side of the bay. She came in near the far headland, arriving at a steady speed, passing on by a wide boulder beach and Shaggy Zawn, where seven pairs of shags nested every spring in spume-damp nests on spume-wet ledges. Progress was by way of a succession of shallow dives. Across the entrance to Waterfall Cave, she swam, drawing out Meinek to check who passed. Finding her in breeding condition, he made a concerted effort to waylay her; but she rejected and evaded every advance until he periscoped high above the surface and performed a perpendicular circle. What he saw galvanised him. Totally forgetting the elusive female and her evasions, he submerged, powering across the bay toward the northerly headland and its scattered stones.

He had glimpsed Balanec motionless at the surface of the sea, his side pressed to the side of a female seal, his upper fore-flipper resting placidly along her flanks. Minutes before, he had mated with one of the Great Seal Hole seal mothers.

Mornalas had swum blindly at the limits of her power away from Martinsfinger Cave the previous morning. Some hours before nightfall, she found herself under lonely, surf-swept Wolf Rock lighthouse, eleven miles offshore. Under the most isolated of the local lighthouses, aware of weariness, yet the madness of fear and pain drove her on. She had not aimed to swim to the seal-haunted rocks of Scilly. She did not want to meet seal, fish, boat, human or anything. All she needed was to swim to an oblivion of exhaustion.

Maintaining a brutal speed, following unbelievably ancient seal sea-tracks, she swam to the waters of Seven Stones Reef, nearby which the red-painted lightship was anchored. There, recognition that the flickering lights were gone flickered into her assaulted sanity. It was night. Other lights marking perilous edges of the world had begun to flash in their various combinations instead.

Sanity juddered back through holes melted by her fading dread. The pain of carrying a burden of too much milk reminded her of Somerledaa. Somerledaa; the name echoed around the numbed interior of herself. With remembrance came also recollection of the promise she had made so recently to Ithian, in the cave. She was needed. The clarion call of it recalled her to her first duty. But where was she?

Amid so much shock, impossibly for a seal she found herself lost. She was hemmed in by familiar landmarks but her mind was mazed. Her weary body, her exhausted mind, her imagination had all closed down. Bobbing at or just below the surface of the sea, she was obliterated by deepest sleep that lasted well beyond the rising of the sun over the distant cliffs. It was the juddering wake generated by a passing Newlyn netter that awakened her.

Wakening, seeing the red lightship, seeing — whenever the waves lifted her — the not so far distant smudges of the Isles of Scilly and the much more distant cliff ranges of the Land's End on the opposite horizon: now she recognised familiar landmarks. Her own self had been returned to her. It was time to return to Martinsfinger Cave and a pup too long neglected.

Again, she harnessed a brutal pace to drive her across the grey and lurching sea. She travelled without thought. Locked on to inner co-ordinates that would bring her home to the great bay, she travelled with an empty mind, enjoying only the flaring motion of her haste.

She came in by the headland cave across the great bay from where Somerledaa had entered the world. She curved around near the approaches to Waterfall Cave, simply for the pleasure of hearing again the chorus of pups crying to be fed by the three mothers who had absented themselves. She saw each of them at rest in breaking waves outside the cave entrance.

Meinek, she knew intimately from past years. He had fathered other pups of hers before fathering Somerledaa. She recognised him very well and was glad to see him again. For now, however, she had no thought for him. Fending off his pestering while she passed was automatic rather than personal. It was a relief when he caught sight of Balanec and streaked away, leaving her to conclude her journey as alone as she desired to be.

She swam by the last promontory without imagining Amaury focussing the camera, capturing images of her as she swam toward and into the cave. He heard the crying of the pup suddenly intensify, rising to a hoarse crescendo before falling abruptly, doubtless greedily, silent.

Deep inside the cave, beyond the Tooth Rock, grounded on a dune of seaweed that was partly afloat on the high tide, Mornalas stranded. Immediately, she settled, rolling over on to one side. Having hastened to her, locking immediately on to a teat, Somerledaa guzzled more greedily than ever before. Before that moment, she had often experienced difficulty locating the teat. Not this time. When five minutes had elapsed, Mornalas shook off the little one with some difficulty and shifted position to make available the other nipple. Somerledaa was already so bloated with milk that some dribbled down her chin when she tried to wail her protest. It was stilled as soon as she locked on to the other nipple and resumed loudly sucking in the thick milk.

Another few minutes passed. It was the longest feed she had secured in more than a week, so it was in a miasma of satisfaction that she fell asleep while still suckling. She did not notice herself become detached, her small, milk-wet chin sliding down across the speckled flanks of her mother and down farther to rest on part-floating, sand-speckled seaweed.

Mornalas did not feel greatly different. She, too, was replete. Now she could allow herself to feel drained by the rigours of her journey and its intense postscript. Like her pup, her chin came to rest on the partly floating seaweed. Her eyes closed. She slept.

Deeper within the cave, forgotten, Ithian lay facing out of the cubby-hole, the short tunnel by the kelp-littered fairway. Her chin also rested on weed but her eyes were open. She made no sound. For once, atmosphere and occasion were song enough.

She saw netting no longer strangled the silvery seal mother. In its place ran a red weal, a broad red necklace, but with no peril in it. She recognised the healing had started already. There was no poison in the wound, no stress in her breathing.

Deepest into the cave of the three adults, Tyrian lay where the fairway narrowed. Still not quite dry, steam was rising from the hairs of his drying coat. His chin lay on scraps of strewn kelp and his eyes were open, too. Unlike Ithian, his main awareness was of an exciting strand in the scent of Mornalas. He recognised she was in breeding condition and for the first time in his life, he was the male waiting close by.

Other seals would have experienced no doubt about what to do and when to do it. In his travelling life, Tyrian had become accustomed to pausing between conceiving the desire to do something and performing the action to secure whatever that might be. This reserve did not apply to his hunting or travelling but to how he related to other seals. Now, he observed, wondered and let her be.

For two more days, the triumvirate of adult seals lingered in the cave. Two days more of drinking mother's milk was enjoyed by Somerledaa. For the rest of the time, there was a peace that became tense whenever Tyrian brushed by Mornalas — when he would involuntarily sniff the area near her tail. She was not discontent to have the careful male nearby. Something about his presence contented her quite as much as, if differently from, the presence of Ithian.

On the final day, Ithian drifted from the cave at first light, glancing at sleeping Mornalas and watchful Tyrian. Somerledaa was snoring quietly, as usual. She swam the length of the long pool for the last time, slapped her heavy body and worn-clawed flippers over the bridge of rock and through the other small entrance pool. Soon afterwards, Tyrian watched her sliding steeply into the sea. She surfaced quite soon thereafter, but did not look back. Her course was set firmly for the south and warmer waters.

One last feed Mornalas gave to the bloated barrel of lard that was her daughter, feeding her to sleep. Somerledaa was considerably moulted already. She was fat, alert and without injury. She had learned to swim. That guaranteed nothing though it should give her some advantage while facing the immense challenges of the near future. These thoughts she experienced as she glanced for the last time at the daughter. Then she wheeled quietly about and made, for the last time this year, for the cave entrance.

As she emerged from the cave, she sensed the nearness of Tyrian, not far behind her. His patience had been unobtrusive and now they would discover what, if anything, lay between them, for he had quickened his pace. His intent had locked on to her. She sensed the intensity of him but, of habit, quickened her own pace in the age-old theatre of eluding him.

His speed surprised her. In the cave and inshore waters, much of his activity had been languid in recent times. Now, transformed by desire, he closed the gap between them faster than she imagined possible. His acceleration sabotaged her only escape. His teeth gathered in the nape of her neck, strangely gentle but firm. His capture achieved, she made no struggle and, because there was no desire to escape him, they became embroiled in sharing one of the fundamental mysteries of a year or a life.

Considering the bulk of them, it was a gentle mating. They made no great commotion. Perhaps Tyrian remembered the proximity of the seal he had learned to fear; but if so, she shared that reserve, desiring no interruption. When the mating was done, they remained clasped together for an hour, quiescent in the still waters, his fore-flippers resting gently on her flanks, his chin on her back, the grip on her nape now loosed. The sea surged about them without making much of an impression on the position they were holding in the sea, for they were not close in under the cliffs.

They did not see a big seal emerging through the confused swell from that entrance to the Great Seal Hole which had given it the name. His colour was brown and he was a big male, but there was something strange about the way he moved. As he dipped down and up, disappearing then reappearing with the exaggerated movement of the swell in the entrance waters, the relaxed Tyrian could no longer avoid noticing him. Without flurry or obvious movement, he released the gentle connection he had shared with Mornalas and began to drift from her.

Inside him, something had changed following the capture and mating. Where, before, he had been a seal observing life, now he was transformed into an invincible seal, the defender of a female and a territory whose bounds he was yet to learn. Intent on challenging Balanec, whom he had recognised, he swung his hind quarters and his hind flippers, achieving slow, powerful acceleration in the direction of this intruder, who lay now like a log on the unstill surface of the sea.

It was clear to Tyrian that Balanec had no thought of yielding ground, even as Tyrian noticed the big new wound on the bulky neck of the larger seal. Simply, he maintained his powerful, steady approach until doubt registered in his wounded rival. Seeing it, instinct kicked in. He accelerated.

Balanec roared his challenge, but even as he roared, he felt the draining of his courage. Unnerved by the so-direct approach of the younger male riding his rising star, Balanec crash-dived and fled. Once submerged, he swerved back toward the cave entrance, streaking away at the last moment between the cliffs and the triangular island beloved of shags outside the big entrance. He had hope of misleading Tyrian.

Behind him, Tyrian following his sense of Balanec found himself, by chance rather than design, driving up behind the hind flippers of the fleeing male. It was a great shock for Balanec, who responded with blind acceleration, but Tyrian was not in deadly earnest. He was

Tyrian, not Meinek who understood so well how to plant seeds of fear in the soul of his rivals, thereby prolonging his hegemony over the other males using the locality. Therefore, he made a theatre of prolonging the chase, but without the intensity that would have necessitated battle and more bloodshed. In the end, he peeled away from the line he had been following, returning at a lesser speed to where he had left Mornalas.

They remained together, making no effort to leave the vicinity though that was imminent now, as both knew. Mornalas was beginning to feel a ravening hunger, having eaten nothing since before Somerledaa had been born. The narrow-waisted, bony seal mother who had mated with Tyrian was a shadow of the resplendent silver-coated seal that had arrived at the nursery cave. That seal, despite her shawl of monofilament netting, had been shaped like a glistening torpedo. This seal was skeletal by comparison; a starveling. When sleeping on the mattress of kelp inside the cave last night, her thigh bone had been jutting into the air and she had a waist where she should have had none.

She had lost just over forty per cent of her body weight during the feeding of Somerledaa. Her strength was spent. Little wonder Tyrian had caught her so easily.

Hunger and freedom gave birth to the germ of restlessness in her, but something yet held her. For two days more she would remain in breeding condition although she was a seal who recognised the moment of conception and felt it had befallen with Tyrian.

As the day closed, the two of them were drifting across the bay, heedless of their progress, locked in the intimacy that bound them. Twice more they had mated before, nearby, the great brown head of savage Meinek broke the surface. His glance took in the tranquil female. His snout reported her condition. but his attention locked ominously on the black seal he had already driven off once this season. Startled, Tyrian yet managed to maintain his composure, returning the pitiless, aggressive glare with antipathy.

Meinek took the initiative in this no-man's-land between the two caves, accelerating as directly toward Tyrian as had Tyrian toward wounded Balanec. However, against all precedent and for no conscious reason, Tyrian held his ground, though instead of continuing to drift upright in the sea, he swirled to the horizontal. When Meinek drove straight toward him and made to rip at his neck with his teeth, Tyrian eddied just out of reach and continued to do the unexpected, driving straight in to inflict a shallow wound along the rippling neck of his opponent. It was a shock, but Meinek was wise, sinking below the surface and launching a diagonal attack from which Tyrian corkscrewed away.

Against all recent precedent, this was not a battle destined to end quickly. Three times, Tyrian managed to inflict shallow wounds, each time in the bulky neck of his opponent, despite fighting defensively.

It developed into a three-dimensional battle of attrition that strayed across the entire bay. Meinek was struggling to bring his superior weight to bear against an opponent so exceptionally sea-wise.

There was another aspect to their battle on which Tyrian was placing hope. Just as Mornalas had lost weight and condition ashore, the same was true for Meinek. His sojourn, dominating the approaches to the cave selected for his base had extended for six weeks. But his very ruthlessness required a massive expenditure of energy. Consequently, the outline of his body had become bony, giving him a derelict appearance. Tired from his long vigil, yet he had not been closely challenged all season, so powerful was his aura of invincibility.

He was wise enough to recognise Tyrian as the first true contender

Tyrian fought carefully, holding his own, growing in confidence the longer their engagement lasted, the longer he avoided debilitating injury. From the first moment, he sought to carry aggressive attack against Meinek.

Twenty minutes passed. Both males were bloodied superficially about the neck without either having managed to inflict a significant wound on the self-confidence or will of the other. In the intensity of the engagement, inevitably they tired, Meinek more than this tenacious challenger.

Tiredness allowed Tyrian his chance. Meinek was veering away after another unsuccessful assault but, this time, and for a little while past, following the same course as in the previous several attacks. It was what Tyrian had been provoking. Now he coiled around and drove in hard, mouth wide open and then snapped shut. Grabbing a great chunk of skin and blubber, he clung on as Meinek, for the first time in years, felt real danger. He tried to burst free but Tyrian predicted the first movement and the second, hanging on so that his jaws ached with the mightiness of his grip. The third evasive movement took Meinek free of the tenacious hold, but at a cost. A great chunk of blubber from his neck came away in Tyrian's jaws, opening a terrible ragged crater of a bloody wound.

Yet, it was now that the indestructible courage and indomitable will of Meinek came more than ever into play. Almost any other male would have weakened fatally having sustained such a wound. Not so Meinek. He corkscrewed around immediately so that before Tyrian could open his clenched jaws to drop the chunk of flesh, he had driven forward and taken an equally powerful hold on Tyrian's throat. Now it was the turn of Tyrian to display indomitable will in extremis. It was the last thing he wanted to do, but he shook his powerful neck to such effect that Meinek's hold was dislodged. Puncture wounds and a tear he suffered, but it was then that he guessed wrong. Meinek, still at close quarters, now took a decisive grip on the side of his neck.

Now, Meinek shook his great head from side to side, as if he was a terrier shaking a great rat but in slow motion. The pain was agonising. Tyrian shook his own head to try to ride the grip of his enemy but this time there was no escape and, in turn, he lost a great chunk of flesh from his neck.

Tyrian now mirrored the counter attack that Meinek had mounted and almost got through his guard but, at the very last, Meinek's head swung around and teeth clashed against teeth, slashing jowls. By now, a lot of blood was coiling in streamers about them but still neither of them was prepared to surrender.

Perhaps slightly less hurt of the two, Tyrian mounted a determined series of attacks but each time Meinek dredged up a counter attack. By now, both seals were suffering from a lack of inspiration. Their battle shrank to a trial of pure will.

Thirty-five minutes had passed since the conflict had begun and still, they circled, probed, attacked and fended off — punch-drunk fighters, careless and desperately weary.

The decisive engagement began well for Tyrian. At last, he found in himself the imagination to feint, feint and feint again before launching himself toward the pitiless black eyes of his enemy where they circled, deep below the waters at the entrance to the bay. In a last-ditch effort to fend off the attack, Meinek swept an aggressive swiping fore-flipper to swat aside the assault, only to suffer excruciating pain as teeth closed over half of the flipper and its broken, worn claws.

The bite was fierce and true. The pain was massive. A chunk of flipper fell from bloody jaws to float down heavily to the sands. Not long afterwards, the crabs would gather to tidy up, but at the time Meinek swerved away and started to try to fly blindly from the pain and the terrible seal that had inflicted it. But even as he began and Tyrian began his triumphant victory chase, he recalled yet again who and what he was. His mind obliterating pain with rage and deadly enmity, he performed the lithest of somersaults in the water more quickly than Tyrian could follow. In the last access of power, he drove upwards and took hold of a chunk of flesh adjacent to where he had already most-bloodied Tyrian. With his last strength, he tore free a chunk smaller than before, but still large and destructive.

Now it was the turn of Tyrian to flee. Blind pain overwhelmed his senses. He had no strength left to respond.

Beaten, zigzagging wildly, he spurted away and upward through the water column, clouded as it was with sand stirred up by the big seas.

Far inshore, Meinek had gone nowhere. In greatest pain, he granted Tyrian the accolade of an escape free from his customary relentless pursuit. There was nothing left. He had battled to the limit of his strength for the first time in his life, suffering wounds the like of which he had never sustained even in the days when he was still an aspirant challenger. All but defeated, he had triumphed through the power of his granite will and, finally, from habit.

Somewhere outside the bay, Tyrian fled no more, drifting limp in the increasing swell. His mind was empty, but his body was working on automatic compass, guiding him toward the great saddle-shaped sea rock sanctuary below Gwennap.

Arriving, it was awash with churning runs of high tide surf. Wave after wave poured across brown granite, gushing down the other side into the narrow channel dividing islet from mainland. Angling in from both ends, replenished in the middle, the channel waters seethed, tugging powerfully in all directions.

To this waiting room came the spent male. Here, with all that was left of his bruised will, he took up station. The buffeting of wind and surf seething in all directions made a noise drowning out all sense of self, providing balm for the pains that wracked the entirety of his body and depressed his imagination.

Later in the night, after the tide had ebbed for five hours, he hauled himself slowly up on the rocks, hurried ashore at the very end by a following wave. There, he found himself not alone but in the company of a motley group of ancient male seals and others too young to risk the kind of encounter from which he had been forced to flee. There was a solitary female. Er-Erie had nursed her pup to the time of weaning, mating first with Balanec and the next day with Meinek after he defeated Balanec. She knew herself pregnant by Meinek, feeling the multiplication of cells that were the microscopic beginnings of another pup. If it survived the year ahead lodged within her, it would be born in late September next year.

No longer in season, she rested on the sea-wet rocks, gathering her strength and quietening her mind for a prolonged hunting trip out to sea. She, too, needed to replenish her haggard self so that she could offer the newly conceived life essential sustenance.

Not all the males on the islet were ancient. One particular seal noticed the arrival of Tyrian. Lifting his head, the friendly rumble of welcome was stilled in his throat when he saw the condition of the seal who had directed him to this safe haven. When he lowered his head back down to its resting place on the night-black rocks, the light of the moon picked out the mending wound at his nape. Lying dark in the darkness, he knew for certain, having experienced the same flinching away from companionship upon arriving at this place, Tyrian had no desire for company.

Bloody, Meinek returned to a sea cave where two females lingered yet with their pups. In the morning, a third female arrived, making her way above the reach of the tide. Her presence did not disturb the females already present. She was able to fall asleep for several hours. It was not just the imminence of the birth of her pup, but the long swim westward along the English Channel that had wearied her. She had left the sandbank between the Dutch islands of Texel and Vlieland two days previously. It was not a swim she had enjoyed until she felt the cleansing influence of the Atlantic on waters in which she swam. Off Looe, she had made a final hunt, being rewarded by the capture of a large monkfish, the tail of which she feasted on with relish.

At one hour after high tide, she gave birth to a little pup but, when she turned to make contact, and helped it escape from the amniotic sac in which it was lightly packaged for entry to the world, she was surprised to see it made no movement. Persevering, she nuzzled it; but it was stillborn. The journey of that little life was over before it had drawn breath.

Later, on the same falling tide, she left the beach. As she departed, the great, injured seal in the entrance waters sniffed her as she passed, learning she had not yet come into season. He did not waylay her.

For a day or two, Irasana travelled as a seal bereft. Having left Waterfall Cave, she made her way across the bay to Martinsfinger Cave. She entered and explored it like one seeking something she had lost. There, she found moulted Somerledaa roving the mattress of kelp, hungry and alone. Fleetingly, the little moulted pup mistook her for Mornalas and hurried toward her, crying with hunger, begging for a feed. She suffered no angry rebuff. Rather, Irasana eddied away from her, startled, recognising this was not the pup she sought. That pup was not to be found. Like one chased, she hastened back over the rocks and into the sea. Abandoned again, Somerledaa watched her go, perplexed by the lack of greeting.

*** *

For one week more, Somerledaa slept, swam and grew hungrier on the kelp-cluttered beach. Between-times, she would slip into the sea making small, exploratory dives. Often, she would pick up a seashell, a piece of seaweed or a stone. This she would bring to the surface, held in her mouth. There, she would drop it only to bank over and dive in pursuit of whatever was tumbling or dropping through the water column. Having retrieved it, she would return to the surface and drop it again, always deliberately. Banking over, she would dive in pursuit of it, retrieve it and return to the surface; for hours on end.

This game was her main activity, her main pleasure of the day. Never did she venture far. As if on a piece of string, having ventured so far, she would hasten back to the only haven she had ever known.

While playing the game, under the water sometimes she dallied, watching the silver glimmerings of fish darting into the sand, rock crevices or algal forests. At other times, catching sight of a crab working sideways across the bottom, she would drift down head first, to watch the creature more closely. Sometimes, the crab would stop, raising heavily armoured claws, pincers open and challenging. She would twirl in a full circle, upside-down above the small show of courage, uncomprehending but hypnotised until the next flashing movement distracted her.

Already she was a powerful swimmer, for her age.

She practised different forms of swimming. This day, she had made her longest journey ever, concentrating on how she moved through the water. Upon entering the sea, her mood was to swim in long, shallow submergences punctuated by visits to the surface for air, counting her heartbeats as she went. In her imagination, she decided to develop a travelling mode of swimming, a rhythm she was capable of sustaining. She had started by taking an irregular series of breaths before submerging and swimming.

She did not travel fast, but was soon in the middle of the bay. It was not that she thought 'I must do this and that'. Indeed, she had few thoughts at this time. Rather, it was as if the stirring of her inner self toward the struggle to survive ran an instinctive check across the inventory of fledgling abilities available to her.

She made a series of travelling-pace trips to the middle of the bay despite the continuing heavy run of surf toward the rocky shores. By good fortune rather than design, her first three trips were uncomplicated. She managed passages to areas where the weight of the waves and turbulence of the surf were least powerful. The fourth time, she found herself being sucked toward a great, rearing, roaring green wheel of a wave. No sooner had she felt the quickening of it than she dived as deep as she could go.

It was the perfect choice. She wove through a sandstorm of churned up sand at the seabed as the wave toppled over with a crisply explosive ripping-zipping sound that transformed into a bouncing, bounding avalanche of running surf.

She was fortunate to remain down until just after the third wave came crashing down, bobbing up fortuitously on its seaward side. There, she felt a twist of anxiety. The waves rearing about her were the biggest she had met yet in all the short days of her life. Before the next wave, she dived a fraction late and failed to submerge to a depth sufficient to reach the calmer places below the commotion. She found herself rolled over and over by the turbulence before being released to the quiet waters of the greater depth.

Confused as to whether she was drifting to the surface or to the seabed, she followed the small trail of bubbles escaping from her sealed nostrils to find the surface. There, she gulped in air and ejected it, gulped it in again, feeling already the quickening tug of the next wave but feeling the need to take just one more breath before the final emptying of her lungs. This time, though, she had made a bad mistake. The sea was already turning upside-down before she endeavoured to dive free of danger.

It was a very big wave. Had Amaury been watching, he would have seen the darkly ovoid smudge of the small seal captured in aspic near the steepling crest of a majestic wave. Being elsewhere, he saw neither that, nor the graceful, almost slow motion, tumbling of the crest. A green wheel of unimaginable power, it came crashing-bouncing down on to the sea it had shallowed just ahead of itself; all along the length of itself, the wave green-wheeled, green-pealed, into brightest surf.

It would have been a dream wave for Neil, Richard or Tom, for the break was steady and fast without being quite too fast. For Somerledaa, now at the most dramatic moment of her life, here was the first big challenge she must answer for herself, if she was to survive. Helpless in the wave itself; helpless in the inescapable green-wheeling of it, and more than helpless in the white water that followed was she. In the white water, her seal self was utterly shaken from her. She became rag. As rag, she was entirely at the mercy of violent water. Had she been visible, she might have resembled a leaf in a gale.

Nothing worked. Her power was gone. Her breath was exhausted by helplessness and fear brought about by the pummelling white waters.

She did not have time to become aware she was going to die. When she came to the end of her strength, she did not become aware of it, neither the sideways slide into a dream state that was not quite consciousness. The waters bowled on, tossing her around their heart while reality swam and blurred for her.

And then she was no longer being tossed like rag. Inexplicably, she was in quiet water. Operating on automatic, but very soon coming to some ghost of alertness, she breathed in gulps of air that she had never thought to breathe again. As she breathed, she noticed the next lithe animal of white water bounding toward her across the surface of the sea. Aware she had failed again to take in enough air she dived deep as she could go. To her alarm, she came too soon to the shallow bottom, where she schooled herself to stillness as the surf poured by overhead, but the surf did not trouble her. Dimly at first, she recognised that she had been ejected from the clutches of the sea at the margins of its main power. She recognised the main power of the wave was in its breaking.

Very soon after the drama of her escape from the waves, she hastened to Martinsfinger Cave where she fell asleep. Sleeping, she twitched and made small crying sounds as she dreamed the horrors of what she had survived. It was not a restful sleep, but it was not without value. Had she known it, this was a learning sleep. Today, she had the luck to survive a great mistake. Never again in all her life, be it long or short, would she make the same mistake again.

The next day, the wind had dropped, the sea was less tempestuous. Swiftly recovered from her ordeal, in the way of the young, Somerledaa tried another kind of travelling. This time, she swam steeply to the seabed and made a serpentine course through waving fronds of seaweeds into deeper water, remaining close to the bottom all the way until she needed to take in air. She continued seaward in this manner for a while, pausing to periscope in the middle of the bay, checking no steepling waves were threatening. Satisfied, she continued seaward in the same manner, low over the bottom. Along the way, she disturbed a flounder sheltering camouflaged by a shallow sheet of sand. It rippled up into open water, accelerating away in a rippling of long-rested fins.

Provoked to curiosity, Somerledaa hastened after the speckled, blotched flatfish. Three times, she tried to touch its dorsal surface with her whiskers. Each time, the flounder changed direction and evaded her, in fear for her life. They continued with what, to Somerledaa, was an underwater dance. At speed, they drifted apart and closed together, the direction changing all the while. Somerledaa made repeated probing approaches from different angles until, growing needful of air, she swerved away upwards to the surface.

She did not immediately forget the interesting play-companion as often had happened already with play-mates of the moment. When she was ready, she dived again and tried to locate the flounder in the desert of flat and unmarked sands. Finding no visible trace, she continued seaward and, abruptly startled Balanec who had been drowsing at the surface, stretched out like a log. Ashamed to have been startled by so small a seal and not being interested in her, he drew himself out to his full length until he resembled a floating plank again and just lay at the surface blowing bubbles of disapproval through his nostrils.

From below, the equally startled Somerledaa came up through the water column more tentatively. As the male re-appeared at the edge of her vision, she sensed no imminent antagonism, nor prospect of chastisement. Having taken some breaths at a respectful distance, she submerged again and swam with great care toward him, trying to behave with courtesy. She stopped slightly more than the length of his body from him, her small body curved respectfully like a comma in the water and her head reaching telescopically toward him as if she was seeking to read the scent of him.

Balanec made no sign of noticing her so she dared move no closer. While, a few days since, she had felt confidence at the proximity of dark Tyrian who had more than once shepherded her from danger, her trustingness had been frayed by her solitude. Now, his complete lack of communication unnerved her. For two minutes she lingered, inquisitive, ready to be friendly.

Balanec opened one unfriendly eye in her direction but then allowed his attention to wane. Both eyes closed, locking Somerledaa out. Discouraged, she allowed the teasing water movements to increase the gap between them. Her body lost its curve, regained its youthful grace. Quietly, she slipped below the waves and returned to her home cave.

That was the way of things for a week. Day after day, she ventured out, constantly trying things that had worked during the previous days, and trying to avoid repeating mistakes she had made. Her swimming grew stronger, but the only sensation growing in her was not confidence but hunger.

Having yet to make essential connections, her instincts did their best to guide her to the answers she needed to find. She found herself spending more time venturing along the seabed through tide-teased seaweed forests and along the wrinkled skirts of cliffs often cluttered with the residue of ancient rockfalls. Often, she brushed her whiskers lightly over the sands, enjoying the sensations. Often, she followed closely above or behind fish or crabs, following clues without realising they were supposed to lead to answers.

Her bloated puppy-fat was dwindling. She had shrunk since Mornalas had weaned her, but she remained mercifully free of injury and, therefore, of debilitating infection.

On the eighth day, a stranger female arrived at the cave. Perzia. She was not peaceful in nature, like Mornalas and Ithian, like dark Tyrian. This female had never given birth to a pup before. She was restless, anxious and frightened of the stirrings of her body. Swimming into the cave, grounding on the litter of stipes and fronds, she looked about her as if seeking deadly enemies. She found none but the bold little female who came swiftly over the kelpy mattress to greet her.

Perzia extended her neck to its full extent and moaned. It was a lingering sound made with whiskers fully cupped in electric hostility. Somerledaa backed off and humped her back as if to resist an attack. She made the mistake of offering her own impolite riposte. It was another learning moment.

Perzia drove forward, snarling open-mouthed, displaying her teeth causing Somerledaa to whirl around and retreat at speed by the Tooth Rock. At that point, some preserving instinct warned her not to retreat deeper into the cave and make more complicated her return to the sea. For a prolonged moment, she was riven by indecision, not realising it was a conflict between her baby self and the self she was trying to become, independent and at home in the world, that wrestled within her.

Following the base of the rock she reversed into a Somerledaa-wide gap there, hunching her back and shrinking into her smallest self.

Perzia did not pursue her and soon forgot her. She entered deeper into the cave, seeking a birthing couch and when she was far enough up the kelpy sandhill, Somerledaa fled fast as she could down to the long pool

In the darkness, three hours after high tide, Perzia gave birth to her pup. It was a difficult birth. She had to meander about the cave while, at the last, the pup simply would not make the final twitch out into the world, but in the end her improvisation had the desired effect. Soon thereafter, the latest thin hunger cries were being uttered breathily into the quiet, damp airs of the seal cave.

It was more than two hours later that the awkward beginning between mother and pup was sealed by the first feed. The young male, Tirquin, experienced great difficulty locating the nipple. In large part, this was because it was a long time before Perzia keeled over on one side, granting him the access he needed. She had not yet felt any connection with this scrap of life so utterly dependent on her.

The rigours of his birth had exhausted him. The first feed was an extended, fumbling affair, satisfactory to neither pup nor mother. The second feed, made in the first light of day, was no better. Uncharacteristically, for the mother of a seal pup so new to the world, Perzia rested in the sea between feeds.

Meanwhile, Somerledaa had come ashore and soon was sleeping in the neighbouring Great Seal Hole.

By the morning sunlight, on the far side of a tidal bar of water, she made out the forms of other seals at rest on the sand, counting four of them. Two were young males; another was a seal mother while the fourth was the moulted male pup, Cerriec.

Watchful of the other seals, who seemed to be sleeping, she moved slowly downhill, remaining close to the cave wall, glad to be moving over sand instead of a slippery-slithery tangle of kelp. At the bottom of the hill, she found herself in a high tunnel that led back out to the sea. On a roosting perch, high above, three rock doves stared down, discussing her in soft, gossipy voices. From the sandhill, Cerriec watched her drift in the shallow, tugging-pushing water out of sight in the direction of the sea. When she moved out of sight, he could not see slaloming languidly through the maze of partly emerged boulders to meet the small successive piles of incoming surf. There, she dived, made a sinuous passage out of the cave and along the root of the headland leading from the entrance.

Having emerged without yet being inspired to follow a plan for the day, she played with the waves, turning it into a happy dance. They bore down on her and she faded before them, eluding them. If a wave was too small to have the power to tumble her, she surfed before it, revelling in the quickening of it, the sensation of speed without effort. She could even change her mind, become still in the water before pirouetting away from or into the next wave.

Heedless of the wider world she played until, suddenly, another small seal was with her. Like the living shadow of her whims, Cerriec found and followed her, always fractions of a pulse behind. Though two days older than her and lacking her water-mastery, he swam like a seal much younger until she touched the length of him lightly in passing. Thereupon, the electricity of her zest for life illuminated his world. He rose above himself and the two seals coiled about one another. About and over one another, they continued to roll and twine, happy with the patterns they created, the trails in the water, the bubble-streams. Once started, it became the game of the day. There was no need to be travelling far.

The hours passed. A succession of heavy showers tracked in from the horizon, hatching soaring, vivid rainbows that spanned their world. None of that made the least difference to the seals. If the condition of happiness could be said to exist in seals, then it existed in Somerledaa and Cerriec that day.

They covered no great distance. Under the headland and, occasionally, out beyond the handsome tip of it, they sleeked the flows of their water dance. Most of the time, it seemed, they maintained some small point of contact between their twining bodies; or, if that was an illusion, they remained bound to their shared dance by invisible ribbons. There were instances, rare instances, where they parted. Such partings were soon mended by a chase. As soon as the pursuer caught up with the pursued, the dance was resumed.

However, toward the end of the day, Somerledaa made a playful attempt to escape. That was when something new and incredibly important happened.

Ahead of her, there was a collapsed wreck of a timber-hulled ship substantially buried in shell-sand beyond the headland. She had foundered more than one hundred and fifty years before. Gliding by, glancing at it, she took in the lovely encrustations of hydroids, sponges and vivid displays of various anemones and Devonshire cup corals along with the waving weed. She glimpsed the furtive movements of cuckoo and ballan wrasse, of pollack, shoals of sand eels and bib. Peering from crevices, sometimes she glimpsed the tiny, watchful eyes of blennies. At once she paused, and then was drawn down towards the long, wand-like antennae of a lobster that showed neither fear nor the least sign of budging from its lair. Then she was flowing on again, catching the glimmer of something silver that flashed and flashed again, irregularly in the distance. It triggered a strange sensation in the whiskers along her muzzle. Compelled by the electricity of it, she accelerated to gain a better look at the silver glimmerings.

Fish. Bass. Approaching them unseen, now the electricity spread to the four or five whiskers above her eyes. Was hunger doing this, the light-headedness that came with having gone so long without food? The reflections were abstract, milling unformed in her mind. Something strange was happening. Of a sudden, one fish stood out clear of the rest. Brilliantly framed in silver, it grew until it filled the entire space before her eyes. Accelerating more, it was twitching its body left-right with no regularity, but she remained locked on to it as though burgling its every intention. Her mouth half-opened without her realising or requiring it; then wider, widest, as she closed in and grabbed it in her jaws, holding it with her small teeth. Veering aside and upward, away from the scattering shoal, Somerledaa spiralled up to the surface.

There, the movements of the broken fish were already weak. Holding it crossways in her jaws, still nothing she did was deliberate. Never before had she bitten into anything. Before, all nourishment had come from sucking. Now, she bit into the silver scales, chewed, watching as the ruined fish went slipping down under the water. Playing the childhood game that was no longer a game, she pealed over and followed it down until she recovered it. Returning with it to the surface, she bobbed there for five minutes. She was aware Cerriec was close by, watching her, but she was no longer interested in their game. She was savouring the flavours of the beautiful silver fish.

She had crossed a threshold crossed previously by millions of seals down through the uncounted millennia of her line. She had hunted. She had chased down the glimmering target. She had feasted. This was the seal way.

Without feeling the elation that might have been, Somerledaa made her way back to the cave. Cerriec, close behind, was considerably awed by the younger female. He had witnessed what she had done and felt the gap widen between what they were. Out of daylight into the quiet gloom of the cave tunnel they swam. Not knowing they were following the route once taken by Tyrian, they followed the flow of the waters left around the bend, their wave depositing them at the foot of the sand-hill.

Light-bodied, up the steep hill they hauled themselves, leaving behind them less well-defined tracks than those left by the heavier adults. They made no effort to make a big evasive arc around the seal mother, who had stirred at their arrival. There was no sense of threat. The only sense either of them received was of haven. They did not know it and neither did their companion seals, but in this cave, no more pups would be born this season. The breeding season, here, was concluded. Now, for many months, there would be an absence of real aggression. The worst that might befall would be grumbling as seal bumped into seal, apologised or complained.

Already, in Somerledaa, the sense of total awed respect she had felt in the presence of unfriendly Balanec, across the bay by the rock off the opposite headland, was slightly outgrown. Already, a ray of belonging to all sealdom was touched to life in her. One ray, it promised her nothing, least of all that she would survive this dangerous first year of life, but she who had been reared on milk with the texture of mayonnaise had gone beyond total dependency. Be it by good fortune or design — and she felt wrongly it had been by good fortune — she had hunted, killed and feasted, achieving an embryonic independence. She dreamed the miracle of it over and over without knowing that she was wearing the groove of the hunting line she had followed and the clues that kept her to it ever-deeper into her eager instincts.

Glimmer; silver glimmer. Hither, thither. Disappearing but no, there again, a little farther on. Silver glimmers in eddying waters where silver bodies slid, leaving the finest silvered slivers of signatures; a trail. Gone again, reappeared again. Glimmer; silver glimmers, the strangest sensations in her mystachial vibrissae. Acceleration. Whiskers calling for acceleration? Surely not? Closer now, a more regular glimmering. Light-filled mirrors winking on and off in irregular illumination. Mystachial vibrissae cupped toward the shoal and the strangest feeling behind her eyes. Above those eyes, clogged with silvered slivers of reflected light, superciliary whiskers standing erect. Now sliding the length of her silver snout — everything so sensitive, the sensitivity of learning a line whereby survival became possible; just possible. Strangest feeling, as if now sight was being taken over by those excited vibrissae. Hallucination? No, there they go, around that angled piece of encrusted metal sticking up out of the sands. Eyes back in control flow on, around the corner and there they are again!

Like a psychedelia about which she had not knowledge but instinct; the strange sensations flowed through her dreams. All had their origin and final home in the various vibrissae, her whiskers. What was going on? Were they seeking all to link up at the same time? Then it happened, as if triggered by the thought. All the sensations touched, sparked, the silver glimmerings merging and vibrating. The vibrations intensified. Inside her head whirled a candelabrum of sparkling, silver lights. For a moment, it occurred that her sanity was spinning out of control.

The superciliary whiskers above her eyes locked in complicity with the two erect vibrissae on the top of her snout and the cupped whiskers about her short muzzle for the first time. Like the sights of a sniper's rifle, they lined up and identified their target. It was a sensation she would never forget.

One great silver fish swam outlined, illuminated. Of the remainder of the shoal, there was no sign. No need to think, now. Something else was thinking her every movement. She did not feel like a seal just then. It was as if she was the silver hunter and silver hunted, seal and bass, both along with the sea between. She was herself and the moving spirit of the hunted fish.

She dreamed of the culmination, when she had more collided with than bitten into the bass. In the very end, returned to control of what she did, she had hardly known what to do. Instinct had kicked in very hard at the last.

And then the dream started all over again, and the groove of it worked one revolution deeper.

Somerledaa remained with Cerriec for a week but they and all other seals avoided Martinsfinger Cave. Therein, the pup grew without bloom, without thriving. He was wary of his disturbed mother, moving about the cave floor as little as possible when she was present for fear of provoking her anger. From the first day, the boundaries of his roaming were extensive because Perzia swam out of the cave on the falling tide and remained sleeping in the entrance waters until about two hours before high tide. Most feeds were squeezed into a period of a few hours around high tide. Tirquin often cried monotonously, miserably, but spent long hours unanswered in his hunger.

It chanced that a storm blew up one day, driving Somerledaa and Cerriec right over the submarine resting place where Perzia was sleeping and into the neighbouring cave. Emboldened by the company of Cerriec, she made one last exploration of her birth-place and so chanced upon wakeful Tirquin. It was an unhappy encounter; he bunching himself up defensively in the same narrow place where once Somerledaa had hidden from Perzia. She saw the poor condition of him and absorbed how woebegone he was as he resisted her friendly cajoling. She persevered with him, but he was not to be persuaded and so, feeling it had not been right to return to this place, she and Cerriec made their getaway before Perzia returned.

It was in her mind that time was imminent to be leaving home. She had learned to hunt and had become a much better swimmer over the past week, so nothing was holding her but habit. More, the unknown and its challenges were exerting their allure.

Somerledaa streamed by familiar rocks and familiar decorations. An orange encrustation of sponge by a green encrustation under that face of rock, the heavyweight, pale green spiny starfish with its five rays spread broadly over that rock. Cerriec was somewhere to the left of her. This was less familiar territory to him but he was playing a favourite travelling game, brushing against the canopy of the kelp forest and catching the occasional glimmerings of fish hastening to hide themselves and the fear they felt at his awful passing. Well, his somewhat less than awful passing, truth be known. But they didn't know that; only that the shape passing was the most dread of all shapes in their dangerous world.

Weed canopy, flowing this way with the run of the waters above, now flowing back again. In again, now out again. He swerved and swayed, much like a good surfer trying to generate pace on a wave that was running in too slowly. Accelerating here, pausing there, and now accelerating again. Swerve around that rock. Drift over that one. This rock looks like a seal! Locked into the joy of his solitary water dance, Cerriec responded not at all at first to the sight of the female sleeping upright at the bottom. Until the very last moment, he took her for a rock, so still was she for once. Only at the very last, when Perzia's eyes opened, did he accelerate blindly upward and away.

His acceleration set off a precautionary acceleration in Somerledaa, though she knew not the reason for it. They did not relent for a long minute, by which time they were out by the headland. Only there did they come together to the surface, Cerriec rotating jerkily, scanning each quarter of his vision. He could not know it but Perzia had swum immediately into the cave rather than in pursuit of intruding pups.

The next morning, after a night at rest on the sands of the Great Cave, the two moulted pups emerged together. Almost immediately, while foraging along the bottom, running his whiskers between sand and a litter of flat boulders, a large edible crab began a sideways getaway. This time, instead of shadowing its movements, Cerriec came in and caught the multi-legged, liver coloured shell and instead of lightly feeling the carapace with his teeth crunched into it.

The remains of it, he brought to the surface where, as Somerledaa had done with the first fish that she had caught, dropped it. As it saucered down through the water column, he recaptured it and returned it to the surface. Not far away, Somerledaa watched his small triumph. Having grown more accomplished as a huntress in the week since her transformation, she recognised that at last he had given himself the beginnings of a fighting chance to survive; but only the beginnings. She had sensed in him no silvery illuminations.

An hour later, the two small seals were playing a game of hide-and-seek. For five minutes or more, now, Somerledaa had evaded her companion. At that moment, somewhere on the far boundary of her vision, another small seal accelerated westward, out to sea. It was another moment of pure illumination. Inside her being, something turned upside down. Luminous as the first bass she had captured, a map of all her limited wanderings was spread across the entirety of her imagination. Superimposed over the top of it was a compass needle, though she did not recognise it as such yet or as anything at all, though she would come to recognise it as the key to everything.

Fascinated, she came corkscrewing up to the surface. Out west and several miles distant, she could make out the familiar dragon ridge of rocks. The dragon ridge had always been there, the nearest faraway place in the very brief span of her young life. She did not know that her mother had swum inshore from those rocks to release her into the world. She knew nothing at all about them except the desire in herself to go there. Now!

She did not seek Cerriec for a last time but surged forward, her back humping before she dived. She swished lithely with the hind end of her body, settling immediately into shallow-diving travelling mode. Her luminous internal map grew more familiar during the crossing. It developed along with her understanding of the movements of the needle. She did not understand it yet. That would come. She knew it would come.

For now, there was only the excitement of beginnings, of moving out into the world, that vast, unfamiliar jigsaw of unconsidered pieces. Eagerness ruled her; eagerness and burgeoning confidence that had no special right to be yet existed in her, even so.

Along the way, she made the acquaintance of the first powerful tide race she had ever encountered. She flirted in and out of it, not daring to thread a track across or under its boisterous, churning turbulence. As she dallied, working her way along its eastern margin, she came face to face with a trio of travelling harbour porpoises. Two of them were larger than her. They glistened and when they breathed, she heard them panting, puffing. The third was not black, like the adults but charcoal-coloured and small. A calf, it was travelling tucked close into the hindmost left flank of its mother. Seven months old, its mother would yet feed it for as long again and more before finally it was weaned and ready to live the independent life.

Playful, not alarmed by the strangeness of them, Somerledaa went down below them and swam there for a little while, coursing along upside down; but the porpoises took little notice beyond registering her unthreatening presence. Nothing deflated, Somerledaa resumed her probing of the water maze until, wearying of her indecision, she took a fix on the lighthouse and began to labour her way toward it.

Once into the flow and the turbulence, she was surprised how comfortable she felt. Swiftly, she learned where to go with the flow, where to burrow deeper into the maze and where to force her way. It was a three-dimensional game, a three-dimensional lesson, as ever in water, so it was almost with disappointment that she reached the far side of a race that ultimately curled away south-westward toward Isles of Scilly decorated in a cotton wool wrapping of sea spray.

Arriving at the Longships Reef, she explored the waters local to it because there could be no hauling out yet. Explosions of surf were geysering skyward. Heavy runs of surf were scouring all the potential haul-out places. No seal, not the mightiest of them, could haul-out under such conditions. But as the tide fell, opportunities might occur. Somerledaa went exploring. Very soon she discovered that, along the outside of the Reef, the sea ran like the clappers in one direction. Returning inside, she found herself being raced along at the speed of an express train the opposite way.

It was fun. She made a game of it. While she played, she noticed other seals continuing to arrive, taking up station in the sea. The tide ebbed at its fastest rate and then began to slow. All the while, more rocks were emerging. The play of surf was diminishing as some rocks created shelter for others. Having made yet another circuit, she was taking her latest express train ride in a northerly direction when she saw one big dark-grey seal had made landfall. Glistening, alert, he stared as she went flowing by.

Other seals hauled out. The movement on to the rocks was slow at first, undertaken only by the most powerful seals. As the tide ebbed more, the pace of hauling out speeded up and among the crowd of seals daring to come to shore surfed Somerledaa. Achieving a place on a flat slab otherwise occupied by mature males, none guessed the pride she felt. Close on the heels of self-satisfaction, weariness welled up, coshing her into restoring sleep.

***

Clad only in surfer's baggies and wet suit boots, he slipped into the sea outside Martinsfinger Cave. Using a relaxed side-stroke allowed him to tow along at the surface beside him the blue dry bag locked inside a larger red one. As ever, he was surprised the water did not feel colder at this time of year. It was the commonplace assumption of those who observed him in the sea and virtually the only question anyone ever asked: 'Isn't it freezing?' or, the same question phrased differently: 'You must be mad!'

For Amaury, it had become a matter of long habit — something good for his soul. Nevertheless, despite all his experience, he went warily with the tug of the waters on this November morning aware he was being sucked into a building wave and hoping he would not take a beating from it.

The conditions had looked marginal from the outset, when he paused at the cliff-top. The north-easterly breeze which that should have lain a calming hand over the bay waters had, after all, done little to suppress the corrugated lines developing outside the bay. Steepening as they steamed in, they disturbed his confidence. Caution was ever to the fore when exploring by himself. The smooth corrugations were incoming from some storm far out in the Atlantic.

His general hope lay in the fact that even the most daunting wave pulses were only intermittent. The gaps were his opportunity.

Obviously, he hoped to launch himself during a relatively quiet spell rather than into waves that would give him a drubbing. He chose his moment after having spent fifteen minutes of observant hesitation, trying to work out the rhythm of the sets. The trouble with making any choice outside Martinsfinger Cave was that there was a direction, hidden beyond the promontory, from which waves could march in unobserved.

Swimming around that promontory, Amaury saw immediately he had guessed wrong so he tried to turn, put on the brakes, and evade the inevitable, but he was not a seal. Seals, in these conditions, seemed to become magic colanders. The power of the suck of the sea seemed to have no effect on them. Many times, he had watched them hold station in surf surges without apparent effort, but he was sucked swiftly seaward. Upward he was sped into the curve of the wave, being lifted precisely to where he least wanted to be. But he was not going up and over a blue wave face. The crest was beginning to tumble over. Having achieved maximum elevation, the crest closed about the head of the man treading water.

Briefly locked in the wild surge of it he was tumbled shoreward, but even at the violent heart of the rude tumbling, his priority was to keep his fingers locked around the dry bag containing the precious, expensive equipment. Before the power of it spat him from its clutches, he had been bounced over a big submerged boulder like a struggling rat in the jaws of a Jack Russell. When he surfaced, looking down he was unsurprised to see he was cut and bruised. Blood coiled thinly in the surface waters from a re-opened scar scored in the thin skin covering the front of his shin. The skin covering that part of his leg had taken such a beating over the years that it was permanently thinned; vulnerable.

In the turbulent shallows, he managed to slide in horizontally, seal-like, to catch hold of a boulder. On the approach, he did not kick his legs at all, for fear of barking them against the submerged boulders — another lesson born of painful experiences. There, regaining his breath, he turned half about and watched again for the right moment. It dawned so immediately that he almost missed the chance, but he went fast as his side-stroke would propel him back toward the little promontory. Between promontory and islet, standing not more than five metres off, he saw another set of steep, hungry waves piling in. Again, the quickening waters caught him, but this time he swam with and slightly across them, deciding his hope lay in catching the knobbed and seamed promontory he was aiming for. He had climbed up out of calms as well as wave-churned seas here countless times in the past. He knew how to use the water movement there.

He had time enough, just, to secure his habitual one-handed hold on the top of a projecting pillar of rock; the only feasible hold. This was achieved while securing a tentative foothold on a small underwater ledge. He had just two seconds before the first wave broke over his head. Prepared for the punishing surge of it, Amaury focussed all effort on maintaining the finger hold in the crevice he had found. He allowed the sea casually — irresistibly — to sweep his feet from the underwater ledge, fully extending his body horizontally from the finger hold. At the far end of its reach, he felt his booted feet dancing against rock, but there was no hope of being able to brace himself at both ends. He willed himself to become a frond of seaweed. He was relaxed. It had happened so often before. Nearly always he managed to maintain his grip.

For long moments, the sea was all turbulence until he felt the inevitable rapid waning of that power. Because he was fully extended horizontally, he moved as the surf willed, even though he could see over one shoulder the next wave smoking in. It was just the first hurdle cleared in a tumultuous steeplechase with an unknowable number of fences.

This next wave seemed even bigger than the one that had just bowled through. Alarmed, Amaury used the very brief quietness of waters ebbing seaward feeding the incoming wave to lever himself up a step, still using the one unencumbered hand. This he achieved, now standing on the crevice where his fingers had been anchored. He was braced, having taken a finger hold in a slightly wider crevice, when the next wave broke about his chest.

Again, he was swept horizontal by the power of it, but for not so long. This time, the main power was sweeping by below him. The boiling waters subsided quickly, giving the moments needed to scamper up to more gently sloping rock. For the time being, he was safe. First base was secured.

Panting, excited by the successful exertion of it, he glanced down at the waters draining heavily over the rock where he had stood. Briefly, he saw the small ledge upon which he had been standing before it was buried by the next swamping wave. His gaze slid on and locked with that of a small seal. A moulted pup, he recognised it was the last-born pup from Martinsfinger Cave. Tirquin was weaned. His restless mother was gone and he had strayed into the ultimate danger zone, also his ultimate hope of life. Amaury wondered if he had learned to hunt, yet, suspecting not.

The seal stared back, apparently equally interested in what he was seeing. He might have been watching television.

What went on in the mind of any seal? Amaury watched the pup for a little while. It looked like a cocoon, upright in the sea, with its face wrinkled around relaxed whiskers, untroubled by the considerable water movement. He wondered: what is happening for you? How does a seal learn? By what means will you survive this first year? Where will your wanderings take you? How will I ever be able to answer questions like this working as a lone wolf? Of course: I won't.

He dared not linger. If he did not drive himself onward along the track he had made his own, who would? Another heavy set of waves was slavering in and, because the tide was still falling, the Atlantic wheels rolled over at the ideal place for sending up perfect geysers of vertical spray against the cliff. They drenched him where he flinched on the periphery but without threatening to drag him in to the sea.

He set off after the final major explosion. He moved fast, with decision, along a sequence of narrow, pool-riddled ledges, leaping over small, deep, watery chasms. One leap of his own height brought him down to a lower system of ledges. This part was easy. He had to remain alert but here were occasional curtains of rock to protect him against the full force of the waves, until he arrived at the last ledge. There, no choice: pause and reassess. Seeing yet another large set of waves tracking in, he fled up a steep slope to a familiar hiding place behind a thin curtain of granite.

Always, he counted them. Thirty-seven waves came bullying in, without respite. He found himself wondering, despairingly, what had happened to sets of four or seven? Only experience reassured him. If he remained patient — not usually a quality of his — the opportunity would occur and he would complete what he had set out to do. After two false starts, from which he drew back just in time, he recognised the moment when it came. He hastily insinuated himself from his refuge down to the flattish platform from which he had to launch himself while a lesser wave slopped up over the ledge.

Stepping into the sea, he went with the slop away from the wall of rock down with the four-metre fall. Once in, he swam strongly for the next point of emergence. It was not far away, but he was more than ever aware of the waves. The shag island stood outside the Great Seal Hole and, between it and the outer wall of the cave, the approaching waves were constricted so that, for a few seconds, they reared disturbingly tall while steaming in. By some alchemy of underwater topography, much of the height and power was lost thereafter and so his body was not smashed against the cliff wall. Instead, he was lifted and carried irresistibly up a ramp of bare rock. There, as the run of water came to its turning point, he grasped an isolated stipe of kelp.

The kelp was anchored to the rock by a holdfast. Amaury had long since learned that if he wished to use it for an anchor when emerging from the swell, he must hold it gently to avoid tearing it from the rock. The temptation, of course, was to grab it, hang on for dear life: wrong! The holdfast would part from its anchorage. Be gentle. As the wave drained away, he found a place to rest one knee, a submerged piece of kelp upon whose holdfast he could rest two toes, a rock slope upon which to press an anchoring forearm. Thus, he spread his weight and kept to a minimum his effect on the kelp held in his seaward hand.

All this took no more than three seconds before, again, he was scurrying upward in the next watery surge like an over-sized, tap-dancing crab to a more secure place. He was certain, now, he would reach the cave.

The last section was comparatively easy, despite a dearth of secure handholds or footholds. The cliff wall was steeply angled down to a ledge that appeared, disappeared. Where his feet felt their way, waves surged along the wall lacking their main power, being secondary waves angling off the main ones.

He had heard sounds earlier, in the forty minutes it had taken to climb down to the beach, traverse it, change into swimming gear, and prepare his equipment and struggle to this point. There were seals in the cave. He had heard them singing; he did now. A lone seal was uttering the long ululation that was one of the outstandingly atmospheric sounds of wildlife in the British Isles.

The singing was one reason for his determination to reach the cave.

With great relief, he entered Great Seal Hole. Moving across the entrance, body bent double, his movements were as near as possible silent. Above him, massive boulders concealed his moving figure from any seals drawn up on the sand-hills within, though not from the inquisitive pup who yet watched him from the moving hills of water at his back. Tirquin did not come ashore but remained alert and curious outside the sea cave.

Amaury worked his way along the west wall, as ever, moving over boulders, along little ledges and bedrock outcrops, wading knee-deep through pools while small fish darted to hide in shadowed margins and clefts. While moving, he absorbed that the sand-hill whaleback of his previous visit was dramatically altered from the previous week. Where the boulders came from was, in part, a wonder. They were huge. Correspondingly huge seas had relocated them. It was not simply a matter of wave action having sucked scores of tons of sand from the cave, thereby, revealing what had always been present. They had not. They had been bulldozed in from the sea floor beyond the cave entrance. It was all part of an aeon-long game of scour-deposit; with wind and wave action the puppeteers.

Finding a comfortable seat, out of possible line of sight of the seals within, he set to work in his notebook, sketching the positions of the largest boulders, the location and measurements of the largest pools.

Sketching, he was aware of the contrast with the exterior world. He had only just made it. Today was one of the most marginal days. A wise man would not have attempted it. Was he an unwise man, then? By any normal measure, what he was doing was folly and the greater for being alone and no-one knowing where he was.

Sitting there, adding brief annotations, Amaury did not feel like a fool. Danger was behind and ahead but not here and now. He had reached this cave thrice-monthly for almost three years. The way-wisdom in him was enormous. Like seals hunting fish, he had developed his own invisible hunting lines, knowing what to do and precisely when, especially in the sea; so far, at least.

Very often, the closest shadow accompanying him on lonely adventures of discovery was fear. He was often afraid but, equally often, in the heart of challenging moments, so far there had been always a way of coming through. He had found ways to relax at critical times, as when he imitated — became — a seaweed frond anchored to a crevice only by his fingers. Often, then, real time seemed to slow right down for him, like the heartbeat of a diving seal. It allowed him to relax, find his way in the heart of tumult.

Having made his latest cave floor plan view diagram, Amaury made his way between the remaining boulders and over the brow of the once-sandy whaleback. The boulders there provided good cover for his stealthy progress downhill toward the light from the other cave entrance.

Today being a spring tide, there was no water in the tunnel used by the seals for accessing and departing the cave. A thinner screen of boulders there allowed him to crawl unseen to the base of the interior sand hill, staying close to the wall.

On a neap tide, the sea would have barred his way, requiring him to wade sometimes neck-deep through water during the critical interlude. Now, on the threshold of the crucial observation period, he could see many seals sprawled over the sand hill. Not all were asleep. The reason he had heard singing was that a dispute was taking place. It was never simply the hauntingly beautiful wild choral music he described occasionally to someone who had never heard it. There was always a reason for it and nearly always that was disputatious.

The closer he crawled to the seals, the greater the likelihood of being observed. At the base of the sand-hill, he paused in deep shadow. Very carefully, he raised himself up until he was kneeling. Using binoculars that were his most expensive possession, he focussed on the seals above.

To find the first pup and to behold the commonplace miracle of new life, and of the latest breeding season getting under way again: no moment in any year could beat that. But to some extent, this did. On the threshold of winter, grey seals came to this cave shore to form the greatest haul-out assemblies. In the final week of another November, he had chanced, as he had hoped, on the beginning of the latest season of gathering.

Behind him, the sun was obliging; having escaped from behind what he had assumed would remain an impenetrable barrier of cloud. Sunlight was always a cheering companion, especially in the morning and most especially in this remote, stormbound cave so redolent of everything primaeval.

Even the dark interior felt the tendrils of light. It did not disturb the seals but it did make the counting easier.

He counted them four times, seeking them out in every nook and cranny they had used for a retreat. Thrice, he achieved the same total number and the same breakdown into categories. Fifty-five adult males and nine immatures. Sixty-four seals. It was a high number, but still almost two score short of the highest number he had ever counted. He had read that elsewhere females assembled ashore first, followed by the males. Here, it appeared otherwise. The males always came ashore first, a sprinkling of immatures and occasional females among them, between the last weeks of November and January. Thereafter, numbers were sometimes high even through to May of some years but never as high as during the most lightless months.

It was not uncommon to visit this cave in mid-November, as he had, finding something between just two and seven seals present, or maybe just a late pup or two with attendant adults. A week or two later, in the last week of the month, there might be thirties or forties of seals and no sign of pups, as now.

Mindful of the continuing levels of seal song and bickering, Amaury settled to his other main reason for being there. He crawled around the corner to be out of sight of the seals, all of whom were at least halfway up the sand-hill. Now, he could straighten his cramped body, return feeling to his limbs and set up the microphone. Having unravelled the cable, he placed the digital recorder on waterproof matting, switched it on and double-checked everything was protected against the ruinous damp. Satisfied, he walked slowly toward the more secret of the sea cave entrances.

He paused often, using his torch to illuminate various anemones anchored to the granite walls or less precariously in hollows. He examined sea squirts, sponges and once a crawling thing that he could not name, but which he photographed to be identified later. Near the entrance, he went leaping from one *Lithophyllum*-encrusted boulder to another, until he came out into the light.

There, above him on the right-hand side, was the familiar fragment of raised beach. Perched on it, neck extended diagonally, stood a sunlit iridescent shag. Its bill and gape were vibrantly deep yellow, enhanced by a filigree of maroon tracery across the gape. Lovely green eyes showed concern but no surprise at seeing a perpendicular rather than a horizontal mammal emerging from this entrance visible only from the sea. Likely the same shag had observed this perpendicular mammal many times before, he supposed silently.

He noticed two more immature seals in the narrow approaches to the cave. A cramped swell was developing into steep, paler turquoise waves there. The pair of seals, as ever tucked beyond harm's way outside the break, bobbed irregularly up and down as if on a slackly-tensioned trampoline. They showed briefly like small, dark flowers sprouting from the apogee of the rolling swell, disappearing only to be lifted again. Beyond, small flights of gannets were flowing along, untroubled by the wind or the confused waves. All were flying south to north.

Behind him, the voices of two seals rose to an extended crescendo of choral disputation, reeling him in from casual exploration. Although the digital recorder was doing the work, he still had to be its shepherd. At any moment, driven by some whim, a seal cavalry might come charging down the sand-hill and around the corner. If there was one thing Amaury had learned about using cameras, flashguns, tape recorders, mini-disc recorders, camcorders — in short, any sensitive instrument requiring batteries — if it could go wrong, it did, and if it could do so the most expensive way possible, then it would. Therefore, he scuttled back to his responsibility. Close to the corner where the tunnel joined the main fairway of the cave, he dropped to all fours and crawled forward. At the junction, he craned his head to the left, peering warily uphill.

At the lowest edge of the assembly, two males were flippering at one another, each having keeled on to one side. Amaury grinned. Whatever they were doing, it appeared to be for appearances only, unlikely to develop into anything serious. In fact, he was glad of it, for it was accompanied by another bouillon of their lovely, evocative choral music.

The microphone extended farther out on to the main fairway than he dared go, but at the thought of the recorder, he checked again that a light was shining, confirming it was switched on. Relieved, he resumed formal watch over the behaviour of the seals, at intervals of three minutes for the next ninety minutes.

Later, when reviewing his harvest of cave behaviour data, the outstanding feature was that nearly all the seals had spent almost the entire period sleeping, but for occasional stretches and looks around before continuing to drowse. There had been but one event of note. Two yearlings had spent a period playing a game of seal-tag which entailed chasing one another through the quite tight maze created by scant spaces left between the bodies of the adults. It caused much adult irritation as they bumped along, scattering sand as they went.

There was a general stirring in their wake, much belated flipping and open-mouthed grumbling; but the yearlings were unperturbed. They roistered on, culminating the game by setting off a stampede having suddenly changed direction and scampered at full speed downhill toward the light.

Amaury had been resisting the temptation to take a sequence of photographs of their behaviour, knowing the flashes would have triggered a stampede. It was the same difference with the camcorder. To generate sufficient illumination, he would have had to shine the torch toward them, with the same inevitable result. Now, as they galumphed downhill and swerved along the corridor to the sea, he delayed no more but captured his sequence of images.

Afterwards, having retrieved the undamaged digital sound recorder, he was happy to leave the cave. He never knew whether he was going to meet even worse sea conditions on the return leg — hoping for the best, prepared for the worst.

He followed his own footprints back to the cave entrance. The view that met his eye was unnerving. A wave burst vertically, explosively, up the cliff.

Still delighted by his experience of cave-time, philosophically, he saw he had time to weave his way to the starting line and the hope of quieter waves. There was a very slender thread of high track he used to traverse the first part of steep slope whenever, as now, the big boomers were putting on their show.

It was always good for morale to be heading for home, though the way be beset with peril; as now. Strange the way impulses bubbled from the unconscious. I am in dread – I am immortal: the bookends of what he might have thought, teetering along high above the slavering sea. Some days, he could not over-ride fear, but never on the way back. There was no other way back.

At this point, he always felt immortal, in contrast with the mortal, vulnerable being that had embarked on the high-drama phase of the outward leg of the expedition. For now, some hunger in him was relishing the challenge of these moments. Inside, he knew there was only one real challenge. It entailed swimming one-armed, if he was lucky, no more than fifteen strokes across a strip of strongest water movement.

He gave it no thought, caring little how big might be the waves running in now he was engaged. In fact, the bigger the better because then the great inshore sweep of water movement should lift him up and, if he made the right set of moves, deposit him up on the crucial ledge. In a smaller sea, he would have struggled to reach it.

In the meantime, lock fingers around the handle of the dry-bag, at all costs. Leap now! Out into space and an ugly submerging. Surface; drive sideways through the water rebounding from the cliffs, accept the swift seaward flow sure that the very next wave would stamp on the brakes, drive him back in just as fast.

It happened. Still sweeping away from the cave, working out the angles, lining up with the ledge, trying to make it easy for the depositing wave, he felt the flood reverse. Now he was being driven in. Too fast! Too fast, he would have thought; had this been the first time. Too fast this would be, but only if the wave had broken to hurl him into the cliff, and that was not going to happen. It swept him in with great power, but the very power of the unbreaking wave created some sort of a cushion that shielded him from harsh abrasion against the cliff-face. Close to, he realised, the wave was not big enough. It was not going to lift him to the ledge. He had a choice. Grab the inner edge of the ledge, which he knew by heart, or kick off from the cliff and go with the backwash of the wave? A split-second. No time to choose.

His free left hand reached out, took the familiar grip and as immediately he braced his body for the sudden incredibly heavy weight of it as the waters drained totally away. His feet were left kicking for a grip, found a tentative one, on the steeply-angled ledge below. It relieved the excruciating downward drag of gravity on his single arm. Prepared for everything, still he grimaced with the drag of it, risking a quick glance over his shoulder at the same time to assess just how stupid an impulse it had been.

It would not have mattered, whatever he had seen. Everything always looked bad in this kind of a sea from this viewpoint.

What he recognised was the first of another set of big boomers. It was bounding in diagonal to the line of cliff, and the only good thing

Amaury managed to see in it was that if it lifted him up, then it could only wash him in the right direction. Trouble was this was a wave with a look of malice about it. He had been caught in such waves before. Yes; they swept you up on to the ledge, but they did it with such grandiose excess that they swilled him around before dragging him right back into churning, air-filled waters.

Committed, he had no choice but to wait. The dice were rolling.

The two seconds preceding his critical moment dragged on for a quite inordinate length of time while he listened to a running boom of exploding surf farther along the cliff-face. A great geyser of spray had exploded up the cliff-face, briefly hanging there like a heavy curtain of fountains. Terribly frail and vulnerable at the full length of his arm, his feet only partly sharing the weight, suddenly and without gradations, the sea was about ankles, knees, waist and then he was being swept upward in an incredibly powerful surge of water.

It was as strong as he feared, but there also the peculiarly slow-motion element in his reactions that allowed him to keep thinking clearly; the seal-heartbeat reflex. His eyes were scanning the rock face along which the water carried him. There? There? There? His eyes took in crevices, knobs of rock, all the inadequate anchorage points he might have grasped. He felt the waters thinning, falling, subsiding over the deeply submerged ledge into the sea and he just one more part of the flow of it all.

Fighting now, he was light-footedly tap-dancing his way along again, still too fast, feeling with his feet even as he searched with his eyes. Suddenly, he had it. He dropped, knees bent, legs angled in toward the cliff, neoprene-booted feet dug in at an angle of at least forty-five degrees like a skier braking on a steep slope of snow. He presented the sideways-on profile of his body to the main flow of the wave. The strain was incredible. For a moment, he thought he couldn't hold the stance but then he was free. No time to think. Run fast; leap the gap; clamber up the next bit, and anchor on to the hand-hold he knew existed above his head. Use both hands. Do it now! Ignore the knocking of the dry-bag against his cheek. Ignore the swirl of water, up around ankles, knees, waist; again. Ignore it because it is not going to reach any farther. Now go down with the ebb of the water. Go fast.

Back to the ledge with the pools. Ignore the sight of the next wave. Just go!

He ran fleetly and reached a wall of rock taller than the height of himself. He reckoned, even as he tossed up the dry-bag with its cushioned contents, he had reached it with three seconds to spare. Still he had to run for another second, reach up to the ledge with his hands, lever himself up, generating a small boost by kicking up from a small protuberance of rock. Even then, he was not quite quick enough. Some malice in the wave accelerated him up over the broad, sharply-barnacled ledge into the wall. He spread his right hand to save himself, but in the unexpected depth of water, found he had to hurl himself left like a goalkeeper across his goal to grab the dry-bag before the wave made any more mischief.

Catching the bag, he submerged momentarily in the retreating flow of water, but it could not drag him over the edge. His bottom and back grounded. Without style or dignity, he scrambled to his feet and ran to refuge in a higher, safer place around a corner.

What next? Around the promontory that had provided first base on the outward leg of the adventure, the tumultuous waters looked deeply unattractive. Neither had he forgotten that just below the surface were very large rocks into or over which he risked being dragged.

Plan B required the hero's leap. This also held potential peril, but also offered the shorter swim to shore and just the one large boulder to avoid.

He was beginning to feel tired and cold. He was aware that in being dragged along the wall of rock and grounding on the ledge from which he had just fled, he had been roughly scraped by barnacles. From myriad shallow abrasions to shoulders, forearms and shins, he was bleeding ribbons of water-thinned blood. Later, he knew taking a bath would be agonising.

Weary of being battered, he chose Plan B. Carefully, he clambered over the edge and down the face of a vertical tower of rock at the inshore edge of his secure refuge. He reached as far as he could go without more drama: the lowest comfortably attainable point. There was no agony in the waiting this time. From this low vantage point, he watched the extended pulses of surf pour by below him. He timed his leap into the rock-strewn waters finely, dropping a second behind a big boiling of surf. In effect, he hitched a ride on the back of an express-wave, coming very soon and without effort to shore. Swept over the one big rock he had feared, he grabbed the next. When the wave had all but drained away, he levered himself up one last time and scampered for safety and relief.

Safe.

It was a blessed relief to towel himself dry, dress, begin the process of warming up, becoming snug again inside his clothes; but he was most aware that the real triumph lay in having reached the Great Seal Hole on such a day: to have secured swag! With luck, the sound recordings would be good, too. These, he would carry to Radio Cornwall as the centre-piece of the interview programmed for later in the week.

***

Having travelled up the Cornish coast, lingering on its sandy beaches and, farther north, in the greatest sea caves she would ever see, Somerledaa crossed the mouth of the Severn bound for the stranded granite hulk of Lundy. Having begun to learn about tide races, she recognised them as magnets for all the great fish hunters in the sea and as magic carpets for riding. Every time she flirted along the edges of such streams, the excitement of the hunt set her whiskers a-tingle. More, just as it was a fine arena in which to hunt, hone erratically developing hunting skills, she was also beginning to notice and enjoy the wondrous submarine decoration. Kelp forest near the surface dipped to the teeming anemone flower gardens or the red algal meadows and the gently writhing acres of brittle star nets on the scoured bottom.

In the race that pours by the south end of the island, under the lighthouse overlooking that dangerous waterway, she corkscrewed lazily down among the glooms of the sea floor. She moved without effort, fanning her hind-parts from side to side, occasionally flexing her flippers so that the webbing between her long toes showed. Her fore-flippers, for the greater part of this prospecting dive, lay along her

170

flanks. Where she needed to exaggerate a lateral movement, then one came into play. Her change of course was accelerated with no squandering of grace.

Most of the time she prospected, her movements were languid. She was not driven by the urge to hunt and feast. Still so new to the world, everything was of compelling interest to her. She was nearly always ready to be distracted and fascinated. Whatever the movement of the waters, she had learned to stop and perform dextrous aquatics to examine more thoroughly whatever caught her eye.

The most compelling feature that caught her imagination here was the living carpet of literally millions of brittle stars, which she felt resembled skeletal star fish. Despite their vast numbers, this multitude consisted almost exclusively of just two species. The seemingly fragile creatures were anchored to the sea floor by two or three legs, leaving the remaining ones free to test the streaming current. By an extraordinary miracle of symbiosis, the myriad brittle stars delicately linked arms to create the finest fishing net in which to catch the miniscule planktonic creatures that teemed or dwindled in the bottom currents, according to the season.

It lent an extraordinary living shimmer to the sea floor as she cruised in slow, serpentine passes upside down above it. It was like observing the one vast organism their beautiful organisation mimicked. Roving above the miracle of what they were doing, it did not occur to her to imagine what a great horde of seals, all guided by one communal mind, might achieve.

She lingered long in the race without making dramatic contact with large fish. At one point, she chanced on a shoal of sand eels, many of which she swallowed without chewing, but they served only as a small snack, taking the sharpest edge off her hunger.

Inshore of the race, under the southern heights of the island, Somerledaa came warily into a cave with a tunnel crooked as the hind leg of a dog. She was wary. The main fairway was narrow, wide enough for an adult seal to move in and out without bumping against the walls, but not wide enough for a small, moulted pup to squeeze by unnoticed in the opposite direction. She moved up the shallow, sandy slope in short bursts, sniffing and listening for other seals, noting mainly inward-bound tracks.

She knew she was not alone but was uncertain of her welcome. Twice already, aggressive immature seals had driven her away when she had sought rest from her journey. Adults had proved more tolerant.

At the top of the slope, she reached an end to the tunnel that was not an end, for she found it shrank to a burrow leading claustrophobically onward. Hardly large enough for an adult seal to squeeze through, tracks marked the sand leading inward to the unknown.

It was not a good moment for Somerledaa. For once, she was indecisive. It would be very bad, trying to turn about if there were seals within who made her unwelcome. Twice, she entered the tunnel; twice she reversed out, spooked by irregular breathing sounds emanating from within.

The third time, she forced herself to continue inward. The tunnel was not much longer, nor much higher, than the length of the body of a big bull seal. At the inner end, finding herself in a small chamber, she looked around anxiously in the crowded gloom. Dark eyes glistened as big seals looked her way. Six big ones, all male, were present. She shuffled in a little farther. No challenge startled her. Glistening eyes closed. A wave of intense relief swept over the weary seal. She had not feasted sufficiently in the race but the yearning for rest proved stronger than mild hunger, as often it did.

Settling as close as she dared to the nearest hulking male, she fell asleep.

When she wakened during the night, briefly, at high tide, she found two more males and a female had swollen the small company in this not-quite secret chamber that had been used by their forebears over thousands of years.

Nor only their forebears. As she lay there, she could sense the faintest tang of tobacco, though she had no way of recognising it. She could not see the ledge above the slumberous seals upon which a rusted tin rested. No longer used for holding tobacco, it held a notepad and pencil. People visited this place, now and then, when the sea was calm.

Some noticed the tin. Still fewer added name and message to the others contained within.

In the thinnest light of morning, penetrating even to this innermost recess of the cave, Somerledaa continued to rest even after she had wakened. Around her, she sensed some seals were awake. It expressed itself in a general twitchiness and the occasional grumbling of a seal that was bumped. Otherwise, the atmosphere was soporific. No sense of energy emanated from the gathered seals.

On the damp sands, there was a considerable litter of hair. She realised the seals were moulting. Other than the time of pup production, this was the time of year when the general community of affected seals was most sensitive. It was a time when fights were few, but there was restlessness, vulnerability, reluctance to venture into the sea unless to avoid a major disturbance. Where dispute flared, the seals involved would not lunge or threaten to bite but would wave fore-flippers at one another in carefully muted irritation. It was a time of shared physical discomfort.

Alone in this small assembly, Somerledaa had not come to shore to moult her fine new coat of silver, patterned with her Somerledaa-pattern of black splodges photographed by Amaury several weeks previously. Alone in this small sea-kennel, its roof polished by centuries of churning white water compressed and accelerated through the small umbilical tunnel connecting it to the outer cave, Somerledaa felt no itchiness. Casually accepted at her resting-place, she felt no restlessness, either. She was content for now simply to rest and soak up the atmosphere, despite the hunger she felt.

It was still hard for her to reach all the decisions she needed to make. Just now, she felt that to understand how to behave with other seals that were, everywhere, in residence when she arrived was as important as learning to capture her first fish. Well; not the learning, exactly, but the vivid illumination that seemed to mark every real moment of learning, when abstract notions all came together and knowledge existed luminously in their place.

The line of the coast, its islands and the smaller skerries, the world she had explored already, were being traced indelibly on her internal, three-dimensional chart of the world. Everywhere she had been she could find her way back to it — even to the beginning: Bay of Seals. Home. The needle pointed the way, at first. Time had added complexity. There was one simple needle for travelling, where her destination was not specific; another needle brought her back to somewhere already known to her.

So many grooves of noticing growing surer, translated into learning and little clusters of learning. Bright-eyed, wondering and eager, she welcomed these treasures in the abode of her restless, wandering water-being.

Already, she had compiled and stored away so many charts and maps. There was the line of the coast, lesser lines of islands and the variably-shaped specks of skerries. There were plan views showing the topography of the sea floor. Here, sand, shingle, gravel, boulders, bedrock, gullies, a chasm, the kelp forest, a wreck of wood or metal. There, the main assembly places, the occasional lodges or empty places she thought seals might use. Fainter lines showed the best place to haul-out on different shores, whatever state of the tide. Others sketched ideas of how to come to shore in onshore or offshore-running seas. Another chart showed where the tide-races ran. But of all the charts and maps she was compiling, the daily record of where the sun and moon rose and set and the slow-turning wheel of the stars and how their travels across the night sky exercised the greatest allure of all to her imagination.

She had noticed, from the first day of her life, the movement of the queen of day. Most mornings, in both her first and second home, the uplifting bounty of her light poured into the caves, even through the murky waters of the long pool. Where sunlight lingered long on still waters, those waters grew warm and there she delighted in resting. There, she had dreamed her first dreams without sensing the movements of sand eels along her flanks. They had known themselves safe, by the sum of all those invisible cues that are everywhere and always abroad, via the medium of all their own wild senses had learned to trust.

Opening her eyes before the sunlight moved on, she had gazed, rapt, at the fuzz of red algal turf growing on the vertical walls below the mark of high tide. The queen of the day breathed such colourful warmth into everything.

The queen of night was otherwise. Like the queen of day, she did not always appear but, like her sister, magic was in her touch. She painted ivory light wherever she chose, charging atmospheres with electricity. Through the succession of spring tides from spring to autumn, her will was that an unimaginable proliferation of life should occur. Uncountable millions of lifelets swam, puffed, spurted and sprayed into being. It was right that it should be so, for where the queen of day was gloriously unique in her high blue domain, the queen of night had countless children of her own. Given dominion over the dark side of the day and the colder half of the year, she had seen fit to decorate the night skies with the uncountable glory of her children. Yet though they were strewn across the sky as far as the eye could see and probably farther still, each one had a name, and all had a road they could use if they wanted to speak with Mother Moon. Some humans call it the Milky Way, but it has names in many languages. To the white-fronted geese flying to summer breeding grounds in Greenland, it is the Egg Road. To the swans with yellow and black bills and necks notably straighter than their mute cousins, it is the Swan Road. To the orcas' haunting the elastic edges of the northern ice fields, it is the Road of Plenty while to their rival white-coated predator hunting other species of seal along the same margins, then it is the Ice Bears' Road.

Among grey seals, it is known sometimes as the Seal's Strand.

There were times when to gaze at the moon, blotched with her waterless seas, pock-marked with craters, scorched the wondering imagination. Sometimes, while travelling along the Cornish coast at night, Somerledaa had simply drifted with the tide, gazing back at the ivory-bright eye, totally surrendered to the lovely mystery of it all and to the stories that came into her head.

She could not spend her life locked away daydreaming in her crowded rock-burrow. When the afternoon high tide came probing, she bestirred herself. Departing the cave was not easy. She needed to pick a careful trail by the great, stranded bodies of her companions. A careful departure caused no offence. Here and there, a seal stirred, noticed her and soon slumbered again.

She emerged into the main cavern, splashing into the strong run and suck of the waters of high tide. It was in contrast with her arrival. Belatedly sensing the bulky body of a seal ahead of her, she dived, rolling at the same time. Her eyes remained open and, as she hastened by, she made out the shape of one more male before the suck of waters accelerated her beyond him.

As ever, it was uplifting to be back in the light. No sun was shining but, cheered by the light, Somerledaa embarked, full of unquenchable energy, on her latest map-making expedition. That afternoon, she made a complete circumnavigation of the island, pausing at every inter-tidal rock and sea cave or cleft to peer up or across to see whether any seals were there or might reasonably be there on another day.

She had chosen to go westward, clockwise under the high cliffs. It had hardly been a choice. The run of the tide grabbed her and she went willingly with the flow. Almost immediately, she was weaving and swerving her way through a litter of islands off Shutter Point and more awaited her as she came around to a more northerly course. To landward, there seemed to be little except a great gauntness of cliff-faces until, submerging and exploring closer to shore, she discovered pocket-sized beaches, some which had cavelets at the back. However, once she was a quarter up the west coast, the beaches ceased. Instead, she found herself exploring wave-worried wrinkling of the cliffs. Sometimes, at the innermost end of narrow indentations, there were sea caves. These, she did not explore for the weight of the swell and the wave-breaks there were forbiddingly heavy.

At the north end, after exploring two major seal caves and a lesser one, she flirted into the other major tide race. Remembering her hunger, she ventured offshore to the North-West Bank where she saw four other seals, all foraging for food but each little more than a passing shadow. Now was not time for being sociable.

She went all the way to the bottom, as was her custom.

Diving to any great depth had been impossible at first. Fledgling huntress that she was, she found when she reached a certain depth, she began to feel anxiety about whether she could return to the surface in time. It was as if her world was fitted with a glass bottom below which she simply could not go, no matter bigger seals dived much deeper, disappearing into the same alarming gloom that daunted her.

In the deepest water, out of the main race in a locality where there was a silty floor; her curiosity gained the better of her again. Down on the bottom, she lay totally still on an elongated slab of encrusted iron, a plate from an old coaster that had foundered nearby. From that slight eminence, she watched a vibrantly reddish-coloured fish mincing along on tiny stalked feet located approximately under its throat. As she watched, it occurred to her the beautiful fish with the steeply triangular head and tapering body was hunting. However, though she noted the technique, she found it more interesting to watch the lovely fanning of the two big 'ears', scallop-like pectoral fins fanning on either side of its body. She was also fascinated by the movements of the dorsal fin, so unimpressive when laid back in rest but so graceful when erect.

It was a red gurnard that was, indeed, hunting. The legs stalks were really modified fin rays functioning, in effect, like metal detectors, except the fish was sensing food. Somerledaa, remaining patiently immobile, watched the gurnard unearth a small crab and consume it.

Somerledaa had forgotten the gurnard was a target of her own hunt, allowing it to disappear around a corner before she surfaced for air.

This time, she drew a blank. She failed to find the glimmerings she sought and no flatfish was stirred by her whisker-ticklings. She had learned not to be disconcerted by hunting failures, learned to recognise when to desist as well as when to proceed with her experiments.

Off the line of steep northern slopes east of the lonely lighthouse at the Welsh end of the island, she continued her explorations. Under Kittiwake Gully and Puffin Gully, pausing at the wave-swept emptiness of Seal's Rock, turning south off North-East Point.

Farther south, swimming through waters mainly sheltered from the fresh south-westerly winds, she came alongside an extensive slab of rock situated below lofty Gannets' Rock. Here, she came upon a large assembly of, predominantly, female grey seals. Having not yet encountered such an assembly in her travels, she hauled out with confidence, surging ashore with a wave that streamed across the lower reaches of the rock. At the far reach of its power, she dug her long, slightly curved claws into a fissure, bracing her body. The backwash of the surf exerted its forceful drag but the gypsy pup held her ground. When the power of the drag weakened, she scampered higher up the slope, trying to reach above the reach of the next run of surf.

The ranks of slumberous bodies remained mainly still, undisturbed by so small an arrival, but two or three females in the immediate vicinity watched her with grave eyes. As she reached an invisible borderline, one of the younger females, Cyridin, began to pulsate an admonitory fore-flipper, in the all-too-familiar gesture of rejection. Uncharacteristically, Somerledaa stopped and telescoped her small neck. Her whiskers cupping in animosity toward the larger female, she snarled aggressively.

More heads lifted at this brazen deviation from etiquette. Elsewhere, eyes opened, focussing on the feisty newcomer. Forced to make a choice, Cyridin stopped waving her fore-flipper, rolling into an upright position. She proved to be larger than Somerledaa had imagined. Nevertheless, moved by the continuing spirit of challenge, Somerledaa darted forward, whiskers continuing to bristle, uttering the most fearsome of her very small baggage of battle-cries.

In the face of an aggression so unexpectedly confident, Cyridin half veered away from the line of Somerledaa's approach, but no farther. The same temper that had reacted to the arrival of the newcomer now reasserted itself. Roaring with infinitely more menace, she started down the wet, rocky slope on a collision course with Somerledaa. Reality trumped theatre. Quickly as she could, Somerledaa wheeled about. Accelerating to her top speed, she rippled seaward without looking back.

Down the slope she galloped and in great fear somersaulted though the air back into the unquiet sea. Surfacing soon thereafter, in her anxiety she crash-dived. This startled a lone female sleeping close by in the sea that awakened, crash-diving in turn although unaware of what threatened.

South of Gannet Rock, hidden from sight of the seals, Somerledaa surfaced. Soon forgetting her humiliation, gazing up at the pale grey heights of the high tower, she could make out three feral goats finding improbably precipitous places to browse, but of gannets, she saw nothing at all. The goats saw the small seal and stared back from wild orange eyes with oblong irises. Haunted eyes, they gave an impression of having seen unspeakable sights. But their primary quest was for food, and once their attention was returned to the foraging that had brought them to the high places of Gannets' Rock, the small seal lost interest and dived.

She swam along the quite steep, partially-silted roots of the island. Close to shore, she quested into surge gullies where she found large numbers of flexible-stalked hydroids, *Tubularia indivisa,* taking small particles of food from the powerful ebb and flow of waters. Among the *Tubularia*, she glimpsed skeleton shrimps, not guessing that, for their size, they were infinitely more voracious in pursuit of prey than the most renowned of hunting seals. They were voracious enough to be entirely capable of hunting and eating their own young.

Also, among the *Tubularia*, she saw species of beautifully-coloured but generally small sea slugs feeding on the hydroids pink polyps, these being a favourite food of theirs.

Gloriously coloured orange-yellow sunset corals waved tentacles, pretending to be anemones. On boulders near the sea floor, as on the floor itself, sea fans bent flexibly at their anchorages in the currents while tiny sea slugs grazed on the polyps that covered them while mimicking their appearance at the same time.

Wrecks always seduced her attention. Performing some of the finer points of her repertoire of underwater ballet, she became still, upside down, to peer through a broken porthole. Again, she witnessed the extraordinary psychedelia of colour that would have been even more vibrant, were sunbeams streaming down through the water column.

It was another windy, grey, showery day. Nevertheless, there was still the perpetual summer of jewel anemones and Devonshire cup corals, impressive spreads of red seaweeds, attendant sea slugs, tube-worms and sea firs to watch. Here, fish to be seen, although often they were little blennies whose main dwelling-places were tiny nooks and crannies where they could remain entirely safe from any seal eager for a snack so small.

Again, Somerledaa paused in her hunt. There was so much to see, some of which she had never seen before, or else had never seen in such profusion. This time, the tiny movements of a Devonshire cup coral caught her eye. So far, she had not watched any jellyfish at close quarters, though she had glimpsed many large white, blue-fringed *Rhizostoma pulmo* pulsing by since leaving Lands End. She was not aware the cup coral was mimicking the hunting style of a jellyfish.

It was extending lovely, transparent tentacles into the water movement. Each tentacle was armed, like the tentacles of a jellyfish, with stinging cells capable of stunning their prey, as she observed.

What she did not observe at that time was a small colony of barnacles gathered about the base of the cup coral using it for an anchorage but also competing with it for food. That was because something more dramatic was happening. Down on the sea floor black tubular animals, sea cucumbers were moving placidly like enormous, cuddly caterpillars. They seemed harmless. A crab was crawling over one of them, clearly intent on subduing it, but things did not turn out as the crab intended. Under attack, the sea cucumber began to expel a stream of long, white, sticky threads. It was the puff of sticky threads coiling on the water and beginning to entangle the would-be crab-assassin that compelled her attention. Hanging upside down not far from where the little drama was being played out, she was transfixed by the progressive entanglement of the crab in the web of threads. Some coiled around a small rock, so the crab was additionally manacled to that.

When it was immobilised, the sea cucumber unhurriedly departed the scene. Only very slowly, the crab struggled to free itself. Somerledaa, driven by the need for air, surfaced before returning to continue her watch. In the end, wearying of it, she departed before the crab recovered its hard-won liberty.

There were a few larger fish flirting in and sometimes out of the shadows of the wreck. Among them, sullen but threatening in its lair, was a middle-sized conger. Somerledaa stopped before it, imitating its stillness for two minutes while debating whether to tug at it. It returned her regard, gunmetal grey and muscular in its chosen gloom. In the end, Somerledaa swirled away to seek an easier catch, making a wise estimation of her hunting ability, knowing she lacked the strength to match such a fish.

In one elongated horizontal crease in the side of the wreck, she found a peculiar fish that reminded her of the Cornish clingfish of which she many under flat stones she had turned over in her earliest hunting days. Then, their maroon bodies had sometimes been anchored to the undersides. Now, here was a Connemara clingfish, a fish only recently settled locally, having ventured northward with the warming waters. Its head looked reddish. As with its Cornish cousin, it also had pelvic fins modified to form a sucker on its undersides that could form a watertight contact with rocks out of the stronger currents, as this one was doing.

Somerledaa pressed her snout against the crack in which it was hiding. The clingfish, tiny by comparison, opened wide its mouth to display a white interior. It was intended to daunt would-be intruders, rivals for this niche. In fact, Somerledaa did not notice it. Instead, tiring of the little distraction, she arched away languidly into the stream of waters and upon her way.

Around the far side of the wreck, through ragged holes in its iron flanks, she glimpsed a shoal of pollack drifting along at no great speed. Knowing herself unseen, it occurred to her to try another strategy. Having guessed where the shoal might have reached; now she came in at her top speed. Over the top of the wreck, she streamed and straight into the heart of the unscattered shoal.

It worked, to the amazement of Somerledaa herself, who snapped at two fish in quick succession, wounding them in passing while locked on to the third and making her kill.

Here was a feast indeed. The smallest of the three fish, being about twenty centimetres long, she swallowed whole. She had not intended to; it simply happened: another of those luminous moments when everything coalesced into a vivid new perspective or, as in this case, an instinctive new action. Somerledaa was an eager noticer of things. She sensed noticing was the crucial ingredient in what was developing in her very life: the noticings just grew and grew until they hatched.

At another time, having swallowed the smallest fish, she might have caught the second and abandoned the third. However, being very hungry by now, after eating the second fish, she dived to retrieve the third, depriving a large spiny spider crab of a meal in the process, for the crabs were always swift to attend the aftermath of these engagements. The doubly unfortunate crab she consumed after the chewed pieces of the third pollack were swallowed.

That night, Somerledaa shared a cave resting place with a moulted female pup on a dispersal pathway heading in the opposite direction, having arrived at Lundy from a sea cave lodge on Ramsey Island, off the south-west coast of Wales. Ellyn was older than she. In the waters adjacent to Ramsey, she had honed her hunting techniques, forgetful of the need to be forever continuing along the next stretch of coast or around the next headland. However, she was driven from her cave refuge by a restless, bad-tempered seal mother.

Her flight brought her south to the great natural breakwater against the south-westerlies that is Lundy. Having arrived and heard stories of more seal coasts to south and west, she saw Lundy as a natural border post situated between Welsh seals and those of the West Country.

In fragments of song, the two seals shared their stories, from the end of day, through the lovely changeover hour of dimpsey into the night when weariness stole in and laid compelling fingers on their eyelids and their songs.

When Ellyn wakened in the morning, her companion of the previous evening was gone from the lonely stretch of shore they had shared. Ellyn was not to know she had slipped into the water on the middle of the ebb, her spirit strong, her compass set for the south-westernmost places of Wales: a balancing journey inspired by her eventide companion.

The squally force six winds had not diminished. A strong swell with plenty of curling white crests was running, grey and forbidding under a low ceiling of obese nimbus clouds heavy with rain.

Steadily travelling, the speck of Somerledaa surfacing was so small that had gulls been abroad in such weather, they would have been hard-pressed to notice her let alone wheel above her raining down their mordant mockery.

Gannets, flying low over the white horses, occasionally swerved up abruptly to avoid drenching from white over falls brimming over the wave-crests. Their questing eyes noticed the gleaming, sea-wet seal head, as did the smaller, low-gliding fulmars, the advance guard of their kind streaming back across the ocean from Greenland waters and the Grand Banks. However, while the gannets sailed serenely on, the fulmars lingered, making long ellipses around her head. They followed lines of curiosity and cold-eyed, dark-eyed assessment. Was she going to survive? How soon might she fail?

Having ellipsed their fill, the fulmars would resume their course, sensing no desperation in the small seal. Recognising the difference between a moulted seal pup in good heart and a struggler, they recognised she was thriving. There was no point lingering.

Somerledaa ploughed steadily into a new day, the high cliffs under the Exmoor coast shrinking behind and the coastline of Wales growing, disappearing, at the whim of the oncoming waves. Throughout, she maintained awareness of the way the great tide was running. When it was ebbing westward, she ran at her fastest travelling speed with it, toward the sea horizon rather than the land. While it flowed, she laboured across the run of it, winning what ground she could.

It was a hard, dreary progress, her longest sea crossing to date and it was not until midday of the following day that she came in toward the Welsh coast. Earlier, she had miscalculated, being swept farther west than she had intended. Tired and chilled from long immersion, she lacked the energy to make landfall on the surf-rimmed shores of Ynys Skokholm, but came instead out of the main flood into a side-stream that carried her in by the Mew Stone to South Haven.

Here, increasingly sheltered by the high cliffs of Ynys Skomer, she could allow herself to surrender to her weariness. Coming to another of the cave beaches she preferred to use, she rested. She slept, long, deep and mercifully undisturbed.

***

It had been a windy, battering, damp autumn; short, dark days. Now, in the approaches to Christmas, a glacial northerly airstream poured down from the Arctic. Even the far west of Cornwall, its oceanic climate differing from that in the east of the Duchy, was not immune from bitter shrouds of frosts that covered the landscape.

The cleanest, largest waves of the year were steaming majestically into the north shore, seemingly getting bigger by the day. They exercised hypnotic allure upon everyone who turned their eyes seaward.

Amaury had spent much time surfing that autumn because so often the conditions rendered sea cave entry impossible. Usually, he rode with Rory, Tom or Neil. They were more skilled than he but he learned from them as the season progressed.

Just over the threshold of December, the exceptional day dawned.

By telephone, Neil summoned the man they had taken, part-teasingly, to calling the Fourth Musketeer to Sennen Cove on a fair day.

When he arrived in the main car park and joined his three companions, the sky was mainly blue, marred only by a few black nimbus clouds. Along the horizon, rainbows were putting on a show. It was windy, blowing force five from the north. The sea outside the bay was dark blue but, the waves, breaking farther out than usual, marched in as a succession of steep walls of green glass.

Amaury looked doubtfully at his companions: "Too big for me! You're not thinking of trying to ride them?"

It was Rory who answered him: "We have conditions like this maybe once in a blue moon. Truth is it won't be easy but we have to try. We thought to head out in maybe another hour. We thought you should come too! You're good enough and we think you are brave enough."

"Even from here, those waves scare the hell out of me."

"They scare us too. But you know this autumn we've all surfed waves almost as big. Anyway, I just don't see you hanging back when the three of us go for it. You're not the type."

They talked, remaining mesmerised by the huge waves. In that hour, they watched occasional, always small, groups of surfers paddle out only to fall at the first fence, unable to get beyond the seething of waves crushed into very heavy surf.

When the three surfers began to change from their clothes into lightweight wet-suits, Amaury did not at first join them. When he became aware that all three were watching him, he spread his hands and asked: "You want me to die?"

"Three guys nearly managed to get outside. Not one of them is as good as you. We know it and so do you,"

"You know I am not a big wave rider. It is so bloody difficult getting out through that broken water. Look at the size of it! Imagine the weight of it!"

In the end, inevitably, Amaury drew on his full length, pale grey wet-suit. Set beside their black wet-suits, as he pointed out to them, his was the uniform of a beginner. But once they tired of the badinage, all four men settled to checking ankle-leashes and the final waxing of surfboards; a last nervous twitch.

There were many people walking on the great sandy beach that gave Whitesand Bay its name. Some were walking their dogs; some were being walked by them. Others searched the heavily littered flotsam lines for treasures, especially beans that had made the ocean crossing from the Caribbean. Most simply stared out at the great waves under the dramatic sky, partly blue but increasingly clouded with dramatic, scudding nimbus towers.

Amber Mellin had noticed the four surfers when they tucked their boards each under one arm and trotted down the granite steps to the beach. She had not heard the previous badinage but did notice none of them spoke or smiled.

She always enjoyed watching wave riders but couldn't imagine them breaching the successive steamrollers of surf to reach the unbroken water that would serve for their launch points. She continued slowly on her way, searching the seaweed line for another improbable bean to join her small collection, finding little other than the dense tangles of torn kelp.

Sometimes, her thoughts strayed across the water to friends in the west, the people living on off-islands in the Isles of Scilly, who were likely temporarily cut off, isolated by the massive seas, maybe going slightly crazy with the confinement of it for, potentially, weeks on end. Mostly her attention was upon the surfers now reaching the challenge of the heavy surf born out of the destruction of those faraway waves. She had a fondness for brave men.

They were Eskimo-rolling under the heavy, churning waters. It didn't always work. Sometimes, one would be caught with the nose of his board at the wrong angle and be dragged tumultuously back toward the shore — the equivalent to landing on snakes-heads of various sizes in a much more dangerous game of snakes and ladders. She supposed the chill of it, along with the distance they had paddled already, must be exhausting.

For the most part, they made slow progress, but a brief lull unexpectedly intervened, allowing them to accelerate seaward. It brought all four to the foot of the great, green waves they had the wild ambition to surmount and ride. She stopped, compelled to stare as they paddled up, up and up the first unbroken giant, the wave seeming to tease them by growing ever higher as the crest thinned. Through the crest in its various phases of curling they burst and she saw nothing of their long slides seaward of the wave, guessing they must be paddling flat out again because now they were totally committed. It was time to do or die. Other waves might not break so close to shore, for they seemed to her to grow bigger in their lines to seaward.

She watched the surfers fork; two heading left, two to the right. It worked for the first wave and the second although for them all it was a close-run thing. All burst through the crests both times, becoming airborne in the process. The third wave was the largest and the farthest out. Now Amaury was beginning to lag behind his companions for, fit as he was, he lacked the extreme paddling-fitness of the others. He saw Tom and Rory surmount it, over to the left. Ahead of him, above him, Neil just made it through the curling crest but he knew there was no way he was going to make it. He was thinking furiously, the strange slow-motion rhythm taking him over without slowing his paddling at all. All he could see piling up above him was the most horrible wipe-out of his life; except something in him had not yet quite accepted it.

Often, waves continue to steam in having reached their apogee without yet breaking and so it was now. It should have broken before he spun around just below the crest and drove powerfully just the once with both hands. Instead, it continued to teeter. Immediately having launched himself, he sprang lightly to very widely-spread feet, squatting very low, much nearer the back of the board than usual but precisely as Neil had advised before they separated near the foot of this very wave. He understood well enough the idea was to dig as much as possible of the fins on the underside of the board into water rather than simply free-fall through air; and because he did not immediately wipe-out, he supposed he must have got something right. The front of the board was bouncing as if experiencing shallow, high speed palpitations; distractingly.

He was locked into something entirely new for him, most of all the extraordinary speed with which he had plunged down the wave-face. Instinct took over. As soon as he reached the less steeply angled part, maybe two-thirds of the way down the face of his monster, he squatted even lower, putting most weight on his right foot close to the tail of the board, trailing one hand in the great wave face as he came swerving around to his right.

Instinct alone had taken him into the manoeuvre and it happened so fast he almost fell off, so sharp was his swerving curve, before the board began to rise again fast across the clean face of the wave. For the long moment, he began to pull away briefly from the stupendous weight of tumbling surf that slavered with monstrous, thunderous noise at his heels and beat upon his hearing. He ran quite high up the face before turning less wildly and settling on a line that he hoped would allow him to outrace the folding waters when an unforeseen section of wave folded over prematurely, engulfing him. Then, although out of the sight of most people on the white beach, he rode for his life within a great living tube of barrelling wave.

It was the fastest ride of his life. Some part of him, the part that wasn't terrified, was ecstatic. He was reminded, improbably, in the heart of the fury of it all, of his first ever ride on a little green wave on a sunlit summer day at Whipsiderry. At fifteen, he had never known a feeling like it. Riding that wave, he had thought it was how it must feel to be a god.

Amber watched the miracle of his reappearance, streaming with a white vapour trail out of the barrel of water, outracing the tumult. She let out breath she had not realised she had been holding. She watched him reach the foot of the wave climbing it again only to disappear again into the reformed tube. All the time she watched, she was sure she waited to see the impression of him being consumed by the wave, perhaps tumbled over on the roof of the barrel before being smashed down with unimaginable force.

But after he defied her thumping heart by steaming out a second time, he attempted no more exploits. Like her, he could see the other end of the wave — the part breaking fast to the left — erratically bouncing toward him — so he went streaming up to the crest and over. Briefly, she saw he was airborne, squatting still, one hand reaching down to hold the board, and then was gone.

For a time, she was distracted as Tom found his feet, surfing another monster a little farther out; then Neil was on his way. At some point, she saw the surfer wearing the pale grey wet-suit Eskimo rolling, gaining ground, losing it, in a primitive water dance until at last he was up and over the sets of clean faces and properly out at the back for the first time.

All four surfers, having ridden each their first wave, were wary in choosing which next to ride. Tom, who was the national longboard champion, rode the most waves over the next hour. The others rode less, Amaury least of all, managing just one more and somehow not coming to grief on his ride or afterwards, struggling seaward. All of them had been helped by the unexpected trustworthiness of the waves and the allowing ways in which they had broken so that if you dared, were competent and lucky, they were just about manageable.

Amaury was very tired when he took off for the last ride. He had not lost an atom of his fear of the waves, knowing he was out of his class here, whatever his friends might wish for him. He had decided that whatever happened, he was heading inshore when it was done. He chose what he took to be a smaller wave, although it was still twice head height.

He followed his previous trails after take-off by swerving back up the wave as soon as its shape permitted. Some distance below the crest, he settled into another long barrel of veiling water, keeping his eyes locked on the exit point, stoked by the headlong, other-worldly wonder of it. But this wave had another character to the others. Glancing upward ahead, he saw the crest coming over too soon, beginning to stop up his exit with an avalanche of water.

Locked in a darkening world with micro-seconds to react, he simply dived to landward trying to kick toward the seabed and the faint hope of quieter conditions. It didn't happen like that. He was kept too buoyant by his ankle leash connection to his green board. The white water caught and consumed him. The force and the malevolent violent confusion of it was everything he had ever feared. Terrified, he relaxed. He knew he had to relax. Inside his head he tried to make a calm, slow count as he submitted to the will of the wave.

It went on for a long time. Without least theatre, he thought he might have remaining to him only so many seconds of life. That fear remained as he reached the end of his long breath, but somehow did not yet gulp in the fatal mouthful of water while still tumbling ever on. He was desperately hoping for but not finding a lessening of the violence of it.

He had swallowed one gulp of water before the white water spat him out. Painfully spluttering water from his lungs, clearing his nose, he took in that he had a board no longer. The wave had smashed it. So, no help returning to shore, only a long hard swim and already the next thunderous plateau of water was upon him. He took his breath and dived, knowing he had left it too late, had spent too long at the surface.

Another prolonged churning, more willing himself to remain relaxed. More water swallowed. More strength drained from his rag doll body — another long slow count before another miraculous, spluttering emergence. He was facing the beach. People there looked tiny. He turned just in time, breathed just in time, alerted by the fizzing water sound and was gathered into a smaller breaking wave that simply heaved him up with it, smashing him down as it smashed down.

Amber imagined his body hitting the hard-packed sand of the seabed. Once more, he seemed to be submerged for an impossible length of time in bright, bouncing surf. Holding her own breath in sympathy again, she gasped when he reappeared, only to be battered down below again by a second wave that was, in effect, a double wave.

No longer was he in massive surf, having been bowled a long way toward the beach but this time he was totally disorientated and had no time to draw breath before being consumed. Under the wave, bowled over and over, he tried to re-orientate himself, regain a sense of which way was up or down. Come to the end of his air supply, he opened his eyes, breathed out, watched the bubbles and followed them, swallowing more water as he went.

Amber thought he had been down so long he must surely be drowned. She was looking toward where the lifeguards would have been in summer, but were not this day. Turning back, she scanned and then, with huge relief, saw his head, saw he was weakly side-stroking with the next but weaker run of broken water in the direction of the shore.

It took a long time. He used the surf to sweep him in for he was bereft of all power. So dynamic at the earlier hour, now he was limp.

The sea took a long time to wash him into shallows where she walked to intercept him because no-one else was doing so. She watched him strand on hands and knees, coughing, choking, being — after a fashion — sick except all he was doing was regurgitating swallowed water. As he suffered, a little wave caught him from behind, washed his listless form into even shallower water where he just struggled up again on to all fours. She saw he was at the end of his strength. Another little wavelet knocked him even closer to shore where again, with stubborn effort, he came to hands and knees.

She called uncertainly: "Can I help? I'm a nurse. That is, I used to be."

From the shallowest of water, from hands and knees, he smiled in her general direction without properly seeing her. Not quite answering her, he said in a blurred voice: "This is your best-ever opportunity to kick sand in my weakling face, you know. I've been eaten by the sea." His voice was almost inaudible.

"Shall I bring you your towel? You might feel better out of that wetsuit."

He crawled the few tentative steps from the shallows to the damp sand: "You are very kind. If you really don't mind, I have a towel and a heavy towelling dressing gown on the passenger seat of my camper van, near the restaurant, just up there." He pointed vaguely: "A dark-green Volkswagen with an S registration. The doors are unlocked." It was articulated very softly in a sea-ravaged voice.

She performed her chore though it took more than ten minutes, returning to where now he was kneeling, just beyond reach of the tide. As she arrived, he smiled and said: "My benefactress! Thank you. I'm Amaury; Amaury Valneuve." He spoke the words while really looking at her for the first time, taking in a serious, sad expression; or so it seemed to him as a first impression.

"I am Amber Mellin. Here is your towel."

"Would you object to unzipping my wetsuit? I really am quite ridiculously cold. My fingers don't seem to be working."

She drew the zip down over smooth skin still dark from summer sunlight. He did not seem particularly muscular but she saw no trace of fat. They co-operated in the removal of the top half of the wetsuit. When he made no attempt to dry himself, she took the towel from him, performed the task and then, as he struggled vainly with the chore, drew off in turn his two wetsuit boots.

Having put on the dressing gown, he just about managed to strip himself of the remainder of his wetsuit without her help. When he was done, she said: "You need a hot drink."

He said, with a small smile: "I have facilities in the campervan."

"Then I will walk you there, make your tea or coffee and then be on my way."

"That is kind of you." They made a slow, halting progress across the great beach. He enquired after where she lived and she answered Newlyn. When she offered no more information, he asked whether she was still practising as a nurse which caused her to smile: "No. I am a lady of leisure indulging in only a few pursuits these days." Again, he felt the sense of sadness and gravity emanating from her; or so it seemed to him.

"Foremost among which is?" he enquired, his smile neither sad nor entirely serious as he tried to draw her into more comfortable conversation.

She did not return his glance. Head bowed, still scanning the sands over which they walked, she answered: "Painting and being in nature, I suppose." Without looking up, she added unexpectedly: "You are limping. What have you damaged?"

"Aside from my ego, you mean? I think my board hit my knee in all the confusion. Nothing serious."

They both glanced down but his knees were concealed by his dressing-gown. Though he was trying to walk off the pain and conceal the limp, she saw through the subterfuge but said no more. She lacked the skills to mend him.

At the van, he opened the back door and moved what needed moving to access and turn on the gas. He lifted a work surface. Gas rings were revealed. He brought a kettle from a cupboard which he filled with water. Thereupon, to his slight surprise, she took it from him, set it on the stove, lighting the ring with a firelighter. Then she said: "After this, I must be on my way."

"Will you not share a biscuit or two with me?"

"I have to be back. I have a friend calling for lunch."

He said that it was a pity and was gratified to see her flush. Then, he noticed the ring on her wedding finger. Talk moved to small things of little consequence until the kettle boiled and the small dish of tea was brewed. Having found the biscuits, she set the packet beside him with the mug of tea. She was turning to go when he rose to not entirely steady feet and said spontaneously, with warmth: "You have been very good to me, my benefactress. I shall not forget you."

She coloured again, but smiled through her small discomfort and said: "And neither, of course, shall I forget you. You rode beautifully this morning." With that, she departed on her way. He watched her walking without haste across the car park.

***

The continuing restlessness driving Somerledaa ever on relented sufficiently to allow her two weeks at the refuge of North Haven. A small window in the run of storms provided the opportunity to go hunting in waters where her Lundy companion, Ellyn, had honed her hunting skills.

She submerged at dusk. Flowing low over the sea floor, she glimpsed a creature she had not noticed before. It was a shape-changer, apparently without fins, oozing across the uneven sea-floor from a cavelet lair at the base of a large boulder. Thick, telescopic tentacles writhed, touching, testing, and probing in the direction of a red-eyed velvet swimming crab. All the while, its colour was in a state of flux.

Every time any of the eight arms moved and extended, Somerledaa saw the double row of powerful suckers arrayed on their undersides, for this was a common octopus. It was a menacing sight.

Aware of the surreptitious approach by the octopus, the doughty crab was not alarmed, but raised high two partly-opened claws to resist whatever challenge was being mounted. Somerledaa watched the shape-changer continue to ripple along the sea floor and then, at the last, throw the cloak over the crab, covering it with its body. She did not see the hidden crab being injected with and paralysed by potent enzymes delivered by the suckers.

She watched the octopus carry its prey back to its lair. There, the crab was eaten, but for its hard parts. These were ejected, later being consumed by other scavengers.

Somerledaa caught some small whiting later, but the next day returned to the lair of the octopus and, for the first time in her young life, had to battle to secure her supper. The octopus had lost three arms before she subdued it sufficiently to bring it to the surface and the light that, during its bandit life, it had tried to shun. More arms were eaten at the surface but, when Somerledaa dropped it, the octopus made one last effort to escape before being recaptured for the final time.

She was not unmarked by the encounter. She acquired two sucker marks on the side of her neck, slightly distorting the pattern of black markings there. These were to remain visible for several months, though she noticed them not.

Generally, it was a peaceable time and never before had she rested among so many grey seals. However, having recovered her strength and energy, she travelled on to nearby Ynys Dewi, that was Ramsey Island to the English.

Here, because the seas remained rough, she made a sea cave her temporary home, shared with a small number of female and immature seals. Although the number was small, the composition of every assembly was always different, as some seals went upon their way and others arrived.

It functioned, or so it seemed to Somerledaa, as a hotel cave. It had no resident seals, only a gypsy population of travellers. She had already discovered some haven haul-out sites, where conflict never occurred but which seemed to serve mainly as places of rest and refuge for male seals. This was something new in her experience.

December month held no significance for her. She felt the shortening day length cease, like the flow of waters at low tide. It would remain thus for two months. The Solstice passed without note, but she was immediately aware of the veering and slackening of the wheel of the wind. For the first time in her short life of slightly less than three months, she felt an Arctic wind brushing across her sea-coarsened coat.

Although tempted to venture across the Celtic Sea to the gannet-haunted Saltees, in the end she held firm to the star she had followed from the outset. She would continue northward, hopping from resting station to resting station along coasts she had heard were riddled with sea caves and isolated beaches where she might rest in this dark part of the year without fear of disturbance.

She stopped several times, sleeping on beaches in sea caves on which the seas only whispered. At first, in what had become alien quietness, she slept poorly.

Under Dinas Head, glossy black choughs and anchor-shaped peregrines, she lingered for two days. Here, hunting in the tide race was successful. She bobbed up one day beside a red-throated diver who had been hunting smaller fish. The local waters exerted great attraction upon divers for the winter hunting here was excellent, even if they must contend with sudden emergences of seals, porpoises, dolphins and sometimes even small minke whales.

It was a clear day. While feeding, Somerledaa had slowly spun about to bring the northern horizon before her. In the far distance, she could see white-peaked mountains including Cadair Idris and the long peninsular of the Llyn extending far to the west.

In the farthest west, separated from the tip of the Llyn by the merest thread of water, or so it seemed, lay a pebble. In English, it was the island called Bardsey, for this was Ynys Enlli, island of currents. She did not know King Arthur was said to have been wrecked on a reef to the south of it or that, in the aftermath, he was healed by druid's resident on the island. She did not know Merlin had hidden the thirteen treasures of Britain there in the shallow island earth. She did not know that, since early mediaeval times, Christians had followed a pilgrim's way along the north coast of Wales as far as the haven at Porth Meudwy. From there, boats powered by sail or oar carried them across the Sound to the shores of Enlli. It was a commonplace saying that three trips to Enlli were equivalent to one to Rome.

It was to that island that her compass was pointing.

Lingering at Dinas Head, Somerledaa was torn between taking a direct route across Bae Ceredigion, without touching land, and continuing her coastwise journey. She had no desire to approach places busy with people, like Aberystwyth. She had no desire to delve into west coast estuaries under backdrops of soaring white mountains like the Rhinogs, scaling the blue skies behind Barmouth and Harlech.

In the end Somerledaa took the innermost of the offshore lines. For the greater part, she travelled over a sandy seabed in a shallow sea not more than fifteen metres deep. Had she travelled south from Lands End rather than north from her nursery place, Somerledaa might have reflected there was some degree of similarity between Mount's Bay, especially that innermost part called Gwavas Lake, and this vastly greater bay.

Gwavas Lake was clearly a land inundated by the sea only in relatively modern times. Had she gone exploring across the bottom there, she would have found the remains of submerged forests. Here was another seabed with similar remains for her to explore.

Three main reefs extended south-westward from the mainland shore; these were Sarnau: Causeways. Somerledaa had been following a course skirting the most southerly of these when the temptation to explore its length overwhelmed her.

This largest and most interesting of the Sarnau extended seaward from Mochras Point and Shell Island. Somerledaa followed the gentle meanderings of massed boulders, cobbles and pebbles of flat-capped Sarn Badrig. Far offshore, her progress was through or beside a forest of sea oak, a lovely brown seaweed. Closer inshore it became a gentle slalom through thickets of bootlace weed rising from the sea floor.

This cruise coincided with a tide that, when she had returned to its tip, almost twenty-five kilometres offshore, had all but ebbed. There, she found what might have been the boiler of a ship protruding above the surface. Seeing two males, a female and two immatures hauled out around it, on impulse she joined them, resting in the cold air. The skies were cloudless, but snow resting on the mountain slopes sent cold air flowing down into the bay.

Hardly had her pelage dried than the little seal felt the comparatively warm waters rising again about her body. As a reflex, she lifted head, tail flippers and one delicately poised fore-flipper out of the reach of the water. In silhouette she resembled a banana.

The tide rose. The angle at which head, tail flippers and fore-flipper were held steepened.

Thus, Somerledaa was putting into practise one of the first lessons she had learned following the departure of her mother, Mornalas. It was not a random movement and she had not learned it from another seal.

Grey seals have approximately the same blood temperature as people. However, the body of every seal must be protected against the chill of the sea by a generous duvet of blubber, several centimetres thick. Although blubber covers the main bulk of the body, only minimal layers cover head and flippers. While hauled out, the seals rearrange heat around their bodies and, when necessary, get rid of it through the least-blubbered places. In fact, did humans perceive the world through infra-red eyes; they would see the hottest spots in the body of a seal ashore were, principally, the head and the flippers. Consequently, when the sea touches a hot spot, it feels startlingly cold to the seal. Once bitten, twice shy, as with Somerledaa. The next time tongues of swell licked toward head and flippers, she had lifted them out of reach and kept them there until, tiring of the losing struggle, rolling over into the sea.

By now, it had become a reflex.

That was why she, the smallest of the seals, was the first to depart Boiler Rock. It was dimpsey already and her course was set north-westward, toward a pair of islands east of the long, pointing finger of Trwyn Cilan, about twenty kilometres distant. Though they did not show against the background cliffs and fields, she was confident that if the sea conditions did not become disturbed — and in the light Force two north-easterly breeze, she sensed no prospect of change — she should reach the Islands in three to four hours, unless distracted to hunt and feast.

Even before she departed Boiler Rock, the lighthouse on Ynys Tudwal West had started transmitting its pattern of white light, as if to guide her safely in. In addition, she marked on her latest chart the pattern of the skyline to either side of the Islands. Almost directly ahead of her, Carn Fadryn was the highest point but there was an attractive peak far to the west. This was Mynydd Rhiw, a hollow mountain stripped of its viscera of manganese, now crowned by a mast as well as a story. It was on this modest, but commanding height that King Arthur had posted scouts to monitor the shining seas off the tip of the peninsular for sea raiders. On the clearest of days, they had scanned waters north beyond the druid island of Ynys Môn to distant Man. They scanned west across the Irish Sea to the Wicklow Mountains beyond Dublin and south across Bae Ceredigion to its farthest outlier, the white summer island of Grassholm where the gannets nested.

To the east, while Somerledaa travelled, were the great mountains of Snowdonia where golden eagles once soared and raised their young. Now, the airs were consistently colder than any Somerledaa had felt before, but she had amassed just sufficient blubber to remain warm enough because the waters were hardly affected by it. They were only about three degrees Celsius colder than when she had departed Lands End, or one degree, if she allowed for the time lag and the degrees of latitude she had moved northward.

The failing light still allowed her to make out the planes of the low cliff walls of her island destination when she was startled by an eruption of moon-ivoried forms about her. They were leaping clear of the surface, accompanied by squeaks and puffs, bringing her to as much of a standstill as the tidal flow permitted. She could make out a conical buoy, tilted by the flow, not far ahead. Just beyond it, she saw three ivoried leapers emerge as one, not fully clearing the water before surging on and downward.

She counted eleven bottlenose dolphins, recognising their exuberance was because they were hunting. Even as she peered through the starlit darkness, she saw a fish flipped through the air, launched from one beaked mouth to another. Clearly, they were herding together a shoal upon which they were inflicting great damage.

In blind panic, spooked beyond any water wisdom by the huge, terrifying hunters, fish were attempting to flee in all directions. Somerledaa felt a small number straying madly by her and found herself infected by the excitement. For once, she submerged with stealth, her own personal hunting radar having read the level at which the fish were escaping. She bided her time. Eight relatively small fish dashed by, heedless because she was not emitting the most horrific impression any could imagine: of being a bottlenose dolphin. She might have been driftwood, so concentrated were their minds.

The ninth fish collided with Somerledaa's shoulder, disorientating itself. A fine, large fish, it gleamed in the full pride of its life, but Somerledaa glimpsed only a target. There was no chase. She wove a swift and fluid figure of eight in the water, down and then up again, at the apex of which she took the fish before it realised what was happening.

While the wild chase continued south-eastward, in the direction from which she had come, Somerledaa feasted on this fine gleaning from the dolphins' royal table. Around her, the waters quietened, eventually becoming completely silent, but for the sounds of her chewing.

She was in no hurry, being uncertain whether there would be a place she might rest ashore at the end of her peregrination. The thinnest sliver of a moon hung like a lop-sided smile above the white ghosts of the mountain peaks across the way. Its reflection showed in both her dark eyes.

She came first to the more seaward of the two islands, south of Ynys Tudwal East. Sliding by, she made out the bottle-shaped heads of at least three seals sleeping off the south-east tip. Around caves to the west, surf worried under heights that would become noisy and bright with guillemots, razorbills and kittiwakes at nesting time. This night, no perpendicular white smears faced outward over the sea.

The journey was nearly over. Crossing the gap between the islands, to the right, she could see the lights of Abersoch. Car headlights showed along the coast road. She came to a point quite near the south end of the island where the stub of a ramp had been hewn by men. The rotating wheel of light almost directly above her, blazing many miles across the hushed waters of Bae Ceredigion, spilled sufficient periodic illumination for her to glimpse hair that had been moulted by seals although none were then present as the tide approached full. Had she not seen the hair, she would have sensed readily enough this was a seal place. Her nose confirmed they had lain here at some time in the last twenty-four hours. Their fishy perfume still clung to damp rock and quiet air.

Somerledaa did not haul out. The air was too cold. She preferred to remain in the sea. She was not alone. Not far away, she sensed other seals sleeping, some of whom had been aware of her quiet passing.

When dawn came, snowflakes were drifting down thickly out of the sky.

Not long thereafter, Somerledaa departed. She turned westward, away from the cold, toward Trwyn Cilan, greatest by far of all the Llyn headlands. Swimming close in under the tip, her attention was caught by a small brown animal flowing over the rocks. Insinuating itself across the horizontal planes, it moved in ripples, but also shinned up vertical planes and leapt across considerable gaps, always without sign of fear. Sometimes, white underparts could be glimpsed and, throughout, it was possible to make out the black tip of its relatively long tail. A stoat, a bold, bloodthirsty fellow, he was quite as fearless as he appeared. When a swooping herring gull lingered just above his grape-sized head, he managed to leap, twisting vertically upward, to take a brief grip on the flesh-coloured webbing of the gull's left foot. Involuntarily, the gull kicked at it while trying, initially without success, to gain height.

To the horror and quickening fear of the weighty seabird, the small hunter was not dislodged but clung on with soulless tenacity. The gull gained height but then, as quickly, lost it because another herring gull came sweeping by, thinking it carried a dainty morsel. Briefly, the gull lost control, coming down near rocks along from where the stoat had taken its grasp.

More fortunately for stoat than gull, both the stoat and a piece of the webbing it was gripping came away as the gull banked, regaining aerial control. Without any great distance to fall, the stoat recovered from the brief tangle of landing. Standing on hind legs to achieve his most commanding height, he chattered imprecations at the departing seabird. The gull had no answer; a crestfallen bully bullied.

The gull gone, the stoat resumed its more customary, four-legged horizontal posture, rippling on to forage among the clifftop rocks. Like many knights of mediaeval times, he gave no thought to the horrible death he might have died had he fallen. The bloodthirstiness of his thoughts was nothing abated. Before long, he happened on the trail of a brown rat.

Down in the quiet sea into which the stoat did not fall and drown, the young seal heard the screaming of the rat tracked to bloody doom in a rocky cul-de-sac. The screaming went on and on, and then went on no more.

Higher up on the face of the same headland, Winwiloe the peregrine falcon stared down in magisterial indifference at the chestnut smear locked to the brown neck of the rat above the red petal of blood.

Drawn back to thoughts of seafaring by the whispering waters, the young seal swam into the great bay marked on most maps and surfing forecasts as Hells Mouth. To the Welsh people living along its shores, it had another, older name, given in mediaeval times. Porth Neigwl was named for the English knight, Nigel, whose drowned body was never washed ashore on the strand of sand, pebbles, and cobbles and, at low tide, submerged forests and peat deposits. It had been armoured.

Somerledaa quested along the line of the headland. Hollows, inlets and caves were explored. About halfway along, she came to Ogof Mulfran, the cave of the cormorants. It had been named, like the bay, long ago but the cormorants or, more precisely, shags remained. They perched in considerable numbers on a long projection of rock extending seaward from the northern margin of the cave.

It was a strange kind of open-plan cave, more a beach almost entirely overhung by the angle of the cliff. At the back, it became more really a cave and, as in caves she had seen so often, derelict plastic fishing floats of all sizes patterned diagonal seams. Otherwise, the floor was broadly triangular, covered with smooth, quite large boulders except near the now incoming tide-line, where small patches of gravelly sand showed.

It was on the most northerly sand patch that Somerledaa grounded, hauling herself ashore. To reach it, she had swum through a maze of larger rocks strewn across the inundated low water mark. Once ashore, on a sub-stratum otherwise empty of seals, she made her way through the more awkward maze of middle-sized boulders. All the while, she moved close as possible to the northerly cave wall, her progress ceasing where a burrow delved downward into a concealed cavelet. At the top of the slope, longest-settled boulders were sparsely bearded with pale green lichens — *Ramalina siliquosa.*

Here she settled, sleeping well-sheltered against the cold air drifting south-westward over the high headland. On those light airs, choughs, ravens and jackdaws played on the wing. Their cries made a rude lullaby before she slept.

She slept while the tide whispered in. Because there was no surf, she was not drenched in her sleep, wakened and driven on her way. She slept while the tide receded but when it had half-ebbed again she wakened with a start. Instinct: a stray scent on the air, unfamiliar, close by. Immediately alert, she stared up out of her burrow, the like of which she had never rested in before. Her whiskers were rigidly cupped.

She found herself looking into the black face of a small seal. Shocked into rudeness, she extended her neck and snarled, long and low, at him.

The male was equally startled. Like her, he had been questing along the north wall of the cave but, unlike her, he had some sense of another, having caught her scent, but there was no seal to be seen. Not expecting to meet a seal in a burrow, never having met a seal in such a place before, he flinched back from her ferocity, realising he must have frightened her. He backed off farther than was customary at such times, hoping to placate her.

In this, he was successful. She stopped snarling and hauled herself, grunting with effort, out of what had seemed so safe a place. Now they faced one another over the three metres or more that separated them.

"Forgive me," he sang, in an accent strange to her. "I was exploring the beach, looking for a place to rest and so I startled you... and you me!"

She stared back, more than just surprised. She had been dreaming of her earliest days, perhaps because her burrow felt so snug and safe, and the faces of Mornalas, Ithian and black Tyrian yet lingered on the blue, snowless afternoon air. That was it. His black face: the blackness reminded her of Tyrian — kindly Tyrian who had, in his quiet way, cared for her. Very swiftly on the heels of recognition came disappointment. Tyrian was but a dream whereas this was a pygmy seal by comparison.

"My name," he offered, quietly, "is Iolair."

Iolair! Iolair? She had heard that name before. Where? She looked away from him, down the beach toward the winter-blue sea. Was it Skomer, Ramsey, Lundy? Had it been the crowded, multi-lingual beach called Beeny?

She returned her attention to the small seal who was, yet, twice as large as she. She guessed he must have come but recently to the age of maturity.

Like hunting a fish, like making a map, the abstract of the unknown blurred and cleared. She saw him afresh, this small echo of black Tyrian, remembering where she had heard the name. In the earliest days it had been, before she understood much at all. She had been resting, wakeful and damp, on her bed of storm-strewn kelp far inside Martinsfinger Cave, listening to murmured seal song as Tyrian and Ithian shared stories. Much of it floated by, unnoticed, but some names had lodged. Iolair the Wise, Tyrian had named him, without mockery. A bardic seal, he said, different in his ways of understanding the world to me and yet of the same rainbow — if that makes sense to you?

In the most reflective and wondering of her voices, small Somerledaa now sang:

"Iolair the Wise," knowing full well that no two seals bear the same name any more than any two seals share identical markings on their coats.

Wise or not, she flabbergasted him and rendered him, for that little while, silent while the trickle of realisation stole in and then flooded him with radiant delight:

"I do not know how this can be! This is your home?"

"Am I speaking to you in the accent of North Wales?"

"No. I hear that. So; you must be from the Land's End, for that was whither he was bound when we made our farewells under the Saltees. His chosen home"

He did not make it sound like a question, but she knew it was, and so she agreed it was so.

"You are kin?" That was eagerly asked, and from the look in his eyes she recognised that while this young seal had made a uniquely favourable impression on Tyrian, clearly it was deeply mutual. Each held the other in highest regard.

"Close as kin," she answered. "I do not know how I appear to you, but I think if it had not been for Tyrian and Ithian..."

"Ithian, too! Can this be so? He never mentioned they had met!"

"I think they had not met before my milk-days. You can guess, I imagine, she attended my birth. Her song was the first sound of my first day and her songs wove a web of loving protection about me, or so I have come to see it. You see, Mornalas my mother was horribly twined in fishing net when I was born and I think she expected to die before my time of weaning. Ithian lingered and Tyrian joined them in the nursery cave. If I ventured out to sea, one or both of them watched over me, always.

"I do not understand: humans came. It seemed they wanted to kill my mother. They hurt her terribly, for she gave the mightiest of roars and fled the cave for more than a day but, when she returned, the net was gone and only a scar remained. She survived. I survived. Then Mornalas-mother mated with Tyrian and after that I saw them no more."

The black seal was silent, taking in what had been said, still wonderstruck by this chance meeting. She ventured less certainly:

"Tyrian always spoke well and warmly of you. He said he would return to the Blasket's, hunting from there, when breeding time was completed at Land's End to seek you out again."

Iolair regarded her with bright happy eyes: "Your name? You have not told me your name?"

"Forgive me! It must be the shock! I am Somerledaa. Somerledaa of the Land's End." She spoke with pride.

"And were you persuaded by Tyrian — am I worthy of your trust?"

"Oh yes!" Her reply was heartfelt and trusting in the way only so young a seal may trust. Hers was a full heart and it gave him pain she should trust so for it made her seem awfully vulnerable to the ill-doings of the world.

"Then tell me where you are bound and allow me to accompany you for a while along the way. This is an interesting coast. The seals seem friendly and I have found good hunting grounds. We could exchange travellers' tales?"

It was the first time such a proposition had been put to her, but she did not answer immediately. Instead, she reflected on what her travels were about and whether she should abandon her fruitful solitude. She looked toward black Iolair, liking and trusting him both, and because of that she was able to answer:

"I think I would like that very much, but I would prefer even more to remain free. You see how young I am and you will remember well what it is like to be this age. I feel I need to continue exploring. I need to make maps that bubble up out of my own questing, not out of collaboration. Might it be we could meet, instead, at whatever resting-place or hunting station calls us?" She fell silent and then she sang out to him, impulsively: "Do you not see? I am too young to be sharing, before I am properly myself. Can you be patient?" She added spontaneously: "Though I am hoping we will meet again, and very soon!"

Iolair stared back, bright-eyed and glad as before, liking very much this so young seal who was, yet, older than she knew. Quietly, he sang back:

"Let it be so. Myself, I will linger for the remainder of this day and through the night. Thereafter, we will part and meet again. I am glad I've met you, Somerledaa of the Land's End."

Somerledaa made her way toward the water. She nursed her own gladness, for to have met Iolair had helped her to a sense of belonging lacking before, except for the fundamental sense of being of the Land's End. He conjured the few seals who had liked her best in her brief time, all of whom glowed in her memory. Even as she passed the small black male, she knew they would meet again. She gave no sign of it, doing the breast-stroke through the gravel and over the boulders with her fore-flippers, entering the sea without commotion. Submerging, she propelled herself seaward between boulders and under the water-blurring of shags who noted her passage without flinching.

Out near the tip of the roughly diagonal swoop of rock into water, she surfaced. Pirouetting slowly, she gazed back toward the cave. Iolair was there. He had hauled himself on to one of the larger boulders, gazing seaward, fore-flippers splayed to keep him from slithering inadvertently.

For perhaps ten seconds, she watched him there. She watched and then watched no more, for the chill air remained and now began to make itself felt. With barely a ripple, she sank into the water, the back of her head going under before the tip of her nose. There, she swished briefly with her left fore-flipper and then her hindermost body, driving back into watery solitude.

Dogs noticed her crossing the bay, now close inshore. Two border collies raced to the water to bark at her, but whatever they communicated did not translate except as noise, even though one started to swim toward her. It soon turned back to shore where, before it shook itself and if you imagined it had flippers rather than legs, Somerledaa noticed it bore a passing resemblance to a seal...

She continued west after that, swimming mainly at the surface, across to the far side of the bay toward the miniscule bouldery haven of Rhiw. Here, a handful of small boats were drawn to the top of the shore, safe from the worst winds, no matter what direction they blew from. She could see two men conversing while seated on a plank mounted on coloured plastic fish boxes outside a small stone building.

In summer, it was partly shaded by a sycamore tree whose branches were now Leonard Cohen's charts of rivers, being bare of leaves.

Just around the corner was a small pile of fish boxes, flotsam rescued from the shores of the bay. On the far side of the building, a partly rusty tractor was probably used to winch boats up across the shore.

The two men in bulky pullovers and woollen hats did not notice her, being engrossed in a conversation about a fishing expedition. Sensing no threat, Somerledaa swam beyond boulder beach, cliffs and the partly-wooded hills above.

Around the point, she saw a crab fisherman working from a catamaran, the front end of which reared like a frisky horse as he steered it at speed from one plastic pot marker to the next. She did not have to stray from her travelling line to watch him; he was working close inshore.

He wore yellow dungarees and was using a mechanical winch to haul up the pots from the seabed. He worked without fuss in the beamy midships part of the boat, throwing back into the sea crabs or lobsters that were too small. He noticed the small seal, wondering in passing if it was one of this year's, born along the local coast or maybe out at Enlli. Every year from August onward, he saw white-coated pups on the breeding beaches without thinking much about them. He would see them on shores he could have predicted through August and September, maybe even October, depending when the bad weather set in. Come October and bad weather, though, they might turn up anywhere as they got washed along the coast. Or they might turn up dead. If pups died, he tended to see the white rags of them on the shores of Porth Ysgo and Porth Llawenan, but he knew they might also be washed up on beaches east of Pwllheli, from what his wife's father had told him.

The shell-fisherman probably knew more about local seals than anyone.

Steve Trebilcock didn't know his local coast had never been studied by seal scientists, but for one fleeting visit in the early 1970s. He would have cared little, had he known. Seals did not trouble him, did not steal his catch. He thought maybe it was them that sometimes tangled his pot lines or even sometimes stole bait from his pots but he was a fair enough man, not having seen them do it and so not holding it against them. To him, at best, they were companions of his working days, maybe even sharers of arcane knowledge. Less fancifully, they were his wallpaper, along with the porpoises and dolphins, the choughs and ravens, the peregrines and, in summer, shearwaters, terns, puffins, guillemots and razorbills.

They moved on in opposite directions, him into the bitter breeze and she, quite soon, to another shore.

Having feasted poorly over Devil's Ridge offshore, she continued to meander about the seabed, getting her bearings, feeling she was near a place where she could linger for a while. She went with the tide, first a slow drift in one direction, then back again; when she wearied of her explorations, she returned to the same coast where she had slept the previous night but this time straying a little father to west. She chanced upon a sea inlet where the cliffs were riddled with sea caves that resembled mouse-holes of varying size. She was drawn, as countless seals before her, to the cave with the largest entrance and its dense water curtain of dripping fresh water. Situated in the right corner of the bay, she was reminded of home. Improbably, Tirquin came to mind.

Poor Tirquin. Since leaving, she had hardly given him a thought. What had become of him? Had he developed as a hunter? Was he travelling in her wake or had another course claimed him? Where were any of them, the seals with whom she had shared time and felt some association?

She floated in quietly through the waterfall of droplets briefly pattering on her wet head and cratering the flanking waters.

Within, she could see the light and dark of rough-cut walls, a pebbled beach with a scattering of boulders, a huge rock over to the right behind which anything might be hiding. Farther back, it was not so gloomy she could not see a barrier of driven seaweed standing more than one metre high. Punctuating her progress into the cave with long searching pauses, Somerledaa moved into Ogof Lleiddiad: the cave of the assassins.

Observing the huge rock over to the right of the main beach, it occurred to her anything might be hiding there. From where or what had the thought originated? Where does any thought come from? In this quiet sea cave, an exceptional event had occurred involving people. It had not acquired the name Ogof Lleiddiaid for no reason. There had been a day when assassins gathered here.

Around the peninsular as well as at Ynys Enlli, locally-rooted stories remembered Arthur the King. It was not the only name by which he was known and maybe realities, dreams and hopes melded together in stories across the long years, to fit changing times.

East across this bay of cliffs, sea caves and beaches, that were difficult to reach even from the sea, was the beach where he fought his last battle. If they were true, fighting on the slippery shore must have been desperate indeed and many boats might have been involved. Battles involving Arthur tend to be remembered as epic affairs, but who survives to say how they really were? Who is left to say with authority what befell on the day hope died?

Some contend Arthur was more a sea lord than the mediaeval king on horseback invented by Malory for the period in which he was writing. In the unruly age in which Arthur lived, to be a successful leader required he be able to move like the wind and attack his enemies from unexpected directions. Might not swift boats, propelled by oar and sail, have been the ideal transport for the forces of such a leader? Being attacked along the east and south-east coasts by dread axe-men pouring out of longboats with dragon prows, might it not be that he saw sense in turning their own fleets, their own tactics, against them? Had he done that, might not his captains and steersmen have acquired the advantage of a better understanding of inshore currents, winds, hazards and landing-places than the would-be invaders?

A story is whispered still. Arthur, lord of battles, owned a homestead inland of Rhiw, under that high, bare top with its loyal, far-seeing watchers. Life did not exist exclusively of the last battle-the next battle. Sometimes, there was for him peace to celebrate the four quarter days of the year. Sometimes, no enemies were in the field keeping him from sharing the rigours, weariness and celebrations of harvest. Sometimes he joined the herders bringing down cattle and sheep to the lowland fields for the winter. There were times to hunt with his fighting companions as well as the huge, faithful hounds that were forebears of Gelert, driving the wolves to take ever deeper refuge in Snowdonia, nest of eagles; protecting the flocks.

Of Ogof Lleiddiaid? In his older years, aged Arthur had been sailing home accompanied by his household warriors only. Enjoying a peaceful interlude, he was returning from visiting friends in Dyfed. The longboat in which they sailed belonged to him — his only ship. Close to home, he was running to shore at the safe corner of the bay where today there stands an old stone storehouse under a solitary sycamore tree.

From afar, rounding Trwyn Cilan, they saw smoke billowing where none should have been. Altering course, they made a scanning pass of shores that should have been empty but for feral goats. East of the first great bay of the peninsular, they saw warriors milling on the shore. There were more than they would have chosen to confront, but Arthur commanded the ship be rowed in at fastest speed to challenge them, believing their best chance lay in catching them before they could concentrate scattered raiding parties.

Without display of banners, he led his men into a desperate battle. To some extent, the perils of the uncertain shore made it more equal than it should have been, but at the end of the killing and maiming, Arthur had secured the shore. Only the small reserve of men who had remained on board to guard Gwynhefar the Queen, her womenfolk and the few children were without wounds.

Moving among the prisoners, discovering from where they had come and why, warriors returned to their king with a strange tale. It seems captives had been taken earlier and marooned in a sea cave to the west to keep them from raising the alarm. After the raid, they were to be carried into slavery. They lay in the cave that came to be known as Ogof Lleiddiaid: Cave of Assassins.

None present on that bloody shore guessed the entire engagement was a trap. Whoever conceived it had known well the lord Arthur, he was not a great man for the delegating. Cutting out one of the smaller boats drawn up on the shore, he rowed west with a handful of men. Entering a little bay, they rowed into the cave with the big rock over to the right side, behind which anything might be hiding. Arthur was, as ever, first over the side. Seeing no-one at first, he heard the low cries of a seal pup issuing from the far side of the rock. Mistaking it for the keening of a woman in great distress, he had run toward the sound of it carefully, for fear of falling. He faltered briefly, though only in horror at the sight that met his eyes. Before him, some seated, others standing, were the cowering captives.

In the very short time left to him, it did not occur that he recognised no-one. Surprise was when he leaned forward to cut the bonds of the first captive, when daggers and axes flashed in the dark. In the shock of pain, he felt a slow-motion sense of being hurt this time to death even as he fell.

Losing consciousness, he did not see the desperate mêlée fought over his body, did not feel himself trampled nor feel the friends and enemies who fell about him nor witness the eventual triumph of the remnant of his bodyguard.

Afterwards, they carried him in the boat back to his queen. Without pause, they rowed with all power beyond Pen y Cil at the tip of the peninsular to Enlli, landing on the seal-haunted, shallow shores of Henllwyn. Gwalchmai, his lifelong friend, having stripped off his armour during the crossing now ran to the place of the druid-healers. Telling the need Arthur had of them, he did not garble his message nor use more words than were necessary.

The druids came with all speed, as they had come many years before when Arthur had been washed up on their shore, one of the few survivors when his first ship was wrecked on Caswenan Rocks. This time, however, they recognised his life had run beyond the place from which it could be recalled. The shield of his peoples had been burst asunder.

Therefore, when Somerledaa wondered what might be concealed behind the wicked rock over to the right of the cave, she was twitching one of those thin curtains between the deathless memories of her kind and those of humankind, where all time thins and is present.

No man waited, club in his hand. She moved in to the wall of flotsam, finding a winding ramp leading upward to a plateau spreading to the back of the cave. Here, the air was dense with small flies. It was unpleasant, trying to breathe as she moved through them. She moved steadily on to the back of the cave but, when she arrived, found it was not what it seemed. Before her, its entrance just high enough for her to squeeze in, lay another secret kennel, resembling that at the back of Seal Hole on the south shore of Lundy; except, there, the floor was sand whereas here it was sea-flung pebbles and cobbles.

Squeezing through, she moved above and beyond the irritating haze of small flies, made her way over the piled cobbles and marine debris littering it. Here, she would be beyond reach of the surf at all states of the tide and in all but the roughest seas. Here was a safe refuge.

She slipped into dreamless sleep.

She did not sense that once a man had waited here, trembling with fear lest he be discovered, having immured himself from within. That man heard the muffled sounds of the slaying of a king and its aftermath.

In the dark of the night, he opened a hole in that screen, slipping out into the comparative light of the moonlit cave. Pausing only to ascertain his companions really were all dead, he swam out into the bay, only to clamber out of the sea at the nearest headland, down to which, even then, ran the thread of a fisherman's track. It was used by local shepherds and horse-herders, but not this night.

Shivering with cold and fear, he clambered up to where he had stowed dry clothes. Once dressed, he escaped overland to the north coast, his progress marked all the way by the barking of farm dogs. In the first light of morning, a small fishing boat stole inshore, picking him up from a sheltered cove where the sands squealed as he crossed them. Only the gulls and a solitary grey heron noticed their departure but not the prospect of imminent war it foretold.

He had a tale to tell his master.

***

Amaury lived quietly above Porthgwarra on good terms with his neighbours and occasionally passing an evening, a day or part of it with friends. Often, many short, midwinter days passed without he met or spoke to a soul but although sometimes solitude remembered itself to him, he was not lonely. He worked hard; he wrote up his notes, and researched what he could using the Internet. Quite often, he went surfing when the weather was bad. Most days ended with him feeling physically tired. He received little mail and so was surprised when, one afternoon, he found a letter on his mat.

As it was an unusual event, he bathed first, made himself a mug of hot chocolate and only then opened it. It contained an unexpected invitation. He found himself invited along the road to Boswithen Manor on the day after Boxing Day, there to stay and participate in a friendly gathering that would run until the 30th.

Jenny Carew had sent the invitation and for the long, bemused moment, he couldn't remember who she was; before he remembered being introduced by Lucas two weeks since to his latest lady friend.

Amaury phoned Lucas who admitted: "I mentioned you to her and the likelihood that you would be making a lonely, unsociable period of it so she insisted you join the small gathering of folk she is calling to Boswithen. Don't sound so dubious. You'll love it."

That was how Amaury came, willingly enough, to the snug little U-shaped manor house, barely large enough to merit the name — a charming place in a snug little coombe with views through the lichened branches of leafless trees down the uneven slopes to the Atlantic.

It was snug to behold from the outside; it was snug inside, especially in the main sitting room with the large wood fire burning bright in the handsome hearth. The atmosphere was happy. Jenny had met him at the door, accompanied by a daughter of maybe six or seven who seemed set fair to grow into a similar dark loveliness,

"Amaury! Welcome to our home!"

Mother and daughter ushered him into the great sitting room with its welcoming fire. Lucas noticed him immediately, disengaging from a small group of people to greet him. They shook hands, smiling, immediately after which, Lucas looked down at the lovely little girl and said: "This is the man I told you about who works with the seals." It elicited a cry of wonder followed by a cascade of questions eventually staunched by her mother hushing her, saying "Later, maybe! First, let us show him his room."

That proved to be small and snug as everything else about the place. Its small windows had deep sills. One offered a sea view. The floor was made from lengths of timber partly covered with rugs. The entire room might have been a chilly haven, but was not. It lacked a shower. He was introduced to the bathroom, two doors along the corridor.

When he re-joined the gathering, he recognised three people, but knew none of them. Conversation seemed to be focussed on the weather for there was an improbable forecast of imminent heavy snowfall. Snow was becoming a rarity in West Penwith, but this was promised to linger.

West Penwith tended to miss snowfall altogether most years. The main question under discussion was whether to take it seriously or were the forecasters covering their backs, as usual, by presenting a worst-case scenario.

People were friendly. Jenny, Lucas had mentioned already, was a local GP but, as he never went to see a doctor, he had never heard of her. Yann and Celine were old friends of hers, long distance sailors visiting from the west of Brittany. They spoke English beautifully but, when he found the chance, Amaury spoke French as fluent as theirs, for his father was Breton. Jenny's nearest neighbour, George, was a mediaeval historian working predominantly in Cornwall while his wife, Elen, was a lecturer in marine archaeology at Bangor University.

There was an actress visiting from London called Beth of whom Amaury, again, knew nothing. Attractive, knowledgeable in gossip and good-natured, it emerged she and Jenny had been school-friends. Robbie, another GP, was another friend since childhood days, as was Ruan, who Amaury had not yet met.

Greta and Lionel owned galleries in Newlyn and St Ives and knew many people. At moments of doubt as to who was who, it soon became evident they were by far the best points of reference. They knew Vanessa and Johnnie very well for they exhibited their works and moved in the same social circle. Vanessa was a handloom weaver. Her man was a potter.

Harry and Ben arrived late. They were deep-voiced, tousle-haired brothers who ran passenger boats out of Penzance and St Ives by summer, primarily looking for marine mammals, but they fished during the winter months using a multi-purpose ten-metre boat. They were friendly and talkative, as might have been expected from their summer work. Amaury had met them before, already got on well with them. The three of them remained yet dark-skinned from the outdoor lives they lived, and despite the pale nibbling of deep midwinter at their heels.

It was dark by the time the final person arrived, apologising to her hostess, having all but decided not to come being so rusty, socially, as she put it. She was accompanied upstairs and settled into her room. There, she wondered again why she had come, when her instincts had warned her to remain safe in her lonely tower. Perhaps, in the end, the subdued familiarity of the tower had swayed her. So long did she linger that Seren was sent to summon her to the room of feasting and merriment, supper being imminent. Seren, of course, was an irresistible force, just like her mother.

Brought to bay, she said to the ageless little girl: "Give me just two minutes to climb into a dress and I will be down, I promise!"

Seren Carew withdrew but then tiptoed back and waited outside the closed door. As Amaury had done, once upon a time, she thought the lady looked sad.

Within, Amber drew a three-quarter length dark blue cotton dress over her head, a pair of black tights and her favourite mid-blue shoes. Briefly regarding herself in the mirror, she decided it would have to do. Running the fingers of both hands back through her hair to ensure the presentation was not too careful, she opened it and smiled, startled, at Seren, who smiled guilelessly back and reached for her hand.

Downstairs in the crowded room, the quiet hubbub briefly muted with her arrival; Lucas, who had known her husband, emerged first to kiss her on both cheeks, saying something about how long it had been since their paths crossed. Cheered to find herself not entirely a stranger, she was greeted by Lionel, with whom she lodged occasional paintings or wood-carvings she had made. He was with Vanessa, who linked a friendly arm through hers, upbraiding her with light insincerity for the gap since last they had met.

If Vanessa was present, Johnnie must be, too, she realised. She didn't want to meet him. It had been a while since he had exercised his charm on her but, quite simply, she disliked him and, for good measure, his ceramic work, too. Therefore, when she turned sideways and found him close by, smiling at her, she simply said "Hello, Johnnie" and would have walked on had he not reached out to catch her by the arm. By then, it was just the two of them as Lionel had spirited Vanessa unhelpfully toward a side-table to replenish their glasses.

"I expect you have been regretting the rebuff you delivered to me a while back," he proposed, seemingly on the same trail as when they had last met.

"No, I meant what I said. It is a point of difference between us, I suspect." It was spoken waspishly, but she found his behaviour claustrophobic. Unused to dealing with a man determined not to understand the word 'no', she was flustered by his persistence.

Someone came into the room carrying an armful of logs for the fire. She half-noticed, distracted by the movement of him, but he recognised her immediately. Perhaps even guessing her dilemma, he slewed around, coming to a standstill beside Johnnie. As he stopped, a displaced log fell directly on Johnnie's foot, causing him to cry out and to jump on the spot. Grave-faced, Amaury apologised profusely, damning his own carelessness, while around them conversation in the room failed. Some faces showed mild concern. Others sought to conceal amusement.

Benignly, Amaury looked at Amber, smiling broadly: "My benefactress! My mermaid, waiting on the far shore of adversity! Surely this is serendipity!" Johnnie was beginning to recover his composure. Amaury glanced at him unflatteringly before asking: "Was this man troubling you... he is known for it, of course!" It was difficult for anyone hearing him speak to distinguish whether he was being playful or in earnest; except Johnnie Hall.

"You did that on purpose. I think I'm going to punch out your adjectival lights!"

"Johnnie, better not talk about it. We both know you haven't the energy so don't make silly mouth-noises!"

Ostentatiously, Amaury turned back to Amber, looking pleased with himself. She had blushed again upon recognising him. He was relaxed: "Do you remember me, the drowned wretch you found washed up on the Sennen shore?"

"I remember you," she agreed, smiling back, "because it was impossible not to."

"I hope you have thought of me occasionally since then."

She thought he was more incorrigible than Johnnie, but far more winningly so. Again, she blushed! He realised he must be gentler with her, accidentally sensing her impression of him. Johnnie was limping off having stopped glaring at his back. She answered comfortably enough: "I didn't entirely forget you".

With another smile, he moved across to the hearth, to deposit the logs into a great, wicker basket without more damage to feet. His action seemingly met with the approval of a relatively small, brindle wolfhound bitch that rose to nuzzle him with her wonderful head while her great tail thumped from side to side. He slapped her rump and gave it a good kneading, securing additional approval, until the flushed mistress of the house intervened. On the threshold of the room, holding a great serving plate laden with food, she announced supper was being served in the dining room.

The dining room had another great hearth, another great fire. The long table dominating the stone-floored room was illuminated by several tall and multi-candled candlesticks. Unexpectedly, cutlery, glasses and even the plates shone. The tall windows were garlanded with holly and ivy under the low ceiling. People took their places in a gentle hubbub of friendly conversation.

Amaury saw that, somewhere ahead of him, Amber was uncertain where to sit so he came to her side and asked, pulling out a chair for her in the central part of the table: "Shall we risk sitting next to one another?"

She smiled her more careful smile, subsiding into the seat. When he settled beside her, he asked "You exhibit?"

"A few not very good paintings and some not very large wood carvings "

"Are you to be believed, about 'not very good'?"

216

"Oh yes. It is more of a hobby. More than anything, I like the links to the old days I feel when working with wood and stone, especially in West Penwith."

"What are your subjects?"

"In one catch-all word? Nature."

She was relaxing. Quite gently, he probed more, not crowding her but cajoling the first trickle of revelation into a gentle flow. People were helping themselves to food. A bright crescent moon shone through the tall windows and smeared the surface of the sea beyond. It was bitter-cold outside. All had felt the keenness of the dry east wind braved between their cars and the great oak door that opened into the hallway at Boswithen.

There was strong scepticism about the forecast, particularly so far as it applied to West Penwith with its oceanic climate. Everyone around the table believed weather forecasts serially exaggerated risks. The trouble with repeated exaggeration was precisely the same as crying wolf too often.

Nevertheless, by the time supper reached its conclusion, the wind had dropped and snow was whispering down, beginning to accumulate on the window sills. Much later, when numbers had thinned and the mood was mellow, Amaury found himself standing by one of the tall windows beside his hostess. They hadn't conversed alone previously but were easy together, liking one another. She said: "I have underestimated the weather people. At this rate, we are going to run short of logs."

"Are you short, also, of wood to cut into logs?"

"I have plenty of wood but my gardener will not be back until after the year has turned."

"Then let me fill in for him. I always carry a bowsaw and a splitting axe with some wedges in the van; so, I am prepared!"

"Absolutely not! You are my guest."

"All the more reason! It wouldn't be a chore. I love sawing and axe-work and it will keep me in shape while I honour your marvellous cuisine. Really; it will be a pleasure."

That was how he came to be laying logs across the saw-horse in the morning light while most of the guests were yet abed. By the time a half-hour passed, he had exerted himself sufficiently to strip to the waist. Nearby, a neatly stacked hedge of logs was growing. He felt no chill. Snow fell steadily, but there was no wind to make mischief with it. A hopeful robin, perched close by, watched him with cocked head and bright eyes, possibly with an air of seasonal goodwill.

In the kitchen, Jenny was taking tea with Amber. Lucas had taken the wolfhound for a walk down through the leafless woods to the sea, accompanied by Seren who was excited by the snow. Somewhere upstairs, they thought they recognised the voice of Harry singing in the shower.

Both women were in the habit of rising early, Jenny being the mother of an early-waking daughter and Amber being locked in a phase of sleeping poorly. They had been gossiping light-heartedly about the happenings of the previous evening and laughing at Amber's account of how Amaury had punctured Johnnie's importunate bubble. Guilelessly, Jenny said: "You liked him, didn't you?"

"Amaury? He put himself out last evening to be kind to me, I felt."

"I was just remembering how happy you looked... and then how long it had been since last I saw you looking happy." That caused a not-unfriendly silence to settle between them. Jenny was thinking maybe she had pushed a touch too hard before Amber said: "It was good to smile and be interested in what someone was talking about, or drawing out of me. I forgot to feel dull for a little while."

"Dull! Why would you feel dull?" Suddenly, Jenny smiled, with mischief; said: "Would you mind performing a dull chore for me? A kindly man is performing a chore for me out in the barn. He deserves a mug of tea and maybe some digestive biscuits. It has been nagging away at me but I need to wait here as the breakfast lady. Would you mind?"

"It isn't Johnnie?"

"I wouldn't do that to you."

Amber was not surprised to see Amaury, skin flecked with sawdust, bent over the saw-horse. Distracted by the small sounds she made, he glanced up then yelped as the saw-blade, the pressure off, bounced lightly across his fore-finger where it held the log steady. Bright red beads of blood showed, begin to seep and then to flow.

Propping the saw against the base of the saw-horse, he held up the finger, placed pressure on the ragged cut with the fingers of his other hand, but he was smiling as she approached close with his tea: "My benefactress!" he repeated.

"Why are you always so careless with yourself?" She hadn't intended it but she sounded exasperated with him.

"Attention-seeking behaviour?" he suggested happily, accepting the mug she held out to him and raising it to his lips to take a tentative sip, but it was yet too hot for him.

She stayed in the barn, ignoring his warning about getting sawdust on the coat she had thrown on over her dress before crossing the snowy yard. They didn't talk much. She just sat there, watching him at work. She saw how he loved splitting the cheeses he had sawed, splitting them into more-or-less equal halves each time. When she rose to go in for breakfast, reading her mind, he paused in the sawing, walking around the saw-horse and over to where she was brushing sawdust from her coat. He came unexpectedly close to her then, kissing her lightly on one cheek and then the other: "I was forgetting my manners. Thank you for the tea."

Surprising herself as well as him, she rested one hand briefly on his shoulder and kissed his cheek once in return, smiling but not meeting his eyes as she turned to walk from the barn. Finding himself liking her more than he had expected, Amaury ruefully remembered: where was her husband?

It was a happy day, especially once the heavy snow ceased and a rare, vast silence settled. Most of the houseguests spent the day outside, making the most of it for Seren, especially, who had never experienced such conditions before. For her, it was magical, filled with snowy constructions, snowball fights and long, mazy walks through the woodland looking for birds or animals sheltering from the cold. They found woodcock, redwings: a host of small, fluffed-up birds. Evening was likewise happy and good-hearted. Dancing followed supper and much later everyone sprawled in chairs or on the floor. There was much laughter still, but people grew quieter and conversation more serious after the light-heartedness of the earlier hours.

The tone was set for the days that followed. Much more snow fell and people grew concerned about how to return home or to work. The forecast was for continuing heavy snowfall and no sign of a change of wind direction. Complicating life additionally, the telephone lines were down.

On the third day, Amaury rose earlier than usual and forged a pathway through waist-deep snow down toward the coastal footpath. Dressed in his most waterproof clothes, in his rucksack he carried a flask of tea, a hunk of bread and some cheese. The long drag before him through the deep snow was going to exhaust him, no matter how tough he might suppose he was.

He tried settling into a slow, steady rhythm, tried not to overheat. It was difficult. Every step, necessarily, was a high one. He was glad no wind was blowing to freeze the sweat on his brow.

Westward along the coastal footpath, bound for Penberth Cove, he met flattish stretches and great sweeping slopes — quite hard work even in good conditions. Chancing on a large sheet of thick plastic, he used it as a makeshift toboggan for the major descent to Porthguarnon. He carried it up the demanding hill on the far side, leaving it at the wayside to serve for the homeward trek.

All the way, he was hoping to meet other people snow-ploughing their way along, to make the going easier. It didn't happen. Hours after he had set out, he trudged up to the door of a granite cottage next to the sea. Behind it, a border collie called Jessie barked furiously until a big man opened it and stared in astonishment at his weary visitor while Jessie leapt up in recognition. Ben Eliot growled her to silence. Stepping aside, he ushered Amaury into the cottage and a wide-eyed greeting from Kirstie as she slid an arm some distance around the considerable waist of her man.

They brought him into a sitting room warmed by a wood-burning stove. Ben helped Amaury divest himself of his boots and his outer covering. Underneath, his clothes were wet with sweat so they also came off, too, requiring he borrow a flannel dressing gown that was far too big for him. The wet clothes were consigned to the clothes horse in front of the stove.

"So, my dear, this is an unexpected surprise, that you should be quite so eager to see us again so soon?" Ben wrapped a big, muscular arm around the shoulders of his friend, guiding him to a chair near the wood-burning stove.

"Well, I am the emissary for some stranded houseguests of Jenny Carew, along the way. I was wondering: are you fishing at the moment?"

"I was thinking to be ashore until the year turns. You know how fish get in a calm sea, especially when the east wind blows. Were you needing some fish?"

"I was thinking if you are not busy, I might take Sea Breeze around to Penzance and take the houseguests with me?" They had long shared ownership of one of the broad-beamed cove boats now hauled well inland beyond the reach of the heaviest waves with the remainder of the little fleet. Ben was the major shareholder and had the greater use of it, but it was an amicable partnership. That showed now: "Course you can, boy! But it'll be cold! When do you reckon to take her round?"

"Tomorrow, we'll be setting off around nine — later, if they make a meal of ploughing through the snow." Both men grinned.

"You should have made a fair-sized track through it by now — that'll help, so long as there is not another heavy fall of snow."

"What do you reckon, about the weather?"

"Reckon there'll be two or three days of no wind and not much snow. After that, a slow thaw." Kirstie thrust a mug of hot chocolate into Amaury's hands. He smiled his thanks. She said: "If your seals are smart, they will stay holed up in their caves for the while."

"If time permits, maybe I'll pay them a visit, too!" The first time ever he had suggested it, Ben wouldn't hear of it, but had long since come to trust his companion-in-arms; so, he did not leap to the bait this time, just spreading wide his palms and shrugging.

Neither man mentioned though both knew that if he planned to do it in the one day, the trudge homeward would likely conclude in the dark; the weather would yet have a major say in what would come to pass.

As direct communications were impossible, the telephone lines being down and the mobile network out of commission, the two men talked half-blindly around the possibilities of precisely when to make the run to Penzance. In the end, they came comfortably to an accord.

They tried to prevail upon him to stay for lunch but once his clothes were dry, he felt he should be getting home as fast as the fallen snow permitted. Those at Boswithen might yet need some persuasion to go along with his plan.

Ben, dressed in matching waterproof gear, accompanied him so far as the top of the long drop into Porthguarnon. There he lingered, watching his eccentric companion toboggan erratically down the snowy slope on his plastic sheet. Down above the boulders and bedrock of Porthguarnon, from whose small and lonely shore he had swum often enough, especially in the new light of dawn, Amaury tumbled off to one side, stood up patched with snow and saluted his friend standing in silhouetted bulk like some standing stone against the skyline. Shaking his head from side to side, Ben waved back. The standing stone turned back homeward.

Amaury imitated him.

He found the woods around the house quiet, but for occasional bursts of birdsong. People had certainly been exploring during the earlier hours for there were many trails of human footprints threading among the trees.

Outside the house, Seren was in a snowball fight that included Lucas, Elen, Yann and Celine. All was noise and laughter as he arrived on the edge of their battleground. Though he had taken them by surprise, it did not prevent them coming together and subjecting him to a fusillade of snowballs, under which he subsided, hands in the air, in snow that crumped under him. That, in turn, brought Seren leaping extrovertly on to his stomach in an extra shower of snow, shouting something incomprehensible.

Somewhere amidst it all, peace was restored and Yann it was who helped him to his feet, asking as he did from where he had materialised; so Amaury related the small story and the ambitious plan for the first time, but it was not until supper that he related his idea to the full complement of the house. He rounded it off by saying: "So, if there are people among us who want or need to get back to Penzance tomorrow or for New Year's Eve, so long as this weather holds, I can take you. What are your thoughts?"

Of course, there was the question of where they would be able to join the boat. He told them he would bring the boat around to a landing place at St Loy he knew would serve at high tide, with the essential proviso that one person had to hold the boat steady while inshore, keeping it from rubbing against rocks or settling on the bottom. Neither Lucas nor Yann needed to make the trip so both volunteered. Amaury was glad of that, knowing they would be competent. Foremost among the people heading for Penzance would be Jenny, who had to attend her surgery — who would have to sleep there, content to leave Seren in the care of Lucas. The remainder of the company was to include Robbie, who also needed to return to work in another surgery, Johnnie and Vanessa, Elen and George, Greta and Lionel as well as Harry and Robbie. It promised to be a very full boat.

As they had contrived to sit next to one another again at supper, Amber said it was a pity the boat would be so full, as the trip sounded enchanting. Amaury was silent for so long she began to wonder whether he had heard her, but he suggested quietly, almost thinking it out word by word as he spoke: "I could take Sea Breeze out again the following day. The weather should hold for that long. I could take you around to Longships, maybe even into the seal caves."

That was unexpected. He glanced sideways to read her face and was surprised by her look of happiness. She was smiling: "So that would be a 'maybe'?" he asked, also smiling.

"Boats scare me," she said. "They scare me, but it sounds irresistible."

"You will need to wrap up very warm."

"I wonder."

"What?"

After a pause, she went on tentatively: "You know who else would like it? Seren! She was talking a lot about you and the seals today."

"With you?" he enquired, the wickedness in the question too well-disguised for her to notice.

"Yes. She was sharing some thoughts about the house-guests. She likes you."

"Of course, she is welcome to come. She will love it."

Which was how, just before eleven in the morning two days later, on New Year's Eve, Amaury came to complete his third walk in successive days to Penberth, twice now having set forth in the dark. Having launched Sea Breeze with the help of Ben and a couple of other villagers, he brought her the short distance around to St Loy. There, for the second day running, Lucas and Yann waded thigh deep into calm water — one wearing waders, the other a dry suit — and hauled Sea Breeze into the shallows. There, they helped Amber into the boat. Then, they left Amaury to leap over the side to take on the anchoring role while between them, having returned to shore, they hoisted Seren to the shoulders of Lucas. Yann steadied him as he progressed across the boulders, to deposit her safely aboard Sea Breeze.

Quite quickly, Amaury hauled himself inboard. Pushing Sea Breeze to seaward, Lucas also leapt aboard, leaving Yann in the shallows making the final, precarious seaward push. The four-stroke inboard engine came immediately to life and Amaury set it straightaway into reverse, to carry them well clear of the rocks before he brought her gently around and into forward gear. On the shore, the dry-suited figure of Yann waved as he dwindled in size.

Amaury set no great speed westward, remaining close inshore as they passed Penberth and around the great cliff-castled headland of Treryn Dinas, just beyond the stump of shag-clad Sighy. They crossed Porthcurno Bay with its several sandy beaches and the ghosts of the basking sharks that browsed there, gape-mouthed, in warmer months. Beyond, they passed below the much-frequented lovely local masterpiece that was the Minack Theatre.

There was minimal wind but, having already warned Amber and Seren to wrap scarves around their faces to fend off the chill, now he wrapped them together in a large sheet of thin tarpaulin, the ends of which Amber secured with a green scrap of binder twine.

He took them out first to Longships whose challenging tides were quiet this day. Already a few seals were hauled out on low-lying rocks south-east of the lighthouse, but Amaury explained he was giving them a wide berth so as not to scare them into the sea. He promised disappointed Seren they would come much closer to seals later in the day.

They circumnavigated the great rocks of the Longships while everywhere gannets sheered up high before diving into their reflections in the vast mirror of the sea. One party tilted their wings above what proved to be a small hunting party of harbour porpoises that might otherwise have passed unseen. Seren's good spirits were much restored as they were able to point out a porpoise calf swimming alongside the little dorsal fin of what they took to be the mother.

While they progressed, Amaury had Lucas trail a long-line over the side so that by the time they were ready to head inshore toward the seal caves, seventeen mackerel had been landed into the big bucket stowed well forward. It was well-known there were big shoals off Land's End in winter, along with anchovies and pilchard. He said he would cook them for supper.

Inshore, under peregrine-haunted headlands, they came quite suddenly to the bay of seals whose caves he knew uniquely well, but he failed to mention he had never tried steer a boat into any of them.

He felt no anxiety at the novelty of the experience now. It was half-tide, approximately, on a spring tide. The air pressure was settled and high; the breeze hardly troubled the surface of the sea. That should ensure sufficient quietness of water under their hull to enter the cave.

He slowed Sea Breeze almost to a standstill beside the headland and said to them quietly: "Two torches for you Lucas. Amber, Seren: time to hatch from the tarpaulin and switch on your cameras." He waited while they emerged from their wrapping, not without muted laughter. When they were done, he said: "We must keep quiet. Once we are in the cave, the seals will be up the sand-hill to the left. Perhaps they will come galumphing down but don't worry. We will be fine; so will they. Try to keep quiet, no matter how exciting it gets."

They nodded and he set the boat with it quietly throbbing engine slowly ahead and in through the cave entrance. There was little free room on either side and in the clear, still waters he could see familiar boulders under the hull. On the flanking walls, they saw closed sea anemones above the waterline, sea squirts and encrusting algae. Ahead in the dark, they heard a squabble. A seal ululated hauntingly.

"Lights!" Amaury whispered to Lucas, steady in the bows. The sea cave was flooded with light, revealing a remarkable amount and variety of colour. The boat slowed to a halt as he set the gears briefly in reverse, then neutral. Everyone stared up to the left at the great, seeming-rugby scrum of shadowy seal shapes resting on the slope. They were black, steaming shapes against the paleness of the sand. The longer they watched, the more seals came to the alert, straining heads and necks upward. From the small, confused movements they were starting to make, they were thinking of moving and milling, seemingly undecided whether to stampede or haul themselves higher into the glooms at the back of the cave. In the event, helpfully, the drift proved to be uphill.

All the while, Amber and Seren reeled off camera shots until Amaury urged them: "Don't just take pictures! Look at them, too. Look at this fantastic place sea palace. Feel the atmosphere!"

The seals gave them that long, but just as Amaury was poling the boat around to face the entrance, fending off the wall and boulders, the great stampede began and so he paused in his labour. Seals rippled down the sand-hill, crashing through the shallows until submergence made them graceful again. Seren clung to Lucas's leg in the bows while Amber clung on to Amaury's arm with a force that surprised him and embarrassed her, causing her to release it abruptly when she realised what she was doing. Under their feet, the boat continued to rock violently on the swift-falling tide.

A few seals lingered yet, alert on the sand-hill while Amaury edged the boat slowly from the cave once the disturbed seal-wake fell still. Outside, sixty-two seal heads, all but three being males, crowded the surface of the sea betraying nervous curiosity as the intruder-boat emerged. They continued to watch as it pulled away slowly from the cave entrance. As they went, everyone aboard watched the audience of watchful seals in turn, but as their size dwindled to pin-pricks, Amaury had Amber wrap Seren and herself once more in the tarpaulin, for there was no longer any sun shining through the uniform clouds, nothing to take the edge off the chill. Once wrapped together, he had them sit, tucking them below the wind. Only when he opened the throttle did they feel the cutting edge of the light breeze whispering off the land.

Thereafter, tucked as close under the cliffs as he dared — which was close indeed for he knew these waters as well as anyone — they made swift headway. They had a second encounter with a pod of five harbour porpoises over the Runnelstone Reef and off Treryn Dinas, some distance to seaward, they glimpsed the lovely silhouettes of common dolphins repeatedly breaching in considerable numbers. Lucas supposed they were hunting a shoal of mackerel. No-one was immune to the enchantment of it, least of all Seren.

He brought them safely back to the great beach of dinosaur eggs that was St Loy. Having been watching for them from the warmth of the house, Yann awaited them.

It was much later that Amaury returned to the path behind the same shore, having hastened as best he could from Penberth. By then, his fleetness was quenched to plodding weariness. Longing was for the day to shrink to some warm place close to a fire. It was with surprise and a lightening heart he met Lucas emerging from the woods ahead, clearly set on meeting him.

"Are you prepared to receive the laurel wreaths that await you?" he enquired, as they came together: "You are lauded! You produced a glut of rabbits from your hat today! Seren has been talking about you for a couple of hours at least!"

"And Amber?" Amaury asked, slyly, smiling.

"We suspect she may have a taking for you. Nothing has been broadcast; she is very private. But Seren repeatedly references her and receives smiles and no discouragement." The men smiled at one another, much being understood between them but nothing more said. So, they trudged uphill through the trees and Amaury arrived back at the little manor house to receive his laurels.

The evening passed in warmth and friendliness. Amaury spent quite a lot of time diverting plaudits. Amber was silent and thought no-one noticed when she slipped out of the room and the house to listen to the noisy wood owls by moonlight. It was something she had always loved and the settled snow greatly added to the magic.

Amaury had been noticing her throughout his visit with an ambivalence owing much to her wedding ring. Soon after her departure, he followed her. Instinct guided him in the right direction. The sudden cry of an owl as he ghosted among shadows of unmoving branches sharpened those instincts. He followed the only trail of fresh footprints until he came upon her, leaning against a tree on the edge of the wood, her back to him. Despite the calling of the owls, she heard the crumping of the snow as he approached her. When he stopped, she turned, knowing who it would be. He was glancing down at her left hand where the moonlight was glancing off the golden band.

"I've been wondering," he said, conversationally: "where your neglectful husband might be."

For a long while, she returned his gaze with what was set in stone as his initial impression of her: sadness and seriousness. When he began to wonder whether she would reply, she said quietly: "He died seven years ago."

There was hardly anything to be said to that so he remained silent. While he reflected how he might phrase his apology for blundering, she said: "He was a generation older than me. I had nursed him for some years before that." Stark and simply stated. "I loved him. He was the love of my life and I for him. As soon as we recognised one another, I moved down from Devon, left my old life behind. I wanted a romantic love affair. That we had; for a long while."

"And since then?" He spoke quietly as she had done.

She sniffed quietly. He recognised the sound, but she did not break down: "Hope of life shrank in me."

"You didn't look shrunken inside today."

She smiled, but still contrived to seem sad: "You shared treasures and atmospheres remorselessly. I blame you."

"Don't give me too much credit. It is my home-world, but I'm glad you were warmed by it."

"I like you. I would always have liked who you are, I think. I don't want to tarnish the memory of my love." These thoughts she articulated, setting the implicit conflict before him, feeling it needed to be said.

When the silence stretched to its limit and him yet silent, she stumbled slightly in her fluency: "I've been wondering whether you, having shared a day of your life and your world with me, might share the same from mine, sometime in the not-too-distant future?" Her voice was shaking a little, betrayingly. Both noticed it. She added with a small smile: "Of course, it wouldn't be so exceptional."

"I'd like that, very much," he answered, smiling. In peroration, perhaps in approval, an owl called from close by. It was answered almost immediately by another, farther distant, causing them both to smile.

***

Somerledaa slept one night in her haunted kennel and emerged at morning. She felt ready, now, to come to a winter resting place. She would swim out to the island she had seen on the many previous days since her arrival at Ramsey.

Without delay, she ventured into the strong running waters of Swnt Enlli where she saw, as she had seen so often in her travels, a little pod of porpoises rolling, grunting and piffing in another tide race. They were always there. Making the crossing, few birds observed her passage except occasional gannets or guillemots in winter plumage. Without misadventure or banners, she followed many centuries in the wake of the stricken lord Arthur to the kindly refuge of Henllwyn.

She cruised into the broad bay, to the weed-draped rocks and shingle gullies of the south-east. During the summer months, these were the busiest seal places, situated below the grass-topped, narrow neck where the two halves of the island married. Only grass showed now but, come late spring, there would be a spread of wild flowers. Today, just five seals witnessed her arrival.

Moving on southward, clockwise around the island, she glimpsed promontories, inlets, small coves but hardly any seals. Her instincts recognised as seal haunts the places she passed. From the south end, under Maen-du, three males noticed her passing. Now, running north, she caught the first faint sounds of seal song. She ventured into a narrow zawn off which ran the two-tunnelled sea cave, Ogof Ystwffwl

Glas, but no seal was resting there and she saw it was no place for her to rest, either.

The restful place she found quite near the square red and white striped tower of the lighthouse whose lantern glass was the doom of many Manx shearwaters that dashed into it every spring and summer. There, at Porth Hadog, the rock slabs were covered with dull-coloured velvet slugs; slugs that sang. She had found the largest seal assembly ashore on the island, gathered at a favourite winter resting place — at least, when the winds blew with easterly in them.

She moved ashore scanning the outer rank of seals — most slept but for those closest to her. The most recently arrived she could recognise because their pelages were yet wet. Three lifted their heads in curiosity when she came slowly by them, settling to rest beside a big, pale-brown male with relatively fresh scars that gave him an alarming appearance. He was one of the three seals who had lifted their heads. Gazing down at her, his head seemed massive and the bulk of his body seemed hardly to taper at all to his hind flippers. The rumbling sound he made deep in the back of his throat gave her pause but gazing up at him Somerledaa sensed he was not unfriendly.

Once more, the male made the low, not unfriendly not friendly rumbling in his throat before he, too, lowered his head. He did not yet close his eyes, continuing to watch the little female whom he recognised as having been born during the latest breeding season. He noted she exuded a glow of vitality. There was something bright about the spirit of the little one toward which he felt a mild tug of friendliness.

His name was Vystar, lately arrived from the inshore territory of a few sea caves he had held on the Calf of Man, a small island not far to the north.

The most successful fighting males who had passed the breeding season controlling waters adjacent to nursery beaches, driving off prospecting males but behaving with solicitude toward the seal mothers, had all but wasted away by the season's end. They were, all of them, in a parlous state. At the last, they were almost relieved to escape their obsession with receptive females, returning to sea and restoring spent bodies to good health. By then, they felt no longer the pain of their wounds for these had sealed into scars and memories.

Vystar was one-such. He had arrived alone, three days previously, having been using nearby Ynysoedd y Moelrhoniaid for a base. Travelling on a course slightly east of south, that island and its attendant islets was the first land he had encountered south of the Isle of Man. During previous years, he had moulted and overwintered on the sea cave shores of the ferocious tides girdling lonely Rathlin Isle, the north gate of the Irish Sea, east from the north coast of Northern Ireland. Now he wanted to try another place, hunt in other races.

Somerledaa, continuing wakeful on the slab of rock beside huge Vystar, wondered: where were the seals special to her?

***

Like Vystar, Mornalas had travelled in a different direction to normal. She was still restless after her entanglement and the incomprehensible aftermath. Feeling she had experienced a rebirth of sorts, she had decided to explore new localities. Initially, she swam to the River Dart but, finding it too busy with human traffic, had travelled on to Portland Bill, the east coast of the chalk Isle of Wight, sand-banks off Sandwich and then into the North Sea until she reached the dune-backed sandy beaches spread between the Wash and the Humber.

There she came to shore, taking her place in an assembly of sandy seals whose patterns were obscured by clinging sand. It took a little while for her to adjust to the fact that the beach inshore of the sandbank she was using was intermittently used as a bombing and strafing range by warplanes. However, she soon adapted to the prevailing atmosphere of indifference displayed by her companions toward the shrieking warplanes and the exploding ordnance. No ill befell them, unless to their eardrums.

Once a week, a warden walked out to count them. Even to this she adapted, for he never came too close. Had he done so, they were resting close enough to the sea to escape easily. It did not occur that he might have nothing in mind but to count them while causing the least possible disturbance.

That was how Mornalas and the youngest of her pups chanced to be on approximately the same line of latitude at the same time, though on opposite sides of the same great island.

Ithian the midwife seal had travelled far south, as she had done during previous winters, lingering briefly on the shores of islands in the Molène archipelago, planted among the ravening tide races of the Mer d'Iroise. She continued south into Biscay following the angled line of the shelf edge, feasting royally there. She followed this track down to Hossegor, between the surf paradise of Biarritz and the entrance to the River Gironde upon whose shores spread the ancient wine port of Bordeaux. Farther south, she turned westward where the shelf ran close in under the mountains of North Spain.

Oftentimes, the seas had been mountainous so there she returned northward. She moulted with eleven other females at the back of the longest sea cave on the north shore of the small, usually uninhabited Île de Keller, itself situated to the north of the largest island of West Brittany: Île d'Ouessant. This place she liked well, perhaps not least because over its entrance some of the last puffins still using burrows delved into French soil reared their young every springtime and made a pretty dance of colours whenever they came down to the nearby waters.

Tyrian had followed her south to another group of islands off the Breton coast, the rocky Sept-Îles archipelago, close to St. Malo. Here, he found solitude for several days before other seals joined him in using it for a hunting base; but by then he had decided also to turn about and return to Ireland's perilous coasts. He would seek young Iolair and perhaps take him travelling to the Hebrides.

Two days later, he was ashore on the Saltee Islands. Another week later, tired of waiting, he pushed westward for a grand hunting expedition out to and along the shelf edge to dive to the deepest depths he had attained in his life

Cerriec had not prospered, had not graduated to eating fish. One day, hungry as usual, he awoke on a beach surrounded by people. Despite presenting them with his most ferocious face, he was herded into a cage and carried off the beach up to a waiting van. He was admitted to a seal sanctuary and, soon thereafter, placed on public display for a period that lasted five months.

Tirquin was found dead on the surfer's beach of Porthtowan. People were appalled that his head had been cut off and news of it was taken up by the media. Accusations and insinuations were made.

He had been washed along the coast for several weeks before ending up on Porthtowan. As he was washed along, his head lolled below the surface. Wherever he was rolled to shore, his head was knocked repeatedly against rock. The bones of the skull of grey seal pups are thin and fragile. He was not battered to death by soulless people but, post mortem, suffered wear and tear while in passage as well as the neatly snipping attentions of scavenging gulls.

Other headless pups were found. Lurid stories were published in the national media but no culprits were found. The result was an embittering of attitudes between local conservationists and inshore fishermen, upon whom fixed the accusatory attention of an ill-informed public.

***

Iolair? Iolair came ashore beside Somerledaa four days later, while she rested beyond the reach of the flooding tides spilling around Carreg yr Honwy, the large rocky islet a few hundred metres to the west of Enlli. The gladness in both seals was revealed in the way they reached toward one another, snout gently reaching to and briefly touching snout.

The weather remained cold but the seas were unusually clear, being both settled and largely empty of the teeming clouds of water sprites that would develop in spring into the annual miracle of algal bloom. Being the first winter of her life, she never imagined it might be different.

Far across the waters of the great bay to the east that stretched almost the full length of the West Wales coast, she grew used to the sight of distant snow-covered mountains. However, she noticed the two islands she had passed just before entering the waters of the Sound were changing colour. They were growing ever whiter but without the chill of snow rolling down off them into the waters of the bay. Without mentioning anything of this to Iolair, who could have explained the mystery, she decided to pay them a visit.

One morning, she slipped into the waters off Henllwyn and struck out for the Gwylans. It was just an easy, uneventful jaunt. She felt this race tugging in one direction, other races in other directions. Untroubled, she wove a passage among them coming, without misadventure, to the more westerly of the islands.

It was another gaunt, sea-wet place like so many shores she had visited. From a great slab at the west end of the island, a lone male of great antiquity opened his eyes, watching her approach the foot of the slope upon which he lay at rest. His name was Gydyr. He bore a latticework of scars inflicted during the years of aspiration, rule and inevitable decline. Now, at thirty-two, oldest of the male seals dwelling in the northern half of Bae Ceredigion, his battles were over. In recent years he had wearied of the company of other seals. His haunts had become solitary as, bit by bit, he withdrew from a world in which, for a few bright years, he had been invincible in battle and had fathered scores of pups.

Pattering about below him was a flock of turnstones, among which roved a pair of yellow-legged purple sandpipers and two watchful oystercatchers. Black and white birds, they always looked immaculately clean, though with the red eyes of perpetual drunkards.

Gydyr registered Somerledaa was not of his line. He was aware of a flicker of appreciation for the bright-eyed curiosity he sensed about her but gave no sign of it. All Somerledaa saw was the most massive and ancient seal that ever she had seen, staring down at her without invitation or expression of any kind. So solid and still did he look, she suspected he was carved from rock. So compelling was the thought that she stopped swimming and stood upright in the quiet waters, staring at him.

She saw the ancient eyes close, and when they did it startled her, causing her to crash-dive in alarm. She surfaced some distance farther out but the ancient eyes had not re-opened. He had lost interest in her, retreating within again, back to comfortable meditations that were the mainstay of his last days.

Relieved to be released from that formidable scrutiny, Somerledaa skirted along the north side of the island and, as she swam, the larger island that had drawn her across the Sound loomed. She was in no hurry, but even as she felt the tug of the race that ran in the divide between the islands, she recognised it was not snow covering the rocky heights beyond.

It was a lovely sight.

Nearest to her, a low-lying rocky finger protruded westward. Settled snugly about halfway up the seaward side of the finger, three female seals lay sleeping like silvery velvet slugs, long dry.

Above the rocky finger and the slumberous seals, there was a great sweep of lawn speckled not with snowflakes but fully open white petals of the tiny, abundant common scurvy grass. This lawn of flowers dwindled up where the rocky heights began. Here, the white paintwork covering the rocks proved to be the accumulation of two months of cormorant droppings. Since January, cormorants had been renovating their nests and since the last week of February they had been laying their eggs. Now, incubation was under way.

Gazing upward from the sea, Somerledaa saw the great colony of serpentine black bird shapes spaced across the patchy white cloth of their own making. The seabirds — once, countryfolk had fancied they were sea ravens — nestled in grass-lined cups atop castles woven from pale sere stems of last year's tree mallow, standing up to thirty centimetres high. Other birds stood upright and watchful on crags from which they could readily launch themselves into flight.

In turn, they were surrounded by watchful gulls. From below, the tableau had the appearance of a wagon-train surrounded by Indians in some old American film. The cormorants were surrounded and also overflown by gulls but there was no conflict. The cormorants appeared to be ignoring them.

As for the end-of-winter whiteness, it had begun as one white chalk patch, and then another. As the weeks passed and the number of cormorant nests increased, so did the chalk patches. Younger birds were still, prospecting for sites and potential partners, felling the dwindling supply of tree mallow stems to build their less immaculate nests. These birds, or their late-laid eggs or late-born young, would become the most likely victims of the tireless gulls. For now, though, there was some safety in numbers for the nesting cormorants. Their eggs would remain safe so long as they were not spooked into hasty evacuation of their shallow nest cups. At such times, there was the extra risk that an egg might be caught by one black, webbed foot and dislodged. Once dislodged, the cormorant would be unable to retrieve it and then the boldest of the gulls would take the prize.

It would be no different for their naked young. Born with the appearance of bulbous-headed, black-skinned, sightless reptiles, they would be safe so long as their attendant parent remained unphased by the proximity of the bandit birds. However, did the parent allow itself to be startled from the nest, their helpless young must contend not only with bandit birds but also the heat of the sun, the chill of the winds and the splatter of rains.

The newborn cormorants resembled their pterodactyl ancestors, in appearance and in the unexpectedly small, frail voices they learned first to use.

Nothing of this extraordinary life-and-death drama communicated itself while the small seal gazed up at the busy island heights.

Having recognised the secret without unravelling it, Somerledaa swam away in a lazy anti-clockwise circuit of the islands and back to Enlli.

Iolair wakened there without the proximity of her. He was not alone at that time because a bright female arrived. She was silvery-coated with a cream throat, vivid markings and a scar grooved along the topmost part of her skull where a bullet had come close to ending her life.

Her name was Marrocha. She had been travelling clockwise about and beyond the Irish Sea since the weaning of her pup on a sea cave beach at remote Rathlin. Iolair recognised her as soon as she periscoped in shallows just offshore, remembering she had been present on another Rathlin sea cave beach when he had arrived with Tyrian, shocked and drained the year previously.

They had narrowly avoided the track of a sinister-looking, matt-black monstrosity of a gigantic nuclear-powered submarine. Looming and quietly thrumming its way through the wintry gloom of those northern waters, it was massively larger than any killer whale. Thinking themselves hunted by the hugest predator in the world, they had fled in blind panic at topmost speed, unaware they had not even been noticed.

The fear and horror had been hard to shake off, even when they began to believe themselves safe. When they arrived on the sea cave beach, both were nervous and prepared to fight for space, if need be, but the need did not exist. They found themselves in assembly of moulting females, among whom the scar made Marrocha distinctive.

Scarred, though she was, the spirit of life was strong in her. When restored to some semblance of normality, Iolair enquired with all he commanded of courtesy, after her scar. She was not shy telling how she came by it. It had been inflicted while she was caring for the first of the seventeen pups she had delivered into the world. That year, she had delayed setting out for the nursery grounds and had been forced to give birth on a remote mainland shore little-known to her.

A bad choice: for the first three days, people had repeatedly passed them by, venturing too close. Beside herself with anxiety, Marrocha had driven them off with a snarling defence of her pup. Several days of poor weather with driving rain followed, making for a miserable existence even though the disturbance ceased and her pup fattened. On the eleventh day, the showers ceased. This day, for the first time since giving birth, she swam off the beach at high tide and so was in no position to defend her pup even had she found in herself sufficient courage. A local salmon netsman who bore an implacable hatred for all seals stumped down to the beach in his rubber boots and clubbed her pup to death.

One moment, he was just another human intruding into the quiet of their day. Next, the club was raised once, twice and a final time. Unbelieving, she had thought to leave the sea, drag herself up the beach to nuzzle the battered remains of her still-warm pup. Fear stayed her. She did nothing but watch as he stumped on down toward the tideline, continuing to watch as he raised the rifle to his shoulder and steadied himself.

The shout and the sound of the shot were not quite simultaneous.

She responded to the shout, the instinct to escape over-riding all. Even as she ducked, she felt the hot pain of the scalp wound from which dark blood was already welling and turning to ribbons in the water. Under the surface, she streamed madly away. When next she surfaced, she was concealed from the shore by a rocky outcrop. She ducked immediately down again because there were the sounds of a shouted altercation coming from the shore where the man without a gun shouted at the man with the gun. She lingered until after dark before daring to return to her pup.

She found it unrecognisable, tangled like a red and white rag on the shingle. Sniffing tentatively, she found even the scent mainly unrecognisable, spoiled by the congealed blood. Thereafter, she remained beside it all night, but as the eastern sky began to admit first light, she moved down the shore. Twice she stopped, looking back over her shoulder, before continuing into the sea.

It was not long before her scalp wound healed, leaving only the scar to mark where it had been.

As for people: they had been peripheral before the bloody day. Now, she shunned them totally. She was always first into the water whenever a boat approached any haul-out site she was using. All tolerance for people was lost but as a seal she flourished. She grew glossy again, produced another pup and, since then, a long line of them.

Now she had come to Carreg yr Honwy, where all seals were alert to the least hint of disturbance, and then to Pen Diban where Iolair the Wise was waiting. It was a friendly reunion. She had forgotten neither him nor Tyrian, appearing out of the wild sea on that wintry morning and disappearing as completely, two days later, having filled the time between with stories of the past told by young Iolair and traveller's tales told by his companion. Vivid days. All her companions remembered them: Iolair, whom they had wanted to mother; Tyrian, whom any would have chosen for a mate and then the two of them, singing songs made on their travels around western Ireland. That had been the most abiding memory of all, the way they encouraged the assembled females to join with them and make the cave itself sing in joy at the lovely remoteness and security of their abode and their welcome company.

Having learned Tyrian was elsewhere, Marrocha settled to answer the questions he asked of her winter travels. She described how she had wandered up into the Inner Hebrides, travelling as far north as orca-haunted Canna before turning back and cove-hopping down the wild west coast of Scotland under flaring hills and across the mouths of great sea lochs. She had lain on shallow rocks in the Sound of Mull while the tide roared by, carrying on it one of the black and white Calmac ferries, northward bound for Barra and the neighbouring Uists. She had run down the south-west coast of Scotland, avoiding the temptation of Rathlin and its seal-friendly tide races, avoiding the Solway and the radioactive flow emanating from the Lake District. In time, she came to the southernmost Cumbrian shore on sands opposite the south-east tip of Walney.

Travelling ever southward, the hunting was good some miles north-west of the Dee, where she found herself among more seals than she had seen at any point in her journey. There, she learned of the sandbanks at the mouth of the Dee, especially of West Hoyle. To that complex she set her course and there rested for several more days before working westward along the North Wales coast, hunting every day but without great appetite, toward the islands off the east coast of Ynys Môn. There, on Ynys Dulas, from a sub-assembly consisting exclusively of females gathered on the east shore, not far from the unpainted stone tower that served for a daymark beacon, she learned of Enlli.

Iolair listened and remembered what she had heard.

Marrocha lingered for three days on the Enlli shore before the familiar restlessness began to nibble again at her heels. On the early morning tide, Iolair watched her slip gracefully into the sea with the backwash of the swell and disappear. Five times after that, he glimpsed her head. Each time it was smaller. When he could see her no more, he unfocussed his gaze and was left with his thoughts.

***

Amber had picked up from the doormat an envelope addressed to Amaury when she arrived for supper. It seemed he had overlooked it at the earlier hour when he had arrived back from a busy sea-visit to the faraway Boscastle coast, taking advantage of a small benison of light south-easterly breezes. It bore a beautiful postage stamp coloured darkly turquoise-green, superimposed on which was a silver dragon with a barbed tongue and uplifted wings. Looking down at the novelty of it, she wondered why stamps so handsome were not readily available for her to stick on envelopes when she wrote one of her infrequent letters.

Someone had mentioned his name to government scientists in Wales organising a survey of grey seals in their little-known haunts there. Back in November, he had received an initial telephone call; enquiring after all he had done in the way of seal studies. A follow-up call had invited him to submit a bid for the survey projected to begin in August. A strange period: he hadn't the foggiest idea what his time was worth, what equipment he might need or how much it would cost to live there. He had learned, also, not to become distracted or too hopeful.

He read of the huge body of work conducted at seal sites in the southern half of the Welsh coast. Nowhere in Britain had such a continuing run of studies been made of a regional population of grey seals, often using methods at modest frontiers of science. The roll call of researchers was an inspiration to him — A.L. Johnston and Ronald Lockley high among them and, more recently, Mick Baines.

Now, he rose to hug and kiss this newly beloved woman who had ceased to be a stranger and, only when they were done, did she tap the sealed envelope against his chest in enquiry. Taking it from her, recognising the origin of the postage stamp, Amaury felt a frisson of excitement. Reaching for the pen-knife on his desk, he slit open the envelope, drawing out sheets of printed paper. Without haste, he read the page in which the remainder of the papers were enclosed.

It invited him to visit the survey organisers without offering him the contract.

She smiled after she had read it. He thought how different she looked to when first he had seen her, at the edge of the drubbing surf. The sadness was less apparent. It came and went. Her past was not a light thing to her, to be casually set aside. She was a woman of abiding loyalties.

***

Riding the big wave of this unlooked-for encouragement, the next week Amaury took the long road north, setting out early and alone. Close to the end of his journey, bowling along a road doing its best to cling to the north coast of Wales by the quiet waters of the Irish Sea, he drew closer to the high mountains where patches of snow yet lingered.

Conwy felt like the truest borderline he crossed in the entire journey, except for his beloved Tamar River. There, he became more really aware he was entering another country, where a road tunnel delved below the waters of the estuary. That brief sojourn through the underworld proved an ordeal for him. It was a habit of his to hold his breath for the duration of every passage made through any tunnel. This was a longer tunnel, requiring he hold his breath for more than a minute while resisting the desire to speed up and make it easier. It was good if irregular practice for being underneath heavyweight Cornish surf.

Leaving behind small private challenges, he elected slip from the flow of traffic at Aber. Leaving the van in the small car park by the bridge over the dipper-haunted stream that flowed from the Falls, he sought to revitalise his humanity, dulled by the hours of driving. Immediately, the riverside trees, the birdsong and the lovely air rolling down off the mountains worked their magic. He smiled as he walked, making the easy drag up to the Falls.

His eyes drank in the novelties of a landscape he was seeing for the first time. However, as he walked, he was scouring dusty places of memory, trying to snout out what he had read about this place in the history books and gazetters through which he had spent the past week grazing.

The waterfall: who could gaze at it and remain indifferent? What dreamer of dreams could fail to be refreshed there? It was a singing place. Birds sang, the waters sang and all the lovely things that had ever happened here had left their trace in the singing of the place.

Down the high, almost sheer face of grey rock, a thin veil of white water, now and then worried by the breeze or rainbowed by sunlight, pulsed down into the bowl hollowed out by ancestor-waters across centuries. From that sculpted place, waters bounced and slithered onward through the valley and under the fine trees below, all the way to the shining shallows of the Menai.

More than seven hundred years before, the magic of this place had been known to the penultimate true Prince of Wales. Llewelyn the Last had walked or ridden here from his home at the bottom of the valley, set back from the dangerous, sometimes flooding waters of Menai. He, too, would have heard the skylark, invisible against the blue sky, whose nest was the goldsmith's crucible from which — at dawn — it poured its boiling of golden song, as Dafydd ap Gwilym had it in his poem. No naturalist or scientist would ever represent the skylark more perfectly than Dafydd ap Gwilym.

Amaury could not help but be interested in history — the history of large events, of place and of the little people. In all his wanderings in wild places, as in the creatures, the form and coverings of the land and the weathers to which they were subject, his curiosity was always initially for the land or sea itself and for the peoples who had dwelt, roved or raided there. How could he relate to the individuals and communities he met lacking such foundations to inform his sensibilities?

And Llewelyn the Last? Llewelyn had travelled with Amaury since before he turned his thoughts to any adventure into Wales. The prince had long fought the reluctant fight he knew neither he nor his descendants could win against his covetous neighbour. An unfortunate prince, supported by his own people of the north, but envied by lordlings with holdings in the south. His only real misfortune was to have the first Plantagenet Edward for his enemy.

The year 1282 was branded on his imagination. That year, Llewelyn spurned the bribe offered by the English Crown to yield up the independence of his people and their enlightened code of laws. The year ended with him lured into a trap, wounded, imprisoned and murdered. 1282 was the year the people lost their protector, going down into a darkness of the soul that lingers yet, felt but rarely understood by strangers. Rights were trampled by martial might. That was why, he realised before ever he crossed the border, and he would understand if he was made to feel like a stranger.

Llewelyn.

242

At the bottom of the valley, he had glimpsed the modernised remnant of the site on which Llewelyn had a home. There, his daughter had been born; Gwenllian. Once her father was slain, they came for her. A baby, just a few months old, hardly yet with lengthening hair, not yet walking, not yet speaking Welsh or French or English. They took her from her English mother, stifling her in sorrow upon sorrow, tragedy upon tragedy. They placed her in Sempringham convent in Lincolnshire, on the east coast of England, there to be held until her death at the age of fifty-four years.

Standing under the waterfall, he wondered had she ever seen it. He wondered if ever she had known love. He wondered if her companions had been kindly or merry or dour. The sadness of it caught his throat. Of course, most human life is freckled with tragedies, great and small, some known, some not. There are many for whom we might grieve. This, he knew; but thought of Gwenllian snared him, even so. Little girl: helpless and in need, faraway, long ago, largely unremembered.

With her and her two cousins incarcerated in Bristol Castle, in the passing of time, the line of the true princes of Wales, whom some might better prefer to call the princes of Gwynedd, ceased. A lordless people came to feel like foreigners in their own land. Long winter, a darkness of spirit, was laid upon people who had previously lived free and strong and bright in ancient poetry under passing shadows cast by the wings of eagles.

He stood there, a Cornishman — not a Welshman, but affected by so forlorn a history — in that place of green and slate-grey under blue and white skies, gazing to the top of the white waterfall. A grey wagtail jinked by in flight and song before his eyes, all citrine and pale grey, landing on a dome of rock protruding from the waters, flirting the white fringes of its bobbing tail like a little bird of paradise. Up above the Falls, above sheep grazing on invisible fragments of ledge, a raven shot into view, flipping over to glide along upside down before righting itself, making the belling, telephone-ringing of a call as it did so.

Thoughtfully, Amaury wheeled away and headed back the way he had come. From the bottom of the valley, he drove away westward in search of an end of journey sunset.

It was mid-afternoon. There was no urgency to be finding a bed to rest his head for the night. In three days' time he had to be in Bangor, to talk with the scientists. So, he came to the most handsome and Byzantine of castles built by command of royal Edward. A red dragon painted on a green and white background floated above the towers under the distant peaks of mountains once the stronghold of the people of Gwynedd. In that remembered year, in 1282, he had ordered the castle built at a river mouth between the mountains and the island across the Straits that had long been regarded as the granary of Wales. Ynys Môn: Anglesey. How people must have hated the place, across the centuries and now, for all the appellation as a World Heritage Site.

He continued westward toward the triple-peaked mountain that served for an obstacle against those who might come raiding into the fertile places of the Llyn Peninsular. Yr Eifl: The Rivals. Feral goats browsed on high sea slopes, among the ghosts of folk who knew the shelter of encampments up there. Choughs flew above wheatears and here Amaury saw the first red kite of his journey, not realising it had strayed north from its normal haunts. Birds of prey are never less than handsome, but he found himself wondering if any of them could compare for grace with this one, working its way through the blue and white airs above the grey, rock-littered slopes of these hills. Not so much a red kite, more a buzzard crossed with a kestrel and then improved some.

It was another place from which to scan far horizons, had he been prepared to stop the car again, but there was no longer enough light remaining in the day. While he drove, he guzzled distance, noticed the tiny pebbles of the Tudwals, where Somerledaa had not dallied. Indeed, surfing down that high and winding road from Llithfaen, one glorious view yielded to another, all the way to sheltered Nefyn.

Here, Amaury was tempted again to break his journey, seek out a place to stay but knowing himself close to the west end of the peninsular, now he felt the tug of it. How could a man of the Lands End resist such a lure? He drove on, still following not only the north coast but the pilgrim's way. A smile, long absent from his face, returned. This was it. Somewhere hereabouts, he felt certain, would be places to which he might bring Amber. Here was so much she might sketch or paint in the water colours she used so well.

At Aberdaron, he found a pub by the sea. Having secured a room there, he covered the last few miles to the tip of the peninsular. Along the way, he passed a place which, translated, was Above-the-Mountain: Uwchmynydd. On to the heights of Mynydd Mawr, out of the car he walked into the spring breeze and then downhill toward the race of Braich y Pwll. Such a sea was spread before him. Here was a race and there were over-falls. Close inshore, as he followed a sheep track southward, were places where only quiet waters ran. The wondrous tidal checkerboard of waters enlivened the Sound.

Following the very edge of the cliffs, he found ravens nesting, feeding young in the luxurious woollen bowl of their nest above the usual sea-footed precipice. He saw choughs using their fine, red, down-curved bills to probe the cliff edge grassland for invertebrate prey. High above, a pale-bellied buzzard wheeled between several-fingered wings angled slightly upwards.

He prostrated himself for a while to scan the pattern of surfaces that together made the Sound. Because he knew how to look, he saw the small party of porpoises Somerledaa had met on an earlier day off Pen y Cil. He saw gannets, oystercatchers, gulls and Manx shearwaters: like reading music made by an orchestra of flight. The deep and effortless power of gannets, the narcissism in the gliding of shearwaters so close to their reflections, the clean black and white of oystercatchers and greater black-backed gulls, all gilded by the setting sun.

On the sea, shag and guillemot dived without dread while, over to the south on a dark rock wearing a restless white ruff about its base, the pale smears of six seals made him feel welcome.

Across the way and slightly to the left, Ynys Enlli: Bardsey. He read its shape as the top half of a guillemot's skull. He could make out no seals on those distant shores, though it was reputed a stronghold of their kind.

It was a clear end to an early spring day. From his vantage point, the coastline of Wales spread all the way to Grassholm-of-the-gannets: Huganod; a fantastic view. When time came to retrace his steps back to the car, he was feeling stirred in a way that he had not foreseen.

Cornwall was the heart of his heart; home. Yet, he knew this place was special, was finding it easy to love.

That evening, he went down to the bar and talked with any local people in the mood to engage. They asked him what was he there for, out-of-season? When he told them he was interested in the seals, the variety of reaction was not greatly different to that in any other relatively remote place. Bloody seals. Best seal is a dead seal. Too many of the damned things. Have you tried flipper pie? There's more around now than there have ever been. Vermin. On the other side, there were one or two who said live and let live. They were here long before us; there should be enough for them and us.

There was a weather-beaten man drinking quietly at the bar who did not join in the conversation though hearing well all that was said: broad-shouldered, broad-chested with a heavy mop of dark curls. Already, Amaury had been struck by the sense of two peoples or two origins sitting side by side in this peninsular. The other people were small, more slender, less dark, and less broad. Amaury asked him if he was a fisherman

"That's right. Out of Porth Meudwy, across the way there." He waved his arm indistinctly toward the south-west.

"Mainly for crab and lobster?"

"Aye."

"Do you see much of seals?"

"As much as anyone, I reckon."

"I come from Cornwall. There, I reckon crabbers know better than anyone the places used by seals. I reckon it's the same here. If I were to open a map, could you show me where they have their pups or where they rest ashore?"

Steve Trebilcock was a good-natured man. Across the bar and its burden of part empty glasses he reached a big hand:

"I am Steve Trebilcock. And you are?"

"Amaury Valneuve, from Cornwall. Your name has a Cornish ring to it, too; for all that, you sound like a Welshman." It was half a question.

"Grandfather was a Cornishman; a fisherman — we were all fisherfolk or farmers hereabouts, before most of us were forced to

246

convert ourselves into holiday home proprietors. He married a local girl, long since. Now I reckon I am about as Welsh as anyone here." He looked around him, smiling broadly, wondering if anyone would take his bait.

Amaury was thinking he looked indestructibly strong. How did someone become so strong?

Someone said something to Steve in Welsh and was answered in the same language, at the end of which the fisherman turned to him and asked: "Are you going to open that map?"

The glasses cleared, the map was opened and spread before Steve. Amaury came to his shoulder, watched one large forefinger stab Aberdaron. Glancing up to be sure Amaury was with him, he said:

"We are here. You know about Bardsey being the main seal haunt on the Llyn? OK? Run east along the north coast as far as Morfa Nefyn. You find seals here, here and on these rocky islets. Run east along the south coast to the Tudwals. That is a site they use in the summer months. Pups? Bardsey, again, and this coast." His finger moved along the south coast east of Aberdaron.

"What about farther east?" Amaury asked.

"Too many people on the beaches. Seals seem to like their privacy. So; all the way to Aberystwyth, did you say? None of it much good for them beyond the Tudwals, I would guess. I may be wrong." He raised a brow, twisted his head again to look at the stranger, assessing.

"I'll let you know. Do you know anything about seals on Anglesey?"

"I don't go there, but you might get lucky around Holy Island — lots of high cliffs, hostile tide races and sea caves. Ideal for the seals... You could check Ynysoedd y Moelrhoniaid — the Skerries — near the nuclear power station. It is surrounded by tide races too. I don't know where else to suggest. There are many dangerous stretches of seaway up there. Be careful even if you have been told before and have escaped the worst consequences of ignoring the warnings."

"What about Ynys Seiriol? Don't they run trips to watch seals from Biwmaris?" One of the men who had spoken for live and let live re-joined the conversation. Amaury looked from him to Steve, who nodded: "Try it. I'd forgotten Seiriol. Loads of wildlife there."

"Where is Ynys Seiriol?" That drew smiles from everyone within earshot. It was one of the better-known landmarks of North Wales. Steve helped him out: "Bottom right-hand corner of Anglesey; at the entrance to the Menai. It is separated from the main island by a narrow strip of water through which the tide runs often like an express train."

"I am getting the impression that tide races dominate everything hereabouts. Otherwise, the Irish Sea seems gentle by comparison with those I'm familiar with, down in Cornwall."

"That is precisely true. Another feature you will notice about these seas is that in the wake of heavy seas, everything calms down a lot quicker than in the Western Approaches. Otherwise, I imagine it is much the same as Cornwall. When the south wind blows, you will look to be working on the north coast, and vice versa. What kind of boat are you planning to use? A RIB?"

Amaury smiled tightly: "I use a wave ski."

"A jet ski?" The fisherman sounded scathingly dismissive but Amaury had anticipated the familiar and, apparently, universal misunderstanding.

"A wave ski. It looks like a large, thick-bodied surfboard. I paddle it much as you might paddle a kayak, and I perch on top of it, much as in a kayak, but without any cover."

"What about your survey equipment?"

"I stow everything inside a dry bag that rests between my legs or can be anchored to a point near the front."

"Sounds dodgy! You will likely find trouble in the tide races hereabouts, although there is usually a stand of water sometime in the tide cycle."

"Can you indicate where I will meet the fiercest tide races?" Seeing Steve draining his glass, he picked it up, took it to the bar, asking for another beer. Once he had conferred it upon the man who knew so much about everything he needed to know, he settled beside him and handed him a felt-tipped pen: "You can mark them on the map, although when I head back through Bangor, I'll buy a chart."

When they parted, the map was extensively annotated. Before parting, they had exchanged telephone numbers and Steve said, as his parting shot: "The day after tomorrow, I'll be departing Porth Meudwy to test new outboards. Nine o'clock. If you like, you can come and I'll take you for a spin around Bardsey, give you a sense of the lie of the land and a close-up view of the friendly waters."

Not knowing the translation, Amaury raised his brows.

"The island of currents. Seven different races girdle the island."

Amaury had only to mount the stairs from the bar, walk along the corridor to find his room and the welcome bed. He was happy. The adventure in North Wales could not have started better. He was aware he could have simply relaxed after the grinding journey up from Lands End, but to have done so was not in his nature. He had felt the need to mark his arrival by making contact with the land. That, he had always done. Making such a good connection with the local people felt like a very big bonus.

The next day, using the annotated map, he meandered through the lanes eastward to Porth Neigwl. Everywhere he went, he referred to a book teaching him how to pronounce the names in Welsh. It was a pleasant task. He liked the softness of the sounds of the language, the same language that had once been spoken across Britain before successive waves of invaders drove it to its remote and upland refuges, including south-west England, of course.

***

On the brown rocks of Carreg yr Honwy, about five hundred metres to the west of Ynys Enlli, about fifty seals lay under the grey skies beside a sea full of small waves. They were not restless. These rocks were the safest of havens, a very strong flow of water racing over the shallows on the landward side. Nearly all the seals were assembled at the north end with just four or five at the south tip.

Most of the seals currently present had grown familiar with one another through the winter months, sharing Enlli sites to mount expeditions northward into the great interrupted eyebrow of races curving round the northern shores of Ynys Môn, where the hunting was always good. In those fertile waters, they met and mixed with seals from the northerly sea caves of Ynys Cybi and open-sky sites at Ynysoedd y Moelrhoniaid.

Now, at Carreg yr Honwy, most of the seals present were adult males or immatures. The immatures, including individuals who had arrived as dispersing moulted pups, had learned to take their positions more comfortably in the winter assemblies, but they did not imitate any hectoring still visited upon them, occasionally, by the big males.

Somerledaa had become more effective as a huntress during her stay. Iolair felt that so long as she suffered no physical misadventure, she looked certain to become one of the survivors of her cadre. She looked well.

The two of them were together often. Many seals at these assemblies had formed friendships or affinities. Such pairs would rest ashore together, synchronise their hunting forays, rest in the sea together. Some, especially but not exclusively younger seals, made sport together in the seas adjacent to the island. They would dance and roll, keeping endless physical contact until one would break away, whereupon a chase would ensue.

There was no pressure at this time except to avoid upsetting seals that were still moulting, for they were uncomfortable in their own bodies. They itched. It made them irritable.

Somerledaa learned the seal etiquette for use of the rocky sites to which they hauled themselves. Moulting seals and those with no intention of making an imminent journey to sea assembled at Henllwyn. At low tide, that part used by seals consisted of gravel-bottomed gullies, extensive spreads of gently undulating rocks covered by fucoid seaweeds and islets.

Seals here had to become habituated to the irregular comings and goings of the charter vessel supplying the lightly-inhabited island. Now, instead of plunging into the sea in alarm whenever it curved around to line up for the final harbour approach, they hardly bothered to come to the alert.

Fifteen years earlier, it had been another story. Then, had the assembled seals caught sight of a human walking anywhere on the shores of the bay, all would have stampeded into the sea. Fifteen years since, they would not have returned to the same site until the following day. Time had mellowed them. The instinct to flee the seal-clubbers was transformed, having developed a degree of trust that people, on land or in boats, meant them no harm. It took aggressive behaviour to drive them from their snug resting places now, such as a fast approach toward the rocks by one of the high-speed fishing boats, especially by one particular fisherman when checking the most inshore of his crab pots. Even in this, there was no great malice, just a young man feeling the need to impose his authority on the 'coddled' seals.

At Carreg yr Honwy, there was an entirely contrasting atmosphere among the gathered seals. Fifteen years previously, like their fellows in sheltered Henllwyn, seals using this gaunt place had gone crashing into the water whenever a boat ventured into their comfort zone. Now, unlike Henllwyn, their reaction was as it had ever been. The boundaries remained as unchanged here as they were changed at Henllwyn. If a boat flirted by too close, all the seals hastened to such security as the sea offered.

Seals spending periods coming to shore at Henllwyn to rest behaved as if their wiring had been totally changed when they swam westward to Carreg yr Honwy. It was as if memories and decisions determining behaviour were made not by the seals themselves but by the stones upon which they lay.

Low tide returned. The seals dozed on the safe, gaunt rocks. Some noticed the small dot of a boat even as it appeared from behind the rocks at the south end of the island, recognising it as one of the high-speed fishing boats and even identifying it as one that did not regularly fish these waters. Somerledaa noticed it. As ever, she was occupying one of the marginal assembly locations, lacking authority to take and hold a more central position. Iolair rested beside her and, as ever, noticed the boat before her. He was the most alert seal she had ever met, but she understood why.

The horrors of what had been, the horrors he feared would occur again as well as the recognition that he was powerless to avert the least part of it, he had shared with her at length. He was deeply scarred by bitter awareness of his limitations. He was also the seal through whom she understood and lived the idea of friendship.

Iolair mentioned always, at some moment in every day, black Tyrian. She knew he believed Tyrian was not only the spirit of odyssey but also that he understood as well as any seal he had ever met the idea

251

of living friendship. Tyrian was talismanic to both seals. Wherever they returned to shore, they scanned for him but he was never there and would have been surprised at their preoccupation.

The dot of a boat grew in size and identity. It acquired a colour; pale blue. Unusually, it was not standing upright in the sea in the usual rearing horse position, but travelling slowly. Steve Trebilcock was pointing to the rocky, low-lying islet ahead of them. To the dark-haired man standing beside him in the small wheelhouse, he shouted:

"This is Carreg yr Honwy — best place on the island for seals, apart from Henllwyn, which we passed earlier. You might get a few photographs as we slide by. I could hold the boat still for a while, if you like."

"Yes, please!" Amaury rummaged in his dry bag, extracting the camera and the powerful, even more expensive lens, both now imperilled by exposure to damp and salt in the air about them.

They made a first pass of the islet at about one hundred and fifty metres, identifying the location of the main assembly of seals. They counted about fifty, all across the north-west corner. Steve brought the boat around, glanced enquiringly at Amaury who gave him the thumbs-up. This time he ran by at just over a hundred metres. Running slowly, he heard the electrical sounds of the motor-drive reeling away.

Amaury shouted: "This time, let's try fifty metres. If you can, it would be great simply to hold your place in the tide, giving me a still platform to work from. Even if the seals do enter the sea, they have a tendency very shortly afterwards to take a periscoping scan around them to determine what is going on. That means they stand high out of the sea as possible, showing as much of the patterning along their chests and necks as I could hope for. Those are the perfect moments for me, what I am hoping to capture."

The fisherman made a circle of forefinger and thumb. The boat began to surge powerfully northward again, punching into the last of the ebb. Amaury glanced down, making a final check. His camera was switched on, the correct settings were in place, and the lens was clean. They drove along parallel first to the tail of the rock, gaining ground until level with the first of the seals.

Here, even as he clicked away, he thought he recognised a small, well-marked female possibly born in the recent breeding season. Next to her rested a handsome black male. He could not be sure whether this was a small mature male or an immature. It was always difficult to tell how to classify seals of either sex while on the cusp between maturity and immaturity. There was no such doubt about the next four: all large males. He was struck, as ever, not so much by the variety of pelage colouring but the lordly variety of snout shapes. As ever when photographing male seals, he reminded himself he must make the effort to identify them on that basis and scarring in addition to any other head and neck markings. It was something he had always neglected to do, always being distracted by whatever was most important at the time. If he was a research team instead of a lone wolf, the task would have been tackled long-since.

The boat moved parallel with the sea-rocks where seals had started working their way laboriously down to the sea. Amaury, kneeling on the small bow deck, continued taking shots, motor-drive whirring, noticing the dearth of females and wondering whether it had something to do with the site. Was this a male-dominant site or was the sex-skewing to do with the moult and its single-sex nature? He smiled to himself. In the year opening before him, here was a question he might get the chance to address if chance actually materialised.

Somerledaa watched it go. Beside her, Iolair watched, also. It had happened only rarely during winter that boats had made such a close passage. More rarely still had boats passed close enough to cause them to retreat to the sea. It had the effect of returning Iolair to his dark reflections, his sense of security frayed.

The effect on Somerledaa was quite different. No great ill had ever befallen her, unless it was the invasion of her nursery cave by the people who had briefly captured her mother. She saw the world through eyes that noticed the light, first learned watching morning sunlight illuminate the west wall of her natal cave. Of shadows, she knew little, from foraging along weedy underwater skirts of these islands and skerries. To her, they were places where fish and crabs took refuge and with which the sunbeams danced.

She was startled when he began then to weave a song of parting for her. But though he made the song of parting, into which he wove images of his own land's end home, he asked her to accompany him, to share more of their journey.

For Somerledaa, it was a beautiful moment. Winter had lingered late in the high mountains beyond the long peninsular, and, only a week before, the lower heights of Yr Eifl had been dusted again with snows dropped by a late shower. It had been a long winter, but now flowers were busy changing the rind of colours above the sands and rocks and cliffs. Choughs were surfing black waves in the sky. Ardour was in their courtship flights. Ravens were feeding their swollen young in the deep nests of woven gorse on cliff ledges above the reach of the sea-spray. Much larger numbers of shearwaters were streaming in now over the sea from winter haunts off the coasts of Ecuador and Galapagos. They returned a long-absent night voice to the slopes of the lonely mountain, where they were spring-cleaning thousands of burrows ready for the imminent business of egg-laying.

The instinct to move had awoken, not yet southward for home, but continuing northward, in the direction Iolair was gazing. In the sea, the two seals looked at one another and understood they would yet travel onward together.

Setting forth, immediately they were in familiar territory, moving with the tide races into the shadow cast by the gauntest winter cliff-faces, beyond South Stack and its massive down-draught of guillemots. It brought them under lichen-bearded cliff walls and renowned climbing places with beautiful names, one of which translated as the Dream of White Horses. Beyond race-kissed North Stack they swam, flowing now out to the low-lying island group of Ynysoedd y Moelrhoniaid. All the way on to Point Lynas and its exceptional glut of scores of foraging porpoises they swam before veering northward to an island yet unseen but which Iolair knew to be there.

The seas of early springtime were still mainly empty of boats, though they had seen big coasters with empty holds moored well off the east coast of Ynys Môn. Of summer birds, there were returning terns, flying buoyant as ever on the breezes while, on the sea itself, rafts of guillemots and razorbills mainly rested. Occasionally, among the more common auks, the seals glimpsed a black guillemot, whose lovely red legs could be recognised below the surface. Of winter birds, a few great northern divers remained, drifting northward mainly to their breeding stronghold of Iceland, though a few might linger on islets or grassy promontories beside the Minch.

Their agreed destination was a smudge that clarified into a chain of islands on the northern horizon in the middle of the Irish Sea. As the seals approached, the number of islands diminished until only two remained. The closer they drew, the more fishing boats speckled the encompassing horizons, along with a scattering of sailing boats and motor cruisers.

Other than the changing scene and increasing traffic, they experienced little distraction although they did take time out from travelling at a steady four miles an hour to hunt when they came to promising ground. This delayed them. They reached the Calf of Man, the big island off the south-western tip of Man, after dark. It was a cloudy night, so their search for a haul-out site was not illuminated, but it did not matter. Faintly at first, on the breeze, their sensitive ears picked up threads of seal song somewhere near the north end of the Calf.

By the lighthouse they came and, keeping the looming tower of Spanish Head away to the right, they came into the channel dividing the main island from the Calf. Ahead of them, to the right but still in the channel, the rocks of Kitterland loomed. Closer to the shores of the main island, they were velvet-patched with seals. Gratefully, the travellers ended their journey, letting the gentle swell deposit them ashore. It was achieved without collision. The seals already in possession of resting places slumbered on.

Somerledaa fell asleep, but Iolair never found sleep easy to come by upon arrival in a new place. As ever, his first interest was in truffling out customs and traditions of the local seals. Spotting another seal that seemed wakeful as he, he shuffled quietly across and was rewarded by meeting another midwife seal, Narienya, who was also local. From her, he learned that at certain times of year there was also a large contingent of Hebridean seals present here. He discovered very early, also, that his Irish accent was almost as familiar on these rocks as those of Welsh and Manx seals. He was no longer out of place.

They had been long-locked in their exchange when Iolair, who continued to scan whenever talking or listening, realised there was something strange about three seals down by the sea. They were resting on a raft of folded kelp fronds that were just about afloat. It was their behaviour that he noticed initially, and then something about their heads, noticed without noticing.

Interpreting his distraction, Narienya sang to him that these were their cousins; the harbour seals, all three being females recently arrived from Strangford Lough, across the way.

Relieved from fretting over something not quite familiar, he was free to notice other details of the assembled sleepers. Six wore shawls of fishing net. It was the highest concentration of such disabled seals he had yet observed in his travels. Narienya explained all had been entangled off the Cornish coast where the spread of fixed nets covering the sea floor was at the highest density.

Why were there no immatures among the netted ones? He sang the thought aloud. Narienya regarded him with gravity, answering coolly:

"Do you have any idea how much physical power and will it takes to burst free of nets holding you to the bottom of the sea? I see you don't. May it be ever so!" She extended her neck telescopically upward, snout pointing toward the stars, and as she did, Iolair saw the long-healed scar marring the pattern of her markings about halfway along its length. Iolair felt the hair rise on the back of his own neck. Uncertain whether he should comment, he remained silent.

Resuming her former posture, the older female continued: "The younger ones lack the power to burst free. They struggle, exhaust their air, lose co-ordination and die in glooms at the bottom of the sea. Scavengers emerge, even as they emerge to eat those fish held in nets left too long between hauls. They feast. You see, there are countless sad deaths died while the occasional gleam of taut netting catches the dull light down there. Are we not the fine ones, with so much tragic dying? Shall I sing it to you, Iolair?"

She sang and it was sad indeed; of all the laments ever he had heard, it was among the saddest. And, all the while she sang, the grumblings and snorings and hissings around them quieted. There was silence, but for the play of the waves over the rocks, as if the entire world about them listened with its soul.

Iolair listened. He listened, absorbing stories and the sorrowing music of her. Like gazing through a telescope back down the long years, he recognised she was singing also the story of her own loss, of loss too great to be borne.

Looking at him when the great music was gone from her and her weary with the making of it, she saw how much he had understood. And because it was simply in them to do so, she recognised the great darkness clouding his soul. His own sorrow was despite all the songs he heard and harvested, it was not given to him to create his own great music. For him, for now, there was yet only a lesser music or remembrances in the great music of others.

Awash with melancholy, the seals locked gazes. Neither moved but they clung to one another, in recognition and relief, under the stars that guided them and decorated the night. Sleep came in the wake of the residue of remembered suffering. It came as a kindness.

The next day dawned blue and white, windier than it had been for some time. For once, Somerledaa found herself unintentionally excluded by Iolair, who was usually impeccably mindful of her sensibilities. Upon her wakening, he had introduced her to Narienya, but soon thereafter, they were locked again in conversation from which she was not excluded. Simply, they were so interested in all they had to say that she was forgotten.

Somerledaa was not dismayed.

Having swum and feasted, she saw that on Kitterland the seals had moved higher up the rocks beyond reach of the surf. Among them, it was easy to pick out the distinctive black seal. Re-joining him proved problematic. Twice she ran for shore and pulled out at the last moment, so heavy was the surf. Annoyed with herself, she determined that whatever happened, she would not pull out a third time. She waited, watching for a smaller set of waves to track in.

By sheer misfortune, the wave that dumped her bruisingly on the rocks had reared up and slammed her down at the very last moment. The backwash would have dragged her into the sea had she not dug her long claws into a cleft. The power of the drag was tremendous, to the point she was sure she must relinquish her hold but, of a sudden, she was free of drag and wise enough to know she must use every moment to scramble higher up the rocks. Like a mechanical caterpillar, she hastened up the uneven slope, only to be caught in the next great sweep of water. It was larger than she expected and of a power greater than her own. She was not dragged over rock back into the sea. She rode a great bucking carpet of surf in a curve up, across and back down over the rocks without ever feeling them, before being obliterated in churning commotion. There, her body washed against another larger seal, she felt a large flipper fending off the sea-driven force of her.

Wary now, Somerledaa made a circuit of the rearing rocks, seeking an easier landing-place. Nowhere looked attractive. There seemed to be no lee shore landing-places so she returned to the place she had selected originally and resumed watch for a set of allowing wave.

It was a long wait during which other seals tried their luck. The larger ones tended to achieve precarious landfall. The immatures had no luck at all.

Somerledaa waited long. In that time, she selected three waves. Each would have been a good wave for her to catch and so with confidence she chose the fourth, surfing up over the rocks with it.

It was not the perfect choice but, as it reached its apogee, she reached and again dug her claws into a crack in a way often lamented by Iolair. Nevertheless, she managed to achieve an initial anchorage and survived the tremendous drag of gravity as it ravened away. Finding no energy to make a dash for higher ground, she secured a firmer hold with her claws.

The next wave was no stronger but described a different flow over the slope. The force caused her body to twist, putting incredible pressure on her claw-hold. The claws of the fore-flipper felt trapped. The pain was excruciating in her old wound, in the redistributed claws that had suffered so extremely once before. Then the water was gone but the pain remained. Tentatively working the claws loose, seeing blood, trying not to think about it, she made haste up the slope toward the crowd of watching seals. They could do nothing to help; she knew that, but she could feel the communal will wishing her higher, higher.

Another, larger wave crashed into her, rolling her, battering her this time, over and over. Hurt and frightened, she reached out with the same left fore-flipper. Once, twice, three times, she tried to grab a chance claw-hold. The fourth time, something held. Amid all the power and pain, she somehow held on. She felt consciousness tremble and dim before recovering herself. Dazed and hurt, she limped higher with all the speed.

She could hear a song sung by the most familiar voice in her world, willing her not to stop, not to look back down, not to dwell yet upon injuries: just to join the crowd above the violence of the surf.

Terribly weary, Somerledaa found her fore-flippers making customary breast-stroke movements ashore, but everything was heavy as lead. Every movement required the drudgery of will supported by enormous physical effort.

The living fence of waiting seals was very close now. With consciousness reduced to the minimum necessity of gaining height, she did not feel herself arrive among them. She did not sense the heat of bodies, did not scent familiar fishy perfume and she did not feel them doing what seals rarely do. They yielded ground, opening the way for her to pass where she would.

When she reached her destination, she sank into an immediacy of healing sleep. Above her, black Iolair gazed down and then beyond her to the white billowing of dangerous waters around their unsafe haven. For a long time, all song in him was rendered dumb. Then, so low that few other seals did hear it, he began a song of healing. But though he sang, he did not yet dare to look at what ruin was wrought upon her left flipper.

Through the shortening night she slept, and well into day. It was as if she had gone into hiding but Iolair was glad, knowing it could only help her. When she did waken, the first thing she saw was his familiar dark head, before the dam burst and pain washed over her. Less squeamish than Iolair, she stared at the bloody mess of her fore-flipper. More than the encrustation of dried blood, she saw the two claws that would now forever protrude at strange angles.

The innermost of her claws had been wrenched so that it sat almost at right angles to the way it should have pointed. The claw next to it had fared less badly but still stood at an angle of forty-five degrees to the remainder around all of which the skin had been pulverised; but the claws had somehow endured, unbroken.

Having absorbed the shock of her most acute injury, she became gingerly aware of pains patterning the remainder of her body. There was bruising to her head and shoulders as well as superficial damage to her hind flippers. Lesser pains elsewhere hardly registered.

She remained ashore for three days. Her mind largely shut down by shock. For all that time, she lay drowned in a total exhaustion of spirit.

And for all that time, the same storm raged. She was hungry but gave no thought to hunting. In her weariness, she mislaid some of the irreducible confidence that had attended her enchanted odyssey across the first months of life. Would her injuries make it harder for her to hunt effectively? There was only one way to find the answer to that.

Iolair found himself preoccupied by the same question. She would have to test her fate. She would not lightly surrender to any challenge. This much, he knew.

On the fourth morning, placing minimal weight on her left fore-flipper, she limped down the rocky slope having decided to put matters to the test. She was extremely hungry. She was tired of fearing what her fate might be. However, though she limped there was a strength of will about her that drew the attention of the few seals still gathered ashore. Once more, she felt the community of them not exactly sending but exuding whatever they had to spare of goodwill and approval. Young, and impressionable, it lifted her spirits, helped her dive cleanly into the sea.

Once submerged, she went immediately down through the water column toward the seabed. She was frightened of what she might discover but, to her overwhelming relief, she found her manoeuvrability in the water uninhibited except most marginally by the injuries to her claws.

After a while, she forgot her injuries altogether and concentrated exclusively on locating fish. However, no sooner had she submerged than she became aware of the activity of three scallopers dredging noisily some distance away. Although recognising they were not close enough to menace her, she remained disturbed by the horrible sounds of the heavy gear they were using. She had met them occasionally before and knew they were destroying the surface layer of the seabed. Without thinking the thought, she determined forever to give them a wide berth. Out on the scalloping grounds, the boats having ploughed onward, she found the seabed mangled by something that left long scars behind it. Some obese dragon might have dragged along its armoured body there, crushing and scarring everything in its path. Here was a wasteland and there was horror in it before she disturbed a surviving flounder. Capturing it while it undulated just above the seabed, without using her flippers to hold it, she swam to the surface where she crunched it. It assuaged, to some extent, her hunger. However, she had been made restless by her jaunt over the seabed so when she returned to the rocks, she was glad to see that Iolair had returned from his own hunting trip. In a high-pitched song, she called out to him:

"Are we for travelling on?"

She knew he must have seen what she had seen, but he swam toward her with a rare gaiety in his eyes. She sensed his gladness that she had hunted again:

"Would you be interested to visit my island, for a change," he enquired, his Irish accent more pronounced than usual; adding: "It is not so far away now."

She had seen the mountains rising far to the west, toward which his attention oftentimes shifted. He had been long from home and now homesickness was upon him. Neither paid much attention to the clouds massing in the north-west. The desire to depart was overwhelming. There had been a surfeit of drama here.

They made a leisurely progress northward, across Little Sound and, thereafter, remained close in under the cliffs as they worked their way north-eastward up the coast. The entire south-west corner of the Isle of Man proved to be a coast of magnificent high cliffs, but there was particular grandeur under the cliffs where they tracked around to Fleshwick Bay.

Here, they were spotted by two people on a shingle beach at the bottom of a deep valley. They gazed from the seaweed and plastic tangle marking the reach of the highest tides across rock pools and islanded rocks protruding above the surface of the sea. What species of seal they were seeing? Were they greys or commons? The temptation was to believe they were commons, because both were small. However, the woman had been leafing through a book about sea mammals only the week before and made the correct identification, based on the appearance of the little silvery female and her black blotchy markings.

Their springer spaniel, having spotted the two sea spaniels, barked at them, inviting them to come closer inshore, to play. The two seals did not enjoy the sound of the barking, or the relative proximity of the people. They did not flee but edged gradually seaward into the freshening north-westerly wind.

Before long, the people and their eager dog were no longer in view. They were alone again in an unpeopled world beyond the great and handsome arch south of Raclay. Far below the flowering gorse and farther below the lovely tumbling flight of the familiar choughs, they swam; onward, under languidly-wheeling buzzards whose stations were lodged even higher in the sky than those of the cliff-loving choughs.

Immediately, north of The Stack, they swam into a wide sea cave. Both felt it was a nursery cave. Seal etiquette required seals avoid using nursery caves except during the breeding season or where they served as all-purpose caves through the year.

This was not one such. Nevertheless, they hauled themselves part-way up the pebble beach as the boulders under the back wall permitted. In the poor light, they watched waves breaking, just beyond the entrance and listened to the deceptively thunderous music of it. Caves always exaggerated. Nevertheless, they recognised the music was changing, the sea growing more turbulent.

They travelled north beyond Stroin Vuigh toward Grinnagh Doo. In boisterous water, they swam by skerries awash that, in quieter times, surely were frequented by seals. Inshore of them, because the tide was sufficiently high, they explored another cave. Shaped like a hammer, the walls had been surf-burnished to a gleam.

Because, primarily, they were following her impulses, Somerledaa was leading and it was she who was first to dip under waves breaking over the few huge boulders situated just outside the entrance. She slalomed in between the boulders, surfacing in relatively quiet waters within. Very soon the black head of Iolair surfaced nearby. Both seals automatically swivelled on the spot, settling their bearings while a secondary swell pulsed in from the cave entrance. The walls and roof were unusually dark and gleaming having been brightly polished by millennia of storm surf. No algal turf could grow here. Light flickering along one wall changed fitfully in quality with each wave movement.

The eyes of the seals gleamed in the dark, both staring toward the inner recesses of the cave. There, it appeared to divide into two tunnels. Both were aware they were not alone, hearing irregular breathing of unseen seals within, the merest whisper of sound amid the beautiful rolling thunder of the wave-break.

Iolair glanced at little Somerledaa, but she gave no sign of having noticed the unspoken question that provoked the look. Rather, she measured her full length along the surface of the water and drifted at her slowest speed toward the interior. Iolair followed, gliding equally slowly in her wake until they came to where the tunnels had appeared to divide. To the left, the cave did little more than bulge, and reach, its end; so, the incumbent seals must be to the right.

Somerledaa could tell that, even at low tide, there must be a big, shallow pool below her, on the far shores of which, and away to the right there rose a shallow pebble beach. It was hard to make out the pebbles, not because of the gloom but because the six bull seals resting there had taken all the available space.

None of the males lifted whiskered heads to examine the newcomers. The small seals listened to the slumberous music of snoring; grunting; groaning, and breathing, knowing there would be no resting place for them here. Indeed, sooner rather than later, the rising tide would force the seals from their beach.

Pressing northward, they were aware they were swimming along an exposed coast in deteriorating conditions.

In the end, they swam beyond a seemingly endless beach, behind which the land appeared to be mainly flat and featureless. Only beyond the lighthouse at the Point of Ayre, having turned south, did they rediscover the cliffs. Still harried by strengthening wind and steepening seas, they went beyond Maughold Head and Gob ny Strona before finding at last the quiet backwaters they sought.

Despite their weariness, they conversed before they slept. Somerledaa had found this most recent leg of her odyssey especially enjoyable, especially now they were safely at rest. She sang to him:

"Sometimes, I wonder: was I born for days like today, to see such things? Not only that. You and I; when we dive to the deepest glooms of the sea, we carry such lights, brightest of candles, planted in the deeps of memory, but everywhere we go we sprinkle the merest seedlets of it all. For me, it brightens the way. So far, if I have understood anything, I feel as if I have been a harvester of all the good, the natural, and the lovely things of life. Surely it must all go somewhere? Is it held in some internal cistern until time arrives for it to be used to serve some fruitful purpose? Is that how it is for you?"

Humbled, he felt acutely the contrast of her vision with the darkness he was forever trying to fend off inside himself. He said softly:

"I think that it is how it will forever be for me, now you have described it so, under these high cliffs. I shall remember your bright candles in my diving and foraging... and doubts. But in truth, I had not thought of it so before. Is that the main difference between us? I am so full of the gathered, cherished wisdom of candle-bright seals I have known, whereas you see the world through your own bright eyes, eager senses; uncluttered. You have not yet shackled your originality into habit and duty. You are spontaneous!"

"Duty?"

"The duty to gather stories, memories, moments that tell us who we are, what and why — or as far as that is possible. That is my variant on your passion for compiling charts, peering into possible futures via the past."

More intensely than ever, he sang: "I fear the future. I should not say it and I should not think it, yet it is the truth. I am supposed to be young but, inside, I am already ancient. I have heard too much of the deaths of seals and I have watched how the noise of the world, of people and their creations, creep ever closer. It is true that on the face of it, we grey seals are doing well. Our numbers in these islands have been increasing for over a hundred years. Maybe we are as numerous again as we were in those far-off days when they began to hunt us with weapons made from bronze. But the same holds true for people. They have withdrawn from a few isolated islands, leaving the shores free for us to dare to use again, but, for the most part, they are more numerous than the stars! I believe they will consume all our privacy long, long before the end."

Somerledaa felt the power of his misgivings, but she was too young and eager for life to be overwhelmed with anxiety. She looked out on the world with brighter eyes and brighter hopes, but she was sensitive enough to her companion not to soothe him with the counter-images of hope crowding her mind, clamouring to be communicated.

To the north, the Galloway Hills darkened above Burrow Head. Farther away, to the east, ranged the wild heights of the Cumbrian hills and between them, the boundary waters of the Solway poured into the sea, but the two seals neither saw nor felt the freshwater influence of them; over the horizon, farther still to the south, were the high Cambrian Mountains that dominated the winter horizon. Lands End and the caves of her beginnings were so much farther away and by now had begun to feel long, long ago.

Somerledaa felt the nostalgic tug of home. It was the first time ever she had felt it and she glanced almost guiltily toward Iolair, but he was sleeping, his black nose tilted toward the ragged clouds racing above them.

She looked again to the north, to the flashing of another far-distant lighthouse. West of the places she could see, there was a sea road to islands where grey seals long-made their most populous strongholds. Uncertain that she need visit that scattering of small, uninhabited islands, still she could feel the nagging of her personal compass pointing north. That was it. Her compass was pointing north, not yet to the south-west.

That night, she did not sleep well. The seas around her were quiet, but she was restless with the realisation that the morning held a parting.

Somerledaa was adamant and so they had their parting. The seas and the winds driving them had abated considerably, enough that they could set out together on the first leg of this next stage of each their own journeys. Off the Point of Ayre, Iolair set course for the Irish north-east coast; Somerledaa set course for the Mull of Galloway.

***

In such a sea, it was not long before both were utterly alone again, nor so very long before Somerledaa was rounding the southernmost point of Scotland under a black and white confetti of auks. It was a harsh coast with few havens for boats, until she rounded the north end of the peninsular and found herself caught in the dwindled wake of a distant ferry accelerating on the outward leg of the short sea crossing to Belfast. Long after the wake had settled, she passed the tip of the Kintyre Peninsular, coming in under Sanda Island lighthouse and, off the long, sandy beaches of Southend, to the sheer cliffs of the Mull of Kintyre, passing below another light.

Not far west, little more than a four-hour swim away, she could see the Antrim cliffs. She remembered Iolair vividly then; he was not a seal easily forgotten.

She was making the longest uninterrupted sea trip of her life, though she was rarely far from the shore. She swam steadily at three or four miles an hour. Often hungry, rarely sated by what she caught, she was travelling through a wonderland of islands, races, weedy shallows, lighthouses, ruinous Celtic duns, and a stupendous teeming of seabirds. She glimpsed, on rocks and in shallows, an increasing number of harbour seals. On the shores, she saw sheep, sometimes goats, foraging. Overhead, the last winter geese were flying northward, bound beyond the Arctic Circle for their nesting grounds, the brief Arctic summer and the threat of hungry Arctic foxes.

She swam northward by the inshore coasts of Islay and then wild, majestic Jura. Squeezing between the north end of Jura and Scarba, she skirted the sometimes-deadly waters of Corryvreckan Whirlpool in which half a fleet of Norwegian longships had once swirled to its doom, when the mists of history were thinning, but the lands about remained debateable. Chance provided her with a gentle north-easterly breeze and a neap tide, so she had an easier time of it than might have been had there been a big sea pouring in from the ocean, given extra bite by a following south-westerly gale.

She hopped from headland to headland, loch entrance to loch entrance, swimming under high, afforested hills and by bleakly rocky shores besieged by small black islands. Everywhere, there were tide races to learn — the picking of their locks. After crossing the ferry-strewn waters beyond Kerrera, she found harbour seals and black guillemots idling by the ferry terminal of handsome Oban but she did not linger there, despite temptations.

Reaching the Firth of Lorne, shining and calm in sunlight, she came also to a cooler world. It was as if spring itself had grown shy, reluctant to keep pace with her. Far, far up Loch Linnhe, she saw snow still whitening the peaks of Ben Nevis and its lofty neighbours. Close by to the north, white-plumaged ptarmigans on the uppermost heights of Ben More might yet remain invisible to the questing eyes of the golden eagles that, in their soaring, reduced the buzzards who sought to harry them to the status of sparrows. On the east shore of the Sound of Mull, no snow covered the lesser heights of remote Morvern.

The Sound exercised its compelling allure. Small, silvery and emblazoned with the same pattern of markings she had carried from birth, Somerledaa reached the southern entrance to the Sound. She lingered by the inviting ledges of Lady's Rock, with its tower-mounted light, drawing herself from the sea for the first time in two days. Once her coat had dried, she basked for hours in the warmth of the sun, not stirring when the black and white Calmac ferry passed by, northward up the Sound. The big ferry, despite giving the impression of slipping graciously and sedately by, was hardly there than she was gone. She progressed between the low-lying rocks on which Somerledaa rested and the grassy headland-island of Eilean Musdile with its lighthouse. Here, some weeks since, Marrocha had rested – Marrocha, who she had met on the shores of Ynys Enlli.

On the decks, enjoying the same sunshine as Somerledaa, a man with binoculars focussed studied her as the big boat passed by. He was a naturalist, living by the shores of Loch Buie and this small rock was where he expected to see seals. Other passengers, following the line of his gaze, saw the same small seal. The children among them expressed their delight in the traditional way. They saw her as a sweet creature, alone and, like them, very small to be all alone in the world beside such dangerous waters.

They remembered her at journeys end when recalling the highlights of their trip, before they slept that evening. Tucked up in bed, they demanded their mother tell them what the seal was doing 'now'. For them, the seal was gatekeeper to a world in such contrast with their home in Kent with its lawns, apple trees and unknown neighbours.

Later in the day, Somerledaa had continued north. It was unique for her to have green sloping slopes with patches of unmelted snow on their northern heights on both sides of her — unusual, too, to experience such quiet waters. There was no surf here; no sense there was ever surf.

There were red-throated divers and red-breasted mergansers on the waters. She swam without haste between Glas Eilean in mid-channel and the larger Eilean Rubha an Ridire close under the quieter Morvern shore. She felt herself watched by a group of seals among whom she would not have felt small. Harbour seals. They watched warily, recognising what she was. All of them had long since learned to behave discreetly in the presence of grey seals.

For the first time in her travels, Somerledaa had a sense of moving into foreign waters. She was aware, also, that for now her progress felt trudging. She had no destination, no sense of what she was being drawn to. Twice, she thought of turning back and taking the west coast road by the stupendous heights of Mull, but both times she decided to press onward, see what the day might hold.

It was late afternoon by the time she was swimming near the dark, squat ruins of Aros castle, partly screened by the waterside trees. She had no interest in castles except insofar as they helped her monitor the headway she was making, for sometimes she forgot to be aware how powerfully a tide was racing against her. However, this time her attention was diverted toward a huge bird and then a second one. They were birds of prey. More than that, they were the most massive birds of prey she had seen or ever would see.

She watched them gain height and, as they reached the sunlight, Somerledaa saw they wore coloured tags on the leading edges of their wings. She tried to recall where she had seen such decoration before. The rude background banter made by boisterous jackdaws jogged her memory. She recalled coloured decorations worn around their ankles by choughs foraging on the kelp-strewn beach at Porth Solfach on Ynys Enlli.

She watched the great birds circle ever higher and, while she watched, a buzzard soared up to challenge them. She was struck by this because, when still a white-coated pup, fattening on her mother's milk, Somerledaa had come to know the buzzard who often — inexplicably, not being a hunter of water-prey — overflew her bay and sometimes even perched on the crags overlooking it. In those skies, the buzzard was the largest bird of prey present, but this did not deter the intermittent harrying bestowed upon it by a variety of tormentors. Ravens and jackdaws were persistent harriers. It seemed to her he spent the most part of his time tipping his wings, climbing higher or losing height to avoid them. She used to wonder if they left him time enough to eat.

It had been the same on the Welsh and Manx coasts, but here things were different. The diffident bird who tolerated so much harassment farther south now emerged as the principal tormentor of birds far larger than itself. Now, just as the southern buzzards absorbed an excess of bullying, these sea eagles showed a lordly tolerance of their northern cousin.

Re-discovering her most purposeful mood, she foraged northward beyond the north entrance to the Sound with some small success. Afterwards, she ran with the current back into the Sound, sleeping below a salmon farm in which she could hear the limited movements and feel the pent-up desire for freedom of the entrapped fish. On the way upstream, she had found diversion in cruising just once along the drapery of armoured nets designed specifically to exclude seals far stronger than she. She had not seen the man, dressed in camouflaged clothing, very slowly move his rifle with its telescopic sights to bring her head into view. It was her sixth or seventh sense that made her dive when she did, causing the watching man to swear sharply under his breath.

She returned, unseen, after dark, thinking the place well-sheltered and quiet, but did not sleep well because she was receiving a stream of hysterical chatter. The unsettling noise of it came from the teeming thousands of closely-confined fish who did not recognise that, for all the remarkable size of themselves, they were but shadow-salmon. She had learned to recognise the glorious silver-gleaming sea-power of wild salmon. However, some escaped shadow-salmon she had met lately in her wanderings and these confused her. She had taken one off the Knapdale coast, noticing the difference in taste, in the texture of its skin, the floppiness and under-development of its fins, the greyness of its flesh.

Having slept poorly, Somerledaa slipped away northward again before the dawn. It was raining but the shower soon passed, only to be followed by another. That proved to be the way of it that day. After sunrise, there was an unending sequence of brief, fierce showers. The mountains appeared, disappeared, re-appeared as if by magic and, in the lovely cycle of it all, rainbows did the same. Before midday, thirty-six had tracked by in a primordial intensity of colours, each guiding in the next gauze curtain of fine rain.

Near the head of the Sound, Somerledaa ventured eastward into Loch Sunart. Near Glenbeg, undulating along the shore, she caught sight of another creature she had never seen before. Its tail was finer and bushier than that of any squirrel. It brought squirrels to mind when climbing deftly up the trunk of an ivy-clad oak. Somerledaa, transfixed, found it almost as wondrous as watching the sea eagles rising ever-upward on airs she assumed they must be too heavy to ride. Suddenly, a smaller creature she did recognise erupted from the ivy, sometimes bounding, sometimes flying through space, to ever-smaller branches in neighbouring trees.

Roiran the pine marten did not see it at first, for he had been searching for the nest of a blackbird he felt sure lived close by, but at the first leap of Tispandel the red squirrel, he felt a small tremor pass through the tree almost like an electric shock. Informed by instinct alone, the pine marten flared after the squirrel. With remorseless, mesmerising intelligence, he closed the gap between them. It was as if the squirrel was disadvantaged by having to think, choosing the way all the time, almost reeling in the yellow-throated marten.

Hunted and hunter swirled in a high-speed spiral around another big trunk down toward the earth. It had become an unequal contest. By now, there was only one possible outcome between them. The rare, yellow-throated pine marten feinted once, twice, a third time. The squirrel, rare, but less so than Roiran's kind, reacted once, twice before, fatally, pausing. He did not see the bright-eyed head of the hunter loom behind him, accelerate, and make the kill.

One rare animal slew another on the ribbed bark of the loch-side oak. Roiran carried the limp body to mossy ground below the tree. Somerledaa dived. Roiran glanced at the ripples, reading the signs correctly and feeling no fear. Somerledaa was wondering whether Roiran owned the same bright radar she used when pursuing fish.

She did not dwell on what she had just seen. Killing and being killed was the hallmark of nature. A pine marten cannot visit the supermarket or the farmer's market with a shopping list and money in pocket. Nature offers no guarantee of a next meal. The red squirrel's flight cannot always have a happy ending.

She swam into the long, narrowing waters of Sunart, the slightly curved northern frontier for the wild hills of Morvern, until she came to the large island that was not an island at low tide. It was situated below Camuschoirk and the magical woodland. Here, she hauled out on rocks already occupied by more than thirty harbour seals.

These seals lay closer to one another than the greys would have. There was a small amount of seal song. It was the first time Somerledaa had heard their language for those she had passed at Kitterland and subsequently had been sleeping. She listened without appearing to. Once her pelage was dry, thirty minutes later, she rested her chin on the warm rock without quite sleeping.

She found she could understand most of what passed between the harbour seals. Interpretation was difficult at first, mainly because of the Scottish accent they used. Nevertheless, the more she listened, the more she understood. Curious to know more, she made educated guesses to fill the gaps.

The dominant theme was wariness and a measure of anxiety. They were unused to seeing a grey seal so far inside this sea loch. Aware a small number of pioneer seals were forever seeking new sites, they wondered if she might be one-such. Neither did they recognise what they called her tartan. Out of their gossip, she wondered whether there might be physical features distinguishing grey seals that indicated from which regions or even localities they came.

One immature seal, a dark-coated male with the finer, harbour seal speckling of pale-ringed markings, came swashbuckling into the conversation between his elders and asked why did no-one speak to her and find out whether she had anything to share with them. He went on to say they would thereby relieve themselves of the need to gossip more with each guess as reliable in determining the truth as the next!

Never had Somerledaa heard an immature seal challenge his elders with such fearless insolence.

Their reaction was unsurprising; one of the males, very dark-brown in colour, surged aggressively toward the youngster who scampered to the nearby margin and dived into the khaki waters. There was growling approval for his chastising of the youngster but Somerledaa felt a pang of disappointment. In the precocious male, she had sensed novelty, something interesting she had not previously met in a seal.

She understood very well by now that seals tended to be conservative, careful.

Opening her eyes without moving her head, she scanned the waters without catching sight of the seal that was even smaller than she. Lifting her head and glancing sidelong at the nearest seals she found many heads returning her regard. They looked eager and friendly, but she was remembering their conversation. They had the good fortune to appear deceptively open-faced. Hearing the miniscule sound of surface waters parting, Somerledaa twisted her head and gazed across at the small head, darker now it was wet, of the small seal.

Alone, Og-dona lacked some of the braggarty courage he had shown on the island. He stared at her, trying to discern her intentions. Her attention disconcerted him. It made him feel like a target. Fearing she might slide into the water and approach him, he crash-dived, unsettling many of the seals on the island. One or two clearly considered stampeding into the water until recognising who had caused the alarm.

Somerledaa continued to stare after returning to the surface farther away, but when he crash-dived again, she knew she must be the cause of his agitation so, resting her chin on the rock once more, closed her eyes.

While she lay there, showers continued to track by, soaking her so that she tired of it and thought of re-entering the water, but then the sun would shine again, dry her again, leaving her with a sense of languor such as she had not felt since her earliest days, resting on the sun-warmed pool waters of the cave.

Most harbour seals lacked her patience, made their way back into the water. Not only were they wearied of repeated drenching, but also it was a time of year when they fed more copiously. In little more than a month, the firstborn pups would be appearing, so they were trying to reach peak condition before the debilitating trials of the nursery season.

Against the run of that tide, and to his own surprise, Og-dona returned to the haul-out site, resting close as he dared to Somerledaa. She sensed his anxiety and was afraid that if she made any move to communicate, he would flee again. They lay so for more than an hour when, after shifting position to make herself more comfortable, she was facing Og-dona. For a little while, she kept her eyes closed, but when she opened them, she caught Og-dona in the act of telescoping his neck and cupping his whiskers toward her as if to better discern her.

Very softly, she sang: "I am happy to talk, if it would please you."

His reaction was dramatic, becoming alert, poised to galumph into the waters of the sea loch. Ignoring it, Somerledaa continued, slowly in case he had difficulty understanding her accent or her language: "It is true I am a stranger here, for I am travelling, learning the world. Here, for example, it is very different from my home, which is far to the south, at the Land's End. Somerledaa is my name. And yours is?"

"Og-dona!" It came out abruptly and more highly-pitched than intended.

"This is your home, Og-dona?"

"Aye! You probably know that we are not great wanderers, like you grey seals. This is home to me. I try to be content with it."

"And with your companions?" she enquired, surrendering to the impulse to prick his anxiety by teasing him.

Og-dona gave a snort of improbable eloquence: "They grumble into their whiskers and talk about the world as if it was always so and ever will be. Maybe I will become like that. They tell me so. They tell me I am full of questions, dreams and opinions because I am young and that is what being young is about. But I look at them and wonder why should life become so dull. I can see it is good to bring pups into the world and it must be a pleasure to mate because that is why all the adult males strive against one another, but I wonder what else I might do. Moreover, I watch the greys and hear tales of their journeys and it makes me wonder whether I should go beyond waters I know, with their secure supply of food and dangers I understand, to explore the world beyond." He paused, and then dared to enquire: "That is what you are doing, you said? I do not know where Land's End is but I can tell from your accent it is nowhere near."

"Land's End is several days to the south, if you travelled without rest. I was born in a sea cave at the end of a peninsular very close to where the ocean divides. I have a sort of friend called Tyrian who told me that to the west, but for one small group of islands, there is no land for thousands of miles." While she was saying it, she wondered how Tyrian would feel at being called her friend, and wondered, for the first time, how he had come by his knowledge.

"It is the same here," Og-dona chorused. "We heard a grey male was caught in a run of storms and washed westward for so long he lost track of time. In the end, he came to a great crescent of sand on the edge of waters where once fish had been uncountable. Here were many tribes of whale, dolphin, porpoise and even seals. He saw great islands of ice creaking through those waters. He spent half a year there before he felt strong and courageous enough to try to find his way back home. In that, he succeeded; his accent changed forever from what it had been before. I cannot swear all that is the truth, but this story is widely known. Probably he came from the Monachs."

"Ah; the Monachs!" Several times, by now, Somerledaa had heard tell of this east-ocean capital of her kind. A seal metropolis they said, at the edge of the known world. Sometimes she wondered if there was more myth to it than reality: "Am I close to it here?" He heard her eagerness.

"For you, I guess it is half a day to the north-west."

Somerledaa fell silent. She carried no intention of visiting the small faraway islands already described so many times in conversations overheard. Now, with them so close, did she really want to go there after all?

Og-dona asked: "So, you understood what they were saying, before I was chased off the island." It was not quite a question.

"Yes. I heard what you said, too. I agreed with you although you didn't make it easy for your elders to hear the rightness."

Og-dona made an indeterminate sound that may have been impatience: "They never take young ones seriously. I spoke so because I am weary of not being taken seriously and because I feel I am right and they are wrong."

"That sounds fair, but I am young, like you. Was there something you wanted to ask me, now that you know I am not hostile?"

"I think you have told me what I might have asked."

"Then answer me this: do grey and harbour seals communicate with one another in these parts — not that I have seen any greys recently?"

"That is because they use more exposed sites; the western shores. We are there, too, but using quieter stretches. There are huge numbers of greys around small islands west of Mull in a long, broken arc as far as the west of Harris. We call it the grey road.

"As for communication: I know of none. I was taught it is best to give greys a wide berth because they can be aggressive. But that is not to say there is no communication, because what are we doing now? Yet, I think the greys like shores that feel the weight of Atlantic waves. Most often, they rest ashore on rocks while we might prefer sheltered rocks, mud or sand for our resting places.

"For the most part, we don't mix. I think we even hunt for different fish. I do not know what you choose to feast upon, given the choice. I prefer sandeels. They are abundant hereabouts, especially in the Minch; at least, there is sufficient during most years."

"What is the farthest place to which you have travelled? Indeed, how old are you?"

"Quite soon, I will begin my third year. As for my travels: that is easy! Just once, I was out in the Minch caught in a southerly gale. I took shelter in a beautiful loch on the east coast of South Uist. Loch Aineort, it is called, under a mountain called Ben More, like the one across the way towering above all the lesser heights of Mull. Just like Mull, I remember sea eagles and golden eagles, inhabiting the same skies. Red deer foraged in small herds across the high places, seemingly smaller than ants. There were red-throated divers, eiders and greylag geese nesting on the shores near common gulls and numbers of harbour seals to make me welcome and hear my traveller's tales. I listened to them in turn. It was they who told me of the grey seal places beyond the western shores of their islands and they it was from whom I heard of the grey road." He added lightly, gladly: "There! You have made me nostalgic and restless again, all in the one question!"

"Was it so good, this Loch Aineort?"

"Like here, with Mull-sized mountains and even more beautiful scenery! There was a great plenitude of fish. I hunted with great success there."

Somerledaa allowed a small pause to develop, for the sake of courtesy, before shifting her weight again:

"I am thinking it is time to be continuing on my way. I have no destination in mind, but I was wondering whether you would share the first part of the way with me, at least so far as the entrance to this loch?"

The little harbour seal did not contain his enthusiasm:

"Oh yes! Oh yes!" Somerledaa guessed correctly at the satisfaction it would give him to be seen travelling in company with the unexpected grey of uncertain temperament; but in doing so, she underestimated the sheer friendliness of this latest companion. Afterwards, when they had gone, each upon their own way, she recognised a difference in the natural friendliness shown by the harbour seals to her own kind, who were generally more reserved.

They went westward along the loch toward the sun at their slowest speed. Along the way, Somerledaa taught him to dance. It was not the most fluent of partnerships for both remained slightly inhibited by the difference between their species, but it was the final piece in the beginning of a lasting understanding. Forever afterwards, their attitudes were altered toward their cousin seals. The other species would never be so unfamiliar, again.

At the entrance to Loch Sunart, they drifted south simply because it was the way the tide carried them. They had a brief glimpse of the painted shops of the Tobermory waterfront until they disappeared behind Calve Island, whereupon with much puffing and snorting, a herd of six harbour porpoises travelling in close formation, bustled down the west side of the Sound, regularly breaking the quiet of the surface waters with breathy exertions.

Not long thereafter, they came through weed to Eilean nan Gabhar. Three harbour seals rested on these rocks, all becoming extremely alert as Somerledaa surged ashore. They reacted almost as sharply to Og-dona. Perhaps the presence of the latter inhibited their unwelcome. Instead, they stared in silence while the two seals sang to one another, continuing their conversation, chins again resting on the rocks. For that small period, the rains held off and the sun shone so that all five seals grew drowsy. Conversation lapsed.

Somerledaa had not closed her eyes, but was watching the movements of the water when she saw a tiny seal pup swimming by, or thought so until it dived, when it was followed underwater by a long, thick tail.

The next time the otter surfaced, it carried a writhing eel in its smiling, whiskered mouth. Somerledaa and, sensing something amiss, Og-dona watched as Mhic-ciara the otter rolled over on to its back, beginning to eat noisily and with relish. Feasting brazenly under the seals, the flow carried it southward until it dived again, carrying the silvery fish with it.

When it re-surfaced, it had propelled itself back upstream, as if its whim was to reprise the feasting run below the watching seals. Once more drifting on its back, still chewing noisily, it drifted by, oblivious to all but the succulence of the eel, of the meal. After a third pass, the otter came out on a lesser rock, not far distant, where he remained preoccupied with his meal. Indeed, so preoccupied was he that he failed entirely to see the eagle gliding along the far shore. Gliding just above the level of the trees, head turning this way and that, far-seeing eyes noted the addition to the regular gathering of seals on the rocks off the east shore of the Sound. Otter. Mhor-Sithean banked around, glimpsing the silver and white of the mainly uneaten eel and came directly across the quiet waters.

The seals saw her immediately and stirred, made restless by the directness of her approach. One harbour seal did not wait, but went crashing immediately into the water. His two companions shuffled to the edge of the water, undecided. Perhaps Somerledaa and Og-dona were tardy in recognising the menacing approach of the sea eagle because they were more completely fascinated by the nearby otter.

Mhor-Sithean was very close, beginning the stall that was her prelude to landing on the rock and, if need be, the wet brown otter. Her great wings were lifted high, catching the wind and stealing the light, scaring Somerledaa and Og-dona so completely they went crashing into the water, Og-dona performing an inadvertent back flip in the process.

For Mhic-ciara, it was different. He turned his small head, fragments of eel clinging to his whiskers, toward the seals in the moment they crashed into the water. Simultaneously, he recognised the sound of wind in the wings of the looming eagle. In the next moment, his head was twisted around in the opposite direction. It was a terrible shock, seeing the eagle almost filling his vision. He gave no more thought to his getaway than had the two small seals but leaped, writhing, through the air into shallow waters on the shoreward side of the rock. The eagle had inadvertently cut off the opportunity to make any other escape.

He leapt, expecting at any moment to feel huge talons pierce his sides, but the waters closed over both his head and unpunctured sides even as the great brown bird, white tail spread, landed on his dining table. The otter surfaced at some distance, now on the seaward side of the rock. Then, when he recognised who had so frightened him and why, he streamed violent invective with bloodcurdling fury at the robber baron who had already placed one proprietorial talon on the stolen booty. It was not the first time he had been robbed and he felt an almost insensate desire to drink the blood of this enormous enemy, but the size of the eagle kept him marginally on the side of reason.

Now the pale head, having scanned the nearby surroundings, lowered to the slender meal. The massive yellow bill tore off a strip of eel larger than that already eaten by the watching otter. As she feasted, her fierce eyes glanced from the heads of the watching seals across to the smaller one of the otters.

In little time, the eel was gone. Having feasted, Mhor-Sithean looked about her as if the audience was over, as if allowing that now the rest of the world might eat. She did not linger long on the small rock because the tide, almost full now, was threatening her talons. With greater difficulty than it had taken to land, she lifted from the rock leaning into the air, bound for the shoreline trees of Mull and a familiar larch bough that offered a quiet perch upon which to digest the plundered meal.

Somerledaa accepted it for a token of the need to be upon her way. Having made a short, friendly farewell to her cousin seal, she ventured with refreshed purpose northward toward the west end of the long Ardnamurchan Peninsular. It was easy going and she went without haste. It was time for her to feast again, to eat, once more, a meal that left her sated. She did so beyond the reach of any eagle.

Farther north than she had ever been she found herself, but then, it had always been so, ever since she had set out from home. No longer close to shore, she ventured out into the clean power of the ocean swell, abounding with auks and shearwaters, as well as gulls and skuas whose trade was robbery brazen as that of Mhor-Sithean. The farther west she travelled, the more she saw of brigand birds alighting on the backs of gannets that had risen from the surface of the sea having made their catch. In the mêlée, the captured fish would be dropped or disgorged, whereupon the remarkably agile and graceful skuas would stoop to retrieve the tribute that had been rendered.

However, despite the glut of extraordinary and different things she seemed to be seeing, she continued to spend at least four-fifths of her travelling time while in the sea submerged in travelling mode. She identified some far mark and travelled toward it with no deviation except that caused by tide or tidal stream. At such times, long periods passed when it seemed she moved hardly at all.

Sometimes, she would deviate to explore novelties.

Most often, her explorations were associated with hunting. If the floor of the sea was flattish, she would glide over the plain of it, glad of any weed-decorated rock or sponge, anemone and hydroid-decorated wreck. There, she would become extraordinarily acrobatic and resourceful in her efforts to examine whatever caught her attention. Then, she might ignore or even try to play with fish or crabs or the wisely unfriendly, hole-anchored lobsters.

Her adventures close to island shores were another source of pleasure. She might spend hours seeking out perfect underwater resting places, often in seaweed forests. At such times, if other seals were about, she might conceal herself to watch what they did. At other times, she would search through the weed as if expecting to find a companion who would share play in and out of the tide-swirl of it all. Most often, after feeding she would identify an underwater rock that offered security from disturbance before taking the deeper of her sleeps. Then, she would sleep underwater for perhaps up to eight minutes at a time before surfacing on automatic. There, she would pass a minute taking in breaths of air before submerging again for a similar period of deep rest. Mostly, this could be achieved without waking, but where some small drama was being played out, part of her mind would come to the alert, feeling around to be sure it contained no menace. Then sleep drew the wakeful element back to itself and she would sink again, slowly, through the shallow water column.

Now far from shore, she concentrated on feeding. Although impulse had brought her to these waters, perhaps the motor driving impulse was instinct, distilled from all the charts she had compiled to date. Unwittingly, she had reached the happiest of hunting grounds, hunting mainly by night because there was an enormous shoal of herring moving through the Minch. For the first time in her life, for days on end the hunting was easy.

For several weeks, she ranged about the Sea of the Hebrides while the days grew longer and the seas slightly warmer. At the northern reach of her roving, she hunted the eel-strewn waters of Little Minch.

Here, she had the impressive peaks of the Outer Hebrides marching along the sunset horizon of her world while the light of each new day spread from behind the even more impressive peaks of Skye and mountains behind the Scottish west coast. These felt like the wildest waters that could ever be, but were not.

She ranged south, too, as far as the gaps between Barra and the nearby fangs of Mingulay and Berneray, at the southern extremity of the Outer Hebrides; then back inshore she hunted, to sunny, fertile Tiree.

Excitingly for Somerledaa, her adventure coincided also with massive seaward movements of sprats that had over-wintered in the sea lochs and elsewhere. She was also marauding across the nursery and rearing ground for many other kinds of fish, some of which she sampled along the way. Despite the ease of her hunting, she remembered to be wary of the silhouettes and sounds of the fishing boats with whom she was sharing this bounty.

For the most part, she conducted her hunting expeditions in the dark hours between dimpsey and midnight. In this, did she realise it, she was another puppet dancing unwittingly to the tune of the myriad plankton.

Every spring, when the sea settles, a bloom of phytoplankton — plant plankton — develops, drawing sustenance from nutrients accumulated in the water column. In that profusion of fertile sea dust, a great struggle determines which species will become dominant in the bloom. That species can literally overshadow its competitors and even produce toxins, deploying a natural form of chemical warfare to help them maintain their dominance.

What glut of anything in life is unattended by predators?

Grazing on the teeming pastures of plant plankton are equally teeming hordes of animal plankton. Among the largest and most distinctive of these is a copepod lacking a common name known as *Calanus finmarchicus.*

Mysterious and obscure as a word, the copepods form the second largest class of crustaceans, with more than twelve hundred species occurring in British waters. Their obscurity is mainly due to their microscopic size, along with wariness people may feel when encountering their name. But how strange is any name? Translated from its Greek origins, it means nothing more than oar-foot while, in appearance, it resembles a twirling moustache.

Calanus finmarchicus is an accidentally important exception to the general obscurity of its kind. Well-known, now, it owes its name to the Evangelical Bishop of Trondheim, Johan Ernst Gunnerus. In the northernmost province of Norway, in 1765, he drew a phial of clear water from an inlet of the sea that contained the tiny creature known thereafter as *Calanus finmarchicus*. Gunnerus, in describing it, was also giving the first-ever description of a planktonic organism.

Visible to the naked eye, it has a segmented body with five pairs of what look like legs and one pair of segmented antennae that are as long as the rest of its body. These are agitated to generate a large vortex in the water all around the body that, in effect, draws the phytoplankton prey to itself.

Why were they so incidentally important to Somerledaa?

Despite being just tiny specks of life, they are capable of stupendous feats of vertical movement through the water column during the cycle of day and night or, more specifically, of light and dark. In effect, from midnight until mid-afternoon, *Calanus* is likely to be at the deepest places of its daily migration and there dispersed randomly. In the waters where Somerledaa was hunting, between mid-afternoon and midnight they were closest to the surface in their greatest numbers, feeding voraciously on the phytoplankton, unaffected by civil war or chemical weaponry.

What glut of anything in life is unattended by predators?

Calanus the Hunter was, in turn, the hunted. Calanus is the favourite food not only of the ubiquitous herring, the silver darlings, but of the huge, rather stately basking sharks. Hunting Calanus, they came. Small, silvery Somerledaa came, too, her strings unwittingly strummed by the dinner gong of Lilliputian dust motes of life, *Calanus* among them.

It was harder to miss a fish than take one and, in the excitement of the fabulous hunt, sometimes the instinct to chase and take outran her appetite. Then, she snapped or tore at fish she would never eat, injuring or killing them.

She was far from being the sole hunter haunting these enormous shoals.

Through the water, clear and ever more familiar came sounds she recognised, like the excitement clicks on a sharply ascending scale of hunting porpoises, so often neighbours in whichever habitat she foraged. She saw much larger, battleship-grey bottlenose dolphins, visiting from more customary haunts at the south end of the Outer Hebrides. Then, she began to notice how the black rolling barrels — her fellow travelling porpoises — and the gypsy dancer white-sided dolphins would go silent and disappear. They knew the bottlenoses as beefy bully boys, capable of giving them a tough time, wounding or even killing them.

She saw other dolphins who, previously, she had recognised only by each their own signature of clicks. Smaller than bottlenoses, white-sided and, more occasionally, white-beaked dolphins sheared along, fast and faraway, surfacing often. In celebration after a fine feeding, up off Canna, eleven white-sided dolphins put on a glorious show of breaching, sometimes somersaulting through the air. It continued without inhibition for almost ten minutes before their joy wearied. Drawing together, they set off at high speed as of one mind toward open water.

This coincided with distant sounds she had heard, without recognition, only twice before that made the hair on her neck stand on end. This time, rather than hasten to a precautionary hiding place, she remained periscoping at the surface.

At the time, her good fortune was to be in shallows adjacent to Hyskeir, far south-west of Canna. Perhaps due to an imprint left by her earliest adventure, daring to swim to the rocks off Lands End, she found herself often choosing to rest on remote sea rocks from which a light stalk sprouted. In her wanderings across the Sea of the Hebrides, whenever she felt the desire to come to shore, she used exclusively the rocks under the lighthouses at Skerryvore and Hyskeir.

She had been hearing the far-distant sounds since the previous evening. Initially hardly noticing them against the commotion of background noise, she became aware of a repetitive sequence of sounds that snared the attention of her bright mind.

She was certain the sounds were closer now and once she felt she saw something briefly stir the distant surface — distant to her from sea-level but, in reality, not far away at all. Or, had it been a wave shadow? Wave shadows, as she had learned, could be such tricksters. She continued to stare.

The sea, she knew had a talent for tricking her eyes. Many were the occasions, already, where her eyes had misled her, in contrast with her vibrissae, which never failed her.

Another wave shadow? Another trick of the eye?

Causing least disturbance to the water, she submerged, still hearing the occasional familiar-strange sounds being broadcast, but now interspersed with other sounds. These were low frequency grunts, thumps, and boings; uttered by what? She had heard them elsewhere, too. Several times she had heard them without, yet, making a visual connection between sounds and sound-makers.

Maybe she had missed the apparent coincidence of the two sets of sound-makers previously. This time, she was sensitive enough to pick up the deeper sounds that she did not fear along with another occasional brief ones that seemed somehow to be insinuated into the otherwise familiar pattern.

Her minutes of attention lengthened to hours. Holding station off the lighthouse, it took time for another impression to register, that an unusual number of seals were crowding on to this resting station. Many times, the usual seals assembling behind her were exuding acute anxiety. Whenever the wash of surf moved her to look at them, she saw they remained alert, staring in the direction of the sounds and the intermittent wave shadows that fascinated her.

What was happening? Tension was flooding her world.

The day had been grey, with only a light wind blowing, but the white cumulus clouds piling in from the west had blue windows through which, eventually, sunlight leaked. It was in the very first sunbeam that the umpteenth wave shadow was illuminated and stripped of its disguise. A fin reflected silvered light and close by another fin silvered soon after.

The temptation, equally irresistible to young dolphins, seals and humans, alike, was to discover what was happening. She succumbed.

She swam slowly northward, toward the west end of Canna, all senses straining.

There was some discomfort inherent in submerging, now. She sensed strain in the sounds she was hearing, an evolution toward desperation; strain and exhaustion. Yet, the unquenchable desire to know lured her onward.

Out of the silvering sunlight, the fins were black and one, maybe two, were upright and exceptionally tall. Here were dolphins, but considerably larger than any she had seen before.

They were hunting. Of that, she was certain. That she continued slowly toward them was because she had been ignored by every dolphin pod she had ever met.

Like trying to understand a foreign language, not knowing the meaning of the sounds, Somerledaa reverted again to instinct. She sensed distress. Great distress, with a very occasional chirrup of hunting language interspersed; and she sensed true.

During the night, eight hungry orcas had been drawn to the low frequency grunts, thumps and boings uttered by a female minke whale closely accompanied by her calf just five months old. Smallest and by far the most abundant of the baleen whales in the Sea of the Hebrides, they had been moving northward off Skerryvore when the pack intercepted them — ever since, the killer whales had been trying to separate mother and calf.

Time passed. The hunters did not relent. Their attacks became more extravagant. Twice in the last hour, the great male, Ob-Zemlya, had breached and landed across the blowhole of the frantic mother while the eldest female, the matriarch of the pod, Oba-Talitscar, attacked the minke calf, inflicting a deep wound near the shoulder of one of his white-banded pectoral fins.

The fresh blood in the water provoked a quickening in the frequency and ferocity of the orca attacks. The change of tempo exhausted both mother and calf and, before long, separated them for the first time. After the first success, the separations became steadily more commonplace. Every time it happened, the calf was attacked and wounded again. The hunting was confusingly swift, remorseless and unfailing.

The tripwire moment came when Ob-Zemlya hurled himself across the blowhole of the minke mother again just as she was surfacing to breathe. Ten seconds after he had floated free of her, the younger male, Ob-Okhtosa, imitated his leader. This time they created such a turmoil of disorientation and fear in the desperate mother that the calf was fatally isolated.

Being transient hunter-killers, the dread attackers knew what would happen and what to do when it did. They co-ordinated a seemingly frenzied group attack on the wallowing distressed calf that was not frenzied. Calculated, clinical and lethally effective it was, born of long, daily practice. These moves they practised repeatedly even when there was nothing to hunt. The females drove in. Oba-Talitskya breached and fell across his blowhole while, almost simultaneously the young whale was savaged on both sides by younger females, raking him with their teeth. As the calf gasped and swallowed water, Oba-Talitskya tore at his tongue. While the two males distracted the minke mother, the kill was made. No single blow ended it but exhaustion, loss of blood and spirit. In extremis, the calf turned toward death as a refuge from the sudden brutal horror of life.

Not so his mother. With unthinking courage, driven by her great mothering instincts, she drove in among the excited, milling killers, and half opening a passageway toward her calf. She had a sharply pointed head. From the tip of her snout back to her twin blowholes, there ran a distinct ridge. Her snout caused a primary parting of the waters as she drove along at the surface. A secondary parting fell away to both sides of the central cranial ridge.

Before the powerful desperation of this progress, the attacking killers fell back. They did not fear her. There was nothing in all the world they had ever thought to fear. They knew the calf was dying or dead. They recognised the last few moves were being played out before the wild feast. The outcome had been pre-ordained, once they had picked up the trail of the couple. This drive to the side of her slain calf was just a late move that changed nothing.

Alone, beyond hope of succour, the minke mother continued to shepherd her dead calf across the wasteland of the afternoon and to the setting of the neutral sun; life giver. It was a long vigil of the heart, but it was not in her gift to alter the outcome, to bestow a second life upon her young. The doom of her calf was written not in the afterglow of this sunset but that of the previous, painless day.

The battle and its long aftermath had brought the orca pod and the two minkes quite close to the Hyskeir shore. Somerledaa had long since surged up out of the sea there, starkly afraid. There she stared, rigidly alert, differing not at all in her attitude from all the other seals about her

After the sun had hidden its face behind the Outer Hebridean mountains, Ob-Zemlya, who was slightly longer than seven metres, came up from underneath the minke mother and drove into her underside, causing her to flinch her pointed snout steeply up out of the sea and then to dive steeply to escape these beautiful pain-bringers. In her flight, some members of the pod harried her while others commenced the feast. The waiting was over. And who is to say that the forlorn death of the minke calf may not have been the reason Somerledaa and her voracious curiosity lived to see the next sunrise from the shallow rocks spread below the white Hyskeir lighthouse?

In that sunrise, Somerledaa was still a small seal in a crowd of anxious grey seals. None yet dared to venture their shallow bastion into the deadly sea to essay a passage into the realm of the pitiless killer whales. They remained terrified.

The black fins were no more to be seen. They had departed under cover of darkness. The minke mother had lethargically gone upon her calfless way. She did not return to the tattered, barely recognisable remnants of her calf after the feast. Her mind, for the time being, was blank. Instead, the remains, floating at the surface, became a food island for gulls, fulmars and skuas. The seals heard and saw them, soullessly riotous and quarrelsome at their lavish banquet.

Inshore, on the wave-lapped rocks, still no seal entered the sea. At the outskirts of the assembly, Somerledaa thought of going to the water's edge and began, slowly, to move in that direction, but still she dared not enter the sea. Her senses had been mazed by the terrifying drama of the last twenty-four hours. She had learned dread. It made her stop, baulking at slipping off the rock into the inviting sea.

Hardly any time passed before the tip of a straight dorsal fin pierced the surface membrane of the sea. There were nicks in the after-edge near its apex. Almost two metres high, it rose steadily until the middle part of the back of Ob-Zemlya came into view. Then a second dorsal fin showed and a third, until eight killer whales were in view about fifty metres from where Somerledaa lay. They were close together and side by side, without quite being in a straight line. Largest of dolphins, the killer whales simply grew until they were massive. Most handsome of dolphins, most deadly of assassins in any ocean, tall-finned and indomitable, they tracked toward where she had frozen.

Her sense of shock electrified, she hardly dared breathe. Likewise, shocked, one hundred and twenty-two other seals dared not move and did not think to breathe.

At their slowest speed, the killer whales paraded around the island, maintaining a constant distance

At close quarters, they looked exquisitely clean in their mainly black and white livery. Now was one of the times Somerledaa was appointed to die. This, she knew with awful certainty, and yet she waited almost with gravity as Ob-Zemlya cruised slowly by, seeming to regard her with an eye that did not seem so deadly or even unfriendly under its flaring elliptical eyebrow.

Fascinated more than fearful, hypnotised by that gaze before it released her, she watched the incredible length of him pass by. She had to look up at the dorsal fin, noticing the detail of it. There was a relatively slender grey saddle immediately behind the fin and then half a body's length of black back, trailing to tail flukes set on the horizontal axis that hardly moved as he drifted beyond her sight.

She did not see them veer seaward. She did not see them gather speed, surging forward with all the grace and power of their kind. This time, they were really going.

Much later in the day, the grip of their spell was slackening. Somerledaa fell asleep. The following morning, she discovered many of her companion seals departed. Now it was her turn. There was delight, not fear, in feeling the lovely salt waters close over her small head again. She set course for a recently-discovered favourite bank beyond the west end of Canna, suddenly aware of sheer empty-bellied hunger. At her comfortable travelling speed of about four miles per hour, she flowed along. Nothing befell her until she was almost there, but when that thing did happen, it was singularly dramatic.

She had been aware of more thumps, grunts and boings as she swam along. These, she could now recognise as belonging to a minke whale. She was not alarmed because there were no hunting sounds among them, but she was briefly extremely alarmed when a great, green trawl net broke the surface less than one hundred metres ahead of her and continued to move directly toward her though there was no trawler in sight. Through the netting she heard, but failed to see, a sharp blow of expelled air before the grey back followed the green-netted head and then, far back, a sharply curving dorsal fin.

After the initial appearance of the netted head, the minke whale continued to make gliding, shallow appearances at the surface. Four more times, the green net and the long male whose head it entangled appeared. Somerledaa had not waited this time, but had swum strongly from the path of the oncoming whale. Consequently, she could better-observe the sharp-pointed head of this adult more than eight times her own scant length.

Seaweed was growing on the net and pieces of marine debris were snagged in its meshes. The topside of the net was pressing into the distinctive ridge running from his twin blow-holes to the tip of the snout.

The whale passed close to Somerledaa who submerged as he passed and swam even closer, the better to see him as he struggled along. That way, she achieved a glimpse of the vivid white central bar across the nearside flipper and the big egg of white ballooning along his central belly. As she swam in brief company, the distressed whale uttered another resonant boing of gravest distress that vibrated through her body so she must forever afterwards recognise the source of it while also remembering this tragic moment.

She was back at the surface when the minke surfaced for a final time. This time he emerged more powerfully, back arching strongly as he readied himself to try for the deeper, longer dive the net was bound to deny him. After he was gone down, she fled at her fastest speed from the waste and pity of it.

It had been her tentative plan to explore the length of the indented and islanded west coast of Mull but this encounter broke her resolve. Too much that was strange and alarming was beginning to crowd her present. She began to hunger for what she felt to be normal.

Later, she hauled ashore on Eilean nan Gabhar. Several harbour seals lifted their small heads, regarding her in a manner the small grey had come to recognise as customary, although one brown adult male had extended his neck over the edge of the rock before she hauled out and growled at her in warning. Not caring much about him, she came directly up on to the rocks at a place not far removed from the nearest female. She did notice Og-dona was absent before she fell deeply asleep, even before her pelage had time to dry.

That night, while the great wheel of stars travelled above her heedless head, she dreamed of home. She saw the bay, the sea caves, the offshore reef and the great lighthouse with the famous name. She saw Mornalas, Ithian and Tyrian. She saw her father, Meinek. She did not see the pups she had encountered in her days of transition to a workable independence. Neither did she imagine the reason she did not dream them was they were gone from the world. While she had wandered far and prospered in herself and in her companions, they had died their unremarked deaths.

The next morning dawned much as the previous one. The breeze was being warmed by the sun. She could hear the voices of songbirds in trees and bushes singing the sweet songs of the season. Not far away, the male who had growled at her was leaning against another brown male of similar size, neck to neck, in a trial of strength. From the leaning, they should learn which of them was the stronger. So long as that happened, they would have no need to engage in a potentially bloody dispute about who had pre-eminence, about who should be recognised as king of the small rocks, their small kingdom. They were like the greys in that: always trying to avoid unnecessary bloodshed, to avoid disabling a fellow seal to the point it was unable thereafter to hunt and, therefore, to survive.

Somerledaa paid them little heed. Her head was turned south. The snows had almost gone from the high places of the island across the

290

Sound. Swallows were swooping low over the waters. Spring was displacing winter, even so far north.

The Monachs were forgotten, set aside for another time. The tug had become too strong. It was time to be heading south, to be returning home.

***

During his adventure in North Wales, Amber heard the sea-wetness and sun-brightness in his voice when they talked on the phone. She had read it in the language he used in the unexpected flurry of letters bearing the silver dragon postage stamps mailed to her from places with the unfamiliar names he had learned to pronounce. They were names she hunted down on the Ordnance Survey maps he had left for her.

Up there, she sensed he had been encouraged to flex previously cramped wings. He had breezed along, serious, focussed, happy and irresistible; sharing with her another of the men he was capable of being.

His adventure was planned to culminate in a series of meetings at the research unit. Meantime, he had given a presentation about grey seals, in effect the story so far, by invitation at the university. Planned in advance, the lecture had drawn a satisfyingly large and diverse audience.

The next day had been the day for signing the contract. Consequently, despite his customary reserve about things existing only once they existed and not while they remained just a dream, he came buoyantly into the building. Upstairs, he walked buoyantly to his appointment with a team of people he believed he had only spoken to by telephone. Arriving, he met the project leader and recognised immediately that he had been in the audience the night before.

Soon thereafter, the bombshell exploded. He was told there had been a technical problem securing the funding and there were unresolved problems with the contracts section. There could be no progress in the current financial year. The gist of the message was 'maybe next year'.

From the ashes, the people to whom he would have answered retrieved what they could. He spent some time with the statistician, running over everything to do with what they wanted to accomplish and how they were going to do it. Crucially, they devised the database in which all detail of the work would be stored. As far as Amaury was concerned, the creation of such a database was sheer magic. Dafydd ap Seimon was the magician. He proved to be not exclusively some pale creature with bulbous eyes dwelling in a subterranean labyrinth, but someone excited also by the physical world.

The database was not, and could not be, created that day. It came in the electronic mail two weeks later to west Cornwall, being batted back and forth for a few weeks to tease out the flaws. The penultimate review was carried out by the chief scientist before Amaury scanned it for the final time.

In the wake of the disappointment, it served for some sort of compensation.

When he came home to Amber, he was as glad to see her as she might have hoped.

After they had returned from the timber and glass studio in her garden where she worked her carvings to life, he startled her by explaining he was committed to two hectic months of wildlife trips out of Dartmouth through June and July. He needed to refresh his coffers. When he asked her if she could make space in her life to share the interlude ahead, she smiled the radiant smile he had discovered was in her gift.

He had arranged to use a caravan for the summer in a combe about ten miles from the sea. It was owned by a friend. Sean Grey had created there one of the largest orchards in Devonshire. Some of the fruits were for eating, some for cooking; the majority were for cider-making. It was the cider-making that was his favourite and most successful enterprise, but he also kept huge numbers of free-range hens, ducks and geese under the trees, sufficient to make him a regionally-important supplier of eggs through the year and of poultry before Christmas.

He was a wealthy man with many interests and inexhaustible energy.

He had invited Amaury back for a nightcap having enjoyed an evening of badger-watching he had organised to add value to the wildlife cruises. They found they liked one another. The seeds of friendship were planted. Soon thereafter, Sean sought out Amaury, asking if he wanted to use the caravan he kept in one of his orchards for accommodation while working on the boats so far from his Cornish home.

On Midsummer's Day, Amaury, accompanied now by Amber, returned like a swallow to the caravan. They looked well together, Sean thought, aloud. He had prepared a light supper. Afterwards, they went out on to his veranda to watch the day turn through dimpsey while damselflies hovered and darted over the still, dark waters of a large pond where, later, Daubenton's bats flittered and swooped to murder moths. Somewhere along the valley through which meandered the stream that replenished the waters of the pond, they heard pheasants returning to their roosts. Closer by, just around the first bend, a tawny owl called, setting the field mice a-tremble and causing Amaury and Amber to exchange a private smile.

Just then, he was sitting on the ground, barefoot, one arm coiled about her shin. It was a secret code they had devised for their time in company, reminding her he had not forgotten her. When his arm moved around both legs, briefly, she smiled and blushed, unseen in the evening shadows. That also belonged in their code book, although the need for small reassurances had dwindled.

In the days following, she shared all his boat trips. In the high season, between late July and Regatta, he made one trip daily in a large passenger boat carrying up to two hundred passengers that lasted for two hours. On those trips, he came aboard solely to give commentaries. However, he had also a skipper's ticket entitling him to carry passengers along the coast.

The family company did not have a boat available to carry large numbers of passengers along the coast. They did own a beamy and very seaworthy little boat with an open wheelhouse, the roof of which extended halfway to the stern. She did not look attractive, despite her cheering pale blue-turquoise and white paintwork, but the roof offered some shelter whenever the summer rains fell.

The clinker-built boat had started life as a crabber in the late 1930s before being converted to serve as a River Dart ferry boat after the outbreak of the Second World War. All her life, she had remained in the same family so now she was regarded as an heirloom; that being so, years passed before it was agreed he be given the chance to see if she could be made profitable.

He found he was able to run two ninety-minute trips either side of the period of low tide. It maximised the prospect of seeing grey seals out on the rocks of the river-mouth archipelago, these being advertised as the likely highlight of any trip. At times, when the weather was fair, he ran a third trip out along the coast in the evening. These trips were mainly for pleasuring in the atmosphere of the Devonshire coast at the end of the day, for the timelessness of it and — for the passengers — something romantic.

In the first year of operation, the success of the small, slow boat was patchy. He had worked from April through to late July and again through September and October. Little effort had been invested in advertising.

The routine made life difficult for Amaury. He had to be prepared to travel the one hundred and twenty miles to Dartmouth, reckoning on taking two and a half hours if he left Porthgwarra at about five in the morning, in response to a phone call received the previous evening. When life was at its busiest, it had been a tight squeeze, fitting in his efforts to collect data on seals using the sites he was monitoring.

Things came good after he tried his hand at advertising. The results were so good that the company stepped in to develop what he had started.

Now, then, Amber was walking hand-in-hand with him along the embankment beside the crowded waters of the Dart. They walked slowly, enjoying the warmth of the sun, the gentle breeze; feeling at home, for this was his second home. In contrast with life at remote Porthgwarra, he seemed to know so many people to speak to and more by sight. He knew where to shop, where to buy lunch or go for supper. He knew where to park their campervan, despite the overwhelming pressure on the summertime parking places. He knew about births and deaths and who had just split up and how they felt about it; in turn, he was known and mainly liked because he had no quarrel with anyone, even boatmen from the rival companies. He intended to keep it that way. When he was alone, it was not quite the same. There were one or two men working to maintain the boats who disliked him. Life had its rougher edges. He noticed Amber had a talent for melting tough men. When she was present, their manners improved.

They stopped to watch herring gulls menacing people eating fish and chips near the Station Café, wondering whether they would land in someone's Styrofoam tray today, spilling their chips. They watched a big man declaiming there was no way it would happen to him when, shockingly, it did. The act of banditry shocked everyone. Chips spilled across a large area of the absurd, impractically scalloped tiling that had changed the character of a quay once used mainly by working boatmen. The man froze while four gulls made smash-and-grab visits to the chips, flying away again before the swiftest reacting person tried to kick the last of the gulls and another flailed his arms to deter more from robbery.

Amaury looked at the loud-mouthed man feeling not the least trace of sympathy for such a fool. Had he been a child, he would have felt differently, not least because gulls were smart enough to have started targeting them.

Aware why he was slightly out of control, Amber squeezed his arm to capture his attention, narrowing her eyes in disapproval. She watched him try to compose a graver face, continuing as the attempt disintegrated. He started to laugh and continued until his eyes began to leak and his sides hurt. It was infectious, causing others around him to smile or laugh, while Amber could not but smile, too. She dragged him on, in front of the café, so that they could no longer be seen by the big man who had been scowling in their direction, clearly recognising he was the likeliest butt of Amaury's mirth.

Having restored him to an acceptable state, they walked on to their meeting with Rob Mariner, who ran the company, sold the tickets and, at need, functioned invaluably as both shipwright and marine engineer.

He was a rock of a man only slightly softened by the ravages of how he had lived his life. Broad chested he was, his shock of grey hair bleached white by the sun and tousled by the wind. He was a

Dartmouth man, through and through, being able to trace his ancestry back to Elizabethan times. It was impossible, knowing his trade, knowing his ancestry or simply looking at him, not to recall Elizabethan times. Surely such men must have skippered the ships sailing out of Dartmouth across the Atlantic to the Newfoundland fishing grounds, trading with the Portuguese or fighting with the Spanish anywhere in the North Atlantic that began with the letter C from Cadiz to the Channel to the Caribbean. Endlessly capable, unflappable, blunt without ever intentionally being rude and always busy; that was Rob Mariner.

Perhaps it was also a mark of his character that though he never got on any better than 'well enough' with Amaury, his real liking that June day he reserved for Amber, having taken to her at first sight. Amaury understood Rob; he was the kind of man with little time for any other man except a small number of lifelong local friends. By the same token, he trusted Amber from the outset, recognising the earthy friendliness and the essential honesty of her.

Excluded, Amaury walked to the edge of the quay. Having climbed down the steel ladder, he rowed the punt easily from the ferry pontoon toward the nearest moorings. The strong, unsubtle reminder of the tide forced him to row harder. His discreet struggle concluded when he drew alongside the faded turquoise and white hull of the Chanticleer. He took a couple of turns of the painter around the midships post, securing the punt before hauling himself aboard and running the few checks on the inboard engine that needed be made. He swabbed the decks, scrubbed the white ceramic gull droppings from the paintwork they were burning.

The essential chores done, he brought Chanticleer across the mainstream to starboard in a sharpening curve, settling her, snug as could be, at the seaward end of the ferry pontoon, bows into the tide.

He was about to jump back up on to the pontoon when a local ferryman forestalled him, boarding and squatting beside him so that their heads were at a level. Amaury liked this man. They had never shared a beer or even a mug of tea but they talked often of wildlife or river life because it was their shared interest. Will Beare was another Dartmouth man from another long line of Dartmouth men and women, but where Rob was a rock, Will lacked physical distinction. He was a softer-seeming man, strong in his convictions but not given to throwing his weight around, as rumour claimed Rob had done in his youth. As capable of shipwrighting as the bigger man, they had in common also their complete passion for the river and the vibrant town of Dartmouth. It showed in that while Will was the ferrymen's representative on the Dart Harbour Navigation Authority, Rob represented the pleasure boat interest.

By now, Amaury's own passions were well understood. He lacked the local pedigree but had made up for that by getting to know every inch of the river by foot and water. Its wildlife he knew especially well as it was his trade. While a small handful of local people might have known the river as well as he, none knew it better. He had talked to almost everyone who worked on it about their work and had visited farms with river boundaries to find out all he could. It was never enough for him to read the mainstream histories — repeated mistakes included — in books on the subject. He had camped by the river, explored it in all seasons along its length and, when one of the radio four local-colour programmes came to the Dart, he had been the man interviewed about local wildlife, aboard Chanticleer — of course.

Because he had spoken with such warm regard for the river and its people, most people who might have resented the upstart voice instead appreciated what he said and the way he said it.

Will said: "Just thought I'd tell you a couple of dolphins are in the river. Folk have seen them as far upstream as the Higher Car Ferry. Thought you might like to know."

"I would! Have you any description?"

"As you can imagine, descriptions vary; however, I saw them myself three mornings since, out by the Castle. They seemed quite interested in me. They fizzed around the ferryboat for a little while, until another boat came in and then they were off to play with that one."

Amaury raised his brows: "What size were they? Any colour or pattern visible?"

"Sure 'nough. Grey they were, on top at least; not very big, maybe eight feet long — hard to tell. You know what they're like. Seemed paler underneath. One of them tipped over as if to peer more closely at me, or so I fancied. Thought there was a pattern on its side and maybe a bit of colour. My impression was they were young ones, having a bit of fun."

"Well; that describes common dolphins." Seeing Will's face drop, he hastened on: "Some people call them the gypsies of the sea. They can appear in huge pods, super-pods, in the Channel some winters, but what these two are doing here and now I haven't much idea, unless they like the sounds of the big chains running to the river-bed from the main mooring buoys in midstream... Did you get any pictures?" He knew Will always carried a digital camera on board.

He looked shame-faced: "I know I should have been snapping away. Tell the truth: it was so fantastic having them so close, I clean forgot. Sorry!"

"No! I'd probably have forgotten, too. Cameras can get in the way as well as help, at times. What else have people said about them?"

"All sorts! I'm never quite sure who to believe. Mike Sawdye, you know, one of the harbour boys, has heard several reports of them playing around the chains of the main mooring buoys, like you were saying. Someone else says they saw them performing acrobatics at dawn not far off the Kingswear ferry pontoon. Other people say they have been swimming round and round some yachts resting at anchor."

Amaury sighed through his closed lips: "They must be commons, though I think your recollection of their size may be a bit on the generous side. Why they are here now, I can't imagine unless they are two youngsters doing their own thing, like you thought. Be sure I'll keep my eyes peeled! Thanks for telling me, Will!"

Straightening up with some effort, Will set his old-fashioned navy-blue cap back on his head, saying: "The mink is still around the seaward side of the castle. Reckon any gull nesting there will have no fledglings this year, which will be a relief of sorts for us living in town. Come 3.30 in the morning these days, they let us know they're awake, big time. I wonder anyone can sleep through such a cacophony! Take care, now." With that, having slapped Amaury on the shoulder, defying his bulk he stepped easily from the boat and strolled away along the pontoon, by the line of people queuing for the next pleasure boat to Totnes.

A few minutes later, Amaury followed him. As usual, he was wearing no shoes and his trousers were rolled almost to his knees. At the top of the ramp, he found Amber awaiting his arrival, smiling and relaxed. Glad, he touched her cheek fondly in passing. Rob had returned to the treadmill of selling tickets to passers-by he had intercepted with offers of watery delights...

Sheila, his wife, emerged from their kiosk as if to confirm the weather for the day would be fine. Smiling at him, she held out a list of twelve names: "Welcome back to Dartmouth! You look well! We have a full complement for the first trip and I think we'll get a second full complement. Do you have everything you need? Fuel? Grease?" The list might have grown but he arrested her flight of customary concerns by holding up both hands:

"I've checked everything. She is running beautifully and I felt her eagerness to be down to the sea again. I felt that," he added, pointedly, wickedly: "through the soles of my feet!"

His refusal to wear shoes had always been an issue of contention between them. Amaury insisted he felt safer at sea without shoes on his feet and claimed, less certainly but not less boldly, that to be barefoot was the traditional way of going to sea and so he was representing old Dartmouth rather than the politically correct modern-Dartmouth-modern-everywhere.

They had always got on well but now her attention flickered back to the quayside walkers who were about to brush by him without buying tickets:

"Are you interested in a trip on the river?" she began, leaving Amaury to fade away with Amber.

"So!" He contemplated her with brazen eyes: "Would you care to join me aboard Chanticleer? She has been longing to meet you"

He held out his arm and they proceeded down the gangway, steep now with the falling of the tide. She noticed him scowl at a man who almost bumped her in passing. The man seemed unaware of his offence but then flinched slightly and hurried on. At the foot of the gangway, turning winningly to her, he said:

"I hope you can forgive my rough waterside ways, my love."

"You know I don't," she retorted hotly, showing a flash of how cross he had made her.

They continued to stroll seaward. She was aware that though he had spoken the words, there was no shred of regret in him. Had he not told her often enough he usually apologised simply to allow the world to keep spinning around its axle-tree?

Arriving at the boat, he leapt aboard. It was something some of the boatmen did, something he had always done. Somewhere in the theatre of it, there was schooling in balance on the water being practiced. Having landed safely as ever, he pirouetted and extended up to her a gallant helping hand. She stepped down more sedately by way of a varnished thwart to painted duck-boards. She did not notice he stepped back to brace the boat against the way it would have rocked with her arrival. With his free hand, he indicated the cushion. He was smiling. She had learned his smiles were not always trustworthy.

Head resting to one side, accepting it, she leaned toward him and kissed his smiling, unresponsive mouth. She said softly to him: "How could I not forgive your rough waterside ways, my Amaury?" She seated herself, staring up at him with an air of expectancy. With a small shrug, he rummaged in the rucksack and held out for her the promised bag of red Italian grapes:

"I have also bread, cheeses and some apples — the ones you like best; and there is tea in the flask, as you will have guessed."

"Is there not a small something for yourself as well?" she enquired with seeming innocence.

He did not meet her gaze but groped until he withdrew a paper bag. With a sly glance at her, he withdrew a coffee-flavoured Swiss roll.

"Would you like a slice?" he asked, politely.

"Certainly not, disgusting man! You are going to eat all of it, aren't you?"

"I might," He was non-committal. Sitting beside her, he opened his penknife and made an incision. Time slipped by. They talked a little and looked about them while eating lunch. She ate mainly fruit. He ate the Swiss roll. She shook her head but anything she might have said by way of comment must perforce wait because a shadow fell across them. They looked up at a father followed by the gaggle of his family. He asked uncertainly:

"Are you running the 11.30 wildlife cruise?"

"Indeed, I am! Would you care to step aboard?"

Amaury uncoiled himself, rising to his feet while speaking. He helped Amber to her feet and moved the cushion to the long thwart running along the starboard side of Chanticleer so that she could be seated comfortably with no need to rise again. As soon as she was settled, he returned to the family, reached up a helping hand and, assisting the father on board, said:

"I am Amaury; Amaury Valneuve. Welcome aboard!"

The boat tilted a little but, Amaury, aware of all the possibilities, steadied the man as he stepped from thwart to deck. In turn, he helped three children and their mother aboard. The youngest girl would not accept the hand he proffered so he stepped aside, looking to the father, saying: "Dad?"

Once the family was aboard, the mother asked:

"Where is the best place to sit?"

"Anywhere!" Amaury answered, with a broad smile. Seeing the shadow of irritation threaten to inform her features, he bolstered his reply: "Really; anywhere. If you sit on this side, you'll be on the seaward side on the outward leg of the trip and the landward side when we return. On the other hand, if we see something interesting along the way, I'll manoeuvre the boat so that it can be seen by the people on the blind side, too. There will be no need to stand up. Everyone will get the best possible view in turn." Amber, temporarily forgotten, watched him soothe the persuaded woman and then, without seeming effort, discover whether they were local or not. It was neatly welcoming.

Clearly, they were inclined to be nervous while also wanting to get their moneys-worth. She knew very well that Amaury, under normal conditions, would have had scant patience for their attitudes and the ways of being that informed them. She was struck by it because it was the first time she saw how, given command, his character changed. On board, his was the responsibility. She knew he was amazed at the prices they paid for their tickets. He found it hard to believe a family could afford them, but she said he had spent so long in sea caves in recent years that he no longer had the least idea of the value of money.

Be that as it may, feeling they had borrowed his time in purchasing their tickets, he would do his best. For her, it made fascinating theatre, aware as she was that even if he made an improbable fortune, he would still have wanted to run these trips precisely as he was running them now.

Ten minutes before they were due to depart, the full complement of twelve passengers was settled aboard. Once the last of them was seated, Amaury addressed them:

"May I have your attention, everyone! As I mentioned, my name is Amaury so, if you need to ask me anything, that name will capture my attention. There are things I need to mention before we set out. Firstly, having sunshine and a gentle breeze, once out of the river in coastal waters, you'll feel hardly more motion than we have here, in harbour. Therefore, if you have any anxiety on that score, allow me to set your mind at rest.

"Secondly, I am required by law to point out to you these two life rafts, behind the central thwart. Lifejackets are stored beside me at the helm and in that locker below the stern thwart or seat. The key detail, however, is not to panic in the extremely unlikely event of an emergency. Simply await my instructions. It may reassure you to know I have lifesaving qualifications additional to the general requirements of a skipper of such a boat. If that sounds daunting or alarming, I can tell you that in the six years of my association with sea trips, we have had no emergencies.

"Thirdly: if anyone cares to borrow a pair of binoculars, I have four pairs and all are pretty good. All I ask is that you don't knock them against anything. The optics are sensitive and expensive to repair."

He handed out two pairs before continuing: "Every time we linger to watch something, today, I would ask you to remain as quiet as possible. Most of the creatures we can hope to see are sensitive to sound and human movement. They are easily disturbed. My aim — I hope our aim — is to observe them being their natural selves. That means we linger, make our observations and then pass on, leaving the place and the creature we have been watching undisturbed. Does anyone object to that way of doing things?"

Unsurprisingly, nobody did so. He added: "You can imagine the pressure on the remote sites we will visit today. In effect, if we cause disturbance today, and I cause disturbance day after day, then we will drive away creatures dwelling in places previously little visited. I am not in business to cause that to happen, so I will appreciate your co-operation in keeping the peace.

"Finally, this may be a cause of deep sorrow to you, but I shall give a commentary only on the outward leg of the trip. Returning, you will be forced to endure peace and quiet, only."

The smiles came then, as usual. A feature of pleasure boat commentaries in recent years had been for those giving them to generate a wall of sound, a flood of information larded with a liberal — in fact, crucial — sprinkling of jokes. Amaury had long since decided that if he was taking a trip, he would like to hear interesting and accurate facts, aware his might be a minority view.

"Right! Does anyone object if we depart five minutes early? We shall still return at the allotted time."

The adventure began. Raising his voice, turning his head to make himself heard above the relative quiet of the engine in its sound-proofed housing, he went on:

"We are heading to sea on an ebb tide, hoping to return at dead low tide. Reason we have timed the departure thus is to maximise the chance of seeing seals on rocks outside the river. Low tide is the best time for seeing them in maximum numbers. Because conditions are so quiet, I am hopeful of seeing them today, so long as no-one has beaten us there and scared them away.

Apart from the seals, there is a pair of common dolphins in the area, so watch out for them. They are small dolphins but extrovert, so if we come quite close to them, they will be easy to see. There are also seabirds and birds of prey to watch out for, so keep alert — mindful that when I am looking to port, the action may well be to starboard! If anyone sees anything interesting, speak up and share it. Best way of indicating that is by using the points of a clock. For example, dead ahead is twelve o'clock. Broadside on to starboard is three o'clock and broadside on to port is nine o'clock; and so on. Any questions, anyone?"

The son of the first family to come aboard asked:

"Will we see sharks?" It was neither an uncommon nor an unexpected question.

"It is the time of year for them to be around, but the answer is: probably not. They are being seen two or three miles offshore presently, maybe closer around Start Point, which I will point out to you later. My licence forces me to remain within one mile of the coast, so we will not see them unless a front has pushed them close inshore, but if we fail to see them today, maybe your folks will take you to Start another day for a few hours of shark-hunting." He glanced around at the mother and father, recognising from their reserve this was the only day of the holiday set aside for nature watching.

They chugged out between the castles guarding the narrows beyond which the coast opened. Before reaching the seaward limit of the river, something he expected caught his eye so came in under a red sandstone cliff. To and over its crumbling edge, huge-girthed Monterey pines grew.

High up on the cliff-face was a long, angled ledge at one end of which he had glimpsed the upright smear of slate-grey and white that was a peregrine falcon, perched above a brighter dribble of white droppings.

He was familiar with the sloping ledge habitually used by the obliging falcon. Often, she or the tiercel, would be perched there, above their vivid giveaway white blazon. While making his slow approach, Amaury reminded his audience quietly: "Remember we are companions trying to keep the peace!"

He lingered for about five minutes, dividing his time between moving from person to person, guiding binocular-aided gazes to where she stood, and returning to the helm to restore Chanticleer to where he needed her to be. When asked to describe more of what the peregrine was doing, he told them of a nest in the river approaches that he was forbidden by law to show them. Its young were hatched and well-grown. He said they might happen upon the youngsters by chance, but if they did not, their plumage was at a halfway stage and they looked like aristocrats dressed in rags.

All the while, the chunky little faded turquoise and white boat rocked gently on kindly dark green waters under the brick-coloured cliff and its dark-green thatch of Montereys. When the curiosity of the passengers was sated, he eased the boat seaward toward a rocky island whose outlying cardinal buoys were given a wide berth. When they progressed in toward it, he pointed out the gradation of colours upward from the sea-level glister of kelp fronds, which showed only around low tide on a spring tide, such as they had this day, to the pale brown barnacle zone, covered twice daily by the full tide. Above the barnacle zone, the black, undulating band of variable thickness was the lichen *Verrucaria*. It gave an indication of the average range between high tide at neaps at base, and to high tide at springs along the top line. Above this black band, on the partly-bare rocks of the splash zone the yellow lichen *Xanthoria parietina* grew in great abundance. But the heights were forgotten when he announced — teasingly, insofar as he knew they were too far distant to be yet distinguished — he could see at least three seals.

He continued his steady approach until they lay about one hundred metres off the archipelago in an area bright with coloured floats marking where crab pots had been set by one of the local boats.

"OK! I think there are six grey seals on the rocks today. Can you all see that there is an outer line of rocks of varying sizes closest to us?" Looking around, he saw they were with him: "I guess you'll have seen the most low-lying rock, broadside on to us, has two dry, dark velvet slugs clinging to it. One is on the top, the other on the right-hand slope? The one on top is a mature male, resting on what I call Seal Rock because, so long as it is showing, it is their favourite resting place in the archipelago. The one closer to sea level is a younger male. Now, if you look across the lagoon waters behind them, you will see two more pale smears very well camouflaged against the rocks, just above sea level more or less to the right of Seal Rock. The one on the left is a female, the other, closer to the water, is immature."

So, it developed. Relaxed in the sun, very happy to be precisely where she was, Amber breathed in the unfamiliar scenery, sometimes listening to Amaury, sometimes to what the passengers were saying, most often day-dreaming. It was in her mind that she had never thought to be living such a life following the death of her husband.

Greatly struck by the dragons-head outline to the main island and its attendant rocks, she drew from her pocket her small, hard-covered sketch book and began making marks with her pencil. At one point, she stared unseeing at the sea until two somethings swam across the blur of her vision.

Looking about her, she realised no-one else had seen it and so poked Amaury in the back with the reverse end of the pencil. He glanced around, mildly surprised, followed her guiding glance, blew her a kiss and announced:

"Just in case anyone is getting bored with seals..." The little girl who had declined his assisting hand when coming aboard was quickest to look at him, frowning as if he was mad. She had not expected her expression to be seen and was disconcerted to find his gaze waiting in ambush. She faded behind her mother's jeans, clutching them with one small hand. The thumb of the other found comforting refuge in her mouth:

"On the seaward side of the boat, we have two small, chocolate brown and white visitors. They look rather like small penguins: a pair of guillemots, cousins of the smaller puffin. Their largest colony on the south coast of England is just a few miles north of here. Unfortunately, we can't go that far because this boat can't get us there and back in the time available.

"If you've had enough of boats, but would like to see it, you can visit the country park above the limestone ledges where they nest. You can get there via Brixham. On site, they have a remotely-operated camera on the cliffs streaming images showing every detail of guillemot nursery life on screens in a viewing centre. I recommend it. It has been well done."

Before they moved on, Amaury guided their eyes up toward the slopes of the main island, to a small forest of straggling greenery speckled with mauve flowers:

"I know from down here it doesn't look impressive, but that is a tree mallow forest. This is one of the sites I monitor every spring to identify the onset of egg-laying by different birds, count the number of eggs laid, the number of hatchlings that appear and the number of fledglings surviving to independence. Believe it or not, that little, straggly forest is very important to seabird youngsters. Once they've left the nest, the shade they offer is where partly-fledged cormorants hide from the heat of the sun, the rain, the wind and even the eyes of predators, especially those handsome, but cruel, black-backed gulls. And it is a good place to hide because the plants typically grow to a height of more than two metres and they have large leaves."

From his rucksack, he drew out a photo album and set it on the thwart: "If anyone is interested, here is the story of the island's seabird breeding season. Pictures accompanied by notes: some facts and figures."

There were more birds and plants to point out while he brought Chanticleer around the great sea rock. There were oystercatchers and the differences between shag and cormorant to point out. There were green patches of deliciously edible sea beet to point out which led on to a discussion on how best to cook their faintly nut-flavoured leaves. Around the last corner, on the shallow rocks arrayed on the landward side of the island, two more seals were waiting, already noted but not yet properly identified.

They strayed seaward thereafter as far as the less impressive blocks of the Eastern Blackstone, then back landward to steep, adder-haunted Scabbacombe, there reaching the far point of the cruise.

The hour and a half raced deceptively by, ending too soon for everyone. They were returned safely to land where twelve more people immediately replaced them. In less than ten minutes, a full turn around had been accomplished. After another ten minutes, the same peregrine falcon was being contemplated by delighted, wondering eyes and Amaury was varying his commentary, as forever he sought to do for fear of becoming dreary to his own ears.

It was a lovely, generous day, the kind when nothing goes wrong and everything was there to be seen. Amber had remained on board for the second trip.

The full cast of wild characters made their appearances and a quiet, happy boat was homeward bound again, very slowly drifting by under the yellow-lichened heights of the main island. The same dry seals remained strewn over the dry rocks. One moment, all was peace and the next, a jet ski came frothing into view from the direction of the Dart.

Scowling, Amaury rummaged inside his rucksack, making his camcorder available. He handed his digital camera with the big lens to Amber. She knew what was needed and felt happy making a team with him.

He hastened Chanticleer over the quiet waters, announcing: "The Shooter Rock, that big tower where the shags are nesting, lies at the entrance to the lagoon. I am going to take up station close by, leaving room for the jet ski to enter if that is the driver's intent. That would be an infringement of rules relating to this voluntary exclusion zone. I hope no-one minds?"

Everyone was happy with so much already seen; they were very much on-side.

Glancing at Amber, he said: "I want you to capture his hunting line. I'll capture the response of the seals." Not forgetting he had twelve passengers to care for, he turned to them and explained:

"It is likely the jet ski will pass close to the rocks. If it does it will scare the seals into the sea. We cannot prevent it so the most useful thing we can do is record the sequence of events. With others, I am working to capture moving and still images of disturbance taking place so that we can produce a brief educational film and booklet showing good practice and also what not to do. It will show also how to approach wildlife discreetly, recognising when to draw no closer. It will be circulated to harbour authorities, all sorts of motor boat, sailboat, canoeing and other organisations, in the hope of reducing current levels of disturbance without recourse to the law. That is what this little cameo is about. I hope you will find it interesting."

The jet ski was close, now, so he made slowing down signals to the driver with both hands. With glorious disdain, the driver surged by, one solitary finger raised from his fist in lordly response.

Amaury leapt around the wheelhouse and down to the deck. The jet ski was not supporting the lordly man alone. Behind him sat a woman while between the two a small boy sat sandwiched. Once in the lagoon, they had no option but to slow dramatically but the intrusion was altogether too aggressive for the previously relaxed seals. All four crashed as one into the lagoon waters, scattering seaward.

Pausing on the disturbed waters of the lagoon, the little party on the jet ski looked about them for about five seconds before surging out through a smaller gap to seaward and speeding away to the next treat. Immediately they were gone from view, Amaury returned to the helm and hurried the boat back the way they had come, to where the two mature females might still lie resting.

Sure enough, there they remained. Both were alert, searching keenly about them, clearly poised for flight. Amaury looked at Amber: "I think he glimpsed them from the lagoon."

He was right. Seconds later, careless of the noise they made, indifferent to the disturbance they were causing, the jet ski was speeding toward the two remaining seals. Even at one hundred metres, it was too much for their frayed nerves. Like the seals in the lagoon, they went crashing into the sea. As the jet ski drew up for a second brief pause, everyone on the boat heard the man shout something and saw the small boy laughing. Only the woman betrayed concern at the pleasure boat passengers looking their way, cameras trained upon them. Recognising it was not flattery, she tapped the shoulder of her man but he responded as before with the lordly, dismissive finger. In a great fan of spray, he accelerated around and away, northward up the coast. In doing so, he narrowly missed hitting a rock barely breaking the surface that he had failed to see.

There was nothing left to see. The magic had been rudely trashed. Looking at the passengers, Amaury said: "Time for home!"

He had just set Chanticleer moving slowly forward when he noticed the big male who had been resting on Seal Rock had returned to its weedy margins. Noticing its colour, some instinct made him reduce speed again. Very slowly, he returned to the lagoon entrance and there trained his binoculars on him.

The seal half hauled out, watchful and clearly prepared to return to the sea at the least concern. The three other seals were all swimming at the surface not far from the black male. Studying them, Amaury saw a short antenna protruding above the head of the smallest seal. It was wearing a satellite tag!

The flow of the tide was carrying the boat very slowly in reverse into the lagoon now the gears were in neutral.

Having raised a finger to his lips, making sure the gesture had been seen by everyone, Amaury bent double and made his way to the stern. Checking the vibration reduction button was in the correct position, he focussed on the black seal. When satisfied with the composition, he began to take pictures.

Stubbornly, the black male refused to turn his head and show his alternative profile until the very last, when the immature seal appeared to be moving up on to the same rock. A brief exchange of views was followed by the abrupt departure of the smaller seal. The altercation revealed, for about three seconds, the left side of the black seal's neck, so Amaury managed to take two pictures of him that also included the right profile of the satellite-tagged youngster.

Thereafter, he had to wait so long he feared he might lose the goodwill of the passengers, but his opportunity came when the tagged seal emerged and flaunted its left profile.

Having secured the images needed, Amaury returned to the wheel, put the boat in gear and eased her out of the lagoon at dead slow speed. Once outside, he turned to tell the passengers he thought he recognised the male, provoking one passenger to ask how he could be so sure.

Amaury explained the photo-identification programme and the way comparisons were run.

Lacking a little of the gaiety and uncluttered happiness of the earlier hour, they made headed back toward the Dart. A general buzz of conversation resumed. Assistance came from the least expected quarter in the form of a fizzing sound just below the gunwales. Amaury's head came sharply around and he blurted one of the most evocative words in the English language: "Dolphins!"

Here was the cavalry riding over the hill indeed. All earlier discipline was forgotten. Everyone lurched to starboard, glimpsing silvery grey backs streaming with water. Two sickle-shaped dorsal fins cut the surface, white water flaring behind them. They saw amused dolphin eyes glancing back at them as they watched in excitement.

Unforgettable moments. Amaury set the recording mechanism of the camcorder in motion once more. Leaning his body against the spokes of the wheel to hold course, he sought, found and focussed on the common dolphins.

They had not come for the brief visit that could have been expected from their bigger cousins, the bottlenoses. These two small, speedy dolphins were exceptionally generous, seeming content to remain in close attendance. They remained so long that Amaury had the rare luxury of being able to swap cameras, taking some still pictures and being far from alone in that.

He was reflecting how, among the so-called charismatic marine animals, seals were regarded as the trusty stand-bys. They were the ones that could be relied on to appear because they had a relationship with the land. Everyone interested knew some could usually be seen ashore at the time of low water.

By contrast, in West Country waters at least, dolphins were the star performers with hardly any great whales present to rival them. Turtles did occur but as needles in a haystack, most often stumbled on by chance by boats working along the Shelf edge. Sharks were laden with terrifying mystique but tended to be met infrequently inshore by the pleasure boat community, at least during most years.

In by the castles they came, attended by their honour guard. The sea anglers on the rocks saw them. Looking up to the peopled heights above the graveyard, Amaury saw others had noticed the dolphins; there was some shouting and pointing. The Castle ferryman glanced their way, saw the dolphins, raised a greeting arm. Amaury returned the salute.

It was a royal progress into the harbour. Everyone noticed them because everyone noticed the companion dolphins. On the quayside, looking the way of Chanticleer from their kiosk, Rob and Sheila Mariner spotted the dolphins and regretted it was happening so late in the afternoon. Most holidaymakers who might have been tempted to take a trip on the river or a wildlife cruise were gone by now. Nevertheless, judging by the number of people remaining to take pictures of the happy spectacle from the quay, it seemed inevitable that one of them would find its way into the Dartmouth Chronicle and, if they were lucky, into the Western Morning News, to be read across the region. Only belatedly did they realise they should catch pictures of their be-dolphined boat.

Having made his farewells to the well-contented passengers, Amaury contacted Rob by radio, telling him of the images he had secured, suggesting he contact the BBC to see if they wanted to run something on the early evening regional news programme.

Having helped his lady ashore, Amaury moored Chanticleer and rowed back to shore. Rob and Sheila were deep in conversation with Amber when he arrived. As ever, they allowed him a few teasing moments to feel completely superfluous, so he slid an arm around the waist of his lady, rested his cheek against her warmer one and looked at Rob and Sheila with an air of exaggerated expectation.

Having become visible to them, he asked: "Is it on?"

Rob glanced at his wife who, normally, did the talking:

"They want it and will pay the standard fee for the use of the film, so long as the quality is good enough, but they want you in Plymouth for a studio interview."

Amaury groaned: "Is there no way we can get them to come here?"

"No. They said they want to have the action on screen behind you. They want you in the foreground, talking them through what is going on."

"Did you mention I captured some stills as well?"

"Sorry! He forgot." She nudged her husband in the ribs. He had the grace to look shame-faced.

"When do they want me?"

"Soonest!"

Amaury looked at Amber; she looked back. Just as they were about to depart, Rob clapped him on the shoulder, tapped the side of his head and said: "Remember! It happened while you were running the Small-boat Wildlife Cruise out of Dartmouth."

Amaury grinned. Somewhere along the road to Halwell, Amber looked at her man and asked: "Why is life never simple for long? After all the excitement, all I wanted was for the two of us to be alone again."

***

Having spent the greater part of late winter and spring hunting along the edge of the Continental Shelf, habituating himself to dive ever-deeper for increasing lengths of time, Tyrian was in the best condition of his life.

Having lingered hoping to link up with Iolair on the Saltees, he had ranged westward along the sunset road. The farther west he swam, the more determined he grew to give a wide berth to the shores of bloody memories; to the Blaskets, but impulse drew him there, even so.

To his surprise, hundreds of seals were hauled out there. They were far down the shore from where the desiccated hulks of the dead seals had been strewn by the highest tides. The higher up the shore he hauled himself, the more obvious it became that he was joining one of the principal moulting assemblies in all Ireland. Perversely, this was the beach he used for his base for what remained of winter and all of springtime.

Initially, his knowledge of the Shelf Edge was patchy. He had probed that far before, never staying for long. This winter, he spent nearly all his time there.

He experienced one great storm that lasted for two weeks. It began just after his arrival at the Edge. He was still there when it passed. In all that time, while at the surface, he was among moving hills of solid water capped with seething foam. He was never able to see far even when swept up and briefly caught at the crest of a wave. When travelling, he swam deeper than usual to avoid being tugged hither and thither by the surface turmoil.

When hunting, he dived repeatedly to the Shelf Edge itself through the faltering, light into such darkness that only his vibrissae were in their element, telling tales of the nature of that world. He might have been blind, so far was he from the light. Sun was no more than ancient memory.

Tyrian was a bold seal endlessly uncovering new layers of self as well as of his world. His curiosity was as insatiable as his courage. At the greatest depths of all, he ranged beyond the Shelf Lip, into the abyss that hinted at writhing, eyeless monsters and faery twinklings of pinprick lights.

He hardly noticed the pressure bearing upon his body in that Stygian place. Sometimes, he supposed he slipped from normal consciousness into an unguessed-at, otherworldly, deep-sea consciousness. On the sensitive canvas of his imagination, his vibrissae painted extraordinary images. At the greatest depths he was saw real sparks and flickers of light. He chose not to believe it, assuming he was hallucinating, but he was not.

The sounds were wonderful. It was a place webbed with sound as varied as all he glimpsed with his eyes of the surface world. Much sound seemed to be in slow motion, being deep and extended. Had he known of such things, the quieter sounds would have reminded him of internal rumblings of elephant digestive systems: creaking, pings, trills, echoes, and bubbling.

Sometimes, he found himself being hurried along in bottom currents and sometimes becalmed in quiet water.

At the surface, he had a close encounter with a fin whale and its calf as they surged through the storm without sign of having noticed him. Like everything else in that long storm, they seemed to plough along grimly, heads down.

In the deeps, the sounds of five young male sperm whales trooping close by caused him to abort a dive. Alarmed by the size of them, sensed rather than glimpsed, he hastened back to the lesser horrors of the surface. Despite the unkind conditions there — he took a considerable battering from some exceptionally heavy whitecaps — he did not submerge again for another hour.

At and near the surface, he met many bustling pods of dolphins. Mainly, they were common dolphins but white-beaked and white-sided dolphins, pilot whales, Northern bottlenose whales and even Sowerby's beaked whales also chanced by. None offered any threat or paid him but passing attention.

More than the cetaceans, it was the submarine world and especially the bottom that held the greatest fascination for him. That, and the slope below, into the true deeps and submarine canyons where lurked uttermost unknowns.

Sometimes, he edged inshore but mainly he inhabited an offshore, impressionistic, abstract world. In the deepest sea, it was remarkable, to be cruising along the right way up but with nothing visible to confirm that. It was more incredible to be in open water with no vision at all and yet to have a sense of direction, proximity and orientation.

It was particularly surreal to engage in combat with a large monkfish that, exceptionally for its breed, had managed to evade the diversity of fishing nets capable of capturing his kind. Until the United Kingdom and Eire entered the Common Market and discovered the appetite in Spain and France for the tails of monkfish, they had usually been thrown back overboard when caught, left to grow in size and wickedness. Since that time, the British appetite had been pampered to greater expectation by memories of meals eaten on foreign holidays. Neither was the media backward singing the praises and possibilities of monk tails, in their ever-increasing obsession with cooking. Monkfish, once the hopeless Foinaven of a fish, surged through the Grand National field to pre-eminence on menus as well as on plates at home.

On the market, monkfish commanded prime prices. Hardly anyone raised their voices against the fact that ninety-eight per cent of landings of the two species were of immature fish that would never breed. Hardly anyone protested the population status of the two species and location of their breeding grounds were inadequately known.

The monkfish on sale in markets and shops were, more correctly, monkfish tails. They were relatively slender, in contrast with the broad, fiercely-toothed head. Neither that nor the peculiar adapted first fin ray that functioned as a lure while the main body of the fish lay buried or camouflaged against the muddy or sandy bottom were persuasive sales-features. The lure had a piece of tattered skin at its tip, entirely unlike the other fin rays.

Tyrian had become adept at locating them but he captured the bigger ones only after struggles that, in the total darkness, were horrifying. Nevertheless, he was a skilful hunter and successful warrior. They had not yet managed to scar him with their wide gapes and fearsome teeth.

Only rarely that season did he set his compass for the Blasket's to take short periods of rest. Finding Iolair absent, he would draw himself across extensive, seal-scented sands to some favourite place and take little notice of the cosmopolitan collection of seals around him. He exuded such quietness that even noisy seals regarded him as a daunting figure. Beyond doubt, he understood he was fully come to his prime.

Not long after he began to feel the urge to be home, against all expectation Iolair arrived and they were reunited. They had a lot of catching up to do. At the outset, Tyrian learned of Somerledaa's extraordinary journey, at least so far as the Isle of Man, amazed she should have travelled so far when all he remembered was the scrap of a silvery seal last seen in Martinsfinger Cave. He heard of Iolair's adventures along the Donegal coast and out toward the Rockall Deep in the same great storm it turned out he had shared.

He told his own story in few words, but the rare underlying luminosity in them fascinated the small seal because it was something only true explorer-seals would ever do. Strangely, his exploits brought Meinek to mind. He had not been greatly different in prowess or curiosity from black Tyrian.

Meinek had journeyed north beyond the volcanoes and geysers of Iceland. Hunting along the edge of the ice, he had met bearded seals, hooded seals, ringed seals and harp seals. He had made great hunting trips and epic captures of the largest fish a grey seal might take. He had seen sea-unicorns. He had even been caught in a trawl and emptied on to the slippery deck of a beam trawler. Fortunately for him, they overlooked his snarling rage, managing to throw him back overboard. The Hebridean skipper had thought it unlucky to kill a seal on his decks.

"What deep thoughts are you thinking, now?" Tyrian had asked, with something akin to the humour that had become a feature of their communication.

Iolair might have dissembled, had he known how. Instead, he told the truth.

Tyrian answered not at all, simply raising his dark head and gazing toward the horizon. He might have protested his difference, but he had his own wisdom, his own baggage of self-knowledge. Perhaps he would go the way of Meinek. In the living was where the truth would be found

Looking again at Iolair, he said: "I will not deny I am excited about the breeding season ahead and I am certain that when I meet Meinek again, he will face me without eagerness. I think I shall vanquish him because of the way the wheel of life turns. Last year, we were almost equal. This year, I feel I must have become more equal. In a way, it seems a shame. He is a great seal and a maker of great seals, as Somerledaa confirms." There, he paused, impressions falling into place. The pause lengthened: "So, perhaps my star will shine this year. Who knows what life holds? Assuming I avoid misadventure and enjoy a period of peerlessness as long as that of Meinek, where does that take us? Surely, then, you will be coming to your fullest power? Will you overthrow my tyranny; perform the kindness of returning me to my lonely, wandering ways? Who will be waiting on the nursery beaches? I wonder if you are carrying a female seal in your heart. It is not uncommon for seals to form exclusive attachments, as you know better than I."

Iolair made to protest but on the brink of laughing off what Tyrian had said, he remembered he was not being teased by some big, stranger seal but by Tyrian, who did not account himself wise, but who surely was.

Wryly, he elected to answer obliquely: "Can you recall your size when you were my age, Tyrian? Look at me? I cannot conceive there will be even one season of peerlessness for me. I flee from fights and when I am of a size to consider offering battle, I think I will continue doing so."

Tyrian continued to exhibit an air of expectancy when he fell silent. Iolair tried not to notice a stare directed at him that was altogether too knowing. He turned away, looking down the long, indented coastline of Kerry and Cork. He looked that way for a long time. When he turned back, still Tyrian watched him; waiting.

"What is it?" Iolair demanded.

"I thought I asked you a question about feelings. You gave me a story about lack of physical prowess. I thought you might have a little more to share? Through winter and spring, I sought you, looking forward to picking up again the threads of our friendship. In you, I found a seal with whom I have affinity; we are brothers more really than brothers in blood. Am I wrong?"

Iolair hung his head, yet unmarked by — maybe destined forever to lack — scars: "You are not wrong. Forgive me. I think I have not so much been hiding something from you as from myself. You see, she is so young. Even now, she has not attained her first birthday. There will be three or four birthdays before she comes into breeding condition. You know what will happen. She will suddenly pass through that glass curtain into maturity, probably while attending a moulting assembly, far from home. Come September, she will be back in the Bay of Seals, maybe even in Martinsfinger Cave.

"Yes! Whenever she passes through that glass partition, I want to be close by. I hope she will choose me for her mate. Not just then, but in all the years thereafter. She is incredibly special for a seal so young, capable of everything and I see others noticing that. I never met a female who so affected me, though I have met several who are exceptional."

Tyrian made a long, low rumble of approval deep in his throat: "Do you mind if I remember something of what it is to be a seal to you, Iolair?" he asked.

Iolair yielded up his fullest attention. Looking at the fine black outline of him against the setting sun, he realised the winter and spring adventure truly had changed him. He was the same Tyrian. His great Roman nose was bowed, broad and full. His eyes were grave and far-seeing, but there was something more. It was as if he had, somewhere in his stormbound solitude, passed through a glass curtain of his own that even he, wise Iolair, had not guessed was there. What was it he had said, one evening, more than a year ago? We are all born to the rainbow, Iolair. You travel on the colour that is sharing, born of knowing, born of asking, born of listening, born of learning; then communicating. Who does not derive pleasure from the songs you sing, from old stories you have retold? You surely sense the way seals on the periphery strain to hear you? It is a bold, brave adventure of mind and soul and you are a true and appreciated seal, young though you are.

Me? We recognise I travel on another colour of the same rainbow. The first love of my heart is to find ways to as many edges of the world as I can reach, pressing against the boundaries to see whether there is something more. Loving life so much, the world I have explored, being at home in my skin, remembering the very few seals that are dear to me: I am content.

It sounds so fine when I put it so, don't you think, Iolair the Bard? And it is fine, you know! Have we not discussed it often enough, the way I live is possible only because I spend most of my time daring to be what I can be. If I turned aside too long, grew too comfortable on the skerries and beaches of south-west Ireland or the Land's End, thinking aloud with a friend, I would soon begin to lose whatever good health it is that allows me to be true to the finer words.

"We know the etiquette of the breeding grounds. Those males who are near their prime take up station close to the nursery sites before the season starts; sometimes, long before. In May, June, July, they can be found, boasting, bickering, engaged in trials of strength or even fighting. Gradually, relative power is established. The peerless males emerge, and take territories for their own which, subsequently, they will defend against all-comers. The females do not enjoy these squabbles. Why they tolerate it at all, I am at a loss to understand. Is it the lesser evil to have a peerless male at hand to drive away nuisance males who might otherwise cause mayhem and even cause injuries to the pups?

"Peerless males dare not rest. Chained to the watchtower, they scan for challengers while discreetly monitoring the females, inhabiting territory they have made their own. They are sea dragons guarding a golden hoard. The glittering females resist the monitoring. The male learns to respect their will. He has no choice because, as all the world knows. A female mates only with a male of her own choosing. A male cannot force a female to mate with him. It is a provoking dilemma, is it not, Iolair?

"Many females — not necessarily the majority, but many — mate with the same male, year after year. All that is required is that he be somewhere close by. He does not need to be the biggest, baddest, boldest seal after all. All he needs is a mutual understanding with a singular female. Had you forgotten that?"

319

"Not forgotten; no! As I said, she is so young and her world will grow with each new year. Simply, I dare not hope too much for now. It all lies too far ahead."

Tyrian stared at him, listening to the faint-hearted sentiments without admiration. They were friends. There would always be friendship between them now, whatever befell either along the way. They were friends not because of the ways in which they were alike. Discordant moments bubbled up, dispersed, on the evening breeze as now, but not before Tyrian observed:

"Perhaps nothing makes us so faint-hearted as the fear a dream might crumble. But what kind of dream is so faint-hearted that it just trembles into fearful imaginings? You are better than that, my friend. I refuse to believe otherwise. You know you must find the way to that other colour of the rainbow — as, perhaps, your own father did before you? I am guessing that you must know. In which case, is there farther to look for inspiration or reassurance?"

Iolair was silent. Somewhere in what his friend had said a rebuke was implicit, but it was a justified and helpful rebuke that he accepted, properly recognising it had been made out of great warmth for him.

For weeks thereafter, the two seals made a slow journey back along the south coast of Ireland to the Saltees of far-wandering gannets. There, they joined a scattered assembly of almost thirty salt-stained seals of whom only two had Irish accents. It was that time of year when seals were scattered across sea areas rather than upon homely nursery or moulting shores. It was the time of feasting, hunting from rocks that became home for a day, a week, a fortnight or even months at a time.

For Iolair and Tyrian, the Saltees served for only one week. Tyrian did not recognise Rra'ik, the gannet when that great bird came in over him to land with food for the latest solitary young with its black plumage on which a galaxy of stars had been sewn. No more did Rra'ik recognise Tyrian. Each was part of the familiar wallpaper of the daily world of the other.

When their hunting was done, they swam south-east for a hundred miles, arriving at the Western Rocks of the Isles of Scilly at first light. They cruised under tall Bishop Rock lighthouse, sweeping up gracefully, defiantly, into the sky as if it had been there since the beginning of time, but that was not so. They bobbed there in the sea at high tide on a big spring tide. Both had swum there before so both remembered it grew from a granite rock seemingly too small to provide a secure foundation for a structure battered by more than one hundred and fifty years' worth of storms. That rock was even now awash.

They wakened later in the morning still under the fine roof that capped the lantern and on which they had seen a helicopter land, bringing essential supplies, including fuel oil. The Trinity House engineers were attempting to convert the lighthouse fully to solar power, but were concerned about the effects of bird droppings on the solar panels and about generating sufficient power for the distance the beam was marked as showing on Admiralty charts. They were currently using a combination of solar power supplemented by fuel oil.

No men maintained a permanent watch inside the light. It was hard to imagine how anyone with imagination might keep watch there when every substantial wave butting into it made the entire structure judder and items fall from shelves. Hard to imagine anyone might be found to man it when the first lighthouse, had been swept clean away by a February storm even before it had been commissioned.

Hard to imagine how anyone with imagination might keep watch there in the knowledge that even the dressed-granite lighthouse built to replace the lost one had subsequently to be encased in a granite sheath following the appearance of cracks in its structure. At the same time, the lighthouse had been considerably heightened. Monstrous waves generated by an exceptional storm had once so damaged the glass of the lantern that the interior of the lighthouse started to fill with water to the extent the keepers thought themselves certain to drown. How do minds cope with such horror?

So, it was empty of men. Only their ghosts remained. The light itself was switched operated remotely now.

Tyrian and Iolair swam to the nearby arc of the Western Rocks where, the greater part of a year ago, Tyrian had taken refuge and licked his wounds. Not needing sanctuary, they prospected around the many rocks, often massive, that comprised Daisy. Scattered at the south end of the westernmost shield of rocks over which the first waves of every south-westerly storm did break, here they found many immature seals, quite a few males but hardly any females. They encountered no aggression. For the most part, seals lay in the sun in twos and threes. It seemed to be serving as an annex to The Rags, the principal safe haven.

Tyrian lay like a log at the surface of quiet waters near the south margin of the rocks while Iolair went visiting. He moved from rock to rock, scanning who might be there, singing songs of greeting, eager to find another seal who wanted to communicate. They gave hardly any response, usually regarding the small, black seal with sun-dazed indifference before continuing to doze.

Having enquired unsuccessfully at every slab, every islet, Iolair returned to where Tyrian lay, blowing streams of quiet bubbles at every breath. He had been waiting at his ease, content in the warmth of the sun while Iolair went hunting for stories. It was not a hunger he shared. Upon occasion, communication between Iolair and a stranger would burgeon at some haul-out site but, for the most part, Tyrian was comfortable in his decorated silence.

There came a time when he tired of doing nothing. He was content to idle after Iolair while he continued his quest northward around a big block of rock into the narrowing channel to the north of which was Rosevean. Here, the atmosphere was the polar-opposite of that prevailing at Daisy. Here, great slabs rose from the sea along the first part of the east shore. Dried to velvet on the granite slopes, but resting at a distance from one another, two strong males came to the alert as Tyrian and Iolair entered the channel. Not far in, they saw a third bigger and more confident male resting on his side, sleeping.

Sleeping he was, but not so oblivious that he had failed to hear the movement of bodies through the water. Wakening, still resting on one side with uppermost fore-flipper folded along the edge of his chest, he came around to watch them in a sequence of slow, on-the-spot, and whole-body movements. A rock pipit that had been resting close by flew away, uttering her alarm cry.

Iolair reacted more strongly than Tyrian, halting upright in the water and scanning for what had disturbed the small bird. Many seals ignore the cries of birds around them. Coming from islands rendered so dangerous by seal killers, Iolair had learned to listen to all the sounds Nature saw fit to utter. It was he who spotted the alert male atop a natural ramp of granite, who first recognised he was staring at the master of the island; the peerless seal of Rosevean.

Like an insolent herald, a herring gull on the heights above suddenly gave voice to a prolonged, ringing cry, challenging all-comers.

In all West Country sealdom, the peerless seals of the Western Rocks were most renowned for their ferocity and courage in combat. They had no fear and acquired their pre-eminence by defeating seals not less ferocious or courageous. Lapis of Rosevean was of that line. Now, he stared down at the larger of the two intruders with fine disdain. There was no sense of challenge but the intruder was floating along the borderline of territory Lapis was prepared to defend.

Tyrian, looking up the honey-coloured sea-wet slope to charcoal-coloured Lapis, recognised his readiness to fight. He knew himself to be in debateable water, but he felt an unfamiliar unwillingness to ignore any more threatening stares or actions. He was not seeking confrontation actively but he would not shrink from it if it came.

Lapis could read from the same radar Tyrian was using. He recognised the fearlessness of the intruder, the confidence of him, but he also recognised he was not receiving a direct challenge. It was up to him to make the decision.

There was a secondary factor of which he chose to take account. For two breeding seasons already, Lapis had controlled this point of access to the Rosevean shore. He was vividly aware of what lay ahead: hunger, tension, threat, chase, battle and mating. Was it worth the energy, to fight a passing seal before the first damp, white-coated pup flopped out on to these gaunt rocks, before the first female came into season and chose to welcome or reject him?

Experience should lead to wisdom; it had in Lapis. He knew there was little to gain and just maybe everything to be lost from fighting Tyrian. He suspected, in any case, Tyrian was not the fleeing type, just a powerful traveller passing by.

Iolair was relieved to exit the channel unscathed and resume his quest for communicative seals. He was relieved Tyrian had been content to drift peacefully in his wake. Few knew better than he the stories told of the peerless seals of the four outermost Atlantic stepping stones of Rosevean, Rosevear, Jacky's Rock and Great Crebawethan.

Passing a small tower, four young razorbills, born in spring, spilled out over his head, dipped down toward the sea and then gained height again. They made an ellipse flying over the black seals not just once, but twice. Aloft in sunlight over clear, quiet water, it was easy to see how shallow was the sea and how close the paler bellies of the seals to the dark honey-colours of the canopy of hydroid-embroidered kelp fronds. They saw the darting of wise, colourful fish into the shadows of that kelp. They glimpsed gleams of trickles of blue-rayed limpets burrowed and then studded into kelp stipes and, here and there, the prickly pink or mauve globes of grazing sea urchins.

At low tide, as it was then, Rosevean is two islets made one by a shallow bridge of boulders. On the far side of that bridge dozed a small collection of immature seals. Each rested on their own small, uncomfortable-looking rock, apparently safe from being chased off by their elders. Now, Iolair led Tyrian to that exposed west shore of the island. Leaving him to doze, bottling in a small cove under ledges where, still later in the year, pups would crawl, cry and behold the enormously powerful surging of the Atlantic, Iolair swam on to make contact with the youngsters.

This time, he was away for a longer time. A four-year old female was lately in from the Blaskets, having followed the same route as the two of them via the Saltees, but a few days earlier. It was a happy surprise, to meet one of his own tribe here on Scilly. Still immature, Mara would come to maturity after the end of the breeding season, at the winter assemblies. However, she had witnessed bloody events on the Blasket's on another occasion to those attended by Tyrian and Iolair the year previously, and there was uncertainty upon her as to whether she should return there to give birth to her own pup this or any other year.

It was a weighty question. Iolair came out of the sea on to the rock beside her. It was not a comfortable subject but her predicament touched him. A central custom of all grey seals since the beginning of time was that females returned to the locality of their birth to give birth to their own pups.

Despite her fears, she was aware that if she did not return, perhaps no seal would return and it followed that the Blaskets could be erased as a nursery ground. Yet no seal had been able to withstand the men when they came with their spiked clubs, their pungent tobacco and their alcohol smells.

"What is in your mind to be doing, at this moment?" he asked.

"At this moment? This is another place. It is a goodly place, guarded by powerful males, although you are not one-such." That recognition appeared to puzzle her momentarily. "But when I hear your accent, I feel a longing within me for home and I suppose it will always be so, wherever I roam. But where does longing fit when set beside the memories I have. I should have died, four years ago. My entire year-group of pups died that morning. They missed me alone because I was in the shallows. It is the strangest feeling; to have survived the day I should have died"

"Have you returned since your weaning?"

"Every year, at the time of the annual moult of females, and again in midsummer before the new breeding season begins. It was what I did before I came here."

"Had you been here before?"

"This is my late summer fishing station. There are many safe places here and although I have heard of seals being caught in nets, yet the fishing is wonderful and I see little of people. They appear infrequently and soon enough are gone without leaving their boats. People are the strangest things, Iolair. Don't you agree?"

The contemplation of people was very high among his preoccupations when alone. They seemed to want to be everywhere: he had seen them on seal beaches, seal rocks and even, though very rarely, inside seal caves. He had seen them swimming at the edges of the sea, walking on paths on top of cliffs and in boats. Rarely, he had seen them dressed in strange skins bearing strange lumps on their backs under the sea, watching the world from behind glass masks. He had been surprised they were such poor swimmers underwater. Twice, he had tested very gently with his teeth the bright fins they wore as feet and once a man had gently placed his gloved hand in his mouth. Iolair remembered gently touching the neoprene with his teeth, that he might

325

remember it. It was a material he chanced upon now and then, both in the sea or among litter strewn along tidemarks. Since that day, he had always recognised it, always associating it with the foolhardy black-suited diver.

"I think," he answered, "it is possible they are not stranger than we are. I find I am surprised by every new thing I see them doing, but why should it not be so? Clearly, though, they are of the land. How great is the land? How many of them are there? How many stars are there in the sky at night? How can I know!

"I think, like us, they vary. It is not everywhere that men come with clubs to kill us. They don't kill us among these islands. If you think of all the people you have seen, how many do you feel came to do you harm?

"I think, mainly, they mean us no harm. Rather, they do us harm by being numerous. They seem to need to use a huge part of the world to survive and so they squeeze other living creatures, like we of the seal tribes, to the edges. How sad it must be for them to be so! How sad it must be for their hearts and souls and dreams and imaginations! I am guessing but I suspect by reducing us and crowding in on our privacy, they are reduced and somehow crowded out of the world they really need."

He looked sideways at her, found she was staring at him wide-eyed because never had she met a seal remotely like him, a seal who thought across so broad a rainbow. Especially, she had never met another seal who thought to conceive what it might be like to be a human being.

Disconcerted by her concentration, he lost confidence and asked quietly: "Shall I stop there? I do tend to talk too much."

"Oh no! Please go on!" Such was the ring of her sincerity that he took heart:

"Often, if I allowed myself, I could feel lonely; I guess if I was brutally honest with myself, then I would admit I am. The trouble is, this is all I am, so far, and if I dwelt on the probability of loneliness, what would become of me? What would become of hope and intent; of life itself? Might I — we — degenerate into self-pity? But that, like fearfulness of people, is only one colour of our rainbow. We must try to remain true to what comes naturally through us. I will continue speaking to strangers, listening to tales they tell, telling them tales I have heard. If I sleep on these rocks tonight, perhaps I shall sing one of the ancient stories of these rocks, of seals that once inhabited them, before I sleep. Before any seal goes to sleep. I will sing the story as a lullaby at the gateway to your dreams and, who knows, it may unlock a door and you may find an answer that has been eluding you."

Beyond Mara, other seals were alert. Others had opened their eyes. Still others listened without opening their eyes. All eleven seals within earshot listened to the beautiful voice, recognising him for a bard, for all he was so young. This, he was aware of and, although he was content that they should hear him, he spoke intensely to Mara alone. Rarely among seals, had she taken the trouble to welcome his greeting and to share her story with him, so maybe he could be of some small assistance to her.

Now, she stunned him: "Are you called Iolair?"

For her, it was a long shot, but he fitted the description she had heard of his colouring, his lack of years and the treasury that was his mind.

"Indeed; that is I! How can you possibly know?"

"I met a seal who spoke at length of you on the Saltees, not more than three weeks since. She had just tracked down from the Outer Hebrides, by Rathlin and the east coast of Ireland. A Cornish seal, eager to be home after long absence, but already incredibly far-travelled for one so young. You reminded me of her, the way you came up to these rocks and started to sing. She did precisely the same thing. Can you guess her name? Small, she was, and silvery, with a pattern of markings that includes the letter Y on the right side of her face, under her ear."

"Somerledaa!" He sang her name softly, with great pleasure and even relief that she had survived whatever perils had been on her way: "Is she here, with you?"

"No! She left two days before me, saying she wanted to go directly to the Land's End albeit possibly pausing at the Isles of Scilly. But she was asking for you, before she came ashore, passing from ledge to islet to skerry; asking, asking. I chanced to be the last in her line of calls so she came ashore by me. There were hours of daylight left. We talked, having a whole lifetime to share.

"She said that, were our paths to cross, you are to know she will look for you at the Land's End."

A rare surge of pure gaiety swept over him before he recalled how their conversation had started, with the bright young female fearful of holding true to the seals way. What would become of her? What would become of their shared home at the edge of the Irish world?

They talked more without reaching a satisfactory destination until, remembering Tyrian, he departed with the tug of the turning tide. Mara watched him until he disappeared around a promontory. She did not see him continue along his way with Tyrian, moving back again to the inshore channel and on to Rosevear.

Of all the wave-scoured places in the Western Rocks, the greenest is Rosevear. Behind its high seaward granite tower, the heart of the island was green with flowering tree mallow and sea beet. Shags had explored the jungle of it with their grey fledgling young, wary of bandit black-backed gulls whose nesting stronghold was the ruin of an old smithy. It had been built at the time of the construction of Bishop light, Rosevear having served as the main staging point. Even the greenery hinted at past human endeavour, being once the vegetable patch.

It was a dangerous place to be, a shag. The rocks and ledges at the margins of the greenery were littered with shag leg and breast-bones picked almost completely clean, with only the feathered wings to help anyone identify what had been eaten on these rude granite platters. It might have been equally dangerous to be a guillemot or razorbill, but only one adult razorbill lay in the litter of gull-slain corpses. Also vulnerable were Manx shearwaters and the smaller storm petrels. They laid their eggs at the end of labyrinthine burrows among pale boulders at the top of the sometimes-lichened boulder dunes. The boulders were glued together by the passage of time. Few moved when trodden on.

The fattened shearwater and petrel young had mainly left. Few strange sounds remained to be heard by the seals prospecting along below jumbled boulder ramparts and intervening ledges of bedrock. Fewer auks remained; the four razorbills had been the only ones still present. Neither did they see any seals. They concluded they had arrived too early and so were spared the huff and puff of territorial angst.

Another impressive bull was asleep just off the north-east tip of the island on a seal-sized rock. As they drifted by, he opened his eyes. Both saw the small wound near the tip of his nose, suggesting he had successfully enjoyed his first engagement. They passed by without disturbance, then onward by the strewn rocks of Silver Carn and the larger bestrewing of even more boulders south of Jacky's Rock and its ledges. Here, several seals in the sea showed mild curiosity at their passing.

Crebawethan Neck was the widest gap in the shield of the Western Rocks, but no great run of tide was pouring through. The black seals circumnavigated both Great and Little Crebawethan. If a peerless male was present, they did not notice him nor suffer from not-noticing. Thereafter, Tyrian took the lead and they crossed more than two kilometres of open water to the seal-friendly boulder shores of Annet, island of recently departed puffins and a glorious spring flowering of thrift. Annet, island of the last-born seal pups of the season, with green, over-running seas rendering the Western Rocks impossible to use as nurseries. Just short of Annet, by a clutter of jagged rocks called the Ranneys, a porpoise calf seeming small and silver as a salmon in the sunlight breached three times, but of its parents — which must have been very close — they saw nothing.

Moving south, now they did meet some tide, but no seals while swimming through the rock-littered shallows of Hellweathers Neck. Thereafter, the Necks grew ever wider as they passed between Isinvrank and Brothers to reach lonely Melledgan with its piled boulder beach and bedrock slabbed shore. From one side, it looked like an extinct volcano. From all sides, the shags and a few cormorants stared back at them.

The last Neck they needed to cross in their circular exploration to reach Gorregan, The Rags and then Rosevean again was Gorregan Neck, and here they felt the force of the flooding tide. But they were grey seals and had met far fiercer races than those of Scilly; for all that the Islands are so exposed. Reaching the broken ground at the south-east corner of Gorregan, they saw more than fifteen adult seals hauled out in close proximity, suggesting no-one had yet laid claim to the territory. Nevertheless, they swam south of it and of The Rags, where they knew there would be no threat. Approaching the gap that had begun to appear between the two wings of Rosevean, they parted temporarily. Tyrian, being hungry, chose to go hunting. Iolair had an appointment to keep with Mara and the other immatures. He had a lullaby to sing.

Tyrian swam southward, leaving Iolair to dawdle to shore, rummaging through his memories to tease out a song appropriate to the occasion.

Once he was re-settled among them, after the tide had gently brushed them off the rocks, they drew quite close together. One of the young ones who had found no voice earlier now dared ask, in a strange accent, had Iolair any stories of seal places sunk under the Breton sea along with the fabled city of Ys.

It was a happy choice. Iolair was no stranger to the Molène archipelago, which was another part of the world where seals felt themselves endangered. Despite having almost faded away, there remained a strong tradition of story-telling. Under crowding stars, from his comfortable place in the whispering sea, he sang a story first in mediaeval French, the language in which he had learned it, then in the common tongue of grey seals everywhere. He did not realise that singing in the two languages, he was creating a rare and precious moment in the lives of these youngsters, none of whom had yet settled into the seal it was in them to be. He sang an ancient story back to life. In the singing, he had sung something to life in each of them.

Thereafter, while the young seals fell asleep, Iolair did no more than doze. He was not tired and occasional shooting stars sheering across the sky provided stimuli for his thoughts. Consequently, he was awake when his friend, night-dark Tyrian, swam quietly to the base of the slab upon which he was resting. There was no need to ask whether the hunting had been good. Indeed, there was no discussion between them. The bigger seal simply settled upright in the nearby waters and slept.

At morning, the presence of so powerful a seal in their midst proved daunting for the seals who had grown in confidence under

Iolair's tutelage the previous evening. They faded before the alarming size and gleaming health of Tyrian, understandably taking him for one of the peerless males, though such males did not use this water area, the island heights behind being inaccessible from the sea. It was the custom of peerless seals to defend gates rather than walls.

This, Tyrian noticed without properly recognising his role in it. It denied him the chance to be as friendly as he was prepared to be, but it had become habitual and, in any case, he was content to ponder upon his own thoughts and impressions as to make connections with seals who behaved so strangely.

He did not recognise the thin, squealing race of his destiny, smoothly reeling him along.

Iolair did. He continued to feel some anxiety about changes that might be wrought in his friend. Before Tyrian wakened, he had been remembering the moments after he had seen the peerless seal resting by the north ramp on Rosevean. He was aware of the complete and genuine self-assurance Tyrian had felt during the brief theatre of it. Another world, probably one he would never know: to be supremely self-confident and at home in one's skin.

When his eyes focussed, he found Tyrian contemplating him with the serious expression that had grown so familiar by now: "Iolair! How was your evening? What am I sensing in the air about you that has changed?"

Startled, because normally he did the seeing, he remembered he had not shared the news he had received of Somerledaa while sharing the sun-bright passage around the western islands yesterday.

Now, he shared the news Mara had brought. Tyrian responded by corkscrewing away lazily through and down in to the shallows. He emerged very soon, head covered with fronds of kelp: "So now you will want to head eastward? Of course! Land's End is just half a day away. Yet, before we leave, I have a proposal. I had been thinking you might be interested to visit the seal places east of Land's End: to recognise better the position of Land's End in this region of sealdom. It might be a journey of seven to ten days, depending on how leisurely a progress we choose to make of it. I think you will find it interesting. There are many estuaries to explore and good hunting to be had in them." He paused, looking at the attentive face of the smaller seal: "It depends whether your compass has become set. Do not answer to what you think I wish to hear. Answer true, as usually you do; for yourself!"

It made all the difference. The word 'true' had its usual effect, drawing him back to the centre of himself, to an open mind. What did he want to do? His mind ran over possibilities until one strand became luminous. He recognised it would be the last trip of this season of life with the black seal that had become so important to him; filling the empty place where he had always yearned friendship might exist.

Ahead lay a reunion with Somerledaa in the sea cave locality that would forever be home to her. Ahead, there was a victory in battle for Tyrian, territory he would control and seal mothers who would welcome his peerless ways. The world would continue to spin but their lives would change; for better, for worse?

It was not such a hard question to answer, after all. With a little effort, he slithered off the rock, entering the sea with a loud splash before bobbing up again close to Tyrian:

"Whither are we bound, navigator?"

"You see this rock of which these islands are made? Granite, they say it is called. You remember the good hunting we had about one day west-north-west of here, on the way over from the Saltees? We hunted deep down over a submerged island of granite?

"Once, most of the lands to the east of us were like that. Once, it was covered by sea and only the highest volcanic places of Dartmoor remained above the surface, spilling lava flows into the sea. These things you can tell from patterns in the rocks. I had a good companion who loved to share such things: Arlandhu. He was my half-brother." Tyrian fell silent.

Quietly, Iolair ventured: "Arlandhu? You have never mentioned him before."

"He died. He was my friend even more than my brother. Not as big as me, nor as small as you, wise in understanding of the rocks to which the sea plants and animals anchor themselves; superb at hunting lobsters. It was his specialty."

"He died, you said?" Iolair asked the question as gently as he could.

"In nets, set on the bottom of the sea, they told me. I searched and even found him, but the feasting of scavengers had rendered him barely recognisable."

"It is a strange and awful thing, when one you love dies. You lose something that you cannot afford to lose, but they are the ones who lose the so-much-more of everything-that-might-have-been. A space comes into existence that can never again be filled. Set beside that, perhaps you gain in responsibility, to life and to their memory. They have been lost to life, but you can carry the afterglow of them not only in your heart but in the course you steer. And in sharing whatever is worth celebration. Thus, they remain, after their fashion.

"Sometimes, I see you looking at me. Sometimes, I hear you thinking well of me, but the truth is what you see is not me alone but also the afterglow of a half-brother and one or two others who I will not mention just now, though they maintain a presence. But we were talking of destinations, were we not?"

"You spoke of the seas and volcanoes of ancient history."

"That was Arlandhu whispering to you! What could I know of such things? I thought we might make another trip, a little longer than that from the Saltees, to the east, but travelling well out to sea. The inshore waters will be crowded with boats and people just now. Are you content to do that?"

"You lead, Tyrian."

***

An easy journey they made of it. A few fishing boats, more yachts and motor cruisers they saw along the way, but the weather was settled and quiet.

More interesting to them than boats were the interrupted columns of basking sharks they met. The smallest sharks were little more than three metres long. Youngsters, they were hardly longer than the largest grey seal. Others were huge, up to ten metres long or similar in length to the largest killer whales, but such giants were very few in number.

They travelled mainly in parties strung out along thermal fronts. Their great white gapes were caverns receiving plankton rich waters

333

that distended their gills; such was the volume of water they were sieving through their gill-rakers. Every so often, each shark would gulp down a knot of sieved plankton. If the food source was exhausted, they would seek the next bounty using their extraordinarily sensitive electrical receptors.

Ancient as dinosaurs, in the time of which their kind had known their beginnings, they swam along with apparent unwitting indifference to everything except the dense floating islands of microscopic zooplankton.

The seals had met them before, in every year of their lives; firstly, as callow yearlings, full of curiosity. Approaching quite close to the huge, slow-gliding fish, they never thought to fear the size of them. Now, bound in different directions, they were aware they offered neither harm nor opportunity.

The sharks took even less notice of the seals, but both had their distinction and sightings were enjoyed by the summer people abroad in their boats, relieving the desert-tedium of the almost changeless view from cockpit or wheelhouse.

Their passage took two days. When they came to the Dart, two hours remained until dark by which time the tide was full again. Despite the number of boats crowding its waters, they entered the river. The noise decided them to proceed, mainly submerged, by the Dartmouth shore where revelry was already in full swing. The gulls were even noisier than the people.

No-one saw them in the densely crowded reach downstream of the Admiralty moorings below the red brick Naval College. The sun was gone behind the high hills by then and they had crossed the broad mouth of Old Mill Creek before a man with dark, curling hair lifted an arm, pointed for the lady beside him, whispering sharply: "Martha! Look!"

As she looked up, the breeze caught her dark hair, blowing it across his face. Catching it in one tanned hand marred, here and there, by sweet-scented stains of dried river mud, he breathed in the scent of it, of wood smoke from their driftwood fire made earlier. They had shared the cooking of a simple supper eaten while grey herons and little egrets flew to roosts in nearby riverside oaks where they made a cacophony of ancient, even pre-historic, sounds of settling. It was crude music, but music all the same and river music at that.

Earlier, the man had pointed out the commotion made of the surface waters where the mackerel were marauding in from the sea, harrying and making slaughter of a shoal of brit. It was that time of year again.

The fire was burning low now. They had eaten their fill. They were full of the lovely, simple happiness you find waiting at such places and times and yet are too rare in a life. It was all they had. They had the fire, a shore empty but for two oystercatchers and three curlews and, for a roof, the darkening sky where, already, the Evening Star was shining bright.

In that place, together, they were utterly at home. Yet they were a secret and the hours they shared were stolen. If anyone had seen them, they would have been cruelly reduced by gossip to a crude, lewd caricature of what they were. She was married and Kevin a newcomer to the small, important, gossipy town.

Even now, her husband was sitting in one of the pubs from which the seals had heard noise emanating. A friendly, generous drinking man who would remain there ensconced with his drinking companions until closing time, he would accompany them to a club afterwards. Their marriage two years previously had been attended by a huge number of local people. As a pleasure boat skipper, he was part of the living core of the town, the waterfront fraternity, among whom no-one was more popular.

He loved his wife, but absent-mindedly. His habits had changed hardly at all since his marriage. He had not noticed the ties between them straining. His meal was on the table when he came home. His clothes were washed, mended, even ironed. If she was quiet most of the time, well, that was her way. So he had no sense of the disappointment and loneliness that caused her to become a refugee watching black seals passing from beside the fragrant warmth of the driftwood fire that was all the home that was left to her.

"We could shadow them upstream?" he suggested, tentatively.

"You know I should be getting back; in case." She did not need to elaborate.

"I know."

Caught in a tide of their own, he lifted her into the white boat, its stern in the water, bows resting on the gravelly mud. He had bought it as soon as he had saved enough from his wages: a little river boat with a shallow draught and a cuddy to keep the wind off them when the evening cooled. It was cooling now. Sending her to sit in the stern, having loaded aboard their few possessions, he lifted the bow and walked the feather-boat into the stream, leaping deftly aboard at the last minute. As able as he was in the management of boats, she released the outboard from its rest so that it measured its full length down and below the transom; stood and, at the second attempt, brought it to life.

They settled on the central thwart to keep the boat balanced. Facing upstream, proceeding at slowest speed, she steered the outboard by the extension he had rigged up. Having placed a soft blanket about her shoulders, he slipped an arm about her waist and drew her to him so they shared warmth. She glanced at him briefly, still shy of what so swiftly they had become, but smiling.

Ahead of them, the seals heard the outboard, but paid it least heed. Not gaining on them, it was no threat. They did not have far to go before they caught up with the mackerel they had been tracking. Near the Anchor Stone Rock, in the deep narrows below the village of Dittisham — once a place of orchards, but now a retreat for the wealthy — the tide gushes through and the riverbed falls away from shallows to the murkiest depths.

Intent on the merry, easy slaughter of tiny brit, the mackerel did not sense the seals until they were upon them. Two hundred metres downstream of the Rock, Kevin saw stressed white waters just above the place where the mackerel were slaying the brit but he had lost sight of the seals. He reached for his camera; the one Amaury had given him at the end of the last river cruise after he had mentioned he would be happy to take photographs of seals he saw in the river. Perhaps because both were outsiders, the two men had always got on well.

The unexpected casual generosity of it had taken Kevin aback. He had protested it was too generous a gift, aware Amaury was, like himself, against the wall financially, but his protests had been waved aside.

Was there enough light, and just how good was the zoom of the little camera? Standing up, moving over to starboard, he explained to Martha what he was aiming to do and how he would like her to manoeuvre the boat. Taking up position, leaning partly against the curve of the cuddy, partly against the lesser curve of the gunwale, he awaited his chance.

The seals had watched the killing frenzy of the mackerel from afar, using it for cover. Mackerel had been a major component in their diet since their reunion on the Blaskets. It was a taste of which neither tired, loving the texture of the firm flesh, loving the sea-turquoise colour and pattern while they held them between their flippers at the surface. Almost telepathically, they agreed to dive deep, to the bottom of the river. Angling steeply down, arriving in the depths they were surprised by what they found in the murk. All sorts of metal things had accumulated above a core of timber clutter. They did not recognise rusted, twisted farm machinery, cars, refrigerators, ovens, washing machines, televisions and more, all being reduced to a reef to which unrecognisable plant and animal life adhered.

Among the ribs of the reef protruded once white bones of cattle, horses, sheep and even people. It was a strange world, not necessarily sinister, but which they were glad to depart. Steeply upwards now, accelerating, they came up in the confused heart of the mixed shoal of mackerel and brit. Iolair swallowed three small mackerel almost by accident while Tyrian caught one more before seizing the largest in the entire shoal.

Deeply satisfied, he caught it in his mouth very close to the surface. He brought it lightly but securely held between his peg-shaped teeth with their flanking barbels. By now, the small white boat was only fifty metres downstream. Surfacing, Tyrian had been facing upstream toward the lights of Dittisham but, hearing the quiet sounds of the approaching boat, he performed a half circle in the water until he was facing downstream. Kevin was able to catch two profile shots in the process. When Iolair surfaced, holding another fish, Tyrian continued to turn; just checking it was his companion and, in so doing, exposed his other profile, allowing Kevin two more gifts along with a right-hand profile shot of Iolair.

That was to be all. Both seals sank under the water, snouts last, suggesting to Kevin they might stay down this time. He had learned quite a lot of seal field-craft from listening to Amaury's commentaries on the river wildlife cruises. When they did surface again, minutes later, they were upstream beyond the Anchor Stone and his searching.

It was a lovely evening. In the boat, the two refugees wanted to follow the seals but knew they must return to their secret landing place near the head of Old Mill Creek. There he kept the boat moored not far below the mill house, lime kilns and the old stone bridge. The herons and egrets, seeing their passing, would keep their secret. Afterwards, he would drive her most of the way homeward to a place where he might bid her a discreet, reluctant, farewell.

Not party to the secret, but having feasted, the seals cruised on the flooding tide upstream across the wide, shallow places of Broad Stream and Long Stream beyond. There, they chose the quietest channel off the Higher Dittisham shore. Still hunting there was a raggetty grey fisher with a heavy spear for a bill in shallows where, for a time, there had been an oyster farm. That was before the extraordinarily successful tributyl tin oxide co-polymer anti-fouling paints had come into common usage on most yachts using the river. They had proved perfect at preventing the growth of unwanted life on the hulls.

The French had raised the alarm. Their commercial oyster fishermen were suffering from the effects of the paint; as in the British estuaries. The shells of the oysters where the ragged grey fisher now plied his trade became deformed. The meat content shrank. The oysters and not only oysters displayed imposex, rendering them incapable of reproduction, and this happening at just a few parts per billion of the active agent in the paints in water.

Subsequent research proved it to be the most toxic compound ever deliberately introduced to the marine environment. Legislation came limply along behind. Use of tri-butyl tin oxide in anti-fouling paint was banned on all vessels less than seventy-five feet long because, of course, it could not have a measurable effect on the sea. When research at Sullom Voe in the Shetlands showed it could? Well, Sullom Voe is far away, and half measures had been taken already. How much TBT is to be found in any kilometre square of the surface layer of the sea today?

The grey heron was not aware the mud about his yellow-green feet was contaminated by tributyl tin oxide. The grey seals were aware or would soon become aware that whenever a flood of freshwater gushed off the granite moor, where this and other rivers had their birth, the mud of the riverbed was churned up. Tributyl tin locked there was re-released into the water column, requiring the agency monitoring the quality of the oysters to review repeatedly their status. Were they still fit for human consumption after their cleansing by ultra-violet light treatment?

For the time being, the river level was low and there was little prospect of floods spilling down from the heights of Dartmoor.

Near Stoke Gabriel, long-time heart of salmon netting on the Dart, two old men were watching the waters, as they had through their lives since they had run wild as small children on the same shores. They sat on a rough plank spanning the gap between two flat-topped rocks. One lifted the slightly gnarled holly stick he had cut for himself thirty years before and held it out horizontally, pointing. Without removing the black pipe rammed between his lips, he swore:

"Bliddy seals! Bliddy vermin!"

He was in his seventies. He could remember when the netting on the river had been good and the size of salmon regularly greater than in recent times. Eighteen licences there had been. Eighteen crews, of three or four men until they started the rot of including womenfolk, there had been. Mainly from Stoke Gabriel, of course. Reckon Stoke Gabriel had grown up where it was courtesy of the mediaeval salmon fishery and being not far from Torre Abbey and Torquay. The netters came from Galmpton, Dittisham, Cornworthy, Tuckenhay, even Duncannon. One boat even worked out of Totnes.

Trouble was no-one would control they rod-and-line men, farther upstream. No rules for the toff, only for the working man; only ever for the working man. Then came all they conservationists fretting about the seals! Didn't they know the damage a seal could do to a net? Didn't they know the difference a seal in or near a net made to their livelihood? 'Course they didn't! All they did was read about things in books and magazines! What did they really know about the outdoors? What did they know about working outside through the seasons in all weathers, as the tide permitted, working together as one? Sod all! They just lived their clean little lives with their clean little principles, office workers interfering with their little understanding burnished by degrees in this and that, manipulated by rabble-rousers.

They started by reducing the number of licenses issued. They shortened the season. Now, there was a moratorium on salmon netting in the river. Stocks had dwindled, the size of the few fish caught dwindling apace. No moratorium on the bliddy seals, though! They could still lord it, take what they chose to take. That wasn't fair. What point having a moratorium if nobody did anything about the seals? How could the stock recover if the buggers were out there, stealing their tithe?

Shoot a few of the buggers! There are enough of them, so they scientists are always saying. Every year: more of them, less of us! Who beats a drum telling how it is for us?

His companion saw the seals, shared the reaction. Rivals, they had been, once upon a time. Time had smoothed the rough edges. Now they shared memories and wisdom in the twilight of their trade:

"Chris, down Dartmouth; he'll know what to do for they!"

The two men chuckled. Let the fair-weather conservationists and scientists make their clack! There were still quiet ways of sorting out seal problems. No sense broadcasting it. Wait until the wind gets up a bit and it starts to rain, with the coast path empty of do-gooders and a fishing boat working out beyond the river-mouth rocks at low tide. What was it that boy running they wildlife cruises out of Dartmouth was always saying? 'These trips are timed to coincide with the period of low water to maximise the chances of seeing grey seals hauled out on their favourite rocks'. But not just in summer, boy; not just in summer!

Above Stoke Gabriel, the estuary narrowed, becoming dramatically serpentine. The river valley hills steepened, crowding closer together. Woodland covered the slopes of the left bank all the way to the pond below the handsome Palladian house on the hilltop built from Portland Stone. As on the estuary slopes of so many West

Country rivers, though, the woodland was predominantly a trick of the eye. Oaks, horse chestnut and other broadleaf trees gave a lovely rind for river users to gaze up at, largely concealing the conifers massed behind and the bare fields beyond.

Into Ham Reach, the seals cruised under the second of the river heronries. Bulky nests were built in the crowns of horse chestnut trees growing one rank or two back from the muddy shore the dredgermen of bygone days had known as Heron's Back. The name commemorated an earlier heronry, built in trees farther up the slopes, felled in the early sixties. They said it had been the largest heronry in the West Country. Young birds, grey necks proclaiming their immaturity, took first fishing lessons in shallows just beyond this mud, then as now.

Farther upstream, the seals passed below a trio of cormorant trees. They were easy to pick out in daylight, but this was the dimpsey hour. The white droppings of the large, ancient-looking birds perched high in these trees had dusted the leaves white. As summer progressed, the whitening became ever heavier as ever more cormorants flew upriver to use the roosts.

Around the sharpest bend, at Ham Point, into Sharpham Reach — Near the top of it — a pale rock called the Bonstone rose from weedy mud. On a riverside ledge near the top of that volcanic plug, a lovely pearly nest was now dilapidated. It had been substantially lined with the silky down Canada geese had plucked from their own breasts to create luxury for their new-born young. Not more than a hundred metres above the stone, a kingfisher stood on a smaller stone proud of the waterside mud and did not startle at the passing of the seals. Neither did three pairs of shelduck and their gaggles of pale grey and black young, dibbling over the mud of The Gut on the opposite shore.

In the light, fickle breezes, they could hear wind in the reeds over the wall, stretching inland from the rusting hulk of a paddle steamer. Under the wall, its iron hull was filled with river ooze. In this fertile ground, sea asters flourished. The old river boat was rotting away against a wall built to span the mouth of what had once been a short, shallow creek. Now a marsh, it was choked with reeds and the small biting things that thrive in such places, stretching inland, dog-legged under steep hills. Sometimes the otter hunted there for eels, afterwards sleeping on a couch of flattened reeds while the barn owl flew its ghostly moth-flights in search of mouse and vole.

In Home Reach, they were not tempted by the hole in the long wall that had been built in the wake of the Napoleonic wars by French and American prisoners marched down from Dartmoor Prison. They paid no heed to the five common sandpipers lined up on the grassy roof of the wall. Later, they flew upstream with umbrella-shaped wings, occasional wing-beats and little sprays of piping calls. The dry-stone wall had been built behind embankments of sandbags by hand. Embanking the river had kept the port of Totnes alive to enjoy an extra century and a half of prosperity, despite its location, ten miles in from the sea.

Once, heavy horses had tramped along the top of that wall, towing sailing ships carrying goods to Totnes. For one summer month of every year, they had been turned out on the Town Marsh, there to relax their hooves and perchance to gambol, recalling long-lost days of foaldom. This evening, no trace of the old towpath remained.

In the early years, towpath and wall were maintained. Latterly, they had been neglected. Now young trees grew where great, sedate hooves had trod. Here and there, a tree had toppled into the river, carrying a section of wall with it. That was how Hole in the Wall had begun to grow into its name. A tree fell; a section of wall fell with it. Thereafter, the hole grew ever greater from the pressure of the stream behind as much as from tidal movements of river water inward. In autumn and winter, almost annually, fierce waters flooded off the saturated moor. On them, sailed battering rams made of tree trunks and boughs of all sizes. There were periods of lesser flooding, with more trees falling, more trees sailing, more trees battering the carefully laid stones. Seeing their state of sorry dilapidation, opportunists removed more stones to use in construction work elsewhere. Cattle, grazing on the marsh, had further marred the sad riverside ruins.

Now, at Hole in the Wall the work of destruction was complete. It was hard to tell a wall had ever spanned what had come to resemble, to be, a creek entrance.

Totnes. What could be said of the handsome, flourishing town that had been left unsaid by the elegantly succinct pen of Defoe after his visit in the eighteenth century?

The passing seals, swimming into ever-sweeter water under quays latterly reinforced with an ugly fence of iron pilings, passed unseen below the manicured grass of Vire Island. From a boat, moored in the mainstream just below the bridge Fowler had designed, a moorhen slipped with a splash on to the water only to catch sight of unexpected whiskery faces heading her way. She ran away from them across the surface in sheer, blind panic before lifting off.

Under two road bridges the seals swam, a railway bridge carrying the main line and almost immediately afterwards, a newer footbridge. It led to the steam railway station that was the Totnes terminus of a lovely little line that ran alongside the Dart through Staverton to Buckfastleigh; through Old Devonshire. Far above the little River Hems that joined the mighty Dart beside the sewage works and the four Totnes bridges, the seals arrived at their concrete terminus separating the salt tide from the moorland drain of the higher Dart. They arrived at a weir awash with the thinnest curtain of lightly chattering sweet waters, its salmon ladder over by the far shore. Stout mallards were standing on the slope in the shallow waters. They had been minded to sleep but the seals disturbed their ambitions. An immature cormorant stood on the raised concrete barrier serving to keep separate weir and salmon ladder, but of salmon the seals sensed nothing. Any salmon of a size to catch their attention were absent.

However, there were fish present, perhaps pushed upstream on a tide now starting to ebb. Neither seal had happened upon grey mullet before but a shoal they found here, in a muddy, shallow inlet. Their behaviour was strange, opening their small mouths with the swollen upper lips to swallow the mud into which they settled to digest whatever it held of animal or plant life. They were slow-moving fish so, in the confusion created by their unexpected arrival, both seals caught a fish apiece. It made unusually dull fare for them. They preferred fish that had lived with zest in the open sea, like the mackerel they had taken down by the salty racing waters around the Anchor Stone.

It spoiled their appetites.

Resting after their feed, they idled at the surface of the dark waters, listening to unfamiliar birdsong and watching the bird-of-paradise tail dance performed by a grey wagtail on a rock sticking up out of the river. A babble of sounds emanated from a small estate of self-built houses ranged alongside and in from the river just upstream of the weir, tangling with the calling of unseen tawny owls. On the woodland floor, just downstream from watery ditches where the earliest kingcups began flowering in January, a stoat pounced on a rabbit. It severed the artery in its neck with savage expertise. The shrill, anguished farewell uttered by the rabbit persisted, growing ever weaker. The seals listened without comprehension, for these were land-sounds; of the interior, of another world.

After a little while, the seals drifted back downstream with the tide. That night, they might have slept in the quiet waters of Ham Reach, free from any pollution of artificial light, but the tide was ebbing strongly so they rode it all the way to the archipelago outside the river limit, sleeping there in the lee instead.

The next day, they were in no hurry to go anywhere for the atmosphere was gentle and peaceful. Tyrian hauled out on Seal Rock while Iolair followed him after the tide had dropped some more. Vyspedaa, an elderly female settled on the reef on the far side of the lagoon, to be joined by an immature seal lately arrived from Brittany. A satellite-relayed data logger was glued to her nape. Having been washed ashore, emaciated and starving, south of Bordeaux, she had been taken into care and transferred to Océanopolis in Brest. Restored there to good health, on Shakespeare's birthday she had been released back into the sea from the shores of the island of Banec.

Now, having first hauled out on a sandy beach in a sea cave near Hope Cove, later hunting over Skerries Bank, she had continued eastward to the place where now she found herself.

A boat full of people idled close by without causing any stir among the seals so it was the jet ski that smashed the quiet of the lagoon. All four seals went crashing into the sea, marginally preceded by the French visitor. Very soon thereafter, the jet ski sped seaward, narrowly missing Iolair where he had been drifting back to the surface.

Tyrian returned almost immediately to the base of Seal Rock, wondering whether to haul out again, whether there was time to justify doing so before the rising tide washed him back off. The little French seal swam over with similar intent. Initially, he did not notice her until she nudged him in passing whereupon he turned toward her with a rumble of irritation that sent her skittering away.

Near the entrance to the Dart, there was a parting. Vyspedaa departed in the direction of the river-mouth, intent on making a sedate progress as far as the Anchor Stone. The black males watched her go, cruising between Inner Froward Point and the submerged rock currently known — less crudely than before — as the Bear's Tail. Weed growing from its cap floated like a nest of leather belts at the surface, showing precisely where it was. She grew ever smaller, never turning. They knew she would swim on like that to the end.

***

They pressed westward by the wide gape of Plymouth Sound to Dodman and beyond, toward the most southerly mainland lighthouse on Lizard Point. By then, they were close inshore rather than shortening the water distance by taking a direct line for the Lizard. That was how they came to Gull Rock.

In the sunniest and calmest of weather, they did not glimpse the man whose white wave ski was lodged discreetly among rocks low on the seaward side of the island. At an earlier hour, he had arrived there. Landing was a little awkward but, once ashore, it had been easy enough to clamber to the top of the island.

The nesting season was over. There were no shags, cormorants, razorbills or guillemots to disturb. During the climb, he had stooped to pick up the skull of a shag as well as four pink sea fans bleached white in the light found in the dilapidated nests of shags. Having landed on many West Country islands, he knew the nests of shags often flaunted surprising construction or decoration materials. It was the primary reason he was there and then.

From his first year studying seals, he had kept field journals recording not just seal data, but everything of interest. In the third

345

month of that first year, he noted two pairs of shags nesting on high ledges inside Martinsfinger Cave.

Initially, he had made the note in passing because it was a cave that required you remain keenly alert. Danger, if it threatened, came from ground level or below water level so the heights merited hardly a glance.

Late in the fifth month, finding two dead partly-fledged shags below a nest and no mark on their bodies suggesting how they might have died, he made the awkward ascent to discover whether it contained survivors. It was a dangerous climb, his wet suit boots achieving uncertain grip on the damp surfaces. The brave shag in residence repeated its ancient challenge, each time supplemented by a vigorous shaking of the head. Finally, losing heart at the climber's approach, it dropped into the air becoming iridescent bottle-green in sunlight as it slewed around out over the sea.

The nest was empty but contained a detail that inspired him to make a long-term study of shag nests. The nest had contained no natural materials being made exclusively of thick, white plastic fishing line. Teetering with tenuous hand-holds and slippery foot-holds, he was chastened to find he had made months of cave visits without noticing this bizarre construction.

In the years since, he had visited nearly all the islands of Devonshire and Cornwall, discovering derelict fishing gear was commonplace in nest construction. The study evolved and he discovered how in some years the onset of egg-laying by shags was as early as January.

So, he climbed to the long, uneven crest noticing on the steep, white-splattered slopes that one of the shags had again used barbed wire for part of its nest construction. As ever, he took the essential confirming photograph and sketched the position on his heavily annotated sketched plan of the slope, its nests, spreads of plants and prominent perching places.

Chores done, he became ensconced in a comfortable skyline place, nestled against a rock so that he offered no human profile to alert his presence to wild creatures or people walking the coastal footpath across the narrow sea.

This day, guillemots were his chore though their nesting time was done. He had discovered that where guillemots and razorbills shared a site with shags, they tended to stray over the dilapidated remains of the shag nests, there becoming entangled. Once entangled, death always ensued: there was no-one to release them. It affected only small numbers annually but was known to no-one other; so, here he roved, collecting evidence.

Down below him, the present intruded in the form of a seal swimming just below the surface above the canopy of sunlit kelp. Submerged and sunlit, the seal looked as if made of mercury. Behind, at some distance, swam a larger, mercury-seal. These he photographed, not in the hope of identifying them but being charmed by their magical appearance.

Later, both seals hauled out briefly on nearby Middle Stone but, after two hours, continued their journey. Once around the stones under Lizard light, they would see the end of their year's journeys, but still they found time to make another detour. Having traversed the great entrance to the Fal, they slipped into Helford estuary and, once more, passage between wooded hills and small villages.

Above the crowded moorings of Helford Passage was a great pool from where water spread in all directions. On the far north slopes, ancient semi-natural western oak-woods had grown since Roman times. Away to the left opened the occasionally osprey-haunted, kingfisher-haunted, grey mullet-haunted quiet of Frenchman's Creek. The seals took neither course but went northward by Groyne Point into the quiet of Polwheveral Creek, making for a small, white-painted boathouse nestled under busy trees.

There were occasional small boats drawn up on the far shore, but none were being rowed, sailed or motored in the creek. Some had lain so for decades, forgotten. It was a place for birds, the first of which were returning from their breeding grounds. Two pairs of shelduck swam, ever wary, with their vulnerable but well-grown creches regarded still by the gulls and crows with covetous eyes. Young herons and egrets practised fishing with increasing aplomb in the creek shallows.

There had long been a heronry in the creek-side trees. In relatively recent times, little egrets joined them. Had the seals been swimming by two months earlier, they would have heard ancient croaking's, beak-tapping's and other noises uttered by the young of both birds, rising to a crescendo every time a parent brought food to the nest.

They swam above the silent heronry across the entrance of Polpenwith Creek, almost to the head of the creek where wastes of soft mud prevented farther progress. On a hill above, at the edge of a copse, a vixen stared down at the two of them. Deciding they were not a threat, she resumed her hunt for beetles.

A lady tending her garden above the head of the creek in the small hamlet of Polwheveral straightened, mopping her brow. She felt the loveliest view in the world was spread below her, especially with the trees were covered with leaves that resembled dense carpet pile under a blue sky. She was aware of the fox on the hill, seeing her most days. She kept chickens, but had suffered no loss; chicken run and hen house were secure against foxes and rats.

It was by watching her, seeing she was staring at something, that she noticed the seals. She hastened into the house, collecting binoculars from the cupboard and focussed on the two heads. Seeing one was much bigger than the other, she assumed he must be a male.

The seals had nowhere to go but back downstream. They felt and saw mullet moving in mud-swirling shallows of their own making. Perhaps remembering the drab meal not savoured at the head of the Dart, neither seal was tempted to hunt them.

They returned to the sea, content to aim for Lizard light, with Iolair setting the pace and making the decisions.

They rounded Lizard Point, seeing seals bottling in sandy-bottomed Housel Bay and Polbream Cove. More were bottling in Polpeor beyond the decaying slipway of the old lifeboat station where several choughs were on the wing. In recent years, they had returned to nest after more than fifty years absence in Cornish sea caves and disused mine adits, initially along this Lizard coast. These were the first choughs they had seen since departing south-west Ireland. It chanced they were of the same line.

The seals reached the serpentine coast. Here, rocks were the most alive either seal had ever seen, exuding vitality. Was the affinity they felt due to some sense they had of it having served, long, long ago, as the sea-floor? Once upon a time, it had been part of the Earth's crust, subsequently uplifted to decorate this once remote and rarely visited shore?

The beaches and caves behind them at Kynance were crowded with people but the seals did not make a wide detour. Many people, on the cliff tops and the beaches, saw them swim by, stopping often to peer shoreward, enjoying the good television of human behaviour. However, when they passed behind the rocky heights of The Bishop and Gull Rock, no-one saw them submerge and swim below the surface over serpentine sands until they were in a narrow defile leading to a dead end.

They followed the defile in the spirit of curiosity and so chanced upon a passage even narrower that delved left into the heart of Asparagus Island. The lure proved irresistible, the more so when they discovered it widened below the surface. Indeed, instead of proceeding into ever-deeper darkness, at the very heart of the small island they came to the surface of a large, deep, sand-bottomed pool in unexpected sunlight. Looking upward, they saw a bright blue window high in the east wall where natural processes had quarried a skylight.

They were made madcap and gay by the miracle of this secret place. Briefly, they performed a dance of sheer delight in the unexpected pool, coiling down to the sandy bottom, later performing a brief chase round and round at the surface before spilling vertically down again to the depths.

In the end, Tyrian led the race back along the narrow passage out of the pool into the blocked defile. Emerging initially as two black impressions of seals, their shadows proceeding side by side over the pale seabed were seen by some of the few people walking the cliff tracks north of Kynance Cove, but after they rounded Rill Ledges, they were seen no more.

Farther north, they discovered a serpentine seal cave. They might have missed it, even though they were mainly close in to the cliffs, but that Iolair saw two immature seals bottling in a shadowy corner of a small bay. Such sightings often indicated the proximity of a place where it was possible to haul out. They radiated no aggressive intent to the two young seals who watched their passing with wary eyes. They reached the gloomy corner of the bay under grassy heights where two more choughs probed the short turf, rolling over pieces of pony dung searching for ants and dung beetles.

As ever, Tyrian led the way through the narrow, steep-walled entrance into the serpentine cave. Within, immediately they could smell on the cave air the fishy perfume of seals present or recently departed.

Here, a mainly inaccessible beach of slippery boulders stretched back into the gloom to the left of a polished serpentine pillar, so Tyrian led the way to the right of it. The waters remained just deep enough for him to reach a narrow shore of serpentine pebbles where he half-emerged, still sniffing the air. The beach was empty, but the sense of at least one seal present remained strong.

Behind him, Iolair was looking to the right, sensing himself watched. Very slowly, he drifted by Tyrian toward the belly of water within. There, he lay at the surface, become still, daring venture no deeper.

With many pauses, Tyrian hauled himself up the beach, all senses alert. Behind him, Iolair came half ashore, but even as he did a seal erupted from the back of the inlet into which he had peered for so long. The water being too shallow to allow for full submergence, the fleeing seal made a great commotion as she went, looking like a mechanical toy in a bath.

Startled fully ashore, Iolair glimpsed the fearful, distended eye of a young mature female as she dashed for the narrows of the entrance and the light beyond. Tyrian came hastening down the beach until he was stationed directly behind Iolair. They exchanged a brief glance; Iolair re-entered the water.

Alone on the beach, Tyrian lifted his head again, no longer sniffing the air but watching the play of light on sea-polished serpentine walls. As it shimmered, he found himself enjoying the rare atmosphere. Only belatedly did he follow Iolair back into the light. As ever, this engendered a lifting of the spirits even though they were never aware of them sinking while in the caves. He swam slowly at the surface, glancing toward Iolair who seemed suddenly frustrated by their desultory progress.

It was time to accelerate on to their destination.

That evening, after dark, they hauled out on Longships Reef in an assembly of more than forty seals, most of them local. Having ascertained Somerledaa was absent, Iolair had leisure to notice that many seals offered Tyrian the standard passing recognition of a local seal returned after long absence.

Iolair recognised Tyrian had, in one sense, not yet fully returned. He knew that in the morning Tyrian would lead him to the Bay of Seals, known so well already through the songs of Somerledaa as well as through Tyrian. He might have travelled that last short leg alone but Tyrian would not hear of it.

He saw the impression Tyrian created. A member of the tribe had returned with the gleaming air of a peerless seal. Other males assessed him, wondering whether there was a fighting heart in the great black body or whether he was one of those gentle seals incapable of being as mercilessly destructive as a peerless seal needed to be.

At one point in the night, when the sea lifted them from the rocks back into the sea, Tyrian rolled over with casual grace and found his way aggressively blocked by a big brown male who was not Meinek. Scath had travelled south from Skomer, seeking a place to settle. At the surface, Tyrian stretched himself out to his full length and gently blew bubbles in the direction of Scath, who mirrored the posture and the bubbles.

It was Iolair who broke the deadlock by speeding over Scath's hind flippers and racing seaward at his top speed. Taken unawares, the brown male came sharply around and began initiating a chase before remembering his confrontation was with lately arrived Tyrian. Too late. When he returned to the sea-washed rocks, Tyrian was nowhere to be found. With a sense of satisfaction that a potential rival had avoided his challenge, Scath settled to doze contentedly under the spokes of revolving light.

Other seals had been aware of the confrontation. The atmosphere on the rocks was restless even though it was not a nursery-territory proper. Rather, it was the main resting place in the locality. The full cast that would hold the stage or inhabit the wings as hopeful understudies for the duration of the imminent breeding season was thrown together here. As ever, this was leading to a jockeying for position. Like Scath, they decided Tyrian had lost face.

Had he allowed his mind to wander, Tyrian could have guessed their feelings, but he had followed Iolair to seaward, passing close to Scath in the darkness without either recognising the other. Farther out, he made a rendezvous with Iolair, thanking him with some irony for protecting him. Thereafter, they made a last hunt together. Tyrian caught such a large ling he was unable to eat it all, leaving it in the end for the gulls to quarrel over where it hung like a floppy scarf at the sea surface.

Iolair feasted on mackerel, aware that somewhere along the perimeter of the same glittering shoal; the usual porpoises were taking their usual tithe.

In the first light of morning, from a place approximately halfway between Longships Reef and the Brisons, a few miles to the north, Tyrian and Iolair swam in toward the long shield of brown cliffs. The propitious sun had risen above the cliffs. They swam south to the Mermaid's Pool because the tide was flooding and here made their parting. For the first time since they had met one another, when and where they might meet again was obscured. Come to the moment, both were quiet. Change was upon them at last.

"When you have secured your territory, will you remain here the year around?" Iolair asked, aware his words sounded a little stilted.

"No!" Absolute certainty: "It is in my mind that once I have returned myself to good health and moulted, to travel far into the north. I am curious to visit the snow country that Ithian has seen; Meinek, too, they say."

Iolair noticed the absolute certainty that he would hold a territory this season. He noticed also he was maintaining an adamantine connection with the Tyrian who loved exploring the far margins.

"Then we shall be travelling separate ways for the full year. I shall look for you out on the Longships, this time next year, if all is well."

"Do I need to ask you what plan you have?" Tyrian asked, gently.

"If Somerledaa allows, we may explore together for part of the year. If I travel for some time alone, I may travel east to the dune islands I have heard described at the south end of the North Sea, off the coasts of the Netherlands; the Mermaid Country. If that happens, then perhaps I will emulate you, venture northward to the Baltic, find a snow country of my own."

"So be it. Perhaps we will meet again before our time here is done. If so, be sure I shall not fight with you; however, mad gossips may make me sound. If not, travel well, Iolair. I will seek my friend at Longships Reef this time next year."

At the very last, neither was immediately able to turn away from so close a companion. They stared at one another in prolonged, intense regard, aware as seals ever are that any parting might be the last. In the end, they swam off together while forking ever farther apart. Tyrian was returning to Longships Reef while Iolair would come, at long last, to the Bay of Seals.

Coming around the headland, Iolair espied the seal entrance into Great Seal Hole where, the year before, Balanec held tenuous sway in the shadow of mighty Meinek. Wary, now, he swam into the sea cave under the gaze of inevitable shags. Just before he came to the junction on the left after which rose the sand-hill beloved of weary seals at journeys end, he glanced upward upon hearing the slow, soft commentary of four rock doves. There was enough light to highlight the iridescent green panels on the sides of their necks.

His first impression was that it was a great cave indeed. His second was that it was unexpectedly full of light and sand. His third was of Somerledaa, quite obliterating the previous two impressions. There were four seals within. Three were yearlings. Smallest and most silvery of them, Somerledaa lay closest to the entrance, some sense causing her to lift her head, strain her eyes. And then she came down the sand-hill, not daring to hasten for fear of setting off a general avalanche of seals.

Happily, he came up the same hill toward her, his sea-smoothed pelage in contrast to the velvet she wore. Meeting, they extended their necks, touched snouts, cupped vibrissae toward one another. Then, she led him back downhill and out into the daylight. The eagerness was back upon her immediately; there was so much to share. They swam together out to the rock-littered waters of the headland where she said:

"Very soon, now, the madness will begin and Great Seal Hole will no longer be a safe lodge in which to rest. I know a place along the coast from here where we will not be troubled. But there is no hurry. Where have you come from? What have you been doing?"

They were too eager to remember to be shy with one another, as they could have been. The sharing began. Other seals passed as they shared their tales. The tide rose to the full and receded again, but none intruded on an intimacy as apparent as something physical between them.

***

At the end of the same afternoon, Tyrian was resting on a low-lying skerry below the camel-shaped rock near the south end of the reef. Stretched to his full length, he was velvety in the sunlight. He was aware his fellow males were less wary of him than on the previous day, but no seal challenged him, even so. Peace endured until the second hour of the flooding tide on which Scath emerged from the rise of the swell. Sending a bow wave before him, he teetered on the edge of the rock, neither quite ashore nor falling back while the wave spent itself against the flanks of Tyrian.

By reflex, Tyrian did the banana, lifting head, tail flippers and one fore-flipper as high as possible from the water. Identifying the source of the disturbance, he understood the big seal would give him no peace until the issue was settled between them. Turning without hesitation, he came directly to confront Scath at a moment most unpropitious for his rival. Scath could do nothing from the position he was holding. He subsided awkwardly backwards, into the sea.

Tyrian settled just back from the edge of the rock. He lay on his belly with his chin resting on the wet slab, making it impossible for Scath to return to the same shore. When the challenger bobbed up close by, Tyrian snarled: long, low and threatening. Scath snarled back until the swallowing of water spoiled the effect.

On surrounding rocks, males of an age to consider making their challenge made hurried reassessments of the black male.

Matters came to a head in the morning. Tyrian was first ashore and, as the tide fell, found his rock shared by ever more seals, most of whom were males. He slept soundly as the sun rose higher, untroubled by their proximity until Scath hauled himself from the sea. It became apparent because, in the fidgeting caused by his aggressive arrival, a young male accidentally nudged Tyrian.

Sleeping on one side, Tyrian wakened, craning his neck to seek the source of the disturbance, rubbing one eye with — then flexing — the same fore-flipper. Across the velvet of several moving bodies and others that were still, he recognised his rival without appearing to do so. Subsiding back to the rock, he closed his eyes again though, around him, few other seals relaxed.

Very soon, the snarling began.

It had not continued for long when two yearlings went splashing down a long basin of rock into the sea. As it continued, three more seals departed. Suddenly, the atmosphere was full of agitation.

It was Scath, of course, but the prime object of his aggression remained apparently oblivious. Time passed and the intermittent stream of departures continued until only seven seals remained. At this point, Scath began to intensify his bellicosity, recognising the seals remaining were not the type to be daunted by simple abuse. Isolating the smallest, he made a sudden rush at him, so discomforting him that he turned hurriedly aside and dived into the sea, followed by his near neighbour, an old, once peerless male who had not held a territory for three seasons. He repeated the tactic against the smallest of the remaining seals and then against the oldest until he was left on the once crowded rock with just two males.

Like Tyrian, Stypic was the same age as Scath, untroubled by rudeness except it meant he would probably have to answer the challenge when his mood had been simple luxuriation in the warmth. When Scath made another aggressive charge in his direction, Stypic answered with a bloodcurdling snarl. Scath drew up short. For a while, they snarled at one another until the stalemate induced Scath to make a second charge ending so close that Stypic yielded a little ground. This

355

led to a renewed bout of ever more aggressive snarling before Scath made another threatening surge that drove Stypic back a little more.

A pattern had developed. Very slowly, though it took fifteen minutes, Stypic was driven across the rock until he was against the far edge. There, though he tried to hold his ground, his hunger to fight was simply not as overweening as that of his rival. It was a longer drop into the sea than normally he would have essayed but he twisted and dived away from Scath's challenge, even so.

Still snarling quietly in the back of his throat, Scath shuffled around and stared at the remaining seal. Buoyant on ripples of easy triumphs, Scath began a long charge across the rock, snarling as he came. Tyrian watched, making no move at all. He watched the brown seal huffing and puffing with exertion as he galumphed toward him. Rolling on to his belly, he drew himself up to his fullest bulk. Scath came on, still snarling but ultimately disconcerted by the lack of reaction on the part of his enemy. Stopping at the very last, almost within touching distance, he extended his neck and snarled into Tyrian's slightly averted face.

For the next five minutes, intermittently, Scath snarled so, only to be confronted by supreme indifference and disconcerting silence. There was no sense of fear about this seal.

Caution snapped. Scath lunged open-mouthed toward Tyrian and this time, Tyrian mirrored the gesture. Imperceptibly, they shuffled forward until they were neck to neck. Still leading the attack, Scath leaned his full weight through his neck against that of Tyrian and was shocked to find himself not only matched but forced into slight retreat.

Tyrian had never behaved so before in his life but understood very well what to do. This was the last engagement short of bloodshed whereby they tested each the respective strength of the other. If either sensed himself the weaker now, he must yield ground and try to escape without being bitten in the attempt.

Some seals who had yielded their places on the rock had lingered in the sea to observe the outcome. They watched them part three times but each time resume the trial of strength. When they had been re-engaged for another minute, Tyrian suddenly blazed into effort. Neck to neck, he bulked himself up and unleashed himself at Scath, driving him more than halfway across the rock before he paused, apparently to draw breath. Scath, surprised and therefore weakened, attempted to counter-surge, but found himself driven backwards again, this time in disorder. Tyrian had paused when he thought it politic, setting the trap into which his rival had fallen.

It was the decisive phase of the encounter. Scath found himself forced to recognise not only the over-mastering strength, but also superior guile of Tyrian. Wheeling, he fled at his fastest speed, unhappily aware Tyrian was in closest pursuit, almost on his hind flippers. He dived steeply into the sea. Above him, Tyrian stood high on his fore-flippers as he came to a standstill at the brink. He had no sense of triumph, having won no territory, but there was satisfaction in driving off bullying Scath. He felt the theatre of the occasion called for it. It meant Scath, at least, would no longer disturb his peace on these rocks. Nor Scath alone; all the seals who had fled would recognise the unwisdom of challenging him.

Settling once more, he fell asleep in the ancient summer sunlight.

***

Having spent four hours paddling his ski along the coast checking every sea cave along the way, Amaury had found the first pup of the season. It was swimming in a chest-deep pool some way into a cave that delved about eighty metres into the cliff. By lamplight, he clambered over huge entrance boulders, some sharp-edged, some slippery, before reaching the pool. There, he spent the statutory ten minutes scanning the murky water.

Straightaway, he had espied the white-coat in shallows on the far side of the pool at the bottom of a steep hill of shingle. He had scanned longer than usual because there was no seal mother on the beach and neither had he seen one outside the cave. Logically, then, she must be submerged in the pool. Nor did he simply scan with his eyes, spending the same amount of time listening for the breathing of a seal returned to the surface.

When caution was exhausted, he edged into the pool, working watchfully along the left-hand wall. He reached the far shore without being ambushed by a submerged seal trudging on through deep shingle up the hill, scanning by torchlight for more pups, sleeping adults or even tracks.

There were no seals, but at the back of the cave was a huge pile of timber. It had been lost from a ship that had foundered and, driven into the coast, finally grounded in the bay outside the cave entrance. Of the five metre lengths of timber washed ashore thirty years previously, many lodged at the back of this cave. Repeatedly battered by storm surf, re-floated at high tide of all the spring tides of the intervening years, the timbers had been smashed, whittled and smoothed. Now, a great bonfire pile of pine-scented wood remained at the back of the same cave, most of the planks greatly shortened, their jagged edges sea-smoothed. The pile was decorated with plastic floats, green trawl netting, aluminium beer barrels, strips of wet suit rubber, pellets of Styrofoam and congealed oil, but the strongest impression yet remained the scent of pine.

Returning to the pool, he took close-up photographs of the tolerant pup by lamplight. Estimating its age, he guessed it had been born just before the middle of July. He had not checked the Land's End or Boscastle caves so this must serve as the firstborn pup of the season.

Pictures secured, he made his way back into the ever-welcome light. Soon, he was paddling again on the quiet sea. Because it was so clear, beyond the margin of sub-littoral boulders he saw pieces of rusted iron wreckage dark against the sands below, only to be startled by a sudden snort. A seal, surfacing very close behind him, cleared water from her nostrils. The absent seal mother, making a belated appearance, surged along close behind him, regarding him with eyes wild and challenging.

Amaury did not alter the rhythm of his paddling, but looked to the bottom no more. Distractingly, the seal mother remained in close, threatening attendance for about a kilometre. He felt like a lumbering transport aircraft that had intruded into unfriendly airspace, from which a fighter plane was now escorting him.

He did not expect the female to veer away. Seal mother escorts were not the norm, but at certain sites, or in the case of certain individuals, they might accompany him until he was well-beyond their notional exclusion zones. This was one of those sites and one of those seals. She dropped back slightly as they drew further from the cave but she did not turn back until he was approaching a great headland with a famous name.

Alone again, he had a long paddle homeward in sunshine before him. He made a beeline for the famous headland, then others.

This day, attended by memories of adventures-past, he paddled on a sea empty but for two crabbers working lines of pots outside the headlands and came without misadventure to his landing place.

When he landed, several people were watching him, but he did not look at them. Having climbed the steps to the low cliff-top, he strode to the cliff edge by which his van was parked. There, he set the dry bags down and lifted the ski to the roof rack despite objections from his muscles. He stowed the dry bag, peeled off his baggies and wet suit boots and set about towelling himself dry.

He was dressed and sipping tea from his flask when his mobile phone rang. It was Amber, telling him that she lay in the grass not more than one hundred metres distant and might he consider sharing his tea with her? Also, she just happened to have two fresh batons, butter, the tomatoes he loved as well as some cheese and pate.

He was laughing happily as he sought and found the waving form of her arm, rose and started walking toward her.

***

Iolair and Somerledaa were in no hurry to travel eastward to her place of refuge, but lingered near the great cave. They made no great journeys but each day swam sedately across the neighbouring bay to spend the hours of low tide in the Mermaids Pool. Sometimes people were sitting in the cliffs above, watching them, being watched in turn; it was a comfortable stand-off.

For the most part, the seals enjoyed a sociable time there for up to eight hours daily before the rising tide called them back across the bay and round the granite headland to the sea cave. There, they would sing much and sometimes sleep.

Offshore, Tyrian was receiving increased respect since his bloodless battle with Scath. Other males, arriving since the dramatic day, sensed the atmosphere and quietly recognised the pre-eminence of the gleaming black male. On the edge of the assembly, no longer contending for the resting place occupied by Tyrian, Scath remained aggressively quarrelsome. Although he had been defeated, he yet hoped to secure a nursery territory. Small sea cave territories offered chances to more seals to mate with females than the great east coast and Scottish beach assemblies. From time to time, he would gaze balefully toward Tyrian, wondering whether to offer battle a second time.

Meinek remained an absentee but his absence loomed like an ominous, threatening cloud over the seals assembled under the lighthouse.

The composition of the assembly changed daily. There were local seals, returned for the nursery season, who ventured to sea on short hunting expeditions. There were travelling seals that played no part in aggressive inter-actions but rested far from potential contender-seals. Among them were pregnant females bound for breeding grounds not only in Cornwall, but Lundy and South Wales in one direction, or Ireland in another. Some were powerful males who might have challenged Tyrian, at the right time and place, who kept their peace as he had while lingering abroad among the Western Rocks.

Apart from trips to other local haul-out sites or water resting places, the bigger males also made occasional trips inshore to prospect around sea cave nursery sites for seal mothers. In fact, Artesyn did come by night to Martinsfinger Cave, giving birth to a sickly pup that survived only long enough to see the light of dawn before drifting quietly out of life again.

Two days later, Stypic ventured into the cave on the high tide and found the drenched remains of the lifeless pup stranded broadside on to the entrance, entangled in salt-stippled kelp. Of the mother who had produced it, there was no sign — not even tracks in the sand. He came half ashore, stretching forward his neck and sniffing gently, first at the poignant remains of the pup and then, more generally, at the air. Finding nothing, he went with the tug of the backwash, wondering where the female might be and whether she had come immediately into season. That night, Tyrian noticed his absence from the rocks of the Longships Reef. He had been ever-present since Tyrian's arrival, a not-unfriendly presence at a time of restlessness.

He had seen Stypic swimming off in the direction of the nursery caves and guessed he was making a prospecting run. Noticing he did not return, Tyrian supposed he might have found a seal mother and wondered, for the first time, whether he should make a prospecting run of his own, though he sensed it was still early for that. Moreover, he was acutely aware Meinek was the best guide as to when and where to swim inshore. In past years, he had always returned before the breeding season had begun in order to assert his authority. His prolonged absence was the lone unsettling feature in Tyrian's world.

One morning, slipping into the sea Tyrian elected to forage around the roots of Wolf Rock on whose brown dressed-granite ledges kittiwakes clung like while petals. On the sea floor, he came upon a wreck remembered from past visits and here took another big ling.

Sensing it was his last feast before the nursery season began, he feasted until he could eat no more, this time leaving only miserly pickings for the gulls. He swam back via the repetitive mournful sounds and the gentle rocking of Runnelstone Buoy even as the white-hulled brightness of Scillonian III came steaming by, outward bound to St. Mary's. Because he was seaward of the ferry, few passengers saw him. Most were leaning against the rails listening to the turgid, taped commentary pointing out landmarks to starboard.

In the wake of the ferry, Tyrian continued inshore toward Porthgwarra. There was not much of a swell. Below him, foraging among the canyons, he did not sense Meinek hunting, Somerledaa hunting, Iolair hunting. He just surged easily along, at or just below the surface, heading directly for Gwennap Head.

In the canyons, Somerledaa was hunting without intensity, happy exploring places she had rarely visited. She explored without caution, failing to sense she was not alone as she drifted down the wall of one of the wider canyons.

Guarn, the great, scarred conger who had been forgotten by Death, the horror of the gullies, the bender and breaker of fish hooks, the doom of the unwary, was watching her. One year previously, he had watched her mother swimming by his sea-sculpted piece of boat iron on top of the canyon-riven plateau. Since seeing Mornalas, he had taken two emaciated moulted seal pups and wounded two more. Ancient in years, learning, in refinement of hunting instincts, he sensed she was well fed and lazy. His great cunning whispered to him that she was an opportunity.

He was thinking of his opportunity as she swam by the iron in which he was resting. He watched her pause, approach tentatively, then veer sharply away having caught some sense of the danger she was in. Guarn did not move nor react in any way at all. He was confident she would return, and that he would have his opportunity.

Somerledaa had glimpsed something in the iron, something that might be alive and alarming. She accelerated over a precipice down into another canyon. She hurried all the way to the bottom where the barrel of an 18th century cannon was wedged, encrusted with anemones: one small place where flower power had vanquished the will to war. Quickly forgetting the horror that had sent her fleeing to this refuge, she drifted back up the wall to the riven plateau, continuing her languid foraging along with occasional visits to the surface.

From time to time, across the clear, sunbeamy waters, Iolair intruded as a distant silhouette, playing the same lazy game as she. Time passed. She forgot the fright she had received from within the sea-sculpted iron relic. Criss-crossing the ground, she ventured close to it again, all the time watched by the fearsome, conger. Once more, she spilled into a wide canyon as Tyrian swam by overhead, his shadow marked only by Guarn. Spiralling downwards, a smaller conger shrank back into his narrow abode. Farther down, she lingered above a small lobster, rightly wary of the heavily armoured claws. At the bottom were the bones of a seal pup Guarn had eaten, though she failed to recognise the white sticks for what they were.

Returning to the plateau rim, she rested her nose on it, watching the movements of a seal that might be Iolair working in her direction. Deciding she would play the hunting game with him, she kicked so that she emerged from the canyon and moved slowly along the edge of the precipice, thinking to hide behind the piece of iron wreckage set back from the edge. Lazily, she came around the curved rim of the iron and face to face with Guarn.

At first, she did not recognise him as a conger, but saw eyes glinting at the edge of a monstrous gape, and then she went spinning as the enormous eel lunged at her. There was a moment of blinding pain in her shoulder, of shock, as she went spinning away, but she could never know this once, Guarn's aim had been flawed. His first lunge should have been fatal for her but, as it was, his teeth had scored a long red line along her shoulder and now he was uncoiling his considerable length and massive power to finish her off.

While she strove feebly to recover her equilibrium, he sailed free of the boat iron and drove in powerful ripples toward her. She found herself paralysed, unable to move as the numbing monstrousness of him fully emerged from concealment. Belatedly, she did try, hindered by the sharp pain of the deep wound in her shoulder and then panicking because of her weakness and his size.

Guarn came on, closing the gap between them. Without thought, she kicked for the sunlit surface but this only narrowed the gap between hunter and hunted for Guarn changed his line of attack. He followed her upward at a steeper angle. Closing, now more swiftly closing, he was certain of taking her.

Meinek struck him hard, just below his massive head, teeth sliding on the surface of gleaming, dull grey skin; then striking again and again. The shock for Guarn was massive. For the first time in several decades, he was dully conscious of pain, of an attack dangerous to him. On the final driving lunge, Meinek had taken a chunk from his neck, making it possible to take a grip of the slippery conger and drive for the surface.

Massively, they burst into sunlight. There, at the earlier hour, six Penberth cove-boats had been fishing. Now, only one remained. The noise of it startled the fisherman who jumped, turning at the same moment. He saw seal and massive eel locked together but made no sense of what they were before they were gone again. Less than a minute later, a young seal bobbed up, not far distant, her shoulder streaming blood, which was a mystery of itself. Fishing forgotten, he wondered what would happen next. Much farther away, he saw Iolair bob to the surface to breathe and look about him, he too having been startled by the strange noises he was hearing. He, too, was mystified.

Both young seals still at the surface, the fisherman having not yet returned to his chores, there was another massive eruption, this time accompanied by a great roar from Meinek, Guarn having secured a grip on the top of his head. Around Guarn's neck, Meinek had inflicted a deep necklace of bites and continued to cling on, though not quite so securely as Guarn. Blood was running into his eyes when the waters closed again over them.

A minute later, the two emerged again with another mighty roar from Meinek. Guarn had maintained his bloody grip while the necklace of bites ringing the neck of the eel was more extensive and deeper than before.

They submerged again while the fisherman stared. Now there was a much longer wait but when it happened, Meinek again broadcast a massive roar as if his intention was to drive dread deep into the heart of his enemy. Both were bearing wounds so dreadful that this battle must end only with the death of one of them, but they remained locked together as they sank under the surface for the fourth time.

The quiet this time was eerie. Four minutes passed before the surface waters parted again, and this time the head of the great-hearted seal was not gripped by the massive conger yet gripped in his teeth. Death had remembered Guarn after all, but doom had been visited upon him only through the agency of a seal as mighty as Meinek.

Meinek remained long in sunlight at the surface, not feasting on the savourless flesh. Blood flowed more slowly from his wounds until it stopped altogether. All the while, he moved not at all but to freshen his grip on his victim.

He did not know Somerledaa was his pup, or that he had saved her life. She did swim slowly across, wary of him because he exuded precisely what he was: a daunting seal of exceptional ferocity. Nevertheless, her body curved into a comma of respectful submissiveness, she dared telescope her neck with vibrissae relaxed to sniff his great snout, knowing what he was to her. Among seals, descent is matrilineal. Rarely does a seal learn the identity of its father, though sometimes it is obvious, as it was then for Somerledaa.

Having paid her tentative respects, she edged away from the great brown seal who seemed to be in a trance after the life-and-death battle. Still troubled by her wound, she eased inshore. Off the Vessacks, Iolair joined her. He telescoped his neck to sniff at the wound, to sense something of the enemy who had inflicted it. Catching the scent of Guarn, he flinched.

They swam slowly in the opposite direction to Tyrian who was flowing on with supple power across a tide race to Longships. His imagination was more than ever filled by the imminent daunting challenge of Meinek despite having no sense of how close they were to one another just then.

Meinek, when he did stir, swam to the granite saddle of Guthensbrâs Island. He came ashore while the small swell was still running over the brown rocks and settled as high up as the rocks allowed, knowing he would be able to rest the maximum length of time there while the tide ebbed, turned, filled again. Settling, weariness flooding over him, he slept deep and dreamless sleep under the healing sun.

Many people, on the coast path near the edge of the adjacent cliff-top, failed to see him sleeping there, so well did he blend with the rocks that were his couch. Nor did another seal haul out while he lay there. Three smaller seals visited the rock, periscoping to see what seal was resting there. All recognised him and so did not haul out, but bottled in the inshore sea channel.

Three days Meinek lingered, recovering his strength. On the fourth morning, the wind was fresher, the sea more stirred up. Lifting his snout, he scented the wind, knowing he had lingered long enough. Time had come to reassert his dominion. He rolled over, rolled again and slid into the frisky swell. There, orientating himself north-westward, he kicked strongly as he made a shallow dive.

At the same time, Tyrian was swimming into the Bay of Seals on his first ever prospecting cruise. It felt like the right time.

He came in by the headland cave where, the previous season, he had lingered with Hythar and adventurous Aleutia. Swimming by, he noticed the beach had been scoured away by eroding surf during winter storms. Even as he watched, a wave broke, bursting against big boulders exposed now the sand was gone, confirming his instinct that no pups would be born there this season.

Continuing into the bay, glancing upward he saw Key-Ki the buzzard, circling ever higher above the sea from which he was neither equipped nor inclined to pluck prey. He did not espy the perpendicular slate grey and white smear of Pellitras, the tiercel, under the overhang of a cliff top above massive, rough-cut black boulders strewn below. Pellitras did not fly up to make sport of Key-Chi for intruding into his own aerial space. His young were grown to a kind of independence, but they would prosper better if Key-Chi remained ignorant of their practice-grounds; so, he kept his peace.

Off the boulder beach, two males rested under the sea, one surfacing to challenge a third who was passing. Immediately recognising Tyrian, the aggressive impulse died. Tyrian swam on, serenely aware of a desire only to meet rather than provoke challenges.

At Waterfall Cave, the tide was high enough for him to swim inside. Here, again was change from the previous year. Then, sand reached all the way out to the entrance, filling in previously permanent entrance waters. It had been driven in by wave action caused by a year of winds blowing from a different quarter to normal, especially during the stormiest interludes. A long ramp of shell-sand had formed, running from outside the cave to the back. This rendered it vulnerable to access by people who would not have thought of climbing down into the previously rocky bay.

This year, all was returned to how it had been before.

He surfed in on the entrance wave-break across a restored entrance pool and by a massive rock on the left. There, once, he had swum in and out again without waking a big, dry male who slept, snoring on top of it, steam rising from his warm body. Of habit, he glanced up as he swam by it. It was empty.

Within, he discovered where the interrupted strewing of boulders ended and the sand began. He recognised the cave fairway, made from sand, as ever. Pups born here would be able to reach the entrance pool unimpeded by any barrier of rocks, just as any prospecting male would find landfall easy to achieve.

He found the sand quite yielding as he hauled himself up the hill, caterpillar-like. This sea cave, of all the caves in the bay, admitted most light. Peering into the gloom, it was clear no seal was yet ashore; but that was as expected. He knew, also, by tradition the firstborn of the bay was never born in this cave.

Returning to the sea, he swam westward toward the sea cave rendered extraordinarily familiar and dear to him from all that had happened in the previous year. Nostalgia peaked when he swam in under the fern-hung lintel, the alarm calls of the bold rock pipits ringing in his ears, the dark shadow of a passing shag on the air between wide-spread wings.

His belly scraped rocks at the outer edge of the Long Pool that, at this state of the tide, spread to Tooth Rock. This year, there was an additional shallow pool between Tooth Rock and the north wall through which he splashed to reach the inner sanctum of the cave.

The sand-hill within was less steep than the previous year. Moving in, he noted first that no seal lay in the cubby-hole off the main fairway. Farther up the sand-hill, he came on some seal tracks that were several days old blurred by the partial erasing action of light waves. Following them, he found what Stypic had found the days before. The dead seal pup was a forlorn discovery. As Stypic had done, he sniffed quite delicately at the corpse and wondered about the female who had given birth here. Where was she? But even as he wondered, he knew such seals and quests to find them were not for him. This was his year to be the peerless seal in this familiar bay and if he could, he would exclude all other bull seals from it in enforcement of his authority.

He was in the full flood of his power and it was not a time for dreaming conservative dreams. It was time for discovering just what he was and that included discovering just how far he could extend his power.

In the Great Seal Hole, he recognised the scent not only of Iolair but Somerledaa, too, among several scents on the inner sand-hill. So intent was he on detecting these, among the several scents — for this was a cave often used as a lodge by seals travelling through from one region to another — he failed until the last to detect that he was not alone in the cave. At the top of the sand-hill and a little beyond, Ithian stared down at him from deep concealing gloom.

When he did become aware of her, she knew the moment precisely because she saw him become very still, sniffing the air with exceptional delicacy as if to conceal he was doing so at all. She felt when he recognised it was she, rather than another seal. Before he could utter sounds of greeting, she sang out to him:

"Tyrian! Have you made this place your territory? I see no new scars marring your fine pelage."

Aware he was being teased, he did not answer her but asked: "Can I smell the sands of Spain on yours? Where did you go after Brittany?"

"South across Biscay, first, then north again. And your travels?"

Tyrian said: "You remember I told you of the wise young seal I met at the Blasket's, and the murderous things that happened?" Glancing up, he continued: "He is a fine seal, though he seems not to know it. He has a huge store of stories and a desire to travel to the far places of grey sealdom. I wonder if he might be persuaded to travel so far south, to meet them the monk seals you told me of — to listen to them. He is the most sensitive male that ever I have met!"

"Well spoken!" Ithian said, approvingly. "You are quite right, of course. He will never be a peerless seal like you; he has neither the stature nor the instinct to fight and prevail. Unlike you! Neither has he the inclination to go to the far margins of where any grey seal has been, and then go farther still. Unlike you! But he is a true bard, and that is both rare and wonderful in a male. It might be best for you both that you travel together."

"There is a fair, tantalising prospect!" Tyrian agreed, glad to hear his friend so appreciated by this exceptional seal; as if she had met him. He asked: "How can you know these things? I thought you had not met him?"

"Wise Tyrian!" she commented, approvingly. "You might have been any kind of seal at all, but you choose to squander your energies becoming a peerless seal and a mapmaker of the far margins! You are right. I have not met him. Yet I have rested ashore three days in this cave and for two of them, Somerledaa and he lay on the sand-hill below, not interested to discover who else might be here. I might have remembered myself to bright, bold little Somerledaa, but she was interested only in Iolair, in swapping travellers' tales. I believe I was mentioned, but your name occurred often. They love you well".

Pleased, nevertheless he demurred: "They are generous. It is the way of the young."

"Friendship, I think they will not outgrow. One another, they will not outgrow."

"When did they leave?"

"Very early this morning."

"Then they might return later?"

"I suspect not. I fancy Somerledaa means to take him from the battleground not across to the Isles of Scilly but around to St. Clements Isle."

"Ah! Good!" He was relieved for them. They should be safe from misadventure the short distance seaward of Mousehole harbour. He returned his full attention to the midwife seal and observed, without really asking the question: "It is beginning, isn't it?"

Ithian was silent. It was her duty to remain silent. He shifted position, coming closer to where she was resting. Gently, he telescoped his neck, vibrissae relaxed in trust and affection, reaching so that there was the briefest touching of snouts:

"Prosper, Ithian! Our meetings are always too short."

It was more than he had intended to say but he was not sorry to have done so. Ithian was silent, so he wheeled easily and made his way with rippling power down the sand-hill to the edge of the tide. There, he paused, looking back. All he could see of her was the glitter of her seeing eyes. When he was about to plunge into the water, the quietest of songs came to his ears, so quiet that, afterwards, he wondered if he might have imagined it.

"Be not cruel to Meinek when his time comes. Allow him his pride. He has a right to it"

It was a strange farewell, remaining at the forefront of his reflections all the way back to Longships Reef. Near the halfway block of rock known as Kettle's Bottom, he saw gannets in the distance beyond the isolated pinnacle of Shark's Fin. Small as white gnats, in the sunlight they were diving, as usual. There must have been twenty of them, folding their wings along their sides, plunging into the sea, bobbing up again with remarkable buoyancy, so different to the seal way of surfacing. He recognised their activity indicated a shoal of fish so he adjusted his course. Carried along by the fierce tide, he soon noticed the gannets were — as usual — not the sole predators at the feast. He had seen a triangular grey fin scarring the surface at one edge of the area in which they were diving. Several fins. Some were firmly triangular but those belonging to the greatest sharks were flopped over, sagging with weight or age. He was seeing not just dorsal fins but the part of their caudal fins as well. Basking sharks: they presented no threat to him.

He had learned to be wary of sharks, but not all of them. Thresher's and Mako's he sought to avoid while Greenland sharks he had heard described only in Iolair's stories. These he would hope to avoid forever. Dwellers in the deep seas, it did not stop them from straying into seal waters and hunting there. The ferocity described by Iolair was the worst nightmare of any grey seal because it happened in the deeps. Being killed in any way was not something to be contemplated, but if attacked by orcas, at least there was a sense of awe competing with the dread.

In the sunlight, the sharks drifted slowly along not in a troop, but with a sense of being fellow travellers. Probably they were feasting on the *Calanus finmarchicus* copepods that were being taken also by the brit who, in turn, were taken by sea-spirited mackerel. They were, in turn, taken in their gleaming glory by the yellow-headed, blue-eyed gannets. From close quarters, Tyrian beheld a glorious mêlée of life and death.

Tyrian took two mackerel and, touched lightly by the frenzy of hunting, killing, escape, was tempted to take more. The spirit of killing was suffusing the minds of the creatures sharing the arena. Tyrian had sensed other seals in the vicinity while he had conducted his simple hunt, but he found no reason to linger once his small appetite was sated. He eased away from the great deformed globes of fish and gannet splashes. As he departed, at one point he found himself swimming straight toward the bright white gape, distended head and gills of an eight-metre-long basking shark. For the briefest moment, he saw how he might swim into that white, vestigial-toothed cavern while the shark just came slowly on, apparently oblivious to his approach. The whim was gone as soon as it occurred. He dived deeply below it. The shark, also, veered away from where Tyrian had been, her own senses working quite as well as Tyrian's, albeit differently.

Below the shark, Tyrian levelled out, becoming horizontal in the water column. He corkscrewed the better to see the passage of the turning shark above him, dark against the bright daylight in which her dorsal and caudal fins yet showed. Attached to her flanks, he made out the eel-like forms of lampreys drawing their sustenance from her.

The sharks were not only at the surface. Their banquet was taking place at all levels. Huge, otherworldly neighbours, he had no sense of how far their line had travelled through time to this latest springtime in the uncounted seasons of their wandering.

He stirred again. A little farther on and to one side, he saw bubbles where a gannet had speared the waters, missing the intended mackerel victim. Soon, its buoyancy had returned it irresistibly to the surface. Thereafter, he set course for the faded grey lighthouse on its stark rock between the express tidal streams. Even from so far away, he could see gathered on the lower-lying rocks strewn out to the south a group of seals already dry and pale in the sun.

He swam steadily under the same sun. He did not know whether it was wish or instinct, but he sensed time quickening; seal-time, quickening.

He swam steadily to the looming rocks whose silhouettes and underwater roots he knew so well by now. He swam prepared to be peaceful, prepared to fight if need be, with a sense that, for all the restlessness of the atmosphere among the seals, this was not the true stage. These rocks were the wings flanking the stage. The true stage was a mixture of sea caves, shell-sands, boulders and bedrock beaches: the Bay of Seals.

South-east of Carn Brâs, in front of a double-humped rock generally known not only to the seals but the seabirds, porpoises, dolphins and even the occasional passing leatherback turtle as the Camel, there are low-lying rocks. They are mainly sheltered from the predominantly south-westerly winds by the Camel and so were favoured by the seals. Tyrian had made them his base during his stay, returning again and again to the same high place where he could sleep easy, undisturbed by the action of the waves, above the comings and goings of his peers.

Given the sea was almost calm, he always surfed up on to a slab at the south end and made a slow passage to his viewpoint. Now, having surged up on to the rocks and achieved comfortable landfall, he was aware immediately of a changed atmosphere. Several seals shuffled a little to one side of the route he liked to take to his resting place. Instead of being a rock littered with at least twenty mainly sleeping seals, he found just seven. All were restless except the huge, brown male seemingly sleeping on the top ledge.

Tyrian came a few shuffles up the bare slope before stopping and shaking the full, impressive length of himself. Water flew in all directions, wetting two seals that reacted not by snarling but by stretching in turn and curving their bodies into perfect bananas, heads and tails as high off the rocks as they could be lifted.

He recognised the moment that had been approaching ever since he had disengaged from Meinek and fled westward from him the previous autumn. He recognised many things. The names of the seals gathered on the rocks: the shape and condition as well as the nature of them. The position of the sun in the sky, ducking behind a cloud, he saw. The dryness of the rocks up to where Meinek lay, he saw. The red-painted crabbing boat not more than a half-mile to seaward, he saw. The gannets, the basking sharks and the extra commotion of surface waters, a little northward of where they had been before, he saw. And, far inshore, the surging drive of the dark-blue and orange painted lifeboat from Sennen Cove, seaward-bound to render assistance to yet another yacht that had suffered engine failure, he saw.

He felt the warmth of the rocks under his fore-flippers and in his nostrils.

He did not feel anger or lust for battle. Only the most foolish seal would feel any eagerness to engage savage Meinek in combat.

Halfway up the slope, he knew Meinek was not asleep. Dark eyes watched his slow, uneven progress. He noticed the recently-healed wound on top of his head guessing, correctly, it had not been inflicted by another seal. He found himself wondering what manner of creature might cause such an injury. Might Meinek have escaped a close encounter with a shark?

Just two body lengths below him, he paused, steadily watching the male who had only ever existed as his nemesis. He did not snarl or utter threats. Simply, he stared into the open eyes of the seal he had to fight. It was his way.

Meinek stared back, emitting a steady flow of lowest level snarling like a purring in the back of his throat. In effect, his opening gambit was crude abuse, recalling his victories. It must be ever so, he implied.

Tyrian understood very well Meinek did not expect him to flee the expression of a few unpleasant sounds. Unimpressed, he looked carefully about him, at this arena where they would have their third encounter. He knew the lie of the land very well and did not need to look, but it did no harm. He could have moved over it without least misadventure in his sleep, but it was as well to refresh his memory one more time.

Tiring of eliciting no reaction, Meinek came to life, drawing himself up to his full height and bulk. Opening his large mouth to its widest gape, he leaned down and half-roared, half-snarled. Tyrian moved not backwards, but forwards by half of his body length. It was not what Meinek had expected and he gathered up his body in response, ready to launch an immediate attack from the advantage of what remained of the slope between them.

There were sounds behind Tyrian, but neither needed to see what was happening. They were departures, culminating in four splashes, which meant only two seals remained. He had noticed Stypic, back after an absence of several days. He had a sleepy, satisfied look that was more eloquent than any verbal communication might be. Clearly, he had found the bereft female and passed the days of her oestrus with her without needing to fight for her.

The abuse impinged: "Do you remember the pain, upstart? Pain made you flee. Are you so eager for more that you come begging me for it now?"

It was the savage voice with which Meinek forever expressed himself, except in the company of seal mothers. They made no complaint about his rough voice or his winning ways, having borne his dynasty of fine pups across the six years of his supremacy.

Watching him, Tyrian was silent, lacking the language or the taste for competing in abuse.

"You can leave now, before I refresh your memory," he went on, "but my hope is that you are too stubborn or stupid to leave. Stay and I will injure you so badly this will be your final challenge to any seal in this life."

He sounded convincing, but Tyrian was not remembering his own pain. He was remembering their last battle, when he had come so close to victory. Then, only the fantastic fighting guile and indomitable will dredged from the core of himself had saved Meinek — fighting guile and a fighting heart. It seemed he had no sense of what defeat might be. Such was Meinek. Tyrian's silence continued, steady as the gaze he bestowed, knowing precisely what he was looking for. There was only one move Meinek could make.

"Look about you. Remember these rocks as a place to avoid forever, after this day. If ever I see you here again, I shall drive you off again. I hear it said you are a great wanderer, a great explorer, even to the edges of the world. I hear it said you are a mighty seal. But I, Meinek of the Land's End, have travelled farther, dived deeper, even during this last year. Look at me!"

Even as he said it, he launched his charge. Half-leaping, half-driving down the slope, he attacked, open-mouthed. Tyrian swerved sharply to one side. He had not, in the end, been distracted by the threats, having been watching the bunching of Meinek's body. His sight and mind were clear. Teeth that might have traced along his neck missed as he made his matador move before the charging bulk. Even as the brown male lurched by, drawing up as he went, Tyrian attacked with a more clinical ferocity. Mouth agape, he darted in, biting at the great rolls of fat softly armouring the neck of his rival and drew blood immediately before drawing back in turn, for Meinek recovered swiftly.

Meinek charged again from close quarters. His intent was not to bite, but to buffet his enemy, upright neck against upright neck, but Tyrian met him with solid, unyielding, aggressive stillness and again, at such close quarters darted in a grazing bite on the other side of the brown seal's neck before backing, wheeling and gaining the higher ground.

Leaving no time for thought, obeying only instincts long-honed in battle, Meinek again crowded belligerently in. Attack, attack, attack! The momentum was his. He drove Tyrian to the highest place of the island, turned him there, driving him down again with repeated attacks aimed at all parts of his body. It was another kind of battle to either that had gone before.

Like Tyrian, Meinek had spent many months between their last encounter and this swimming to a different quarter of the Shelf Edge. He had experienced a brief dip in confidence following their last battle and had prepared for this inevitable battle by spending nearly the entire year at sea. Though his years weighed against him, his body was in the best condition of his life.

Tyrian, on the other hand, retreated, retreated and bided his time, trusting Meinek must surely tire, being the heavier animal.

He was chased about the slopes and ledges of the rock for fully five minutes, without a break, with just a single thought luminous in his mind. They were both panting, tiring in the unbroken run of violent action but, as soon as Meinek paused, he intended to counter-attack with all his power.

The moment arrived near the bottom of the south slope, near his landing place. Meinek had driven home another attack, another near miss and before he could shuffle round to pursue it, Tyrian launched his counter-assault. Hitherto, he had avoided any more counter-attacks than those two initial ones. Now, wedged against a substantial ledge, as he had seen he would be, he used it to generate extra power to launch head-on into Meinek's side.

He bit and tore once, twice, a third time, making a big wound in Meinek's neck. He was lunging to bite again when, somehow, Meinek managed to sweep up a defensive flipper. It was not the one Tyrian had ruined last autumn, but the one that was entire. The wicked claws raked in an arc along the long, black converse bow of Tyrian's snout and so close to his eye that, afterwards, Tyrian wondered how he survived with both eyes intact.

Now, at last, there was a longer pause than either had yet allowed. Meinek's neck was thick with blubber so despite having received a deep and ugly wound, he was not losing much blood. Tyrian, however, found blood running into his left eye, for the claw had sliced open a long red eyebrow that began halfway down his snout. He tried to wipe it away with a fore-flipper, achieving only partial success.

That conceded a rare opportunity to Meinek, who attacked again in the moment the flipper was covering the eye. He drove in with a bellow of rage, a war cry, and bit hard into Tyrian's neck, but Tyrian was already fading and, although Meinek drew blood, the wound was only glancing. However, at this point, Tyrian was cornered with minimal freedom of movement. Gathering together all he had of courage, he met Meinek at closest quarters, mouth snapping, tearing at mouth, while both reared as high as they could go, leaning their fullest power each into the other with flippers frantically clawing.

There ensued a prolonged stalemate as they strained together, both trying to avoid the mutilating injury that might now be suffered by chance. They undulated, striving to launch bites lower down, until suddenly Tyrian was above his enemy and surging over him, crushing him below his bulk and slashing with his own scrabbling fore-flippers as he went. By chance, in the confusion, he slashed open the recent scalp wound that Guarn had inflicted so that suddenly Meinek's head was a spider's web of blood. In the ensuing confusion, both seals fled not in dread, but to create space to review their positions.

Meinek, who had suffered several wounds, found himself more inconvenienced by the blood running into his eyes than Tyrian, who was only partly inconvenienced, but Meinek continued to exude an irreducible, savage confidence that was draining for his opponent, who lacked experience in battle-craft. Tyrian was fighting well with a clear mind for the most part, but still without the deadly intent of the other.

Both seals continued to hold their ground and launch attacks, in the case of Meinek, and counter-attacks. ten minutes grew to fifteen, moved on to twenty. They grew weary; desperately weary, sustained only by their superb condition and, in both cases, by the certainty of achieving eventual victory.

The rock on which they fought was bloody in places and emptied of other seals. None wanted to be anywhere near such formidable seals but they watched from the sea. Battle-royals such as this happened not more than once in a lifetime at the Longships. Few doubted that Meinek would win, such was his reputation.

They persevered with manoeuvrings. Engagements were shorter now. More often, the two were leaning together, neck to extended neck, no longer trying to inflict wounds but to exhaust the other. Their panting was hoarse and tortured. Neither was in a condition to feign any counterfeit fraction of freshness. Longing for it to end, neither dared imagine disengaging and fleeing the encounter. In their extremis, they had become primordial beings, hardly seals anymore, fighting on instinct and reserves of strength alone.

Throughout, Meinek was the attacker. Just twice had Tyrian mounted his own bullocking attacks, achieving successes that were slowly clawed back by battle-wise Meinek.

They reached the decisive moments having, again, long leaned against one another, struggling ever higher against the other so one might bear exhaustingly down on the other. It was from the stalemate that, unexpectedly, Tyrian disengaged and started to galumph, fast as he could go, down the uneven rocky slope. He was admitting defeat, desiring to fight no more.

The battle-wisdom that had made Meinek so destructive and long-lasting a dominant male was due, in part, to his behaviour in victory. Then, no matter how weary or wounded, he dredged a final surge of energy and pursued his enemy as fiercely as lay within his power. Such chases would see him pursuing his broken enemy not only into the sea but for miles across it. Nor was it a token chase. At every point where he gained some aquatic advantage, he would inflict another wounding bite so that his opponent feared he would be pursued even to death. Such battles are extremely rare in the grey seal world, but Meinek was an exceptional warrior.

Aware of those tactics, Tyrian fled down the slope. This once, Meinek was slow in following up his advantage. Perhaps he had become convinced he was entangled in an encounter where neither could prevail. However, when it sank into his embattled imagination that the spirit of his opponent had broken, he drew on those secret reserves, flying down in thunderous pursuit, gaining speed all the while. Down near the waters-edge, Tyrian came swerving powerfully around and went driving up a side slope before swinging fully around, hard and true. Meinek had faltered, unable immediately to continue the chase back up the slope, trying to gather his breath and recover from the shocking disappointment of not yet having triumphed after all.

When Tyrian came charging down upon him, he was very poorly positioned to meet him. With full power, open-mouthed again, Tyrian drove into his strong but bloodied neck, buffeting, biting and tearing. Drawing on a great surge of energy, he sustained the attack. Meinek was in the worst possible position to counter-attack, but he had no instinct how to submit so he sustained such heavy wounds that he had no choice, but to break away and make an untidy escape into the sea. But, even there, he found he had not escaped his opponent.

Understanding well the mind of this enemy with whom he had been so closely engaged, body to body, will to will, fighting intelligence to fighting intelligence, Tyrian drove into the sea, submerging right behind him. On top of Meinek, he bit and tore again before they surfaced. So closely had they fought, so close had their minds and bodies wrestled for ascendancy, it was as if they were no longer separate seals or separate minds. The curtain between them was drawn back and Tyrian had no choice but to hunt him down as ferociously as ever Meinek had hunted his own vanquished enemies. He did this without thought because he was certain that making him fall into the sea would never count as a defeat in Meinek's mind. It would lead to more fighting later; a second engagement.

Therefore, he attacked and redoubled it until he broke the will of the other and drove him before him while other seals scattered from their bloody path.

He did not pursue him beyond the tidal stream to which Meinek's bruised instincts guided him, now he had the need. Tyrian watched him disappear into the turbulent waters and wheeled away. Not lingering, he swam straight back to the islet upon which he had fought and, without pause, surged ashore. Wearily now, he hauled himself up slopes he had fought over for so long. When he reached the high platform that was his customary resting place, the place Meinek had briefly usurped, he drew himself to his maximum height and roared. He roared and roared again, and no seal bottling or logging thereabouts doubted, but that another peerless seal had taken his place for the forthcoming season, one who would never be easily displaced.

***

Thereafter, daily, Tyrian made the easy cruise inshore to inspect the breeding places of his domain. On the fifth day, he did not return to the Reef because Hythar, who he remembered warmly from the previous nursery season, took up station at the top of the Great Seal Hole sand-hill. In the night, she gave birth to another female pup. Two days later, Veriaana arrived on the sandy beach of Waterfall Cave. This, he did not notice until three days had elapsed, and Veriaana's pup had reached the second evening of her life. Then, as he cruised around the bay, he swam through the shallows and saw what was to be seen. Balanec was guarding the entrance to the cave beach.

He came very directly toward Balanec who fled at his greatest speed, hoping Tyrian would be unlike Meinek, but it was not so. While Meinek had been his nemesis, Tyrian feared him, but had still been able to recognise how he maintained dominance. Now, he imitated him because it was proven the best way of dealing with intruders and keeping subsequent intrusion to a minimum. In one way, he improved upon his teacher in that his pursuit was silent. Over the season that followed, seals fleeing him would find that the most unnerving threat of all. It made him a potential shadow at all times. He might be there or not.

The first weeks of the nursery season saw quiet weather and quiet seas. It was a quiet time for Tyrian, too. He swam between the caves, discreetly monitoring the condition of the females so he could know when they came into breeding condition. Everything was well and, as part of that, every pup born in the sea caves prospered to the time of weaning.

In turn, Tyrian mated with Hythar, Veriaana, Adjac, Perzia and Celira, all of whom had given birth to pups before the middle of

379

September. A lull followed so it seemed the season was over almost before it had started. In that window, the weather worsened. Moderate seas ran into the bay. The surf would have made life difficult for pups of a week or less, had they been on the cave beaches.

However, although the sea conditions did not abate, with October came a stream of pregnant females to the three caves. In the vanguard came a well-marked female, on one side of whose neck was a mark resembling an inverted number seven and around whose throat was the scar left by strands of netting.

She came to the cave in early evening, before it was too dark to note the changes since her last visit. Landing, she listened for the cries of pups already using the site, but heard none. Thinking herself alone, she came slowly across the Long Pool, up to and around Tooth Rock to where Ithian awaited. In the quiet of the deeps of the cave, they sang late into the night. Much had happened since their parting and now the imminence of the birth of Tyrian's firstborn was upon them.

Swimming from the Great Cave across the bay to Waterfall Cave, Tyrian heard and recognised them but did not alter his course. He was wise enough to recognise they would have no use for him this night. Instead, he rested ashore in Waterfall Cave, remaining just beyond the reach of the surf racing back and forth across the shellsands. In the morning, Elorin came in through the surf. Seeing Tyrian at rest in mid-beach, she snarled at his sleeping form. He wakened with a start and shuffled meekly away, observing traditional seal etiquette for such occasions.

He was still gleaming with health despite his prolonged watch as the peerless seal. Now, drifting to the far side of the cave shallows, he made his way slowly deeper into the salt water.

Passing well beyond the halfway point of the suckling period, once the female had come into season, usually she became increasingly tolerant of and receptive to the male who kept all others from the nursery beach. However, a large minority of seal mothers formed a lifelong bond with single males. In effect, theirs was a marriage uniquely marked by fidelity. Then, although Tyrian's behaviour remained respectful, there was electricity in the atmosphere and a sense of imminence from which he came to recognise he was excluded; he had no power to cajole such females from their choice.

In Martinsfinger Cave, that time came for Mornalas. She had said her farewell to Ithian a week before. Ithian was bound for Boscastle, there to rendezvous in one of the great caves with a young female seal she had promised to support through her first delivery period.

Mornalas was not alone this year, sharing the nursery beach amicably with two other females and their pups. Her own pup, Melorian, was a miniature reproduction of his father. Entirely black, he had been a greedy, exhausting feeder and a good sleeper. He had gone early, without fear, into the Long Pool and achieved a dominant position in games he played with the two younger seal pups with whom he shared his first weeks.

Now, with only two suckling days left, she was relieved that it would soon be over and increasingly conscious of the huge, quiet figure of Tyrian resting now at the inshore end of the Long Pool. She had noticed his patience with the pups, even when they bumped into him. She noticed how it communicated itself to them, engendering in them greater confidence in their own explorations and endeavours.

She did not know if he guessed he had shared in the making of Melorian. It was obvious, but it was not part of seal etiquette to acknowledge such a detail because it might have led to even more bickering and battles between the males. She was glad in herself that it was he who was there awaiting her rather than any other. Had they been two seals wandering the world that had chanced to meet at any time on any shore, she would have been happy to make an exclusive bond with him. As it was, she found him much more silent than during the previous year.

She sensed he had much to share and the desire to share it, but there was awkwardness between them because of his changed status because of the number of females to whom he was attentive and of whose pups he was being so solicitous. Nevertheless, since Ithian had departed, he had rested each night in Martinsfinger Cave, clearly wanting to be near her. Very occasionally, they sang to one other, but each time something broke the spell, and now Nature entered the conspiracy.

She came into season.

He recognised the change immediately, so receptive was he to her moods, movements and the general atmosphere. Arriving on a middling tide from his dimpsey tour of the sea caves and beaches, finding no need to drive off contender-seals or to mate, he swam into the cave watched by O'Sîana. She was on a grassy slope surrounded by white and grey feathers plucked from the breast of a rock dove taken in the last hour of daylight. The dove had not seen her. He had been flying in a small flock that used the Great Cave for a roost. Out from the seals' entrance they had issued, flying in a big, unwary swirl around the bay. They had checked the skies overhead for the small, dark, deadly star of the high airs but, seeing nothing, had proceeded blithely on their way.

O'Sîana had spent the afternoon perched at another favourite viewing station. It was high on the headland, a rocky ledge fringed with posies of thrift flowers that had long since lost their pinkness. The flower heads were transparent, silvering in the sunlight. She heard the clap of the wings of the doves sallying forth below her even before she had seen them. As soon as they came into view, it was clear they were making an unwary circuit of the bay. Once their backs showed, she slipped from her perch and swept very low over the grey sea. Beating her way along, almost invisible from above, when she was not far behind and below the flock, she began a steady, shallow ascent. This developed until she might have been the last dove in their formation. From there she infiltrated herself among them.

They failed completely to notice her. All their focus was on flight, was otherwise snugly ensconced in the group mind. Even when the cruel talons of O'Sîana audibly punctured the seemingly hollow body cavity of her chosen quarry, they did not notice her. That happened only when she began to wheel out of the flock with wingbeats much more muscular than theirs. She was the sight they dreaded most. The lethal terror had been invisible in their midst. At the shock of it, the group mind shattered and individual doves scattered. Too late. O'Sîana flew inshore carrying her load in one talon to her nearest plucking post, on the grassy slope above the shadowy cave entrance in the corner of the bay.

She had plucked almost enough breast feathers to begin to feed when the mobile chevron of parting waters below distracted her for a brief eye-flicker of time. She recognised the black seal. He had been the largest and only permanent resident of the bay for the last two months, swimming backwards and forwards, patrolling the inshore arc of the bay, venturing into caves, bottling in their entrances.

He was without significance to her. After the all-seeing eye-flicker, she resumed the plucking of breast feathers, liberating them to float on the wind and land where they would. Below her, having noticed the labours of the falcon and the feathers floating on the wind, Tyrian swam into the cave. Even as he was passing below the lintel, a solitary, white feather floated down and settled on his snout. He blinked and sneezed. The feather drifted on down, becoming a tiny white boat, rocking violently on the waters Tyrian parted.

The sneeze of surprise alerted the three seal mothers inside the cave to his arrival and Mornalas came down to the narrows between the cave wall and the Tooth Rock to watch his slow, respectful approach. He had cause. The previous day, he had tried to lean forward and sniff her mouth. She had been resting on one side by the edge of the water and had made it clear she was not in the mood to be sniffed. She had violently vibrated her uppermost fore-flipper in his face and uttered a sustained, ululating rebuff of his tentative advance.

Now, she settled again on her side, reminding him of the previous day. She watched him curve round to the very edge of the pool, to where she was waiting. He was not tentative when he leaned forward and sniffed her mouth again. She made the beginning of a small ululation in her throat, but it lacked the intent of yesterday. This he recognised. Taking confidence from it, he came half out of the water, not looking directly at her, but acutely conscious of how she was reacting in the corner of his eye.

They remained there, blocking the route to and from the inner cave, where the pups were sleeping or slowly moving about the sandy floor. The tide ebbed. The beach below them increased in size, the shallowest of streams trickled through small sand canyons from the shallow pool at the base of Tooth Rock down to the Long Pool. From time to time, one or other of them moved, but none of the pups thought to pass by them to play in the Pool. The remaining two females slept. The tide reached its lowest point and began, imperceptibly at first, to flood in again.

Between Tyrian and Mornalas, electricity and tension intensified until Mornalas began to shuffle down toward the Long Pool. No sooner did she start to move than Tyrian swung around. Very briefly, he watched her before beginning to galumph after her. He was moving the faster and as she was beginning to throw up spray, progressing awkwardly through the shallows, he caught her and took her nape in his teeth. It was not a cruel hold and did not break the skin, but he held her firmly and felt the surrender of her through his teeth and every part of his body.

As one, they proceeded deeper into the pool until they floated at the deepest part, over to the left above the litter of boulders covering the bottom.

Mornalas was subdued, but content. Tyrian waited, waited and then waited no more. As one at the surface of the pool, he mated with her, and when the mating was done, he continued to rest his fore-flippers along her flanks. The two seals remained as one, entirely quiescent in the murky water beside the orange-pink sea squirts and above the occasional cushion star and strawberry anemone. They floated together, hardly moving, their hindmost parts curving downward and resting rather deeper in the water than the rest of them.

They were at peace.

There is no greater peace for a seal than the post-coital period. The minutes passed; an hour passed, and still they did not separate. One hour and twenty minutes passed before another black seal picked the lock of their mutual contentment. Young Melorian began to utter plainting hunger cries.

Mornalas had begun to weary of his cries and his milk-greed. She was among the most generous of seal mothers but inevitably the feeds shortened in their duration. She was feeding him less each day. The ties between them were loosening in the age-old, necessary way; in the seal way. Nevertheless, she recognised his right and so gently drifted clear, reluctantly disengaging from Tyrian.

He made no attempt to stay her. He had learned much during this nursery season from intimate contact enjoyed with the seal mothers and their pups. He accepted his role among them was a modest one. He had not needed to learn to be tolerant of or occasionally helpful to the tiny, awkward pups. That had always been in him.

What he had needed to learn was the courtly dance that for about fourteen days was led exclusively by the females. At all times, he had to be heedful and respectful of their demands. He must never seek to force them to do anything against their will, against their notions of motherhood. If he came ashore, he must remain closest to the waterline. If another male came prospecting for females in season, he was to be driven away. If two mothers saw fit to quarrel, even violently, he was to stand aside and not intervene. If a pup came close to him, he must be tolerant. Had he behaved otherwise, they would have driven him from the beach, banished him to the entrance waters.

That he had been tolerated ashore indicated how quickly he learned, or how natural he was on that demanding stage. That he was a natural was hardly a surprise to the females, who remembered the companionship of Meinek from the recent years. He had been as courteous to them as Tyrian, for all his reputation for savagery. He had been free to concentrate on them and their needs for the most part, creating a peaceable atmosphere that Tyrian was also well able to sustain.

In Martinsfinger Cave, Tyrian and Mornalas mated many times over the next five days. All their mating occurred in water, sometimes in the Long Pool, more often in the shallows outside the cave after the abrupt weaning of Melorian. However, while most seal mothers departed the vicinity of the nursery site immediately her period in season concluded, Mornalas was delayed by her tie to Tyrian. Then, she did not depart the bay but slept in the sea and hauled out, when sea conditions allowed her, on one flat skerry situated close in to the cliffs.

In that period, the other two females who had used Martinsfinger Cave, two more who had used Waterfall Cave and a lone female using the shadowy, open sky inlet of Zawn Pyg in the neighbouring bay all came into season. Tyrian did not neglect them, mating with all as the delicate etiquette of his position required. He was nothing loathe to do so; it helped him better understand the small differences that made intimacy with one seal so different from that with another.

He returned, again and again, to Mornalas.

With her, especially following coition, the curtain between their two beings wore thin. Only openness, sharing and interest in one another existed between them.

Tyrian was mindful that, very soon, she must depart, head out to sea to feast and restore her emaciated body to good condition, partly to help the infinitely tiny new life inside her to prosper. He wanted to ask her to return before the month of shortest light but, for once, was at a loss, sensing it should not be asked.

Their time came; a dark day. Bruised clouds filled the sky, overlapping one another. Fierce rain fell intermittently. A moderate sea was running that would render the swimming and hunting lessons of the remaining pups difficult; but if they could proceed from such unpromising beginnings, then they stood a chance of surviving the most challenging year.

Bobbing in the sea together, neither wanted to be first to depart. Tyrian tried several times to find the magic of song-words, but they eluded him. Mornalas did not try to communicate. The tension escalated until it became unbearable. Recognising the moment for what it was, Tyrian found the question he had wanted to ask.

Her response was to crash-dive. When she bobbed up again, for he did not chase her, she was at the edge of his hearing. He heard her answer:

"At the second new moon, I will return to the bay to look for you." With that and no other farewell, she was gone. Watching the place where she might surface again, Tyrian found a place of happy relief in himself. Six weeks is not a lifetime for a seal as solitary as he knew how to be. Perhaps she would allow herself to be persuaded to accompany him on his winter Arctic wanderings…

***

On the landward shore of St. Clement's Island, there is a generous bay where the sea is calm when the east breeze blows. Ledges are to be found there on to which it is easy for even the smallest seal to climb. The ledges are brown and often sharp but even young seals are normally so well padded with blubber that they experience no discomfort resting there.

Above the places that Iolair and Somerledaa learned through that late summer into autumn, the rocks were heavily patterned with white gull droppings. Herring gulls and greater black-backed gulls roosted there. The young of the year who had survived swelled their numbers. Many of them continued to beg for food, but their parents had grown weary of satisfying their needs. The begging cries that, in the early days, had been satisfied at the earliest opportunity were now an irritation only. The background noise of their bickering, quarrels and begging filled the days the seals spent there. However, their alarm cries the seals did learn to heed.

Once, people had come ashore from a boat and all the gulls had taken to the wing. By then, the two seals had already slipped into the sea where they had a talent for remaining invisible by keeping their heads as flat at the surface as possible. They had not remained to watch what was happening but headed into the bay, submerged and only surfaced for the shortest possible time when they had need of air. This response, Somerledaa copied from Iolair, who had no trust in human beings.

As well as the gulls and shags, an increasing number of cormorants used the rocks for a resting place, along with many turnstones and a smaller number of oystercatchers. Then, when the two seals had first arrived, migrating common sandpipers were passing through, but now purple sandpipers were hunkering down for a long winter of foraging, along with a few passing dunlin and a lone whimbrel among scores of curlew.

In a way, the Island was a strange kind of refuge for the seals. Inshore, little more than three hundred metres across the sea, was a harbour. Behind the curves of its granite walls, there was a busy granite village nestled under slate roofs yellowed by lichen and by the green hills behind. Village and island both were the first stations on the west shore of Mounts Bay, barely but sufficiently sheltered from the predominating south-westerly winds off the Atlantic.

On the seaward side of the island, commercial fishing boats of all sizes and colours sailed by to and from Newlyn as angler and dive boats passed to and from Penzance. At rest on that side of the rocks, the seals would watch them, assessing always the degree of danger they posed. Aboard the big beam trawlers, they saw little of men. Aboard the smallest boats, men were always visible, often steering while standing upright in the stern.

Through the year, the chunky blue work-horse called Gry Maritha laboured by at no great distance, hold and decks packed with the supplies that sustained the communities on the Isles of Scilly.

At first light, in the evenings and weekends while baulks were not yet blocking the harbour entrance, small boats issued from across the way, carrying local anglers to nearby fishing marks. Through autumn, many trolled for bass while others checked small strings of pots. Most noticed the ubiquitous seals.

The seals did not remain to witness glorious winter displays of common dolphins hunting, successively, pilchard, anchovies and mackerel. The days shortened drearily but weather and sea remained warm. Iolair and Somerledaa had arrived just after the hottest days of the year and remained long enough to feel the evenings closing in.

Several seals visited their island retreat. There was little communication between them. A minority hauling themselves ashore had been born this season. They were small, carefully respectful of all seals older than them and, if they were not exhausted, curious about everything. Although so small, some were Welsh, some Irish and one had come from South Devonshire, but the majority originated from the sea caves and secret beaches of north Cornwall.

Not a single moulted pup failed to explore every nook and cranny of especially the sub-littoral of the island. Here, many discovered how sharp are the spines of sea urchins but how tasty the spiny spider crabs. They made their small circumnavigations alone or, more often, in small parties of two or three. That way, if they wearied of exploring, they could chase one another, hide, pounce on unwary companions, play hunting games, perhaps swallow some small, fatally unwary blenny or rockling and afterwards pretend they had feasted royally.

By late October, the seals felt their tenure at this restful place drawing to an end. Even Iolair, with his bottomless baggage of stories, knew he was beginning to sound stale. Wearying of the sound of himself, he dared not ask if Somerledaa felt the same.

They were in good condition, but restlessness possessed them. Departing without intent one day, they swam around to the Lands End waters under the arched stack of Enys Dodnan.

Here, Somerledaa felt the lovely sense of home married to the intense tug of the offshore sea, both at the same time. She was alive, the milestone of her first birthday having been passed on the Island. She had learned she was not immortal, needing only look over her shoulder at the scar Guarn had branded or down at the ruin of two claws that would cause her forever to limp slightly when moving to or from the sea.

But she felt alive more than she was not immortal. All around her, an endlessly interesting water world was eager to be explored while, beside her, she had the companion of her own heart and spirit and outlook.

Offshore were tide races to cross and familiar Longships Reef at which to pause and briefly linger, for old time's sake. It was misty. The foghorn was sounding, its tireless light roving but forever showing a bleary red eye to the inshore place from which they watched.

More than ever alive, she turned in the water to face Iolair. He had been awaiting the familiar movement, for it was a habit of hers. He recognised her vivid, tumultuous enthusiasm for the moment, felt the tide of it infecting him, too. As one, they turned seaward, toward all the adventures that life could never cease from offering them.

GEOFFREY GUY'S
WAR

GEOFFREY GUY'S
WAR

MEMOIRS OF A SPITFIRE PILOT 1941–46

Edited by JENNIFER BARRACLOUGH
and DAVID GUY

AMBERLEY

First published 2011

Amberley Publishing
The Hill, Stroud
Gloucestershire, GL5 4EP

www.amberleybooks.com

British Library Cataloguing in Publication Data.
A catalogue record for this book is available from the British Library.

ISBN 978-1-4456-0022-2

Typesetting and Origination by Amberley Publishing.
Printed in Great Britain.

Contents

List of Illustrations

Preface and Acknowledgements

Early in the Second World War a young Englishman, Geoffrey Colin Guy, left his university studies to join the RAF. He learned to fly in Canada, trained as a photographic reconnaissance pilot back in England, and then was posted to the Middle and Far East. He was among the few members of his squadron to survive the conflict in the skies over Burma. Later, he went on to a career in the Colonial Service. This man was our uncle. He died in 2006 leaving the manuscript of his war memoirs, which in accordance with his wishes we have now edited for publication.

Geoffrey begins his story in the spring of 1940, at the time of the Dunkirk landings and just before the Battle of Britain. Still a schoolboy, he is evacuated away from his home in Kent to escape the threat of German invasion. In the autumn, he goes up to Oxford, and besides reading history he attends the University Air Squadron, plays cricket and falls in love. A year later, he joins the RAF and sails to Canada where he discovers both the joys and the dangers of flying. After returning to England on the *Queen Mary*, he trains for photographic reconnaissance and meets the other great love of his life, the Spitfire Mark I. In 1943, he is posted to the Middle East and describes a challenging flight in search of his squadron in Egypt. He serves in Palestine and India, flying both Spitfires and Hurricanes, then volunteers for aerial photography with 28 Squadron, making long sorties flying unarmed aircraft low over the enemy-occupied jungle of Burma. Despite his aversion to killing, Geoffrey becomes a combat pilot during the Battle of Imphal in 1944, and goes through many harrowing ordeals which include witnessing the crash of his closest friend, and narrowly surviving attack by Japanese anti-aircraft fire near the Ava Bridge at Mandalay. The highs and lows of service life – excitement and terror, humour and hardship, comradeship and loss – are vividly described. His account ends in 1945, when he returns from the war 'shrunk and yellow'.

The text closely follows Geoffrey's original manuscript. The introductory first chapter has been shortened, while retaining enough personal background material to convey something of Geoffrey's character and of the impact of war on family life. The final sections of the book have been supplemented from tape-recorded interviews carried out towards the end of Geoffrey's life; for this we thank the Second World War Experience Centre in Leeds. Thanks also to the archives office at Brasenose College for details of Geoffrey's studies at Oxford, and to David Pinder, who arranged for drawing of the maps.

We appreciate the assistance received from within the family. Geoffrey's sister, Doreen Collins, helped with verifying information about the wartime years. Jennifer's husband, Brian Barraclough, gave much advice and encouragement. We especially thank Geoffrey's son, Benjamin Guy, for supplying the photographs and for his ready co-operation with the project as a whole.

Jennifer Barraclough, Auckland, New Zealand
David Guy, London, England
2011

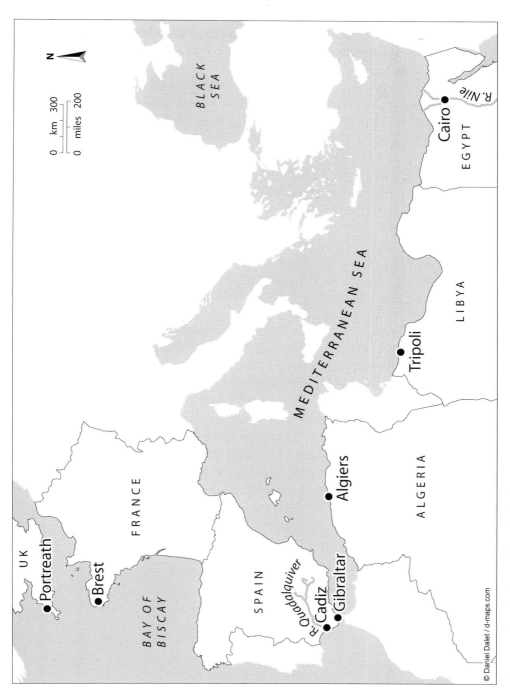

Places associated with Geoffrey's flight from England to Egypt.

9

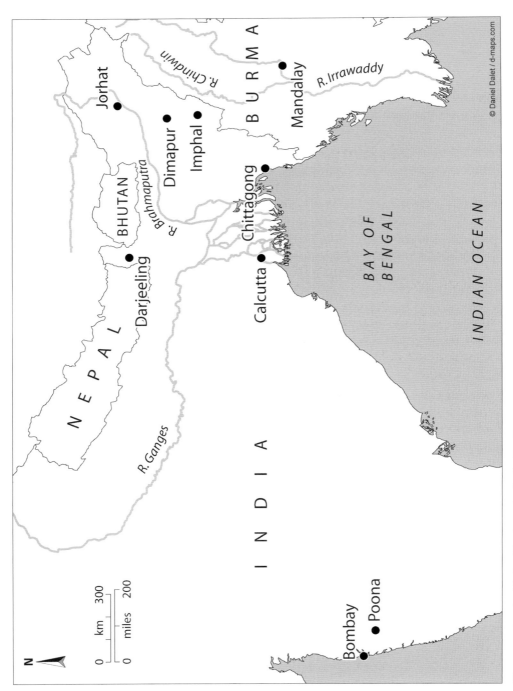

Places associated with Geoffrey's service in the Far East.

CHAPTER ONE

In the Beginning

Ramsgate, May 1940. Chatham House School is being evacuated from the danger zone of south-east Kent to the comparative safety of the Midlands. At the railway station we encounter long lines of soldiers, queuing, waiting for trains. Most are without their rifles or packs, many without tin hats, all are dirty, unshaven, tired, dishevelled, standing dazed and dejected. They are English, French, Belgian, the army rescued from the defeat of Dunkirk at least in part by the miracle of the small boats worked by the fisher folk and the part-time sailors of Kent. As we pass by, the skies are alive with aircraft, out of sight except for their vapour trails though they can be heard plainly enough. In that sky and with those aircraft Britain will soon be fighting for her life.

Our train is waiting and we embark, very orderly and disciplined, although excited by this sudden leap into the unknown; then the rhythm of the wheels takes us away from the grim realities of distressed soldiers and active aircraft and we try to anticipate what will happen to ourselves. Although I was school captain, little responsibility devolved on me during the journey; we were all on our best behaviour, the older ones somewhat subdued in our excitement by the serious events of the last few weeks, wondering when we should see our parents and our homes again. In due course the train stopped at Stafford, we got out and were taken to our billets. The whole operation went with clockwork precision; we were fed, transported, received at the other end in one smooth operation and were not hungry, uncomfortable nor made uncertain and frustrated by delay. There were, as so often, unknown and unthanked heroes behind the scenes, volunteers doing more than their duty and organizing the emergency with selfless devotion.

A friend and I were billeted in a large Victorian house where lived two elderly maiden ladies. They treated the two young men who had been dumped upon them with great warmth and kindness, becoming surrogate mothers during the few months that we were with them. They had a lawn at the back of the house where we played bowls; they made beautiful custard with real eggs. Kind and hospitable though they were, it was a dull summer for me and I was at a loose end, for it was my last term at school, my scholarship exams for Oxford had been taken in the previous winter and I could not now get the books or the tuition I needed to do any serious work. Cricket was my great interest but there was none to be had, so I solaced myself occasionally by swimming in the cold Staffordshire rivers. I was restless and anxious to be off, either to Oxford or to the war, which had become so grim and desperate. I did not much mind which, though on my father's advice I was going to Oxford for one year's academic work to safeguard my place there should I return after the war was over.

* * *

At the end of term I moved some fourteen miles to Westward Ho, a large Edwardian house in Uttoxeter. My mother had rented this so she could keep an eye on my younger brother David and sister Doreen, whose schools had been evacuated to Uttoxeter and Stafford respectively. The house, being shared with another family from Ramsgate, was uncomfortably crowded. This must have been a hard and fearful time for my parents. Camping out in Westward Ho, my mother found the responsibilities heavy on her own, with two younger children still at school, me due in a short time for the war, my elder sister Joan in her final year at college in London and elder brother Bernard, who had a chemistry degree, in a reserved occupation in a munitions factory. And she had cause for concern about my father.

He had stayed behind in Ramsgate to continue his organisation of technical and adult education throughout the Isle of Thanet, and his work with Civil Defence. He was a man of valour and the strain on him must have been immense, dynamic though his energy was. He lived under siege conditions, managing the house and the catering on his own, short of food, short-handed at work, every night driving many miles in the blackout giving evening classes and lectures to troops. The Britain of

1940 must have had many like him whose entire selves were emptied in their devotion to duty and whose diligence built the bulwarks of survival, each playing his own small part to the full.

My first term at Oxford, the autumn or Michaelmas term, was exploratory; finding my feet, joining clubs, making friends, learning how to cope with my work. My college Brasenose, familiarly called BNC, had been evacuated to Christ Church and I had rooms in the Meadow Buildings. The next two terms, the Hilary and the Trinity, were overfull. I had joined the University Air Squadron and enlisted in the RAF in February 1941. This ate up valuable time for I had to spend all but three weeks of the next vacation at the Air Squadron, which was relatively comfortable compared to what was to come later. It had a well endowed Mess with leather arm chairs, where beer was drunk out of silver tankards. Several senior RAF officers from nearby units used it as a club and lunched there regularly. Enthusiastic about every aspect of my new life I was prepared to give the RAF of my best though, alas, the promise of the Air Squadron did not survive for long after I donned uniform in August. And three weeks' training there in the vacation meant that I had to compress all my vacation work into the other three weeks remaining to me.

Three afternoons a week I went to the gymnasium to train as a welterweight in the hope of reaching the University Boxing Team. I sparred with other aspirants and with the trainer, an ex-professional. 'Go on. Try to hit me,' he would say, weaving and bobbing and ducking on clever feet. When I did, I apologised, which took us both aback. Every morning at 6.45 a.m. the trainer took the team on a run around Christ Church meadows. He was first class; who paid for his services I had no idea, for it certainly cost me nothing; if it had I could not have afforded it. I was fitter than ever in my life, walking on air. A superb feeling.

Boxing was a new sport to me and I never really started to try until my opponent had hit me enough to hurt. My lack of physical aggression was to be a disadvantage to me as my war career progressed; it fitted me well enough as the reconnaissance pilot which I became, but had I been a fighter pilot, waiting for the opponent to strike first would not have helped my survival.

In addition to boxing, I believe I could have had a place in the University running team but I had no time for the track. The attraction of boxing was to improve my footwork for cricket and speed my reactions. The gym, the Air Squadron, cricket in the summer, and the demands of my weekly essay were enough even for my ambition.

During March, in the vacation I was spending much time at the Air Squadron where I came second with 86 per cent in an exam on law and organisation. Not that that meant anything much, then or later. One evening I dined with the Principal of Brasenose, famous for his parties. This one went on until 4 a.m. I wrote 'I wasn't able to get back into Christ Church in any orthodox manner, as in the vacation there are no night porters and the great gates were barred. So I had to climb in – rather a feat as I did no damage to my clothes, it was a dark night with no moon during the blackout, and the deed was entirely unpremeditated. Bear in mind that enormous precautions are taken against climbing in, with bars, barbed wire, high walls topped with broken glass, etc. I was relatively sober and in the morning quite fresh and up for breakfast at 8 a.m.'

That year at Oxford was perhaps the most heady and intoxicating in all my life. In the background, behind everything else, was the war to which I must soon go. That was exciting. So was the prospect of flying. But I did not dwell on such thoughts – the interests and activities of each day were sufficient. The immense liberty of a grown up world dissolved all my horizons. I had never been on my own and away from home before. Suddenly gone were the parental disciplines, the school disciplines, the restrictions of family life with close proximity of brothers and sisters. I felt I could do anything, dare anything, try anything; the world was my oyster.

Meals were taken in the spacious magnificent Hall. Drinks could be had in the Buttery or Common Room; if I could afford them, for I was always conscious that my parents were having a hard time financing households in Ramsgate and Uttoxeter and me at Oxford, and there could be no luxuries. The first time I got drunk was in my first term. We were always in each others' rooms, talking until the late hours on ethics or philosophy or politics or college gossip or any subject under the sun. On this occasion a friend had bought some Christ Church Audit Ale from the college Buttery and we drank as we talked. His rooms were on a different staircase to mine and, as I walked back, the solid wall of Meadow Buildings leaned over and struck me on the side of the head several times before I got to the safety of my own room, and even there the world was unstable.

It was in my bedroom at Meadow Buildings that an assault was made on my virginity. I was changing for bed and just getting into my pyjamas when an acquaintance came into my room. I said I was in the bedroom just changing. In he came, put his arms round me and said that he got affectionate this time of night. Did I mind? I said yes I did rather. He said he had been on his way to see another friend, and I said he had better go and see him then. Obediently off he went. I found it hard to sleep, feeling unclean, sullied, dirty all over. Next day I could not shake off this feeling until I had gone to swim at the swimming baths which cleansed and relaxed me.

Once a week we had a one-hour tutorial in History, and lest it should be thought that life was all sweetness, excitement and honey, let me say that this was an ordeal of the first order. The tutor would set a subject and give a list of books to be read and digested before the weekly essay was written. He had a talent for sarcasm and a biting wit and we feared him greatly. He would call upon us in turn to read aloud the ripe fruits of our study. As I read the silence deepened and I realised how bad the essay was, what a poor attempt, how weak the reasoning, how inadequate the language, and the reading faltered, but there was nothing to do but to go on to the bitter end. One early attempt of mine was on some such subject as 'Discuss the Anglo Saxon concept of democracy and its practical implication'. Of the books on the list he gave us only one was well printed and easy to read. So on this I founded my essay. But I had built on sand. As I read it aloud the silence deepened around me and my confidence oozed out of my shoes and away. After I had finished reading, the silence continued for some minutes, a seeming eternity. Then 'Really,' the tutor said. 'Well, really,' and called for the next. I never took the first and easiest route again.

* * *

Back at Westward Ho in April, an event occurred which was to change my life. During the previous summer I had visited the Food Office in Uttoxeter with the family ration books. There I met a young lady named Edith Smith, full of vitality and sparkle. I had been brought up with two sisters, Joan older and Doreen younger, and once in a while had met their friends, so girls were not to me an arcane mystery but ordinary human beings, subject to the same sort of limitations as myself, sometimes friendly and helpful, sometimes mean and spiteful. At childhood parties, girls were always wanting to play kissing games like Postman's Knock, to my acute embarrassment, and I did my best therefore to keep out of their way. There were always more interesting things to do, like playing cricket or reading a good book than wasting time on a useless distraction like talking to girls. Except of course that my sisters usually talked with more sense and wit than I did and thank goodness never wanted to play kissing games, at least with me.

During that brief summer of 1940 there was a War Comforts Ball in Uttoxeter Town Hall. Like many such occasions at that epoch it was an evening dress affair, by today's standards rather formal but most pleasant, and I was persuaded to wear my father's dinner jacket. My mother had some years before insisted that Doreen and I attended ballroom dancing lessons so that we should know the elementary steps of the waltz, foxtrot and tango. I danced with the lovely Edith Smith; and also on the dance floor was a young woman whose looks entranced me and I asked Edith to introduce us. So it came about that I danced with her younger sister Joan, known as Jonathan. I remember that we passed close to Edith, at this time with someone else for these girls were never wallflowers, who said to Joan as we went by 'Tell your partner his shirt tail is hanging out'. That was nothing unusual, mind you; it often did, particularly on the cricket field. Though I did not forget this ballroom encounter, I thought no more of it then for I was on the brink of going up to Oxford and each day was new with excitement and fresh endeavour. Joan Smith also was going away, to Bishop Otter Teacher Training College in Chichester, and her world was expanding as was mine.

* * *

Two terms, the Michaelmas and the Hilary, had passed and I was back for my shortened vacation in April. Wednesday was market day in Uttoxeter and I always enjoyed walking round the town, seeing the stalls, the bustle, the farmers' wives selling eggs, or fowls, or home-made butter, and the cattle market. In the main street, amongst the crowds near the Town Hall, I passed Joan Smith; a petite figure with brown hair and sparkling green eyes. It was the Queen of Heaven. She turned her head and smiled at me over her shoulder. Time stood still, the world turned upside down. She walked on, but several more times that morning I contrived to see her. She said later that I followed her all around the town. I had not thought it could have seemed so obvious and I was sorry, but she drew me as a magnet draws a helpless fragment of iron.

I went home and wrote her a letter asking her to meet me at the Elite Cinema at 6 p.m. the next day to see *Night Train to Munich*. I took the letter to the Food Office, and ran after Edith who was just leaving on her bicycle. I learnt later that Edith expressed indignation as she had supposed the letter would be for her. Nevertheless she must have delivered it, for next evening her little sister Joan cycled the seven miles to Uttoxeter from her home in the deep country, and she must have cycled home again after the cinema, presumably in the dark.

We arranged to meet the following day, but she overslept. Did we meet again in the few brief days of freedom left to me? At any rate we promised to write. Poor correspondent that I was, I kept my word and sent her a letter three weeks before the final exam for my wartime degree, describing a good game of cricket. In this same letter I wrote with some prescience 'it does not look as though the war will ever end. We are not strong enough to meet Germany in the field and unless America comes in it seems doubtful if we shall ever be. On the seas and in the air we may hope for supremacy, but not on land. So we seem doomed to a slow war of exhaustion and blockade. The question at issue is: can we smash Germany into submission with our Air Force any more effectively than she has done us? Apart from America the only hope is in Russia and whether Russia turns against Germany depends on the actions of Germany herself.' In early May the outlook looked sombre even to a nineteen-year-old; to my surprise one month later on 22 June my prophecy came true, for Germany invaded Russia and changed the course of the war, although for a time the German advance was so huge that prospects looked even worse. But I did not brood over what the future held for me or for my country. My final examination loomed and there was cricket.

Cricket was the great passion of my life and even Joan Smith was at that time less important. I had cut short my vacation in order to practise at the nets before the Trinity term began. In this I was following the footsteps of my elder brother Bernard, who had been at Brasenose before me and established a high reputation.

My father had been an excellent games player himself. He played with Bernard and later with me in the garden with a tennis ball as soon as we were big enough to hold the smallest possible bat, to the destruction of the flowers and my mother's periodic attempts to create a garden. Brilliantly gifted at ball games, Bernard would excel in tennis, table tennis and football, but was directed into cricket because this was the high road to glory. Our headmaster at school, where my father at this time was the senior science master, did everything he could to build up the school's cricketing prowess. On several occasions the Headmaster turned out all 500 boys to watch Bernard in full swing and on his way to yet another century; one such day I remember when he made two hundred – one hundred before lunch and one hundred before tea, the only time in the school's history this had been done – and I lay with all the other boys in the long grass of the boundary swelling with love and pride: 'That's my brother; what a lovely shot; oh how I wish I could play like that.' I had a long way to go, for I lacked his gifts though I tried hard and single-mindedly, spending all my spare time in the summer at the nets.

Though I, like Bernard, had been captain of the school first eleven, I never approached the standard he had set. I trailed brilliance I could never attain myself and always knew it. But cricketing ambition explains why I curtailed my brief holiday that Easter of 1941, to return to Oxford before term started to play at the nets in the parks or the college grounds. As I write I can smell the sweet new cut grass, see the gleam of white shirts and flannels, the hard red ball curving through the air and hear the satisfying clunk of the ball meeting the sweet part of the bat. These things were mine once and I am grateful.

* * *

So began the last term of my first year at Oxford, before the war swallowed me up down its long dark tunnel. All the year at Oxford is a delight but the summer is supreme. The sun of course was always shining. The foliage on the trees, young leaves tender and green, the may, the hawthorn blossom, the quickening pulse of all life coming to fruition, the lazy punts on the river, overarched with trees above the shining placid waters. But I had little time for the river, for I was dedicated to play cricket and take my final examination, the first part of the History School which would give me a wartime degree.

About that examination I mercifully remember little, except waiting tensely for papers to be distributed and then the rapid and intense scribbling to cram as much as one could onto paper in the time allotted. Getting a reasonable degree was vital. I could not have envisaged failure, nor have I ever done so, though there were to be some dark hard times ahead.

When challenged for survival as in examinations, as in a sortie against an enemy determined to destroy one, or as in other such desperate occasions which test the whole of one's being, it is often the accumulated disciplines of one's previous life that come to the rescue. The dull and prosaic secret of all such tests and challenges is to work steadily to prepare oneself in the months beforehand; to be, like a good Scout, prepared. Then, a day or two before the event, to relax and quiet your mind as best you may. It is now too late to worry. You have prepared; your conscience is clear. Put your trust in God and your guardian angel. Then next day let battle start.

My subject was Modern History. During my childhood I had loved history, but now the romance seemed to have gone out of it and in a letter home I lamented that if I came back after the war I would take another subject, as I saw no point in this tedious struggle to absorb facts which were of little relevance today. I was of course wrong; history is a grand subject and as important and relevant as anything else which one can study for it is of life itself that has been lived up to this point of time, and what can be more important to the living than that? And I did achieve a sound second class, which was as much as a devoted cricketer like myself could expect.

* * *

At the end of June I was back at Westward Ho. My first priority was to get myself some games of cricket, so I joined up with the Uttoxeter Grasshoppers, but at the most we would only have had two games a week. That left time on my hands, so taking hold of my courage I mounted my bicycle and set off for Grindley, the home of Edith and Joan Smith and as rural a place as could be imagined. It was hidden away along byroads, and as all signposts had been removed to defeat possible German parachute attack, and as the countryman from whom I sought direction must have suspected me of being a German parachutist and sent me the wrong way, it was hard to find. But at last I succeeded, left my bike by the hedge, walked up the garden to the door and asked if Miss Joan Smith was there. 'Yes, she is somewhere about,' said a lady I took to be her mother. 'Let me find her for you.' But she was nowhere to be found. Years later I learned that seeing me coming she had felt panic, fled upstairs to her room and hidden under the bed.

Our fate and fortune however were not to be defeated for long. Very soon after my failed mission to Grindley, the two Smith sisters joined us on a family picnic, and Joan and I lay side by side on the grassy river bank and read the book of Border Ballads I had taken with me. That day was the start of Paradise. We met as often as we could and explored the Derbyshire Peak District, sometimes bicycling, sometimes by train. My father was home, on holiday from the battle zone in Kent. He was about to go to Gravesend where he had been appointed to run the Technical Institute, providing education for adults, a big boys' school and through a headmistress a girls' school as well. A giant task, well suited to his huge energy, and when at last the time came for him to retire he was replaced by three people. A great lover of the country, it was he who first took me to the Peak District where later I took Joan Smith. Once we had a family excursion; at other times we adventured on our own. Often it rained; we got wet and sheltered under trees and in caves. She had told me that her hair was naturally curly but then when it rained I found it became straight and straggled. We laughed about that and about most things. We kissed once, sheltering under a moss-covered tree, and I expect we held hands at times. But this was an innocent relationship, belonging to the days before Eve had given Adam the apple to eat from the Tree of Knowledge. We were entirely happy exploring the countryside and each other's personality; we would have shrunk from close physical contact. Indeed, throughout my life I could not contemplate physical contact without complete commitment to the partner, which in many a later wartime episode would leave me disappointed and frustrated, though with integrity intact, while my companions were enjoying themselves. But in the sweet freshness of our companionship that brief summer of 1941 no such thought or impulse arose. We had no contact and except deep within us and unexpressed, no commitment. And then alas, the idyll ended. Paradise was lost – I went to war.

CHAPTER TWO

I Join the RAF

In August 1941, together with friends from the Oxford University Air Squadron, I joined the Aircrew Reception Centre at St John's Wood in London. Before leaving Westward Ho my father, who had just taken up his post at Gravesend, sent me the following letter.

The Technical Institute

Darnley Rd

Gravesend

11 August

My dear Geoffrey,

I am really writing this in my bedroom before retiring for the night, but the above address is one which you can remember and use until we get settled.

Your mother has told me that you go on Saturday. Well, God be with you my lad. It is an old old phrase but it is all that comes to me now. I wish you all the best in your new life and I feel that you will come through safely and well. You have youth and pluck, any amount of perseverance and a good brain. You have a fine body to stand exertion and strain, and a pleasant manner with others which will stand you in good stead. Look after yourself. Don't be led into temptations, and you will be tempted in various ways. You cannot expect or wish for a sheltered life, but temptations can be resisted. Don't get the idea so common in the Army that drink and girls are all that matter. Your body is too fine and precious for that. I don't think I need say any more on those lines, because you already know what I believe. I was brought up much more strictly than you have been, and now at my age I am thankful. But you have been left with much more freedom. It is up to you to show that this has been a good thing. It is funny but as I write this all sorts of religious sayings and teachings crowd into my mind. What a pity it is that we ever lost the old faith! It was a sure shield and protection.

And now let me know where you go and how you get on. Write as often as you can and remember that your mother and I have really only one wish and hope in life and that is for the well being and real happiness of our children. You can rely on us to give you help if ever you need it and we know that we can rely on you to do well in whatever work you are called upon to do.

I hope you will keep in touch with your little girl friend. She seemed to me very pleasant and 'nice'.

Good hunting and a safe return,

With much love,

Dad.

Thus fortified I presented myself at Bentinck Close, a block of flats near Regent's Park which had been commandeered for the purpose, full of self-confidence, of anticipation and eagerness for the new life, keen to throw my entire self into whatever lay before me. I was soon sobered by the cold waters of reality. No. 1 ARC, Aircrew Reception Centre, was just simply that, a reception centre. All of us were awaiting postings. Most to go to the Initial Training Wing or ITW to receive basic ground instruction; we from the University Air Squadrons had already been through this stage and were to go direct to EFTS, Elementary Flying Training School. In the meantime we received a stringent medical examination, inoculations, vaccinations, and were given our uniform. Mine had to be taken back for alterations and I was not able to put it on until the end of the week, when I donned this uncomfortable and still somewhat ill-fitting blue serge and a forage cap which sported a white flash to show that I was cadet aircrew. We were told our rank was Acting AC2 though substantively we were already LAC or Leading Aircraftsmen. To act AC2 was to act in the lowest possible rank of His Majesty's Royal Air Force. Later I was to boast that I had held every rank in the RAF from AC2 to Flight Lieutenant except that of Corporal, and judging from the corporals I encountered in those first few weeks of my service I must say the rank of corporal was not one to which I ever aspired.

Apart from being jabbed and kitted out there was absolutely nothing to do. We were woken at 6 a.m. and not allowed out on the town until after 6 p.m. We scrubbed the floor of our bedroom which must have been shared with I suppose half a dozen others, and an orderly officer came round on inspection, screamed at us that it wasn't clean, and though in fact it was clean as clean could be we were made to scrub it again. But most of our time we spent queuing for food. We were fed in a canteen at Regents Park Zoo and any passerby would have seen long columns of us in Regents Park, waiting for breakfast, lunch or tea. The average wait for each meal was from two to two and a half hours and thus we spent at least seven hours a day standing waiting to be fed. And when at long last we got it, the food was not very good. An orderly officer came round every day to ask for complaints. Eventually we resolved that we owed it to ourselves and the RAF to offer our views on the food with which we had been served, so the entire table of us poor young recruits stood up. We were then told that this constituted mutiny and that only one person was allowed to stand up and complain at a time.

I make no criticism of the authorities who evidently had to improvise administration for huge numbers of people to be clothed, housed, fed and transported; no doubt they did the best they could. I sympathise with their difficulties. However I find completely inexcusable the shouting, screaming attitude of the junior NCOs and orderly officers who did all they could to make life unpleasant. Presumably they thought they were inculcating discipline but personally I, like most others, react very badly to being shouted at. We were all volunteers for dangerous employment and we all knew that many of us would not survive the next few years. It was not necessary to treat us with hostility.

I became friendly with a man named Deane who had been a full-time lieutenant serving in the Royal Marines, had volunteered for aircrew, was told to resign his commission and re-enlist in the RAF. This he had done. Now he found our treatment intolerable. Recruits would not have been treated like this in his service and he bitterly regretted the step he had taken. 'It is all very well for you,' he said to me. 'You just retreat to an ivory tower of indifference, separating yourself from the discomforts all around you. But it is different for me. I can't do that. I am going to resign.'

I counselled patience. 'You cannot spend all your war resigning from one service after another. Anyway I don't suppose they will let you. Put up with it for a few weeks longer and we shall be away to flying training and things will be different. Anyway you can have an ivory tower for yourself if you want, but the price paid for it is lack of personal involvement and this can be a high price.'

Some of us were due to go to America and some to Canada under the Empire Air Training Scheme, and off Deane went to the States with about four-fifths of my friends. There I was later told the discipline was even worse, with bullying and harassment from instructors and pupils on the course just in front, designed supposedly to test one's moral fibre. It was said the daily kit inspections were so frightful, with every item possessed by each pupil having to be laid out on his bed every day in precise order and polished, that many left theirs so arranged permanently and slept on the floor. Whether Deane ever survived this training I never knew, but I very much doubt it.

Often have I wondered whether the shouting and bullying to which we were subjected by the NCOs and orderly officers was a sign of a sense of inferiority on their part. We were the elite, the cream of British youth, all volunteers, young, eager. Were they not jealous because they themselves could never become what we were, and therefore would make use of the little brief authority in which they were dressed to assert themselves in compensation for what they could never be, and for their narrow, dull and constricted roles during this great war of their lifetimes? But we did not take it all lying down. On one occasion we were summoned to an Odeon Cinema, which we filled entirely, to listen to a pep talk given by an Air Commodore who had before the war been big in greyhound racing. He kept us waiting for about forty-five minutes and we started to sing 'Why are we waiting?' an impressive sound from the lusty lungs of some five hundred young men. No-one charged us with mutiny. Perhaps we were too many for the orderly officer, whose courage may have failed him. The speech when it came wasn't very good. I could have done better myself. The 'Why are we waiting?' chant became common usage in the days ahead.

For the first time in my life I was faced with the need to wash my socks, handkerchiefs and collars. This I discovered was not difficult, but the prospect of darning holes in the socks filled me with horror. Though doubtless long ago some mighty genius invented the way to darn socks, this information had never been passed to me and I was left to my own invention. Inventing mathematics or language might have been easy in comparison. For years I experimented, but it was not until I reached the Imphal Plain in 1943 that my friend Ken Draycott took pity on me and demonstrated how a sock should be mended. Ken was a gifted painter who had been at art school and knew about practical things, and from then on I would have comfortable feet. But that was a mercy to unfold in the future and until then I suffered in ignorance.

The monotony of boots and buttons, of standing on your feet for seven hours each day queuing for food, was broken by occasional evenings out. There was a persistent rumour that each day we were being dosed with bromide in the tea, or perhaps in the food, to subdue our sexual impulses. No one could advise whether any particular bromides could in fact do this and I thought the whole story very unlikely. But 'beating the bromide' became a standard expression. Ask anyone who was set for an evening out what he was going to do, and 'Beat the bromide' was the reply. One Saturday we were allowed out from noon to midnight. Mervyn Wingfield, an old Etonian and one of my few friends of Air Squadron days who had not gone off to the States, was a member of the Junior Carlton Club in Pall Mall. There he took me and showed me the swimming pool. We went to the cinema to see a film of Nazi Germany, dined in the West End, went to see another film called *Lady Hamilton* and ended up in a night club. I recorded that we had spent six pounds each and that I was without a penny until the following Thursday which was pay-day. It sounds dull enough now but perhaps it was exciting at the time. At least neither of us tried to beat the bromide.

Such spare time as I had I wrote letters to Jonathan, my girl friend. Three sonnets I composed for her, generally when I was on guard duty from 2 to 4.30 a.m. watching over a London where in daytime, or when illuminated by searchlight, the barrage balloons looked like silver toys in the wind. They were not very good sonnets and did less than justice to what I felt for my little friend. We made pledges of fidelity and I asked for a promise that she would forget all about me as quickly as she could if I did not come back or was disabled. But I found writing difficult; in fact throughout my Air Force career I found the lack of privacy a great handicap; people were around you all day and there was nowhere to retreat on one's own in moments of leisure, though this became a little easier when commissioned. My friends did not write letters and were always wanting to be off and away from camp whenever chance offered. In such circumstances the example of your acquaintances can be very compelling. Others perhaps overcame this problem but I was soon to feel as my flying career progressed that I wanted my family and my loved ones to write me off; to forget about me. If I thought they were worrying about me I should be weakened, and indeed it would weaken me to think of them. So after I left ARC my letters became few and far between.

During the five weeks that I was in London, my mother had given up the house in Uttoxeter and had gone to join my father in Gravesend and it was there that I went on pre-embarkation leave at the beginning of September. I wrote to Jonathan suggesting that I go to meet her in Staffordshire or that she come to stay with us in Gravesend; alternatively that we could meet in London on her way through to her new term at Chichester on 15 September. Then I received orders that during this leave I was not to leave my home address as I might at any time be recalled at very short notice. My lady would not come to Gravesend and did not tell me the arrival time of her train in London. When she arrived at St Pancras she nevertheless searched the station diligently for me but of course I was not there. So I sailed away to the New World and to the Aurora Borealis without seeing her again.

CHAPTER THREE

Canada

This was the first time I had left England, and I left from the Liverpool Docks. In later years after the war I was to leave England several times from Liverpool for Sierra Leone and the impression the docks gave me is an abiding one, ever the same. The waters lapping at the dock and ship side are grey and muddy; the skies are dull and leaden. There is dirt and grime in the air and all around; there is a raw damp cold which penetrates through you. Overhead a few miserable gulls, floating and wheeling, desperate for trifles, confirm the scene as one of desolation. This no doubt is mercifully ordained by providence, for the grim aspect of land, air and sea is such as to overcome any sentiment about leaving the country of your birth; you are glad to leave such a place. Nor indeed when you arrive back in England at Liverpool Docks is the welcome any warmer than was the farewell, nor the scene any friendlier. Perhaps I am unkind to Liverpool for I have never in truth known a British dock that was a jolly place.

The ship that was to carry us over this great and stormy ocean where the German U-boats lurked was the MV *Highland Princess* of the Royal Mail Steam Packet Company, a ship of some 14,000 gross tons and capable of fifteen knots. Built in 1929 for the South American trade, she was intended to carry both passengers and meat cargoes. Her designed accommodation was for 135 in the first class, 66 in the intermediate, and 600 in steerage to cope with emigrants and the flow of labour between Spain and Portugal and South America. How many she carried on our journey I do not know but there were a great many more than that. Nor do I know if there was any first class accommodation on board for anyone, but there certainly was not for me and my friends.

It must have been late afternoon when we embarked and the ship's canteen was open. A mad scramble started amongst my companions for chocolates, which had not been seen in British shops for many a long month and most bought slabs and boxes of chocolate. Not me; I do not have sweet tooth. We sailed shortly after embarking, and as soon as we met the rough Irish Sea those who had stuffed themselves had speedy cause for regret, as I have never seen so many people seasick at one time. In our cramped conditions this was less than pleasant though luckily for me I happen to be a good sailor. Our accommodation was three decks down, in the bottom hold right under the stern of the ship. It had been a refrigerated compartment for the carriage of meat and the walls were lined with the pipes that had carried coolant. The ship was equipped with twin screws and every time she lifted in the long Atlantic swells, which was often, her stern rose high in the water and we could hear them thrashing above our heads vibrating through the whole of our compartment. We were issued with hammocks and blankets which every evening had to be slung and every morning rolled up tidily, for underneath the hammocks were the mess tables on which we ate. The hammock is a marvellous invention, for it holds you still while the ship moves as though in gimbals, and in it you may snuggle up and sleep sound. But when all the hammocks were slung they filled the entire space, touching one another. When one hammock moved, they all moved and the scene inside the hold was one of hammocks gently swaying backwards and forwards in unison. Once in there was no prospect of getting out; you were there for the night. Some slept on the mess tables beneath the hammocks and some on the floor below them. Those who were sick in the night – and there were many – could not get out and perforce vomited over those on the mess decks or those on the floor. The two decks above us were similarly packed, so that even if you could have made your way in the middle of the night out of your hammock and up the wooden stairs you would have to fight your way through the same conditions in both of them. In fact no-one was allowed on deck after dusk, in case a light was shown by a careless smoker, for we travelled under the strictest blackout and many lives in the convoy were at risk. It was very plain to me at the time that had we been struck by a torpedo we should have all feasted the fish, for from the third deck down below the shelter deck we should none of us get out, nor from the second or even the first deck down. Now, I thought, this is how the sailors in Nelson's navy lived, sleeping in hammocks above the tables of their mess decks with neither room, privacy or hope of survival in disaster, but the thought was not much help.

The convoy was a large one. There were many ships all around us, dark shapes on the grey tossing sea and the destroyer screen was ever active, backwards and forwards, but the visibility was often poor in driving rain and we were not encouraged to linger on deck where there was neither space nor comfort. After queuing for food, cleaning up afterwards and then queuing to use the lavatories perhaps there was not much daylight left for there was nowhere to spend time except on the mess decks. And progress was slow and the days multiplied; the speed of a convoy is well known to be that of its slowest ship and I do not suppose we sailed at anything like the fifteen knots of which our vessel was allegedly capable. The sea was certainly not calm but nor was it unduly rough, though I learnt my lesson early on that slops and waste – perhaps it was the water in which I had washed and shaved or it may have been the washing-up water after the first breakfast – must be flung over the lee and not the windward side or it would come straight back in your face. Food was plentiful, for with all but two of us at our mess table sick, I was issued an abundance and was at a loss to know what to do with twenty-four hard boiled eggs which were too much for me to eat unaided. We were young; we were tough and prepared to rough it but every one of us was glad when the journey had come to an end, as it did one darkening afternoon as we glided into the great harbour of Halifax, Nova Scotia. Shortly after we dropped anchor the lights of the town came on, for it was dusk and all the houses which were hidden in the wooded slopes overlooking the harbour gaily twinkled at us. After two years of the British blackout and the continuing and even stricter blackout across the Atlantic, this was truly fairyland, startling us with sudden surprise.

* * *

After the ship, the train. Trains in Canada are larger than those we had left at home, suitable to carry passengers over the long journeys of thousands of miles. As we sped along I was entranced by this large and spacious land, of great woods and lakes and few people. We were handsomely fed on the train, for Canada was still a land of milk and honey though we were later to find that the food in our RAF camps was not particularly distinguished, efforts being made we presumed to keep down costs and to keep us accustomed to the sparse British standards to which we must return. Then one night on our journey we saw the Aurora Borealis. For hours I sat gazing at the sky, at great waving, folding, shifting curtains of light, green and greenish white and yellow and fawn. I have since been told this is caused by the solar wind, a hot gas streaming from the sun towards the earth; if this wind is disturbed and made stormy by solar flares there can be a display of splendour and perhaps this was the cause of my astonished delight. Apparently the earth's magnetic field can act as a giant cathode ray tube, projecting light on to the great screen of the upper atmosphere near the Pole. Sometimes the curtains were folded into pleats, sometimes becoming an arc reaching from the horizon, then folding and waving, changing colour, taking my breath away and leaving me spellbound.

At Winnipeg we were met by a civic reception. There was a band, the mayor, town dignitaries and a large crowd were there to meet us and we were paraded for them on the platform. This made us forget the discomforts of the sea journey although, as is the way of youth, that was already receding behind us and the reception was but an indication of the warmth and hospitality with which we were treated throughout our stay in this great new land of Canada. Feeling good after this we set forth into the rolling, undulating, treeless expanses of the prairie, towards the towns of the romantic frontier names which were to be our homes for the next few months: Swift Current, Moose Jaw, Medicine Hat, Red Deer, names rather more romantic than the reality, though the boyhood thrills which Fennimore Cooper and Longfellow's Hiawatha had given me lay only just below the surface. The prairies seemed largely waterless and except for the creek at Swift Current which I thought disappointing and only a brook, there was no running water for many miles in any direction. Here I found the people tough but very kind; tough, so they said, they had to be to stand the extremes of temperature which in the summer could rise to 110 °F and in winter to 40 below zero. Being in the middle of the continent there was little rain, and the snow when it came in the Fall was generally light, only an inch or two thick and this would be the main moisture for the ground throughout the year. Occasionally in the summer there would be terrible dust storms which banished all visibility so that you could hardly see to move, and when they were over the fine tilth and topsoil of the prairie was piled many feet high against the perimeter fence, like huge snow drifts.

Apart from dust storms it was wonderful flying country. The land was thinly populated and there were few settlements to cause confusion. One main road and one railway ran from east to west through the prairie so it was difficult to get lost. It was only necessary to remember whether you had flown north or south, east or west of the airstrip, north or south of the road or railway line. Find them again and they would lead you home. How different from England with its seemingly infinite network of little roads and railways which offer the poor lost pilot only a confused jumble of conflicting signs. And as for the weather, generally this was clear, and only a very few days throughout the year were not suitable for flying training.

But when we reached our destination, Swift Current, there was no flying to be done. Courses were in training ahead of us and we had to bide our time for five weeks. I was put to shovelling coal out of railway wagons, needful to keep the camp warm. At this time, late October and early November, there was already snow and with temperatures of some degrees below zero one tended to keep at one's work of shovelling in order to stay warm. Canadian civilians were also employed in this work and I suppose they did the bulk of it. In fact there was good company and good humour and I did not resent what we had to do. I later discovered this to be a recurrent pattern of my wartime life. Training, adventure, excitement or great endeavour were suddenly to end in an unexpected blank period of waiting and inactivity; geared to great things we were suddenly landed in anticlimax, a trough of dullness and depression, which had we been older and more worldly-wise might have cooled our ardour and blunted our eagerness. Instead we rejoiced in our surroundings and the prairie town and the large T-bone steaks served in the cafés. Our turn would come.

But it was at Swift Current during this waiting period I was introduced to the dodges of avoiding work. 'Take a wheelbarrow,' it was said, 'Wheel it from one side of the camp to the other; sit on it for half an hour and then wheel it back again to the other side where you sit on it again, and repeat the process throughout the day. No-one will trouble you or question you.' Similar advice was to equip yourself with a folder of papers and walk briskly from one end of the camp to the other as if with purpose. Conceal yourself, wait a while and repeat your journey, and so on through the day. I found it easier to shovel coal which I much preferred to do. These ways of avoiding work seemed to be harder work in themselves than legitimate activity and only worthwhile if determined to spite authority, for which I had no reason. But one lesson learned from our contemporaries was hard not to absorb. This was to avoid the limelight, not to thrust yourself forward or to attract attention in any way, or you risked being singled out for some unpleasant task. You even tried to shrink yourself and make yourself look less tall so you would not be chosen to be a marker on parade. This was not a good lesson nor was I ever happy with it, for it ran counter to all I had ever learned, or been taught, or been brought up to believe, though I must confess that when I am with a large number of other people, like most of us, I tend to adopt the protective colouring of my environment as does the chameleon. A natural instinct which needs either strong force of character or the strong grip of circumstance to overcome and squeeze you out like the pip out of a lemon.

* * *

Jim and Beatrice Ironside of Swift Current, middle-aged, warm-hearted, kept open house for my friends and me. They were business people and ran the Cold Store in the town. Where distances are large and temperatures extreme, the proper keeping of food supplies assumes considerable importance, as we were to discover years later in Sierra Leone when the arrival by train of the weekly Cold Store Box from Freetown was a major event of the week for much of the expatriate community. On the Canadian Prairie, our needs for food and shelter being provided by His Majesty's Royal Air Force without effort or concern by us, no such thoughts about the significance of a Cold Store troubled us as we luxuriated in the Ironsides' hospitality; often we came back to visit them from further afield and some of my friends planned to spend leave with them. I bless the memory of the Ironsides, and of those other kind souls whom I met later, who lit lamps for us in the darkness of the war.

Memories of Prohibition must have been strong on the prairies, for liquor was hard to come by. Not that we were depraved; we were young men experimenting with life and finding our feet. There were Servicemen's Clubs but these were inclined to be dull places which served only beer. Anything else had to be obtained from a Liquor Store. This had a counter with an iron grille above, like a Bank. The precious bottles were behind the grille. One filled in a slip of paper, giving name and address and possibly a reference or two, then took it to the counter and slipped it together with the money under the grille. The bottle was slipped back underneath. Having got it, the next problem was to drink from it. No drinking was allowed in public places so there were two alternatives. One was to walk out of town into the prairie and, ensconced out of the wind behind some dune, sip from the bottle. Without glasses or water or ice this was not to be recommended. The other alternative was to rent a room in the local hotel and order glasses, ice and Canada Dry or other fizzy drink and taste the alcohol there. This wasn't much fun either. The equivalent of the English pub which is really what we should have wished to find did not seem to exist. And indeed there was not a great deal of time for such diversion, for we worked hard.

* * *

At the end of November we moved to Bowden near Red Deer, Alberta, in the foothills of the Rockies. That too was under snow but it was beautiful country and the distant white peaks of the mountains would be rosy in the early morning and evenings. Outside, the air was clear and cold. Inside, the barrack dormitories heated by steam-filled radiators were without ventilation. This was No. 32 EFTS – Elementary Flying Training School – and there began the course for which we had long waited and travelled far to get.

Shortly after arriving in Bowden we were assembled and addressed by the Commanding Officer who admonished us to be careful and do our best. 'You must remember that flying is a dangerous business. If it were a natural thing to do, God would have equipped us with wings like the birds. Instead you have to earn them and when you get them pinned on your chest – if you get that far – it is still an unnatural business. And I have to tell you,' he said, 'no matter how hard we try to teach you, despite all our care and precautions and safety measures, by the time that most of you qualify for your wings at least five of you who are here present will be dead.'

We looked at each other, uncertain whether this dire prediction was meant to be a joke, a true prophecy, an admonition to be careful, or even a mixture of all three. Anyway even if it were true it wouldn't happen to me or you but to someone else, so we forgot about it for the time being.

* * *

There is no exhilaration in the world to compare to this, I thought on my first flight on 4 December. The cold winter air rushed with great fury past the open cockpit of the De Havilland Tiger Moth, the DH 82c, as we sped through the sky at about 80 miles per hour, the instructor in front bellowing instructions through a speaking tube to the pupil strapped into the cockpit behind. To the west were the Rocky Mountains; below the road and railway went north to Edmonton and south to Calgary, not east and west as at Swift Current and Moose Jaw. Marvellous flying country. How could anyone manage to kill themselves if they did what they were told? The exhilaration continued throughout the flying on Tiger Moths – like driving an open sports car – though familiarity in the end diminished its intensity. 'We shall have to call you Smiler,' one of my friends said to me in the dormitories after work, when I was exuberantly describing the exploits of the day, 'You're always so happy and excited after flying.' In part perhaps it was the release of nervous tension.

Flights were generally of short duration, rarely more than forty minutes and usually between twenty and thirty. Sometimes one flew more than once in the day but this was exceptional. Flying was sometimes in the mornings and sometimes in the afternoons, and one would wait in the crew room to be called for a half hour flight at any time during the period, sitting waiting with suppressed excitement and some nervous tension. It was then that I started to smoke cigarettes, never knowing when my turn would come or whether when I had already flown I would be called to fly again. This may have been good practice for an eventual fighter pilot on standby, but I might have become a better pilot had things been a little less haphazard. Flying times were short and very exciting; waiting times were long and nerve wracking. Boom and slump, climax and anti-climax, the recurrent pattern of the RAF both in training and in action. But what care the instructors took. Entered into my log book in precise detail are the matters taught in each flight – straight and level, effect of controls, climbing, gliding and stalling, medium turns, taxiing and take-off into wind, gliding approach and landing, spinning (importantly underlined in red), cloud flying, power approach and landing. Each item numbered and each repeated many times.

My first instructor was a fiery young Texan, Pilot Officer Jones. He had joined the RAF as a great adventure in the eager anticipation of becoming a fighter pilot. Instead he had been made an instructor, to his intense frustration, and he would express this by shooting up the control tower now and again or by crazy aerobatics at a low level to call the attention of the authorities to his plight and induce them to give him a posting. He was, as far as I could then judge such things, an excellent pilot but I found him a poor instructor; perhaps because he did not want to be one, or perhaps he wanted to do it badly in the hope of getting posted to the action for which he had joined up. He would shout at his pupils and unless they grasped what they were told immediately would show no patience. Admittedly it was necessary to shout over the intercom of a Tiger Moth in order to be heard, but there is all the difference in the world between shouting in kindness and sympathy, and in shouting in anger and irritation. I will also admit that instructing must require nerves of steel especially if a pupil is slow to learn or a trifle inept, for flying is a dangerous business, particularly when close to the ground and in take-off or landing. 'Now dear, mind you fly carefully, very low and slow,' the old lady said to her aspiring offspring – an old Air Force joke, for there is no more dangerous way to fly. So it is possible to find excuses for the shouting ill-tempered instructor. Unfortunately most of us react badly when subjected to it, become confused and tend to do the wrong thing. This together with the long hours of waiting for one's turn to fly made me fear my progress was slow, and that I would fail the course despite the intense exhilaration I felt when airborne. My flying hours mounted up and I had not been allowed near the great hurdle of the first solo; it was said the better pilots make it in seven hours or even less and I had this already and no indication of when or whether I would be allowed up on my own. Was I about to fail for the first time in my life?

In its wisdom the RAF did not rely on the judgement of one instructor alone, particularly on that of one such as Pilot Officer Jones whose temperament was a camp byword, and I flew occasionally with other pilots including the Flight Commander. Then after two weeks of the course and seven hours flying, my instructor was changed and Sgt Richardson took me over. He was tall and quiet, gentle in manner and kind. With patient good humour he explained, unruffled he coped with any predicament in which you might have inadvertently placed the two of you; he spoke little but gave you confidence. Three flights with him were devoted to take-offs and landings. Then I was given a short test by a Flying Officer Dew but still nothing was said to me. Oh dear, am I about to be failed in disappointment and disgrace? A night of suspense. Then next day another flight of forty minutes with Sgt Richardson, a flight of take-offs and landings. After, as I taxied into dispersal he told me to keep the engine going. Then quite unexpectedly and without any warning he got out of the aircraft, unbuckled his parachute, slung it over his shoulder. 'Alright,' he said, 'Off you go.'

And he stood there outside in the sub-zero temperature to watch what happened.

I turned the aircraft and taxied into the wind. As I opened the throttle a great surge of joy engulfed me. Singing at the top of my voice I sped over the packed snow of the airfield, the tail wheel lifted, I had flying speed and like a bird she lifted without conscious effort her front wheels off the ground. It was what she was made for. Me too. For this moment I also had been made. I was airborne. In continuing ecstasy, singing and shouting in the exhilaration and glory of it all, I climbed steadily to circuit height, throttled back to cruising speed, banked to the left and turned. There below was the airfield and the camp, all around the winter landscape, white snow to the horizon with the western sky limited by the peaks of the Rocky Mountains. I was alone and in command; everything was in my hand, survival or death, safety or disaster. This was life and freedom and power, no longer shackled and trammelled by the earth and the poor limitations of the body; the spirit soared and the cold air rushed past me. But now it is time to turn and land. Gliding approach and landing as taught me so often during the last two weeks. The airfield is below my left wing tip; I bank and turn to the left again until I am aligned with the windsock and throttle back. Tiger Moth DH 82c No 5074 floats like a fairy; ought to be called a Fairy Moth. But it is alright; I have not overshot; plenty of room. The ground is getting close now. I level out, the height looks about right, I am losing flying speed, I ease the control column back into my tummy and stall the aircraft onto the ground, smooth as silk. As pretty a landing as I was ever to make. I taxied in to my waiting instructor, swung the aircraft round and switched off the engine.

'That was alright. Well done,' said Richie as I climbed out. I beamed my thanks at him, for words failed me. I was over the first great hurdle of my flying career and had had one of its greatest thrills. It was 19 December, the course was two weeks old and I had been given ten hours dual instruction, the last three hours with Richardson. I was to have a further four hours with him until the end of the month when I was changed again to other instructors. In all I flew with twelve different instructors, and I presume this may have been part of a deliberate policy to provide several independent assessments of the pupil's ability and to ensure that the same essential flying knowledge and techniques were hammered home by many different hands and voices. But of them all none was sure and gentle like my Sgt Richardson whose name I bless.

The flying training in fact was superb. Aircraft were valuable even if young pupil pilots were not, and the RAF took endless care to teach flying, rehearsing the same lessons over and over again so that any reasonably apt pupil would react automatically with the right responses when faced with an emergency on his own. Emergency actions such as Abandoning Aircraft, and Action in the Event of Fire were underlined in red in the log book as was Spinning. I did not much care for Spinning for of course the aircraft was out of control until the spin was corrected. When you reach a safe height with plenty of air room to recover from mistakes, you stall the aircraft by reducing the power or putting up the nose until flying speed is lost then, when she starts to fall from the sky, kick the left rudder to spin to the left or the right to spin to the right, and down she will go, slewing round in sickening lurches. Stick forward and opposite rudder is the answer, and sweet and easy she comes out of her distress. No less than thirteen entries for Spinning are underlined in red in this short course, some solo, greatly daring. There are also thirteen entries for aerobatics. First to be taught was looping the loop. Put the stick forward and dive to gain speed and then pull it back in an easy and gradual movement into the stomach. The horizon falls away and you are on your back pointing straight into the heaven; in an easy curve the aircraft continues its course and you are upside down, hanging with all your weight on the straps round your shoulders. The blood rushes to your head, the horizon is strangely upside down, there is no cockpit cover, the cold air goes past you, there is nothing between your head and the ground thousands of feet below and you feel grateful for the comfort of your straps. But the aircraft continues her easy curve and you are right way up with the horizon where it ought to be and the blood returning to where it ought to be too. Then after loops there were rolls to the right and to the left, rolls off the top and stall turns.

No less than twenty-four times did we practise forced landings. Suddenly the instructor would switch the engine off and tell you the engine had failed so you must force land the aircraft. Desperately you search for an open space, a handy level field, or a gap in the trees into which you try to glide, turning the machine into wind; within a few feet of the ground the instructor would switch on the engine, the force of the wind would turn the propeller and the engine would come to life – always I wondered if it would and always it did. The usual take-offs were into wind but we practised also taking off out of wind, whilst the emphasis on landings was always the safe way by gliding approach; only twice, when the course was a month old, were we shown a power approach and landing, though this is the usual heavy aircraft method. The traditional and safe way for the lighter single-engine aircraft was the gliding approach when no use is made of the engine; when you judge the airfield is the right distance below your left wing, you close your throttle and turn, gliding all the way into a landing, though sometimes advisedly giving a little burst of power just to ensure the engine does not oil up, in case something goes wrong and you have to open it up to go round again, making another circuit and another landing attempt. Once much later when I was forced into making a powered approach in a Hurricane I met with disaster; gliding approach, as tradition says, was far the best way for the likes of me.

* * *

All our thought and our talk was of flying but there were ground lessons too. Some like Navigation, Map Reading or Meteorology – especially what clouds looked like when bad weather was coming up – were of obvious importance. Some were not so relevant and perhaps were relics of the peacetime Air Force when such knowledge may have been desirable. How to strip a machine gun, for example, taking it to pieces and reassembling it. I never thought I should need to know this and I never did. We had to learn the Morse code and achieve ten words per minute, both receiving and sending at this rate. Easy though it is to transmit faster than you can receive we were carefully warned never to do this, since others would send to you at the rate at which you send to them. I was never able to read Morse except in flashes; I tried hard to make the dots and dashes automatically form their letters in my mind, but without success. By the time I had remembered one letter, several others had winged past me, lost forever. I have always had the same difficulty in hearing foreign languages, struggling to recover the meaning of one word whilst the others that follow and the gist of the sentence get lost. Barely did I scrape through the final Morse test and even then the examiner must have been indulgent. I comforted myself with the thought that I should never need it in practice. Had I become a bomber pilot I might conceivably have had need of Morse, but the aircraft which I flew were equipped with R/T (radio telephone) voice transmission only, and a clear speaking voice was important. One pupil failed our course on no other grounds but that he spoke with a heavy Northern Irish brogue which made him difficult to hear clearly over the R/T.

* * *

Flying continued until Christmas Eve and started again on 29 December. Mervyn Wingfield and I decided to spend two nights at Banff, the resort in the Rockies not far away. It was of course his idea. You could not have guessed Mervyn's adventurous, even reckless spirit from his demure appearance and quiet unassuming manner. He seemed somehow less mature than his contemporaries; never in the forefront of any group, he remained in the background and a little apart, not swayed by group opinion or group action, very much an individual who thought and acted for himself and with the innocence of a child who had never learned to be afraid. He did not talk of his parents or background, which was evidently upper-class, though I formed an idea his father was a Colonel. His attitude to money, which I had learned when he took me out in London to the Junior Carlton Club, obviously derived from an affluent home; money was to be spent and enjoyed as it came, for there would always be more. For me, money was a commodity which had always been scarce and was to be saved. His schooling at Eton and Christ Church must have been expensive but I had not known him at Oxford except as a casual Air Squadron acquaintance, for even though my college of Brasenose shared the Christ Church premises, my circle was largely that of my own college and of the cricketers and athletes whom Brasenose encouraged. And Mervyn was certainly no games-playing hearty. But now that circumstances had brought us together we discovered we had more in common with each other than with any of our associates. Christmas at Banff was Mervyn's idea and a good one.

The little town of Banff is high in the Rockies, neatly laid out by the side of the Bow river on a small flat plain, surrounded by the mountains whose peaks we could see from Red Deer and up whose sides the pine forests marched for a while before giving place to bare rock, now at this time of year draped in snow. A delightful place at any time and now with Christmas lights and deep in snow it had the quintessence of Christmas atmosphere. For reason of economy we shared a bedroom at the hotel, discovering to our dismay that it was equipped with one double bed. I was later to find that in general all hotel rooms in America seem so furnished. But having shared adjacent bunks at Bowden we thought we could rough it together for two nights, and we marched to dinner in step down a broad carpeted stairway into the dining room. It was a luxurious hotel but Mervyn was not the sort to search for cheaper accommodation, even if any were to be had at such short notice and for so short a time. The next two days we spent on the nursery ski slopes. Mervyn had evidently skied before; I had not and every few yards I would fall, as my skis slipped under me with my legs and ankles twisted in absurd and unlikely positions attached to these long and ungainly pieces of wood which then had to be undone to enable me to get up and start again. I was thankful that we were to spend no longer than two days at Banff as otherwise I should have needed several weeks of sick leave to recover from the strains on my knees and ankles. I am persuaded that like other skills skiing can be learned, but perhaps it is best to be instructed and to start young.

* * *

We were back flying again on 29 December, excited, invigorated and slightly crippled. The course resumed; sideslipping, climbing, gliding, stalling, climbing turns, steep turns, instrument flying, sideslipping, medium turns, take-off into wind and gliding approach and landing. Then spinning, forced landings and on one or two occasions only low flying. I suspect we did not need encouragement to low fly which is always an exciting and of course a highly dangerous performance. Then a test towards the end of the course by the Chief Flying Instructor. Flying ended on 23 January; I had a total of sixty hours flying time, thirty dual, thirty solo.

Ground lessons meanwhile had continued, and once Mervyn astonished me when lessons were over for the day by approaching a machine gun on which we were waiting to be instructed, and without prompting or rehearsal took it to pieces and assembled it again. I was greatly impressed by the mechanical ability of which obviously he was in quiet possession; to me it was an intricate mechanism like a Chinese puzzle, but perhaps Mervyn had seen machine guns before at an OTC, though he never referred to his background, family or previous history. None of us did; we were an anonymous society, meeting and living together under the same conditions, sharing the same immediate interests and facing the same prospects with an indefinite war stretching ahead of us. I suppose we were all in the process of breaking free from our home environment, and there was no looking back over our shoulders at what we had been or where we had come from. Our destination, the place where we were going, if we ever got there, was all-important.

About this time I started to receive anxious letters from home. I had not written; I did not wish to write. Lack of privacy was not conducive to writing. Thoughts of home would arouse sentiments I did not wish to encourage and the thought which came increasingly to occupy my mind was that I was unlikely to survive the war. Therefore I wished my family to write me off; to worry no more on my behalf, to shed no tears when I was no more. It was of course too late really for such sentiments, for you cannot be born and raised in a family and suddenly cut yourself adrift without causing pain to those to whom you owe everything, from life itself to all you know and can do. And even my brief acquaintance with Jonathan had set up bonds which could not lightly be disregarded. Now she too sent me despairing letters assuming she had been forgotten. Guilty and uncomfortable I was to remain on this score throughout the war, and though when the war was over and I was safe I wrote regularly, I could never wipe out the sorrow and anxiety I caused to those I loved in the Air Force years. Deeds and misdeeds, sins of commission and omission, there they all lie in the past forever preserved like flies in amber. Christianity teaches the forgiveness of sins, but it is the forgiveness of those one hurt or offended that is needed, and it is usually too late to seek it.

But my parents for their part were not discouraged and wrote regularly. One letter dated 11 December 1941 I received at Bowden from my father, which after his usual encouragement to keep up the correspondence, said:

I hope that by now you have started your actual training. Shovelling coal may be good exercise but it is at least a rather wasteful way of using men trained at Oxford. Write soon and let me know what you are doing and how you are getting on.

Things here are settling down. For the last month I have not felt that my ordinary work was extending me as I like it to do and so I have taken on additional jobs. First of all I am acting as tutor (by correspondence) to twelve men of HM Forces. Then I am lecturing to various Army groups. Some of my lectures are to audiences packed in cinemas, sometimes to lonely groups of AA men. Generally they involve long journeys and to drive back sixty miles in the pitch dark after giving say two lectures is not a picnic. Then why do I do it when the whole of the work is entirely unpaid? I sometimes wonder, because as you know when I am preparing a talk and before I give it, I am intensely irritable and nervous. Also before a long night run in the pitch darkness I feel the same nervous strain. Yet I do it and never refuse, though at the moment requests have poured in from Margate, Broadstairs, Folkestone, Dover, as well as dozens of country districts. Why then? Well I suppose that really and truly I like to pitch myself against conditions. In the same way years ago I used to be intensely nervous before boxing – but I did it. I suppose it is the response to a challenge that I cannot resist.

Well I have told you all that about myself because it may help you. You are very like me in many ways, but I do not think you are quite so much afraid as I am in advance, though you undoubtedly get a little nervous. But you need not worry. It all passes in the action. You may feel nervous beforehand and feel collapse after, but during the trial the nervous energy stored up will carry you through. I never felt nervous during an actual fight; nor do I feel nervous while driving now in very difficult conditions, but only before I start. So too you will find in the much more dangerous job you have to do that the nervous energy you stored up will carry you through the times of trial without any faltering.

My time is nearly up, so I must close with all our love and best wishes.

I have said nothing about the news, but I am afraid it is far from good and that at the best we can look forward to another year or two of struggle and effort.

Bernard is quite well but very busy. I don't think I should like his job of making explosives. One of my lectures was on explosives and finished up at a Divisional HQ with a mighty bang which left ear drums painful for days and hurt my eyes. The sixty mile drive home in the blackout following was not too good as I was deaf and my eyes were smarting, but by taking things easily I got through without difficulty.

Mother and the others are all quite well. This is just a personal letter from me. I expect your Mother has given you all the news.

It was not often that he let down the curtain between us; I was always in awe of him, and when I returned after the war was over I was never able to establish the intimacy which I would have dearly loved to have had, and which I had sometimes glimpsed in evening walks and talks along the sea front in Ramsgate during my boyhood. Somehow the opportunity for this was lost between us and I am the poorer, for he was of the best of his generation.

* * *

Our course at 32 EFTS Bowden, Alberta, had just ended and we faced a critical crossroads of our flying careers. Were we to be posted to Moose Jaw on single-engined Harvards, or to twin engines at Medicine Hat? Was it to be fighters or bombers? Whilst the fateful decision quivered in the balance, I was awakened one early morning in a dazed condition. The long narrow dormitory in which we slept in bunks one above the other was unhealthy. Heated by radiators it was without outside ventilation so as to keep out the cold of the Canadian winter. Every morning in the dark of 6 a.m. a burly NCO would switch on the lights and stride through the dormitory along the space at the foot of the bunks shouting in a voice loud enough to wake the dead:

'Wakey, wakey, coffee and cakey, arise and show a leg there, arise and shine. Anyone sick?'

Anybody who was sick was supposed to know and report at this early hour as our awakener stormed through the dormitory. This morning as I tried to get up I felt peculiar; I was flushed, with a temperature; my throat was sore and, sure proof of illness, I was unable to eat any breakfast. So I took myself to the sick bay. There I was promptly questioned as to why I had not reported sick at Reveille. I said in simple truth that I had not realised I was sick until I tried to get up. Scarlet fever was diagnosed and I was put to bed. There within the next few days I was joined by several others, including Mervyn. Meanwhile the rest of the course was posted on to their SFTS, Senior Flying Training School, some to Moose Jaw, others to Medicine Hat. Those of my friends who had been with me from the Oxford University Air Squadron now disappeared together with the majority of my acquaintance from the course. Alone of them remained Mervyn, companion in misfortune. Although we recovered quickly from the infection, being young and fit, we were held in the sick bay until the authorities were confident there would be no relapse and then we were granted two weeks sick leave. This time a party of us took ourselves to Vancouver, the other side of the Rockies and at this season of course under snow. No luxury hotels for us for so long a spell as two weeks, which on our pay we could not possibly have afforded, but we found accommodation at a YMCA or Serviceman's hostel. We soon made contacts and found hospitality. I remember our host of one evening shaking cocktails for us in a large silver cocktail shaker; I thought I was drinking some spicy iced fruit drink and not until I had had several did I begin to suspect they were in fact alcoholic. It may well have been him who introduced us to some girl companions. In one of my infrequent letters home I said I had been mixing with film stars and allowing for my youthful exaggeration I suspect that these young ladies were connected perhaps as starlets or extras in the film industry. My companion for the evening was dark haired, of medium height, slender and very attractive. We went dancing where the hit tune of the time was *Deep in the Heart of Texas* which everyone present danced with joyful exuberance, singing. Afterwards the girls took us to their apartment. I sat uneasily on a sofa at the end of the room with my new friend and not knowing what was expected of me I lit cigarette after cigarette continually, talking vigorously about Dunkirk and the progress of the war, subjects which were, I would think, of little interest to her. I got up to get a drink and discovered one of my colleagues lying on another settee with his girl friend, locked in an embrace, her skirt up round her waist exposing long lengths of stocking, suspender and bare flesh. I averted my eyes, hurried back with my drink and lit another cigarette.

'Darling,' said my young friend, 'must you smoke so much?' I said I supposed not and put it out. Whereupon she put her arms around me and kissed me with such a kiss as I had never previously known, mouth open, tongue exploring. Strange sensations arose in me, new in my experience. I said I was sorry but I should have to go now as it was getting late. I grabbed my coat and fled into the snow-covered street. I must have spoilt her evening and I hope she has long since forgiven and forgotten the callow ignorant youth I then was.

* * *

We arrived back in Bowden in early March very little fitter, alas, than when we had left for our sick leave. For a few days whilst waiting onward posting, we were put back in the cockpit. I had two days of flying, one short refreshment exercise in dual for twenty minutes and then two hours solo. By now the course coming behind had caught up with us and Mervyn and I were posted to the single-engined SFTS at Moose Jaw, again No. 32. The die was cast. We were to be single-engined pilots and hopefully would end up with fighter aircraft. As I wrote in one of my infrequent letters home I should have hated to be a bomber pilot carrying destruction to civilians; as a fighter pilot I should be matched with other young men under equal conditions, and trying to shoot down someone who is trying to shoot you down is altogether a different thing than dropping bombs on women and children.

Whether I should now see things in the same light is another matter, for though all war is detestable it has continued through time for as long as mankind itself; surely the aggressive, the competitive, the fighting spirit is part of the grim process for the selection and survival of the species that runs through the whole of nature; all we can hope to do is to try to channel it to constructive use, modifying it with compassion and justice if we are to endure on the face of the planet.

Still, once you are committed to war then all that counts is the survival and the victory of your side, and you must fight with everything at your disposal. From the air, civilian and military targets may be indistinguishable – even if they are, a civilian target may yet be a military one if it is supporting and supplying the military. If you grant the morality of fighting at all, you may find you have little option but to destroy civilians, the innocent along with the guilty; but then if they support and supply the fighting man, are they innocent? Are there any innocent in a total war save infants only? Terrible it is to let loose the dogs of war; terrible for those who suffer; terrible for idealistic young men to be confronted with such choices. The prospect of being an instrument of wholesale destruction appalled me, but as I wrote at the time I supposed if I had to do it, I would. All the same, though knightly chivalry may not help you win a total war, you must be kind to the captured and the helpless, for this will not cost you the victory, and you must be merciful to the conquered.

Now in addition to Mervyn and a few other companions from the scarlet fever epidemic there were new friends and associates, the old ones having gone on before. And there was a new aircraft, the Harvard 2. A low wing monoplane with stubby radial engine, it was, I suppose, a good machine for instructing and a sound preparation for flying combat aircraft. The cockpits were enclosed and the intercom was much better. Gone was the thrill of the open cockpit and the rush of cold air past you, gone were the manoeuvrability and security of two wings, one above and one below you, and the slow landing speed. Gone too was the thrill of starting; in a Tiger Moth, in the chill of the early mornings of the Canadian winter, you sat strapped into the cockpit whilst a member of the ground crew swung the propeller by hand, first with switches off, then after the engine had been loosened up and fuel drawn into the carburettor which may have become flooded; so switches off again whilst he swung the propeller in the reverse direction. When once the engine had come to life, he would stoop down by the side of the spinning prop and pull from in front of the wheels the wooden chocks to which ropes had been attached; he would signal all clear and you would blithely taxi away. There was no such thrilling ritual with the Harvard. Not until on my Operational Training Unit (OTU) I was introduced to the Spitfire Mark I, that most wonderful of all aircraft, did I experience again the sheer joy and exhilaration in flight that I had felt with the Tiger Moth.

My instructor, Flying Officer Sparks, was a kindly man and a competent pilot; unfortunately he too would shout at you when you started to do something wrong, which naturally was often, and this was unnerving as I have always found it. I remember once when making an approach to land he said to keep the airspeed constant at 85 miles per hour; when the speed dropped down to 82 or rose to 87 he would then bellow through the intercom saying 'I told you to keep it at 85', whereupon my airspeed would wobble even more erratically. It must indeed have been unnerving for the instructor too. Although I did fly occasionally with others, at Moose Jaw we kept to the same instructor all the way through, so I had to struggle on with Flying Officer Sparks until the end of the course, which ran from 15 March to 4 July. We seem to have worked long hours, from 7.45 a.m. to 7 p.m., and there were ground lessons on such subjects as the theory of flight which was interesting and important, and stripping machine and other guns which was not. But it was the flying which was all-important, the cream on the cake and the reason for our existence. The day after arriving from Bowden we were in the air, making our first acquaintance with the horribly noisy and vibrating Harvard, and by the 22 March after six hours' dual instruction I had gone solo, a relatively long flight of forty-five minutes to my surprise. Mother Air Force still demonstrated concern for her pupils and her aircraft, for there are little certificates in my log book, one to say that I had passed an examination in cockpit drill and one by me to certify that I understood the petrol system, brakes, use of the hydraulic system including the emergency operation, and action to be taken in the event of fire in air in a Harvard aircraft, dated on the occasion of my first solo.

The flying exercises were much the same as at EFTS; take-offs and landing, climbing, gliding, stalling, spinning, forced landings, action in event of fire, abandoning aircraft, engine assisted approach and landing – proportionately more of these than at EFTS – aerobatics and low flying;

but now to these were added instrument flying and navigational exercises, some with instructors and some solo, long flights of about two hours' duration and covering some hundreds of miles. And after six weeks, at the end of April, night flying started. This was something that I never learnt to enjoy, perhaps because I was never secure in my ability as a pilot without a visible horizon and with the difficulty of judging one's distance from the ground. At first I was horrified when, throttling back to land, blue flames shot out of the exhaust by the cockpit – a phenomenon one does not notice in daylight but which at night was at first disconcerting. Everything seemed more difficult at night; take-off was not too bad as you had to rely upon your instruments, level out at circuit height, bank and turn, fly still on your instruments to the other side of the lighted runway below you, then judging your position in relation to these lights, throttle back with flame from the exhaust blinding and unnerving you and come in to land, being prepared to overshoot and go round again to make another circuit if you had got it wrong. Judging the right height by the runway lights at which to stall the aircraft onto the ground was also not easy; nevertheless after two hours' dual instruction and nine landings I went solo for twenty-five minutes, making two landings on my own. A few days later I flew a night solo for one hour thirty minutes, making seven landings. I imagine that I slept well that night. The next day I flew with the Squadron Commander who after a general test put a certificate in my log book that I was qualified to spin solo which I duly did, two spins to the left, then two to the right, having first climbed to some 10,000 feet to put a safe distance between me and the ever dangerous ground. There was practice too in the use of the radio telephone from air to ground. Once, indeed, there was a night flying cross country exercise, but this was dual and not solo. Solo night flights seemed to concentrate on landings and surely these were enough.

* * *

Side by side with the flying exercises was the use of the Link Trainer. We had been introduced at Bowden to this miserable machine, useful adjunct to flying training though it was, and its use continued at Moose Jaw. As I did not enjoy night or instrument flying, so I did not enjoy being in the Link Trainer. This ingenious machine of torture was attached to the ground; one sat in the cockpit with aircraft instruments in front, sometimes with the hood off but often with the hood on, covered up, with nothing to see but the instruments and you must try to keep the beastly thing steady, straight and level, or execute various manoeuvres by the help of instruments alone – turning, recovering from unusual positions, ascent and descent with instruments, changing from 300 feet per minute descent to 300 feet per minute ascent with constant airspeed, turning on to compass headings, climbing and descending at a constant rate with the vertical speed indicator covered, night flying circuit and emergency pull up procedure and ditto without gyro horizon, controlled approach to landings, beam approach, figures of eight. I used to find more tension in trying to control the Link Trainer than in actual flying, and indeed I believe it was more sensitive than any aircraft I ever flew, and when covered, flying blind in it, I used to sweat a great deal for it was claustrophobic and probably poorly ventilated. It is all for your own good, I told myself, for useful it obviously was and good training. But it was not fun.

Fun was to be had when flying solo, experimenting with the aircraft or trying to fly in formation with one's friends. Or finding a fair weather cumulus cloud, small and fluffy, to loop right round it, steep turns around it, dive at it and through it, do a roll inside it, and then go on to the next, which had probably enough difference in shape to make for variety and encourage you to adapt your play to get the most out of it. Tumbling about the clouds like puppies or indulging in dog fights with one's friends were favourite amusements. The game was to turn inside one another, putting down fifteen degrees of flap, pull the throttle back to reduce your airspeed and pull the stick hard back into your tummy to turn in a tight circle difficult for anyone to match though, mind you, you might black out doing it. After one such day of aerial pleasures Mervyn said to me 'Geoff, I frightened the wits out of myself today. I was doing flick rolls at 100 feet, lost more height than I should have done and damn near ended up in the ground.'

To do a flick roll, you first reduce the forward speed until almost stalling, pull the stick back into your tummy, and apply top rudder, when the aircraft will flick round very fast on its horizontal axis, generally without losing height though you must be careful not to stall immediately afterwards. It was not an exercise I cared for much even at a safe height, for it was said to put strain on the fuselage and gave me an uncomfortable thrill I usually felt I could do without.

So I admonished him, 'That's damn dangerous Mervyn. For God's sake, don't kill yourself just to get a thrill. If you must do flick rolls, then please do them at a safe height and not at ground level risking your neck for the fun of it. If you don't succeed in killing yourself and if the instructors find out you have been flying like that, you will be slung off the course.'

He chuckled 'Well, they'll have to find out first and I shan't be the one to tell them.'

But it was at this time that the prediction made at the start of our EFTS, that a goodly proportion of us would kill ourselves before we got our wings, started to come true. A friend of mine, whom I had known well at Oxford and with whom I had been in company all along until I went down with scarlet fever, when he was posted to Medicine Hat onto twin-engined aircraft, was killed. Medicine Hat is nearer to high ground and to the Rockies than is Moose Jaw; apparently he was flying in cloud, got iced up, tried to descend below cloud base and hit ground which was some 2,500 feet higher than the landing field at his base. But this seemed far away, the incident somehow unreal, making little impact on me, perhaps because we had not been in close comradeship for a while. Accidents could happen to anyone, I said, but I was not worried about anything like that happening to me or to Mervyn or my present friends. With all the unjustified confidence of youth we felt luck would ever be with us.

Yet even so I had a suspicion deep within me that it might not always be, and I felt the need to avoid emotional entanglement of any kind. So when I received a letter from Jonathan telling me that her father had died and that they were having to move from their farm at Grindley to Abbots Bromley, losing the scenes of her happy carefree girlhood, I did not reply. She said she had heard from a mutual friend in Uttoxeter to whom my mother had written that I had been ill and if that was the reason for my not having written before, she would forgive me. And she ended with a sonnet which began:

> Are you forgotten? Yes, I think you are,
> Forgotten with most other lovely things,
> Since but a stifled echo faint and far
> Is all distracted recollection brings.

But it ended on a note of hope:

And Night's dark players make their entrance where
The shadowy stage of dreams is dimly set
Then I remember – how should I forget?

I hardened my heart. Better, I thought, that you are disappointed in me now, rather than I give you cause to weep for me later on. Besides, I argued with myself, what do I know of women? How do I know this is the right one for me? I have not met anyone else; there may be many others I shall like better. And meanwhile there is a war on and if I am to play my part in it I need to be free, not fettered by bonds of affection or silken cords of love and longing. I have always been single minded, able to do only one thing at once, and now my aim was to be a pilot and fight for my country and to this end I must discard all distractions. Looking back now I can see that a kind and courteous reply, a word of sympathy for her father's death, need not have bound me and would have saved her distress.

The course moved on a month and on 4 June I wrote a gloomy letter home. We had been told there was very little chance of returning to England for another nine months and possibly not until the end of the war. The story was that there was a vast surplus of pilots in England and the intention was to open up Operational Training Units in Canada so that pilots could be sent straight out to the East. As yet however these OTUs were not in commission and there was a great danger of being taken on as an instructor or staff pilot, which was what had happened to everyone on the course preceding ours. That day we had had interviews with the Squadron Commander to find out where we wanted to go and what we wanted to fly, and I was asked if I would be particularly annoyed if I stayed out in Canada as a flying instructor. I had replied that I was sorry but I would be. By now we had taken the final ground subject examinations and had completed the flying for our wings course. But since there was this current surplus of pilots, the course had been lengthened by another thirty hours flying and we were given an additional month to do it in.

So I waited in trepidation to see what would happen. This would probably be the only war in which I should be involved and I felt the need to match myself with the ultimate challenge which battle would bring; I wanted the adventure and glamour and excitement; but above all I think I felt the need to stand up and be counted; my country was still in danger and I wanted to be of service; that if I were to be taken as an instructor to remain in comparative safety and in the comfort of Canada till the end of the war I should lose my self-respect. In his reply to my letter my father said:

> You sound very disappointed at the possibility of staying in Canada but on the whole I think you would be lucky to be taken on as an instructor. Of course I understand your feelings; there is the wish to share the adventure of risking life with others; the tingle of desire as well as the fear of physical hurt. But all the same we naturally want you to come through unhurt and so I don't think either your mother or myself would have many regrets if you were to remain in a comparatively safe position.
>
> I did not much like your reference to whisky and worthless women, two of my aversions. I should be greatly distressed if I thought you had fallen to temptation in that way. Life is too big and fine a thing to be prostituted like that. You come of clean stock and I think you can be trusted to live a clean and healthy life. [N.B. I had made a silly remark without any foundation in fact, trying as young men will to look grown up, which I wasn't.]
>
> The news is very very serious. It is nearly time we had a victory to cheer us up. The actual direction of the campaign I expected as I suppose other people did also. Some weeks ago I argued that the thrust would come to the oilfields, that probably Sebastopol would fall; that Egypt would probably be over-run, that Malta and Cyprus could not then be defended, that the Germans would break their teeth in Syria and the Caucasus. It sounded very pessimistic then but it has come pretty true. Of course I hope that the outcome of the battle in Egypt will be a success for us and that Malta will not fall, but even if they do, though the consequences will be serious they will not be disastrous, as the Germans will never have the necessary reserves to break through to the oilfields.
>
> We have decided at last to send Doreen to the London School of Economics. She is very keen on this and she will take a three year course – goodness knows how it will be financed! – but still things have a way of working out alright.

* * *

On 2 July I made my last flight at Moose Jaw, one hour fifteen minutes of dual with Flying Officer Sparks, devoted entirely to aerobatics, in celebration of the end of course. My last flight before receiving my wings. I had been given 82 hours dual instruction, had flown 85 hours solo and had had 16 hours of night flying, a total flying experience of 183 hours plus 26 hours on the Link Trainer. But now came a heavy blow. Sparks told me that I was not going to receive a commission. The sudden shock seemed to drain the blood from my head.

'But,' I said, 'when I joined the University Air Squadron I was told, we were all told, that we should all get commissions. Commissions would be guaranteed.'

'Well, I don't know about that,' replied Sparks, 'you've only been classified as an average pilot and on those grounds you won't get a commission. You would have been quite suitable in other ways of course,' he added kindly. 'Now you take your friend Mervyn Wingfield. He is a brilliant young pilot but he won't get a commission either, because we don't think he has the personality – not mature enough.'

So there it was. There was no argument. For the first time in my life, I had failed and the RAF had not kept its promise, had gone back on its word. A double shock of frustration and failure, and totally unexpected. That night at the Passing Out party, I kept plying Sparks with beer, and whilst my friends all round me were rejoicing I was not drinking myself. Sparks noticed this and said to me kindly 'You are not enjoying yourself. Why don't you go to bed?' But I shook my head, determined to see the evening out and to conceal my disappointment as best I could, though evidently not very successfully.

Winston Churchill said 'You can never tell whether bad luck may not after all turn out to be good luck ... You must never forget that when misfortunes come it is quite possible they are saving one from much worse, or that when you make some great mistake it may very easily serve you better than the best advised decision. Life is a whole and luck is a whole and no part of them can be separated from the rest.' Had I been commissioned, my story would have been a different one and I might not have lived to tell it. I should not have mixed with so many other ranks and learnt so broad a tolerance, so wide a sympathy with all sorts and conditions of my fellow humans which was to stand me in good stead later on, not learnt how oppressively rank can be used by those who have it; I should never have reached 28 Squadron at Imphal to which I gave my love and loyalty; not learnt to endure bitter loneliness and isolation during the closing stages of the battle of Imphal, a lesson which I needed to have had when the great test of the Time riots came to me in Sierra Leone many years later on in my career.

But all that was hidden from me then and I was deeply disappointed. I wrote home to explain that of course I could have had a commission if I had agreed to be an instructor. Out of our course, I said, they wanted half for instructors; they were keen to make me one and a commission would have gone with it. However that was not what I had joined up for and I wanted to go to a fighter squadron. Unfortunately there were no vacancies at the time at OTUs so I expected to have to fill in a few months as staff pilot, and I thought it likely I should not be home until the end of the war as there were too many pilots already in England.

It was not true that I failed to get a commission because I refused to instruct; the truth was that I had not received one because I was not regarded as a good enough pilot, and my belief in myself and my trust in RAF promises were alike sadly shaken.

* * *

We had two weeks leave at the end of our course, and with a party of friends I went for a holiday in Banff where it was now high summer. On our way we halted at Calgary where 'the greatest Rodeo Show in the North American Continent' was about to take place. The Calgary Stampede was a premier event of its kind. Proceedings started with a parade through the streets, a march of military men and naval units followed by Blackfeet and Stoney Indians, the chiefs on horseback with their long feather bonnets trailing low behind them. To me, brought up from early childhood on stories of the Wild West, this was enthralling, stories coming alive. At the rodeo itself the highlight of the entertainment late in the day was reputed to be the chuck wagon races; these were light wagons with canvas tops drawn by teams of horses and driven furiously around the arena, often colliding with one another, an exciting spectacle indeed. But for me the greatest thrills were earlier in the day, the steer decorating and the calf roping competitions. Courage, speed, skill and superb horsemanship, the breath of the wild prairie, not in fiction but for real. There must have been accidents and serious injuries, for it was gladiatorial combat, the pitting of man against beast which would have been in place in Rome's Coliseum in ancient days. Wonderful performances which held me glued to my seat. In those days I never stopped to think how terrified the poor animals must have been, who all their lives had wandered wild over the vast plains and were now subject to such a contest before thousands of spectators.

Then on to the pine woods and mountain slopes of Banff. I had an ambition to disappear into the woods, just taking a comb and toothbrush with me and to sleep out for a few days, but when faced with the reality of the cold nights and lack of gear this did not seem practical. Instead I slept on the floor of the place in which we stayed. No hotel this time, for funds would not allow it; this may have been a serviceman's hostel or a boarding house. At any event the beds were too soft for me. In camp I had been accustomed to the hard mattresses which were composed of three square sections known for some reason as biscuits. Every morning the bed had to be stripped, the biscuits piled up and the blankets folded one on top of the other neatly. In the evening before you went to bed – preferably before you went out to amuse yourself for the evening – you made up the bed to sleep on once more. The beds and biscuits between them were hard and unyielding but I was used to them and I found the soft bed in Banff not conducive to sleep; therefore my mattress was the floor boards and not as I would have wished the pine needles of the forest.

Summertime in Banff was even more entrancing than the winter; there was fishing and horse riding and walking and climbing and canoeing. One day, going for a stroll before breakfast we started the ascent of a small mountain and having invested an hour or so of effort, decided we must go on to the top and did so, eventually reaching back in Banff at 6 p.m., very tired, very thirsty and very very hungry; we went to a café and ordered huge porterhouse steaks with fried eggs and mushrooms.

Another day we came across a trading post full of the most beautiful furs. I bought myself a superb moose hide jacket redolent of aromatic wood smoke, again of pine, with fringes on the back and front and sleeves, and beaded moccasins and gloves to go with it. The jacket I wore throughout my stay in Banff though rarely since. Once after the war when I went to meet my young brother from school I wore this jacket and he refused to acknowledge me and walked by, highly embarrassed.

Then up we went to Lake Louise and canoed to the far end where the great glacier comes down to the water. For active and fit young men it was a holiday which would be hard to beat but alas in its latter stages Mervyn became unwell. Back at Moose Jaw, he reported sick and was diagnosed as having mumps. We left him there in the sick bay whilst the rest of us were posted off to the transit camp at Monkton in New Brunswick to await shipment back to the United Kingdom and, we hoped, to the war which awaited us. There, just a few days before sailing, came the shock news that Mervyn was dead. I found it hard to believe. There were no details so we did not know whether the mumps had developed into some more serious complication or, having made the quick recovery which I would have expected, he was encouraged to fly again as we had been at EFTS at Bowden when we had returned from the scarlet fever sick leave. I recalled our conversation about flick rolls at ground level and I was afraid. That night I lay sleepless on my barrack bed, healthy young men sleeping soundly all round me, whilst I stared unseeing into the darkness. I grieved for Mervyn and for his family. We were I thought in the hands of God. What God? What Divinity would allow such waste? His gentle, fearless nature had obviously been the product of much love and care, though who his family was I had no idea. An expensive education, Eton (which I visited after the war and saw his name inscribed on a Roll of Honour), and Christ Church Oxford, an upbringing costly in love and money both, and it was all gone, wasted from a world which was in such need of his qualities, gone for nothing; so what was the purpose of it all, what was the value of life and to whom? Perhaps if truly we are all in the hands of God to whom the past and the present and the future are forever in continuous view, to whom there is no such thing as death, Mervyn lives forever in his gaiety and courage and gentleness. But there is no evidence, and perhaps all that he was and all that he was brought up to be, all that his parents had hoped for him, were gone, extinguished as though they had never been. Such thoughts were to recur many times in one form or another in the years ahead but this was the first impact of the waste of war and of young men's lives, the first intimation of mortality to youth which feels itself immortal, invulnerable, at least for years to come. Thus I wrestled with the dark angel through the long sleepless hours of the night.

Next day I wished to write to his parents, or if he had none, to his next of kin, but I did not know who they were. In retrospect, I could I suppose have sent a letter to the officer commanding 32 SFTS Moose Jaw asking for it to be forwarded but that did not then occur to me. So I wrote instead to Mrs Ironside who had been so kind to us in our days at Swift Current. She had made Mervyn's stay in Canada, as well as my own, very much happier than it would otherwise have been. Mervyn had been happy in his life and had given much to his friends and companions; now he was safe in the hands of God whose divine purposes we may not always understand. Her reply reached me after I had returned to England; she had been in daily expectation of hearing from him for he had promised to visit her again before leaving Canada and she was much distressed though somewhat comforted by my letter and by the thought that she had given some happiness to him, to me and to others during our stay in her country. She added that it was a beautiful letter I had written her; that I must have had wonderful parents and a splendid home life to be able to write like that and she was glad that my philosophy of life and faith were strong enough to stand the test of such an experience. She urged me to take no needless risks, for my work would be hazardous enough without that. Little did she know that the words of comfort I had tried to give her did not reflect my sense of loss and inner turmoil; these I should have to carry with me. Mervyn I must leave behind in Canada forever.

* * *

For now it was time to move and in expectation we went back across the Atlantic in August 1942, back to the still beleaguered Britain, back to the black-out, back to where a young woman waited, half forgetting, half forgotten, and back to the gates of the great adventure. Our return was not as our outward journey had been in the cramped squalor of the *Highland Princess*. This time we were on the *Queen Mary* along with 15,125 troops, all American except for our small contingent of newly-fledged aircrew. The total on board was 15,988, the largest number ever carried on one ship on any occasion. Among the US soldiery one bunk was shared amongst three, each having it in turn for eight hours. But we on this journey had no such pressures, for by now we were sergeants in rank and privileged to have a cabin between six or eight of us, of whom some no doubt slept on the floor but were at least spared the indignity of sharing sleeping space, floor or bunk, in strict eight hourly rotations. No doubt we queued for food and for lavatories but the journey time was short, perhaps only four or five days. No convoys for the *Queen Mary*. Her great speed of nearly 30 knots and her zig-zag pattern of sailing were her protection, putting her destroyer escort hard put to it to keep up. This journey had no acute discomforts; the sea was calm and the great ship stable. Nevertheless, as someone remarked, never since the times of the slave trade had so many humans been packed so tightly on board a ship. Maybe, but we had the dignity of free men, volunteers, travelling under the volition of our will, though not under conditions of our choosing. And so home.

CHAPTER FOUR

Back to England

We landed at Southampton and were sent to a transit camp at Bournemouth whilst the powers that be pondered our destination. Whilst waiting we were asked our preference and given a form to fill in; I wrote Fighter Command as a first choice but as a second, not having the slightest idea in what I might be involving myself, put down General Reconnaissance. It sounded a gentlemanly option in which I should probably not have to kill others, and I thought vaguely that long cruises over the sea in Short Sunderlands seemed an agreeably cushy option, even though as a single-engined pilot I could not be conceivably qualified to fly one. I thought no more about it. Obviously I was destined for Fighter Command to which I looked forward with both fear and fascination.

Five days' leave saw me back at Gravesend with my parents and young Doreen and even younger David, who the previous winter had made himself a reputation on the rugger field at his new school. Badly I wanted to go to Abbots Bromley to see Jonathan and tell her all about Canada, but there was no time and I was under the usual orders not to leave my home address in case of early recall. I hoped that perhaps I might get a posting in the Midlands and sent her words of affection such as might keep expectations high in a girl's heart. The fates in the shape of the Air Ministry seemed to be fighting for us when in early September I was sent to No. 5 AFU (Advanced Flying Unit) at Tern Hill in Shropshire, not far from Market Drayton and as close to Abbots Bromley as I had any right to expect, though an awkward cross-country journey in those days of restricted public transport, few cars and rationed petrol. It seemed we must meet and soon, so I wrote to her rejoicing.

As far as I could gather the purpose of the AFU was twofold. Firstly to prepare pilots for the flying of Spitfires or Hurricanes by flying Masters, an inline engined aircraft which was allegedly not dissimilar to them but in which, as it was a training aircraft, dual instruction was possible which it was not in the single-seated fighters. These had to be flown without any preliminary dual instruction. Secondly, to help pilots trained overseas to become accustomed to English conditions. In Canada skies were clear and navigation easy; one found the road or railway, and often they were both together, side by side, and followed them home. Here in England towns and villages were thickly clustered, railways, roads and canals ran crazily in every direction and there were funny little fields in this toy landscape. And there was frequent obliterating cloud. Oh dear, I thought, I shall get hopelessly lost above this maze of contradictory landmarks; what if I cross the Channel by mistake when above cloud and end up in a prisoner of war camp? But strangely we did seem always to find our way, perhaps because we took particular care and because England, though crowded, is also small after the vastness of the Canadian prairie.

Once again Mother Air Force took good care of her aircraft and therefore of her pilots. My instructor pasted into my logbook before any flying started the usual certificates of competence in safety procedures, in cockpit drill and sundry other techniques, such as correcting spinning, certificates which I also had to sign as having learnt. No chances were taken and I received ten hours' dual instruction before being allowed up solo. The established torture of the oh-so-good-for-you Link Trainer was continued and to this was added the new horror of sodium flying, also no doubt very good for you. This was a simulation of night flying carried out in the full and blessed light of day, avoiding the need for a lighted runway at night. The pilot was fitted with yellow-tinted opaque goggles which allowed him to see the instruments in his cockpit and the flare path, lit by the bright yellow sodium flares, but that is all. No horizon visible, no sweet countryside below. It was flying in the dark dark night with no visibility and none of us enjoyed it.

There was an urgency about wartime England that had been lacking in Canada and I grumbled that this was a poor sort of camp with no time off. We work from 7.45 a.m. to 7.30 p.m., I said, we get half an hour for meals and we never know until mid-day whether we are flying that night; we are on duty seven days a week and there are no weekend passes; it is like being in prison in that we have no control over our movements, our liberties confined to the camp perimeter. This would have mattered little had not one part of me been drawn to Abbots Bromley, so short a distance as the crow flies, yet a world away and out of reach. Yet there was fun and comradeship as always; I played some games of squash and rugger and shot on the range, enjoying the use of the new Springfield automatic rifle and the acrid smell of gunsmoke, poor shot though I always was. And we went to two dances at Market Drayton, which we enjoyed. But day by day I felt the war was drawing ever closer to me as my training proceeded and my doubts about whether I would survive increased. Youth habitually considers itself immortal and that disasters happen to others and not to oneself; this I discounted and reckoned that though I feared the war and had a healthy instinct for survival, I would be fascinated by and irresistibly drawn to accept whatever challenge offered, so the odds would be against me. So I said to my parents and so I said to Jonathan who wrote loving, hopeful and confident letters in reply.

It was at Tern Hill that the letter from Mrs Ironside arrived, having been forwarded from Canada. As it contained complimentary remarks about my parents and upbringing I sent it home for them to see, adding that I had just met a friend who had left Moose Jaw after I had and who told me that the Court of Inquiry on Mervyn's death concluded that he had been doing slow rolls at 20 feet; I had myself done aerobatics in formation with him at 500 feet and that was quite enough for me. Never had I met anyone so brilliant or so utterly fearless. My father replied:

18 September

Dear Geoffrey

I was pleased to read the letter you enclosed – not because of its references to your parents – but because it implied you had developed some philosophy of life which could act as a consolation in times of difficulty. It is not easy to reach such an abiding place. Formerly it could be obtained through religion and many people still find peace and comfort through the Church and Chapel. But I said formerly, because I think it is much harder to accept the fundamental tenets of Christianity today than it was thirty or forty years ago. Scientific knowledge has developed so considerably and has shown our affinity to the animals in both body and mind to such a degree that special creation has become an untenable idea. Yet somehow we still believe we are better than 'sheep or goats that nourish a blind life within the mind', and so we strive to reach some fundamental faith on which we can rest content; – or else we let the whole thing slide and attempt to live in the present and in the little material things of life ...

I wished I had reached such an abiding place; alas I had but put on a front with which to comfort others. Nor could I be content to live in the present and little material things of life if events were repeatedly to confront me with the ultimate questions of death and of the ultimate purpose of one's own life and of the lives of one's friends. Writing now so long after these events, it seems obvious that there have always been war and combat, with other animal species and with one's own from the time when the creatures that were to become men still lived in the trees – today we know that bands of chimpanzees fight one another for territory, hunt and kill each other. From the time we came down from the trees, families and clans have been fighting each other, driving out the weaker to harsher environments, so that man has spread all over the world adapting himself alike to the scorching deserts as to the freezing wastes of the Arctic. And in all this the young male has been expendable, though not of course the young female, for the clan, the tribe, the society, the culture, must go on or be extinguished and supplanted by another. We can look for no other purpose in the tragic deaths of young men than the survival and success in biological terms of the social groupings they represent. Any other meaning or purpose is hidden behind the veil which we cannot penetrate, so we can do nothing else but leave everything in the hands of God, hoping that He is a good fellow and all will be well.

Though I can see this now clearly enough, at the time it was beyond me and I certainly did not see myself as simply the young male driven, as young males before me throughout several million years of evolution, by the fatal fascination of combat and the need to protect family, friends and country which over-rode the individual fears of hurt or death. I steeled myself to accept disaster to myself; disaster to my friends I could not. Never could I come to terms with the sense of loss which each successive death brought until it was dulled by repetition as the months and years went by.

* * *

60

After three weeks at Tern Hill I received news that I was to be posted to No. 3 School of General Reconnaissance at Squires Gate, Lytham St Annes near Blackpool, which for a while made me indignant. My friends would be going on to Spitfire OTUs and thence to Fighter Command; I wanted to be with them and went to see the CO to complain. There was nothing he could do, for the posting had come from the Air Ministry and could not be changed by ordinary mortals. Did this mean I was destined for PRU? No one seemed to know though it seemed highly probable. PRU – Photographic Reconnaissance Unit, flying either Spitfires or twin-engined Mosquitoes – was highly specialised and was reputed dangerous. Rumour had it that in previous years it had suffered 80 per cent casualties. The aircraft were equipped with only cameras, and long-range fuel tanks in the wings to replace the normal guns and ammunition. No armaments at all but stripped of every inessential for the sake of range and speed – no night flying equipment such as headlights, not even IFF – Identification Friend or Foe which could tell the home radar you were one of ours. These aircraft penetrated deep into enemy territory wherever pictures were required, photographing targets for Bomber Command both before a raid and after it to assess whatever damage had been done, when you might expect the enemy ack-ack to be particularly lively and hostile, not to mention the fighter patrols that would be waiting for you. There were horrific stories of maximum endurance sorties with pilots back from Berlin or Rostock, or even further afield, just landing with wheels up on the north-east coast, out of fuel but with the precious pictures intact. If one survived a tour of such adventures, one then went on a rest tour on Short Sutherlands as second pilot/navigator, soothing one's nerves by endlessly flying over the restless and interminable sea. Well, I reflected, it is supposed to be an elite occupation is PRU, and there are worse things to learn than how to navigate; it may be a useful asset one day. And meanwhile I can do nothing about it. By now I had been long enough in the RAF to resign myself to the inevitable and accept what I could not alter.

Whilst waiting for the posting due in early October I was sent to a small dispersed flight at Calveley, Nantwich near Crewe, and no sooner had I got there than the tortures of sodium flying and the Link Trainer resumed. Badly I wanted time off to get to Abbots Bromley, though indeed I was nervous and curiously reluctant about seeing Jonathan again – a feeling which she said she also shared. I applied for a weekend pass only to be told once more that there was a war on, a fact which I understood but was beginning to regret. I wanted and I didn't want to see her, I could not get time off, I did not know how to get there and if she came to see me there was nowhere nearby where she could stay nor could I be sure of getting time off to enjoy her company. And I feared entanglement, for I was not free and my future was uncertain to say the least.

But I did get to see my elder brother Bernard in Wrexham, and met his fiancée. The uncertainties of the future, while they interposed barriers between Jonathan and me, drew the family together. Every opportunity to see brother and sister, mother and father must be taken, for there might never be another. So one evening, not being on night flying duty I took the bus to Chester and another bus to Wrexham, met Bernard and his Alice, drank beer together until after the last bus to Chester had left and set off on the long march home, some eighteen miles, arriving back rather footsore but stone cold sober at 4 a.m. and ready to fly once more after breakfast. My mother wrote to say how glad she was that at least the war seemed to be drawing the family closer. But was this at the expense of excluding my little girlfriend? asked my conscience guiltily.

She wrote saying she had a week's holiday starting on 16 October and she would come to see me. And then she thought she would apply for a job in Birmingham or join the WRNS. The letter was forwarded, reaching me after I had moved to Squire's Gate and was settling in to the new station, to a new routine, to new companions. We again were working long hours and the town seemed full, accommodation difficult to find. I discouraged her from coming, or from joining the WRNS – no doubt the best of the women's services, but I feared the loss of her innocence and her sweet loving ways; her reply was one of distress. 'I still think about you a great deal,' she said, 'and am beginning to feel that I am rather a fool. One day you will perhaps convince me that the past year has not been wasted and that I have not been building up a fool's paradise round a photograph and a few letters. My feelings for you will never alter even though I think you are very selfish.' But shortly after came another letter to say she was sorry for what she had said, but had written out of disappointment and fear that I did not really want to see her. Her holiday she had spent at home cleaning up the house her mother and she had taken in Abbots Bromley, where she invited me to spend my next time off.

* * *

Out of the mists and shadows of that October and November at Squires Gate now emerge figures, taking shape, solidifying; they are to be my companions for the next stage of the journey though as yet I do not know this. There are two New Zealanders, Wal Clarke and Ru Smith, both rather small and though from different backgrounds, Wal being a townsman and Ru a countryman bred on the farm, sharing a common outlook. Both were independent, self-reliant and versatile – especially Ru whose early life had made him intensely practical – both were open and friendly in nature, full of enthusiasms and, refreshingly, neither thought nor spoke of women, for Wal was engaged to a girl back home and Ru already married. Other girls were not for them and they took little part in the talk of sex which dominated the topics of conversation of our company. With them I played several games of rugger for the station team against nearby Army Commando units which we trounced handsomely. They were a formidable combination, Ru as scrum half though troubled by an old knee injury and Wal at stand-off, which had been my position at school, whilst I played in the pack as a second or third row forward, which I had never done before and enjoyed myself thoroughly without having the responsibilities of getting the three-quarter line moving that a stand-off half has.

Then there were the Canadians. Nunton, rather older than most of us, inclined to romanticise and exaggerate, who later got into disgrace for drawing pictures and over-dramatising the entries in his flying log book, and Richards, large and good natured but one of the most dissolute persons I ever met. Women were his preoccupation, any woman, any size shape or age, and for him, drunk or sober – and he was often drunk – they existed for only one purpose. Eventually his lifestyle caused his posting away from the operational squadron to which we were sent in due time.

And then I met Ken Draycott. I first saw him sitting as part of a group in the railway carriage on the journey to Blackpool and Squires Gate and I wondered whether we were to share a posting. 'Oh dear,' I thought 'how very unprepossessing they look. I shall never get on with that lot.' Ken was taller than average, dark hair and sallow complexion, olive skinned, and had a small toothbrush black moustache. A good deal later I learnt that he had been a student of art before joining the Air Force and was gifted, viewing all he saw with a painter's eye, sensitive to the colours about him and seeing shades which I could not distinguish.

But he was not the athletic outdoor type like the two New Zealanders, nor an extreme womaniser like the Canadians. For the duration of the course I had little to do with him. My closest friend was Joe Pack who, having survived a tour on Halifaxes when he was shot down over France and helped by the Resistance to escape, had now been posted to Coastal Command. Aircrew who had thus escaped from occupied territory were normally never again given operational duties where they risked falling once more into enemy hands, lest under pressure they betray those who had helped them. In Coastal Command they would be safe. Joe was quiet and kindly, full of good humour and good sense; he was also a fellow countryman, coming from the same part of Kent as I did myself.

We were billeted in what had been a small private hotel in Lytham St Annes, and Joe and I spent our free evenings drinking a pleasant and non-competitive pint of beer whilst we discussed his adventures in France – though he was always guarded in what he would say about this, for lives were at stake should information leak – about his operational tour, about the course and the problems we had with it. For many of us, and certainly for me, the course was not easy. I had taken maths at school to General Schools standard, and had had a C pass with exemption from matriculation, but maths was not a favoured subject. I suspect a greater facility with trigonometry would have helped. We sweated over astronavigation and sextants, which we were supposed to use to plot our position in the air. I consoled myself that in the PRU Spitfire for which I was destined there would be no possibility of using a sextant. As for an eventual posting to flying boats, it was no use worrying about that until the time came, if ever it did. But I never understood how the harassed navigator of Bomber Command on his way home from a sortie could use a sextant in the air, work out his tables and plot a position with accuracy – perhaps he never did. A Coastal Command pilot on the other hand would have all the time in the world if only he had a calm hand to keep the sextant bubble steady. No doubt practice would make more perfect.

Much easier than the bubble sextant was the Dalton Computer, which you wore strapped to your knee. It was a sort of circular slide rule, with a rotatable rim and setting the variables of wind speed and magnetic variation it would convert your desired track into the course you needed to steer. You played with it in your leisure time with the manual of Air Navigation by your side. 'You will use this on ops,' we were told, but I never did nor did anyone I knew, nor indeed as far as I can recall was I ever offered one.

The aircraft in which we flew as navigators, sometimes as first and sometimes as second navigators, were Ansons and Bothas, both twin engined. The Avro Anson was slow but comfortable, safe and steady as houses. All our night flying was done in these and I have vivid memories of approaching one, clad in a Mae West (life jacket) and parachute with dinghy attached slung over the shoulder, as the mists of a November evening closed round us. The Bothas in which we flew by day were much faster aircraft but had the reputation of being vicious and difficult to control if power were lost on one engine; they were also noisy and uncomfortable and I remember them with no affection at all. Most of the pilots were nervous of them. The man who was the outstanding personality amongst the instructors seemed more nervous than any of us; he had been a regular naval officer before the war and had retired as a Commander. By what means he became a pilot and Flight Lieutenant in the RAF I do not know, but he had an expansive personality, a game leg and a booming voice as he taught us his method of swinging an aircraft compass and the principles of dead reckoning navigation. In the air, flying a Botha, his geniality and confidence disappeared and he became a short tempered, nervous and obviously frightened old man with whom none of us much wanted to fly.

Invariably our sorties took us over the grey Irish Sea; the first leg was landfall over Chicken Rock off the Calf of Man, then to the Skerries off Anglesey and the third leg back to Lytham St Annes and the warmth and comfort of our billet. On these stretches, which lasted between two and three hours, we practised what we had been taught in the classroom, how to find the wind force and recalculating the course to fly from it, square and other searches, and even such exotica as the radius of action from a moving base in bad weather, though the weather that November was usually bad. It was always deeply satisfying to make a landfall dead on target, turning with Chicken Rock or the Skerries directly below. On one flight the wind kept veering and I could not make a proper calculation as we navigated over the sea for some two hours, during which time we saw neither land nor lightships to fix our position, and as we were under wireless silence we could not get a W/T bearing. When we eventually decided to go home, I gave the pilot a course and estimated time of arrival; soon we ran into low cloud above which the pilot had to keep, descending through it dead on the ETA to the second to find the airfield directly below us. Pure fluke. I received the warm congratulations of the pilot, the second pilot and the wireless operator. 'How did you find the wind?' asked the pilot. In my trusting innocence I replied that I couldn't satisfactorily but had used the wind given by the meteorological forecast. Whereupon the warmth evaporated and gave place to wrath. 'You are not supposed to do that. That is not what you are here for.' I thought myself that I had not done too badly with the met wind though never again did I admit to using it, even if in fact I often did, especially at night. But as the course continued so did my accuracy and confidence improve.

* * *

My twenty-first birthday came and went unremarked in a swirl of November mist; feeling sentimental I wrote my mother a letter thanking her for a happy childhood and my life to date, which she said was very beautiful and which she would keep amongst her treasured possessions; I had been the middle one of five children and she had sometimes thought that I had not had all the attention which she would have wished to give me. When I replied I said that soon I would have a forty-eight hour pass, my first since disembarkation leave, and that I thought I must go to Wrexham to congratulate my elder brother Bernard and his fiancée who were to get married early in the New Year, when I was unlikely to get time off. I liked his choice, though I added how anyone can get married I didn't know for it seemed such a compromising and irrevocable step. My elder sister Joan had just got herself engaged too and I thought (not that anyone took any notice) that as her fiancé was in the Forces she should not get married while the war lasted. For myself I could not dream of making any attachments until it was over; this might not apply to everyone, for not everyone may be required to fly an unarmed Spitfire over the heart of Germany, but there will be a lot of casualties everywhere before the end. Underlying this attitude was no little guilt and unease, for a young lady who would have liked very much to see me was waiting in vain in Abbots Bromley. But I was frightened of seeing her again and frightened of deepening our association. So to Wrexham I went.

* * *

I was still running scared of Jonathan when we were given a few days leave over Christmas and I invited Wal Clarke to come home with me to Gravesend to spend Christmas with my family. Gravesend was new territory to all of us and time rather hung on our hands, so we went up to London to meet some of Wal's New Zealand friends. To Jonathan I sent as a Christmas present my copy of an anthology of modern verse which contained some favourite poems I had quoted to her and which I wished to share with her, asking her not to think hardly of me this Christmastide; I had not wished to be cruel but felt I had been unfortunate. Her present to me which arrived on Christmas Eve consisted of one volume of Browning's works and one of Keats, leather bound with my name embossed in gold on the front cover. Lavish and beautiful presents which I felt she could not afford and which embarrassed me. I hid them under my bed so as not to expose myself to the ribald comments of the family, and I wrote to chide her for sending something so nice and so expensive which I had not been able to reciprocate.

The time for plain speaking seemed to have come. So I said I had been immensely attracted to her as to no-one else but as we had had but three weeks' companionship I did not know if I was in love; you have to know someone more intimately than that before you can decide whether to spend the rest of your life with them. I simply did not know, and I did not want her to base hopes on uncertainty. Even if I had decided that I wanted to marry her, what hope did I have of that? Before the end of the war I may be dead or crippled; if not, I should have to return to Oxford for at least two years to finish my degree and then perhaps two or three years of intensive effort afterwards before I was in a position to support anyone other than myself. This would be five years from the time I was demobilised. So what now was she going to do? Would she continue a friendship, the most significant one I had ever had, which might later develop and, though the way was long and hard, might be infinitely pleasant at the last, or would she now give me up in disgust and despair? It now rested with her. She should not mistake me; the books she sent me were a marvellous present but I had felt that such a happy association as ours had been would be unbearable if it were to have a tragic conclusion. I needed her friendship and sympathy but did not want her love until I could give her mine. She should attach no significance to the fact that I had not been to see her, for I had not been a free agent and was governed by circumstances which I could not control. As I wrote I felt mean, betraying a trust, a friendship, a loving impulse never before met which had opened for me unparalleled vistas of a new world. But what else was I to do? Looking back now I see that I should have plucked flowers whilst I may, as everyone else seemed to be doing, but I was young and inexperienced and I had ideals.

* * *

Back at Squires Gate we had news of our posting which pleased and puzzled us. We had expected to go to the OTU for PRU which was at Fraserburgh, but all of us single-engined pilots were being sent instead to 61 OTU at Rednall in Shropshire. Rednall was purely for training fighter pilots, no teaching of how to take photographs from the air which was what PRU was all about. But, we reasoned, the RAF did not give reconnaissance courses for nothing, nor yet to fighter pilots; once on Coastal Command, always on Coastal Command. If Fraserburgh were full up, were we perhaps just going to Rednall to learn to fly Spitfires whilst waiting for vacancies? As against this the postings had come through from Air Ministry and not from Group, so were definite postings and not just temporary attachments. So we formulated a theory that perhaps we were not to go to PRU at all, but that instead a new scheme was being tried out and that we would be taken to form an entirely new kind of Fighter Reconnaissance squadron. No doubt we should find out once we got there. We were to move soon. Bernard was getting married and Wrexham was not far from Rednall. By this time I knew better than to expect time off to go to the wedding but I told the family that if they saw a solitary Spitfire circling the vicinity it would be me.

In the third week of January 1943 we arrived at Rednall; there was snow on the ground and it was very cold. But our hearts leapt up when we saw the low sleek Spitfires which we were to fly, on the ground at dispersal. This had been our ambition. This is what we had long awaited, the crown of the lengthy period of careful training. I could not then think of anything more beautiful than the Spitfire Mark I and after all these years I cannot now. Mankind has created many works of art throughout his recorded history, aspirations of the spirit like the Acropolis or a great mediaeval church, aspirations of the flesh like Michelangelo's *David* or of compassion like da Vinci's *Mona Lisa*, and surely the Spitfire Mark I in its own time and in its own way was as great a triumph as the spire of Salisbury cathedral. Lyrical in its perfect proportions, with its slim fuselage and rounded elliptical wings, it sat on its wheels, its nose angled and pointing confidently at the sky to which it belonged and of which it was the mistress – like Britannia I can only think of her as female – who matched, faultless as a lover, all who had the great good fortune to fly her. Strap yourself into her cockpit and you felt she was part of you, responsive to your every mood, touch, whim. Love at first sight developed on further acquaintance. Later marks of Spitfire, the five and the nine, added a more powerful engine so the nose grew longer to give greater speed, a higher altitude and a faster rate of climb but the symmetry and balance of the Mark I were inevitably lost; fine aircraft they were, these later marks, and needed to match the later versions of the Messerschmitt and Focke-Wulf that the Germans were putting into the sky, but they were not aircraft to love and to which you lost your heart like the marvellous Mark I.

No time was wasted at Rednall. Once again in my flying logbook there appear certificates of proficiency, one by me to say that I understand the petrol, oil, ignition, hydraulic and pneumatic systems of the Spitfire aircraft, that I was considered proficient in cockpit drill, that I had been instructed in and understood the use of oxygen and in particular the oxygen system of the Spitfire and finally that I was considered proficient in the use of the VHF type of R/T set. Mother Air Force once again was taking no chances with her precious aircraft being misused by brash and ignorant pupils. Next day we were in the air.

First a check flight with an instructor in a Master for forty-five minutes, then a check solo also in a Master for fifty minutes, then without time to think or worry about it I was fastening my straps in Spitfire Mark I No. A, taxiing out to the runway, asking permission to take off from the control tower, then turning into wind in the middle of the runway and opening the throttle. Down the runway she went like a perfect little lady, straight and true, no tendency to swing, eager for the air, trembling buoyantly on her wheels as the air took hold of her. Easy now, don't hurry to leave the ground, so keep her nose down for another moment, then lift her gently. We are airborne; wait another moment, now select the wheels up; climb straight for another moment now turn to the left and here we are at circuit height circling the airfield. What a lovely girl you are; how sweetly you handle. Why, I can do anything in the world in this aircraft. I had looked at the shape of the countryside and identified landmarks in the two earlier flights this morning in the Masters, so I shall not get lost in the vicinity. Now I will climb, and up she goes effortlessly like a bird, like in the old RAF phrase 'a homesick angel' and swiftly the altimeter's hand swings round telling off the thousands. At 10,000 feet I level off. This must be a safe height. I tell myself that come what may I must be able to master this aircraft in any position, put it through any manoeuvres. Only so shall I have any real confidence in it and in myself. And there is no time like the present. I feel determination rising firm within me, steady and strong, surprising myself. I pull back the throttle, put the nose up into the sky and stall her, and she stalls straight and true with no tendency to spin. So now to spin; I stall again and this time kick rudder to spin to the left; down she goes in a shallow easy spin. One turn, two turns, that's enough, she has no tendency to tighten in the spin, stick forward and opposite rudder and out of the spin she comes sweetly and easily and without any fuss. Oh what a perfect little beauty. We have lost a little height so climb again to 10,000 feet – angels 10 they call it – and spin to the right. And again she handles like a dream. A child could fly this. A few more manoeuvres, a tight turn or two, shall I try a roll? Enough for one day, I have been up an hour and it is time to go home. Down to 1,000 feet and back into the circuit. Ask and receive permission to land; position the end of the airstrip under your left wing, cut the throttle, gliding approach turning onto the runway which comes up to meet me, level off just above the ground, I am losing flying speed, ease the stick back into my tummy, gently now and she is down on the ground, nice landing, no bouncing and now she runs straight and true down the runway, no tendency to swing either to the left or to the right as she loses speed. Gently apply brake, turn and taxi off the runway. What a thrill, only beaten by the first solo of all in the Tiger Moth. What a wonderful aircraft, what a doll, what luck to be flying it here at Rednall.

Not all first solos went as smoothly as mine. For safety reasons we were supposed to land with the canopy open, sliding it back as you started the final approach. Poor Nunton could not get his to open and in panic called the control tower who had him circle the airfield while giving him advice and calm counsel. The solo pilot has to solve or at least come to terms himself with his difficulties in the air. He cannot stop and get out as you can in a car to make adjustments or take a breather. Either you make a go of it or you bale out and that is the last thing to do, especially in winter time and especially on your first solo.

Every day we flew and always under grey skies and sometimes under low cloud. Every day would start with what was euphemistically called by the station commander a weather test, when either Flight Lieutenant Stanforth, previously test pilot at Vickers where Spitfires are made and who had more than 10,000 flying hours on the type and who after the war was to break the world speed record, or Flight Lieutenant Hesslyn DFC DFM and bar, a New Zealander and ace from the battle over Malta with nineteen enemy aircraft to his credit, would take off nominally to 'test the weather'. Never had I seen such flying before and I was never to see the like again. Alternately, one morning Stanforth, Hesslyn the next, would take-off in one of the normal ordinary little Spitfires that we were flying, not fitted with special devices like inverted carburettors to make it possible to fly upside down using the power of the engine; they would climb to two or three thousand feet, power dive onto the airfield to build up speed, roll over within a few feet of the unyielding earth and fly across the airfield upside down with the propeller seemingly only inches from the ground, so low that standing beside a stationary Spitfire I have seen them pass out of sight behind it; I have seen also an airman riding his bicycle across the airfield fling himself onto the ground to avoid having his head cut off by the propeller of an aircraft flying upside down. Upside down they would aim for the control tower, climb inverted over it, then roll over right way up with the engine at last coming to life, climb up again before coming down to pleasure us once more with low level aerobatics. 'It's not so hard perhaps,' I thought to myself 'if you have ten thousand hours on the type and have flown upside down so often at height without losing an inch that you are confident in your ability.' Meanwhile this was something I could only gaze at with awe from a safe distance.

Then the weather having been pronounced fit, even if it wasn't very, it was our turn. Sector reconnaissance to explore the countryside and practise D/F homings (being directed back to the airfield by radio), cloud flying, aerobatics, dog fighting – exciting this, trying to turn inside each other, knees drawn up as high as possible above the rudder bar to lessen the effect of G, the force of gravity, which would drain the blood from your head, turning the world grey around you, black if you turned tight enough. It was Hesslyn who taught us the trick of turning, momentarily shutting off the throttle, banking over and then slamming throttle and pitch forward together for a sudden spurt of maximum power whilst pulling the stick back into the stomach. 'You PRU chaps will be all on

71

your own and you won't have guns to protect yourselves from enemy fighters; you can expect to run into standing fighter patrols often enough and this will be all you can do to help yourselves. But no one on your tail will be able to follow you round in a turn like that; you will shake him off even though you will black out, and he may sheer off thinking you have guns to fight him with. Then dive and he probably won't catch you, especially if there is any cloud to hide in.' Life saving advice to those of us who were later to feel the uneasy thud of bullets into the armour plating at the back of our seats.

Low flying was exciting too, though for my part I dared not fly as low right way up as the 'weather testers' flew every morning upside down. And formation flying. Desperado Hesslyn would shout at you over the R/T 'Come on, man, you're supposed to be part of this formation not a bleeding spectator,' and he would not be satisfied until your wingtip was gently rubbing the fuselage below his cockpit. It was right enough a school for fighter pilots was 61 OTU Rednall.

It continued to snow, the weather was bitter and the barrack rooms were uncomfortably cold, our blankets thin and insufficient. I shared a room with Ken Draycott who invented an intricate way of making a sleeping bag, laying out the blankets one on top of the other, folding the edges of the top one lengthwise, then turning it upside down and folding similarly the one underneath on top of it and then reversing the bundle. If there was another blanket that would be treated similarly. I found this complex and difficult to do; when it was done and you crawled in you found either that it was too tight and you could not move with comfort, or the whole thing fell to pieces as you moved and exposed vital portions to the unheated night air. Our two New Zealanders, Wal Clarke and Ru Smith, also shared a room and conceived the notion that it should be better furnished. So on an evening out to a nearby pub they would acquire whatever might be handy for the purpose, whether it be a beer mat or an ash tray bearing the name of the hostelry or even brewery; all was grist to their mill and we had to discourage them from trying to remove a rug; no doubt it would have gone beautifully into their room; no doubt the proprietor did not really need it and would have been willing to surrender it to them in such a good cause, but the odds against this seemed too great to be worth a try.

* * *

72

On our first Saturday night we took a liberty truck to Oswestry, some six miles away, and went to a dance. This was a grand small town affair like the ones I had enjoyed so much in Uttoxeter when I had first met Jonathan. There were Paul Joneses to mix people up, fun dances like doing the hokey-pokey and knees up to Mother Brown and the Lancers, as well as the conventional slow waltz, foxtrot and tango. I met up with a slim young lady of about my own age, wearing a pink jumper, who was the most superb dancer I have ever met. She seemed to have no feet but simply melted into you as you moved in rhythm to the band. I knew when I was in luck, so for much of the evening she became my partner. 'That's a nice little thing you've got hold of. You must take her home,' said Richards to me in an interval. 'She'll fuck like a rabbit.' Eager though my young flesh is, avid for this experience around which much of our talk seemed to centre and which seemed to be regarded as the supreme event which life had to offer, the years of my upbringing are now reinforced by my long line of Puritan forebears from the stern north country; all unite in saying NO. 'But,' I ask them, 'suppose I should die before I have had this experience?' 'That will be your bad luck,' they answer. So I murmur to Dick in reply that I don't want to fuck like a rabbit, not knowing next day with whom I may have mated, but like a human instead. And I let my light-foot lady, gentle as gossamer, warm and melting in movement, go home unescorted by me. I go back with my company.

But we are late and have missed the return liberty truck to camp. We shall have to walk but at this time of night there is no-one about of whom we can inquire the way. Empty of people, the town is under heavy blackout, dark and shuttered. We come to a place near the town centre where road repairs have been in progress, marked off by warning red lamps. 'Just the thing we have always wanted,' cried Wal Clarke, 'splendid décor.' He and Ru take one each and their example is followed by others, though not by Draycott and me who have not taken to this room-decorating fashion. Just then we see light from underneath a door; someone must be up and about from whom we can inquire the way. We knock and the door is opened by a large policeman. It is the local police station. 'Please can you tell us the way back to Rednall?' we inquire. He starts to do so; then 'What are you doing with those lamps? You had better all come inside.' So meekly we did and it took an hour or so of sweet talking and promises to be good and to restore the lamps to their proper place before we were allowed to tramp home. Perhaps I would have been better employed to have taken my gossamer girl back to her house and found my own way back to the camp; perhaps not.

They were happy carefree days at Rednall; we were flying the finest aircraft ever made, which we had longed to do, and our instructors were brilliant pilots who carried with them the camaraderie, the friendship and informality of the best fighter squadrons; we had no responsibilities ourselves except to fly and learn the techniques of combat and we had good companionship, making close friends. To Jonathan I wrote briefly to tell her where I was, to complain about the lack of facilities way out in the countryside with no transport and no shops so that I even had to write home for a toothbrush and toothpaste which I could not get in camp, to describe the glory of flying a Spitfire and to make a definite promise that I would come and see her at the next opportunity. Alas, there was not to be one. For Rednall days lasted a scant three weeks; time and events were winding up tighter than we knew. In the wartime RAF one never knew what was to come and perhaps that was as well. We were but arrows to be shot at the enemy in the hands of some unknown bowman, shuffling us unseen in the Air Ministry, and the best arrows are unfeeling without prior knowledge of what the future may have in store.

* * *

By the end of the first week in February we learned we were posted to Operational Squadron No. 541, formerly part of No. 1 PRU at Benson in Oxfordshire. Much excitement. At long last we were to take part in great events. We were ready. Not one of us reflected that we were not really PRU trained, that we knew nothing of the techniques of taking photographs from the air, and if we had so thought we should merely have concluded that we were to learn on the job, by doing it, which is the best way of all to learn.

At Benson we fancied ourselves members of a real squadron at last. With the other pilots we attended briefings by the meteorological officer and briefings for sorties given by the Squadron Commander, a young man with a carefully tended ginger moustache, obviously an athlete who walked light as a cat on the balls of his feet and was we were told a superb squash player. I remember him instructing the met officer, after one pilot had returned from a sortie deep into the heart of Germany without photographs for the target had been covered in cloud, to describe any condition of seven tenths cloud or more as ten tenths, as he would not risk the lives of pilots for no result. Years later we heard that he had been killed flying in formation in some victory parade and found it hard to believe that so fit and quick a person could have died so. When there was no flying to be done, the pilots of the flight would pile into transport and go to drink coffee or hot chocolate at a nearby café. But we were kept occupied. Here were no certificates of competence pasted into the log book, no preliminary flights of dual instruction in a Master. No, for we were now grown up, were mature, had the key of the door; the day after our arrival I was taking a Spitfire V off the ground quite happily. It was not the same as a Mark I but there was a sufficient family resemblance for me to feel confident, and in the days to come there were practice flights at high level, photography, cross country, altitude tests, where in the thin air of 35,000 feet the nose in level flight would be pointed up at the sky, obliterating a great deal of the ground below.

One of our number, Jock Power, a tall Scots lad with curly hair, asked to borrow my watch which was a Rolex to which I had treated myself in Canada and of which I was proud. His own watch had failed and he was off to do an altitude and consumption test; we were a socialist little society, holding much in common, lending to one another as need occurred. But I never saw my watch, or Jack Power, again. His aircraft dived straight into the ground from 27,000 feet. When flying we sat on our parachutes in the cockpit as on a cushion and on top of the parachute was a dinghy in case we went down over the sea. To inflate the dinghy was a small bottle of carbon dioxide gas under pressure. The theory was that the bottle attached to his dinghy was flawed and that the bottle exploded at altitude when the outside pressure was less, inflating his dinghy with irresistible pressure, filling up all the space in the tiny cockpit, jamming him in and forcing the stick forward; unable to get out, for the parachute was underneath the expanding dingy, unable to puncture it and release the gas, he could do nothing but wait for death to take him as the ground got remorselessly closer and closer. Jock had been too pleasant a lad to be wasted in this way. Next day I got myself a commando type dagger, its top secured with a loop of elastic so it would not fall out of its sheath when I was upside down, and I wore this strapped to my right calf, outside all clothing so that it would be immediately available to my right hand. Never again did I fly without it.

A prize squadron possession at Benson was a prototype Spitfire. This had been built in 1939 for air races which had never taken place. It was painted sky blue like all our aircraft for camouflage in the heights of heaven but was beautifully finished, no rivet being visible but all flush under coats of paint. No one was allowed to approach it unless he was wearing tennis shoes, otherwise in socks or bare feet. Its performance at its rated altitude was considered to be better than the latest Mark XI which had just come into service on the squadron, but no one was allowed to fly it except the Squadron Commander. He took off in it one day and did a battle climb from leaving the ground, climbing at what seemed an impossible angle.

Pleasant though squadron life was now that we had finished training and were members at last of the real world, we sensed the atmosphere of the PRU was not all that we had hoped for or imagined. The friendships and easy free-for-all of the life of a combat squadron to which we had looked forward did not seem prominent; here no pilot depended upon another for his life, for all flew alone as individuals, and as individuals there was competition between them, as to who should get the best or the most sorties, or the best aircraft, or any of the decorations that might be going. Later we found other PRU squadrons even more flawed in this respect, with jealousies rampant.

Ten days after we joined 541 Squadron came surprise news. The Squadron Commander called me to his office. I was posted to 680 Squadron PRU in the Middle East. 'Where in the Middle East?' I asked. 'No-one knows,' was the reply. 'Or perhaps someone does but I don't. You are to fly a Spitfire out to them. First stop Gibraltar and then you ask the way. You are to go at once but you can have twenty-four hours leave to go home and say goodbye to your folk. Wal Clarke is to go first and you next. I expect the others will follow a few days later.' This was great excitement; it was now 20 February 1943. Operation 'Torch' had secured North Africa and Algiers in November and at the same time the Germans had been driven back from Egypt at El Alamein and were building themselves a fortress in Tunisia; the tide of defeat had turned and here in the Middle East was where the action was to be found.

I packed my toothbrush and caught the first train home to Gravesend. Wartime railway connections were poor and I did not reach home until about 4 a.m. I climbed through the unlatched sitting-room window and went to sleep fully clothed on the settee, where my father found me much to his surprise when he came down at 7 a.m. to open up the house. There was little time but after breakfast I sat down and wrote a brief note to Jonathan.

Sunday

My darling Jonathan,

A brief note to say goodbye, a lot of water has gone under many bridges since I last wrote, but I have really been very busy and on edge. Now having been on an operational squadron I am due to fly a Spitfire out East immediately. I am now at home saying farewells; I catch the train back to my Spitfire in an hour and then it is goodbye to England for a long time, perhaps forever.

I am sorry that I have not seen you – sorrier perhaps than you will ever know; sorry that I made excuses you did not believe; sorry that I said things you did not like. There is little more for me to say. Goodbye, good luck; forget me for the duration, and if I return after the war – perhaps ——

Yours with love

Geoffrey

My mother and younger brother came down to Gravesend station to see me off. Both wept as the train drew out. I had never seen my mother cry before, nor had I expected anyone to cry for me and I wished they wouldn't, for it made me want to cry myself. I always disliked being the centre of attention and concern, and I have never been able to put much value on myself; receiving presents or any token of worth had always been a source of embarrassment to me. But I pulled myself together as the excitement of the coming journey took hold of me whilst the wheels of the train distanced me now irrevocably from my childhood, from my youth, from my family and from all that had gone before.

CHAPTER FIVE

The Adventure Starts

'The Spitfire pilot will take off first.'

There is a ripple of interest amongst the assembled aircrew of the Wellington, Hudson and Blenheim bombers, all multi-engined aircraft, who are gathered in the briefing room at Portreath in Cornwall preparing for take-off the following morning for Gibraltar.

'Spitfire pilot, who's the Spitfire pilot?' asked the captain of a Wellington. Modestly I indicate that it is I. The wintry late afternoon light of this 25 February 1943 gleams through the window and outside the sea looks untroubled, more inviting than threatening.

'You'll never make it, chum. Much too far for you.' I smile but do not explain that I have a PRU Spitfire, fitted with long-range tanks and the journey should be well within range.

It can only be about forty-eight hours since I left home and parents behind in Gravesend and since my arrival back on 541 Squadron at Benson I had been very busy; but to my surprise Wal Clarke and a couple of the Canadians who had been with us from the School of General Reconnaissance at Squires Gate and the Spitfire OTU at Rednall had been busy before me. Having no family in the UK they had not been given a twenty-four hour leave to say goodbye. In the day I had been absent they had received and tested their aircraft and on the morning after my return from Gravesend they had left for Portreath, near Redruth in Cornwall, the jumping-off place and last stop in England; there Wal planned to wait for me if he could.

Meanwhile I was introduced to Spitfire V BR652 which I flew at 25,000 feet, its rated altitude, for an hour and a half on a consumption test, carefully checking the amount of fuel used. On landing I pronounced myself satisfied and packed the few belongings that I could take with me, a change of underclothes and shirts, washing and shaving kit and my precious flying log book; all went into a small cardboard box which was tied with string onto the top of the vertical camera behind the armour. We were given our R/T call signs and another package of escape aids which included maps on silk of the territory over which we would fly, together with Spanish and Portuguese currency, to add to the aids with which we had been issued on the squadron – such as cunning little compasses disguised as buttons to be sewn on one's clothing and another little compass concealed in the stem of a pipe, amongst other items which would be of interest in time of need. And in accordance with the usual operational practice we handed in all items of a personal nature, including our identity cards, the lack of which was to embarrass me a few days later. We dispersed chatting in the darkening evening, the Blenheim, Wellington and Hudson crews and the lonely Spitfire pilot who, full of the untried confidence of youth and with all of some two hundred flying hours to his credit, was not frightened of being alone. Nervous, yes, apprehensive at first, but this soon gave way to a feeling of quiet relaxed tension. It was exhilarating, exciting, and yet seemed so improbable that it was hard to make myself believe that this was really happening. Yet this is what I had waited for during the long training; this was now to be the start of the great adventure. The future beckoned full of limitless opportunities. From this day forth wherever I shall be, whatever shall I become? Will tomorrow find me swimming in the Bay of Biscay or in the Mediterranean sunshine of Gibraltar; and after Gib, what then? 680 Squadron where are you? I shall find you without doubt. Though eager with anticipation that night I sleep well, as I had done the night before the University Boxing match against Cambridge two years before, and as I have since done on the eve of other testing occasions, knowing that it is too late to alter the course of events, too late to worry and that now I must put my trust in God, myself and my previous training.

I am awoken in the dark at 4 a.m. feeling alert and very much on my toes; a quick breakfast and the final briefing, weather reports and new courses allowing for the newly estimated wind strength and direction. This was to be the first and last time in my operational career that my course was calculated for me; evidently the briefing officer was taking no chances on this solitary pilot. I have to take-off first and at first light.

In the semi-dark I strap myself into the cockpit, but the engine refuses to fire. My heart sinks. An anticlimax for the taut strung nerves of a young man about to start on his first great adventure. I try again and again until the battery is depleted. Perhaps a minor blessing in disguise, allowing me to smile at myself and relax tension a little. One by one the others take off in their order but instead of leading the field, the unfortunate Spitfire pilot has to take-off last, having had to wait for ground help with a battery charger to get his engine turning. But once the propeller has swung into life there is no problem. I run the engine up to zero boost and check instruments, before throttling back and waving chocks away. I taxi out onto the runway and take-off, pick up my wheels and climb steadily on course through 8/10ths strato-cumulus, now pink edged in the early light. The sun rises higher, the clouds disperse leaving a few wispy ones here and there; I look back and below, England has fallen away and the sea shines blue far beneath me. 'Lovely weather we are having,' I say to myself as we, Spitfire and I, head out towards the Bay of Biscay and I break out into song with the excitement of it all. I level out at 25,000 feet, my rated altitude – the height at which the aircraft will perform best. Time went by.

It seems very easy sitting up here in the blue sky, the earth spread out below me, but I must not forget to keep a good look out, particularly as I might run into a German fighter patrol off the French coast as I pass Brest. Round my head goes to the left, to the right and above, my hand up to obscure the sun so that I can look in its direction and detect any aircraft lurking there; keep a good look out, I say to myself, even though the briefing officer said I was unlikely to meet either anti-aircraft fire or hostile fighters once I crossed the Spanish coast. So far so good. I am all alone in the blue sky.

I cross the coast of Spain fifteen minutes before schedule though appear to be on course, so the forecast wind direction and speed which I was given this morning is probably right. Spain is displayed underneath and a limitless heaven above. How grim the Spanish mountains look and how rough the country – not encouraging to any who might have to force land but what a wonderful place it must be to visit on foot in other times. Another half hour passes and I begin to worry that I cannot identify any landmarks, so comfort myself in the belief that I have flown an accurate course and should not be far wrong. But I cannot study the map too much or watch the compass too closely, keeping my head inside the cockpit, for I must watch the sky to each side, behind and above, screening the sun with my hand to be sure nothing hostile lurks there; a quick glance at the map spread out on my knee, at the compass, at the fuel gauge and back again to the great reaches of the sky.

I have been flying using in rotation the fuel in the wing tanks which PRU Spitfires carried within their wings instead of guns, half an hour on one, half an hour on the other, then back to the first, in order to keep the aircraft trim in balance and the fuel usage constant from both sides. But now more than a third of the way into Spain on switching to the port wing tank the red fuel warning light comes on and the engine coughs, splutters and stops; there is still some fuel left in the tank so I must have an airlock, and hastily I switch on to the mains. A look at the map and a brief calculation of time needed to complete the journey. I doubt if mains and reserve alone will get me beyond Spain's southern coast, so I continue to switch between mains and wing tank to try to break the airlock. With a slight feeling of anxiety hollow beneath my belt, I continue to scan the sky which remains blessedly empty of life.

More than three hours have gone by since I left Portreath and England behind me and I can now see approaching the Quadalquiver estuary west of Cadiz and the south coast of Spain. I remember the briefing officer had said to let them know that I am coming. 'What is the best way of doing that?' I wonder. Later I would know simply to call flying control, give my call sign to identify myself and then to say 'Listening out'. But I do not know this and in my innocence I ask for a homing.

'Streamline 7 this is Ransom. Can you see the coast of Spain?' was the reply.

'Yes, clearly and coming up fast.'

Curtly, 'Then follow it.'

It sounded like my elder brother talking. Somewhat chastened I followed it with speed for fifteen minutes, gently losing height all the way, until I rounded the tip of Spain and saw the great rock standing up out of the sea. I came with gladness to circuit height, sought permission to land and came down onto the long strip which is usually cross wind and which protrudes out into the ocean, landing I am afraid very bumpily. But I was there, intact, with my aircraft in one piece and with only twenty gallons of useable fuel left in my tanks. I gave a deep sigh of relief as I taxied off the runway which seemed to be lined with a great number of large aircraft, undid my straps and climbed out of the cockpit. It had taken three hours forty minutes and it was good to stretch my limbs; good to feel firm mother earth beneath my feet now that my first serious journey was successfully over; satisfaction and fulfilment at passing the first test; anticipation of the next, and before that of seeing Gibraltar.

I reported in to the PRU detachment there. They were pleased to see me and were kind. No, no-one knew where 680 Squadron was. Certainly it was not this side of Tunisia. I should have to go on tomorrow to Maison Blanche, the airport for Algiers and ask again. Spend the night here and take-off tomorrow morning they said. It's only a short hop of some 500 miles but keep low over the sea for the Germans have over a quarter million troops in Tunisia and are not short of aircraft. But fly low and your blue camouflage for the sky will do nicely against the blue sea too. No, we cannot give you a map; you won't really need one flying over the sea and we don't have any to spare.

'But,' I expostulate, shocked, 'I can't fly without a map and I have never done so. This part of the world is strange to me anyway.'

But I was told I had no choice. No maps were available. I wondered what the tough young commander of 541 Squadron would have done had he been here in my place and whether he would have sanctioned such a flight by one of his pilots. Then I thought that if I protest again I shall only be told there's a war on. With some anxiety I looked intently at the map on the wall in the operations room, doing my best to memorise the coastline, both east and west of Algiers so that I might know which way to go if I made landfall one side or the other. I decided the only safe way would be to fly a course to bring me well to the west of the town and simply follow the coast round to Maison Blanche; otherwise had I the misfortune to strike the coast to its east without knowing it I would follow the coast until I received German hospitality until the war's end. There was nothing for it but to trust my luck. Fancy risking a pilot and an aircraft for the sake of a map worth a few pence, I thought to myself, but no doubt there will be greater risks and wastes in store.

It was now afternoon and I wandered off for the rest of the day to sample the delights of Gibraltar which looked very much a rock, gaunt and bare against a very blue sky. I wandered into the town where I chanced into the Wellington pilot, who looked surprised to see me. 'Oh, so you did make it then?' he said. Looking as nonchalant and as matter of course as I could and as though I did this sort of thing every day, 'Yes of course. Nothing to it you know. A piece of cake.' Then I met up with a soldier who had been stationed there for some years and who took me round to show me all there was to see in the little town nestling into the Rock, the steep narrow winding streets, past the white houses, cartloads of oranges, mules, shops. I looked for some memento to send home but the only things that took my fancy were the enormous Spanish shawls, black silk mantillas, and these were too expensive. Anyhow, I had no means of sending one home nor anywhere to put it to carry with me, unless I either wore it under my flying clothes or unscrewed the fuselage panel and put it on top of the camera with my necessities. So shopping was abandoned and we visited some bars where girls in Spanish costume were dancing flamenco to a clicking of castanets, had a meal of steak and eggs – a treat out of wartime England – and went early to bed. The promised sights had not been much but I had had my first glimpse of palm trees and of the blue Mediterranean. It had been a long day.

Next morning found me and my blue Spitfire low over the very blue sea, a few feet above the waves, on my way to Algiers. I had anxiously studied the map of the North African coast to the west of Algiers in the briefing room at Gibraltar, trying to memorise notable features – a technique I was to practise more and more throughout my career on reconnaissance, for map reading is easy enough at 30,000 feet when the world is spread out below, but it is entirely different when flying low, close to the ground, when the margins for error are very small and when ground and sky alike need constant attention. No time then to pore over the map on your knee; try to learn the salient features of the map before you go. But at this first attempt there were no landmarks on the sea, only boundless shining moving water, so half way there I called flying control at Gibraltar to give me a bearing; to this I added 180°. Good. This coincided with the track I had plotted; I was on course and would strike the coast of Africa well to the west of Algiers.

After some two hours I could see the coast and turned left, eastwards; then in a little while, there was white Algiers with a large convoy lying offshore. Skirt this, giving it a generous berth for I should not wish to begin my operational career by being shot down by our own gunners. Thirteen miles to the east lies Maison Blanche. I circle the airfield at circuit height, obtain permission to land, make a classic approach and then as perfect a three point landing as I have ever made. The noise of the aircraft, of engine and wind, is drowned out by the most hideous and frightening clattering. 'Oh my God,' I pray – many of my thoughts whilst flying in those days were truly prayers – 'the aircraft has fallen to pieces.' And so it sounded. I had for the first time landed, quite unexpectedly and totally unprepared, in interlocking strips of steel mesh put down hastily to make an airfield surface. But Spitfire V BR652 was made of sterner stuff than its pilot, slowed gently to the end of its landing run and I taxied still in one piece to dispersal. There Wal Clark was waiting for me, having put his aircraft unserviceable until I caught up with him whilst the others had gone on.

* * *

We were getting close to the war. It was the end of February; North Africa had only been ours since the British and American landings of Operation Torch in the previous November, which, coinciding with the great El Alamein victory in the Egyptian desert, more than 16,000 miles away to the east of Algiers had forced the Germans to retreat into Tunisia where they were now threatened with attack from two directions, both from the east and from the west. But the rough terrain was to their advantage, they were behind fortifications like the Mareth line, they were plentifully supplied with airfields, and Hitler, determined on a policy of no surrender, was flying in reinforcements of men and aircraft. Churchill and his staff returning from the January conference at Casablanca with President Roosevelt and his advisers, from which he had gone on to visit Cairo and Turkey, had been through Maison Blanche on his way home on 5 February, only twenty-two days before my wheels awoke the clamour of the steel mesh strip. I wondered if their aircraft had felt and sounded like mine. Doubtless we were on the brink of great events, into which Wal and I felt we were being drawn to play our humble part. It was at once frightening, exhilarating, and good to be alive.

Of course no-one knew where 680 Squadron was; certainly not this side of Tunisia, so it must be on the other side, somewhere in the Western Desert and to get there we should have to fly over territory held by the Germans and held in strength. We asked for maps; again none were to be had, being more precious than fine gold. We begged, and eventually were grudgingly given between us just one set of the two maps required to cover the journey from Algiers across Tunisia. So we decided to fly in formation, that Wal would have the map and would lead for the first part of the journey which would take us south over land in Allied hands, and I would have the map and would lead over the second part over enemy lines until we reached the other side. The extent of the desert shown on the maps looked formidable so we each resolved to obtain an empty bottle from the mess, fill it with drinking water and fly with it tucked into our Mae Wests so that should we have the misfortune to be brought down in the desert we should have at least some water with us. Later, much later, I was told that these Spitfires carried a container of drinking water in the wings against such an emergency. I was then not able to verify this; if it were true it would have been nice if someone had told us about it before we set out. But there was a war on.

We were billeted for the night in what must have been the chateau of a prosperous man. It had loggias, arches, great palms and beautiful gardens. Whereas I had travelled with a toothbrush in my pocket, Wal had carried an open razor in his and borrowing this I shaved off three days growth of beard, only cutting my face twice. Then we hitched a ride into Algiers. We saw a beautiful town of gracious houses, green shrubs and palm trees and of course very French. With the aid of what French we had retained from schooldays and the help of many gestures we obtained some white wine at a café with tables on the street, and watched the pretty girls go by of whom Algiers seemed to have many. We reckoned that to get along adequately with any of them would need more French than we possessed and we would not be there long enough to learn it, even if Wal had not his fiancée back in Auckland to blind him to all other girls, and I on my own would be uninterested and far too shy. I had flown that day and would be flying tomorrow, absorbing my attention and energy, and we were there only for the one night. Even so the passing show was pleasant to admire and to speculate upon. Then we moved to another café, had a meal of three eggs each (eggs seemed the most easily come by food in North Africa and was the invariable meal when eating out in Cairo) and split a bottle of champagne between us. It was a beautiful night to be in a strange city, a pure sky of dark velvet bright with stars and the air heavy with the scent of flowers. After Canada and the austerities of wartime Britain it seemed like paradise. It was as well that the night was so fair, for we had to walk most of the way back to the chateau, somewhat hampered by knowing neither its name nor the way to get there.

Next morning, having briefed ourselves with the weather forecast and the estimated wind strength and direction and plotted our course, we went to our aircraft. Alas mine was listing to one side.

Blast it, a puncture. There must have been a sharp piece of steel sticking up in that wretched steel matting, so I sought out a flight sergeant in charge of maintenance; could he kindly mend my puncture for me. He said he would see what he could do. I persisted: 'We are all ready to take off and we have to try to get across Tunisia in the first part of the day to make allowance for mishaps. It is supposed to be urgent that we get to 680 Squadron as soon as we can.'

'Look, Chiefy,' he said, 'I am very busy and everything is urgent. If you bother me you just won't get it done at all.'

I replied I was sorry, but we were on our own without anyone to help but him. Realising he was under pressure I would just leave it with him knowing he would help as soon as he could. Even so, despite my sweet talking, it was not until early afternoon that the puncture was mended and we were able to taxi out into the noisy talkative steel mesh airstrip, signal to each other with thumbs up that we were ready to go, steadily push the throttle forward and take off in formation.

We climbed steadily up into the clear blue sky, Wal leading, for he had the map for this leg of the journey; we levelled off at 25,000 feet, the rated altitude at which our Spitfires performed best and would cover the most ground with the least consumption of fuel. His task was to find the way; mine to watch the sky which remained empty so far. We came to the end of Allied territory and of his map; we had to keep R/T silence so he just waggled his wings and I took over the lead, flying a course for Gabez with all the accuracy I could.

Suddenly R/T silence was broken by the English voice of a flying controller. 'Scramble blank squadron. Two bogies angels 25' (two unidentified aircraft at 25,000 feet). That's our height. I look round nervously. There is nothing to be seen in the sky. I remember that the PRU Spitfires are stripped for long distance flying and carry no IFF, the little machine that codes and retransmits the radar impulse and identifies you as a friend. Perhaps the controller means us. I climb to 27,000 feet. The controller's voice comes over 'Bogies now angels 27'. Still nothing in sight. Yes they do mean us. But they won't catch us; our stripped machines already at operational height will not be caught by heavily armed fighters which would have to climb to reach us; a standing patrol at a greater height than ours would have been a different matter. A fragment of an old nursery tale comes into my mind 'Run, run, run fast as you can, you can't catch me, I'm the gingerbread man'. But to hear yourself being hunted by your own side gives you an eerie feeling, uncomfortable in the pit of your stomach. That is if it really is us they are after and there are not two other hostile aircraft up there in the sun. I screen the sun once more, the sky remains empty. I put the nose down a little to build up speed and the chase fades, for we hear no more on the R/T. Before long we pass over the top of Gabez, true on course, turn east and follow the coast for the next two hundred miles to Tripoli, losing height and collecting speed all the way.

Outside Tripoli is the airfield Castel Benito, built I suppose for the Italian Air Force by Benito Mussolini. Churchill had spent three days there only three weeks before, when he had reviewed the victorious Eighth Army in a ceremony charged with emotion. I decided to land and refuel before pushing on, for there was still plenty of daylight left. Wal decided to fly on without refuelling; as I put down my wheels to make my landing approach, he waggled his wings and went on to Marble Arch. I taxied to dispersal over what appeared to be firm sand, an airman standing in front of me waving his arms. What a nice warm welcome, I thought, how friendly. When I stopped, switched off, undid my straps and got out, he said, 'You've just taxied through an uncleared minefield. I was trying to stop you.' It seems I never do think of the obvious meanings that people try to convey. But all's well that ends well.

Next I was greeted by the PRU Flight Commander. What a pleasant surprise. This was a detached flight of the 680 Squadron I had come to join. The rest of the squadron was at Kilo 8, 8 kilometres outside Cairo, and there I should have to go to deliver my aircraft. I wanted to refuel and go on to join Wal, but they would not hear of it and insisted I spend the night with them. The opportunity to make friends with my own squadron was too good to miss. Their mess was in a pretty white house with an avenue of cypress trees. They plied me with drink and though they were all officers treated me as one of themselves. This is splendid I thought; I am having a wizard time and I shall enjoy 680 Squadron now that I have found it; a home-coming worth training for, worth waiting for, worth flying for, worth the discomforts of the journey. A snatch of their talk remains in memory. They said that in the Italian Air Force mess nearby were a number of little cubicles leading off the main sitting room, approached through a door over which was a clock. As fancy took them, the officers would enter a cubicle to enjoy female company; the mess steward would time them by the clock and the charge per minute would be entered on the officer's mess bill. This struck me as bizarre and no way to win a war, nor could I imagine the RAF providing such facilities.

No doubt the ladies were there no longer and the building put to more warlike purpose.

Early next morning Wal came back to find me and together we set off on the next, the last and longest stage of our journey. Surely our troubles were now over and we would enjoy easy flying in the clear air, following for most of the way the coast and the coastal road, apart from a stretch of over two hundred miles across the Libyan Desert to El Adem near Tobruk where we would need to refuel. In formation we flew low over the seashore for hundreds of miles, admiring the engineering of the long coastal road and astonished by the number of our trucks moving up in constant procession throughout its length; truly an impressive sight and boding no good for the German Army entrenched in Tunisia. A strange sight too was Marble Arch, the triumphal arch in true Roman pattern erected by Mussolini, standing aloof and lonely over the coastal road. From there we cut across Cyrenaica and the grim, empty desert, me leading, towards El Adem. A slim chance one would have of survival if forced down in the middle of this I thought, taking small comfort from the bottle of water making a lump under my Mae West.

But what a wonderful place to fight a war. Wheel tracks abounded and strewn along our course was a colossal amount of wreckage, trucks, tanks, aircraft. A tragic show of the waste of war without reckoning on the dead humans, the young lives spoiled and ended that the wreckage must have involved. Yet if men must fight then the desert must be the best place for it, where tanks can manoeuvre and artillery hurl shells without doing much damage to anything except to the opposing soldiery. Let the warring nations come to the desert and fight it out. I wondered how long the wreckage would remain there or whether at any future time it would be cleared and the minefields too, or whether they would remain to destroy unwary travellers in a hundred years' time.

After about four hours flying I looked down and saw the words 'El Adem' outlined in the desert in whitewashed stones. Having flown many miles over the featureless desert we had arrived directly over the airfield – an exact landfall, such as throughout my flying career never ceased to give me a thrill of pleasure and satisfaction whenever I managed to achieve it. It was virtually an abandoned airfield on which we landed, and which the tide of war had passed by; it was littered with many wrecked aircraft and there were many signs of the recent German occupation, graffiti and inscriptions on walls, as well as the shattered buildings and aircraft that would never fly again. Similar signs had existed at Castel Benito.

We refuelled and stretched our legs, necessary after sitting for four hours strapped into a tiny cramped cockpit. El Adem was almost deserted and it was evident that hospitality would not be available; to have stayed there would have meant a rough night. It was only some 450 miles to Cairo and we ought to get there we reckoned in about two and a half hours; it seemed early afternoon and we looked forward to being with 680 Squadron, to a good hot meal and a night's sleep in comfort. This was a great mistake. Since leaving Portreath, no-one had briefed us on our journey except for the weather forecasts, even maps had been hard to get. No-one therefore had told us to put our clocks forward as we flew east, crossing time zones, and in our ignorance we were still using the same British time as we had when leaving Cornwall. Had we been really clever we might have thought of it ourselves – after all the clocks had gone back when we went to Canada and forward again when we returned, but there had been much else to think about during the journey.

So we took off from El Adem, Wal with his wing tip tucked in close to my side, as tight a formation take-off as you would wish to see, had there been anyone there who would wish to see it, into what we thought was the early afternoon. As there seemed plenty of time we again flew low, sightseeing, admiring the long stretches of golden sand along the coast and the curling surf, and the traffic still busily travelling west along the coastal road. After a while I noticed that the little white cumulus clouds in the sky were turning pink; surely the sun cannot be setting already. We are a long way from the battlefront and strict R/T silence is perhaps not so necessary, so I ask Wal what he thinks about it, but there is no reply. We are still in formation so I gesture to him, but he cannot communicate on the R/T. Obviously his radio has packed up and he will have to rely on me even more for he has no map either, the only one between us is with me.

We passed over the battlefield of El Alamein, more wreckage on a grand scale – I had had no idea that the battle had been so close to Egypt, only a few minutes flying from Alexandria, and how near the great German General Rommel had come to driving us into the sea; again the distance from El Alamein to Tunisia is staggering – what a retreat Rommel had then had to make and what a hugely long supply line he had once had and which we now had in turn, no wonder trucks had been nose to tail along its length.

By now the sunset was fading from the clouds and the ground was becoming dark. Wal without a radio and without a map was flying desperately close to me; we put our navigation lights on; other lights we did not have for PRU Spitfires are stripped of all non-essentials for speed and we had no cockpit lights with which to see our instruments, nor landing lights with which to switch on and illumine our landing path, even if we should find the airfield in the dark. We had neither of us before flown a Spitfire at night. I reached the Nile and followed the Delta south, the water glimmering in the dark land, reflecting the last light of day. I repeatedly asked Kilo 8 for homings. I was told to keep on course; they would switch on the flare path for us once they heard us overhead. All Wal could see were my navigation lights; he told me later that he was really and truly frightened and was prepared to bale out. Flying control told me we were overhead and suddenly out of the corner of my eye I saw Wal spiralling down and below him a windsock on which light was shining. I followed him, put wheels and flaps down, wondered why there was no flare path put on for us, landed as close as we could to the windsock for we could see nothing else, and judging our height by the windsock felt in the dark for the ground. Quite by chance, a good landing. It was pitch dark. Someone shone a light and we taxied towards it, parked the aircraft and switched off in great relief. We had been airborne for nearly seven hours that day. It had been the closest shave that we had either of us ever had; a real shaky do, we said. And it was not Kilo 8 after all at which we had landed but Almaza about four miles away, a civil field in use by the Egyptian Air Force. We picketed down our machines for the night while they kindly rang flying control at Kilo 8; the Egyptian officers were very kind and hospitable and I remember their well equipped mess with very ornately carved wooden chairs.

After a little while a truck with the squadron warrant officer, bluff, kindly, red-faced, who introduced himself as Pinky, came to collect us. At Kilo 8 we were found beds and though we had not eaten since leaving Castel Benito in the morning, went straight to sleep. The journey was over. I had not been frightened unduly at any time, not even during the last hour, perhaps because Wal was depending on me, but I had been highly strung and keyed up for six days; now pressure was relaxed.

Next day I awoke more tired than I ever remember being before, the first fatigue that I had felt on the journey, but we had arrived at the squadron which we had come to join and to which we had so much looked forward after the years of waiting and training.

Next morning we reported ourselves to the Commanding Officer. 'Thanks for the aircraft,' he said. 'Now what are you going to do?'

We were puzzled, not understanding. 'Sir?'

'I said what are you going to do?'

'Do, sir? We've come to join you.'

'I need the aircraft but I don't want you. I don't have sergeant pilots on my squadron. Only officers.'

We were dumbfounded and had nothing to say. I remembered that the flight at Castel Benito had been all officers.

'Well, that's all,' he said dismissively. And then a crowning unkindness 'Oh and by the way, get yourselves cleaned up before you go to town.'

We had travelled light for six days, Wal with his razor in his pocket and me with my toothbrush in mine, all other necessaries and changes of clothing in a cardboard box screwed within the fuselage on top of the camera and inaccessible until now. Although I have always been a little careless of my personal appearance, Wal was dapper, neat and smartly turned out. We would have no more thought of going into Cairo without being reasonably smart than we would have started to walk back to England.

We left the CO's office in silence whilst we went to retrieve our belongings. Then said Wal after a while 'I suppose that's what the Air Force call being shat on from a great height.'

I did not reply at once for the shock and disappointment was heavy in me. Then all at once illumination came. 'You remember that we didn't understand why we had gone to a fighter OTU briefly and not to the PRU one and we had thought we might be going into some newly devised fighter reconnaissance outfit. Well, that's it. They just wanted ferry pilots to bring aircraft out and now we are to be thrown away. I suppose something will turn up in the end. Anyhow let's get changed and go down to have a look at Cairo.' The further indignity that was to come upon us that day in Cairo would be almost an anticlimax.

We wandered the Cairo streets a little and the dirt and squalor did not impress us, the streets crowded with servicemen, full of Arabs and aggressive vendors of trinkets. We thought it time for some local colour and went into a bar where we chatted a while to one of Wal's Kiwis from the New Zealand division of whom there were many in Cairo, waiting to be shipped home to New Zealand which was then being menaced by Japan. 'Be careful of the bar hostesses,' he said. 'They will come up to you in the bar and ask you to buy them a drink. All they will drink will be coloured water, which will cost you plenty, for that's how they earn their living. And then five minutes before closing time when you are looking for the companionship to continue, she will disappear and you won't see her again. You will have wasted your evening and your money for nothing.' It wasn't really as if Wal and I would have been much interested, but it was as well to be forewarned. We sat at a table sipping a glass of beer each, thinking the passing show had little to commend it in comparison with Algiers, when in walked two Army Military Policemen. We heard later that there were supposed to be many deserters in Cairo and imposters pretending to be what they were not. The MPs started checking identity cards and papers of the service personnel. They came to us. 'We only just arrived yesterday,' we said, 'flew out from England and they took our identity cards from us before we left. The RAF will not let you carry them over enemy occupied territory.'

But they would not believe a word of it. 'If you can't account for yourselves you must come with us.' So we were arrested, bundled into the back of the Black Maria, taken through the streets of Cairo to the military jail and locked up behind bars.

'You had better ring 680 Squadron at Kilo 8 and ask for the warrant officer called Pinky. He will vouch for us,' we said.

We sat looking out through the bars of the cell onto a dimly lit long corridor with a red cardinal polished floor. We did not talk much after observing that you never knew where high flying would get you and wondering what next we would be required to do for our country. We had to wait for a while for Pinky was not at once available. We felt depressed, tired after the excitement and stress of the journey but more tired from the shocks and disappointments that had fallen on us since we landed. At least we could not blame the arrogant little godling in charge of 680 Squadron for the imprisonment; that we supposed was not really anyone's fault. It was just bad luck, just the way the cookie crumbled as the Americans would have said; the MPs were doing their duty, looking for deserters and imposters and certainly we were there without papers or means of identity. Nevertheless it was with some satisfaction that after an hour or so we heard Pinky's voice booming down the corridor 'Wish I could get my hands on those bloody MPs' and boots echoing in a sharp staccato as they came to unlock the cell door and let us go back with Pinky, tired and chastened to Kilo 8, where even if the squadron did not want us, it was at least the only place we had to go for the time being.

I sat down and wrote a long letter home describing the flight out and promising to send some silver filigree bracelets which we had seen very small children making in the bazaar, but I said nothing about the humiliations that had met us on arrival. I promised also to send another letter to describe Egypt, but I never wrote it. I did not feel proud of myself and I did not want to upset my parents by conveying to them anything of the sense of shame that I felt. That's when I stopped writing home and very few letters came from me for the rest of the war, much to the distress of my family and that of the young woman in Staffordshire who so much wanted a letter from me.

***

For a few days there was little to do. We went to see the pyramids and the Sphinx, rode on camels, sat in cafés in Heliopolis, frequented by Egyptians wearing red fezzes, drinking the thick black Arab coffee in little cups, always served together with a glass of cold water, presumably to drink afterwards to take the taste away. We spent some time in a Serviceman's Club in Cairo where through Wal I met many more of the magnificent New Zealand division, large men in their desert hats and high morale; I had never been so impressed with anyone as with them, their outgoing friendliness, camaraderie, willingness to help, their instant identification of themselves with you. Rommel is reported to have said that with twelve such divisions he could conquer the world, but I doubt if any of them would have been interested in world conquest. Often we would tune in to the German forces' radio in order to hear 'Lili Marlene' sung in German, as it was night after night, for it was the marching song of the Afrika Corps and had been adopted by the Eighth Army with whom it was equally popular.

After two weeks news came that Wal was to take his aircraft on to India to 681 Squadron which was at Dum Dum, outside Calcutta; my aircraft was to stay at Kilo 8. I was sad to see Wal go, though there were others of our company from Squires Gate and Rednall now: Ru Smith, like Wal from Auckland, Ken Draycott, and the Canadians Nunton and Richards, none of us officers, none of us wanted by 680 Squadron.

One fine starry night Ken Draycott, Nunton and I were walking back from Heliopolis to our quarters when we were accosted by an Arab who asked if we wanted a woman. 'Sure,' said Nunton, 'where and how much?' A pitiably small price was quoted and we were led off the main road to a square surrounded by mud buildings. 'In here. Come,' and Nunton was led off out of sight. Ken and I waited quietly in the moonlit square, alert in case of some unspecified trouble. In a little while Nunton returned buttoning up his trousers and licking his moustache, satisfaction across his lean face.

'Well, who goes next?' he asked.

'Not me,' I said quickly.

'Not me,' said Ken. 'Do you think I would go after you, you dirty fellow?'

'You are a couple of so-and-so's.' And he cursed us with some deep Canadian curses. Then suddenly he saw the joke was on him and burst out laughing. Amicably we made our way back to camp.

We had not liked what we had seen of Cairo. On reflection there may have been resentment at the presence of the Allied Forces there and we heard rumours of tanks having been used to surround King Farouk's palace to induce him to be conciliatory; certainly a ribald derisory song about Farouk was in circulation amongst the troops. Perhaps it was because of this that we found hostility in the streets, where we were warned not to walk alone, even in daylight and preferably in groups of more than two for protection against assault. One particular nuisance were the boys with boot and shoe cleaning materials who would offer a shine and when you refused, your boots having already been shone by yourself before you came to town, would then threaten to throw the liquid polish over your clothes. On your own you might well be robbed and knifed into the bargain. Often we mused it was a pity that the Germans had not taken Egypt after all, for it is certain they would not have put up with such nonsense and would have cleaned the place up, ready for re-occupation for the more pacific, more tolerant but therefore less efficient British.

After a few days we were sent to a transit camp, way out in the desert, too far away to easily reach Cairo or other places of amusement, a place where we could do no harm and in which we were left to our own devices.

Living in tents pitched amongst the harsh sterility of sand and rock, I was astonished at the number of flies everywhere, infesting the food and crawling black over the inner walls of the tents; wherever did they manage to breed in such numbers under desert conditions? I never did learn. Apart from the flies, life in the desert was healthy enough, hot dry sunshine during the day and cold at night needing a blanket or two for warmth. Knowing that sooner or later someone would wake up to our presence and recruit us to the distant battle, we thought it wise to spend our days hardening ourselves to desert conditions. I took to walking barefoot during the heat of the day over the sand and rock to toughen my feet; they at least should not betray me if I were brought down in the desert far from home and had to walk back. And we practised water discipline. Ru Smith, from the farm background in way off Auckland, ever the practical man, said:

'It's silly to drink during the heat of the day when the water comes straight out of you again, for then you have to keep drinking. We've got to practise for the time when water is short and every drop counts; just rinse out your mouth during the day and drink in the evening when the day is cool; then the water will stay in the body and not be lost straight away through the pores of the skin.'

This seemed good sense, so we practised ignoring our thirst during the day. We tried our best to be ready for the battle, even if the battle was not ready for us.

Then through the traditional grapevine – how the news travelled I never knew – we heard that Wal Clark was dead. He never reached 681 Squadron. The story we heard was that at Karachi he had met up with some like-minded fellows and promised them a demonstration of what a PRU Spitfire could accomplish. When taking off before their admiring gaze he had gone into a steep climbing turn, alas too steeply before he had built up sufficient forward impetus, had stalled, spun into the ground and was killed instantly. Wal with his erect carriage, a little man who always walked straight and tall, smart and well dressed, whose eyes had twinkled when he adjusted his sock to show which way he was breaking from the rugger scrum if he got the ball; Wal who had come home with me at Christmas to meet my family, loyal companion in adventure; Wal of the high standards who reproached people who made a noise drinking their soup with 'soup is not to be played like a musical instrument'; Wal so honourable and strict in all his dealings, who never looked at a girl because he was engaged to one back home in Wellington; Wal was dead and I should not see him again. I wanted to write to his folk at home and to the girl who would now wait in vain for his return but I did not have his home address. Had I been on a squadron I could have found out his next of kin from the squadron adjutant but we were not on a squadron; we were in a mindless, nameless transit camp miles from anywhere; how could I make an inquiry, how could I get a reply if I wrote say to 680 Squadron, for day by day we expected to learn our posting and day by day we remained ignorant of it. But we might move tomorrow and then it might take months for a reply to reach me. Thus I could not write to Wal's parents to say he had been my friend, that I had loved him and had been lessened by his death, and so be able to share a little in their grief, nor could I write to the girl to whom he had been so faithful. First Mervyn Wingfield and now Wal Clark, both tragedies had happened when I was in transit and unable to find an address to which to write and help unburden my sorrow a little in praising my dead friend.

* * *

Distant rumours of the war reached us and made us restless. On 6 March, Rommel's attack on Montgomery at Medinine had failed, on 26 March the Mareth Line was taken and on 7 April the First Army from the west and the Eighth Army from the east joined hands for the final push on Tunis and Bizerta, and in all this excitement and success here we were, left to rot in a transit camp. Youth is resilient and somehow this did not diminish our enthusiasm or our desire to play a part in the great drama taking place. It would have been easier if someone had said 'You are just waiting for places at an Operational Training Unit in Palestine where you will finally be trained for a highly skilled job'. But no-one did tell us and we had no way of finding out; faceless, anonymous clerks were shuffling our papers in some military headquarters and deciding our fate – perhaps it had all been worked out at the Air Ministry many months before. But we did not know what was to happen to us, victory was being won without our help, and the waiting was irksome.

The RAF of the single-engined pilot was very much a man's world. Each had to work out his own problems for himself. Any attempt to express the hollow inside oneself, whether of fear or frustration or distress, would be received coldly and without sympathy, for doubtless we all felt the same and few had the strength to comfort another.

Right: 1. Geoffrey's parents, Ernest and Constance, in 1912.

Below: 2. Guy family portrait, 1930s. Left to right: David, Constance, Geoffrey, Joan, Ernest, Bernard, Doreen.

3. Geoffrey (front) running in Chatham House School grounds, 1939.

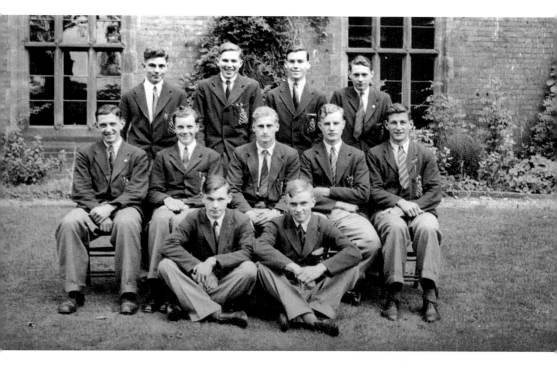

4. Geoffrey (middle) as Chatham House School Captain, 1939.

5. Geoffrey (middle) on leave in Canada, 1941.

6. Geoffrey (left) on leave in Canada, 1941.

7. Geoffrey on leave in Egypt, 1942 or 1943.

8. Men of 28 Squadron in India, 1944.

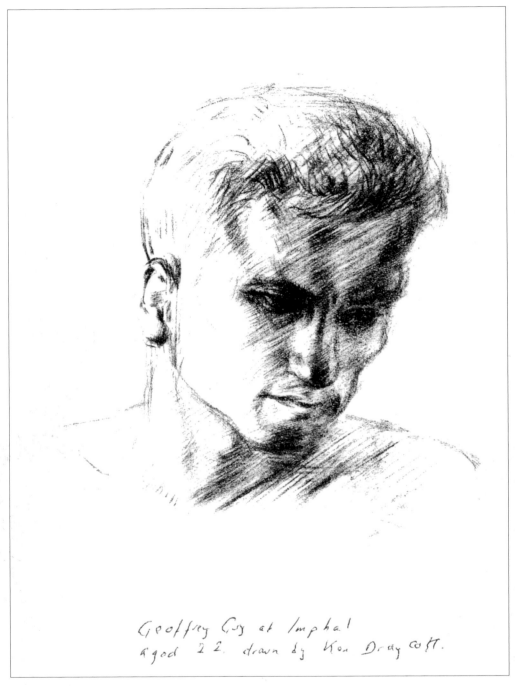

Geoffrey Cox at Imphal
Aged 22. drawn by Ken Draycott.

9. Charcoal sketch of Geoffrey by Ken Draycott, 1943.

10. Wedding of Geoffrey and Joan, 3 September 1946.

It was no use complaining of being left to rot in the transit camp or, unless you were talking to an intimate companion on the same wavelength, trying to express your sorrow at the death of a friend. You would be met by an indifferent shrug and the phrase 'Bad luck, chum. You shouldn't have joined'. Similarly, if trouble came to you in the air you had to sort it out yourself; you could not stop as you can in a car, get out and stretch your legs or get an expert mechanic to come and help. And if trouble did come to one of our company whilst he was airborne, the standard remark throughout the Air Force was 'Well, what goes up must come down'. Cold comfort indeed, but we knew it was true. The classic story which illustrates this attitude was related about the inexperienced pilot on a fighter sweep over France who told his flight leader that he was running out of fuel. The flight leader relayed the question to the Squadron Commander 'What should he do?' 'Tell him to come and see me in my office at 9 a.m. tomorrow morning,' was the cool rejoinder. You were alone, in command of your own aircraft, and hopefully of yourself as well, so perforce you yourself had to settle your own problems which no-one else could solve for you.

The days were idle in the transit camp, the nights in the Mess usually ended with a sing-song. Grouped round an old piano which had come from heaven knows where, we would on occasion sing limericks relating to one or other member of our company, made up on the spur of the moment or more likely thought out the day, linking each one with the chorus, 'That was a nice little song, sing us another one, just like the other one, do.' Perhaps we might start with a classic like:

There was a young girl from Australia
Who went to a dance dressed in a dahlia
The dress as a dress
Was not a success
And the dance, as a dance, was a failure.

And then the chorus, 'That was a nice little song, sing us another one, just like the other one, do.'

Then perhaps a personal one about one of the group:

There was a young man called Chase
Whose nose was too big for his face

When his friends told him so
He replied 'Oh blow
You chaps are a perfect disgrace'.

Followed by the chorus once again, 'That was a nice little song ...'

This game needed a quick and ingenious wit to keep up for long and would soon be abandoned for the standard Air Force favourites like the 'Ball of Kirriemuir', or 'The Blacksmith', 'Lulu', 'As I was sitting by Riley's fire' and a host of others; more innocent ones sometimes like 'Caviar comes from the Virgin Sturgeon' or 'You can't go to heaven in a Tiger Moth, for the engine stops and the wings fall off' and so on through other makes and marks of aircraft, like the Wimpey Ten, the Spitfire One and the Hurricane. And thus to bed. Then tomorrow would be another day, when we would gossip and tell stories, count the flies crawling on the side of the tent, practise water discipline and walking barefoot over the hot sand.

* * *

At last after some six weeks came the news of our posting. To Palestine, 74 Operational Training Unit at Aqir where we were to be trained to take photographs for PRU. At last the operational training which had been omitted in England. But what the hell for, we wanted to know, when they would not have us on a squadron? Perhaps they would commission us all; the improbability made us all roar with laughter. Anyhow ours not to reason why, ours but to do (as we were told) and die (very like). Off we were sent in the verminous third-class carriage of a train with hard slatted wooden seats across the Sinai Desert with a ration of a tin of bully beef each and a packet of hard ship's biscuit. We dozed intermittently and at 4 a.m. were woken when the train pulled into Gaza. Across the cool night air came the fragrance of orange blossom and of jasmine to welcome us to this promised land of milk and honey, and we felt an infinite relief after the flies, the dirt and the diarrhoea, the lack of water and the pestering and persecution by the town Arabs that had been our unfortunate experience of Egypt.

Aqir was not far from Tel Aviv where we spent our free time, such as it was. The Jewish town was modern, new buildings, thoroughly European in feeling and atmosphere; cafés were decent and clean and during a meal you might well be serenaded by a violinist from the symphony orchestra who had to supplement his earnings; and there were young Jewish girls with long shining blue-black hair, perhaps they would be fat and matronly in a few years time but now superb. In this town we felt at ease and at home. But cross from the Jewish to the Arab quarter and you were back in the dirt and filth that we had hoped had been left behind in Egypt. It was there I saw an Arab boy asleep on the pavement with his mouth open and his lips and mouth crawling with flies.

Our quarters at Aqir were roomy and pleasant though one morning I woke and as I got out of bed felt an itching inside my pyjamas; I scratched and out fell a foot-long centipede which must have cuddled up for the warmth during the cold night; obviously a warning against the wearing of pyjamas which I did not heed for many years to come, though I was told I was lucky not to have been severely bitten. It was spring time, the days were delightful, the nights cool, citrus abounded and there were vendors in Tel Aviv with barrows laden with fruit who would squeeze you a glass of orange juice before your eyes. And each day we flew Hurricanes, learning to take photographs, practising and sometimes spoiling film on places whose names were familiar to us, names ringing down the centuries from the crusades and from the Bible – Tyre and Sidon, Acre, Haifa, Damascus, Gaza, Suez, Qantara, Ismailia, Hebron and Bethlehem, names wholly Jewish and names like the Arabian Nights, El Arish, Rosh Pinna and mixed romantic names like St Jean Ramat David. On all these and more we cut our photographic teeth.

It needed practice to take good aerial photographs from a single-engine machine like a Hurricane or Spitfire. The camera was fixed in position behind the armour plating of your seat and was inaccessible once you were airborne. You had therefore to position your aircraft exactly over the target before you switched the camera on. At 25,000 feet which was then the standard height for vertical photographs taken by PRU, being the optimum operational height for the Spitfire V, you see a wide panorama of the country spread out below you but you are handicapped in that the great nose, the mighty engine and the spread of your wings blots out all that is immediately below. To know when you are precisely over the target needs a great deal of practice. The technique was to bank the wing hard over and when the target appeared to be directly underneath, you put the aircraft nose vertically up into the sky, kick either the left or the right rudder and swing down in a stall turn, pointing directly down into the target. Then straighten up, set the gyro compass to zero so that you may keep an exactly straight course, and fly at an indicated airspeed of 180 knots, for at that speed the cameras were set to take pictures that, when viewed on the ground through a special lens, had a 60° overlap. Then everything would be seen in stereo depth and every minute detail could be picked out.

A small target like an airfield might be covered in one run only; but one such as a city either before or after a bombing raid would need a mosaic formed by a series of parallel photographic runs; at the end of each run you turn fairly widely and then do a stall turn over the target once more and fly back on a reverse course, repeating the procedure until the target is covered. If the target were defended by ack-ack, and on operations most were, the guns would predict on you at their leisure, even if you were making a single run; flying a set course and speed you were a sitting duck, though the sky is a big place and you were a small object; but it was much worse when you were making a mosaic, unable to take evasive action but of necessity repeatedly flying straight and level on constant courses, a live Aunt Sally in a shooting gallery giving the boys below practice and hoping against hope that they would not hit you. If the guns were silent it would be perhaps because there was a standing fighter patrol up there in the sun, just waiting for you to level out and fly your constant course and speed for the photographs.

Taking low level oblique pictures was another matter though that too had its share of risk. You approached your target flying low, hopefully escaping enemy radar and taking your photographs before the enemy was alert to your presence; even if the enemy was alert and you drew fire, there was comfort in the thought that a low flying fast aircraft is difficult to hit. Once alongside and close to the target you switched on your camera and tried to fly a constant course and speed whilst your camera was working, though the 60 per cent overlap as in vertical photography was not required. Obliques did not require much practice and out of the 80 flying hours spent taking photographs at Aqir, only 3 were spent practising them.

The weather was always fine and we flew every day, day in, day out. Until 19 May when I had my accident. Returning from a two-hour flight I made the usual circuit of the airfield, discovering a large multi-engined aircraft ahead of me, preparing to land. I had been taught and habitually practised a steep gliding approach – from a thousand feet when the end of the airstrip appears under the left wing, wheels and flaps down, throttle back and come in gliding without the use of engine. On this occasion, with a large aircraft in front of me making the traditional bomber approach using engine all the way in, I should have made another circuit until he was out of the way. Instead I too made a bomber approach coming in behind him, at a low airspeed, close to stalling, hanging in the air on my engine. Suddenly at about 500 feet I remembered that I was still using my auxiliary drop tanks and had not switched onto mains as I should have done. Better late than never, I thought, and switched over. Promptly the engine cut and I simply fell out of the sky, digging a nice deep hole in a ploughed field several hundred yards from the beginning of the runway. My straps broke on impact and I was flung forward, striking my head on the Hurricane reflector sight, always a hazard in such circumstances. With a huge effort, before I lost consciousness, I reached up my hand and switched off the ignition to lessen the chance of fire. Then I was dimly aware of people running towards me across the field. I knew no more until I awoke in hospital, with my nose and forehead covered in bandages. Concussion and a broken nose, they said, and I was lucky to be alive.

I was the only person in the sick bay, where I was left to my own devices for two weeks. Then I was sent to an Army Colonel, a plastic surgeon in Haifa. He removed the bandages, handed me a mirror and asked 'Did your nose always look like that?' I looked carefully into the mirror. Honestly I couldn't remember. I had never taken particular note of my nose, or of my face for that matter, and anyway for the last two weeks it had been covered up in bandages and I had not seen it, so I had recently lost whatever familiarity I may have had with it.

'Well, sir, no I don't think so.'

'Then let me re-break it for you and make it any shape you like.'

'Oh thank you sir, but I think it will do very nicely as it is and I shall soon get used to it again.'

So whether my nose is the shape I was born with or not I shall never know but it still carries the scar from the Hurricane reflector sight. The Hurricane I am sorry to say came off worse than I did and had to be written off.

The day after my visit to the surgeon in Haifa, the Flight Commander kindly took me for a thirty minute flight with him in a Harvard to give me confidence, and the day following I set off on my own in another Hurricane to take more vertical pictures. Without a care or worry in the world I carried my parachute to the aircraft, got in, started up, taxied out, swung onto the runway and opened the throttle. No sooner had the wheels left the ground and I had become airborne on my own once more when, for the first and only time in my life, I froze with sudden terror. All confidence disappeared. My tongue stuck to the roof of my mouth, my movements petrified. 'Oh my God. The engine is going to stop.' I waited for the catastrophe; luckily I had frozen with my hand on the control column in the right position for take-off and climb, and the aircraft was well trimmed. Nothing happened. The engine continued to give full take-off power; we climbed. By the time we got to 800 feet I managed to control myself sufficiently to lift up my wheels and pull back the throttle and pitch from the take-off position. And with the movement fear left me almost as suddenly and unexpectedly as it had come. It did not come again. But now I know why they say if you fall from a horse you should get back on again at once; had I been able to fly straight away after the accident, I doubt if terror would have come to me, but the two weeks in hospital had given my mind a chance to fix firmly its last impression of flying, which was of sudden engine failure and of disaster.

Just before the course ended the powers that be decided to muster most of the aircraft in the neighbourhood for a formation fly-past over Jerusalem to celebrate victory in the desert. I was flying rear centre in a box, fifty feet or so below the man ahead to avoid his slipstream. We went low over the city when suddenly I saw, luckily just in time, a tall and slender minaret looming up the same height as me. It was my only acquaintance with the Holy City of earthly troubles; during the course I had the opportunity for a visit over a weekend but had not taken it, feeling wartime not appropriate and my mood not in keeping. Later and in other times I would perhaps make a proper pilgrimage.

Then the course was over and again no-one seemed to know what our future was to be – except for Pilot Officer Huggins, the son of the then prime Minister of Rhodesia and a nice fellow whom we all liked. Being commissioned he went to join those lords of the air in 680 Squadron whilst we, the non-commissioned rejects, feeding on the rumours of a posting to India, again languished in a transit camp, once more in the harsh desert, this time near Ismailia where we swam in the salt and surprisingly buoyant waters of the great Bitter Lake.

Again we slept in tents amongst the flies though not the flesh pots of Egypt. Here though my companions slept on the desert floor, I was rich, having inherited a very rickety camp bed from a friend who had just been posted away. But I was only able to enjoy my superiority for a few days before a party of so-called friends, led by a New Zealander, who because his name was Steed was naturally known as Horse, came to visit me and all sat on my bed together. Of course it collapsed and thereafter I slept on the same sand of the desert as everyone else, to their satisfaction. It appears a common human tendency to wish to pull down to your own level anyone who enjoys an advantage over you.

Weeks passed before we heard that we were to be posted to India to join 681 Squadron PRU and would sail on the SS *Batory* down the Red Sea during the fierce heat of August. Crowded eight to a cabin, not allowed on deck after dusk for fear that someone might light a cigarette or otherwise inadvertently show a light to a prowling, hunting, hostile submarine, heat is the memory of that journey that abides, heat which even before the time of the noon-day sun drains the colour from the sea, from the shore and from the horizon, turning all to a milky white. The Canadians Nunton and Richards spent the journey playing crap. I was never able to follow the rules of this or of poker, though Nunton offered to teach me both, adding that it would of course cost me something, whereupon I disclaimed anything but academic interest. To play crap you apparently roll two dice around in your hand covering them from exposure to the air, or perhaps to the view, blow on them muttering words of encouragement like 'Come on you beauties, you will do it this time,' and then roll them against the wall of the cabin. In a very short time they would have lost their week's pay; they would then immediately approach their friends for a loan, resume pay and lose that also. As soon as they were paid again, their first action was to repay the money they had borrowed, then promptly proceed to lose whatever they had left at the roll of the dice, and come to you to borrow once more what they had repaid to you only a brief hour before. It seemed a pointless proceeding but their idea of fun was not mine and the Services taught you tolerance even when they were teaching you nothing else.

CHAPTER SIX

India and Burma

At last Bombay and its gateway to India. India pleased us very much. The contrast with Egypt was great; there was even more crowding and bustle, even more beggars and destitution, but none of the aggression, the overt enmity that we had found in Cairo; the hands outstretched for alms were held out in silence, or perhaps a gentle 'Rajah Sahib' to call your attention. Inevitably there was dirt and squalor but people made efforts to keep clean, and wash themselves under standpipes when available. The constant prevailing impression was one of courtesy, of law and order, of a direct descent from some 4,000 years of unbroken civilisation, whereas in Egypt nothing in the manner of the people reminded you of the even older times of the Pharaohs, nor yet of the courtesies of the nomads of the desert. In fairness I must add that Egypt had been close to the war and overrun with soldiery on leave, regrouping, reassembling, and perhaps it was unfair though inevitable to contrast it with a land much more remote from the war and which enjoyed the ordered calm which the British Raj had created during the last two hundred years. Besides I was to be long enough in India to become fascinated by its diversity and its culture.

We were sent briefly to a transit camp at Poona, a name which evoked memories of the Indian Army, and there we were issued tropical gear such as sun helmets which were never worn, for the British troops arriving in the Indian theatre exposed themselves bareheaded and bare-chested to the sun, refusing the helmets and the wearing of flannel next to the skin which conventional wisdom ordained. An elderly gentleman once stopped me whilst walking on a Calcutta street 'My boy I hope you won't mind an old man's advice. But you must in this country never go out without a sun helmet if you want to stay healthy.' But we were none the worse for our hardihood.

Another piece of equipment with which we were issued was a bed roll. This was a splendid invention for which we found the use as soon as we took our first train journey. A canvas cover about seven foot long in which you folded your bedding, sheets, blanket, pillow, and rolled it all up. When night came and it was time to go to bed, you undid the straps and rolled out the bed wherever there was space to lie down. And there already made up and to hand was your bed into which you crawled.

The railway on which we were embarked was broad gauge and the carriages much larger than in England, as was the landscape. English trains and landscape seemed all tidy and all in miniature when I eventually arrived back home at the end of the war. Indian railways seemed well run and organised. It takes several days to travel from Bombay to Calcutta and although more persons might be allowed in each carriage during the day if they were making only a daytime journey, at night only as many persons were allowed in the carriage as there were bunks, when the top racks on each side were let down to make beds. As the carriages were not interconnecting, each carriage had its own WC and shower compartment making it self-contained, preventing one from promenading in the corridor to stretch one's legs and relieve the monotony. That had to await a stop at a major station which was well equipped with a restaurant where one disembarked and took breakfast, lunch and dinner whilst the train waited. Like much in India it seemed a civilised progression, but even so the journeys seemed interminable and I swore to myself after days imprisoned on board a train that I would never again be impatient over an English train journey.

No sooner had we arrived in Calcutta than we were told we could have a few days leave. This would give time for our documentation to catch up with us and because the monsoon was in full flood, covering the earth with immense clouds, aerial activity was at a minimum and the taking of aerial photographs impossible more often than not; and so the squadron was in no hurry to receive us. We decided to try Darjeeling which was the nearest and most accessible hill station, though we were to expect that at its height of about 6,000 feet the days there would be wetter and gloomier even than at Calcutta.

As far as we were concerned the military situation was very quiet. The ease and speed with which the Japanese had overrun Burma in 1942 had taken them by surprise; they had outrun their communications and supplies and they needed time in which to build up their strength for the next thrust, the attempt to conquer India. For their part the British and Indian Armies too needed time to regroup and rebuild their strength, as did the RAF. Ill-equipped and unprepared, we had been overwhelmed by the ferocity of the Japanese, whose mobility in the jungle enabled them to throw road blocks at will behind our troops, unused to jungle fighting and heavily dependent upon their motorised transport and upon the few roads. The enemy too had command of the air, for the Burma theatre came last in priority to the Middle East and to Europe. All agreed that Germany must first be defeated. Thus all the RAF had, in 1942, to meet the Japanese Zeros were a few outdated and inferior aircraft, like the Brewster Buffalo and Mohawk and a few early mark Hurricanes. The saying current amongst the Air Force pilots at this time was 'if you see a Zero twice you will be shot down once'. Thus in a fighting retreat we had abandoned the Burmese plain to shelter behind the mountain shield that runs in a great arc behind the Burma–India border. Here the heavy jungle, the steep-sided hills up to 7,000 feet, the few roads and tracks and generally poor communications in this wild and remote part of the world, the onset of the monsoon and the needs of both sides for a breathing space, had caused fighting to languish.

But behind the mountain shield the British and Indian Armies were learning the new arts of jungle patrolling and mobility, rebuilding morale as well as their numerical strength. The RAF too was building up for the struggle to come. In August 1943, the same month that we had arrived in India, Lord Louis Mountbatten had been appointed as Supreme Commander of the newly created South East Asia Command and though the Burma front continued to be the Cinderella, taking last place behind the other theatres of war, the build-up continued and great effort was put into improving the roads to Manipur, the airfields and the Bengal-Assam railway along which all supplies to the northern front had to come.

Of all this we then knew nothing except that with the monsoon in progress there was no urgency for photographic reconnaissance and we thankfully took ourselves off to Darjeeling with a clear conscience. After the furnace of the Red Sea in August, aboard a crowded and airless troop carrier and then the steamy heat of the Indian plains, we took great lungfuls of the cold mountain air and could see when the weather was clear the plume of snow that blows from the top of Mount Everest. Our young appetites rejoiced too in the fresh food that was available; having breakfasted sumptuously on fresh eggs and half a pound of bacon which we procured from Keventers Restaurant, mid-morning found us again at Keventers drinking warm milk lavishly mixed with honey, discovering afterwards to our disappointment that we had little interest in lunch. Walking by myself through Darjeeling's main street I was accosted by an Indian who tried to sell me an opal necklace and matching bracelet. India was always full of street vendors and this in itself was no surprise though the price of 200 rupees (then about 30 pounds) seemed very cheap. I gazed at these stones, large, brimming with fire and changing colours as you moved them in the light and thought I had rarely seen anything so beautiful. Alas I had no need then for jewellery and anyway I did not have 200 rupees to spare, so did not buy them. Looking back now it seems obvious they must have been stolen and I wonder what great lady, Maharanee or Memsahib, had mourned their loss.

Refreshed, with eager anticipation of enjoying the friendliness and informality of an operational squadron and in high hopes of being at last allowed to take part in the war for which we had trained long and travelled far, we reported ourselves to 681 Squadron at Dum Dum, a large airfield in the outskirts of Calcutta. It was good to see the sleek silhouettes of Spitfires on the ground, together with a few Hurricanes. These we learned were the only Spitfires at that time in the India–Burma theatre and were more precious than fine gold. Their spare parts were at a premium. A story was current, perhaps apocryphal, that a consignment of spares had arrived by sea from the Middle East, preparatory to the arrival of Spitfire fighter squadrons which were to follow, but an equipment officer at Bombay, knowing there were none but the PRU Spits in the country, decided a mistake had been made and sent them back again. However true that may be, the spares that the squadron had were jealously guarded; when a Spitfire fighter squadron arrived a little while after we did, and its Commanding Officer came to visit us to see what he could borrow, he was invited to inspect our empty stores building, for our spare tyres, wheels and other consumables had been taken out and hidden in the long grass before he came.

Our reception at 681 Squadron was characterised by indifference. We were marched in to meet the Commanding Officer, Wing Commander Wise DFC and Bar, who was friendly enough; a kind and gentle person we thought him, but we were not to see him again until we were on the brink of our departure, for the Flight Commander and the rest of the pilots, all commissioned officers, seemed curt and not over-friendly or helpful. We concluded that the nature of PRU work when the pilots flew alone on their sorties led inevitably to jockeying for position, to the jealous search for the best aircraft and the favourite sorties and to the inevitable competition for medals, which effectively precluded the forming of team spirit and a happy atmosphere; this had not been apparent during our brief stay at 541 Squadron at Benson in far-off Oxfordshire but presumably any such tendency had been overcome by the vivid and outgoing personality of the Squadron Commander.

Poor Nunton and Richards received short shrift and were rapidly posted away – where, we never knew – as being unsuitable persons to stay on the squadron and risk their lives for King and Country; Nunton's log book was embellished with drawings and fanciful accounts of his exploits; Richards' lifestyle was devoted to drink and to the conquest of women, following whatever sexual fantasy occurred to him; neither were considered reliable and indeed anyone whose life in an emergency had depended upon the steadfastness or loyalty of either of them would likely have been out of luck. We did not miss them, though their departure reduced those of us who had been together since the navigator training at Squires Gate to three: Ken Draycott, Ru Smith and me. It was company enough, together with the NCO ground staff, whilst the other pilots, all officers, kept themselves apart.

The monsoon was still diminishing activity in the air, though on two occasions I was allowed local flights in one of the old Hurricanes to familiarise myself with the surrounding terrain. On the second occasion I ran into the worst monsoon weather, when clouds mounting up right from ground level to over 30,000 feet barred my way back to Dum Dum; I could neither climb over nor fly under them and was forced to go round them, landing eventually at Jessore, some 50 miles north-east of Calcutta which was occupied by the American Air Force. As I taxied in to dispersal, parked the aircraft and switched off, a mechanic came up:

'Gee, what kind of aircraft is this?' he said.

Still sitting in the cockpit I said it was a Hurricane.

'My, I've never seen one like this before. Mind if I have a look?'

And before anything more could be said he pulled a screwdriver out of his pocket and removed one of the panels covering the engine which he examined with deep professional interest. They were kind and hospitable of course. I was fed and given a bed for a very wakeful and uncomfortable night, for they had no mosquito nets such as we always slept under in India; instead I was given a bottle of some substance to rub on myself to keep insects away, a lotion which seemed to need renewing every half hour or so, and even when it did keep the mosquitoes away it did not stop them singing all night at a distance of about six inches away from my ear drum. 'If I were God, I would not have made mosquitoes,' I thought to myself. Soon after first light the weather cleared and I took myself thankfully back to Dum Dum.

* * *

On 27 September I flew my first photographic sortie, a fairly short mission to take a mosaic of the Kaledan River area in the Arakan. I did not then know that in November the 81st West African Division were to start making their way down the road-less forest of the Kaledan River valley to guard the flank of the next and soon-to-be-launched offensive down the Burma Arakan coast to which it runs parallel, separated by the Mayu range of precipitous jungle clad slopes. 81 Division were to be supplied entirely by air. I was able to cover most of the area before being defeated by gathering cloud and decided to return by flying the reciprocal course to the one that had taken me to the target area. The technique of flying a compass course was to rotate the movable grid ring of the compass to the course and turn the aircraft so that the compass needle lay between the parallel lines across the compass face. Above cloud and being unable to orientate myself from the ground I did this; five minutes later I looked again at the compass and saw to my horror that I had set the compass needle the wrong way round and that instead of heading for home I was flying further and further into Japanese territory. I hastily turned 180°for home. Luckily the sky remained empty of offence and I thankfully reached Chittagong and refuelled.

These PRU sorties from Dum Dum were exhausting affairs. Between Calcutta and Chittagong, at the head of the Bay of Bengal, lies an alluvial floodplain where the many mouths of the mighty Ganges and Brahmaputra rivers came out to the sea – the Sunderbans, more than two hundred miles across, a flat land of swamp and plain and water. An early morning start and an hour and three-quarters flying time at a fairly low level to Chittagong, where one landed and refuelled. PRU pilots who were called on to make long journeys in single-engined aircraft were always most conscious of their fuel supplies, never losing an opportunity of topping up. By the time the aircraft had been refuelled the heat of the day would be on us, but as soon as possible we would be airborne and into our sorties over Burma; another two or three hours flying requiring intense and unremitting concentration to find the targets, avoiding enemy fire and aircraft; then back to Chittagong to refuel once more; then without losing time take off again immediately for home, for the photographs were urgently awaited at Dum Dum where they would be developed forthwith, analysed by the Intelligence Officers and operational decisions taken at once on what they might reveal.

But it meant seven or more hours away, from early morning until late afternoon, in a very hot and humid climate, without food or more importantly water, and no opportunity to ease oneself, the whole time keyed to a pitch of mental and physical alertness and two extra landings thrown in for good measure. Exhausted and in a state of collapse at the end of the day, one pulled the pin out of the straps to release oneself, climbed out of the cramped and narrow cockpit, blessing the absence of noise, vibration and the whirring propeller, thankfully feeling the solid earth beneath one's feet once more. Neither the physical discomfort nor the risk would have mattered had we returned to a happy atmosphere of human warmth and comradeship.

Besides, by the end of September we had only been allowed to fly the aged Hurricanes of the squadron and we felt resentful. We had been thought good enough to fly Spitfires out from England; why now were these being reserved for officers only? Though next month we came to realise that this conclusion was unjustified when we were allowed to fly the Spitfires, the bad feeling remained. Had someone explained that for the first month whilst we found our feet, accustomed ourselves to the local flying conditions and did an easy sortie or two, we would fly the Hurricanes and after that we would be allowed to fly the very precious Spitfires, we would have understood the policy to be reasonable; but nobody did explain and after our rejection in Egypt it rankled deeply.

The Spitfire sorties which we flew in October were even more arduous than the Hurricane ones. True the flying time to Chittagong was reduced to an hour and a quarter but from Chittagong the operation deep into Burma would take four hours or more, the specialised Spitfire Vs with their wing tanks instead of guns having a much greater range; the lack of refreshment facilities at Chittagong continued and one was still exhausted when one climbed out of the cockpit at Dum Dum. 'Whoever shall give you a cup of cold water in my name,' said Jesus3 'shall not lose his reward.' A cup of cold water would have been a gift of great value at Chittagong in the afternoon heat after a four-hour sortie but no-one earned their promised reward. There was a war on.

For my first Spitfire sortie the Flight Commander gave me a summary, curt and dismissive briefing.

'Just the usual round, mainly the airfield targets you know,' he gestured towards the wall map on which the airfields were circled and rattled off a few unfamiliar names which I had never heard before and walked out of the room. I felt hopelessly lost but went over to the map and noted down as carefully as I could the places which I thought he had mentioned. Off I went. It was a good clear day; I found the places on my list without much trouble, though I was surprised by little grey puffs of cloud in the sky at about my height; clouds? No, it's smoke. Gosh, it's anti-aircraft fire; someone is shooting at me, trying to kill me. A sinking feeling in the pit of my stomach. Remote and impersonal it may be but someone is seriously trying to kill me. A strange feeling, but I covered all the targets on my list, weaving a little to throw off the guns when not doing a photographic run and keeping a good lookout for enemy aircraft above and behind me. It was impossible not to think of some of the gruesome stories one had heard about the tortures meted out by the Japanese to those they had captured and especially aircrew; one squadron indeed issued instructions to its pilots to stand by their aircraft if they force landed behind Japanese lines, so their mates could come and machine gun them to save them from the Japanese hostility. This did not apply to PRU who flew alone and had no guns.

Sortie completed I returned to Dum Dum. When the photographs were developed the Flight Commander said to me:

'You didn't take all the targets.'

I said I thought I had taken all those he had told me in his briefing.

'Well you didn't. Oh Christ, now they will have to be done again.'

I said nothing; young and inexperienced, I was not able to tell a senior officer the fault was entirely his for the totally inadequate briefing which had left me floundering. Had I been wiser I would have called him back after the briefing and asked him to go over it again. Now someone else would have to undergo the long hot day of exhaustion and risk because he had not bothered to tell me properly what was required. This was almost the longest conversation the Flight Commander ever had with me. My resentment increased.

For my next sortie I made sure I was properly and painstakingly briefed and I covered all the airfields in northern Burma as far south as Meiktila. I also did a mosaic of Mandalay. There was some isolated cloud about, and over Mandalay I thought I saw an aircraft on my tail in my rear mirror. Must be a standing fighter patrol I said, and immediately did what fighter ace Hesslyn, my instructor at Rednall, had told me to do. I closed the throttle, put the wing over, pulled the stick back into my stomach at the same time opening the throttle and putting the propeller into fully fine pitch, thus kicking the aircraft round into the tightest turn it could do, whilst everything went dark grey as the blood drained away from my head. There was nothing to be seen. Perhaps it had only been my own rudder fin that had momentarily caught my eye as I was turning. But I pulled up into cloud just to be sure. I had my photographs anyway and it was time to go home.

'You found a train at Mandalay,' said the Intelligence Officer to me a little while after I had got back to Dum Dum and the photographs had been developed. 'We think it is an ammunition train.' When next night I heard a radio news broadcast that there had been an air strike on the railway facilities at Mandalay and an ammunition train had been blown up, I felt a modest glow of satisfaction. At last I had made a small contribution towards the war effort.

* * *

Whilst life on 681 Squadron had its ups and downs, I was entranced by India. Whereas in Egypt we had not dared go out onto the streets except in groups, convoys, banded together for protection, what a pleasure it was here to be able to walk the streets alone, without fear of molestation or assault, enjoying the nights of dark warm velvet lit by innumerable fireflies as one walked under the great trees which lined the major roads, or looked at the little shops or bazaars which were open to the street, lit by small oil lamps with the proprietor sitting cross-legged among his wares. There was oriental luxury to be had at the base too, for in the morning many of the senior NCOs would stay in bed whilst the Nappy

Wallah came round with his razor, towel and can of hot water to shave them. To this I never submitted; it seemed a trifle insanitary to be shaved with the same brush, water and razor as everyone else and anyway I always liked to preserve my independence in such matters.

Several times we went to explore Calcutta. The aftermath of the terrible Bengal famine which had begun in May 1943 was still to be seen and people were dying in the streets. There had not been such a catastrophe in British India for very many years; but somehow at the time this made little personal impact. We found it difficult to understand why all these cattle were regarded as sacred and allowed to roam everywhere at will, instead of being slaughtered and eaten. It was explained to us that the people would only eat rice and there was none; but surely we thought if you are starving you would eat meat, even turn cannibal but evidently the taboos which are installed in our early years are hard to break, even when life itself is at risk. The pitiable sights did not stir me emotionally, as ten years on in my career they would have done had such a disaster befallen the district in Africa for which I was responsible. But for these poor folk in Bengal I had no responsibility and my friends and I were entirely concerned with our flying and the daily danger in which we stood.

There was an ugly story current at Dum Dum. A pilot walking to his aircraft had the misfortune to pull by mistake the ripcord of his parachute. Instead of the parachute, out fell a blanket. Doubtless someone's girlfriend would be wearing silk underwear at the expense of some unfortunate aircrew. Imagine baling out from 20,000 feet to discover a blanket where the parachute should be; you would have ten minutes or so of free fall to contemplate your end and curse the infamy of man. Hearing this story I felt tempted to pull my own ripcord (by mistake of course) to see if there was a parachute inside; but then of course it would have to be repacked and one still would not know what was really there. No help for it but to trust one's luck, the discipline and the essential goodness of the nameless others on whose honest and reliable work one's life depended.

A happier tale from Dum Dum was that of the sacred white bull which wandered the airfield at will. No-one must touch or restrain it or there would be a local outcry. This was all very well but the animal had taken to scratching its huge self against the vulnerable aircraft pitot heads. Now the pitot head projected below the wing and measured the velocity of the oncoming airflow in flight, working several instruments, most notably the air speed indicator, without which flying and particularly landing was hazardous, for it is essential to keep the aircraft speed above the stalling point until the moment of touch-down. When the aircraft was parked for the night, a cover, generally green canvas with a red streamer attached, was put over the pitot head to protect it from insects or dust and woe betide the pilot who forgot to check next day before take-off that the cover had been removed. Spitfire spares such as replacement pitot heads being hard to come by, the white bull's need to scratch his back was making no contribution to the war effort whatsoever. Yet the animal must not be molested, impounded or restrained.

A friendly Dakota pilot, who had been flying mules about for the Army, happened to be temporarily at Dum Dum and after being regaled in the mess, offered his help. Under the cover of darkness with as little noise and commotion as possible, the bull was rounded up, pushed, pulled and otherwise coaxed up the ramp into the aircraft which promptly took off for Chittagong. The pilot gave a fictitious call sign to flying control at Chittagong, announced his intention of landing, refused to answer further calls for information from flying control, taxied to the end of the runway, and keeping his engines running, let down the ramp and discharged the bull, turned round and took off again forthwith, leaving flying control to sort out this mysterious behaviour as best it could. Meanwhile back at Dum Dum the local Hindu population was equally mystified at the sudden and total disappearance of the white bull. It had vanished into thin air. There was no evidence that it had been killed or in any way ill-treated. It just suddenly was not there. Those in the squadron who had taken part in this venture were tight lipped except among themselves and presumably the news of what had happened never got out. What happened at Chittagong, whether the aircraft there were molested by a white bull which had arrived suddenly out of the blue, or whether the animal wandered off and made himself at home elsewhere we never knew.

* * *

681 Squadron remained a disappointment to the three of us and we had little pleasure or satisfaction in our life there. So when towards the end of September a notice was circulated asking for volunteer pilots to serve

on 28 Squadron, we all applied. Forthwith we were marched in to see the Commanding Officer, Wing Commander Wise, who had been kind to us when we arrived.

'I see the three of you wish to volunteer to fly with 28 Squadron,' he said. 'Do you know anything about it?'

'No, sir.'

'Well, it's a tactical reconnaissance squadron. Whereas our work on PRU is mainly strategic, concerned with the overall movement and direction of the war, Tac/R is always in close cooperation with the Army; the eyes of the XIV Army they are sometimes called. You will fly Hurricane 2s with long range tanks, which you flew here when you first came, cumbrous brutes compared with the Spitfire Vs as you well know. You will do some photographic work, so your training there will not be wasted, but it will be mostly verticals from about 5,000 feet, at which height you will attract ground fire, and also some obliques. But most of the work will be low level visual reconnaissance, at tree top height, looking for enemy patrols or columns in the jungle, or locating our own troops, dropping them messages or spotting for the artillery. The squadron operates always in the forward areas, as close as possible to the front line, and at present they are working in very bad flying country, jungles and steep mountains, dangerous enough in good weather but sheer murder in the monsoons. It is very highly dangerous work and they have many more casualties than we do. That is why they only take volunteers. After having told you that, are you still sure that you want to go?'

'Yes Sir,' we said in unison.

He tried again. 'You should also know that you will be living rough, generally under canvas, sometimes perhaps spending your nights in a slit trench for fear of Jap patrols and your rations will only be similar to the basics which the front line troops get. As well as doing very dangerous work, you will find it all very uncomfortable. Now here at Dum Dum you have all the pleasures and diversions of Calcutta on your doorstep, you are housed in permanent buildings and you can sleep sound o'nights. Your work is not too onerous, only a few sorties each month whereas on 28 Squadron you will be flying every day and perhaps several times a day. Here as you know the Japs have no aircraft which can match our PRU Spit Vs, their ack-ack fire at height is not too accurate, and your chances here of survival are very much higher. Are you still sure you want to go?'

'Yes Sir.'

'Then perhaps you will tell me why. Is there anything wrong with this squadron which is making you unhappy?'

We did not reply.

We should have told him about the lack of friendship, the cold atmosphere, the jealousies among the pilots, the way in which we NCO pilots felt ostracised so that we were not part of the squadron which, apart from its treatment of NCO pilots, had little cohesion or fellow feeling even amongst the commissioned aircrew. But we remained silent and I was sorry that we did, for it might have helped him to know. There was a long-standing tradition that one did not volunteer such information in case it led to reprisals of one sort or another and we had no wish to be telling tales out of school. If only the Flight Commanders had talked to us as had the CO we should never have wished to leave.

'Very well then,' he said after the silence had deepened, 'I won't stand in your way. Off you can go. But don't say that I didn't warn you. Now I suppose you can have a few days' leave before you make your way to the Burma front. You are not likely to get any more time off for a long while.'

We thanked him and we marched out of his office, remembering him as the only kindly, friendly person on the squadron, and as one who had treated us as human and not as something the cat had brought in.

So we said goodbye to 681 Squadron and took our offered leave. Darjeeling we had already tried; this time we thought we would make for Naini Tal, another Himalayan hill station, further away, where the town is built alongside a lake cupped in hills, with an open square at the north end and a crowded bazaar area at the south end, a walk and bridleway between the western side of the lake and a wooded hillside, the town being on the east side. To get a view of the majestic mountains you walked out of the hotel and mounted the hills which surrounded the lake.

We arrived in the early afternoon. Strolling round the open plaza at the north end of the lake, we encountered a group of sleek looking, lively ponies for hire. Neither Draycott nor I had ridden before and there was no time like the present. In the square was a bandstand with a brass band preparing for its afternoon performance. No sooner had I uncertainly seated myself in the saddle when the band struck up with a mighty blare of trumpets and wind instruments. The horse bolted. I lost reins and stirrups and clung desperately to its mane as it set off at a gallop across the square and down the wooded ride at the western side of the lake. It seemed like flying in an open cockpit with the air rushing past but not nearly so safe. Round the bottom of the lake we clattered as the hooves struck the tarmac surface into the open stalls of the bazaars, scattering the shoppers, before the foolish horse decided to slow its errant course. Rather shamefacedly I returned the animal to its owners, but no such disaster had struck Ken Draycott who was trotting round as to the manor born. 'What a beautiful seat your friend has,' said one of a group of nursing sisters, also on leave. 'I suppose it looks more prominent when seen on a horse,' I replied, 'but normally I wouldn't have thought it more beautiful than anyone else's.'

That evening Ken spent in the company of one of the nursing sisters. When I asked him how he had got on he replied in his loftiest manner, 'We both decided it was too beautiful an experience to discuss with anyone else.' Meanwhile I had teamed up with some American pilots, also on leave, who had been flying over the Hump. Operating from Ledo in the far east of Assam, they had been flying Dakotas or DC3s over the Himalayas to Kunming, the only way the Allies could get supplies to Chiang Kai Shek so that he could continue his war against the Japanese. The supplies had to get to Ledo over the same narrow-gauge Bengal-Assam railway as the supplies to the XIV Army at Imphal. Once at Ledo they were loaded onto Dakotas, such a wonderful workhorse of an aircraft, and flown across the highest mountains in the world and in the worst of weathers. Gallant indeed were those pilots, coaxing the last ounce of effort from their overloaded and highly taxed machines. It was they who taught me the little ditty about Cocaine Bill and Morphine Sue, long before we had an inkling of the drugs problem which besets the modern world. As far as I remember it went like this to a catchy little tune:

> Oh Cocaine Bill and Morphine Sue
> Were walking down Fifth Avenue
> Oh Honey have a sniff, have a sniff on me,
> Honey have a sniff on me.

> From Old New York to the State of Maine
> They went in search of more cocaine,
> Oh Honey have a sniff, have a sniff on me,
> Honey have a sniff on me.

They came to a drug store painted green
Which hung a sign 'No more morphine'
So Honey have a sniff, have a sniff on me,
Honey have a sniff on me.

Now in a graveyard on a hill
Lies the body of Cocaine Bill,
And in the grave right by his side,
Lies the body of his morphine bride.
Oh Honey have a sniff, have a sniff on me,
Honey have a sniff on me.

The moral of this story is plain to show,
There ain't no sense in snuffing snow,
So Honey have a sniff, have a sniff on me,
Honey have a sniff on me.

I was no doubt better occupied learning this highly moral little ditty than I would have been spending the night with a nursing sister, but I owned to a little jealousy. I was always shy with women, did not know the ropes and despite having been brought up with two sisters, lacked all confidence in the matter, envying the success of my more accomplished friends, especially in India where compared to the numbers of male troops, women were in short supply and where sexual prowess and opportunity were a staple of the conversation amongst one's peers.

It was only a brief stay we had at Naini Tal and it was back to Calcutta to embark on the next long train journey into Assam. My birthday was fast approaching and on the day before, far off in England my mother was thinking of me and was prompted to give me the best birthday present possible by writing to Jonathan to give her news of me, to explain that even my letters home were very infrequent and that apparently I wrote to no-one but her and my father, for all my brothers and sisters complained that I never answered their letters. If she did not hear from me it did not mean that I did not care for her. My leave the previous Christmas had been on a 'standby' basis and I had been expecting a telegram of recall at any moment, so could not leave home. 'I know he is fond of you,' she added, 'but he thought his immediate future so full of danger and his prospects uncertain, and this accounts for his apparent casualness. There is rather too much of the Sir Galahad about Geoffrey. Perhaps his experiences will harden him a bit. I hope all this doesn't bore you, but I felt sure you would be interested to hear of him and I know he would be delighted to hear from you. He loves having letters even if he cannot write often.'

My mother's letter caused Jonathan herself to write to me, saying she had not done so before for she thought I did not want her letters, describing how she had written and torn them up, telling me of mutual acquaintances now, like me, in India, and ending with a pen picture of the autumn woods near her home. She followed this letter within a few days by a Christmas Greetings message: 'A very, very happy Christmas and all the luck in the world for the New Year. I am hoping for your return and hope it will be in the not too distant future. Take care of yourself and have a good time. All my love and thoughts, Jonathan.'

These letters reached me together at Imphal, just before Christmas, when in fact I was having a good time, in ignorance of what lay just ahead when surely all the luck in the world which my lady had wished for me was indeed mine and was sorely needed.

* * *

Meanwhile the journey, from Calcutta to Dimapur in the Assam valley at the foot of the Naga Hills, was uncomfortable and seemed never-ending; a more than 600-mile journey, along a railway which had been constructed just to serve the Assam tea gardens, with a daily capacity of only 600 tons. It was now carrying 3,000 tons each day, but even this was greatly less than the need for supplies to the front at Imphal, to the Chinese forces led by General Stilwell who was pressing down into Burma via Ledo and to the Americans who were flying supplies to China 'Over the Hump' of the huge Himalayas. For the first 235 miles the railway was broad gauge; thereafter hordes of coolies would offload the wagons and transfer everything to the waiting metre-gauge train. Two hundred miles later on, when a river had to be crossed, coaches and wagons were uncoupled and pushed onto barges. Once over they were coupled up again; at last after another slow 150 miles the train reached Dimapur. It was a journey to be endured, not enjoyed and we envied the Gurkha Regiment travelling with us, whose little men at each of the very frequent stops would run up to the engine driver and beg boiling water to brew tea. We could have done with some ourselves.

Eventually we stretched our weary selves when we reached the transit camp at Dimapur.

'Welcome to Penis Park,' said the tired old warrant officer in charge of arrangements.

'What are you talking about?' we asked.

'When you've dumped your kit, just go and look around you. These people worship the penis you know, have little models of it in their temples and houses, offering it fruit and flowers and even say their prayers to it. Disgusting I call it,' he said with some relish.

So we found our beds, dumped our kit and strolled round the camp. Sure enough there were columns of marble phalli, I suppose ten or twelve feet high, interspersed every now and then with V shaped blocks to represent the female sex organ; they must have covered an acre or even more. We gazed in wonder and disbelief; doubtless this should be a historical monument; what old rajah, we asked ourselves, lusting after the vigour of his vanished youth had created such a monument to his passion? We did not know then of the great god Shiva, the Lord of Creation and Destruction, he to whom the white bull we had transported from Dum Dum was especially sacred; Shiva whose most evocative representation I was later to find was as Nataraja, the Lord of the Dance, in which, surrounded by flames, he dances the cosmic dance of death and renewal, of evolution and decay; the flames destroy, purify, create the ash from which new life springs. In the hand of one of his four arms he holds the fire, in another he beats the drum of creation and renewal, the third hand is raised in reassurance and the fourth points downwards in a gesture of the giving of energy. The right foot tramples down the demon of ignorance and the left swings in the air in the rhythm of the dance. Continually the generations pass before him as he dances their cycle of birth and death and birth again, of decay and renewal and again decay, with the purifying flame and the throbbing drum, the endless dance from the beginning of time to its last finish when all things shall fall silent. A powerful and haunting image indeed. One of Shiva's symbols is the erect phallus, symbolising the creative power of the universe and as such it is the object of veneration. But none of this we knew as we stared and marvelled at these marble ranks of curious columns.

When we woke next morning our minds were on other things. There before us, crushing the skyline, were the towering Somra and Naga Hills; maps of them for flying, which we were given later, showed white patches marked 'Unsurveyed'. Jungle clad, steep, inhospitable, often blanketed with cloud, we were to become familiar (though never friendly) with them in the months ahead. This was part of the mountain shield to which our Army had retreated from Burma eighteen months before, and through this country wound the road to Imphal, rising to 5,000 feet with peaks of 9,000 feet towering over it. Since the retreat, the tea planters of Assam had supplied IV Corps at Imphal with 70,000 labourers who with pick, shovel and basket had improved the roads from Dimapur to Imphal and from Imphal south to Tiddim and Fort White and from Imphal to Tamu, which would give us access back into central Burma through the Kalewa gap on the River Chindwin. Along these roads, now all weather and largely metalled, came all the supplies for the Imphal front. The scenery was no doubt wild, forbidding and superb, though this day, packed tight beneath the canopy of a 3-ton Army truck, we saw little of it. Halfway along the road we passed Kohima, a pleasant hospital hill station and a district headquarters for some lucky administrative officer, a place of cool refreshment where roses grew. Later, from the air we were to know it well.

From then on, the road wound down hill to the Manipur gap where the river bursts from the hills to the plain of Manipur and the township of Imphal. After the discomfort of the day's journey, confined to the truck, we found ourselves again in a transit camp. The night was cold and the beds, made of lengths of bamboo six inches apart and without mattresses, were instruments of torture rather than repose but at least they kept us off the ground beyond the reach of tick, snake and scorpion. Huddled on these racks, wearing all our clothes and blankets we passed a sleepless night, and when we got up in the morning the ground was white with frost whilst the air sparkled diamond fresh. We had come at last to Imphal plain, 2,600 feet above sea level, oval in shape and 650 square miles in area, with the centre covered in a large reedy lake full of wildfowl. As far south as we could see, the land was flat; around us near at hand towered the high hills. By mid-morning the frost had gone and we could have sunbathed. By common consent, we all thought that we had come to Shangri-La, that dream valley of the Himalayas where all life is in harmony with itself and where age does not weary.

'This is the best squadron in the RAF and I intend to keep it so,' said Henry next morning when we went in to see him. Squadron Leader Henry Larsen, Commanding Officer of 28 Squadron, was then twenty-eight years old. A man of middle height, with fair hair, pale blue eyes and a big hooked nose, he had a mercurial, emotional temperament allied to a quick mind and he was devoted above all else to the well-being and efficiency of all ranks of his squadron, which earned him wide respect. Affectionately known as Henry by all ranks behind his back, he was called Henry to his face by his friends amongst the pilots and certainly by most of the officers, for although he enjoyed his authority he was also eager for affection. He claimed to have been a stockbroker before the war; 'stockbroker's clerk more likely' said the knowing.

'You boys have joined the squadron at a good time, for the rains have just ended, flying conditions are good and you will have a good opportunity to learn the skills of this job before things start to build up militarily, as they are likely to do before the end of the dry season.

'Let me explain some things about the squadron. We have been called the eyes and ears of the XIV Army and we work very closely with 4 Corps HQ which is just on that hill behind the airstrip, together with 221 Group. There is mountainous jungle over all the area of our operations and intelligence of the enemy's movements is hard to come by, especially since he likes to move at night to avoid us. It is our job to let the Army know what he is up to and how the various tracks in these wild hills are being used. Often we get requests for photographs of particular areas, sometimes verticals, sometimes obliques and you PRU boys will be good at that, though we share out the work equally amongst the pilots of the squadron and you will get your turn along with everyone else, specialist photographers though you may be, though an exceptionally important job might come your way. Much of our work is simply the examination of the ground behind enemy lines to keep an eye on troop movements, but we may be asked to do other jobs as the Army needs; perhaps dropping parcels of letters or messages or medicines to cut-off or distant units, some of which may be operating behind enemy lines. Or we may be asked to spot for the guns, directing artillery fire onto a target – this too needs a bit of practice, but you will soon get it.

'I know the three of you have been together for a while but I shall have to split you up; Draycott and Guy will go to A Flight and Smith to B Flight, which has just come up from detachment at Cox's Bazaar down in the Arakan where they have been very busy. But we are lucky at this quiet time here, for we have the airstrip very much to ourselves, apart from No. 1 Squadron Indian Air Force, which is also Tac/R, and indeed you will have to take your turns as duty pilots in the control tower from time to time.

'We always fly operations in pairs, one to work and one to watch, number one who does the work with his eyes on the ground, and number two who watches the sky and keeps his eye on number one who cannot watch out for himself. You will generally fly with the same person with whom you will develop a close understanding, but of course you may have to fly with anyone. We don't make any distinction in the air between Officers and NCOs; you will each get equal turns to lead a sortie and fly as number two – everything of course being subject to operational requirements and I can only tell you of our general rules.

'There is one thing more that it is important to tell you. This work is very dangerous and we have a high casualty rate. We have a saying on the squadron that there are only two kinds of reconnaissance pilot, the quick and the dead. That's why we always ask for volunteers and each and every one of our aircrew has volunteered for this work. Not all pilots are good at it, and if you are no good I shall get rid of you. If you are good and fit in with everyone, you can stay as long as you want. But remember, the moment you feel that you want a break, or you feel that your nerve is going, or your luck is running out, let me know and I will send you off at once. Now that's a long speech for you. Good luck and enjoy yourselves.'

We stepped out joyous into the sunshine; could this really be the squadron that we had all longed to join after so much disappointment along the way? We made our way down to the flights to meet the company with whom we would share so much in the months ahead. Our total strength was about thirty-two pilots in all at any one time, approximately sixteen in each flight, most of whom were commissioned, but with a good sprinkling of NCOs. On A Flight there were the two Canadians, warrant officers Sam Walker and Chuck Watt, Sam rather quiet and reserved, Chuck short, ebullient and outgoing; very much a complementary couple who always flew together and shared a close understanding both in the air and on the ground. There was Flight-Sgt Nigel Sinclair-Hill, a charming young man of leonine appearance, much of whose childhood had been spent in India and who, like Ken Draycott, had been an artist before he joined up; Nigel had specialised in painting stage scenery. There was a tall and willowy young man whose name was Wilde, so was inevitably called Oscar, and there was me, an Oxford student whose interests were largely in history, literature and poetry.

We were ordinary young men, of a similar age and background, sharing common conditions and a common purpose; nothing evidently heroic about any of us; yet – bind them to you with hoops of steel, these companions of yours with whom you break bread. Your life will be in their hands, as theirs will be in yours as you fly over enemy territory. Their kindness and courage will buoy you in rough waters and their humour lessen the impact of fear, danger and hardship. You will feel for them a love greater than the love of women, as between David and Jonathan, for there is a very special relationship between men in a war band, as there has been from the beginning of time. 'We few, we happy few, we band of brothers, For whoso sheds his blood this day with me, Shall be my brother,' says Shakespeare's Henry V before Agincourt. And with your brother, your comrade in arms, you will feel that you can go to the end of the earth, for your confidence and trust in him is without limit. Then when the fighting quickens and your friends fall, you will grieve with a sorrow as intense as was your love.

As NCOs we shared a basha – a long house traditional in the Naga Hills – built of sticks and mud with a thatched roof, still carrying the soot from fires which previous occupants had lit, a house into which extra windows had been let. It was roomy and comfortable, a mile or more away from the airstrip. Down on the flights on the airstrip the accommodation was in both bashas and tents, at various times, and there the camaraderie continued amongst officers and NCOs alike; soon we were all on first name terms, for in our work of operational flying we were all equal, using the same machines and entering into the same dangers. But with the officers our friendships were inevitably less close, because when work was done they ate and drank and rejoiced in a separate place.

Our Flight Commander was Flight Lieutenant Jack Wales. Like Henry Larsen he was twenty-eight – far too old, both of them, for this job we thought in the arrogance of our twenty-two or twenty-three years – a lean Lancashire man with an engineering background and a red wrinkled face, who was kindness itself.

'You boys coming to the Army film show in Imphal tonight?' he asked us shortly after our arrival.

'No, sir,' we said, puzzled. 'It's for officers only.'

'Oh don't be so silly,' Jack replied in his high pitched voice and with his characteristic grin. 'You *are* a bunch of innocents. What do you think they've given you Irvin jackets for? Nice anonymous Irvin jackets, which you'll need to wear these cold and frosty nights.' And for that too we would have followed Jack to the end of the world. Dear Jack Wales. Had he remained A Flight Commander for the next six months my lot might have been easier.

One morning he drove up to the flights in a brand new American Willys Jeep with which as Flight Commander he had just been issued. A great acquisition of which he was inordinately proud, and he spent several minutes showing it off to his admiring pilots. Shortly after he took off on a short sortie, and we, having nothing to do whilst waiting for more demands for sorties to come in from the Army, decided we should teach Nigel Sinclair-Hill who was the only one of us who could not drive a motor vehicle. So we sat him in the driving seat and showed him how to start the engine, put it into gear and release the clutch. 'Like this?' Nigel said, and the vehicle gave a great leap forward and landed in the middle of a clump of bamboos. Shortly after, Jack returned and having been debriefed by Major Taffy Hughes, our Army liaison officer, came out of the tent to find a group of abashed and shamefaced pilots and the jeep in a thicket. No word said, no question asked, withdrawn brow and compressed lips, he gave us such a look as though to turn us to stone, got into the jeep and by skilful manoeuvring for several minutes, managed to extricate it, still serviceable and not much damaged after all. Still no word said, except by us who said we were sorry, and that we had only been trying to teach Nigel to drive. Five minutes later Jack was his old humorous whimsical self again. The incident was closed. But Nigel never did learn to drive on that, or indeed any, vehicle.

* * *

Taffy Hughes was a short, broad Welshman who had been a rugger player of distinction and who was very popular with us all. Ru Smith and I, who shared memories of our rugger matches at Squires Gate, had conversations about having a team in this delightful secluded valley of Imphal but concluded that the ground would at present be so hard that we might injure ourselves in a tackle; we would have to wait until the rains. Taffy agreed. It was Taffy together with the Flight Commander who gave us our briefings before we flew and was usually there to debrief us when we returned. When the first briefings of the day were done and the first sorties airborne, following the dawn sorties which had been organized overnight, Taffy would get into his jeep and take himself off to the 4 Corps HQ on the nearby hill, to keep himself informed of the latest military position and to receive requests for new sorties, for information on this track or that, for photographs of one place or another, or material to be dropped in some forward position, or artillery fire to be directed – spotting for the guns it was called – and back he would come with the Army instructions as to what was wanted. He would tell us what we needed to know to carry out a particular task and the disposition of our patrols in that area, but rarely did he or the Squadron Commander (if indeed he himself knew) give any hint of the Army thinking or of overall strategy; the less we knew, the less we could betray if we fell into enemy hands and were tortured.

These were halcyon months at Imphal, from November 1943 until March 1944, golden days when the sun shone warm and the nights and early mornings at our altitude were crisp and cool, with frost on the ground. Apart from dust haze over Imphal Plain, flying conditions were good; it was thrilling to fly down the steep jungle clad valleys, twisting and turning, reconnoitring tracks, trusting one's luck in being able to clear the hills at the end of the valley, or else have room to turn round and go back the way one came. A time of laughter and comradeship, with sufficient excitement and a constant hint of danger, which had not yet become a menace, to keep us on our toes and sharpen our enjoyment of the passing days. It was good to be alive and to be a member of this 28 Squadron.

We did not then know, for neither Taffy nor anyone else had told us, that these months were a breathing space for the opposing armies; in 1942 the Japanese in conquering Burma had outrun their supplies and communications, they had needed a quiet time to build up their strength for an assault on India; whilst on their side, the British and Indian Armies needed to come to terms with the reasons for their defeat and learn the techniques of jungle warfare, and they too needed to build up the railway to Dimapur, improve the roads to Imphal and beyond and build airstrips in the Imphal valley from which to launch the attack to drive the enemy from Burma. We guessed that our attack would be through the Kalewa gap where, about 100 miles south of Imphal, the tributary Myitha River had cut a valley through the hills to join the Chindwin. There had been a peacetime crossing of the river at Kalewa and it was through there that the XIV Army had retreated the previous year.

The other way back into Burma was along the coastal strip of the Arakan. There also the Army had built up a striking force and had launched an attack without much success at the end of 1943. Widely separating the Arakan and Imphal fronts was a high, broad range of mountains which swept around Imphal Plain until it reached the mighty Chindwin River which was the effective boundary between the enemy and ourselves. There was much patrol activity on both sides in the mountains between Imphal and the Chindwin and in the jungle-clad Burmese Plain on the other side of the river, both sides crossing it to explore, to obtain information and to test the enemy dispositions, both sides becoming poised for attack in strength.

*** *

On my first sorties I flew as number two to one or other of the experienced squadron pilots, whilst I learned the techniques of tactical reconnaissance and I see from my log book that the first was to the area of Fort White where 17 Indian Division held the heights commanding Kalemyo and the Kalewa gap, and the sorties following were along the villages bordering the Chindwin. Very soon Ken Draycott and I teamed up, taking turn and turn about to lead the sorties. He was a much more daring pilot than I was, flying lower and taking risks which I avoided; flying a little higher at a more comfortable level I maintained I saw more and brought home more information. Once flying in the squadron Harvard together to practise instrument flying, Ken did a flick roll at circuit height, which was his idea of fun but not mine.

Off duty Ken would get out his sketch book and charcoal and set to work; once he drew me and asked if I thought it was a good likeness. 'Not much,' I replied. 'Oh, thanks very much,' he said, offended. I hastily added that I thought it a very good drawing but that it flattered me and I was not as good-looking as he seemed to think. But I did like it and could I please keep it? Whilst he was painting or drawing, I would read my Oxford Book of English Verse which was my constant companion. Frequently we would have long conversations on serious subjects, often religious, for his mind would turn that way; subconsciously, underneath our flippancies and sometimes coarse humours, the risks which we daily took made each one of us sensitive, when we cared to admit it, to such issues as the purpose of life, the significance of death, and why we or the world should have been made. Apart from drinks in the evenings and the occasional singing of bawdy songs at parties, our lives were very chaste, and though there was a young lady that frequented the camp precincts who was known as 'Do Anna Dekko' because for two annas she would cast aside her sari and give a very brief and momentary glimpse of the flesh beneath, not one of us paid our two annas or had a dekko.

One golden morning we were surprised to see a large white woman, tall and broad, towering over a party of little Naga village headmen from the remote surrounding hills over which we were flying. There were perhaps a dozen of them, perhaps twenty, all clad in their finery. Bead necklaces drooped on their bare brown chests, back kilts with lines of cowrie shells around their hips and plaids of vivid colours hung on their bare copper shoulders. Here and there was sported the red blanket which was the government issued sign of authority. In their hands they carried tall spears. Chattering between themselves with eager interest, they visited each parked aircraft, climbing up on the wings to see where the pilot sat, cooped and cramped, surrounded by his dials, instruments, handles and levers, whilst it was explained to them that in these strange machines which they now saw flying overhead so often, there was a man, and if one crashed in their neighbourhood they should immediately go to the scene to see if they could help and rescue the pilot. If they could, they must of course return him in as good a condition as possible; a procedure with which we were in entire and hearty agreement.

Their patroness and their shepherd was the celebrated Naga Queen, Ursula Graham Bower. We had heard of her. Since the beginning of the war she had been living on her own amongst the hill Nagas, studying their customs and becoming a revered and legendary figure amongst them; indeed, some even regarded her as a goddess. At this time she must have been about thirty years old and was certainly very much at home with this party of headmen whom in a sense I suppose she regarded as her children; she recruited scouts for V Force, an irregular formation which maintained an intelligence network in forward areas and behind Japanese lines, and kept a watch and ward operation over a large area of wild hills and foot tracks that during the Japanese onslaught became the front line south and east of Kohima. Self reliant, self contained and resourceful; a most remarkable woman.

There were many different tribes living in these distant Naga and Somra Hills, almost untouched by western civilisation and only in recent years discouraged from their head hunting habits. During the Japanese incursions they mostly remained loyal to the Allied cause and if sometimes they reverted to head hunting they were not perhaps to be discouraged if the heads were Japanese. In general the hill people of the India–Burma border and of Burma itself remained devoted and loyal, many at severe risk to themselves; not only the Nagas and their related tribes, but the Chins and Kachins and in particular perhaps the Karens; whereas the loyalty of those living in the plains of Burma was not to be trusted, for they would hand you over to the nearest Japanese unit without any hesitation. They knew on what side their bread was buttered even if the hill people did not. It is difficult to blame them, for the Japanese were ruthless and severe in their reprisals and were in strength on the plains, but were less evident in the hills. Besides, the hill people had until recent times a continuous history of warfare in contrast to the plains of Burma which had been relatively peaceful and secure for much longer. It seemed a poor recompense for the hill people's trust and loyalty when after the war Burma was granted its independence and they were handed over to a government composed of the plains folk who had little knowledge and no sympathy with the hills and their aspirations.

So we all heartily approved of the effort to make us human to the Nagas. Many remote peoples – though I do not believe this to be true of the Nagas – had a habit of castrating foreigners or infidels who fell into their hands. Because of this we all carried what was known as a 'ghouli chit' – a message printed on hard-wearing cloth in several languages and scripts, promising a reward if the bearer of the note was returned intact to Allied hands, and this we all carried as a matter of course.

As well as the ghouli chit, we carried an emergency pack which contained a few Horlicks tablets, water sterilising tablets, a small flat chargal, which was a leather or plastic envelope for carrying water, packed flat when empty and becoming a bottle when filled, two or three fishing hooks and a length of fine fishing line. In addition we also wore a jungle knife – I always carried a Kukri, the Ghurka knife, with which I became very skilled as we spent much of our spare time in practising jungle craft – and a small knife beside; I had as well the small commando dagger which I had strapped to my right calf, a hangover from the fear in my PRU days of the pressure bottle in my dinghy exploding at high altitude and expanding the dinghy which would require puncturing before it filled the cockpit. We would of course always carry a revolver and ammunition; some would even add a Sten gun, together with ammunition for it, as well as a grenade or two, vowing if they were brought down to sell their lives dearly and not attempt to walk back. One pilot, Boris Buckland of B Flight, an old Etonian, was a walking arsenal; a snake was caught and killed and propped up around the entrance to the flight tent, early in the morning before the majority of the pilots arrived. When they did, 'Look Boris a snake' they shouted and Boris, armed cap-a-pie, obliged with a burst of Sten gun fire at the poor dead creature to the amused alarm of everyone nearby. But even without Sten gun and hand grenades there was enough to carry and bestow about the pockets of the green overalls which we wore. We also wore Army boots which we took care to break in and make comfortable for long walking and our trouser legs would be gathered neatly around the tops of our boots, over which and binding in the trouser legs, we would carefully wind puttees and tie them tightly, because these gave excellent and firm support to the ankles, but mostly because the jungle was full of leeches which would fasten on to you anywhere, though of course your legs were particularly vulnerable; sometimes leeches would even find their way through the lace holes of the boots. Once they fastened themselves to you they were best removed, we were told, by the lighted end of a cigarette which would cause them to lose their hold; if you tried to brush them off their heads would be left to fester in your flesh.

As well as the survival equipment and armaments, we had instructions for survival, being issued with booklets, telling how to find game trails which normally follow the tops of the ridges, not to eat unless we had water (in the very unlikely event of finding anything to eat), to travel at night, at dusk and dawn, but with caution along the bridleways, for the Japanese were active at night. But it would be too cold to sleep at night without a blanket or covering unless one could make use of part of the parachute, so the advice was to rest concealed during the heat of the day when sleep might be possible and to walk at night when it was too cold to sleep. Some of what we learned was hard-earned knowledge, gained by pilots who had been brought down behind enemy lines and who had made the journey back. The possibility of having to do likewise was ever before us.

It was early in December when I had my next, and last, accident. The main road from the Assam Plain starts at Dimapur, runs through the mountains to Kohima and enters the Imphal valley following the gap carved by the Imphal River, to which it keeps close. Road and river are thus sandwiched between hills and the airstrip of Imphal Main was sandwiched between river and road, running parallel to the road but a few feet below it. From the airstrip one climbed an earth bank of perhaps ten or twelve feet to reach the surface of the road. The strip had been sited of course in the space available without any thought as to the prevailing wind, and often there was a fierce cross wind blowing from west to east. Normally one had this much in mind and kept a wing down into wind until levelling out at the last moment; after touchdown you needed to remain alert in case the aircraft started to swing. Our Hurricane 11Cs, fitted with long-range tanks, were heavy to handle and ponderous, compared to their agility without tanks. And though the aircraft was without vice in flight, once it started to swing on landing it was difficult to control – impossible unless one corrected the swing at the very moment it started. On this occasion I had returned from a sortie and having made a reasonable landing relaxed my attention. Too late I saw the nose of the aircraft starting to swing towards the bank and the road; desperately I opened my throttle and applied opposite rudder to try to hold the swing and bring the nose round, but it was too late; I swung round, helplessly ground looping until the aircraft struck the bank. It was still travelling at speed, my straps broke and my forehead was thrown against the reflector sight. I switched off the engine, as always in case of fire, staggered out and stood on top of the bank, feeling shocked and desolate, with blood pouring down my face. A few moments later Flight Commander Jack Wales arrived in his precious Willys Jeep and, taking one look at the scene, said, 'Oh Geoffrey, that was our best aircraft. Well I suppose it can't be helped. Hop in and we will get you stitched up.'

Henry Larsen was not pleased. This had happened several times before and aircraft were too scarce to be squandered in this fashion. He issued an edict that the next pilot who was unfortunate enough to swing his aircraft into the side of the road would be forthwith posted from the squadron. And of course it did happen again, only a few days later. The luckless Oscar Wilde, fellow Flight-Sgt pilot of A Flight, was posted forthwith. On all future occasions, the technique was to release one's straps as soon as one had touched down, lift oneself in the seat with one's feet in the rudder pedals and anxiously observe the slightest movement of the nose whilst the aircraft slowed down.

Another skill which we had to learn was that of firing guns. The aircraft were fitted with eight machine guns at this time, fixed to fire forward and set so that the bullets would converge on the target at a distance of 250 yards. Since the guns had a fixed position you could only hit a target when the aircraft was pointing at it; this was all very well in the aerial combat for which it was designed, but hitting a target on the ground was not so easy. Flying at speeds of up to 200 miles an hour, a distance of 250 yards is really very small and it was a matter of nice judgement as to when you had the maximum impact on your target and when you should pull out of the shallow dive in which you were. The interval between the two was very small indeed and many met their end by delaying the pull out a fraction too long. Since the Japanese usually moved at night we found few targets in these days on which to practise our guns, though one instruction we received was to shoot elephants if we should see any on the far side of the Chindwin.

The Companies which before the Japanese arrival had been engaged in extracting teak from the Burmese forests had left behind the elephants which they used extensively in their work, and these the Japanese were putting to use in constructing roads, making road blocks or bridges, towing broken lorries or any other work which a huge and intelligent beast could do. Many said they would refuse to shoot elephant if they saw them; luckily I never saw one, but if I did I think I would have pretended not to see it. War is war, and though I would feel no compunction about shooting at Japanese who in turn would shoot at me and kill me without mercy if they could, to destroy a magnificent, useful and inoffensive animal would be another matter. Perhaps if the occasion arose, I could satisfy my conscience by shooting near it so that it would stampede, and I would only be speaking the truth if I said in explanation that I was not a very good shot, air to ground. But it never happened.

* * *

Christmas was coming; the squadron Harvard was sent back to Calcutta and returned laden with Christmas goodies, mostly drink I suspect. The Scotch whisky ration was only one or two bottles per squadron per month, beer was not obtainable, Indian whisky and rum we thought unpalatable, but Indian gin was available and drinkable, so this we consumed, preferably with fresh lime juice. And we were introduced to the Bun Club. Each component part of the squadron, A Flight, B Flight and maintenance unit, set up its own marquee. I suppose we each contributed so many days' pay to the general kitty, to cover the expenses of a continuous party which started on Christmas Eve, and certainly lasted during Christmas Day and Boxing Day, subject to operational emergencies. My last sortie was on 22 December; the one following was a photo reconnaissance of the nearby Tamu area on Boxing Day. Not a particularly demanding task, nor likely to be a very dangerous one, though that one could never tell, but as I taxied onto the airstrip in the bright morning, slid back my canopy for take-off, put up my thumb to show my companion that I was ready to go and to give assurance and good luck, opened the throttle and went tearing down the runway under full power, I thought I must be young and very fit to be able to fly after two days of partying and being short of sleep on Christmas Eve and Christmas Night. Nevertheless, I told myself, this is stupid. Silly to give yourself a hangover and perhaps slow your reactions should you be bounced by the enemy, or take the wrong decision if something should go awry with your own aircraft, or have to start off the long walk back through the jungle and enemy lines in an imperfect state with your body thirsting for water, all for the sake of a few hours' extra comradeship in the Bun Club, and I reminded myself that I must not do this again. As for now, I will turn on the oxygen and though I shall only be at 5,000 feet and oxygen will not be required, it will help cure my hangover and keep me alert.

Nevertheless such parties for all ranks were good for morale and increased our affection for each other; each Bun Club of course would welcome visitors from other parts of the squadron. So we ate and drank, relaxed and sang songs as we wandered from Bun Club to Bun Club, making and renewing acquaintance.

When we joined the squadron at Imphal Main, we were the only unit there and, as Henry had warned us, we had to take turns at being duty pilot isolated in the control tower with a telephone to the squadron and with one to flying control, which was called Brimstone. We were armed with a Verey pistol, with cartridges both red and green ready to fire if a pilot was making a dangerous approach. When other squadrons joined us in the next month or two, we lost this job as professionals took over.

Then after Christmas we were joined by No. 1 Squadron of the Indian Air Force, also a tactical reconnaissance squadron, who had some brilliant pilots but also many indifferent ones. We were always enjoined to keep operational silence on the R/T, for a pilot might need it in an emergency. And we found their chatter very annoying. There was one incident when an Indian pilot called up his Flight Commander to say his oil pressure had gone off the clock and his radiator was overheating;

what should he do? Whilst his Flight Commander was deliberating, I heard the unmistakable voice of Ginger Wragg, one of our B Flight pilots, cut in 'Just bale out you silly fellow'.

At the beginning of February my squadron sent me down to the other side of the Burma front to brief 81 Division, a West African division, who were about to take part in a thrust down the Arakan. They were newly arrived on the front and were to be supplied by air; my task was to brief them about what help they could expect from air reconnaissance. I spent several days with the division who were very kind to me and I was introduced to Ground Nut Chop (chicken cooked in a soup of roasted ground peanuts) which I had never had before and thoroughly enjoyed. This visit was important to me personally, although I didn't know it at the time, because my commission was to be backdated to then. Presumably, someone thought that if I was fit to brief 81 Division, I was fit for a commission and so they put in a recommendation. When I eventually was commissioned some six months later, it was backdated to the beginning of February; too late to save me from the two months of misery, deprivation and isolation that I was to suffer at Jorhat.

During the first part of February, whilst I was away from the squadron, we lost our beloved Flight Commander, Jack Wales. He was posted away. His place was taken by Arch Guymer, a former school teacher. My log book entries for January had been made by me day by day; Arch kindly added up the totals and signed it for me – very thoughtful of him.

Having rejoined the squadron in mid-February, I was flying as number two to my friend Ken Draycott who was leading this sortie. This was to cover the Chindits who had landed at Broadway some twenty-four hours before. The intention was to drop them letters of instructions as well as take some photographs for High Command to see how their strip was placed.

But I started to become nervous about my fuel supply. Being PRU trained, one was always very particular about one's fuel level; these were long, long journeys which we flew and our fuel supply was not endless. About halfway there, before we reached the target area I said, 'Look, Ken, I am going to have to go back, I am afraid I am running out of fuel.' He said, 'Alright, I will go on and do the sortie by myself.' He went on to complete the mission. I returned having had to turn on my mains, my long-range tanks being exhausted. By the time I crossed the Chindwin River I had to switch onto my reserve which held only twenty-five gallons; to eke this out I was flying with the propeller in fully coarse pitch climbing very slowly to the 8,000 feet necessary to cross the Manipore hills. I can recall my voice echoing in my ear as I called up Brimstone, the controller: 'Hello, Brimstone, hello, Brimstone, this is Pussy Red 2, request-emergency, repeat, emergency, homing.' Every syllable was clear, cold, precise, exactly as I wanted. Brimstone said, 'Just keep your course and height you are now on.' So I did, pressing the fuel button every two or three minutes. I was down to twenty gallons, fifteen gallons, ten gallons, five gallons. I thought well, I am going to have to bale out. I knew that the Japanese were at this time infiltrating through all the valleys, and I recited the 23rd Psalm to myself: 'The Lord is my Shepherd. I shall not want. He makes me to lie down in green pastures; he leadeth me beside the still waters, and though I walk through the valley of death, I shall fear no evil.' I thought, 'Well, I shall get home, however many enemy divisions there are between me and home.' I felt a resolve, an unusual resolve within me like a column of steel building up. I decided I would just clear the top of this hill and then I would jump. My fuel level was nothing. As I opened the cockpit, I had my hand on the pin to release my straps, I cleared the top of the hill and there below me was an airstrip which had just been rolled out of the Imphal valley.

The engine cut out, of course, having run out of fuel and the Palel strip was about 6,000 feet below me, so I just circled the airstrip, losing height and landed with a dead engine, making perhaps the best landing I have ever made in my life. It was only a dirt strip and I came to a halt in the middle of it. A Spitfire pilot came up to me and said to me would I please move my aircraft, because I was blocking the airstrip and they wouldn't be able to scramble. And I said, well, I am sorry, I can't move. I want to go home to Imphal Main, but I can't move until you have put some petrol in my aircraft for me.

'Oh, yes,' the pilot said, 'Brimstone were just asking about you.' I said, 'Well, tell them thankfully I have landed and I am safe.'

Speedily refuelled, I took off again and went back to my home strip at Imphal Main, where I made this time a very bad landing.

Of course I reported the problem I had with this aircraft, and the mechanics examined it carefully, but could find nothing wrong. It was given an air test and a consumption test by another pilot, who again decided there was nothing wrong. It was put again on a sortie but this time never came back.

We had not been asked to do much in the New Year. My log book records only eleven sorties – mostly fairly short ones during January – a meagre total of some thirteen hours. We were well aware the enemy was on the move, preparing to throw his noose around Imphal and again at Kohima. But this was not reflected in our activity. Ominously we waited for them.

At Imphal, the Japanese were getting closer, and their air activity increased. Previously the Japanese Air Force were not often to be seen, they were at the end of a very long supply chain and found it difficult to produce and service their aircraft and provide fuel for them. All the same the Zero were formidable aircraft, very much more manoeuvrable than the Hurricane, and in March or April there was a lot of Japanese air activity and we lost Sam Walker, one of our two Canadian pilots from A flight. They got bounced by a flight of Zeros and Sam was struck down and killed, which was very upsetting. I remember Ken Draycott saying to me, 'Well it can't happen to us though, can it Geoff?'

'No, of course it can't. You know, Psalm 91 says "Thou shall not be afraid for the terror by night, nor the arrow that flyeth by day." No, we shall be alright, Ken. "A thousand shall fall by thy side and ten thousand at thy right hand, but it shall not come nigh thee." No, we will be alright, Ken.'

But I knew as I spoke that it wasn't so, and that neither of us could expect a long life, unless we had an undue amount of luck.

The Japanese were now so close that there were nightly gun battles going on, and artillery were ranging on the hills round us all through the night. We were brought into a sort of covered shelter on the airstrip called Box Sardine. As 5.5 inch guns were stationed just behind and were firing salvoes all night long, the nights were sleepless. It was not very pleasant flying under those conditions.

Then there was an episode when the Japanese broke through onto Imphal plain. Very early on in the battle, they had captured some army trucks and were pouring down towards Four Corps Headquarters. The Headquarters was on a little knoll by the side of Imphal Main Airstrip. Four Corps HQ set our daily tasks and we worked with them very closely. The Japanese were now racing towards the Headquarters and there were no British troops in the way to stop them. They were completely unguarded. I was in my canvas bath when a jeep rushed by with the Squadron Commander shouting out 'All pilots airborne. All pilots airborne'. I wrapped a towel around myself and jumped on the next jeep, but when I got down to the flight I found that I was too late, that all our aircraft had gone to join the other aircraft in the valley, for all the squadrons in the valley had been alerted; we stopped this Japanese incursion dead in its tracks, and destroyed the army trucks. Somebody described how as they shot up a lorry people started jumping out, the bullets hitting them as they jumped and sent the bodies spinning in the air.

If I had had an aircraft, I should have flown with the towel wrapped around me to take part in this. The pilots were just told to follow each other, not knowing what the target was, though obviously somebody knew that the targets were these trucks heading for Four Corps Headquarters. This incursion was highly dangerous flying, with uncoordinated aircraft coming from every direction.

* * *

Flying from Box Sardine was not very comfortable because one didn't have much sleep at night, and next day would probably have to do two, three or four sorties at maximum effort. A day or so later, Ken told me that he wanted to fly with another partner, and proposed to ask for a change. I suppose he found me too cautious a companion, averse to taking the risks he took. I was disappointed and shrugged my shoulders. But then he changed his mind, told me to forget it. In retrospect I wish he had asked for a change, for I should have been spared what followed.

Ken and I had set off on a sortie to Kohima following a trail to a place called Jessami which is at a junction of two valleys, deep in ravines. Ken, seeing a Japanese patrol, went down to shoot them up. We had recently been equipped with two cannon. Our previous armament had been eight machine guns, but now we had been equipped with two cannon in place of four of these. Ken made a run at the patrol, firing at them, but this was the first time he had ever fired cannon. He had not allowed for any recoil, as there was almost no recoil in a Hurricane from firing machine guns, but when you fired cannon there was a noticeable judder, a hesitation in flight. He went very close to his target, the aircraft juddered and this was fatal. He struck his radiator coolant glycol system, which was underneath the engine cowling, on a tree. He called and said, 'I have damaged the aircraft.' As he climbed up to about 1,000 feet, with the engine streaming glycol, he said, 'I have got to bale out.' I was flying close to him but I could think of nothing to say. I was just dumbstruck, horror-struck; all words failed me. I could not even say 'Goodbye and good luck'.

He baled out and his parachute opened, so he got down safely, landing somewhere to the south of Jessami near a ravine. I had the thought that I could land beside him or bale out myself, but then I thought how silly of you, just wasting another aircraft and there isn't much you could do. If there was anywhere to have landed, I would have done so to pick him up, but there was no way, it was all trees, thick jungle.

So I went back to report this to the unit; we had an army intelligence officer with us who briefed me and showed me the routes that the Japanese were taking towards Kohima and he gave me a marked map to drop for Ken, to show which way to go to avoid the Japanese. We had emergency rations which we always flew with, and I took up a spare pack of those, and I took his battledress top which was a heavy garment, because it gets very cold at night. I flew back over the area with a chap called Willy McKilligan, a brilliant pilot, and I found the place where he had crashed.

I could see the wreckage of Ken's aircraft, and his parachute, which had opened and been folded presumably to use as a covering. Ken himself had disappeared. I searched and searched. They used to say you mustn't spend too long on such a mission, lest you just alert the enemy to the disaster. You don't want to attract suspicion. All the same I searched over the thick jungle for as long as I dared, but I could not see any trace of him at all. I thought he would probably have walked along one of the ridges and then turned east to avoid Jessami where the Japanese would be. So I dropped my parcel a few miles along this ridge and waggled my wings to attract his attention. Then I started to fly back, and on my route I crossed a large plateau, heavily wooded as was the whole area. Halfway along this I saw a flash, and my immediate reaction was that this was small arms fire. I took evasive action, kicking a rudder to swing the aircraft. Then I realised what it probably had been; we had been issued with emergency packs with shiny bottoms which could be used to reflect the sun. I guessed that Ken had been flashing his pack at me and it had not been small arms fire at all. The flash of a rifle looks very like it. Alas, I had already dropped my parcel many miles away, far out of Ken's reach if this really had been him.

Ken was never heard of again. I imagine, knowing him and his character, that he walked boldly straight into the Japanese and would not bother to take any evasive action. And I only hope that they finished him off quickly. They sometimes didn't.

Some years later, in the deep jungle in Sierra Leone, I shot a large bird, one of a pair. Its mate circled and circled looking for its companion but could not find him. I was disconsolate, for I had wantonly taken a life, which I could not restore. My mind went back to when I had searched, circling, looking for my lost friend.

Again I would have written to his relatives, but there was no opportunity, for next day we were posted. My flight, A Flight, was moved up to Assam, to a place called Jorhat, so that we could cover Kohima. Jorhat was a strip which had just been rolled out of some tea gardens and its approaches. Kohima was a very wild country and the maps that we had showed large sections of it as un-surveyed, a blank white.

When I had joined A Flight originally there had been half a dozen or more NCO pilots, but by now there was only myself and Nigel Sinclair Hill. He said to me 'Never mind, there are just two of us. I will teach you Hindustani.' I said, 'That would be lovely, Nigel, thank you.'

We continued our sorties from Jorhat. I didn't fly with Nigel, but teamed up with a chap called George Evatt, who was an Australian, the nephew of the Australian Foreign Minister at the time and also a keen cricketer.

Nigel was flying on a sortie over Kohima when he went down from some height, plunging straight into the ground, presumably having been hit by small arms fire. So I never did learn any Hindustani, and Nigel never learnt to drive. Now I was entirely alone as the only non-commissioned pilot on A Flight. There was no flying companion in the evening with whom to exchange reminiscences about the day or discuss prospects for the morrow. This was a dreadful deprivation. Somehow you had to contain, unexpressed, your worries and frustration.

Arch Guymer, Flight Commander, did not know what to do with me, so I was bundled off to spend two nights at a tea plantation near Jorhat. I had left in a hurry, so Chuck Watt flew over to drop some spare clothes which I had had no time to pack. He selected a large, green, flat area in the middle of the lawn; it was, in fact, a lily pond covered in leaves, though there was no way of telling this from the air. The clothes were duly retrieved and dried out. I was given a luxurious bedroom with a large double bed and a fine quality mosquito net. However, I was extremely uncomfortable with my hosts at the plantation. Whatever the intention had been, I was completely ignored. I should have loved to explore, to learn something about the production of tea and its manufacture, but no invitation was given. Perhaps they may have been expecting an officer and not a mere NCO pilot. At mealtimes the couple quarrelled and I felt increasingly unwelcome, an unhappy helpless spectator of domestic misery. I was glad to return to my bleak and lonely A Flight, for Chuck Watt had now been posted away at the end of his tour – dropping my clothes had been his last flight with the squadron.

To cheer me up Willy MacKilligan would frequently challenge me to wrestling matches on the floor of the flight hut, though he was bigger and stronger than me, and he always won. Then Willy also was posted away, to instruct the Fleet Air arm. Another friend gone.

The weather was deteriorating; the monsoon was early this year and getting worse. A monsoon storm is highly dangerous and to be avoided at all costs for it can turn an aircraft upside down, tear its wings off, or spin it like a leaf in a gale. Controls may seize up and instruments go haywire. Yet it was vital to reconnoitre these tracks in the valleys, to see what use the Japanese were making of them. The clouds would now be right over the hills; if you were lucky, you found a gap through them, taking a huge risk of not being able to get out of the valley again. If out of luck you would have to climb through cloud, hoping against hope that you would not hit the hillside. Although it was cold in the cloud, the sweat would be pouring down my face and I would be sucking it off my top lip under my oxygen mask. This was the most arduous and very dangerous flying. You knew very well that you were going to have to do it the next day and the day after that. Every time you took off you thought, as you lifted your wheels, that you would probably never come back: that this might be your last knowing contact with Mother Earth before bequeathing your body to the Manipore Hills. And this went on for long time.

I remember one sortie in the company of George Evatt. I was leading and could not find a way through the clouds. I spoke to George and said it was hopeless, and we must turn back. George suggested that he take over to see if he could find a way through. I agreed and he took over the lead, but cloud was everywhere and very solid; no help for it but to turn back.

Our Flight Commander at A Flight, Arch Guymer, was a very nice fatherly kindly fellow, but he was one of these people who always abides by the rules. Personally, I have always set the rules aside when they seemed to be no longer necessary or not to apply. I was sharing a tent with Flight Sergeant Clarke in charge of A Flight, the senior fitter, who had once worked for Rolls-Royce and knew all about our Merlin engines. We were walking past outside the officers' mess one evening. I heard the voice of one of my friends, saying, 'Look, chaps, we ought to bring Geoffrey Guy into the mess.'

Clarke said, 'I think we are about to overhear something we shouldn't.'

So we walked off. I never was brought into the mess.

***

This was the worst time of my life. The flying conditions day by day were deteriorating. There was no one to talk to at night. The ground crew, who had been my friends for a long time now, were very kind to me. Clarke said that I had been keeping him awake at night because I had been restless and talking in my sleep. I said I was sorry and offered to sleep elsewhere, but Clarke would not hear of it. One night there was a severe storm and the tent, which had not been properly dug out with a surrounding trench, was damaged. All our bedding, goods and chattels were floating in a foot of water. We had to go and sleep on the floor of the mess, an added discomfort. I could have asked for a transfer to B Flight where I had good friends, but the thought never occurred to me. I belonged to A Flight. The ground crew I trusted implicitly. It was my home, my substitute family.

All this time my personal luck continued, my guardian angel shielding me from danger. For we ourselves were a target, mostly of small arms fire and sometimes of machine guns. One often came home with bullet holes in one's wings or fuselage, which were immediately patched up. A Hurricane is of geodetic construction which is really very sturdy. You can patch it up easily as it is fabric covered, and requires just a piece of canvas over a hole with a bit of dope on to cover it. Sometimes, when damage was structural, the struts inside the fuselage could be repaired by lashing in a piece of bamboo.

I was lucky to escape personal injury, though I was struck by spent ammunition several times, mostly in the arms. Spent ammunition is at the end of its range. By the time it hits you it has travelled through part of the aircraft, and fails to penetrate your clothing because it no longer has the velocity to do so.

I never overcame my aversion to killing. At the least, I might not mind shooting at people, when they had been shooting at me. Otherwise I would refrain. I did not use my guns often. I shot at Japanese sometimes at Kohima, when I met a Japanese patrol coming up or going down the road. On one occasion I saw a group of Japanese soldiers on retreat from Kohima. They had no rifles and must have been very hungry. They were about a dozen and sat waiting for death, staring at me. I did not shoot because they were under an overhang of cliff, and I told my number two it was too dangerous. But it was not so in truth, for I could have shot them easily enough. They would die anyway, probably of hunger.

At the end of May, Ru Smith, who was at Imphal on B Flight, borrowed an aircraft and came to see me, making a special journey up from Imphal. I was delighted to see him.

Ru said, 'Look, the Japanese are beat. They are in retreat, and the squadron is going to be pulled out on leave, on rest, because it has been active in the front line ever since 1942. We have applied for leave, Micky Dewing and I, we are going up to Kashmir. Would you like to come with us?'

And I said, 'Yes, I would, very much.'

I applied for leave which, of course, the squadron was only too happy to grant me and off we went to Kashmir, where we took a houseboat. Then after a week or so we found a contractor who organised an expedition for us into the high mountain, hiring carriers and supplying tents, food, a cook and all we needed. We eventually traversed a pass over 17,000 feet high, which was all fun.

When we came back, the squadron had moved to Rachi in Bihar and was on rest. We did a bit of practice flying, but not very much for a couple of months. We formed a cricket team, which I captained as I had played for a representative team at Oxford. George Evatt, the Australian I used to fly with, and I opened the batting. And none of the sides we played against ever got us out. We used to make 150 or so and I would declare. Neither of us bowled, but we had quite a few bowlers and so we won every match. It wasn't very fair. But it was quite fun.

Reminiscing one evening in the mess, Henry said that we had lost ninety-seven pilots in the two years he had spent with the squadron, three times the number of our establishment. The great majority from our squadron, though some had been lost on other squadrons to which they had been posted. Even two thirds of the number was more than twice the number of our pilots. But still they came forward, eager young men in the flush of their youth, avid for the excitement of war, anxious to take their place in the fighting, whereas the more experienced, having buried their comrades, disillusioned, would tend to drop behind. The supply of new pilots seemed inexhaustible.

It was at Ranchi that we hunted a man-eating tiger. I had the end room of a dormitory block and one night there was the spoor of a tiger which locals said was a man-eater. So we took rifles and ammunition from our armoury and waited for it the next night, but it did not come. We gave up, returned the rifles and I went to bed. Suddenly, I awoke: there was a rustling in the room. It must be an animal. I felt for the gun under my pillow, but it was not there – we were on a rest posting, far away from Japanese marauders. I lay awake, wondering if my mosquito netting would deter a hungry tiger and decided it would not. Cautiously, I lifted the netting, found matches by my bedside and struck a light. Two mangy looking dogs were scavenging and ran off. So much for my tiger.

During this rest period I made Ru Smith go home, back to New Zealand and his wife. He had a bad knee, with a damaged cartilage, and would never be able to walk back if he was brought down behind the lines. I persuaded him that New Zealand was crying out for its people to return, for the Japanese were still at their throat. He applied and went off. I lent him some money to go with, which of course he repaid as soon as he could and before he left India.

It was also during this rest period that my commission came through, backdated to the beginning of February. All this isolation, being in Coventry and denied the company of my fellow pilots in leisure hours, had been entirely unnecessary. I had already served my six months as a Pilot Officer and was now automatically a Flying Officer.

In December we returned to the front, flying over Imphal on our way back. The B Flight Commander, Kenneth MacVicar, looked down and said, 'Aha, my beloved Shangri-la'; we had been very happy at Imphal originally, before the battle started. We went on to the next station, called Tamu, in the Kabaw (Death) Valley. There one morning I was late down to the flight, when I saw a column of smoke arising from the foot of the airstrip. I was told it was George Evatt. He had met some disaster taking off and had been killed.

At Tamu our tents were pitched in a teak forest under magnificent great trees. We were always alert for any marauding Japanese patrol, and I slept with a loaded revolver under my pillow and a drawn Kukri, or Ghurka knife, by my bedside. You would sleep, lulled by the jungle noises which would suddenly cease, everything going quiet. Then you wake at once; insects and frogs have warned of the possible approach of an intruder. You listen, wondering whether the noise is the falling of dew drops from the giant leaves or something worse. The gun under your pillow gives you comfort. But then you can go back to sleep, for the jungle noises have started up again.

We were hopping down various airstrips as the Japanese retreated so we went forward, to be as close to the front line as we could; we moved to Kalemyo and then to Yeo. At Kalemyo I was left in charge of a detachment, for the rest of the squadron had gone on to Yeu and I was in charge of the rear party. The night before our final departure I left my chaps, about half dozen in all, sitting around a camp fire as I walked back to where I was sleeping. A lone Japanese aircraft came over and started to strafe us. The airfield was deserted apart from ourselves and I was terrified it would go for the people sitting round the fire. But having taken cover, they were unharmed. I threw myself into a ditch while the bullets rattled around. It was an eerie experience being on the receiving end.

On leaving Kalemyo the next morning, my aircraft failed. I had run up my Hurricane, testing the engine on the usual pre-flight check, and it seemed faultless. The Dakota duly arrived about mid-morning to take our party and I saw them off. I climbed into my Hurricane, started up and took off to Yeu leaving an empty airfield behind me. After a few miles I looked at my oil pressure. The gauge was sinking; I had an oil leak. I looked at it again after a few minutes, and it was down still further. I thought, now either I turn back to Kalemyo where there is an empty strip and no-one to help me, or I go on and try to find the squadron and take the risk of not being able to get there. I went on, found the squadron, and landed safely but with my oil much depleted.

Lord Mountbatten, now recently appointed Commander-in-Chief, came to visit the squadron on three occasions in different locations. Each time, we pilots were lined up to meet him and after shaking hands and a few encouraging words – a pep talk – off he went. After this procedure had been repeated for the third time, he said to Henry Larsen, 'Haven't I met some of these men before?'

On one memorable sortie, I was flying with a chap called Cyril Merrit, who was a tennis player of Wimbledon standard and altogether very good at games. I used to play badminton with him occasionally and he was far, far my superior. I never beat Cyril. One day we were reconnoitring a track down to the west of Mandalay towards Pagan and I was in the lead. As I flew down this track, I saw bushes move in front of me; they were concealing guns, ack-ack guns. As the gun crew flung the covering branches away, I screamed 'Break, Cyril, break', at the top of my voice, at the same time jamming on my rudder. The aircraft swung just in time: the shells went over my wing and I could almost have touched them. Cyril was unlucky. He was hit and climbed to about 300 or 400 feet and tried to bale out, but he wasn't high enough for his parachute to open and he died.

It was also at Yeu that we lost Ralph Hunter, who had been a professional pilot in peacetime and had many years of experience of flying, mostly in the Canadian bush. At his request, Henry Larsen allowed him to fly solo at night, hunting Japanese. One night I overheard B Flight Commander Kenneth MacVicar, an ebullient, outgoing Scot who some months earlier had walked back through enemy lines and rejoined us a few days later, saying in a neighbouring tent, 'Ralph has not returned. We must go and look for him at first light.' But no sign of Ralph or his aircraft was ever found.

The last sortie which I will describe led, much to my regret, to my leaving 28 Squadron. The Army's 19 Division, which was advancing down the Irrawaddy River, wanted low level oblique photographs of the Ava Bridge at Mandalay in order to bring up decking material. They needed to know the length of timber required, for the piers of the bridge were still standing although the decking had been wrecked, and they asked for low level obliques. I volunteered for this. As I guessed it would be a highly defended target, I climbed up a few hundred feet and dived over the bridge, going very fast and low. I took my photographs and pulled up to get over the river bank on the other side. Ahead of me was a tall stand of trees, probably teak trees, which must have been at least 150 feet high, towering above me and above the bank. As I pulled up over the bank, there on the top was a battery of Japanese ack-ack directly below me. I saw the gun crews about fifty feet below and their shells must have been loaded with instantaneous fuses. The sky went all black and grey and the aircraft gave a terrific jolt. I am not sure if it turned upside down or not, but I believe it did. I thought 'Oh God, they have shot my tail off, I am going to die'. I switched my ignition off so that the aircraft would not burst into flames when it struck the earth. Then I committed myself to God; and was at once engulfed in a wave of deep serenity. A few seconds later I was flying right way up about ten feet above the ground with my propeller just wind-milling because the engine wasn't going. I was flying through a gap in the trees I had not even seen was there. Hastily I switched my ignition back on. The air speed picked up, I cleared the ground and I was up and away. Inexplicably there was no damage to my aircraft.

Back at the unit we had a new Flight Commander who was rather unsure of himself. He said, 'I want you to fly again this afternoon.' I said, 'I'd rather not fly this afternoon. I had a shake-up this morning, and I would just like to get over it quietly.' 'No,' he said, 'I want you to fly.' I replied, 'Well, I will fly today since you have told me to, but I will not fly for you again.' And I didn't. That afternoon I flew as number two to the Squadron Adjutant, Roger Quixley. We found an oil dump in a village by the side of the Irrawaddy and destroyed it.

We came back, and I said, 'No, that's it.' I told the Squadron Commander that I wanted to pack up. Promptly, he said I was not to fly again. I felt tremendous relief and that evening I found myself singing in the bath. I left the squadron after a day or two. I couldn't bear to say goodbye to the ground crew, else I should have wept, so I just slunk away.

CHAPTER SEVEN

Afterwards

When I got back to Calcutta, I was told, 'You are being posted as ADC to the Governor of the North West Frontier Province.' I said, 'Oh, that is wonderful. That's a lovely posting. I will enjoy that.' I went up to Delhi and was interviewed and was told they were awfully sorry but the Governor was not ready for me. He had asked for an RAF ADC instead of an Army one, so we sent him one. But now he said he wasn't expecting anyone for about three months, and I would have to go back to Calcutta.

I arrived there in March 1945 and was posted as a personal assistant to the commanding officer of 228 Group, a charming old chap called Air Commodore Battle, and his brother-in-law Group Captain Culley, who was his second in command. They both had been First World War pilots. And their talk would be of Sopwith Camels and when I tried to intervene and say something about Spitfires, they would say, 'Oh my boy, this war is nothing, why you have even got parachutes in this war.'

They were very kind to me. But it wasn't really my metier, and I wasn't really a very good ADC. Air Commodore Battle asked me if I would like a permanent commission in the Air Force. But I refused, saying, 'No, I would really rather return to Oxford to complete my degree and try something else. I have had enough of the Air Force and flying.' So, he said, 'Yes, alright.'

I continued as ADC for a short while. But I was missing the squadron, the activity, the excitement, and the comradeship very much, so I volunteered again. This time there was a request for volunteers for Special Force 136. I went for parachute training in Jessore, where I met the most reckless and unruly bunch of people you could ever imagine. I had never taken unnecessary risks because flying is basically dangerous and unnatural. But they would dice for drinks, rounds of drinks, before flying and before going off to parachute. I thought this was very reckless but could hardly avoid being a part of it, even though I tried to restrict the amount of alcohol I took. After parachute jumping I was trained with Special Forces in all sorts of tricks of the trade. How to handle explosives and blow down trees with them, and how to throw grenades, which I had not done before. Also some unarmed combat. I was given a team, a wireless set, and an operator; there were five of us altogether. We were sent to Ceylon, where we had a camp in a coconut plantation, not far from Colombo.

We were due to parachute with my team in to Malaya and were on a twenty-four hour standby, but we had not been told what the mission would be. Then they dropped the atom bomb, and my mission was switched. I was told I would probably be going to Siam but again that was altered. Then the next thing I was to go to Jakarta and get people out of the prison there. A Wing Commander, an administrative officer with Special Force, said, 'The war's ending, I want some more excitement before it does. I am going to take your team.' So, he took my team and went off with them. I was pleased to say that, as I heard later, he and the entire team were incarcerated by the Indonesians who didn't wish to be re-colonised by anybody, and they were all put in jail. I don't know how long they stayed there but I thought it served him right.

I survived the loss of many friends. Was it luck, blind chance? A very fast reaction time may have helped, but that did not account for the miracle at the Ava Bridge when only my guardian angel could have saved me. I later joined the Colonial Service and was involved in 1955 and 1956 in civil disturbances in Sierra Leone, with continuous rioting. In the beginning, at a place called Roruks, I had one clash with the rioters in which we had to use weapons; I had a lot of police with me who shot and killed seven people. From then on, I refused to take any police with me. This rioting went on for many months, going from one chiefdom to another. It was all to do with the threat of self-government, for people did not want the British to leave. It was a tremendous disturbance. People were pulling down the chief's houses, setting fire, doing what damage they could. And I used to go by myself generally, with my wife and with one interpreter, quieten them down until evening came and they were too tired to be mischievous. I promised to come and listen to all they had to say as soon as I could. The thought did strike me that at last I was doing some good, and that my guardian angel might have preserved me for this very purpose. I ended up by being crowned as an Honorary Paramount Chief by the remaining chiefs of my district. This was a great honour; I never heard of such an event happening to anyone else in Sierra Leone.

I took a Class-B release from the RAF to continue my studies at Brasenose College, Oxford. First to a transit camp near Bombay, then I boarded a large troop ship, the *Ile de France*, for the trip home. We called for about four hours at Durban and were entertained continuously by a lady wearing a red hat and a white gown, who sang magnificently, most memorably 'Land of Hope and Glory', and also much else. This lady, Perla Sieble Gibson, became famous as Durban's lady in white who sang to every large troop ship and 350 hospital ships from 1940 to 1946, not missing once whatever the weather. She worked in the dockside canteen as a volunteer, her white gown was her canteen overall and her red hat was waterproof. She had a vast repertoire of songs and her wonderful voice was a rich vibrant contralto. She had been a singer of international renown and a classical pianist. Now she devoted herself to singing troop ships in and singing them out again. Later she received much international recognition, deservedly, as the quality of the performance she gave was truly memorable.

The other thing that stayed in my memory about the voyage home was a large soft bag which I had to leave in a corridor outside the cabin, in which were stowed a few pairs of ladies' sheer silk stockings. They were near the top of the bag, which was not locked. They disappeared one night – the only things I had stolen in all my RAF days.

There did not seem much hope and glory left in the England to which we returned in January 1946. After landing in Liverpool, we were sent to the RAF demobilisation centre at Hednesford, from which we were cleared within forty-eight hours. Still in uniform, I found myself walking up and down the single main street of Abbots Bromley with the voices singing in my ears that this was all folly. I had once told Joan, or Jonathan, to put me out of her mind, to forget she ever knew me and that one day I would come back to her if I could. She will not remember me; there will have been other boyfriends. In truth, I had not consciously thought much about her, but I had always carried her image in my mind, and her photograph in my wallet. It was now too much to hope that she would want to see me. I walked up and down the street, wondering which house was hers; then about fifty yards north of the market cross a young woman, her elder sister, ran down the steps of her house. 'Are you Mr Guy?' she asked. I said I was. She directed me to a house about 100 yards down the street. I knocked.

Never was there such a welcome. I had truly come home at last. I had lost Paradise. It had been forfeited, forgotten, postponed to the never-never land of 'after-the-war'. Now, suddenly, it was here, warm, vivid and living, full of promise for the future. We were after all only twenty-five years old and life was for living and was truly ours. We were married on 3 September 1946 and are now approaching our diamond wedding. Never has there been so loving and generous a woman, who has suffered many privations and tribulations on my account, success and triumphs as well. What I am I owe to her, a debt I can never repay except with my love.

When at last I reached home in Gravesend my young brother, who had just reached my shoulder in February 1943, was towering above me. He recorded in his diary at the time, 'Geoffrey has come home. He is shrunk, and is all yellow.' The effect of my daily medicine – an anti-malaria drug.

Chronology of Geoffrey's Life

Geoffrey was born on 4 November 1921 in Ramsgate, Kent, third of five children of Ernest and Constance Guy. He attended Chatham House Grammar School, Ramsgate, where his father was headmaster, and became school captain. In May 1940, the school was evacuated to Staffordshire, where Geoffrey was to meet his future wife, Joan (Jonathan, Johnny) Smith.

In October 1940, on a university scholarship, he went up to Oxford to read Modern History at Brasenose College. He took a wartime degree in one year, being awarded his BA in 1943. Meanwhile, in 1941, he had volunteered to become a pilot with the Royal Air Force. His training in Canada, England and Palestine, and photographic reconnaissance service in the Middle and Far East, are described in this memoir.

After the war ended in 1945, Geoffrey returned to Brasenose College to study Philosophy, Politics and Economics and was awarded his MA in 1947.

He married on 3 September 1946.

Following a period in a management position with the firm of Scribbans-Kemp, biscuit makers, Geoffrey joined the Colonial Service. He held the posts of District Commissioner, Sierra Leone (1951–58); Administrator, Turks and Caicos Islands (1958–64); Administrator, then Governor, Dominica (1965–73); Administrator, Ascension Island (1973–76); and Governor, St Helena (1976–81).

He received a series of civil honours, being appointed MBE (1957), OBE (1962), CMG (1964) and CVO (1966).

The first years of his retirement, from 1982–92, were spent in St Helena where he and Johnny remained active in island affairs. In 1992, they returned to England, to the village of Kirk Hammerton in Yorkshire, where they remained for the rest of their lives.

Geoffrey died at home on 1 December 2006. Johnny died in hospital a few weeks later. They are survived by their son Benjamin.

Summary of Geoffrey's RAF Service Record

Date of enlistment: 1.3.1941

Non-commissioned rankings:
1.3.1941   Aircraftsman Second Class
18.9.1941   Leading Aircraftsman
4.7.1943   Flight Sergeant

Commissioned rankings:
18.7.1944   Pilot Officer
27.10.1944 Flying Officer
3.8.1945   Flight Lieutenant

Character: 'VG' throughout

Last day of service: 1.2.1946